A BIBLIOGRAPHY ON TEMPLES OF THE ANCIENT NEAR EAST AND MEDITERRANEAN WORLD

Arranged by Subject and by Author

Compiled by

Donald W. Parry
Stephen D. Ricks
John W. Welch

Ancient Near Eastern Texts and Studies
Volume 9

The Edwin Mellen Press
Lewiston/Queenston/Lampeter

Library of Congress Cataloging-in-Publication Data

This book has been registered with the Library of Congress.

This is volume 9 in the continuing series
Ancient Near Eastern Texts and Studies
Volume 9   ISBN 0-7734-9775-7
ANETS Series ISBN 0-88946-085-X

A CIP catalog record for this book
is available from the British Library.

The Edwin Mellen Press
Box 450
Lewiston, New York
USA 14092

The Edwin Mellen Press
Box 67
Queenston, Ontario
CANADA L0S 1L0

The Edwin Mellen Press, Ltd.
Lampeter, Dyfed, Wales
UNITED KINGDOM SA48 7DY

Printed in the United States of America

A BIBLIOGRAPHY ON TEMPLES OF THE ANCIENT NEAR EAST AND MEDITERRANEAN WORLD

Arranged by Subject and by Author

Contents

Key to Abbreviations

AJA	American Journal of Archaeology
AJSL	American Journal of Semitic Languages and Literatures
ASAE	Annales du Service des Antiquités de l'Égypte
BA	Biblical Archaeologist
BAR	Biblical Archaeology Review
BASOR	Bulletin of American Schools of Oriental Research
BIFAO	Bulletin de l'Institut français d'archéologie orientale
BCH	Bulletin de correspondance hellénique
BTB	Biblical Theology Bulletin
BJRL	Bulletin of the John Rylands Library
CBQ	Catholic Biblical Quarterly
ET	Expository Times
GUOST	Glasgow University Oriental Society Transactions
HUCA	Hebrew Union College Annual
IEJ	Israel Exploration Journal
JAOS	Journal of the American Oriental Society
JBL	Journal of Biblical Literature
JEA	Journal of Egyptian Archaeology
JJS	Journal of Jewish Studies
JNES	Journal of Near Eastern Studies
JPOS	Journal of the Palestine Oriental Society
JQR	Jewish Quarterly Review
JTS	Journal of Theological Studies
MDAI.A	Mitteilungen des Deutschen Archäologischen Instituts, Athenische Abteilung
MDAI.K	Mitteilungen des Deutschen Archäologishen Instituts für ägyptische Altertumskunde in Kairo
MDAI.R	Mitteilungen des Deutschen Archäologischen Instituts, Römische Abteilung
MGWJ	Monatsschrift für die Geschichte und Wissenschaft des Judentums

NT	Novum Testamentum
NTS	New Testament Studies: An International Journal
PEFQ	Palestine Exploration Fund Quarterly Statement
PEQ	Palestine Exploration Quarterly
RB	Revue biblique
REJ	Revue d'Études Juives
RHR	Revue de l'histoire des religions
SBLSP	Society of Biblical Literature Seminar Papers
Syria	Syria: Revue d'art oriental et d'archéologie
VT	Vetus Testamentum
ZAW	Zeitschrift für die alttestamentliche Wissenschaft
ZÄS	Zeitschrift für ägyptische Sprache und Altertumskunde
ZDMG	Zeitschrift der Deutschen Morgenländischen Gesellschaft
ZDPV	Zeitschift des Deutschen Palästina-Vereins
ZNTW	Zeitschrift für die neutestamentlischen Wissenschaft

Encyclopedias and Dictionaries Cited

Encyclopaedia Biblica, edited by T. K. Cheyne and J. S. Black. 4 vols. New York: Macmillan, 1899-1903.

Encyclopaedia Judaica, edited by Cecil Roth. 17 vols. Jerusalem: Macmillan, 1971-1982.

The Encyclopedia of Religion, edited by Mircea Eliade et al. 16 vols. New York: Macmillan, 1987.

Encyclopaedia of Religion and Ethics, edited by James Hastings et al. 13 vols. New York: Scribner's, 1951.

Harper's Bible Dictionary, edited by Paul J. Achtemeier et al. San Francisco: Harper and Row, 1985.

The Interpreter's Dictionary of the Bible, edited by George A. Buttrick et al. 4 vols. New York: Abingdon, 1962.

The Interpreter's Dictionary of the Bible, edited by Keith Crim et al. Supplementary volume. Nashville: Abingdon, 1976.

The Jewish Encyclopedia, edited by Isodore Singer. 16 vols. New York and London: Funk and Wagnalls, 1901-1095.

Theological Dictionary of the Old Testament, edited by G. Johannes Botterweck and Helmer Ringgren. Grand Rapids, MI: Eerdmans, 1974-.

Introduction

The preparation of a bibliography on temples of the ancient Near East, as well as the Greco-Roman world, requires little justification. The temple was the central feature on the religious landscape in the ancient Mediterranean area, and one of the most important on the political landscape as well. The maintenance of the temple and the rites associated with it were viewed as essential to the well-being of the society in which the temple was built. On the other hand, harm to the temple, whether by man or by natural forces, often spelled disaster for the community if it was not corrected.

John M. Lundquist,[1] in a series of seminal studies on the typology of the temple in the ancient Near East, has noted certain features that occur with striking frequency in these temples, among which are the following:

    1. The temple is the architectural embodiment of the cosmic mountain.

    2. The temple is often associated with the waters of life which flow forth from a spring within the building itself—or rather the temple is viewed as incorporating within itself or as having been built upon a spring.

    3. The temple is built on separate, sacral, set-apart space.

    4. The temple is oriented toward the four world regions or cardinal directions.

---

[1] John M. Lundquist, "The Legitimizing Role of the Temple in the Origin of the State," in Kent H. Richards, ed., *Society of Biblical Literature 1982 Seminar Papers* (Chico, CA: Scholars, 1983), 276-78; cf. id., "What Is a Temple? A Preliminary Typology," in H. B. Huffmon, F. A. Spina, and A. R. W. Green, eds., *The Quest for the Kingdom of God: Studies in Honor of George E. Mendenhall* (Winona Lake, IN: Eisenbrauns, 1983), 205-19; and "The Common Temple Ideology of the Ancient Near East," in Truman G. Madsen, ed., *The Temple in Antiquity* (Provo: Brigham Young University Press, 1984), 53-76.

5.   The plan and measurements of the temple are revealed by God to the king, and the plan must be carefully carried out.

6.   The temple is the central, organizing, unifying institution in ancient Near Eastern society. A. The temple is associated with abundance and prosperity, indeed is perceived as the giver of these. B. The destruction or loss of the temple is seen as calamitous and fatal to the community in which the temple stood. The destruction is viewed as the result of social and moral decadence and disobedience to God's word.

7.   Inside the temple and in temple workshops images of deities as well as living kings, temple priests, and worshippers are washed, anointed, clothed, fed, enthroned, and symbolically initiated into the presence of deity, and thus into eternal life. Further, New Year rites are held, at which time texts are read and dramatically portrayed which recite a pre-earthly war in heaven, the victory in the war by the forces of good, led by a chief deity, the creation and establishment of the cosmos, cities, temples, and the social order. The sacred marriage is carried out at this time.

8.   There is a close interrelationship between the temple and law in the ancient Near East.

9.   The temple is a place of sacrifice.

10.   The temple and its ritual are enshrouded in secrecy. This secrecy relates to the sacredness of the temple precinct and the strict division in ancient times between sacred and profane space.

11.   The temple and its cult are central to the economic structure of ancient Near Eastern society.

We have incorporated several features of Lundquist's typology into this bibliography. Thus, we have cited articles treating archaeological and literary evidence that bear on the layout, design, and physical accoutrements (such as the altar and Holy of Holies) of the temples of Israel, Egypt, Mesopotamia, and the Greco-Roman world. In addition, we have treated certain recurring features of the temple (and other sacred space)—such as the role of the priesthood in the operation of the temple, the sacred vestments of the priests, sacrifice and other priestly rituals, the cosmic associations of the temple, the temple as the locus of kingly authority and the site of his coronation—which are manifested in the ancient Near East, in the Greco-Roman world, and elsewhere. In certain instances, where the phenomenon connected with the temples of the ancient Near East and the Greco-Roman world might be further elucidated by examples from beyond that region and period of time, we have included representative literature from other sources as well. Thus, the section treating "Ablution and Anointing" contains several articles and books dealing with aspects of Christian baptism and anointing—from both the ancient as well as more recent periods of time—that were deemed helpful in understanding the phenomenon better. Under "Ritual, Liturgy, and Worship" are general studies of ritual as well as specific investigations of the worship and liturgical practices of peoples of the ancient Near East—including pilgrimage and festivals—as well as in Christianity. The section entitled "Tabernacle" also includes literature dealing with the Ark of the section entitled "Tabernacle" also includes literature dealing with the Ark of the Covenant and the Holy of Holies. Under "Kingship and Coronation," studies that treat various aspects of the ideology of kingship and the rites associated with coronation from a variety of cultures have been included. The category "Temples of Israel and Canaan," by far the largest in this bibliography, deserves special discussion. It includes studies on the temples of Jerusalem, Israelite temples outside of the Land of Israel (e.g., Elephantine), non-Israelite temples of the Levant (e.g., Ugarit and Phoenicia), as well as eschatological and visionary temples in the Jewish (e.g., the Temple Scroll) and Christian (e.g., Epistle to the Hebrews and Revelation) traditions.

The bibliography is divided into other specific categories, such as "Temples of Egypt," "Temples of Mesopotamia," "Priesthood," and "Sacrifice and Offerings." Within each of these categories, the relevant bibliography is listed alphabetically by author. Given the vast and diffuse nature of the material, we have tried to be representative rather than comprehensive. This bibliography, consisting of over 2700 entries, is designed to serve as an introduction to research on ancient temples in general, to specific temples of the ancient Near East, and to the ideology and practices associated with temples and other sacred space.

We wish to express our thanks to those who assisted us in verifying the accuracy of the references in this bibliography—Ann Adams, Brett Holbrook, Frank Judd, Yvonne Knudsen, Tyler Moulton, Ryan Parr, and Andrew Teasdale, as well as Fran Hafen, Brenda Miles, and Shirley Ricks for their indispensable efforts in the production of the volume. We also wish to express appreciation to the Foundation for Ancient Research and Mormon Studies (F.A.R.M.S.) for its financial support in the preparation of this volume.

General Studies of Temples in the Ancient Near East and Mediterranean World Arranged by Subject

Temples of Egypt

Abd el-Raziq, Mahmud. *Die Darstellungen und Text des Sanktuars Alexanders des Grossen im Tempel von Luxor.* Mainz: von Zabern, 1984. [Egypt]

Alliot, Maurice. *Le Culte d'Horus à Edfou au temps des Ptolémées.* Beirut: Librairie du Liban, 1979. [Egypt]

Alt, Albrecht. "Ägyptische Tempel in Palästina und die Landnahme der Philister." *ZDPV* 67 (1944-45): 1-20. [Egypt]

Arnold, Dieter. *Der Tempel des Königs Mentuhotep von Deir el-Bahari.* Cairo: Mainz, 1974. [Egypt]

Arnold, Dieter. *Der Tempel Qasr El-Sagha.* Mainz: von Zabern, 1979. [Egypt]

Arnold, Dieter. *Wandrelief und Raumfunktion in ägyptischen Tempeln des Neuen Reiches.* Berlin: Hessling, 1962. [Egypt]

Badawy, Alexander M. "The Approach to the Egyptian Temple in the Late and Graeco-Roman Periods." *ZÄS* 102 (1975): 79-90. [Egypt]

Badawy, Alexander M. "Maru-Aten: Pleasure Resort or Temple?" *JEA* 42 (1956): 58-64. [Egypt]

Baillet, J. "Le Temple d'Apet à Karnak." *Bibliothèque égyptologique* 16 (1905): 93-111. [Egypt]

Bakry, H. S. K. "The Discovery of a Temple of Sobk in Upper Egypt." *MDAI.K* 27 (1969): 131-46. [Egypt]

Barguet, Paul. "Note sur le grand temple d'Aton à el-Amarna." *Revue d'Égyptologie* 28 (1976): 148-51. [Egypt]

Barguet, Paul. "La structure du temple Ipet-Sout d'Amon à Karnak du Moyen Empire à Aménophis II." *BIFAO* 52 (1953): 145-55. [Egypt]

Benson, Margaret. *The Temple of Mut in Asher.* London: Murray, 1899. [Egypt]

Bissing, Friedrich W. *Die Baugeschichte des südlichen Tempels von Buhen.* Munich: Bayerische Akademie der Wissenschaften, 1942. [Egypt]

Bissing, Friedrich W. "La chambre des trois saisons du sanctuaire solaire du roi Rathourès à Abousir." *ASAE* 53 (1955): 319-38. [Egypt]

Bissing, Friedrich W. *Das Re-Heiligtum des Königs Ne-woser-re (Rathures).* 3 vols. Berlin, 1905-23. [Egypt]

Blackman, Aylward M. "A Group of Texts Inscribed on the Façade of the Sanctuary in the Temple of Horus at Edfou." *Miscellanea Gregoriana* 10 (1946): 397-428. [Egypt]

Blackman, Aylward M. "The House of the Morning." *JEA* 5 (1918): 148-65. [Egypt]

Blackman, Aylward M. *Luxor and Its Temples.* London: Black, 1923. [Egypt]

Blackman, Aylward M. *The Temple of Bigeh.* Cairo: Imprimerie de l'Institut français d'archéologie orientale du Caire, 1915. [Egypt]

Blackman, Aylward M. *The Temple of Dendur.* Cairo: Imprimerie de l'Institut français d'archéologie orientale du Caire, 1911. [Egypt]

Blackman, Aylward M. *The Temple of Derr.* Imprimerie de l'Institut français d'archéologie orientale du Caire, 1913. [Egypt]

Blackman, Aylward M., and H. F. Fairman. "The Consecration of an Egyptian Temple according to the Use of Edfu." *JEA* 32 (1946): 75-91. [Egypt]

Bleeker, Claas J. *Egyptian Festivals.* Leiden: Brill, 1967. [Egypt]

Boak, Arthur E. R., ed. *Karanis, the Temples, Coin Hoards, Botanical and Zoological Reports, Seasons 1924-31.* Ann Arbor: University of Michigan Press, 1933. [Egypt]

Borchardt, Ludwig. *Der ägyptische Tempel mit Umgang.* In *Beiträge zur ägyptischen Bauforschung and Altertumskunde* 2 (1938). [Egypt]

Borchardt, Ludwig. "Der Augustustempel auf Philae." *Jahrbuch des Deutschen Archäologischen Instituts* 18 (1903): 73-90. [Egypt]

Borchardt, Ludwig. *Zur Baugeschichte des Amonstempels von Karnak.* Leipzig: Hinrichs, 1905. [Egypt]

Breasted, James H. *The Temples of Lower Nubia: Report of the Work of the Egyptian Expedition.* Chicago: Oriental Exploration Fund, 1906. [Egypt]

Brugsch, H. "Bau und Maasse des Tempels von Edfu." *ZÄS* 8 (1870): 153-61; 9 (1871): 32-45; 10 (1872): 1-16. [Egypt]

Brugsch, H. "Eine neue Bauurkunde des Tempels von Edfu." *ZÄS* 13 (1875): 113-23. [Egypt]

Brunner, A. "Die Sonnenbahn in ägyptischen Tempeln." In *Archäologie und Altes Testament, Festschrift für Kurt Galling.* 27-34. Tübingen: Mohr, 1970. [Egypt]

Budge, E. A. Wallis. *Liturgy of Funeral Offerings*. London: Paul, Trench, Trübner, 1909. [Egypt]

Budge, E. A. Wallis. *Osiris and the Egyptian Resurrection*. New York: Putman's Sons, 1911. [Egypt]

Calverley, Amice M. *The Temple of King Sethos I at Abydos*, edited by Alan H. Gardiner. Chicago: University of Chicago Press, 1933. [Egypt]

Caminos, Ricardo A. *The New Kingdom Temples of Buhen*. London: Oxford University Press, 1974. [Egypt]

Caminos, Ricardo A. *Two Stelae in the Kurnah Temple of Sethos I*. Berlin: Akademie, 1955. [Egypt]

Capart, Jean. *Abydos, Le temple de Seti Ier*. Brussels: Rossignol & Van den Bril, 1912. [Egypt]

Capart, Jean. *Le temple des muses*. Brussels: Musées royaux d'art et d'histoire, 1932; 2d ed., 1936. [Egypt]

Cenival, F. "Les associations dans les temples égyptiens d'après les données fournies par les papyrus démotiques." In *Religions en Egypte hellénistique et romaine, Colloque de Strasbourg, 16-18 mai 1967*. 5-19. Paris: Paris universitaires de France, 1969. [Egypt]

Chassinat, Émile. *Le mammisi d'Edfou*. Cairo: Imprimerie de l'Institut français d'archéologie orientale du Caire, 1939. [Egypt]

Chassinat, Émile. *Le temple de Dendara*. Cairo: Imprimerie de l'Institut français d'archéologie orientale du Caire, 1934. [Egypt]

Chassinat, Émile. *Le temple d'Edfou*. Cairo: Imprimerie de l'Institut français d'archéologie orientale du Caire, 1934. [Egypt]

Chevrier, Henri. *Le temple reposoir de Ramsès à Karnak*. Cairo: Imprimerie de l'Institut français d'archéologie orientale du Caire, 1933. [Egypt]

Chevrier, Henri. *Le temple reposoir de Seti II à Karnak*. Cairo: Imprimerie nationale, 1940. [Egypt]

Daumas, Francois. *Les mammisis des temples l'égyptiens*. Paris: Les belles lettres, 1958. [Egypt]

Daumas, Francois. "Les propylées du Temple d'Hathor à Philae et le culte de la déese." *ZÄS* 95 (1968): 1-17. [Egypt]

Daumas, Francois. "Les textes géographiques du Trésor D' du temple de Dendara." In *State and Temple Economy in the Ancient Near East*, edited by Edward Lipiński. 2 vols., 2:689-706. Louvain: Departement Orientalistiek, 1979. [Egypt]

David, A. Rosalie. *The Ancient Egyptians: Religious Beliefs and Practices*. London: Routledge and Kegan Paul, 1982. [Egypt]

Davies, N. de Garis. "Two Pictures of Temples." *JEA* 41 (1955): 80-82. [Egypt]

de Buck, Adriaan. *De Egyptische voorstellingen betreffende den Oerheuvel*. Leiden: Ijdo, 1922. [Egypt]

Degardin, J. "Correspondances osiriennes entre les temples d'Opet et de Khonsou." *JNES* 44 (1985): 115-32. [Egypt]

de Wit, Constant. "Einige Bemerkungen zu den Inschriften des Epet-Tempels zu Karnak." *Wiener Zeitschrift für die Kunde des Morgenlandes* 54 (1957): 234-39. [Egypt]

de Wit, Constant. "Inscriptions dedicatoires du temple d'Edfou." *Chronique d'Égypte* 36 (1961): 56-97, 277-320. [Egypt]

de Wit, Constant. "Les inscriptions des lions-gargouilles du temple d'Edfou." *Chronique d'Égypte* 29 (1954): 29-45. [Egypt]

de Wit, Constant. *Les inscriptions du temple d'Opet à Karnak,* 3 vols. Brussels: Fondation de la Reine Élisabeth, 1958-68. [Egypt]

Doresse, M. "Les temples atoniens de la région thébaine." *Orientalia* 24 (1955): 113-35. [Egypt]

Drioton, E. *Le texte dramatique d'Edfou.* Cairo: Imprimerie de l'Institut français d'archéologie orientale du Caire, 1948. [Egypt]

Drioton, E. "Un temple égyptien." *Revue du Caire* 5 (1942): 132-43. [Egypt]

Dümichen, Johannes. *Der ägyptische Felsentempel von Abu-Simbel und seine Bildwerke und Inschriften.* Berlin: Hempel, 1869. [Egypt]

Dümichen, Johannes. *Baugeschichte des Denderatempels und Beschreibung der einzelnen Theile des Bauwerkes nach den an seinen Mauern befindlichen Inschriften.* Strassburg: Trübner, 1877. [Egypt]

Dümichen, Johannes. *Bauurkunde der Tempelanlagen von Dendera.* Bad Honnef: LTR, 1982. [Egypt]

Dümichen, Johannes. *Die kalendarischen Opferfest-listen im Tempel von Medinet-Habu.* Leipzig: Hinrichs, 1881. [Egypt]

Dümichen, Johannes. *Über die Tempel und Gräber im alten Ägypten und ihre Bildwerke und Inschriften.* Strasburg: Trübner, 1872. [Egypt]

Dunham, Dows. *The Barkal Temples.* Boston: Museum of Fine Arts, 1970. [Egypt]

El-Adly, Sanaa. A. "Das Gründungs- und Weiheritual des ägyptischen Tempels von der frühgeschichtlichen Zeit bis zum Ende des neuen Reiches," Ph.D. diss., Tübingen University, 1981. [Egypt]

El-Sawy, A. "The Nile-God: An Unusual Representation in the Temple of Sety I at Abydos." *Egitto e Vicino Oriente* 6 (1983): 7-13. [Egypt]

Engelbach, R. "A Foundation-Scene of the Second Dynasty." *JEA* 20 (1934): 183-84. [Egypt]

Evans, J. A. S. "A Social and Economic History of an Egyptian Temple in Greco-Roman Period." *Yale Classical Studies* 17 (1961): 143-283. [Egypt]

Fairman, H. W. "A Scene of the Offering of Truth in the Temple of Edfu." *MDAI.K* 16 (1958): 86-92. [Egypt]

Fairman, H. W. "Worship and Festivals in an Egyptian Temple." *BJRL* 37 (1954-55): 165-203. [Egypt]

Frankfort, Henri, et al. *The Cenotaph of Seti I at Abydos.* 2 vols. London: Egyptian Exploration Society, 1933. [Egypt]

Fraser, P. M. "A Temple of Hathor at Kusae." *JEA* 42 (1956): 97-98. [Egypt]

Gardiner, Alan H. "The House of Life." *JEA* 24 (1938): 157-79. [Egypt]

Gardiner, Alan H. *The Temple of King Sethos I at Abydos.* Chicago: University of Chicago Press, 1933. [Egypt]

Gauthier, Henri. *Les temples immergés de la Nubie. Le temple d'Amada.* Cairo: Imprimerie de l'Institut français d'archéologie orientale du Caire, 1913. [Egypt]

Gauthier, Henri. *Les temples immergés de la Nubie. Le temple de Kalabchah.* 2 vols. Cairo: Imprimerie de l'Institut français d'archéologie orientale du Caire, 1911-27. [Egypt]

Gessler-Löhr, Beatrix. *Die heiligen Seen ägyptischer Tempel.* Hildesheim: Gerstenberg, 1983. [Egypt]

Goedicke, H. "Cult-Temple and 'State' during the Old Kingdom in Egypt." In *State and Temple Economy in the Ancient Near East,* edited by Edward Lipiński. 2 vols., 1:113-32. Louvain: Departement Orientalistiek, 1979. [Egypt]

Goosens, G. "Le temple de Ptah à Memphis." *Chronique d'Égypt* 21 (1945): 49-53. [Egypt]

Grdseloff, B. "Nouvelles données concernant la tente de purification." *ASAE* 51 (1951): 129-50. [Egypt]

Grelot, P. "La réconstruction du temple juif d'Eléphantine." *Orientalia* n.s. 36 (1967): 173-77. [Egypt]

Grünhut, L. "Der Raum des Tempels nach Estori hep-Parchi." *ZDPV* 31 (1908): 281-96. [Egypt]

Habachi, Labib. *The Sanctuary of Heqaib.* Mainz am Rhein: von Zabern, 1985. [Egypt]

Haeny, H. Gerhard. *Untersuchungen im Totentempel Amenophis III.* Wiesbaden: Steiner, 1981. [Egypt]

Hayes, W. C. "Royal Decrees from the Temple of Min at Coptus." *JEA* 32 (1946): 3-23. [Egypt]

Holscher, Uro. *Excavations at Ancient Thebes.* Chicago: University of Chicago Press, 1932. [Egypt]

Holscher, Uro. *The Mortuary Temple of Ramses III.* London: Cambridge University Press, 1940-45. [Egypt]

Hornblower, G. D. "Temples and Kings in Ancient Egypt." *Journal of Manchester Egyptian and Oriental Society* 17 (1932): 21-39. [Egypt]

Hornblower, G. D. "A Temple Seal and Its Connections." *ASAE* 34 (1934): 99-106. [Egypt]

Ibrahim, Mohiy ed-Din. "The God of the Great Temple of Edfu." In *Orbis Aegyptiorum Speculum—Glimpses of Ancient Egypt: Studies in Honour of H. W. Fairman*, edited by Johann Ruffle, G. A. Gaballa, and K. A. Kitchen. 170-73. Warminster: Aris and Phillips, 1979. [Egypt]

Janssen, J. J. "The Role of the Temple in the Egyptian Economy during the New Kingdom." In *State and Temple Economy in the Ancient Near East*, edited by Edward Lipiński. 2 vols., 2:505-16. Louvain: Departement Orientalistiek, 1979. [Egypt]

Jaritz, Horst. *Die Terrassen von den Tempeln des Chnum und der Satet.* Mainz: von Zabern, 1980. [Egypt]

Jequier, G. *L'architecture et la décoration dans l'ancienne Égypte: Les temples memphites et thébains des origines à la XVIII Dynastie.* Paris: Morancé, 1920. [Egypt]

Junker, Hermann. *Der grosse Pylon des Tempels der Isis in Philä.* Wien: Rohrer, 1958. [Egypt]

Junker, Hermann, ed. *Das Geburtshaus des Tempels der Isis in Philä.* Wien: Nachf, 1965. [Egypt]

Kaiser, W., D. Bidoli, P. Grossmann, G. Haeny, H. Jaritz, and R. Stadelmann. "Stadt und Tempel von Elephantine: Dritter Grabungsbericht." *MDAI.K* 28 (1972): 157-200. [Egypt]

Kaiser, W., P. Grossmann, G. Haeny, and H. Jaritz. "Stadt und Tempel von Elephantine: Erster Grabungsbericht." *MDAI.K* 26 (1970): 87-167. [Egypt]

Kaiser, W., P. Grossmann, G. Haeny, H. Jaritz, and R. Stadelmann. "Stadt und Tempel von Elephantine: Zweiter Grabungsbericht." *MDAI.K* 27 (1971): 181-201. [Egypt]

Keel, Othmar. "Kanaanäische Sühneriten auf ägyptischen Tempelreliefs." *VT* 25 (1975): 413-69. [Egypt]

Kees, Hermann. "Ein Sonnenheiligtum im Amonstempel von Karnak." *Orientalia* 18 (1949): 427-42. [Egypt]

Klimkeit, Hans J. "Spatial Orientation in Mythical Thinking as Exemplified in Ancient Egypt: Considerations toward a Geography of Religions." *History of Religions* 14 (1975): 266-81. [Egypt]

Kurth, Dieter. *Edfu.* Wiesbaden: Harrassowitz, 1990. [Egypt]

Kurth, Dieter. *Den Himmel Stützen: Die "Tw3 pt"—Szenen in den ägyptischen Tempeln der griechisch-römischen Epoche.* Brussels: Fondation égyptologique Reine Élisabeth, 1975. [Egypt]

Labrousse, A. *Le temple haut du complexe funéraire du roi Ounas.* Cairo: Imprimerie de l'Institut français d'archéologie orientale du Caire, 1977. [Egypt]

Lacau, P. "Notes sur les plans des temples d'Edfou et de Kôm-Ombo." *ASAE* 52 (1954): 215-28. [Egypt]

Leeuwenburg, L. "Oversichten van de geschiedenis en opgravingen in het Nabije Oosten: Het tempel complex van Medinet Haboe." *Ex Oriente Lux: Jaarbericht van het vooraziatisch-egyptisch Gezelschap* 6 (1939): 43-59. [Egypt]

Legrain, Georges A. *Les temples de Karnak.* Paris: Vromant, 1929. [Egypt]

Lipinska, J. *Deir-el-Habhari II: The Temple of Tuthmosis III Architecture.* Warsaw: Naukowz, 1977. [Egypt]

Lockyer, J. Norman. *The Dawn of Astronomy: A Study of the Temple-Worship and Mythology of the Ancient Egyptians.* London: Macmillan, 1894. [Egypt]

MacQuitty, William. *Abu Simbel.* New York: Putnam, 1965. [Egypt]

MacRae, George. "The Temple as a House of Revelation in the Nag Hammadi Texts." In *The Temple in Antiquity,* edited by Truman G. Madsen. 175-90. Provo: Brigham Young University Press, 1984. [Egypt]

Mallakh, Kamal. *Treasures of the Nile.* New York: Newsweek, 1980. [Egypt]

Mariette, Auguste. *Abydos,* 2 vols. Paris: Frank, 1869-80. [Egypt]

Mariette, Auguste. *Dendérah: Description générale du grand Temple de cette ville,* 6 vols. Paris: Frank, 1870-73. [Egypt]

Mariette, Auguste. *Karnak.* Leipzig: Hinrichs, 1875. [Egypt]

Martiny, V. G. "Le temple périptère en Égypt." *Chronique d'Égypte* 44 (1947): 305-8. [Egypt]

Maspero, G. "Le temple de louxor et ce qu'on apprend à le bien visiter." *Revue du Caire* 16 (1946): 308-29. [Egypt]

Mayassis, S. *Le livre des morts de l'Égypte ancienne est un livre d'initiation.* Athens: B.A.O.A., 1955. [Egypt]

Mayassis, S. *Mystères et initiations de l'Égypte ancienne.* Athens: B.A.O.A., 1957. [Egypt]

Meeks, D. "Les donations aux temples dans l'Égypte du Ier millénaire avant J.-C." In *State and Temple Economy in the Ancient Near East,* edited by Edward Lipiński. 2 vols., 2:605-88. Louvain: Departement Orientalistiek, 1979. [Egypt]

Mees, M. "Der geistige Tempel: Einige Überlegungen zu Klemens von Alexandrien." *Vetera Christianorum* 1 (1964): 83-89. [Egypt]

Mertz, Barbara. *Temples, Tombs, and Hieroglyphs.* New York: Dodd, Mead, 1978. [Egypt]

Mond, Robert. *Temples of Armant.* London: Egypt Exploration Society, 1940. [Egypt]

Montet, Pierre. "Les divinités du temple de Behbeit el hagar." *Kêmi* 10 (1949): 43-49. [Egypt]

Montet, Pierre. "Le rituel de fondation des temples égyptiens." *Kêmi* 17 (1964): 74-100. [Egypt]

Morenz, Siegfried. "Cult and Piety: The Conduct of Men." In Morenz, *Egyptian Religion*, translated by Ann E. Keep. 81-109. New York: Barnes and Noble, 1972. [Egypt]

Moret, Alexandre. "Le rite de briser les vases rouges au temple de Louxor." *Revue d'Égyptologie* 3 (1938): 167. [Egypt]

Moret, Alexandre. *Le rituel de culte divin journalier en Égypte.* Paris: Leroux, 1902. [Egypt]

Murray, Margaret A. *Egyptian Temples.* London: Low, Marston, 1931. [Egypt]

Naville, Edouard H. *The Temple of Deir el Bahari,* 6 vols. London: Egypt Exploration Fund, 1894-1908. [Egypt]

Nelson, Harold H. "The Egyptian Temple." *BA* 7 (1944): 44-53. [Egypt]

Nelson, Harold H. "The Identity of Amon Re of United-with-Eternity." *JNES* 1 (1942): 127-55. [Egypt]

Nelson, Harold H. *Key Plans Showing Locations of Theban Temple Decorations.* Chicago: University of Chicago Press, 1941. [Egypt]

Nelson, Harold H., et al. *Ramses III's Temple within the Great Inclosure of Amon.* Chicago: University of Chicago Press, 1936. [Egypt]

Nibley, Hugh W. *The Message of the Joseph Smith Papyri: An Egyptian Endowment.* Salt Lake City: Deseret Book, 1975. [Egypt]

Osburn, William, Jr. *The Monumental History of Egypt, as Recorded on the Ruins of Her Temples, Palaces and Tombs.* London: Trübner, 1854. [Egypt]

Osing, Jürgen. *Der Tempel Sethos I in Gurna.* Mainz: von Zabern, 1977. [Egypt]

Otto, Eberhard. "Les Inscriptions du Temple d'Opet, à Karnak III: Traduction intégrale des texts rituels." *Biblitheca Orientalis* 28 (1971): 41-42. [Egypt]

Otto, Eberhard. *Osiris und Amon: Kult und heilige Stätten.* Munich: Hirmer, 1966; also in English as *Ancient Egyptian Art: The Cults of Osiris and Amon,* translated by Kate B. Griffiths. New York: Abrams, 1967. [Egypt]

Otto, Walter G. A. *Priester und Tempel im hellenistischen Ägypten,* 2 vols. Leipzig: Teubner, 1905-8. [Egypt]

Peterson, B. J. *Fornegyptisk tempelarkitektur 3000-1000 F. K. R.* Stockholm: Medelhausmuseet, 1976. [Egypt]

Petrie, W. M. Flinders. *The Pyramids and Temples of Gizeh.* New York: Scribner & Welford, 1883. [Egypt]

Petrie, W. M. Flinders. *Six Temples at Thebes.* London: Quaritch, 1897. [Egypt]

Piankoff, Alexandre. *The Shrines of Tut-Ankh-Amon*. New York: Pantheon Books, 1955. [Egypt]

Pillet, Maurice. "Les scènes de naissance et de circoncision dans le temple nordest de Mout, a Karnak." *ASAE* 52 (1952): 77-104. [Egypt]

Porter, Bertha, and Rosalind L. B. Moss. *Topographical Bibliography of Ancient Egyptian Hieroglyphic Texts, Reliefs, and Paintings*, 2d ed. 7 vols. London: Oxford University Press, 1976-82. [Egypt]

Posener-Kriéger, Paule. *Les archives du temple funéraire de Néferirkarê-Kakäi*. Cairo: Imprimerie de l'Institut français d'archéologie orientale du Caire, 1976. [Egypt]

Posener-Kriéger, Paule. "Les papyrus d'Abousir et l'économie des temple funéraires de l'Ancien Empire." In *State and Temple Economy in the Ancient Near East*, edited by Edward Lipiński. 2 vols., 1:133-52. Louvain: Departement Orientalistiek, 1979. [Egypt]

Randall-MacIver, David, and A. C. Mace. *El Amrah and Abydos, 1899-1901*. London: Egypt Exploration Fund, 1902. [Egypt]

Reisner, George A. *The Barkal Temples*. Boston: Museum of Fine Arts, 1970. [Egypt]

Reisner, George A. "The Barkal Temples in 1916." *JEA* 4 (1917): 213-27; 5 (1918): 99-112; 6 (1920): 247-64. [Egypt]

Reisner, George A. *Mycerinus. The Temples of the Third Pyramid at Giza*. Cambridge: Harvard University Press, 1931. [Egypt]

Reymond, Eve A. "The Children of Tanen." *ZÄS* 96 (1969): 36-44. [Egypt]

Reymond, Eve A. *The Mythical Origin of the Egyptian Temple*. New York: Barnes and Noble, 1969. [Egypt]

Ricke, Herbert. *Der Harmachistempel des Chefren in Giseh*. Wiesbaden: Steiner, 1970. [Egypt]

Ricke, Herbert, G. R. Hughes, and E. F. Wente. *The Beit el-Wali Temple of Ramses II*. Chicago: University of Chicago Press, 1967. [Egypt]

Saleh, A. A. "The So-Called 'Primeval Hill' and Other Related Elevations in Ancient Egyptian Mythology." *MDAI.K* 25 (1969): 110-20. [Egypt]

Saleh, Janine M. "Les représentations de temples sur plates-formes à pieux, de la poterie gerzéenne d'Égypte." *BIFAO* 83 (1983): 263-96. [Egypt]

Sauneron, Serge. *Edfou et Philae*. Paris: Chene, 1975. [Egypt]

Sauneron, Serge. *Die letzten Tempel Ägyptens*. Zurich: Atlantis, 1978. [Egypt]

Scenes and Inscriptions in the Court and the First Hypostyle Hall, vol. 1; *Temple of Khonsu—The Epigraphic Survey*, vol. 2. Chicago: Oriental Institute of the University of Chicago, 1979-81. [Egypt]

Schott, Siegfried. *Die Reinigung Pharaohs in einem memphitischen Tempel*. Göttingen: Vandenhoeck and Ruprecht, 1957. [Egypt]

Schwaller de Lubicz, R. A. *The Temple in Man: The Secrets of Ancient Egypt.* Brookline: Autumn, 1977. [Egypt]

Schwaller de Lubicz, R. A. *Les temples de Karnak.* Paris: Dervy-Livres, 1982. [Egypt]

Sethe, Kurt. *Thebanische Tempelinschriften aus griechisch-römischer Zeit, I.* Berlin: Akademie, 1957. [Egypt]

Seton-Williams, M. V. *Ptolemaic Temples.* London: Waterloo, 1978. [Egypt]

Sety, Omm, and Hanny El Zeini. *Abydos: Holy City of Ancient Egypt.* Los Angeles: L. L., 1981. [Egypt]

Smith, Joseph L. *Tombs, Temples and Ancient Art.* Norman, OK: University of Oklahoma Press, 1956. [Egypt]

Spencer, A. J. "The Brick Foundations of Late Period Peripteral Temples and Their Mythological Origin." In *Orbis Aegyptiorum Speculum—Glimpses of Ancient Egypt: Studies in Honour of H. W. Fairman,* edited by Johann Ruffle, G. A. Gaballa, and K. A. Kitchen. 132-37. Warminster: Aris and Phillips, 1979. [Egypt]

Spencer, Patricia. *The Egyptian Temple: A Lexicographical Study.* Boston: Kegan Paul International, 1984. [Egypt]

Teichmann, Frank. *Der Mensch und sein Tempel: Ägypten.* Stuttgart: Urachhaus, 1978. [Egypt]

Uphill, Eric P. *The Temples of Per Rameses.* Warminster: Aris and Phillips, 1984. [Egypt]

Van Siclen, Charles C. *Two Theban Monuments from the Reign of Amenhotep II.* San Antonio: Van Siclen Books, 1982. [Egypt]

Varille, A. "La grande porte du temple d'Apet à Karnak." *ASAE* 53 (1956): 79-118. [Egypt]

Ventura, Raphael. "Bent Axis or Wrong Direction? Studies on the Temple of Serabit el-Khadim." *IEJ* 38/3 (1988): 128-38. [Egypt]

Weinfeld, Moshe. "Instructions for Temple Visitors in the Bible and in Ancient Egypt." In *Scripta Hierosolymitana,* edited by Sarah Israel-Groll, vol. 28. Jerusalem: Magnes Press, 1984. [Egypt]

Werbrouck, Marcelle. *Le Temple de Hatshepsut à Deir-el-Bahari.* Brussels: Fondation ègyptologique reine Elisabeth, 1949. [Egypt]

Whitehorne, J. E. G. "New Light on Temple and State in Roman Egypt." *Journal of Religious History* 11 (December 1980): 218-26. [Egypt]

Winlock, H. E. *The Temple of Hibis in el Khargeh Oasis.* New York: Arno, 1973. [Egypt]

Winter, Eric. *Untersuchungen zu den ägyptischen Tempelreliefs der griechisch-römischen Zeit.* Wien: Bohlau in Kommissions, 1968. [Egypt]

Wolf, W. *Das schöne Fest von Opet: Die Festzugsdarstellungen im grossen römischen Säulengang des Tempels von Luksor.* Wien: Böhlav, 1931. [Egypt]

Wright, G. R. H. *Kalabsha: The Preserving of the Temple.* Berlin: Mann, 1972. [Egypt]

Žabkar, L. V. "Adaptation of Ancient Egyptian Texts to the Temple Ritual of Philae." *JEA* 66 (1980): 127-35. [Egypt]

Žabkar, L. V. "A Hymn to Osiris Pantocrator at Philae." *ZÄS* 108 (1981): 141-71. [Egypt]

Žabkar, L. V. "Six Hymns to Isis in the Sanctuary of Her Temple at Philae and Their Theological Significance." *JEA* 69 (1983): 115-37. [Egypt]

Temples of the Greco-Roman World

Albertson, F. "An Augustan Temple on a Julio-Claudian Relief." *AJA* 88 (April 1984): 236. [Greece/Rome]

Alles, Gregory D. "Surface, Space, and Intention: the Parthenon and the Kandariya Mahadeva." *History of Religions* 28 (August 1988): 1-36. [Greece/Rome]

Andren, Arvid. *Architectural Terracottas from Etrusco-Italic Temples.* Lund: Gleerup, 1940. [Greece/Rome]

Arendt, Erich. *Griechische Tempel.* Leipzig: Insel, 1970. [Greece/Rome]

Aviam, M. "The Roman Temple at Kedesh in the Light of Certain Northern Syrian City Coins." *Tel Aviv* 12 (1985): 212-14. [Greece/Rome]

Ayrton, Elisabeth. *The Doric Temple.* New York: Potter, 1961. [Greece/Rome]

Bergquist, Birgitta. *The Archaic Greek Temenos.* Lund: Gleerup, 1967. [Greece/Rome]

Berve, Helmut. *Greek Temples, Theatres, and Shrines.* New York: Abrams, 1963. [Greece/Rome]

Betancourt, P. H. "An Aeolic Shrine in Philadelphia." *AJA* 75 (1971): 427-28. [Greece/Rome]

Bianchi, R. S. "The Greek Temples of Sicily." *Archaeology* 37/2 (1984): 26-32. [Greece/Rome]

Birge, Darice E. "Sacred Groves in the Ancient Greek World." Ph.D. diss., University of California at Berkeley, 1982. [Greece/Rome]

Bogaers, Julianus E. A. T. *De Gallo - Romeinse Tempels te Elst in de Over-Betuwe.* 'S-Gravenhage, Staatsdrukkerij-en Uitgeverijbedrijf, 1955. [Greece/Rome]

Bookidis, Nancy. "The Sanctuary of Demeter and Kore: An Archaeological Approach to Ancient Religion." *AJA* 91 (July 1987): 480-81. [Greece/Rome]

Broneer, Oscar T. *Temple of Poseidon.* Princeton: American School of Classical Studies at Athens, 1971. [Greece/Rome]

Broneer, Oscar T. *Topography and Architecture.* Princeton: American School of Classical Studies at Athens, 1973. [Greece/Rome]

Burkert, Walter. "The Meaning and Function of the Temple in Classical Greece." In *Temple in Society*, edited by Michael V. Fox. 27-47. Winona Lake: Eisenbrauns, 1988. [Greece/Rome]

Cali, François. *L'ordre grec: Essai sur le temple dorique.* Paris: Arthaud, 1958. [Greece/Rome]

Carter, Jane. "The Masks of Ortheia." *AJA* 91 (July 1987): 355-83. [Greece/Rome]

Carter, Joseph C. *The Sculpture of the Sanctuary of Athena Polias at Priene.* London: Thames and Hudson, 1983. [Greece/Rome]

Cassano, R., et al. *Tempio di Adriano.* Roma: de Luca, 1982. [Greece/Rome]

Caton, Richard. *The Temples and Ritual of Asklepios at Epidauros and Athens.* London: Clay and Sons, 1900. [Greece/Rome]

Cipriano, Palmira. *Templum.* Rome: Prima cattedra di glottologia Università "La Spienza," 1983. [Greece/Rome]

Conti, Flavio. *Shrines of Power*, translated by Pat Craegh. London: Cassell, 1978. [Greece/Rome]

Cooper, Frederick A. *The Temple of Apollo at Bassai: A Preliminary Study.* New York: Garland, 1978. [Greece/Rome]

Cooper, Frederick A., et al. *The Temple of Zeus at Nemea.* Athens: Benaki Museum, 1983. [Greece/Rome]

Coulton, J. J. "Towards Understanding Greek Temple Design: General Considerations." *Annual of the British School at Athens* 70 (1975): 59-99. [Greece/Rome]

Dar, S., and J. Mintzker. "A Roman Temple at Senaim, Mount Hermon" (in Hebrew; *English summary). *Eretz-Israel* 19 (1987): 30-45, *74. [Greece/Rome]

Davies, John G. *Temples, Churches, and Mosques—Religious Architecture.* New York: Pilgrim, 1982. [Greece/Rome]

Dawkins, Richard M. *The Sanctuary of Artemis Orthia at Sparta.* London: Council of the Society for the Promotion of Hellenic Studies, 1929. [Greece/Rome]

Delcourt, Marie. *Les grands sanctuaires de la Grèce.* Paris: Presses universitaires de France, 1947. [Greece/Rome]

Demangel, Robert. *Le sanctuaire d'Athèna Pronaia.* Paris: de Boccard 1926. [Greece/Rome]

de Ruyt, C. "L'ordre de construction du temple périptère grec: état de la question et arguments nouveaux." *Les Études Classiques* 51 (1983): 63-70. [Greece/Rome]

Dinsmoor, William B. *The Temple of Apollo at Bassae.* New York: Metropolitan Museum, 1933. [Greece/Rome]

Doumato, Lamia. *The Temple of Athena Nike.* Monticello: Vance Bibliographies, 1980. [Greece/Rome]

Downey, Robert R. *The Roman Temple on Hayling Island.* London: Robert Downey, 1977. [Greece/Rome]

Dussaud, René. "Le temple de Jupiter damascénien et ses transformations aux époques chrétienne et musulmane." *Syria* 3 (1922): 219-50. [Greece/Rome]

Dussaud, René. "Temples et cultes de la triade héliopolitaine à Ba'albeck." *Syria* 23 (1942-43): 33-77. [Greece/Rome]

Dyggve, Ejnar. *Das Laphrion, der Tempelbezirk von Kalydon.* Copenhagen: Munksgaard, 1948. [Greece/Rome]

Eisenberg, Emmanuel. "The Temples at Tell Kittan." *BA* 40 (1977): 78-81. [Greece/Rome]

Eissfeldt, Otto. "Tempel und Kulte syrischer Städte in hellenistisch-römischer Zeit." *Forschungen und Fortschritte* 17 (1941): 5-7; also in *Kleine Schriften*, edited by Rudolf Sellheim and Fritz Maass. 6 vols., 2:306-8. Tübingen: Mohr, 1963. [Greece/Rome]

Elderkin, George W. *The First Three Temples at Delphi: Their Religious and Historical Significance.* Princeton: n.p., 1962. [Greece/Rome]

Falkener, Edward. *On the Hypaethron of Greek Temples.* London: Longmans, Green, and Roberts, 1861. [Greece/Rome]

Farnell, Lewis R. *The Cults of the Greek States,* 5 vols. Chicago: Aegaean, 1971. [Greece/Rome]

Fasolo, F., and Gullini, G. *Il sanctuario della Fortuna Primigenia a Palestrina.* Rome: Istituto di Archeologia, 1953. [Greece/Rome]

Faure, Paul. "Nouvelles recherches sur trois sortes de sanctuaries crétois." *BCH* 91 (1967): 114-50. [Greece/Rome]

Faure, Paul. "Sur trois sortes de sanctuaires crétois." *BCH* 93 (1969): 174-213. [Greece/Rome]

Fennelly, James M. "The Temple of Dendur." *SBLSP* 21 (1982): 129-34. [Greece/Rome]

Fischer, M., et al. "The Roman Temple at Kedesh, Upper Galilee: A Preliminary Study." *Tel Aviv* 11 (1984): 146-72. [Greece/Rome]

Fowden, Garth. "Bishops and Temples in the Eastern Roman Empire AD 320-435." *JTS* 29 (1978): 53-78. [Greece/Rome]

Gasparri, Carlo. *Temple of Concord.* Rome: Instituto di studi romani, 1979. [Greece/Rome]

Gawlikowski, Michel. *Le temple palmyrénien.* Warszawa: Editions scientifiques de Pologne, 1973. [Greece/Rome]

Gawlikowski, Michel, and M. Pietrzykiwski. "Les sculptures du temple de Baalshamin à Palmyre." *Syria* 57 (1980): 421-52. [Greece/Rome]

Gebhard, Elizabeth R. "The Early Sanctuary of Poseidon at Isthmia (Corinth, Greece)." *AJA* 91 (July 1987): 475-76. [Greece/Rome]

Gilliam, E. H. *The Archives of the Temple of Soknobraisis at Bacchias.* New Haven: Yale University Press, 1947. [Greece/Rome]

Goldberg, M. Y. "Greek Temples and Chinese Roofs." *AJA* 87 (1983): 305-10. [Greece/Rome]

Gose, Erich. *Der Tempelbezirk des Lenus Mars in Trier.* Berlin: Mann, 1955. [Greece/Rome]

Gregory, T. E. "Julian and the Last Oracle at Delphi." *Greek, Roman, and Byzantine Studies* 24 (1983): 355-66. [Greece/Rome]

Griffiths, Anna H. "Temple Treasures: A Study Based on the Works of Cicero and the Fasti of Ovid." Ph.D. diss., University of Philadelphia, 1943. [Greece/Rome]

Grinnell, Isabel H. *Greek Temples.* New York: Arno, 1943. [Greece/Rome]

Gros, Pierre. *Aurea Templa.* Rome: École française de Rome, 1976. [Greece/Rome]

Gros, Pierre. "Trois temples de la Fortune des Ier et IIe siècles de notre ere: Remarques sur l'origine des sanctuaires romains a abside." *Melita Historia* 79 (1967): 503-66. [Greece/Rome]

Gruben, Gottfried. *Die Tempel der Griechen.* Munich: Hirmer, 1980. [Greece/Rome]

Haegg, R. "Mykenische Kultstätten im archäologischen Material." *Opuscula Atheniensia* 14 (1968): 39-60. [Greece/Rome]

Hagg, Robin, and N. Marinatos, eds. *Sanctuaries and Cults in the Aegean Bronze Age.* Stockholm: Astroms, 1981. [Greece/Rome]

Hambridge, Jay. *The Parthenon and Other Greek Temples: Their Dynamic Symmetry.* New Haven: Yale University Press, 1924. [Greece/Rome]

Hanson, John. A. *Roman Theater Temples.* Westport: Greenwood, 1978. [Greece/Rome]

Hanson, Richard P. C. "Transformation of Pagan Temples into Churches in the Early Christian Centuries." *Journal of Semitic Studies* 23 (1978): 257-67. [Greece/Rome]

Hedrick, Charles. W. "The Temple and Cult of Apollo Patroos in Athens." *AJA* 88 (1984): 247-48 (summary of a presentation); also in *AJA* 92 (1988): 185-210. [Greece/Rome]

Helbig, Konrad. *Tempel Siziliens.* Frankfort: Insel, 1963. [Greece/Rome]

Hellstrom, Pontus. *The Temple of Zeus.* Lund: Aström, 1982. [Greece/Rome]

Henderson, Arthur E. "Temple of Diana." *Records of the Past* 8 (1909): 194-206. [Greece/Rome]

Herbert, Sharon C. "The Orientation of Greek Temples." *PEQ* 116 (1984): 31-34. [Greece/Rome]

Hill, Bert H. *The Temple of Zeus at Nemea.* Princeton: American School of Classical Studies at Athens, 1966. [Greece/Rome]

Hollingshead, Mary B. B. *Legend, Cult, and Architecture at Three Sanctuaries of Artemis.* n.p., n.p., 1980. [Greece/Rome]

Hood, S. "Minoan Town-Shrines." In *Greece and the Eastern Mediterranean in Ancient History and Prehistory. Studies Presented to Fritz Schachermeyr on the Occasion of His 80th Birthday,* edited by K. H. Kinzl. 156-72. Berlin: de Gruyter, 1977. [Greece/Rome]

Hummel, Charles. *Die dorischen Tempel Grossgriechenlands.* Basel: Vineta, 1951. [Greece/Rome]

Hussey, George B. "The Distribution of Hellenic Temples." *AJA* 6 (1890): 59-64. [Greece/Rome]

Isenberg, Sheldon R. "Power through Temple and Torah in Greco-Roman Palestine." In *Christianity, Judaism, and Other Greco-Roman Cults: Studies for Morton Smith at Sixty,* edited by Jacob Neusner. 3 vols., 2:24-52. Leiden: Brill, 1975. [Greece/Rome]

Kähler, Heinz. *Der griechische Tempel: Wesen und Gestalt.* Berlin: Mann, 1964. [Greece/Rome]

Kähler, Heinz. *Der römische Tempel.* Berlin: Mann, 1970. [Greece/Rome]

Koch, Herbert. *Der griechisch-dorische Tempel.* Stuttgart: Metzler, 1951. [Greece/Rome]

Koch, Herbert. *Studien zum Theseustempel in Athen.* Berlin: Akademie, 1955. [Greece/Rome]

Koldewey, Robert. *Die griechischen Tempel in Unteritalien und Sicilien.* Berlin: Asher, 1899. [Greece/Rome]

Krencker, Daniel M. *Römische Tempel in Syrien.* Berlin: de Gruyter, 1938. [Greece/Rome]

Launey, Marcel. *Le sanctuaire et le culte d'Héraklés à Thasos.* Paris: de Boccard, 1944. [Greece/Rome]

Lavas, Georg P. *Altgriechisches Temenos: Baukörper und Raumbildung: Ideogramma der baulichen Gruppenorganisation.* Basel: Birkhäuser, 1974. [Greece/Rome]

Lehmann, Phyllis W. "The Setting of Hellenistic Temples." *Journal of the Society of Architectural Historians* 13/4 (1954): 15-20. [Greece/Rome]

Lugli, G. "Il culto ed i tempi di Apollo in Roma prima di Augusto." *MDAI.R* 58 (1943): 27-47. [Greece/Rome]

MacCulloch, J. A. "Temples." In *Encyclopaedia of Religion and Ethics.* 12:236-46. [Greece/Rome]

Mallwitz, A. "Cella und Adyton des Apollontempels in Bassai." *MDAI.A* 77 (1962): 140-77. [Greece/Rome]

Marquand, Allan. "Temple of Apollo." *Records of the Past* 4 (1905): 1-15. [Greece/Rome]

Martienssen, Rex D. *The Idea of Space in Greek Architecture.* Johannesburg: Witwatersrand University Press, 1958. [Greece/Rome]

Melas, Evi, ed. *Tempel und Stätten der Götter Griechenlands.* Köln: Schauberg, 1970; also in English as *The Greek Experience: A Companion Guide to the Major Architectural Sites and an Introduction to Ancient History and Myth*, edited by Evi Melas and translated by F. Maxwell Brownjohn. New York: Dutton, 1974. [Greece/Rome]

Mertens, Dieter. *Der Tempel von Segesta und die dorische Tempelbaukunst des griechischen Westens in klassischer Zeit.* Mainz: Phillip von Zabern, 1984. [Greece/Rome]

Miller, Stephen G. *The Prytaneion: Its Function and Architectural Form.* Berkeley: University of California Press, 1978. [Greece/Rome]

Muchau, Hermann. *Pfahlhausbau und Griechentempel.* Jena: Costenolbe, 1909. [Greece/Rome]

Mussche, H. F. *Religious Architecture.* Leiden: Brill, 1968. [Greece/Rome]

Norman, Naomi J. *The 'Ionic' Cella: A Preliminary Study of Fourth Century B.C. Temple Architecture.* n.p., n.p., 1980. [Greece/Rome]

Orlandos, Anastasios K. *Les materiaux de construction et la technique architecturale des anciens Grecs.* Paris: de Boccard, 1966-68. [Greece/Rome]

Pallu de Lessert, Augustin C. *De la formule 'Translata de sordentibus locis': trouvée sur des monuments de cherchel.* Paris: Leroux, 1888. [Greece/Rome]

Paribeni, R. *I grandi santuari dell "Antica Grecia."* Milano: Societa editrice "Vita e pensiero," 1947. [Greece/Rome]

Pernier, Luigi. *Il tempio e l'altare di Apollo a Cirene.* Bergamo: Istituto Italiano d'arti grafiche, 1935. [Greece/Rome]

Plommer, W. "The Temple of Poseidon on Cape Sunium: Some Further Questions." *Annual of the British School at Athens* 55 (1960): 218-33. [Greece/Rome]

Powell, B. "The Temple of Apollo at Corinth." *AJA* 9 (1905): 44-63. [Greece/Rome]

Quibell, James E. *Hierakonpolis.* London: Quaritch, 1900-1902. [Greece/Rome]

Reichel, Wolfgang. *Über vorhellenische Götterculte.* Vienna: Hölder, 1897. [Greece/Rome]

Reuther, Oskar. *Der Heratempel von Samos: Der Bau seit der Zeit des Polykrates.* Berlin: Mann, 1957. [Greece/Rome]

Rhodes, Robin F. "Early Corinthian Architecture and the Origins of the Doric Order." *AJA* 91 (July 1987): 477-80. [Greece/Rome]

Richard, Heinrich. *Vom Ursprung des dorischen Tempels.* Bonn: Habelt, 1970. [Greece/Rome]

Riemann, Hans. "Zum griechischen Peripteraltempel; Seine Planidee und ihre Entwicklung bis zum Ende des 5. Jahrhunderts." Ph.D. diss., University of Frankfurt, 1935. [Greece/Rome]

Rigsby, Kent J. "Megara and Tripodiscus." *Greek, Roman, and Byzantine Studies* 28 (Spring 1987): 93-102. [Greece/Rome]

Robertson, Donald. *A Handbook of Greek and Roman Architecture.* Cambridge: Cambridge University Press, 1959. [Greece/Rome]

Rodenwalt, Gerhart. *Die Bildwerke des Artemistempels.* Berlin: n.p., 1949. [Greece/Rome]

Rodenwaldt, Gerhart. *Griechische Tempel.* Munich: Deutscher Kunstverlag, 1951. [Greece/Rome]

Rodwell, Warwick, ed. *Temples, Churches, and Religion.* Oxford: BAR, 1980. [Greece/Rome]

Ruggieri Tricoli, Maria C. *Acropoli e Mito.* Palermo: Flaccovio, 1979. [Greece/Rome]

Salditt-Trappmann, Regina. *Tempel der ägyptischen Götter in Griechenland und an der Westküste Kleinasiens.* Leiden: Brill, 1970. [Greece/Rome]

Schaber, Wilfried. *Die archäischen Tempel der Artemis von Ephesos.* Waldsassen-Bayern: Stiftland-verlag, 1982. [Greece/Rome]

Schlatter, A. "Die Bauten am Tempel in der griechischen Zeit. In *Zur Topographie und Geschichte Palästinas.* 188-202. Stuttgart: Calwer, 1893. [Greece/Rome]

Schleif, Hans. *Der Artemistempel.* Berlin: Mann, 1940. [Greece/Rome]

Scranton, R. L. "Interior Design of Greek Temples." *AJA* 50 (1946): 39-51. [Greece/Rome]

Scully, Vincent J. *The Earth, the Temple, and the Gods: Greek Sacred Architecture.* New Haven: Yale University Press, 1979. [Greece/Rome]

Seigne, Jacques. "Notes préliminaires sur l'évolution architecturale du Sanctuaire de Zeus à Jérash." *Syria* 62 (1985): 162-64. [Greece/Rome]

Seigne, Jacques. "Le sanctuaire de Zeus à Jérash: éléments de chronologie." *Syria* 62 (1985): 287-95. [Greece/Rome]

Seyrig, Henri. *Le Temple de Bel à Palmyre.* 2 vols. Paris: Geuthner, 1975. [Greece/Rome]

Shaw, J. W. "Evidence for the Minoan Tripartite Shrine." *AJA* 82 (1978): 429-48. [Greece/Rome]

Smith, James K. *The Temple of Zeus at Olympia.* Bergamo: n.p., 1924. [Greece/Rome]

Stewart, A. F. "Some Observations on the West Akroteria of the Temple of Asklepios at Epidauros." *AJA* 88 (1984): 261. [Greece/Rome]

Stillwell, R. "The Siting of Classical Greek Temples." *Society of Architectural Historians Journal* 13/4 (1954): 3-8. [Greece/Rome]

Stoll, Heinrich A. *Griechische Tempel.* Leipzig: Köhler and Amelang, 1963. [Greece/Rome]

Suarès, André. *Temples Grecs; Maisons des dieux.* Paris: Dantan, 1937. [Greece/Rome]

Tataki, A. B. *Sounion.* Athens: Ekdotike Athenon, 1978. [Greece/Rome]

Taylor, George. *The Roman Temples of Lebanon.* Beirut: Darel-Mashreq, 1971. [Greece/Rome]

Le Temple: Representations de l'architecture sacrée. Paris: Ministère de la Culture, 1982. [Greece/Rome]

Theuer, Max. *Der griechisch-dorische Peripteral Tempel.* Berlin: Wasmuth, 1918. [Greece/Rome]

Thiersch, H. "Ein altmediterraner Tempeltyp." *ZAW* 50 (1932): 73-86. [Greece/Rome]

Tomlinson, Richard A. *Greek Sanctuaries.* London: Elek, 1976. [Greece/Rome]

Trell, Bluma L. *The Temple of Artemis at Ephesos.* New York: American Numismatic Society, 1945. [Greece/Rome]

Trendelenburg, Adolf. *Der grosse Altar des Zeus in Olympia.* Berlin: Gaertners, 1902. [Greece/Rome]

Van Buren, Elizabeth (Douglas). *Greek Fictile Revêtments in the Archaic Period.* London: Murray, 1926. [Greece/Rome]

Weller, Charles H. *Athens and Its Monuments.* New York: Macmillan, 1913. [Greece/Rome]

Will, Ernest. "Un problème d'*interpretatio graeca*: la pseudo-tribune d'Echmoun à Sidon." *Syria* 62/1-2 (1985): 105-24. [Greece/Rome]

Wolfer-Sulzer, Lucie. *Das geometrische Prinzip der griechischdorischen Tempel.* Winterthur: Vogel, 1939. [Greece/Rome]

Wright, James C. "The Old Temple Terrace at the Argive Heraeum and the Early Cult of Hera in the Argolid." *Journal of Hellenic Studies* 102 (1982): 186-201. [Greece/Rome]

Zinserling, G. "Griechische Tempel als Raumschöpfungen." *Annales archéologiques arabes de Syrie* 21 (1971): 293-300. [Greece/Rome]

Zinserling, G. "Zeus-Tempel zu Olympia und Parthenon zu Athen—Kulttempel?: Ein Beitrag zum Raumproblem griechischer Architektur." *Acta Antiqua* 13 (1965): 41-80. [Greece/Rome]

Temples of Israel and Canaan

Abbott, E. A. "John 11:20." *Classical Review* 8 (1894): 89-93. [Israel/Canaan]

Abbott, Lyman. *The Temple.* New York: Macmillan, 1909. [Israel/Canaan]

Abecassis, A. "Les Pharisiens et le temple." *Le Monde de la Bible* 13 (1980): 39-40. [Israel/Canaan]

Abel, Felix-Marie. "La reconstruction du temple de Jérusalem." In Abel, *Histoire de la Palestine, depuis la conquête d'Alexandre jusqu'à l'invasion arabe.* 2 vols., 1:372-79. Paris: Lecoffre, 1952. [Israel/Canaan]

Abel, Felix-Marie, and G. A. Barrois. "Dédicace d'un temple à Jérusalem." *RB* 40 (1931): 292-94. [Israel/Canaan]

Ackroyd, Peter R. "The Temple Vessels—A Continuity Theme." In *Studies in the Religion of Ancient Israel.* 166-81. Leiden: Brill, 1972. [Israel/Canaan]

Adler, Yankel. "Borders of the Temple Mount" (in Hebrew). *The Spring* 9 (1969): 33-34. [Israel/Canaan]

Adrat, Abraham. "Destruction of the Second Temple" (in Hebrew). Ph.D. diss., Hebrew University, 1984. [Israel/Canaan]

Aharoni, Yohanan. "Arad: Its Inscriptions and Temple." *BA* 31 (1968): 2-32. [Israel/Canaan]

Aharoni, Yohanan. "The Building Activities of David and Solomon." *IEJ* 24 (1974): 13-16. [Israel/Canaan]

Aharoni, Yohanan. "Excavations at Tel Arad." *IEJ* 17 (1967): 247-49. [Israel/Canaan]

Aharoni, Yohanan. "The Horned Altar of Beer-sheba." *BA* 37 (1974): 2-6. [Israel/Canaan]

Aharoni, Yohanan. "The Israelite Sanctuary at Arad." In *New Directions in Biblical Archaeology*, edited by David N. Freedman and Jonas C. Greenfield. 29-36. New York: Doubleday, 1969. [Israel/Canaan]

Aharoni, Yohanan. "Israelite Temples in the Period of the Monarchy." In *Proceedings of the Fifth World Congress of Jewish Studies, 1969*, edited by P. Peli. 69-74. Jerusalem: World Union of Jewish Studies, 1972. [Israel/Canaan]

Aharoni, Yohanan. "Lakhish." *RB* 75 (July 1968): 401-2. [Israel/Canaan]

Aharoni, Yohanan. "The Solomonic Temple, the Tabernacle and the Arad Sanctuary" (in Hebrew; *English summary). *Beer-Sheva* 1 (1973): 79-86, *240-41; also in English in *Orient and Occident: Essays Presented to Cyrus H. Gordon*, edited by Harry A. Hoffner, Jr. 1-8. Neukirchen-Vluyn: Neukirchen, 1973. [Israel/Canaan]

Aharoni, Yohanan. "Temples, Semitic." In *The Interpreter's Dictionary of the Bible*, supp vol., 874-75. [Israel/Canaan]

Aharoni, Yohanan. "Trial Excavation in the 'Solar Shrine' at Lachish: Preliminary Report." *IEJ* 18 (1968): 157-69. [Israel/Canaan]

Ahlström, Gösta W. *Aspects of Syncretism in Israelite Religion*. Lund: Gleerup, 1963. [Israel/Canaan]

Ahlström, Gösta W. *Joel and the Temple Cult of Jerusalem*. Leiden: Brill, 1971. [Israel/Canaan]

Ahlström, Gösta W. "Der Prophet Nathan und der Tempelbau." *VT* 11 (April 1961): 113-27. [Israel/Canaan]

Ahlström, Gösta W. "Some Remarks on Prophet and Cult." In *Transitions in Biblical Scholarship. Essays in Divinity*, edited by J. Coert Rylaarsdam. 113-29. Chicago: University of Chicago Press, 1968. [Israel/Canaan]

Albeck, Hanoch. "The Sanhedrin and Its President" (in Hebrew). *Zion* 8/4 (1943): 165-78. [Israel/Canaan]

Albright, William F. "The Place of the Temple of Solomon in the History of Israelite Religion." In *Archaeology and the Religion of Israel*. 5th ed. 138-50. Garden City: Doubleday, 1969. [Israel/Canaan]

Albright, William F. "Two Cressets from Marisa and the Pillars of Jachin and Boaz." *BASOR* 85 (1942): 18-27. [Israel/Canaan]

Albright, William F., and G. E. Wright. "Comments on Professor Garber's Article." *JBL* 77 (1958): 129-32. [Israel/Canaan]

Alon, Gedalyahu. "The Burning of the Temple." In Alon, *Jews, Judaism, and the Classical World: Studies in Jewish History in the Times of the Second Temple and Talmud*, translated by Israel Abrahams. 252-69. Jerusalem: Magnes, 1977. [Israel/Canaan]

Alt, Albrecht. "Verbreitung und Herkunft des syrischen Tempeltypus." *Palästinajahrbuch* 35 (1939): 83-99. [Israel/Canaan]

Amiot, F. "Temple." In *Dictionary of Biblical Theology*, edited by Xavier Léon-Dufour. 594-97. New York: Seabury, 1973. [Israel/Canaan]

Amiran, Ruth. *Ancient Arad*. Jerusalem: Israel Museum, 1967. [Israel/Canaan]

Amiran, Ruth. "Tel Arad." *RB* 75 (July 1968): 388-92. [Israel/Canaan]

Andersen, F. I. "Who Built the Second Temple?" *Australian Biblical Review* 6/1-4 (1958): 1-35. [Israel/Canaan]

Andrae, Walter. *Das Gotteshaus und die Urformen des Bauens im Alten Orient*. Berlin: Schötz, 1930. [Israel/Canaan]

Arai, Sasagu. "Zum 'Tempelwort' Jesu in Apostelgeschichte 6:14." *NTS* 34 (1988): 397-410. [Israel/Canaan]

Arranz, S. J. Miguel. "La liturgie pénitentielle juive après la déstruction du temple." In *Liturgie et rémission des péchés. Conferences Saint-Serge, Paris, 1973*, edited by A. Pistoia. 39-55. Rome: Edizioni Liturgiche, 1975. [Israel/Canaan]

Artom, Menachem E. "Idee profetiche sul Santuario." *Annuario di Studi Ebraici* 2 (1964): 31-38. [Israel/Canaan]

Asami, S. "The Central Sanctuary in Israel in the Ninth Century B.C." Ph.D. diss., Harvard University, 1965. [Israel/Canaan]

Ashkenazi, Malchiel. *The Dedication of the Temple* (in Hebrew). Jerusalem: Hatchia, 1963. [Israel/Canaan]

Assaf, Simcha. *Sources and Research of Israel through the Ages* (in Hebrew). Jerusalem: Mosad ha-Rav Kook, 1946. [Israel/Canaan]

Aucler, P. "Le Temple de Jérusalem au temps de N.-S. Jésus-Christ: Critique des sources." *RB* 7 (1898): 193-206. [Israel/Canaan]

Audin, A. "Les piliers jumeaux dans le monde sémitique." *Archiv Orientální* 21 (1953): 430-39. [Israel/Canaan]

Auerbach, E. "Die Herkunft der Sadokiden." *ZAW* 49 (1931): 327-28. [Israel/Canaan]

Auerbach, Jacob, and Zvi Kaplan. "Temple-Mount." In *Encyclopaedia Judaica* 15:988-94. [Israel/Canaan]

Avi-Yonah, Michael. "The Facade of Herod's Temple: An Attempted Reconstruction." In *Religions in Antiquity—Essays in Memory of E. R. Goodenough*, edited by Jacob Neusner. 327-35. Leiden: Brill, 1968. [Israel/Canaan]

Avi-Yonah, Michael. "Jérusalem du temps d'Hérode." *Bible et Terre Sainte* 117 (1970): 7-13. [Israel/Canaan]

Avi-Yonah, Michael. "King Herod's Work on the Temple and Temple Mount." In *And to Jerusalem*. 318-24. Jerusalem: Union of Hebrew Writers in Israel, 1968. [Israel/Canaan]

Avi-Yonah, Michael. "Places of Worship in the Roman and Byzantine Periods." *Antiquity and Survival* 2 (1957): 262-72. [Israel/Canaan]

Avi-Yonah, Michael. "Reply to the Article by Joshua Brand" (in Hebrew). *Tarbiz* 29 (1960): 218-21. [Israel/Canaan]

Avi-Yonah, Michael. "The Second Temple" (in Hebrew). In *Sefer Yerushalayim*, edited by M. Avi-Yonah. 392-418. Jerusalem: Bialik Institute, 1956. [Israel/Canaan]

Avi-Yonah, Michael, and Menahem Stern. "Jerusalem: Second Temple Period." In *Encyclopaedia Judaica* 9:1384-405. [Israel/Canaan]

Avigad, Nahman. "The Architecture of Jerusalem in the Second Temple Period" (in Hebrew). *Qadmoniot* 1/1-2 (1968): 28-36; also in English in *Jerusalem*

Revealed: Archaeology in the Holy City, 1968-1974, edited by Yigael Yadin. 14-20. New Haven: Yale University Press, 1976. [Israel/Canaan]

Ayali, Meir. "Gottes und Israels Trauer über die Zerstörung des Tempels." *Kairos* 23 (1981): 215-31. [Israel/Canaan]

Bachmann, Michael. *Jerusalem und der Tempel.* Stuttgart: Kohlhammer, 1980. [Israel/Canaan]

Bacon, Benjamin W. "Among the Sun-Temples of Coele-Syria." *Records of the Past* 5 (1906): 67-83. [Israel/Canaan]

Baer, Y. "Jerusalem in the Times of the Great Revolt (Based on Source Criticism of Josephus and Talmudic-Midrashic Legends of the Temple Destruction)" (in Hebrew; English summary). *Zion* 36 (1971): 127-90. [Israel/Canaan]

Bagatti, Bellarmino. "La posizione del tempio erodiano di Gerusalemme." *Biblica* 46 (1965): 428-44. [Israel/Canaan]

Bagatti, Bellarmino. *Recherches sur le site du temple de Jérusalem, Ier-VIIe siècle.* Jerusalem: Franciscan, 1979. [Israel/Canaan]

Bagatti, Bellarmino. "Il 'Tempio di Gerusalemme' dal II all' VIII secolo." *Biblica* 43 (1962): 1-21. [Israel/Canaan]

Baier, W. "Der zweite Tempel." In *Bibel-Lexikon*, edited by Herbert Haag. 1722-26. Zurich: Benzinger, 1968. [Israel/Canaan]

Baltzer, Klaus. "The Meaning of the Temple in the Lukan Writings." *Harvard Theological Review* 58 (1965): 262-77. [Israel/Canaan]

Bammel, Ernst. "Nicanor and His Gate." *JJS* 7 (1956): 77-78. [Israel/Canaan]

Banvard, John. *The Origin of the Building of Solomon's Temple: An Oriental Tradition.* Boston: Gannett, 1880. [Israel/Canaan]

Barclay, Joseph. *The Talmud, with Illustrations and Plan of the Temple.* London: Murray, 1878. [Israel/Canaan]

Bardtke, H. "Der Tempel von Jerusalem." *Theologische Literaturzeitung* 97 (1972): 801-10. [Israel/Canaan]

Barnard, L. W. "The Testimonium Concerning the Stone in the New Testament and the Epistle of Barnabas." In *Studia Evangelica*, edited by F. L. Cross, vol. 3 of *Papers Presented to the Second International Congress on New Testament Studies, 2: The New Testament Message.* 306-13. Berlin: Akademie-Verlag, 1964. [Israel/Canaan]

Barnard, Will J. *De tempel van Herodes.* Amsterdam: Bijbelwerkplats i.o. Nederlandse Zondagsschool Vereniging, 1972. [Israel/Canaan]

Barnes, W. E. "Joachin and Boaz." *JTS* 5/19 (1904): 447-51. [Israel/Canaan]

Barnett, R. D. "Bringing the God into the Temple." In *Temples and High Places in Biblical Times*, edited by Avraham Biran. 10-20. Jerusalem: Nelson Glueck School of Biblical Archaeology, 1981. [Israel/Canaan]

Barnett, R. D. "Reminiscences of Herod's Temple." *Christian News from Israel* 12/3 (1961): 13-24. [Israel/Canaan]

Barrett, C. K. "The House of Prayer and the Den of Thieves." In *Jesus und Paulus: Festschrift Georg Kümmel,* edited by E. Earle Ellis, 13-20. Göttingen: Vandenhoeck and Ruprecht, 1975. [Israel/Canaan]

Barrois, Georges A. "Cultes et sanctuaires Israélites: Les sanctuaires." In *Manuel d'archéologie biblique,* 2:426-56. Paris: Picard, 1953. [Israel/Canaan]

Barrois, Georges A. *Jesus Christ and the Temple.* Crestwood: St. Vladimir's Seminary, 1980. [Israel/Canaan]

Barrois, Georges A. "Le Temple d'Hérode." In *Manuel d'archéologie biblique,* 1:449-52. Paris: Picard, 1953. [Israel/Canaan]

Bartlett, J. R. "Zadok and His Successors at Jerusalem." *JTS* 19 (1968): 1-18. [Israel/Canaan]

Barton, George A. "Temple." In *The Jewish Encyclopedia* 12:81-101. [Israel/Canaan]

Bar-Yosef, Mordechai. *Jerusalem and the Temple: Past and Present* (in Hebrew). Tel Aviv: Mordechai, 1974. [Israel/Canaan]

Bauer, Johannes B. "Zion's Flüsse, Ps. 45 (46), 5." In *Memoria Jerusalem: Festschrift Franz Sauer zum 70. Geburtstag,* edited by Johannes B. Bauer and Johannes Marböck. 59-91. Graz: Akademische Druck- und Verlagsanstalt, 1977. [Israel/Canaan]

Baumgarten, Joseph M. "The Calendars of the Book of Jubilees and the Temple Scroll." *VT* 37 (January 1987): 71-78. [Israel/Canaan]

Baumgarten, Joseph M. "Exclusions from the Temple: Proselytes and Agrippa I." *JJS* 33 (1982): 215-25. [Israel/Canaan]

Baumgarten, Joseph M. "4Q500 and the Ancient Conception of the Lord's Vineyard." *JJS* 40 (Spring 1989): 1-6. [Israel/Canaan]

Beaucamp, Evode. "Psaume 87: A la Jérusalem nouvelle." *Laval théologique et philosophique* 35 (1979): 279-88. [Israel/Canaan]

Beet, J. A. "Another Solution of Revelation XX-XXII." *ET* 26 (1914-15): 217-20. [Israel/Canaan]

Ben-Dov, Meir. "Daily Life in the Second Temple Period, Public Buildings and Institutions." In *In the Shadow of the Temple: The Discovery of Ancient Jerusalem,* 148-83. Jerusalem: Keter, 1985. [Israel/Canaan]

Ben-Dov, Meir. "Herod's Mighty Temple Mount." *BAR* 12/6 (1986): 40-49. [Israel/Canaan]

Ben-Dov, Meir. "Herod's Monumental Enterprise, The Walls of the Temple Mount, The First Overpass in History, The Gates of the Temple Mount." In *In the Shadow of the Temple: The Discovery of Ancient Jerusalem,* 148-83. Jerusalem: Keter, 1985. [Israel/Canaan]

Ben-Dov, Meir. "Temple of Herod." In *The Interpreter's Dictionary of the Bible,* supp. vol., 870-72. [Israel/Canaan]

Ben-Mordecai, C. A. "The Iniquity of the Sanctuary: A Study of the Hebrew Term ' ʿāwôn.' " *JBL* 60 (1941): 310-14. [Israel/Canaan]

Ben-Shammai, M. H. "The Legends of the Destruction of the Temple among the Paintings of the Dura Synagogue" (in Hebrew). *Bulletin of the Jewish Palestine Exploration Society* 9 (1942): 93-97. [Israel/Canaan]

BenTor, A. "Plans of Dwellings and Temples in Early Bronze Age Palestine" (in Hebrew). *Eretz-Israel* 11 (1975): 92-98. [Israel/Canaan]

Bentzen, Aage. "Zur Geschichte der Sadokiden." *ZAW* 51 (1933): 173-76. [Israel/Canaan]

Ben-Yashar, Menachem. "Noch zum Miqdaš ʾĀdām in 4 Q Florilegium." *Revue de Qumrân* 10 (1981): 587-88. [Israel/Canaan]

Benzinger, Immanuel. *Hebräische Archäologie*. Leipzig: Pfeiffer, 1927; repr. Hildescheim: Olms, 1974. [Israel/Canaan]

Benzinger, Immanuel. "Temple, Temple Service." In *Encyclopaedia Biblica* 4:4923-48, 4956. [Israel/Canaan]

Bergman, J., Helmer Ringgren, and B. Lang. "*zebhach*." In *Theological Dictionary of the Old Testament* 4:8-29. [Israel/Canaan]

Berkovits, E. "From the Temple to Synagogue and Back." *Judaica* 8 (1959): 303-11. [Israel/Canaan]

Berry, G. R. "The Glory of Yahweh and the Temple." *JBL* 56 (1937): 115-17. [Israel/Canaan]

Bertholet, Alfred. "Die fertige Ordnung der künftigen Dinge (Hesekiels Verfassungsentwurf), Cap. 40-48." In *Das Buch Hesekiel*. 195-252. Freiburg: Mohr, 1897. [Israel/Canaan]

Berto, P. "Le temple de Jerusalem." *REJ* 59 (1910): 14-35, 161-87; 60 (1911): 1-23. [Israel/Canaan]

Bertrand, Alexandre. "L'enciente du Haram-Ech-Chérif et le temple de Salomon à Jérusalem." *Revue archéologique* n.s/7 (1863): 12-31. [Israel/Canaan]

Bertrand, Alexandre. "Le Temple de Jérusalem—opinion de M. de Vogüe," *Revue archéologique* n.s./9 (1864): 428-33. [Israel/Canaan]

Betteridge, W. R. "The Builders of the Second Temple." *Bibliotheca Sacra* 53 (1896): 231-49. [Israel/Canaan]

Betz, Otto. "Felsenmann und Felsengemeinde (Eine Paralle zu Mt. 16. 17-19 in den Qumranpsalmen)." *ZNTW* 48 (1957): 49-77. [Israel/Canaan]

Betz, Otto. "Le ministère cultuel dans la secte de Qumrân et dans le Christianisme." In *La secte de Qumrân et les origines du Christianisme*, 4:163-202. Paris: Descelée de Brouwer, 1959. [Israel/Canaan]

Betz, Otto. "The *Temple Scroll* and the Trial of Jesus." *Southwestern Journal of Theology* 30 (Summer 1988): 5-8. [Israel/Canaan]

Beuker, W. A. M. "God's Presence in Salem: A Study of Psalm 76." In *Loven en geloven* (Festschrift N. H. Ridderbos), edited by A. Ridderbos-Boersma. 135-50. Amsterdam: Ton Bolland, 1975. [Israel/Canaan]

Bewer, J. A. "Vision of the New Jerusalem." In *The Prophets. Harper's Annotated Bible Series*, 438-67. New York: Harper and Brothers, 1949. [Israel/Canaan]

Bezzant, Reginald, and Reginald Poole-Pridham. *The Promise of Ezekiel's City*. Norwich: Jarrold and Sons, 1952. [Israel/Canaan]

Bialik, C. N., and Y. H. Ravnitzki. "The Second Temple—Its Structure and Services," and "The Destruction of the Second Temple" (in Hebrew). In *The Book of Legends*. 120-42. Tel Aviv: Dvir, 1955. [Israel/Canaan]

Biberfeld, Pinhas. "The Chosen House" (in Hebrew). In *Yad Shaul—Memorial Volume for S. Weingort.* 193-211. Tel Aviv: Ha-Merkaz, 1943. [Israel/Canaan]

Bic, M. "Betel—le sanctuaire du roi." *Archiv Orientální* 17 (1949): 46-63. [Israel/Canaan]

Bickerman, Elias J. "Héliodore au temple de Jérusalem." In *Studies in Jewish and Christian History*. 3 vols., 2:159-91. Leiden: Brill, 1980. [Israel/Canaan]

Bickerman, Elias J. (Bikerman, Elie). "Une proclamation seleucide relative au temple de Jerusalem." *Syria* 25 (1946-48): 67-85. [Israel/Canaan]

Bickerman, Elias J. "The Warning Inscriptions of Herod's Temple." *JQR* 37 (April 1947): 387-405. [Israel/Canaan]

Biguzzi, Giancarlo. "Mc 14, 58: Un tempio archeiropoiētos," *Rivista Biblica* 26 (1978): 225-40. [Israel/Canaan]

Bilde, Per. "The Roman Emperor Gaius (Caligula)'s Attempt to Erect His Statue in the Temple of Jerusalem." *Studia Theologica* 32 (1978): 67-93. [Israel/Canaan]

Billerbeck, P. "Ein Tempelgottesdienst in Jesu Tagen." *ZNTW* 55/1-2 (1964): 1-17. [Israel/Canaan]

Biran, Avraham. "An Israelite Horned Altar at Dan." *BA* 37 (1974): 106-7. [Israel/Canaan]

Biran, Avraham. "The Temenos at Dan" (in Hebrew; *English summary). *Eretz-Israel* 16 (1982): 15-43, *252-53. [Israel/Canaan]

Birch, W. F. "The Levelling of the Akra." *PEFQ* 35 (1903): 353-55. [Israel/Canaan]

Blanchetière, F. "Julien Philhèllene, Philosémite, Antichrétien: L'affaire du Temple de Jerusalem." *JJS* 31 (1980): 61-81. [Israel/Canaan]

Blum, Felix. *Le Sanhédrin ou Grand Conseil de Jérusalem*. Strassbourg: Dumont-Schauberg, 1889. [Israel/Canaan]

Bobichon, M. "Du temple au cénacle." *Bible et Terre Sainte* 98 (1968): 2-5. [Israel/Canaan]

Bockel, P. "Jésus et le Temple: Il parlait du sanctuaire de son corps." *Bible et Terre Sainte* 122 (1970): 16-18. [Israel/Canaan]

Boling, R. G. "Bronze Age Buildings at the Shechem High Place." *BA* 32 (1969): 82-103. [Israel/Canaan]

Boswell, R. B. "Destroying and Rebuilding the Temple." *ET* 26 (1914-15): 140-41. [Israel/Canaan]

Bowman, J. "Temple and Festivals in the Persian Diatessaron." In *In Memoriam Paul Kahle*, edited by Matthew Black and Georg Fohrer. 53-61. Berlin: Töpelmann, 1968. [Israel/Canaan]

Box, G. H. "The Temple Service." In *Encyclopaedia Biblica* 4:4948-56. [Israel/Canaan]

Brand, Joshua. "The Gates of Nicanor (a Contribution to Talmudic Archeology)" (in Hebrew). In *Minchah li-Yehudah* (Festchrift J. L. Zlotnik), edited by S. Assaf et al. 5-14. Jerusalem: Mossad Harav Kook, 1950. [Israel/Canaan]

Brand, Joshua. "Remarks on the Temple of Solomon" (in Hebrew). *Tarbiz* 34 (1964-65): 323-32. [Israel/Canaan]

Brand, Joshua. "Some Remarks on the Second Temple Edifice" (in Hebrew). *Tarbiz* 29 (1960): 210-17. [Israel/Canaan]

Brandon, Samuel G. F. *The Fall of Jerusalem and the Christian Church*. London: SPCK, 1957. [Israel/Canaan]

Braun, F.-M. "L'expulsion des vendeurs du Temple (Mat., XXI, 12-17, 23-27, Mc., XI, 15-19, 27-33; Lc. XIX, 45-XX, 8; Jo., II, 13-22)." *RB* 38 (1929): 178-200. [Israel/Canaan]

Braun, R. L. "The Message of Chronicles: Rally 'Round the Temple." *Concordia Theological Monthly* 42 (1971): 502-14. [Israel/Canaan]

Braun, R. L. "Solomon, the Chosen Temple Builder." *JBL* 95 (1976): 581-90. [Israel/Canaan]

Briend, Jacques. "Le Temple d' Hérode le Grand." *Le Monde de la Bible* 13 (1930): 12-13. [Israel/Canaan]

Bright, J. "The Restoration of the Jewish Community in Palestine, The Completion of the Temple." In *A History of Israel*, 3d ed. 360-72. Philadelphia: Westminster, 1981. [Israel/Canaan]

Brin, Gershon. "Concerning Some of the Uses of the Bible in the *Temple Scroll.*" *Revue de Qumran* 12 (November 1987): 519-28. [Israel/Canaan]

Brinker, R. *The Influence of Sanctuaries in Early Israel*. Manchester: Manchester University Press, 1946. [Israel/Canaan]

Brock, Sebastian. "The Rebuilding of the Temple under Julian: A New Source." *PEQ* 108 (1976): 103-7. [Israel/Canaan]

Brodie, L. T. "A New Temple and a New Law: The Unity and Chronicler-Based Nature of Luke 1:1-4: 22a." *Journal for the Study of the New Testament* 5 (1979): 21-45. [Israel/Canaan]

Broshi, M. "The Gigantic Dimensions of the Visionary Temple in the Temple Scroll." *BAR* 13/6 (1987): 36-37. [Israel/Canaan]

Broshi, M. "The Role of the Temple in the Herodian Economy." *JJS* 38 (Spring 1987): 31-37. [Israel/Canaan]

Brousseau, Gerald B. "The Source and Development of High Place Worship (Bamah) of Israel." Ph.D. diss., Ludwig Maximilian University, Munich, 1968. [Israel/Canaan]

Brown, D. "The Veil of the Temple Rent in Twain from the Top to the Bottom." *Expositor* 5 (1895): 158-60. [Israel/Canaan]

Bruce, F. F. "New Wine in Old Wine Skins: 3. The Corner Stone." *ET* 84 (1972-73): 231-35. [Israel/Canaan]

Brueggemann, Walter A. "Presence of God, Cultic." In *The Interpreter's Dictionary of the Bible*, supp. vol., 680-83. [Israel/Canaan]

Bruston, C. "L'inscription des deux colonnes du temple de Salomon." *ZAW* 42 (1924): 153-54. [Israel/Canaan]

Buchanan, George W. "Mark 11:15-19: Brigands in the Temple." *HUCA* 30 (1959): 169-77; 31 (1960): 103-5. [Israel/Canaan]

Büchler, Adolph. "The Fore-Court of Women and the Brass Gate in the Temple of Jerusalem." *JQR* 10 (1898): 678-718. [Israel/Canaan]

Büchler, Adolph. "The Nicanor Gate and the Brass Gate." *JQR* 11 (1899): 46-63. [Israel/Canaan]

Büchler, Adolph. "On the History of the Temple Worship in Jerusalem." In *Studies in Jewish History—The Adolph Büchler Memorial Volume*, edited by I. Brodie and J. Rabbinowitz. 24-63. London: Oxford University Press, 1956. [Israel/Canaan]

Büchler, Adolph. *Die Priester und der Cultus im letzten Jahrzehnt des jerusalemischen Tempels.* Vienna: Israel-Theologische Lehranstalt, 1895. [Israel/Canaan]

Büchler, Adolph. *Das Synedrion in Jerusalem und das grosse Beth-Din in der Quaderkammer des jerusalemischen Tempels.* Vienna: Israelitisch-Theologische Lehranstalt, 1902; reprinted in English as *The Sanhedrin in Jerusalem.* Jerusalem: Mossad Harav Kook, 1974. [Israel/Canaan]

Büchler, Adolph. "The Visits of Gentiles to the Temple." *JQR* 17 (1926-27): 31-38. [Israel/Canaan]

Büchler, Adolph. "Zur Geschichte der Tempelmusik und der Tempelpsalmen." *ZAW* 19 (1899): 96-133, 329-44; 20 (1900): 97-135. [Israel/Canaan]

Budde, K. "Das Deuteronomium und die Reform König Josias." *ZAW* 44 (1926): 177-224. [Israel/Canaan]

Budde, K. "Die Herkunft Ṣadok's." *ZAW* 52 (1934): 42-50. [Israel/Canaan]

Budde, K. "Die ursprüngliche Bedeutung Lade Jahwes." *ZAW* 21 (1901): 193-97. [Israel/Canaan]

Budde, K. "War die Lade Jahwes ein leerer Thron?" *Theologische Studien und Kritiken* 79 (1906): 489-507. [Israel/Canaan]

Buis, Pierre. "Écriture et prédication. 31-Le Seigneur libère et hommes: Psaume 76." *Études théologiques et religieuses* 55 (1980): 412-15. [Israel/Canaan]

Buis, Pierre. "Écriture et prédication. 43-Jérusalem, un chaudron rouillé. Ez. 24/3-14." *Études théologiques et religieuses* 56 (1981): 446-48. [Israel/Canaan]

Bull, R. J. "The Excavation of Tell er-Ras on Mt. Gerizim." *Biblical Archaeology* 31 (1968): 58-72. [Israel/Canaan]

Bull, R. J. "A Re-examination of the Shechem Temple." *BA* 23 (1960): 110-19. [Israel/Canaan]

Bultmann, R. "Die Frage nach der Echtheit von Mt. 16, 17-19." *Theologische Blätter* 20 (1941): 265-79. [Israel/Canaan]

Burch, V. "The 'Stone' and the 'Keys' (Mt. 16:18f)." *JBL* 52 (1933): 147-52. [Israel/Canaan]

Burdajewicz, M. "A propos des temples philistins de Qasileh." *RB* 93 (April 1986): 222-35. [Israel/Canaan]

Burkitt, F. C. "The Cleansing of the Temple." *JTS* 25 (1923-24): 386-90. [Israel/Canaan]

Buse, I. "The Cleansing of the Temple in the Synoptics and in John." *ET* 70 (1958): 22-24. [Israel/Canaan]

Busink, Th. A. "Les Origines du Temple de Solomon." *Ex Oriente Lux: Jaarbericht van het vooraziatisch-egyptisch Gezelschap* 17 (1963): 165-92. [Israel/Canaan]

Busink, Th. A. *Der Tempel von Jerusalem*, 2 vols. Leiden: Brill, 1970-80. [Israel/Canaan]

Busse, H. "Die arabischen Inschriften im und am Felsendom in Jerusalem." *Das heilige Land* 109/1-2 (1977): 8-24. [Israel/Canaan]

Caird, G. B. "The Mind of Christ, Christ's Attitude to Institutions: The Temple." *ET* 62 (1950-51): 259-61. [Israel/Canaan]

Caldecott, A. "The Significance of the Cleansing of the Temple." *JTS* 24 (1923): 382-86. [Israel/Canaan]

Caldecott, W. (William) Shaw. *Herod's Temple: Its New Testament Associations and Its Actual Structure.* Philadelphia: Union, [1914?]. [Israel/Canaan]

Caldecott, W. (William) Shaw. *The Second Temple in Jerusalem: Its History and Its Structure.* London: Murray, 1908. [Israel/Canaan]

Caldecott, W. (William) Shaw. *Solomon's Temple: Its History and Its Structure.* Philadelphia: Union, 1907. [Israel/Canaan]

Caldecott, W. (William) Shaw. "The Temple Spoils Represented on the Arch of Titus." *PEFQ* 38 (1906): 306-15. [Israel/Canaan]

Caldecott, W. (William) Shaw, and J. Orr. "The Temple of Herod." In *The International Standard Bible Encyclopaedia*, edited by J. Orr. 5:2937-40. Michigan: Eerdmans, 1955. [Israel/Canaan]

Callaway, Phillip. "Exegetische Erwägungen zur Tempelrolle XXIX, 7-10." *Revue de Qumran* 12 (1985): 95-104. [Israel/Canaan]

Callaway, Phillip. "*ʾRbyh* in the Temple Scroll 24, 8." *Revue de Qumran* 12 (1986): 269-70. [Israel/Canaan]

Callaway, Phillip. "Source Criticism of the Temple Scroll: The Purity Laws." *Revue de Qumran* 12 (1986): 213-22. [Israel/Canaan]

Campbell, Anthony F. "Yahweh and the Ark: A Case Study in Narrative." *Journal of Biblical Literature* 98 (1979): 31-43. [Israel/Canaan]

Campbell, Edward F. "Jewish Shrines of the Hellenistic and Persian Periods." In *Symposia*, edited by Frank M. Cross. 159-67. Cambridge: American Schools of Oriental Research, 1979. [Israel/Canaan]

Campbell, Edward F., and G. Wright. "Tribal League Shrines in Amman and Shechem." *BA* 32 (1969): 104-16. [Israel/Canaan]

Campbell, K. M. "The New Jerusalem in Matthew 5:14." *Scottish Journal of Theology* 31 (1978): 335-63. [Israel/Canaan]

Capt, E. Raymond. *King Solomon's Temple*. Thousand Oaks: Artisan Sales, 1979. [Israel/Canaan]

Caquot, André. "Le Psaume 47 et la royauté de Yahwe." *Revue d'histoire et de philosophie religieuses* 39 (1959): 311-37. [Israel/Canaan]

Caquot, André. "Le Rouleau du Temple de Qumrân." *Etudes théologiques et religieuses* 53 (1978): 443-50. [Israel/Canaan]

Carreira, José N. *A plano e a arquitectura do Templo de Salomão à Luz dos paralelos orientais*. Porto: Livraria Tavares Martins, 1969. [Israel/Canaan]

Casalegno, Alberto. *Gesù e il Tempio: Studio redazionale di Luca-Atti*. Brescia: Morcelliana, 1984. [Israel/Canaan]

Cases, Moses ben Samuel. *Beʾur ʿal masekhet Middot*. Jerusalem: Hatchiya, 1963. [Israel/Canaan]

Castelot, John J. "Religious Institutions of Israel." In *The Jerome Biblical Commentary*, edited by R. E. Brown, J. A. Fitzmyer, and R. E. Murphy. 703-35. Englewood Cliffs, NJ: Prentice-Hall, 1968. [Israel/Canaan]

Caubet-Iturbe, J. "Jerusalén y el Templo del Señor en los manuscriptos de Qumran y en el Nuevo Testamento." *Sacra Pagina: Miscellanea Biblica Congressus Internationalis Catholici de Re Biblica*, edited by J. Coppens, A. Descamps, and E. Massaux. 2 vols. 28-46. Paris: Gabalda, 1959. [Israel/Canaan]

Causse, Antonin. "De la Jérusalem terrestre à la Jérusalem céleste." *Revue d'histoire et de philosophie religieuses* 27 (1947): 12-36. [Israel/Canaan]

Causse, Antonin. *La vision de la Nouvelle Jérusalem*. Gembloux: n.p., 1939. [Israel/Canaan]

Cazelles, Henri. "Le Temple de Salomon." *Le Monde de la Bible* 13 (1980): 6-7. [Israel/Canaan]

Chance, James B. "Jerusalem and the Temple in Lucan Eschatology." Ph.D. diss., Duke University, 1984. [Israel/Canaan]

Chaplin, T. "The Stone of Foundation and the Site of the Temple." *PEQ* 8 (1876): 23-28. [Israel/Canaan]

Charles, R. H. "A Solution of the Chief Difficulties in Revelation XX-XXII." *ET* 26 (1914-15): 54-57, 119-23. [Israel/Canaan]

Chary, T. "Le Temple d'Ezéchiel." *Le Monde de la Bible* 40 (1985): 34-38. [Israel/Canaan]

Chavel, C. B. "An Additional Surname for the Sanctuary in Jerusalem" (in Hebrew). *Hadorom* 38 (1974): 45-46. [Israel/Canaan]

Cheetham, F. P. "Destroy This Temple and in Three Days I Will Raise It Up (St. John ii, 19)." *JTS* 24 (1922-23): 315-17. [Israel/Canaan]

Chen, Doron. "The Design of the Dome of the Rock in Jerusalem." *PEQ* 112 (1980): 41-50. [Israel/Canaan]

Chipiez, Charles. *Le Temple de Jérusalem et la Maison du Bois-Liban restitués d'après Ézéchiel et le livre des Rois.* Paris: Hachette, 1889. [Israel/Canaan]

Chopineau, J. "Les prophètes et le temple." *Le Monde de la Bible* 13 (1980): 10-13. [Israel/Canaan]

Chronis, H. L. "The Torn Veil: Cultus and Christology in Mark 15:37-39." *JBL* 101 (March 1982): 97-114. [Israel/Canaan]

Clark, K. W. "Worship in the Jerusalem Temple after A.D. 70." *NTS* 6 (1960): 269-80. [Israel/Canaan]

Clements, Ronald E. "Deuteronomy and the Jerusalem Cult-Tradition." *VT* 15 (1965): 300-12. [Israel/Canaan]

Clements, Ronald E. "Temple and Land." *GUOST* 19 (1961/1962): 16-28. [Israel/Canaan]

Clermont-Ganneau, Charles. "Archaeological and Epigraphic Notes on Palestine: The 'Gate of Nicanor' in the Temple of Jerusalem." *PEQ* 35 (1903): 125-31. [Israel/Canaan]

Clermont-Ganneau, Charles. "A Column of Herod's Temple." In *Archaeological Researches in Palestine during the Years 1873-1874*, translated by Aubrey Stewart. 1:254-58. London: Palestine Exploration Fund, 1896. [Israel/Canaan]

Clermont-Ganneau, Charles. "Découverte à Jérusalem d'une synagogue de l'époque hérodienne." *Syria* 1 (1920): 190-97. [Israel/Canaan]

Clermont-Ganneau, Charles. "Discovery of a Tableau from Herod's Temple." *PEFQ* 3 (1871): 132-33. [Israel/Canaan]

Clermont-Ganneau, Charles. "La fausse stèle du Temple de Jérusalem." In Clermont-Ganneau, *Les fraudes archéologiques en Palestine*. 39-48. Paris: Leroux, 1885. [Israel/Canaan]

Clermont-Ganneau, Charles. "La Porte de Nicanor du temple de Jérusalem." *Recueil d'archeologie orientale* 5 (1903): 334-40. [Israel/Canaan]

Clermont-Ganneau, Charles. "The Statue of Hadrian Placed in the Temple of Jerusalem." *PEFQ* (1874): 207-10. [Israel/Canaan]

Clermont-Ganneau, Charles. "Une stèle du Temple de Jérusalem." *Revue archéologique* n.s./23 (1872): 214-34, 290-96. [Israel/Canaan]

Clermont-Ganneau, Charles. "The Veil of the Temple." In *The Survey of Western Palestine*, edited by C. Warren and C. R. Conder. 9 vols., 5:340-41. London: Palestine Exploration Fund, 1881-89. [Israel/Canaan]

Clermont-Ganneau, Charles. "The Veil of the Temple of Jerusalem at Olympia." *PEFQ* 10 (1878): 79-81. [Israel/Canaan]

Clermont-Ganneau, Charles, and C. Warren. "*Aven Hash-Sheteyah*." *PEFQ* 7 (1875): 182-83. [Israel/Canaan]

Clifford, Richard J. "The Temple in the Ugaritic Myth of Baal." In *Symposia*, edited by Frank M. Cross. 137-45. Cambridge: American Schools of Oriental Research, 1979. [Israel/Canaan]

Clowney, E. P. "The Final Temple." *Westminster Theological Journal* 35 (1973): 156-89. [Israel/Canaan]

Cody, Aelred. *Heavenly Sanctuary and Liturgy in the Epistle to the Hebrews*. St. Meinrad, IN: Grail, 1960. [Israel/Canaan]

Cohen, J. "Les pélerinages au Temple de Jérusalem." *Le Monde de la Bible* 13 (1980): 29-32. [Israel/Canaan]

Cohen, Shaye J. D. "The Temple and the Synagogue." In *The Temple in Antiquity*, edited by Truman G. Madsen. 151-74. Provo: Brigham Young University Press, 1984. [Israel/Canaan]

Cohn, Erich W. "Second Thoughts about the Perforated Stone on the Haram of Jerusalem." *PEQ* 114 (1982): 143-46. [Israel/Canaan]

Cohn-Wiener, Ernst. "Der Tempel des Herodes." In Cohn-Wiener, *Die jüdische Kunst, ihre Geschichte von den Anfängen bis zur Gegenwart*. 71-75. Berlin: Wasservogel, 1929. [Israel/Canaan]

Cole, Harold F. G. *Concerning Solomon's Temple*. London: Roberts, 1920. [Israel/Canaan]

Cole, Robert A. *The New Temple: A Study in the Origins of the Catechetical 'Form' of the Church in the New Testament*. London: Tyndale, 1950. [Israel/Canaan]

Collins, Alvin O. "The Significance of the Temple in the Religion of the Canonical Prophets." Ph.D. diss., Southern Baptist Theological Seminary, 1952. [Israel/Canaan]

Comblin, J. "La liturgie de la Nouvelle Jérusalem (Apoc. XXI, 1-XXII, 5)." *Ephemerides theologicae lovanienses* 29 (1953): 15-40. [Israel/Canaan]

Conder, Claude R. "Age of the Temple Wall: Pilasters of the West Haram Wall." *PEQ* 9 (1877): 135-37. [Israel/Canaan]

Conder, Claude R. "Herod's Temple." In *The City of Jerusalem*. 123-32. London: Murray, 1909. [Israel/Canaan]

Conder, Claude R. "The High Sanctuary of Jerusalem." *Transactions of the Royal Institute of British Architects* (1879): 25-60. [Israel/Canaan]

Conder, Claude R. "The Temple and Calvary." In *Tent Work in Palestine—A Record Discovery and Adventure*. 1:346-76. London: Bentley, 1879. [Israel/Canaan]

Congar, Yves M. *The Mystery of the Temple*. Westminster: Newman, 1962. [Israel/Canaan]

Cook, S. A. "The Synagogue of Theodotus at Jerusalem." *PEFQ* 53 (1921): 22-23. [Israel/Canaan]

Cooke, F. A. "The Cleansing of the Temple." *ET* 63/10 (1952): 321-22. [Israel/Canaan]

Cooke, George A. "Some Considerations on the Text and Teaching of Ezekiel 40-48." *ZAW* 42 (1924): 105-15. [Israel/Canaan]

Cooke, George A. "The Temple and the Community of the Future." In *A Critical and Exegetical Commentary on the Book of Ezekiel*. 425-541. Edinburgh: Clark, 1936. [Israel/Canaan]

Coppens, J. "The Spiritual Temple in the Pauline Letters and Its Background." *Studia Evangelica* 6 (1973): 53-66. [Israel/Canaan]

Corbett, S. "Some Observations on the Gateways to the Herodian Temple in Jerusalem." *PEQ* 84 (1952): 7-14. [Israel/Canaan]

Cornfeld, Gaalyahu. *Bet ha-Mikdash Tamun mi-Darom le-Khipat ha-Sela'*. Tel Aviv: Cornfeld, 1985/1987. [Israel/Canaan]

Cornfeld, Gaalyahu, ed. "Description of the Temple." In Josephus, *The Jewish War*, contributing editors Benjamin Mazar and Paul Maier. 346-64. Grand Rapids: Zondervan, 1982. [Israel/Canaan]

Cothenet, E. "Attitude de l'église naissante à l'égard du Temple de Jérusalem." In *Liturgie et l'église particulière et liturgie de l'église universelle. Conférences Saint-Serge XXIIe Semaine d'Études Liturgiques, Paris, 1975*, edited by A. Pistoia and A. M. Triacca. 89-111. Rome: Edizioni Liturgiche, 1977. [Israel/Canaan]

Couroyer, B. "Le temple de Yaho et l'orientation dans les papyrus araméens d'Éléphantine." *RB* 68 (1961): 525-40; 75 (January 1968): 80-85. [Israel/Canaan]

Cullmann, Oscar. "A New Approach to the Interpretation of the Fourth Gospel." *ET* 71 (1959): 8-12, 39-43. [Israel/Canaan]

Cullmann, Oscar. "L'opposition contre le Temple de Jérusalem, motif commun de la théologie Johannique et du monde ambiant." *NTS* 5 (1958-59): 157-73. [Israel/Canaan]

Dalmais, I. H. "Le souvenir du Temple dans la liturgie chrétienne." *Bible et Terre Sainte* 122 (1970): 6-7. [Israel/Canaan]

Dalman, Gustaf. "Der Felsen als Fundament des Altars." In *Neue Petra-Forschungen und der heilige Felsen von Jerusalem*, edited by Gustaf Dalman. 137-45. Leipzig: Hinrichs, 1912. [Israel/Canaan]

Dalman, Gustaf. "Der östliche Stadthügel." In Dalman, *Jerusalem und sein Gelände*. 112-38. Hildesheim: Olms, 1972. [Israel/Canaan]

Dalman, Gustaf. "The Search for the Temple Treasure at Jerusalem." *PEQ* 44 (1912): 35-39. [Israel/Canaan]

Dalman, Gustaf. "Der zweite Tempel zu Jerusalem." *Palästinajahrbuch* 5 (1909): 29-57. [Israel/Canaan]

Daniélou, Jean. *Le Signe du Temple*. Paris: Gallimard, 1942. [Israel/Canaan]

Daniélou, Jean. "La symbolique du temple de Jérusalem chez Philon et Josèphe." In *Le symbolisme cosmique des monuments religieux*. 83-90. Rome: Istituto Italiano par il Medio ed Estremo Oriente, 1957. [Israel/Canaan]

Davey, C. J. "Temples of the Levant and the Buildings of Solomon." *Tyndale Bulletin* 31 (1980): 107-46. [Israel/Canaan]

Davies, G. Henton. "Presence of God." In *The Interpreter's Dictionary of the Bible* 3:874-75. [Israel/Canaan]

Davies, P. R. "The Ideology of the Temple in the Damascus Document." *JJS* 33/1-2 (1982): 287-301. [Israel/Canaan]

Davies, T. W. "Temple." In *Dictionary of the Bible* 4:695-716. [Israel/Canaan]

Davies, William D. *The Gospel and the Land: Early Christianity and Jewish Territorial Doctrine*. Los Angeles: University of California Press, 1974. [Israel/Canaan]

Davies, William D. "Jerusalem et la terre dans la tradition chretienne." *Revue de l'histoire et de philosophie religieuses* 55 (1975): 491-533. [Israel/Canaan]

Dawsey, J. M. "Confrontation in the Temple (Luke 19:45–20:47)." *Perspectives in Religious Studies* 11 (1984): 153-65. [Israel/Canaan]

de Groot, J. *Die Altäre des salomonischen Tempelhofes: Beiträge zur Wissenschaft vom alten Testament*. Stuttgart: Kohlhammer, 1924. [Israel/Canaan]

de Jonge, M. "Het motief van het gescheurde voorhangsel van der Tempel in een aantal vroegchristlijke geschriften." *Nederlands Theologisch Tijdschrift* 22 (1967): 257-76. [Israel/Canaan]

Del Alamo, M. "Las medidas de la Jerusalem celeste (Apoc. 21, 16)." *Cultura biblica* 3 (1946): 136-38. [Israel/Canaan]

de Langhe, R. "L'autel d'or du Temple de Jérusalem." *Biblica* 40 (1959): 476-94. [Israel/Canaan]

Delcor, Mathias. "Reflexions sur la fête de la xylophorie dans le *Rouleau du Temple* et les textes parallèles." *Revue de Qumran* 12 (November 1987): 561-69. [Israel/Canaan]

Delcor, Mathias. "Le statut du roi d'après le Rouleau du Temple." *Henoch* 3 (1981): 47-68. [Israel/Canaan]

Delcor, Mathias. "Le temple d'Onias en Égypte." *RB* 75 (1968): 188-203, with Post-Scriptum by Roland de Vaux, 204-5. [Israel/Canaan]

Delcor, Mathias. "Le trésor de la maison de Yahweh des origines à l'exil." *VT* 12 (1962): 353-77. [Israel/Canaan]

Delekat, Lienhard. *Asylie und Schutzorakel am Zionheiligtum*. Leiden: Brill, 1967. [Israel/Canaan]

de Moor, F. "Le temple reconstruit par Zorobabel." *Le Muséon* 8 (1889): 364-371, 467-73, 514-51; 9 (1890): 5-15. [Israel/Canaan]

Demsky, A. "When the Priests Trumpeted the Onset of the Sabbath: A Monumental Hebrew Inscription from the Ancient Temple Mount Recalls the Sacred Signal." *BAR* 12/6 (1986): 50-52. [Israel/Canaan]

Derenbourg, J. "Une stèle du Temple d'Hérode." *Journal Asiatique* 6 (1872): 178-95. [Israel/Canaan]

Derfler, Steven. "A Terracotta Figurine from the Hellenistic Temple at Tel Beer-sheba." *IEJ* 31 (1981): 97-99. [Israel/Canaan]

Derrett, J. Duncan M. "No Stone upon Another: Leprosy and the Temple." *Journal for the Study of the New Testament* 30 (1987): 3-20. [Israel/Canaan]

Derrett, J. Duncan M. "The Zeal of the House and the Cleansing of the Temple." *Downside Review* 95/319 (1977): 79-94. [Israel/Canaan]

de Salignac Fénelon, F. "Note on the Site of the Temple." *PEFQ* 31 (1899): 272. [Israel/Canaan]

Dever, William G. "Monumental Architecture in Ancient Israel in the Period of the United Monarchy." In *Studies in the Period of David and Solomon*, edited by T. Ishida. 269-306. Winona Lake, IN: Eisenbrauns, 1982. [Israel/Canaan]

de Vogüe, M. "Note sur le temple de Jérusalem." *Revue archéologique* n.s./7 (1863): 281-92. [Israel/Canaan]

de Young, James C. *Jerusalem in the New Testament: The Significance of the City in the History of Redemption and in Eschatology*. Kampen: Kok, 1960. [Israel/Canaan]

Diebner, B. "Die Orientierung des Jerusalemer Tempels und die 'Sacred Direction' der frühchristlichen Kirchen." *ZDPV* 87 (1971): 153-66. [Israel/Canaan]

Dieulafoy, M. "Le rythme modulaire du temple de Salomon." *Comptes rendus des séances de l'Académie des Inscriptions et Belles Lettres* (1913): 332-47. [Israel/Canaan]

Dion, P. E. "Early Evidence for the Ritual Significance of the "Base of the Altar." *JBL* 106 (1987): 487-90. [Israel/Canaan]

Doeve, J. W. "Le domaine du temple de Jérusalem." In *La Littérature Juive entre Tenach et Mischna*, edited by Willem C. Van Unnik. 9:118-63. Leiden: Brill, 1974. [Israel/Canaan]

Doll, Mary A. "The Temple: Symbolic Form in Scripture." *Soundings: An Interdisciplinary Journal* 70 (Spring-Summer 1987): 145-54. [Israel/Canaan]

Donner, Herbert. "Der Felsen und der Tempel." *ZDPV* 93 (1977): 1-11. [Israel/Canaan]

Doran, Robert. *Temple Propaganda: The Purpose and Character of 2 Maccabees.* Washington, D.C.: Catholic Bilbical Association of America, 1981. [Israel/Canaan]

Doran, Robert. "*T Mos* 4:8 and the Second Temple." *JBL* 106 (1987): 491-92. [Israel/Canaan]

Dothan, Trude, and Seymour Gitin. "Khirbet el-Muqannah (Migné-Ekrôn) 1985-1986." *RB* 95 (April 1988): 228-39. [Israel/Canaan]

Douglas, G. C. M. "Ezekiel's Temple." *ET* 9 (1897-98): 365-67, 420-22, 468-70, 515-18. [Israel/Canaan]

Douglas, G. C. M. "Ezekiel's Vision of the Temple." *ET* 14 (1902-3): 365-68; 424-27. [Israel/Canaan]

Doumato, Lamia. *The Temple Ruins of Baalbek.* Monticello: Vance Bibliographies, 1979. [Israel/Canaan]

Dowda, Robert E. "The Cleansing of the Temple in the Synoptic Gospels." Ph.D. diss., Duke University, 1972. [Israel/Canaan]

Dubarle, André-Marie. "Le signe du Temple (Jo ii, 19)." *RB* 48 (1939): 21-44. [Israel/Canaan]

Du Brul, P. "Jerusalem in the Apocalypse of John." In *Jerusalem: Seat of Theology. Yearbook of the Ecumenical Institute for Theological Research*, edited by D. Burrell, P. Du Brul, and W. Dalton. 55-77. Tantur, Jerusalem: Ecumenical Institute for Theological Research, 1982. [Israel/Canaan]

Du Buit, M. "Les rochers se fendirent." *Bible et Terre Sainte* 149 (1973): 7-8. [Israel/Canaan]

Dunand, M. "Byblos, Sidon, Jérusalem: Monuments apparentés des temps achémenides." In *International Organization for the Study of the Old Testament, Congress Volume, Rome 1968.* 64-70. Leiden: Brill, 1969. [Israel/Canaan]

Dunand, M. "Le temple d'Echmoun à Sidon." *Bulletin du Musée de Beyrouth* 26 (1973): 5-25. [Israel/Canaan]

Dunayevsky, I., and A. Kempinski. "The Megiddo Temples." *ZDPV* 89 (1973): 161-87. [Israel/Canaan]

Duncan, Alistair. *The Noble Sanctuary: Portrait of a Holy Place in Arab Jerusalem.* London: Longman, 1972. [Israel/Canaan]

Dupont, J. "Ruine du Temple et la fin des temps dans le discours de Marc 13." In *Apocalypses et théologie de l'espérance. Association Catholique Française pour l'Étude de la Bible, Congress de Toulouse, 1975* (Festschrift Louis Monoloubou), edited by Henri Cazelles. 207-69. Paris: Editions du Cerf, 1977. [Israel/Canaan]

Dupont-Sommer, A. " 'Maison de Yahvé' et vêtements sacrés à Éléphantine d'après un ostracon araméen du musée du Caire." *Journal asiatique* 235 (1946-47): 79-87. [Israel/Canaan]

Duri, Abdel Aziz. "Bayt al-Maqdis in Islam." In *Studies in the History and Archaeology of Jordan 1*, edited by Adnan Hadidi. 351-55. Amman: Department of Antiquities, 1982. [Israel/Canaan]

Dussaud, René. "Des fouilles à entreprendre sur l'emplacement du Temple de Jérusalem." *RHR* 79 (1919): 319-27. [Israel/Canaan]

Dussaud, René. "Le sanctuaire et les dieux phénicians de Ras Shamra." *RHR* 105 (1932): 245-302. [Israel/Canaan]

Eckert, E. E. *Der Tempel Salomonis.* Prague: n.p., 1855. [Israel/Canaan]

Edersheim, Alfred. *The Temple, Its Ministry and Services as They Were at the Time of Jesus Christ.* Boston: Bradley and Woodruff, 1904; repr. Grand Rapids: Eerdmans, 1951. [Israel/Canaan]

Efron, Y. "The Sanhedrin as an Ideal and as Reality in the Period of the Second Temple." *Immanuel* 2 (1973): 44-49. [Israel/Canaan]

Eibschitz, E. "The Hekhal and the Ulam in the Second Temple" (in Hebrew). *Sinai* 87 (1980): 226-37. [Israel/Canaan]

Eichrodt, Walther. "Der neue Tempel in der Heilshoffnung Hesekiels." In *Das ferne und nahe Wort*, edited by Fritz Maass. 37-48. Berlin: Toepelmann, 1967. [Israel/Canaan]

Eichrodt, Walther. "Tempel und Tempelsatzungen, Land und Volk im Israel der Heilszeit." In *Der Prophet Hesekiel, Kapitel 19-48.* 372-421. Göttingen: Vandenhoeck & Ruprecht, 1966; also in English as "The Temple and Its Ordinances; The Land and the People in the New Israel of the Time of Salvation." In *Ezekiel: A Commentary*, translated by C. Quin. 530-94. Philadelphia: Westminster, 1970. [Israel/Canaan]

Eisenstein, J. D. "Temple, Administration and Service of." In *The Jewish Encyclopedia* 12:81-85. [Israel/Canaan]

Eisenstein, J. D. "Temple in Rabbinical Literature." In *The Jewish Encyclopedia* 12:92-97. [Israel/Canaan]

Eisenstein, J. D. "Temple, Plan of Second." In *The Jewish Encyclopedia* 12:89-92. [Israel/Canaan]

Eissfeldt, Otto. "Eine Einschmelzstelle am Tempel zu Jerusalem." *Forschungen und Fortschritte* 13 (1937): 165-64; also in *Kleine Schriften*, edited by Rudolf Sellheim and Fritz Maass. 6 vols., 2:107-9. Tübingen: Mohr, 1963. [Israel/Canaan]

Eissfeldt, Otto. "Der Gott Bethel." *Archiv für Religionswissenschaft* 28 (1938): 1-30; also in *Kleine Schriften*, edited by Rudolf Sellheim and Fritz Maass. 6 vols., 1:206-33. Tübingen: Mohr, 1962. [Israel/Canaan]

Elliger, Karl. "Die grossen Tempelsakristeien im Verfassungsentwurf des Ezechiel (42: 1ff)." In *Geschichte und Alten Testament* (Festschrift Albrecht Alt). 79-102. Tübingen: Mohr, 1953. [Israel/Canaan]

Eltester, W. "Der Siebenarmige Leuchter und der Titus-bogen." In *Judentum, Urchristentum, Kirche: Festschrift für Joachim Jeremias*, edited by Walter Eltester. 62-76. Berlin: Töpelmann, 1960. [Israel/Canaan]

Emery, D. L. "Ezra 4: Is Josephus Right After All?" *Journal of Northwest Semitic Languages* 13 (1987): 33-44. [Israel/Canaan]

Emmanuele da S. Marco. "Lo pseudo-Aristea e il Siracida (Ecclo 50) sulla cittadella e il tempio de Gerusalemme." In *La distruzione di Gerusalemme del 70: nei suoi riflessi storico-letterari. Atti del V. Convegno biblico francescano, Roma, 22 sett. 1969.* 194-207. Assisi: Studio Teologico "Porziuncolo," 1971. [Israel/Canaan]

Engelkemper, Wilhelm. *Heiligtum und Opferstätten in den Gesetzen des Pentateuch.* Paderborn: Schöningh, 1908. [Israel/Canaan]

Eppstein, V. "The Historicity of the Gospel Account of the Cleansing of the Temple." *ZNTW* 55 (1964): 42-58. [Israel/Canaan]

Epstein, J. N. "Die Zeiten des Holzopfers." *MGWJ* 78 (1934): 97-103. [Israel/Canaan]

Etsyon, Yehuda. *Har ha-Bayit.* Jerusalem: n.p. 1984 or 1985. [Israel/Canaan]

Eybeschuetz, Jonathan. *Tavnit Binyan Bet ha-Mikdash shebi-Nevu'at Yeḥezk'el (40-43).* Jerusalem: Pe'er ha-Ḥasidut, 1965 or 1966. [Israel/Canaan]

Farrar, F. W. "The Last Nine Chapters of Ezekiel." *Expositor* 3/9 (1889): 1-15. [Israel/Canaan]

Fergusson, James. "Herod's Temple." In Fergusson, *The Holy Sepulchre and the Temple at Jerusalem.* 91-97. London: Murray, 1865. [Israel/Canaan]

Fergusson, James. *The Temples of the Jews and the Other Buildings in the Haram Area at Jersualem.* London: Murray, 1878. [Israel/Canaan]

Fernández, A. "El Profeta Ageo 2, 15-18 y la fundación del segundo templo." *Biblica* 2 (1921): 206-15. [Israel/Canaan]

Feuillet, A. "Le discours de Jésus sur la ruine du Temple, d'après Marc xiii et Luc xxi:5-36." *RB* 55 (1948): 481-502; 56 (1949): 61-92. [Israel/Canaan]

Filson, Floyd V. "Temple, Synagogue and Church." *BA* 7/4 (1944): 66-88; also in *Biblical Archaeologist Reader*, edited by David N. Freedman. 3 vols., 1:185-200. Garden City: Doubleday, 1961. [Israel/Canaan]

Finegan, J. "The Pinnacle of the Temple," "The Double Gate," "The Triple Gate," "The Golden Gate," "Robinson's Arch," and "Wilson's Arch." In Finegan, *Archaeology of the New Testament: The Life of Jesus and the Beginnings of the Early Church.* 125-32. Princeton: Princeton University Press, 1969. [Israel/Canaan]

Finegan, J. "Plan of the Temple of Herod," and "Fragment of a Warning Inscription from Herod's Temple." In Finegan, *Archaeology of the New Testament: The Life of Jesus and the Beginnings of the Early Church.* 117-20. Princeton: Princeton University Press, 1969. [Israel/Canaan]

Finkel, Asher. "The Theme of God's Presence and the Qumrân Temple Scroll." In *God and His Temple,* edited by L. E. Frizzel. 39-47. South Orange, NJ: Seton Hall University Institute for Judaeo-Christian Studies, 1980. [Israel/Canaan]

Finn, E. A. "The Rock (Sakhrah) Foundation of Solomon's Temple." *PEQ* 21 (1889): 156-57. [Israel/Canaan]

Fiorenza, E. S. "Cultic Language in Qumran and in the New Testament." *CBQ* 38 (1976): 159-77. [Israel/Canaan]

Fisher, Elliot. *The Temple as It Appeared in the Time of Our Saviour, with Full Description of Its Location, Construction and Service. To Accompany "The Temple in Miniature."* Rock Island, IL: Kramer, 1901. [Israel/Canaan]

Fisher, Loren R. "The Temple Quarter," edited by C. F. Beckingham and E. Ullerdorf. *Journal of Semitic Studies* 8 (1963): 34-41. [Israel/Canaan]

Flanagan, N. M. "Mark and the Temple Cleansing." *Bible Today* 63 (1972): 980-84. [Israel/Canaan]

Fleming, J. "The Undiscovered Gate beneath Jerusalem's Golden Gate." *Biblical Archaeology Review* 9 (1983): 24-37. [Israel/Canaan]

Flusser, David. "Temple Scroll." *Numen* 26 (1979): 271-74. [Israel/Canaan]

Flusser, David. "The Temple Scroll from Qumran." *Immanuel* 9 (1979): 49-52. [Israel/Canaan]

Flusser, David. "Two Notes on the Midrash on 2 Sam. vii: 1. The Temple 'Not Made with Hands' in the Qumrân Doctrine." *IEJ* 9 (1959): 99-104. [Israel/Canaan]

Fohrer, Georg. "Jeremias Tempelwort 7:1-15." *Theologische Zeitschrift* 5 (1949): 401-17. [Israel/Canaan]

Fohrer, Georg. "Kritik an Tempel, Kultus und Kultusausübung in nachexilischer." In *Archäologie und altes Testament: Festschrift für Kurt Galling,* edited by Arnulf Kuschke and Ernst Kutsch. 101-16. Tübingen: Mohr, 1970. [Israel/Canaan]

Ford, J. M. "The Heavenly Jerusalem and Orthodox Judaism." In *Donum Gentilicium: New Testment Studies in Honour of David Daube,* edited by Ernst Bammel, C. K. Barrett, and W. D. Davies. 215-26. Oxford: Clarendon, 1978. [Israel/Canaan]

Fowler, Mervyn D. "A Closer Look at the 'Temple of El-berith' at Shechem." *PEQ* 115 (1983): 49-53. [Israel/Canaan]

Fraeyman, M. "La Spiritualisation de l'idée du Temple dans les épîtres pauliniennes." *Ephemerides theologicae lovanienses* 33 (1947): 378-412. [Israel/Canaan]

Frank, Zevi P. *Sefer Mikdash Melekh.* Jerusalem: Ya'ad Le'hotsa maran ha-Rav Tsevi Pesah Frank, 1967 or 1968. [Israel/Canaan]

Franklin, John H. *The Rebuilding of King Solomon's Temple.* Omaha: Douglas, 1910. [Israel/Canaan]

Fransen, I. "Jésus pontife parfait du parfait sanctuaire (Epitre aux Hebreux)." *Bible et vie chrétienne* 20 (1957-58): 79-91. [Israel/Canaan]

Freedman, David N. "A Letter to the Readers." *BA* 40 (1977): 46-48. [Israel/Canaan]

Freedman, David N. "Temple without Hands." In *Temples and High Places in Biblical Times*, edited by Avraham Biran. Jerusalem: Jewish Institute of Religion, 1977. 21-30. [Israel/Canaan]

Fretheim, Terence E. "The Ark in Deuteronomy." *CBQ* 30 (1968): 1-14. [Israel/Canaan]

Fretheim, Terence E. "The Cultic Use of the Ark of the Covenant in the Monarchical Period." Th.D. diss., Princeton Theological Seminary, 1967. [Israel/Canaan]

Fretheim, Terence E. "The Priestly Document: Anti-Temple?" *VT* 18 (1968): 313-29. [Israel/Canaan]

Fritz, Volkmar. "Der Tempel Salamos im Licht der neueren Forschung." *Mitteilungen der Deutschen Morgenländischen Gesellschaft* 112 (1980): 53-68. [Israel/Canaan]

Fritz, Volkmar. *Tempel und Zelt.* Neukirchen-Vluyn: Neukirchener, 1977. [Israel/Canaan]

Fritz, Volkmar. "Temple Architecture: What Can Archaeology Tell Us about Solomon's Temple." *BAR* 13/4 (1987): 38-49. [Israel/Canaan]

Frizzell, Lawrence E., ed. *God and His Temple.* South Orange: Institute of Judaeo-Christian Studies, 1981. [Israel/Canaan]

Fromer, Jacob. *Maimonides' Commentar zum Tractat Middoth mit der hebräischen Uebersetzung des Natanel Almoli* (in Hebrew). Breslau: Schatzky, 1898. [Israel/Canaan]

Fry, Euan. "The Temple in the Gospels and Acts." *Bible Translator* 38 (April 1987): 213-21. [Israel/Canaan]

Fry, V. R. L. "The Warning Inscriptions from the Herodian Temple." Ph.D. diss., Southern Baptist Theology Seminary, 1974. [Israel/Canaan]

Frymer-Kensky, Tivka. "Pollution, Purification, and Purgation in Biblical Israel." In *The Word of the Lord Shall Go Forth: Essays in Honor of David Noel Freedman*, edited by C. L. Meyers and M. O'Connor. 399-414. Winona Lake: Eisenbrauns, 1983. [Israel/Canaan]

Fujita, S. "Temple Theology in the Second Book of Maccabees." *Bible Today* 64 (1973): 1066-71. [Israel/Canaan]

Fujita, S. "The Temple Theology of the Qumran Sect and the Book of Ezekiel." Ph.D. diss., Princeton University, 1970. [Israel/Canaan]

Fullerton, Kemper. "The Stone of Foundation." *AJSL* 37 (1920-21): 1-12. [Israel/Canaan]

Furneaux, Rupert. *The Roman Siege of Jerusalem.* London: Hart-Davis MacGibbon, 1973. [Israel/Canaan]

Gabriel, Johann. *Zorobabel. Ein Beitrag zur Geschichte der Juden in der ersten Zeit nach dem Exil.* Wien: Mayer, 1927. [Israel/Canaan]

Gaechter, Paul. "The Original Sequence of Apocalypse 20-22." *Theological Studies* 10 (1949): 485-521. [Israel/Canaan]

Galling, Kurt. "Das Allerheiligste im Salomos Tempel, ein christlicher 'Thoraschrein': Zwei archäologische Bemerkungen." *JPOS* 12 (1932): 43-46. [Israel/Canaan]

Galling, Kurt. "Die Beschreibung des Kultortes." In *Hesekiel*, edited by Alfred Bertholet. 135-55. Tübingen: Mohr, 1936. [Israel/Canaan]

Galling, Kurt. "Die Halle des Schreibers." *Palästinajahrbuch* 27 (1931): 51-57. [Israel/Canaan]

Galling, Kurt. "Herodianischer Tempel." In *Die Religion in Geschichte und Gegenwart*, edited by H. Campenhausen et al. 6 vols., 5:1045-46. Tübingen: Mohr, 1931. [Israel/Canaan]

Galling, Kurt. "Königliche und nichtkönigliche Stifter beim Tempel von Jerusalem. *ZDPV* 68 (1950): 134-42. [Israel/Canaan]

Galling, Kurt. "Serubbabel und der Hohepriester beim Wiederaufbau des Tempels in Jerusalem." In Galling, *Studien zur Geschichte Israels im persischen Zeitalter.* 127-48. Tübingen: Mohr, 1964. [Israel/Canaan]

Galling, Kurt. "Serubbabel und der Wiederaufbau des Tempels in Jerusalem." In *Verbannung und Heimkehr: Beiträge zur Geschichte und Theologie Israels in 6. und 5. Jahrhundert v. Chr. Wilhelm Rudolph zum 70. Geburtstag*, edited by Arnulf Kuschke. 67-96. Tübingen: Mohr, 1961. [Israel/Canaan]

Galling, Kurt. "Tempel." In *Die Religion in Geschichte und Gegenwart*, edited by H. Campenhausen et al., 3d ed. 7 vols., 6:681-86. Tübingen: Mohr, 1962. [Israel/Canaan]

Galling, Kurt. "Tempelgeräte in Israel." In *Die Religion in Geschichte und Gegenwart*, edited by H. Campenhausen et al., 3d ed. 6 vols., 6:686-87. Tübingen: Mohr, 1962. [Israel/Canaan]

Galling, Kurt. "Tempel in Palästina." *ZDPV* 55 (1932): 245-50. [Israel/Canaan]

Galling, Kurt. "Der Tempelschatz nach Berichten und Urkunden im Buche Esra." *ZDPV* 60 (1937): 177-83. [Israel/Canaan]

Galling, Kurt. "Zur Lokalisierung von Debir." *ZDPV* 70 (1954): 135-41. [Israel/Canaan]

Gamberoni, J. "Der nachexilische Tempel und der nachexilische Kult." *Bibel und Liturgie* 45 (1972): 94-108. [Israel/Canaan]

Garber, Paul L. "Reconsidering the Reconstruction of Solomon's Temple." *JBL* 77 (1958): 123-33. [Israel/Canaan]

Garber, Paul L. "Reconstructing Solomon's Temple." *BA* 14 (1951): 2-24. [Israel/Canaan]

Garber, Paul L. "A Reconstruction of Solomon's Temple." In *Archaeological Discoveries in the Holy Land*. 101-11. New York: Crowell, 1967. [Israel/Canaan]

Garber, Paul L. *Solomon's Temple*. Troy: Howland, 1950. [Israel/Canaan]

García López, Félix. "Construction et destruction de Jérusalem: histoire et prophétie dans les cadres rédactionnels des Livres des Rois." *RB* 94 (April 1987): 222-32. [Israel/Canaan]

García Martínez, F. "El Rollo del Templo 11 Q Temple: Bibliografía sistemática." *Revue de Qumran* 12 (December 1986): 425-40. [Israel/Canaan]

García Martínez, F. "El Rollo de Templo: Traduccion y notas." *Estudios Bíblicos* 36 (1977): 247-92. [Israel/Canaan]

Garcia-Treto, F. O. "Bethel: The History and Traditions of an Israelite Sanctuary." Th.D diss., Princeton Theological Seminary, 1967. [Israel/Canaan]

Gari-Jaune, L. " 'Desacralizzazione' neotestamentarie del tempio di Gerusalemme." In *La distruzione di Gerusalemme del 70: nei suoi riflessi storico-letterarie*. 135-44. Assisi: Studio Teologico, 1971. [Israel/Canaan]

Garland, David E. "Matthew's Understanding of the Temple Tax (Matt 17:24-27)." *SBLSP* 26 (1987): 190-209. [Israel/Canaan]

Gärtner, Bertil. *The Temple and the Community in Qumran and the New Testament*, edited by M. Black. Cambridge: Cambridge University Press, 1965. [Israel/Canaan]

Gaster, Theodor H. "The Service of the Sanctuary: A Study in Hebrew Survivals." In *A Mélanges syriens offerts à Monsieur René Dussaud*, II. 577-82. Paris: Geuthner, 1939. [Israel/Canaan]

Gaston, Lloyd. *No Stone on Another*. Leiden: Brill, 1970. [Israel/Canaan]

Gaston, Lloyd. "The Theology of the Temple: The New Testament Fulfillment of the Promise of Old Testament Heilsgeschichte." In *Oikonomia: Heilsgeschichte als Thema der Theologie. Festschrift Oscar Cullman*. 32-41. Hamburg: Herbert Reich, 1967. [Israel/Canaan]

Gatt, G. "Zion." *Das heilige Land* 25 (1881): 143-201. [Israel/Canaan]

Geisinger, Marion. *The House of God*. New York: A and W, 1979. [Israel/Canaan]

Gelston, A. "The Foundations of the Second Temple." *VT* 16 (1966): 232-35. [Israel/Canaan]

Georgi, D. "Die Visionen vom himmlischen Jerusalem in Apk. 21 und 22." In *Kirche: Festschrift für Günther Bornkamm zum 75. Geburtstag*, edited by Dieter Lührmann and Georg Strecker. 351-72. Tübingen: Mohr, 1980. [Israel/Canaan]

Gervitz, S. "Jachin and Boaz." In *Harper's Dictionary of the Bible*, 443. [Israel/Canaan]

Gese, Hartmut. *Der Verfassungsentwurf des Ezechiel (Kap. 40-48) traditionsgeschichtlichen Untersucht* Tübingen: Mohr, 1957. [Israel/Canaan]

Gese, Hartmut. "Zur Geschichte der Kultsänger am zweiten Tempel." In *Abraham Unser Vater: Juden and Christen im Gesprach über die Bibel: Festschrift für Otto Michel*, edited by O. Betz. 222-34. Leiden: Brill, 1963. [Israel/Canaan]

Giblin, Charles H. *The Destruction of Jerusalem according to Luke's Gospel: A Historical-Theological Model*. Rome: Biblical Institute Press, 1985. [Israel/Canaan]

Gittlen, B. M. "Form and Function in the New Late Bronze Age Temple at Lachish." *Eretz-Israel* 16 (1982): 67-69. [Israel/Canaan]

Goguel, M. "La parole de Jésus sur la déstruction et la reconstruction du Temple." In *Congrès d'Histoire du Christianisme*. 1:117-36. Paris: Éditions Rieder, 1928. [Israel/Canaan]

Goldenberg, Robert. "Early Rabbinic Explanations for the Destruction of Jerusalem." *JJS* 33 (1982): 517-25. [Israel/Canaan]

Goldschmidt-Lehmann, R. P. "The Second (Herodian) Temple: Selected Bibliography." *Jerusalem Cathedra* 1 (1981): 336-59. [Israel/Canaan]

Goldstein, N. "Worship at the Temple in Jerusalem—Rabbinic Interpretation and Influence" (in Hebrew). Ph.D. diss., Hebrew University, 1977. [Israel/Canaan]

Gonen, R. "Was the Site of the Jerusalem Temple Originally a Cemetery?" *BAR* 11/3 (1985): 44-55. [Israel/Canaan]

Gooding, David W. "An Impossible Shrine." *VT* 15 (1965): 405-20. [Israel/Canaan]

Gooding, David W. "Temple Specifications: A Dispute in Logical Arrangement between the MT and the LXX." *VT* 17 (1967): 143-72. [Israel/Canaan]

Görg, Manfred. "Die Gattung des sogenannten Tempelweihespruchs (I Kgs. 8, 12f)." In *Ugarit-Forschungen* 6 (1974): 55-63. [Israel/Canaan]

Görg, Manfred. "Lexikalisches zur Beschreibung des salomonischen Palastbezirks (I Kön 7, 1-12)." *Biblische Notizen: Beiträge zur exegetischen Diskussion* 11 (1980): 7-13. [Israel/Canaan]

Görg, Manfred. "Weiteres zur Gestalt des Tempelbaus." *Biblische Notizen: Beiträge zur exegetischen Diskussion* 13 (1980): 22-25. [Israel/Canaan]

Görg, Manfred. *Das Zelt der Begegnung*. Bonn: Hanstein, 1967. [Israel/Canaan]

Görg, Manfred. "Zur Dekoration der Tempelsäulen." *Biblische Notizen: Beiträge zur exegetischen Diskussion* 13 (1980): 17-21. [Israel/Canaan]

Görg, Manfred. "Zur Dekoration des Leuchters." *Biblische Notizen: Beiträge zur exegetischen Diskussion* 15 (1981): 21-29. [Israel/Canaan]

Görg, Manfred. "Zwei bautechnische Begriffe in I Kön 6, 9." *Biblische Notizen: Beiträge zur exegetischen Diskussion* 10 (1979): 12-15. [Israel/Canaan]

Gottlieb, Hans. "Amos und Jerusalem." *VT* 17 (1967): 430-63. [Israel/Canaan]

Graetz, Heinrich. *Dauer der gewaltsamen Hellenisierung der Juden und der Tempelentweihung durch Antiochus Epiphanes.* Breslau: Grass, Barth, 1864. [Israel/Canaan]

Graetz, Heinrich. "Die Höfe und Thore des zweiten Tempels." *MGWJ* 25 (1876): 385-97. [Israel/Canaan]

Graetz, Heinrich. "Die musikalischen Instrumente im jerusalemischen Tempel und der musikalische Chor der Leveiten." *MGWJ* 30 (1881): 241-59. [Israel/Canaan]

Graetz, Heinrich. "Die Tempelpsalmen." *MGWJ* 27 (1878): 217-22. [Israel/Canaan]

Gray, John. "The Building and Dedication of the Temple." In *I and II Kings: A Commentary.* 2d ed. 149-238. London: SCM, 1970. [Israel/Canaan]

Gray, John. "Hazor." *VT* 16 (1966): 26-52. [Israel/Canaan]

Gray, L. "La ruïne du Temple par Titus." *RB* 55 (1948): 215-26. [Israel/Canaan]

Greenberg, Moshe. "The Design and Themes of Ezekiel's Program of Restoration." *Interpretation* 38 (1984): 181-208. [Israel/Canaan]

Greenwald, Leopold. *Le-Toldot ha-Sanhedrin bi-Yisrael.* New York: Shoulson, 1950. [Israel/Canaan]

Grelot, P. "La reconstruction du temple juif d'Éléphantine." *Orientalia* 36 (1967): 173-77. [Israel/Canaan]

Gressmann, Hugo. *Die Lade Jahves und das Allerheiligste des Salomonischen Tempels.* Berlin: Kohlhammer, 1920. [Israel/Canaan]

Grigsby, Bruce. "Gematria and John 21:11—Another Look at Ezekiel 47:10." *ET* 95 (1984): 177-78. [Israel/Canaan]

Grintz, Yehoshua (Joshua) M. "The Temple" (in Hebrew). In *Encyclopaedia Hebraica*, edited by B. Natanyahu. 35 vols., 8:555-91. Jerusalem: Encyclopaedia Printing, 1957. [Israel/Canaan]

Grintz, Yehoshua M., and Yigael Yadin. "Temple: First Temple." In *Encyclopaedia Judaica* 15:943-55. [Israel/Canaan]

Gry, L. "La ruine du temple par Titus—quelques traditions juives plus anciennes et primitives à la base de Pesikta Rabbathi xxvi." *RB* 55 (1948): 215-26. [Israel/Canaan]

Guérin, Victor. "Jérusalem a l'epoche d'Hérode le Grand." In *La Terre Sainte—Jérusalem* . 63-76. Paris: Plon, 1897. [Israel/Canaan]

Gulston, C. "Herod's Masterpiece." In *Jerusalem—the Tragedy and the Triumph.* 99-103 Michigan: Zondervan, 1978. [Israel/Canaan]

Güterbock, H. G. "The Hittite Temple according to Written Sources." In *Le temple et le culte: Compte rendu de la vingtième recontre assyriologique internationale organisée à Leiden du 3 au 7 juillet 1972.* 125-32. Istanbul: Nederlands Historisch-Archeologisch Instituut te Istambul 1975. [Israel/Canaan]

Gutmann, Joseph. "A Note on the Temple Menorah." *ZNTW* 60 (1969): 289-91. [Israel/Canaan]

Gutmann, Joseph, ed. *The Temple of Solomon.* Missoula: Scholars, 1976. [Israel/Canaan]

Gutmann, S. B. Z. *Ha-Kotel ha-Maʿaravi.* Tel-Aviv: Omonuth, 1929. [Israel/Canaan]

Haak, R. D. "The 'Shoulder' of the Temple." *VT* 33 (1983): 271-78. [Israel/Canaan]

Haase, Julius. *Der siebenarmige Leuchter des alten Bundes, seine Geschichte und Symbolik.* Munich: Asokthebu, 1922. [Israel/Canaan]

Hachlili, Rachel. "The Architecture of Nabataean Temples" (in Hebrew; *English summary). *Eretz-Israel* 12 (1975): 95-106, *121. [Israel/Canaan]

Hachlili, Rachel, and R. Merhav. "The *Menorah* in First and Second Temple Times in the Light of the Sources and Archaeology" (in Hebrew; *English summary). *Eretz-Israel* 18 (1985): 256-67, *74. [Israel/Canaan]

Hacohen, Mordecai. *Ha-Bayit veha-ʿAliyah.* Jerusalem: Yad Ramah, 1978. [Israel/Canaan]

Hadey Jean. "Jéremie et la temple: le conflit de la parole prophétique et de la tradition religieuse: Jér. 7: 1-15; 26: 1-19." *Études théologiques et religieuses* 54 (1979): 438-43. [Israel/Canaan]

Halevy, Yitshak. "The Sanhedrin in the Chamber of Hewn Stone." In Halevy, *Dorot Harishonim—Die Geschichte und Literatur Israels*, sect. 1, vol. 5 (in Hebrew). 112-16. Berlin: Harz, 1923. [Israel/Canaan]

Halivni, D. W. "Surrejoinder to E. Feldman." *Tradition: A Journal of Orthodox Jewish Thought* 23 (Winter 1988): 101-6. [Israel/Canaan]

Halpern, Baruch. "The Centralization Formula in Deuteronomy." *VT* 31 (1981): 20-38. [Israel/Canaan]

Hamerton-Kelly, R. G. "The Temple and the Origins of Jewish Apocalyptic." *VT* 20 (1970): 1-15. [Israel/Canaan]

Hamilton, N. Q. "Temple Cleansing and Temple Bank." *JBL* 83 (1964): 365-72. [Israel/Canaan]

Hamilton, R. W. "Jerusalem: Patterns of Holiness." In *Archaeology in the Levant: Essays for Kathleen Kenyon*, edited by Roger Moorey and Peter Parr. 194-201. Warminster: Aris and Phillips, 1978. [Israel/Canaan]

Hanauer, J. E. "Julian's Attempt to Restore the Temple, and Other Notes." *PEQ* 34 (1902): 389-93. [Israel/Canaan]

Hani, Jean. *Le symbolisme du temple chrétien*. Paris: Tredaniel, 1978. [Israel/Canaan]

Hannay, T. "The Temple." *Scottish Journal of Theology* 3 (1950): 278-87. [Israel/Canaan]

Hanselman, Robert W. "An Architecturosymbolic Interpretation of the Ancient Jewish Temples." M.A. thesis, University of Florida, 1983. [Israel/Canaan]

Har, Moshe David. *The Temple and the Priests at the End of the 2nd Temple, According to Rabbinic Literature* (in Hebrew). Jerusalem: Hebrew University of Jerusalem, 1972 or 1973. [Israel/Canaan]

Haran, Menahem. "Biblical Studies: The Idea of the Divine Presence in Israelite Cult." *Tarbiz* 38 (1968): 105-19. [Israel/Canaan]

Haran, Menahem. "The Censer Incense and Tamid Incense." *Tarbiz* 26 (1956): 115-25. [Israel/Canaan]

Haran, Menahem. "The Disappearance of the Ark." *IEJ* 13 (1963): 46-58. [Israel/Canaan]

Haran, Menahem. "The Gibeonites, the Nethinim and the Servants of Solomon" (in Hebrew). In *Judah and Jerusalem: The Twelfth Archaeological Convention*. 37-45. Jerusalem: Israel Exploration Society, 1957. [Israel/Canaan]

Haran, Menahem. "Temple and Community in Ancient Israel." In *Temple in Society*, edited by Michael V. Fox. 17-25. Winona Lake: Eisenbrauns, 1988. [Israel/Canaan]

Haran, Menahem. "A Temple at Dor?" *IEJ* 27 (1977): 12-15. [Israel/Canaan]

Haran, Menahem. *Temples and Temple-Service in Ancient Israel*. Oxford: Clarendon, 1977. [Israel/Canaan]

Harel, Menashe. "Water and the Temple in Jerusalem." *Ariel* 70 (1987): 71-88. [Israel/Canaan]

Harel, Menashe. "Water for Purification, Hygiene and Cult at the Temple in Jerusalem" (in Hebrew; *English summary). *Eretz-Israel* 19 (1987): 310-13, *82-83. [Israel/Canaan]

Hayward, R. "The Jewish Temple at Leontopolis: A Reconsideration." *JJS* 33 (1982): 429-43. [Israel/Canaan]

Hengel, Martin. "Der Eifer für die Reinheit des Heiligtums." In Hengel, *Die Zeloten—Untersuchungen zur jüdischen Freiheits-Bewegung in der Zeit von Herodes I. bis 70 N. Chr.* 211-29. Leiden: Brill, 1961. [Israel/Canaan]

Hengel, Martin, James H. Charlesworth, and D. Mendels. "The Polemical Character of 'On Kingship' in the Temple Scroll: An Attempt at Dating 11QTemple." *JJS* 37 (1986): 28-38. [Israel/Canaan]

Hennessy, Basil. "Amman." *RB* 73 (1966): 561-64. [Israel/Canaan]

Hennessy, J. B. "Excavation of a Late Bronze Age Temple at Amman." *PEQ* 98 (1966): 155-62. [Israel/Canaan]

Henson, Ralph B. "The Central Sanctuary in Ancient Israel." Th.D. diss., New Orleans Baptist Theological Seminary, 1984. [Israel/Canaan]

"The Herodian Temple, according to the Treatise Middoth and Flavius Josephus." *PEFQ* 18 (1886): 92-113. [Israel/Canaan]

Herr, M. D. "Jerusalem, the Temple and Its Cult: Reality and Concepts in Second Temple Times—Jerusalem in the Second Temple Period." In *Jerusalem in the Second Temple Period: Abraham Schalit Memorial Volume* (in Hebrew; English summaries), edited by A. Oppenheimer et al. 166-67. Jerusalem: Yad Izhaq Ben-Avi, 1980. [Israel/Canaan]

Herrmann, Joseph. *Le temple de Jérusalem d'après les travaux des archéologues modernes.* Valenciennes: Prignet, 1882. [Israel/Canaan]

Herrmann, W. "Unknown Designs for the 'Temple of Jerusalem' by Claude Perrault." In *Essays in the History of Architecture Presented to Rudolf Wittkower*, edited by D. Fraser. 143-58. London: Phaidon, 1967. [Israel/Canaan]

Hertzberg, H. W. "Der heilige Fels und das Alte Testament." *JPOS* 12 (1932): 32-42. [Israel/Canaan]

Herzog, Ze'ev, Miriam Aharoni, and Anson F. Rainey. "Arad: An Ancient Israelite Fortress with a Temple to Yahweh." *BAR* 13 (1987): 16-35. [Israel/Canaan]

Herzog, Ze'ev, Miriam Aharoni, Anson F. Rainey, and S. Moshkovitz. "The Israelite Fortress at Arad." *BASOR* 254 (1984): 1-34. [Israel/Canaan]

Hiers, Richard. "Purification of the Temple: Preparation for the Kingdom of God." *JBL* 90 (1971): 82-90. [Israel/Canaan]

Hillers, Delbert R. "MŠKN 'Temple' in an Inscription from Hatra." *BASOR* 206 (1972): 54-56. [Israel/Canaan]

Himmelfarb, Martha. "Apocalyptic Ascent and the Heavenly Temple." *SBLSP* 26 (1987): 210-17. [Israel/Canaan]

Hirsch, S. A. "The Temple of Onias." In *Jews' College Jubilee Volume*, edited by I. Harris. 39-80. London: Luzac, 1906. [Israel/Canaan]

Hoenig, Sidney B. "The End of the Great Sanhedrin during the Second Temple Period" (in Hebrew). *Horeb* 3 (1936): 169-75. [Israel/Canaan]

Hoenig, Sidney B. "The Meeting Place." In *The Great Sanhedrin* (in Hebrew), 74-84. Philadelphia: Dropsie College, 1953. [Israel/Canaan]

Hoenig, Sidney B. "Suppositous Temple-Synagogue." *JQR* 54 (1963): 115-31. [Israel/Canaan]

Hoffmann, Richard A. "Das Wort Jesu von der Zerstörung und dem Wiederaufbau des Tempels." In *Neustamentliche Studien Georg Heinrici zu seinem 70. Geburtstag*. 130-39. Leipzig: 1914. [Israel/Canaan]

Hofius, Otfried. *Der Vorhang vor dem Thron Gottes: Eine exegetisch-religionsgeschichtliche Untersuchung zu Hebräer 6, 19f und 10, 19f.* Tübingen: Mohr, 1972. [Israel/Canaan]

Hollis, C., and R. Brownrigg. "The Third Temple." In Hollis and Brownrigg, *Holy Places*, 52-54. New York: Praeger, 1969. [Israel/Canaan]

Hollis, F. J. "The Sun-Cult and the Temple at Jerusalem." In *Myth and Ritual*, edited by Samuel H. Hooke. 87-110. London: Oxford University Press, 1933. [Israel/Canaan]

Hollis, F. J. *The Archaeology of Herods Temple*. London: Dent & Sons, 1934. [Israel/Canaan]

Holtzmann, O. "Tore und Terrassen des herodianschen Tempels." *ZNTW* 8-9 (1908): 71-74. [Israel/Canaan]

Holzinger, H. "Der Schaubrottisch des Titusbogens." *ZAW* 21 (1901): 341-42. [Israel/Canaan]

Hooke, Samuel H. "The Corner-Stone of Scripture." In Hooke, *The Siege Perilous: Essays in Biblical Anthropology and Kindred Subjects*. 235-49. London: SCM, 1956. [Israel/Canaan]

Hooker, Morna D. "Traditions about the Temple in the Sayings of Jesus." *BJRL* 70 (Spring 1988): 7-19. [Israel/Canaan]

Hoonacker, Albin van. *Le sacerdoce lévitique dans la loi et dans l'histoire des Hebreux*. London: Williams and Norgate, 1899. [Israel/Canaan]

Hoonacker, Albin van. "Zorobabel et le second temple." *Le Muséon* 10 (1891): 379-97, 489-515, 634-44. [Israel/Canaan]

Hoonacker, Albin van. *Zorobabel et le second temple: Étude sur la chronologie des six premiers chapitres du livre d'Esdras*. Gand: Engelcke, 1892. [Israel/Canaan]

Horbury, William. "New Wine in Old Wine-Skins: IX. The Temple." *ET* 86 (1974): 36-42. [Israel/Canaan]

Horbury, William. "The Temple Tax." In *Jesus and the Politics of His Day*, edited by Ernst Bammel and C. F. D. Moule. 265-86. Cambridge: Cambridge University Press, 1984. [Israel/Canaan]

Horbury, William. *Templum Amicitiae: Essays on the Second Temple Presented to Ernst Bammel*. Sheffield: JSOT, 1990. [Israel/Canaan]

Horne, Alexander. *King Solomon's Temple in the Masonic Tradition*. London: Aquarian, 1972. [Israel/Canaan]

Horowitz, I. S. "The Temple Administration and the Divine Services" (in Hebrew). In *Jerusalem—a Geographical, Topographical, and Historical Encyclopaedia of Jerusalem*. 389-435. Jerusalem: Mass, 1964. [Israel/Canaan]

Horst, Friedrich. "Die Kultusreform des Königs Josia (II RG. 22-23)." *ZDMG* 77 (1923): 220-38. [Israel/Canaan]

Howie, C. G. "The East Gate of Ezekiel's Temple Enclosure and the Solomonic Gateway of Megiddo." *BASOR* 117 (1950): 13-19. [Israel/Canaan]

Howland, E. G. *Solomon's Temple.* Troy: Howland, 1950. [Israel/Canaan]

Hubmann, Franz D. "Der 'Weg' zum Zion: Literar- und stilkritische Beobachtungen zu Jes. 35: 8-10." In *Memoria Jerusalem: Freundesgabe Franz Sauer zum 70. Geburtstag,* edited by Johannes B. Bauer and Johannes Marböck. 29-41. Graz: Akademische Druck- und Verlagsanstalt, 1977. [Israel/Canaan]

Hudry-Clergeon, J. "Jésus et le Sanctuaire: Étude de Jn. 2, 12-22." *Nouvelle Revue Théologique* 105 (1983): 535-48. [Israel/Canaan]

Hull, E. "Where Are the Sacred Vessels of the Temples?" *PEFQ* 28 (1896): 344. [Israel/Canaan]

Hull, William E. "The Background of the New Temple Concept in Early Christianity." Ph.D. diss., Southern Baptist Theological Seminary, 1960. [Israel/Canaan]

Hurowitz, Avigdor (Victor). "Temple Building in the Bible in Light of Mesopotamian and North-West Semitic Writings" (in Hebrew). Ph.D. diss., Hebrew University, 1983. [Israel/Canaan]

Hurst, L. D. "Eschatology and 'Platonism' in the Epistle to the Hebrews." *SBLSP* (1984): 41-74. [Israel/Canaan]

Hurvitz, Avi. "The Term *lishkat sharîm* (Ezek. 40:44) and Its Position in the Cultic Terminology of the Temple" (in Hebrew; *English summary). *Eretz-Israel* 14 (1978): 100-104, *126. [Israel/Canaan]

Hyatt, J. P. "The Deity Bethel and the Old Testament." *JAOS* 59 (1939): 81-98. [Israel/Canaan]

Hyldahl, N. "Die Versuchung auf der Zinne des Tempels (Matt. 4:5-7=Luke 4:9-12)." *Studia Theologica* 15 (1961): 113-27. [Israel/Canaan]

Idelsohn, Abraham Z. ". . .Second Temple. . ." In *Jewish Music in Its Historical Development.* 9-21. New York: Tudor, 1948. [Israel/Canaan]

Iliffe, J. H. "A Model Shrine of Phoenician Style." *Quarterly of the Department of Antiquities in Palestine* 11 (1945): 91-92. [Israel/Canaan]

Iliffe, J. H. "The Thanatos Inscription from Herod's Temple—Fragments of a Second Copy." *Quarterly of the Department of Antiquities in Palestine* 6 (1938): 1-3. [Israel/Canaan]

Imbert, J. "Le temple reconstruit par Zorobabel." *Le Muséon* 7 (1888): 77-87, 221-35, 302-14, 584-92; 8 (1889): 51-66, 520-21. [Israel/Canaan]

Irshai, O. "Concerning the Purpose and Location of the Chamber of the Curtains in the Second Temple" (in Hebrew). *Morashah* 8 (1974): 56-65. [Israel/Canaan]

Isaac, B. H. "A Donation for Herod's Temple in Jerusalem." *IEJ* 33/1-2 (1983): 86-92; also in Hebrew with *English summary in *Eretz-Israel* 18 (1985): 1-4, *65. [Israel/Canaan]

Ivry, A. L. "Nehemiah 6:10; Politics and the Temple." *Journal for the Study of Judaism* 3 (1974): 35-45. [Israel/Canaan]

Jacobson, D. M. "The Golden Section and the Design of the Dome of the Rock." *PEQ* 115 (1983): 145-77. [Israel/Canaan]

Jacobson, D. M. "Ideas Concerning the Plan of Herod's Temple." *PEQ* 112 (1980): 33-40. [Israel/Canaan]

Jacoby, Adolf. "Der angebliche Eselskult der Juden und Christen," *Archiv für Religionswissenschaft* 25 (1927): 264-82. [Israel/Canaan]

Japhet, Sara. "Sheshbazzar and Zerubbabel against the Background of the Historical and Religious Tendencies of Ezra-Nehemiah." *ZAW* 95 (1983): 218-29. [Israel/Canaan]

Jeremias, Joachim. "Abba." In *Studien zur neutestamentlichen Theologie und Zeitgeschichte*. 353-60. Göttingen: Vandenhoeck and Ruprecht, 1966. [Israel/Canaan]

Jeremias, Joachim. "Der Eckstein." *Angelos* 1 (1925): 65-70. [Israel/Canaan]

Jeremias, Joachim. "Eckstein-Schlusstein." *ZTNW* 36 (1937): 154-60. [Israel/Canaan]

Jeremias, Joachim. "Hesekieltempel und Serubbabeltempel." *ZAW* 52 (1934): 109-12. [Israel/Canaan]

Jeremias, Joachim. *Jerusalem in the Time of Jesus*. London SCM, 1969. [Israel/Canaan]

Jeremias, Joachim. "*Kephalè gonìas-akrogoviaios.*" *ZNTW* 29 (1930): 264-80. [Israel/Canaan]

Jeremias, Joachim. "Lade und Zion: Zur Entstehung der Ziontradition." In *Probleme biblischer Theologie: Gerhard von Rad zum 70. Geburtstag*, edited by Hans W. Wolff. 183-98. Munich: Kaiser, 1971. [Israel/Canaan]

Jeremias, Joachim. "Die 'Zinne' des Tempels (Mt. 4. 5; Lk. 4.9)." *ZDPV* 59 (1936): 195-208. [Israel/Canaan]

Jeremias, Joachim, and A. M. Schneider. "Das westliche Südtor des herodianischen Tempels." *ZDPV* 65 (1942): 112-21. [Israel/Canaan]

Johns, C. N. "Excavations at the Citadel, Jerusalem: 1934-39." *PEQ* 72 (1940): 36-58. [Israel/Canaan]

Johnsson, William G. "The Cultus of Hebrews in Twentieth-Century Scholarship." *ET* 89 (1977-78): 104-8. [Israel/Canaan]

Jongeling, B. "A propos de la colonne XXIII du rouleau du temple." *Revue de Qumran* 10 (1981): 593-95. [Israel/Canaan]

Jouon, Paul. Les mots employes pour designer 'les temple' dans l'ancien testament, le Nouveau Testament et Josephe." *Recherches de science religieuse* 265 (1935): 329-43. [Israel/Canaan]

Junker, Hubert. "Sancta Civitas, Jerusalem Nova: Eine formcritische und überlieferungsgeschichtliche Studie zu Is. 2." In *Ekklesia: Festschrift für Matthias Wehr*, edited by H. Gross and F. Musser. 17-33. Trier: Paulinus, 1962. [Israel/Canaan]

Kapelrud, Arvid S. "The Gates of Hell and the Guardian Angels of Paradise." *JAOS* 70 (1950): 151-56. [Israel/Canaan]

Kaufman, Asher S. "The Eastern Wall of the Second Temple at Jerusalem Revealed." *BA* 44 (1981): 108-15. [Israel/Canaan]

Kaufman, Asher S. "New Light on the Ancient Temple of Jerusalem." *Christian News from Israel* 27/2 (1979): 54-58. [Israel/Canaan]

Kaufman, Asher S. "A Note on Artistic Representations of the Second Temple of Jerusalem." *BA* 47 (1984): 253-54. [Israel/Canaan]

Kaufman, Asher S. "The Second Temple—Description and Location." In *The Temple Mount—Its Locations and Limits* (in Hebrew). 39-46. Jerusalem: Municipality of Jerusalem, 1975. [Israel/Canaan]

Kaufman, Asher S. "Temple." In *Encyclopaedia Judaica Yearbook, 1975/76*. 393-97. Jerusalem: Encyclopaedia Judaica, 1976. [Israel/Canaan]

Kaufman, Asher S. "Temple." In *Encyclopaedia Judaica* 17:577-80. [Israel/Canaan]

Kaufman, Asher S. "Where the Ancient Temple of Jerusalem Stood." *BAR* 9/2 (1983): 40-59. [Israel/Canaan]

Kaufman, Stephen. "The Temple Scroll and Higher Criticism." *HUCA* 53 (1982): 29-43. [Israel/Canaan]

Kaufmann, Yehezkel. "The Cult." In *The Religion of Israel from the Beginnings to the Babylonian Exile*, translated and abridged by Moshe Greenberg. 101-21. Chicago: University of Chicago Press, 1960. [Israel/Canaan]

Kaufmann, Yehezkel. "Zerubbabel and the Building of the Temple," translated by Moshe Greenberg. In *The Religion of Israel*. 4 vols. 4:223-52. Chicago: University of Chicago Press, 1960. [Israel/Canaan]

Kearney, P. J. "Altar in the Bible." *New Catholic Encyclopedia* 1 (1967): 344-46. [Israel/Canaan]

Keathley, Naymond H. "The Concept of the Temple in Luke-Acts." Th.D. diss., Southern Baptist Theological Seminary, 1971. [Israel/Canaan]

Kedar-Kopfstein, B., and G. Johannes Botterweck. "*chagh; ḥgg.*" In *Theological Dictionary of the Old Testament* 4:201-13. [Israel/Canaan]

Kee, H. C. "Tell-er-Ras and the Samaritan Temple." *NTS* 13 (1967): 401-2. [Israel/Canaan]

Keel, Othmar. "The Temple: Place of Yahweh's Presence and Sphere of Life." In *Symbolism of the Biblical World: Ancient Near Eastern Iconography and the Book of Psalms*. 111-76. New York: Seabury, 1978. [Israel/Canaan]

Kelchner, John W. *Unequaled for 3000 Years: Reproduction of King Solomon's Temple and Citadel*. Chicago: Century of Progress Exposition, 1933. [Israel/Canaan]

Keller, C. A. "Über einige alttestamentliche Heiligtumslegenden." *ZAW* 67 (1955): 141-68. [Israel/Canaan]

Kelso, J. A. "The Unity of the Sanctuary in the Light of the Elephantine Papyri." *JBL* 28 (1909): 71-81. [Israel/Canaan]

Kelso, James L. "Bethel (Sanctuary)." In *The Interpreter's Dictionary of the Bible*, 1:391-93. [Israel/Canaan]

Kempinski, A. "The Sin Temple at Khafaje and the En-Gedi Temple." *IEJ* 22 (1972): 10-15. [Israel/Canaan]

Kennard, Joseph S. *Jesus in the Temple*. Tokyo: n.p., 1935. [Israel/Canaan]

Kennedy, A. R. S. "Some Problems of Herod's Temple." *ET* 20 (1908-9): 24-27, 66-69, 181-83, 270-73. [Israel/Canaan]

Kennedy, A. R. S., and N. H. Snaith. "Temple." In *Dictionary of the Bible*, 961-68 (1963 ed.). [Israel/Canaan]

Kenyon, Kathleen M. "New Evidence on Solomon's Temple." In *Mélanges offerts à M. Maurice Dunand*, 2. Beirut: Université Saint-Joseph, 1972. [Israel/Canaan]

Kenyon, Kathleen M. "Solomon and the Building of the Temple." In *Jerusalem: Excavating 3,000 Years of History*, edited by M. Wheeler. 54-62. New York: McGraw-Hill, 1967. [Israel/Canaan]

Kimura, Hiroshi. "Isaiah 6:1–9:6: A Theatrical Section of the Book of Isaiah." Ph.D. diss., Uppsala University, 1981. [Israel/Canaan]

King, James. *Recent Discoveries on the Temple Hill at Jerusalem*. London: The Religious Tract Society, 1884. [Israel/Canaan]

Kirkbride, D. "Le temple nabatéen de Ramm: son évolution architecturale." *RB* 67 (1960): 65-92. [Israel/Canaan]

Kittel, R. "Der heilige Fels auf dem Moria: Seine Geschichte und seine Altäre." In Kittel, *Studien zur hebräischen Archäologie und Religionsgeschichte*. 1-96. Leipzig: Hinrichs, 1908. [Israel/Canaan]

Kittel, R. "Der herodianische Tempel." In *Realencyklopädie für protestantische Theologie und Kirche*, edited by A. Hauck. 24 vols., 19:498-500. Leipzig: Akademische, 1907. [Israel/Canaan]

Klagsbald, Victor A. "The Menorah as Symbol: Its Meaning and Origin in Early Jewish Art." *Journal of Jewish Art* 12/13 (1987): 126-34. [Israel/Canaan]

Klamroth, Erich. *Lade und Tempel*. Gütersloh: Bertelsmann, 1932. [Israel/Canaan]

Klausner, Joseph. *Ha-Bayit ha-Sheni bi-Gedulato.* Tel-Aviv: Devir, 1930. [Israel/Canaan]

Klausner, Joseph. *Historiyah shel ha-Bayit ha-Sheni.* 5 vols. Jerusalem: Ahi'asaf, 1949-51. [Israel/Canaan]

Klausner, Joseph. "Jesus in Jerusalem: the Cleansing of the Temple and the Debate in the Temple Courts." In *The World History of the Jewish People,* edited by Michael Avi-Yonah and Zvi Baras. Jerusalem: Massada, 1977. 227-33. [Israel/Canaan]

Klein, Mina C., and H. A. Klein. *Temple beyond Time: The Story of the Site of Solomon's Temple at Jerusalem.* New York: Van Nostrand Reinhold, 1970. [Israel/Canaan]

Kliers, Moses. *Ha-Mikdash u-Kedoshav: Berurim ve-ʿIyunim ba-ʿAvodat Bet ha-Beḥirah ba-Zeman ha-Zeh.* Jerusalem: Mekhon Hari Fishel li-Derishat ha-Talmud u-Mishpat ha-Torah, 1970. [Israel/Canaan]

Klingele, O. H. "Der Tempel von Jerusalem." *Das heilige Land* 90 (1958): 77-91. [Israel/Canaan]

Klyne, Sylvester S. "The Temple at Jerusalem—Its History and Its Influence on the Religion of the Hebrews." Ph.D. diss., Boston University, 1906. [Israel/Canaan]

Koch, K. "Tempeleinlassliturgien und Dekaloge." In *Studien zur Theologie der alttestamentlichen Überlieferungen,* edited by Rolf Rendtorff and Klaus Koch, 45-60. Neukirchen-Vluyn: Neukirchener, 1961. [Israel/Canaan]

Koeberle, Justus. *Die Tempelsänger im alten Testament.* Erlangen: Junge, 1899. [Israel/Canaan]

Kolbe, Joshua J. *The Temple and City of Jerusalem.* London: Saunders Brothers, 1884. [Israel/Canaan]

Kolenkow, Anitra B. "The Fall of the Temple and the Coming of the End: The Spectrum and Process of Apocalyptic Argument in 2 Baruch and Other Authors." *SBLSP* 21 (1982): 243-50. [Israel/Canaan]

Kon, Maximilian. "Jewish Art at the Time of the Second Temple." In *Jewish Art: An Illustrated History,* edited by Cecil Roth. 51-64. London: Allen, 1961. [Israel/Canaan]

Kon, Maximilian. "The Menorah of the Arch of Titus." *PEFQ* 82 (1950): 25-30. [Israel/Canaan]

König, Eduard. *Zentralkultstätte und Kultuszentralisierung im alten Israel.* Gütersloh: Bertelsmann, 1931. [Israel/Canaan]

Kopp, C. "Jerusalem I: The Temple." In *The Holy Places of the Gospels,* translated by Ronald Walls. 283-86. New York: Herder and Herder, 1963. [Israel/Canaan]

Kopp, C. "Der Tempelplatz unter Julian." *Das heilige Land* 91/1-2 (1959): 17-24. [Israel/Canaan]

Koren (Winkler), M. "Is the Zakrah the Foundation Stone?" (in Hebrew). *Ha-Maayan* 8/4 (1968): 27-31. [Israel/Canaan]

Kornfeld, W. "Der Symbolismus der Tempelsäulen." *ZAW* 74 (1962): 50-57. [Israel/Canaan]

Krauss, Samuel. "Die Synagoge auf dem Tempelberge." In *Synagogale Altertümer*. 66-72. Berlin-Wien: Harz, 1922. [Israel/Canaan]

Krauss, Samuel. "Der Tempel des Herodes." In *Jüdisches Lexikon*, edited by G. Herlitz and B. Kirschner. 4 vols. in 5, 4:2:915-17. Berlin: Jüdisch, 1930. [Israel/Canaan]

Krinetzki, Leo. "Zur Poetik und Exegese von Ps. 48." *Biblische Zeitschrift* 4 (1960): 70-97. [Israel/Canaan]

Krinsky, C. H. "Representations of the Temple of Jerusalem before 1500." *Journal of the Warburg and Courtauld Institutes* 33 (1970): 1-19. [Israel/Canaan]

Kühn, Ernst. "Ezechiels Gesicht vom Tempel der Vollendungszeit, Kap. 40-42; 43:13-17; 46:19-24." *Theologische Studien und Kritiken* 55 (1882): 601-88. [Israel/Canaan]

Kühnel, Bianca. "Jewish Symbolism of the Temple and the Tabernacle and Christian Symbolism of the Holy Sepulchre and the Heavenly Tabernacle." *Journal of Jewish Art* 12/13 (1987): 147-68. [Israel/Canaan]

Kumaki, Francis K. "The Temple Sermon: Jeremiah's Polemic against the Deuteronomists." Ph.D. diss, Union Theological Seminary, 1980. [Israel/Canaan]

Kurth, Dieter. *Die Dekoration der Säulen im Pronaos des Tempels von Edfou*. Wiesbaden: Harrassowitz, 1983. [Israel/Canaan]

Kuschke, Arnulf. "Tempel." In *Biblisches Reallexikon*, edited by Kurt Galling. 333-42. Tübingen: Mohr, 1927. [Israel/Canaan]

Kuschke, Arnulf. "Der Tempel Salomos und der 'syrische Tempeltypus.' " In *Das ferne und nahe Wort*, edited by F. Maass. 124-32. Berlin: Töpelmann, 1967. [Israel/Canaan]

Lachs, S. T. "Why Was the 'Amen' Response Interdicted in the Temple?" *Journal for the Study of Judaism in the Persian, Hellenistic and Roman Period* 19 (1988): 230-40. [Israel/Canaan]

Laconi, Mauro. "Gerusalemme e la liturgia del tempio nel quarto vangelo." In *Gerusalemme. Atti della XXVI Settimana Biblica. Associazione Biblica Italiana*, edited by M. Borrmans. 251-60. Brescia: Paideia, 1982. [Israel/Canaan]

Lagrange, F. J. "Comment s'est formée l'enceinte du Temple de Jérusalem." *RB* 2 (1893): 90-113. [Israel/Canaan]

Lamarche, P. "La mort du Christ et le voile du Temple selon Marc." *Nouvelle revue théologique* 96 (1974): 583-99. [Israel/Canaan]

Lancellotti, A. "La distruzione di Gerusalemme e del suo tempio nel discorso eschatologico secondo una recente interpretatzione." In *La distruzione di Gerusalemme del 70: nei suoi riflessi storico-letterari*, edited by S. Gozzo. 69-78. Assisi: Studio teologico "porziuncolo." 1971. [Israel/Canaan]

Lande-Nash, I. "Der herodianische Tempel." In *3000 Jahre Jerusalem: Eine Geschichte der Stadt von den Anfängen bis zur Eroberung durch die Kreuzfahrer.* 101-11. Tübingen: Wasmuth, 1964. [Israel/Canaan]

Landsberger, F. "In the Days of the Second Temple." In *A History of Jewish Art.* 125-39. Cincinnati: Union of American Hebrew Congregations, 1946. [Israel/Canaan]

Laperrousaz, E.-M. "Angle sud-est du 'Temple de Salomon' ou vestiges de l'Acra des Séleucides?" *Syria* 52 (1975): 241‡59. [Israel/Canaan]

Laperrousaz, E.-M. "A-t-on dégagé l'angle sud-est du 'Temple de Salomon'?" *Syria* 50 (1973): 355-59. [Israel/Canaan]

Laperrousaz, E.-M. "La discontinuité (*seam, straight joint*) visible près de l'extrémité sud du mur oriental du Haram esh-Shérif marque-t-elle l'angle sud-est du 'temple de Salomon'?" *VT* 38 (October 1988): 399-406. [Israel/Canaan]

Laperrousaz, E.-M. "King Solomon's Wall Still Supports the Temple Mount." *BAR* 13/3 (1987): 34-44. [Israel/Canaan]

Läpple, A. "Das neue Jerusalem: Die Eschatologie der Offenbarung des Johannes." *Bibel und Kirche* 39 (1984): 75-81. [Israel/Canaan]

Laughlin, John C. H. "The Remarkable Discoveries at Tel Dah." *Biblical Archaeology Review* 7 (1981): 20-37. [Israel/Canaan]

Lauterbach, J. Z. "The Pharisees and Their Teachings." *HUCA* 6 (1929): 69-139. [Israel/Canaan]

Lauterbach, J. Z. "A Significant Controversy between the Sadducees and the Pharisees." In *Rabbinic Essays.* 51-83. Cincinnati: Hebrew Union College Press, 1951. [Israel/Canaan]

Le Bas, E. E. "Was the Corner-Stone of Scripture a Pyramidion?" *PEQ* 78 (1946): 103-15. [Israel/Canaan]

Le Bas, E. E. "Zechariah's Climax to the Career of the Corner-Stone." *PEQ* 83 (1951): 139-55. [Israel/Canaan]

Le Bas, E. E. "Zechariah's Enigmatical Contribution to the Corner-Stone." *PEQ* 82 (1950): 102-22. [Israel/Canaan]

Lehmann, M. R. "The Temple Scroll as a Source of Sectarian Halakhah." *Revue de Qumran* 9 (1978): 579-88. [Israel/Canaan]

Lemaire, André. "Une inscription paléo-hébraïque sur grenade en ivoire." *RB* 88 (1981): 236-39. [Israel/Canaan]

Léon-Dufour, Xavier. "Le signe du Temple selon saint Jean." *Revue des sciences religieuses* 39 (1951-52): 155-75. [Israel/Canaan]

Levenson, David B. "A Source and Tradition Critical Study of the Stories of Julian's Attempt to Rebuild the Jerusalem Temple." Ph.D. diss, Harvard University, 1980. [Israel/Canaan]

Levenson, Jon D. "From Temple to Synagogue: I Kings 8." In *Traditions in Transformation: Turning Points in Biblical Faith*, edited by Baruch Halpern and Jon D. Levenson. 143-66. Winona Lake: Eisenbrauns, 1981. [Israel/Canaan]

Levenson, Jon D. *Sinai and Zion*. Minneapolis: Winston, 1985. [Israel/Canaan]

Levenson, Jon D. "The Temple and the World." *Journal of Religion* 64 (1984): 275-98. [Israel/Canaan]

Levenson, Jon D. *Theology of the Program of Restoration of Ezekiel 40-48*, *Harvard Semitic Monographs*, vol. 10. Missoula, MT: Scholars, 1976. [Israel/Canaan]

Lévi, Israel. "Le temple du dieu Yahou et la colonie juive d'Éléphantine au Ve siècle avant l'ère chrétienne." *Revue des études juives* 54 (1907): 153-65; 56 (1908): 161-68. [Israel/Canaan]

Levine, Baruch A. "On the Presence of God in Biblical Religion." In *Religions in Antiquity: Essays in Memory of E. R. Goodenough*, edited by Jacob Neusner. 71-87. Leiden: Brill: 1968. [Israel/Canaan]

Levine, Baruch A. "The Temple Scroll: Aspects of Its Historical Provenance and Literary Character." *BASOR* 232 (1978): 5-23. [Israel/Canaan]

Levinsky, Y.-T., ed. "The Destruction of the Temple" (in Hebrew). In *The Book of Festivals*. 8 vols., 7:207-452. Tel-Aviv: Dvir, 1957. [Israel/Canaan]

Levinson, N. Peter. "Tempel und Synagoge." In *Die Kultusymbolik im Alten Testament und im nachbiblischen Judentum. Symbolik der Religionen*. 17:15-45. Stuttgart: Hiersemann, 1972. [Israel/Canaan]

Levy, Abraham J., ed. *Rashi's Commentary on Ezekiel 40-48*. Philadelphia: Dropsie College, 1931. [Israel/Canaan]

Lewin, T. "Observations on the Probable Sites of the Jewish Temple and Antonia, and the Acra, with Reference to the Results of the Recent Palestine Explorations." *Archaeologia* 44 (1873): 17-62. [Israel/Canaan]

Lewis, George W. *From Bible Data of the House Which King Solomon Built for Jehovah*. Cincinnati: Standard, 1927. [Israel/Canaan]

Lewittes, M., tr. *The Book of Temple Service*, by Moses Maimonides. New Haven: Yale University Press, 1957. [Israel/Canaan]

Lewy, Julius. "The Šulmān Temple in Jerusalem." *JBL* 59 (1940): 519-22. [Israel/Canaan]

Lewy, Yohanan. "Julian the Apostate and the Building of the Temple." In *Jerusalem Cathedra*, edited by L. I. Levine, 3 vols., 3:70-96. Detroit: Wayne State University Press, 1983. [Israel/Canaan]

Licht, Jacob. "An Ideal Town Plan from Qumran—The Description of the New Jerusalem." *IEJ* 29 (1979): 45-59. [Israel/Canaan]

Lieberman, S. "The Temple: Its Layout and Procedure." In *Hellenism in Jewish Palestine*. 164-79. New York: Jewish Theological Seminary of America, 1950. [Israel/Canaan]

Liebreich, Y. A. "The Psalms of the Levites for the Days of the Week" (in Hebrew). *Eretz-Israel* 3 (1954): 170-73. [Israel/Canaan]

Lightfoot, R. H. "The Cleansing of the Temple in St. John's Gospel." *ET* 60/3 (1948): 64-68. [Israel/Canaan]

Lignée, Hubert. *The Living Temple*. Baltimore: Helicon, 1966. [Israel/Canaan]

Lignée, Hubert. *Zelt Gottes unter den Menschen: Welt der Bibel*. Duesseldorf: Patmos, 1961; also in English as *The Temple of Yahweh*. Baltimore: Helicon, 1966. [Israel/Canaan]

Lindblom, J. "Theophanies in Holy Places in Hebrew Religion." *HUCA* 32 (1961): 91-106. [Israel/Canaan]

Lindeskog, G. "The Veil of the Temple." In *Coniectanea Neotestamentica, II: In Honorem A. Fridrichsen*. 132-37. Lund: Gleerup, 1947. [Israel/Canaan]

Lipiński, Edward. "Beth-Schemisch und der Tempel der Herrin der Grabkammer in den Amaran-Briefen." *VT* 23 (1973): 443-45. [Israel/Canaan]

Lipiński, Edward. *La royauté de Yahwé dans la poésie et le culte de l'ancien Israel*. Brussels: Paleis der Academien, 1965. [Israel/Canaan]

Lods, Adolphe. "Les cuisines du Temple de Jeursalem." *RHR* 127 (1944): 30-54. [Israel/Canaan]

Lofthouse, W. F. "The City and the Sanctuary." *ET* 34 (1922-23): 198-202. [Israel/Canaan]

Lohmeyer, Ernst. "Die Reinigung des Tempels." *Theologische Blätter* 20 (1941): 257-64. [Israel/Canaan]

Lohse, Ernst. "Temple and Synagogue." In *Jesus in his Time*, edited by H. J. Schultz and translated by B. Watchorn. 75-83. Philadelpha: Fortress, 1971. [Israel/Canaan]

Losie, Lynn A. "The Cleansing of the Temple: A History of a Gospel Tradition in Light of Its Background in the Old Testament and in Early Judaism." Ph.D. diss., Fuller Theological Seminary, 1985. [Israel/Canaan]

Lowy, S. "The Confutation of Judaism in the Epistle of Barnabas." *JJS* 11 (1960): 1-33. [Israel/Canaan]

Lührmann, D. "Markus 14:55-64: Christologie und Zerstörung des Tempels im Markusevangelium." *NTS* 27 (1981): 457-74. [Israel/Canaan]

Luke, Harry C. *Ceremonies at the Holy Places*. Milwaukee: Morehouse, 1932. [Israel/Canaan]

Luria, Ben Zion. "And a Fountain Shall Come Forth of the House of the Lord" (in Hebrew). *Beth Mikra* 15/40 (1970): 3-13. [Israel/Canaan]

Luria, Ben Zion. "Comments on the Scroll of the Sanctuary" (in Hebrew). *Beth Mikra* 74 (1978): 370-86. [Israel/Canaan]

Luria, Ben Zion. "Temple in the First Generation after the Exile." In *Proceedings, 8th World Congress of Jewish Studies, August 16-21, 1981.* 41-45. Jerusalem: World Union of Jewish Studies, 1982. [Israel/Canaan]

Luria, Ben Zion. "The Temple Mount at the Time of the Return to Zion" (in Hebrew). *Beth Mikra* 26 (1981): 206-18. [Israel/Canaan]

Maag, Victor. "Erwägungen zur deuteronomischen Kultzentralisation." *VT* 6 (1956): 10-18. [Israel/Canaan]

Maas, Anthony J. *A Day in the Temple.* St. Louis, MO: Herder, 1892. [Israel/Canaan]

Macalister, Robert A. S. *A Century of Excavation in Palestine.* London: Religious Tract Society, 1925. [Israel/Canaan]

McCall, Thomas S. *Israel and Tomorrow's Temple,* rev. ed. Chicago: Moody, 1977. [Israel/Canaan]

McCall, Thomas S., and Zola Levitt. *Satan in the Sanctuary: Israel's Four Temples.* Chicago: Moody, 1973. [Israel/Canaan]

McConkie, Bruce R. "The Olivet Discourse: Jerusalem and the Temple." In McConkie, *The Mortal Messiah.* 4 vols, 3:421-35. Salt Lake City: Deseret Book, 1980. [Israel/Canaan]

McCready, Wayne O. "The Sectarian Status of Qumran: The Temple Scroll." *Revue de Qumran* 11 (1983): 183-91. [Israel/Canaan]

Macholz, G. Ch. "Noch Einmal: Planungen für den Wiederaufbau nach der Katastrophe von 587 (Erwägungen zum Schlussteil des sog. 'Verfassungsentwurfs des Hesekiel')." *VT* 19 (1969): 322-52. [Israel/Canaan]

Mackay, C. M. "The City and the Sanctuary." *ET* 34 (1922-23): 475-76. [Israel/Canaan]

Mackay, C. M. "The City and Sanctuary—Ezekiel 48." *Princeton Theological Review* 20 (1922): 399-417. [Israel/Canaan]

Mackay, C. M. "The City of Ezekiel's Oblation." *Princeton Theological Review* 21 (1923): 372-88. [Israel/Canaan]

Mackay, C. M. "The Key to the Old Testament (Ezek. 40-48)." *Church Quarterly Review* 199 (1935): 173-96. [Israel/Canaan]

Mackay, C. M. "Prolegomena to Ezekiel 40-48." *ET* 55 (1943-44): 292-95. [Israel/Canaan]

Mackay, C. M. "Zechariah's Relation to Ezek. 40-48." *Evangelical Quarterly* 40 (1968): 197-210. [Israel/Canaan]

McKay, J. W. "Further Light on the Horses and Chariot of the Sun in the Jerusalem Temple (2 Kings 23:11)." *PEQ* 105 (1973): 167-69. [Israel/Canaan]

McKelvey, R. J. " 'Temple' in the New Testament." In *The New Bible Dictionary*, edited by J. D. Douglas. 1247-50. Grand Rapids: Eerdmans, 1962. [Israel/Canaan]

McKelvey, R. J. "Christ the Cornerstone." *NTS* 8 (1961-62): 352-59. [Israel/Canaan]

McKelvey, R. J. *The New Temple: The Church in the New Testament.* London: Oxford University Press, 1969. [Israel/Canaan]

McKenzie, John L. "The Presence in the Temple: God as Tenant." In *God and His Temple*, edited by L. E. Frizzell. 30-38. South Orange, NJ: Seton Hall University/Institute for Judaeo-Christian Studies, 1980. [Israel/Canaan]

McKenzie, Leon. "Of Rocks and Stones and Temples Rare." *The Bible Today* 23 (1966): 1522-27. [Israel/Canaan]

McNicol, A. J. "The Eschatological Temple in the Qumrân Pesher 4Q Florilegium 1: 1-7." *Ohio Journal of Religious Studies* 5 (1977): 133-41. [Israel/Canaan]

McQueen, D. H. "The New Jerusalem and Town Planning." *Expositor* 9 (1924): 220-26. [Israel/Canaan]

MacRae, G. W. "Building of the House of the Lord." *American Ecclesiastical Review* 140 (1959): 361-76. [Israel/Canaan]

MacRae, G. W. "Heavenly Temple and Eschatology in the Letter to the Hebrews." *Semeia* 12 (1978): 179-99. [Israel/Canaan]

MacRae, G. W. "A Kingdom That Cannot Be Shaken: The Heavenly Jerusalem in the Letter to the Hebrews." In *Spirituality and Ecumenism. Yearbook of the Ecumenical Institute for Theological Research, 1979/1980*, edited by P. Bonnard, G. MacRae, and J. Cobb. 27-40. Tantur, Jerusalem: Ecumenical Institute for Theological Research, 1980. [Israel/Canaan]

Madsen, Truman G. "The Temple and the Restoration." In *The Temple in Antiquity*, edited by Truman G. Madsen. 1-18. Provo: Brigham Young University Press, 1984. [Israel/Canaan]

Magen, Yizhaq. "*Bet Ha-Mesibah* in the Temple Scroll and in the Mishnah" (in Hebrew; *English summary). *Eretz-Israel* 17 (1984): 226-35, *10. [Israel/Canaan]

Mah-Tov, G. *Ha-Mikdashim ve-Kodshehem: Korot, Toldot va-Atidot Har ha-Bayit, ha-Mishkan, Bate-ha-Mikdash, Kele ha-Mishkan veha-Mikdashim, ha-Korbanot, ha-Kotel ha-Maaravi ve-Sipure Pelaim odotehem be-Divre Yeme Yisrael.* Jerusalem: Oraita, 1983. [Israel/Canaan]

Maier, Johann. "Gottesdienst in der Zeit des salomonischen Tempels." *Bibel und Liturgie* 44 (1971): 237-51. [Israel/Canaan]

Maier, Johann. "Die Hofanlagen im Tempel-Entwurf des Ezechiel im Licht der 'Tempelrolle' von Qumran." In *Prophecy: Essays Presented to Georg Fohrer*, edited by J. A. Emerton. 55-68. Berlin: de Gruyter, 1980. [Israel/Canaan]

Maier, Johann. "Religiongeschichtliche Aspekte frühjüdischer Institutionen: Tempel und Tempelkult." In *Literatur und Religion des Frühjudentums*, edited by J. Maier and J. Schreiner. 371-90. Würzburg: Echter, 1973. [Israel/Canaan]

Maier, Johann. *Die Tempelrolle vom Toten Meer.* Munich: Reinhardt, 1978; also in English as *The Temple Scroll.* Sheffield: JSOT, 1985. [Israel/Canaan]

Maigret, Jacques. "Le Temple au coeur de la Bible." *Le Monde de la Bible* 13 (1980): 3-5. [Israel/Canaan]

Manson, T. W. "The Cleansing of the Temple." *BJRL* 33 (1950-51): 271-82. [Israel/Canaan]

Mantel, Chaim D. (Hugo). *Studies in the History of the Sanhedrin.* Cambridge: Harvard University Press, 1961; also in Hebrew, *Studies in the History of the Sanhedrin.* Tel Aviv: Dvir, 1969. [Israel/Canaan]

Marböck, Johannes. "Das Gebet um die Rettung Zions Sir. 36, 1-22 (G: 33, 1-13a; 36, 16b-22) im Zusammenhang der Geschichtsschau Ben Siras." In *Memoria Jerusalem: Freundesgabe Franz Sauer zum 70. Geburtstag,* edited by Johannes B. Bauer and Johannes Marböck. 93-115. Graz: Akademische, 1977. [Israel/Canaan]

Margueron, Jean. "Les origins syriennes du Temple de Jérusalem." *Le Monde de la Bible* 20 (August-September 1981): 31-33. [Israel/Canaan]

Martin-Achard, Robert. "Esaïe LIV et la nouvelle Jérusalem." In *International Organization for the Study of the Old Testament, Congress Volume, Vienna, 1980* 238-62. Leiden: Brill, 1981. [Israel/Canaan]

Matthiae, Paolo. "Unité et Développement du Temple dans la Syrie du Bronze Moyen." In *Le temple et le culte: Compte rendu de la vingtième recontre assyriologique internationale organisée à Leiden du 3 au 7 juillet 1972.* 43-72. Istanbul: Nederlands Historisch-Archeologisch Instituut te Istambul 1975. [Israel/Canaan]

May, G. L. "Temple or Shrine?" *ET* 62 (1950-51): 346-47. [Israel/Canaan]

May, Herbert G. "The Departure of the Glory of Yahweh." *JBL* 56 (1937): 309-21. [Israel/Canaan]

May, Herbert G. "Ezekiel, Exegesis: Vision of the Restored Community (40:1-48:35)." In *The Interpreter's Bible* 6:282-38. New York: Abingdon, 1956. [Israel/Canaan]

May, Herbert G. "Ruth's Visit to the High Place at Bethlehem." *Journal of the Royal Asiatic Society* (1939): 75-78. [Israel/Canaan]

May, Herbert G. "Some Aspects of Solar Worship at Jerusalem." *ZAW* 55 (1937): 269-81. [Israel/Canaan]

May, Herbert G. "The Two Pillars before the Temple of Solomon." *BASOR* 88 (1942): 19-27. [Israel/Canaan]

Mayer, H. "Das Bauholz des Tempels Salomos." *Biblische Zeitschrift* 11 (1967): 53-66. [Israel/Canaan]

Mazar, Amihai. "Additional Philistine Temples at Tell Qasile." *BA* 40 (1977): 82-87. [Israel/Canaan]

Mazar, Amihai. "Bronze Bull Found in Israelite 'High Place' from the Time of the Judges." *BAR* 9 (1983): 34-40. [Israel/Canaan]

Mazar, Amihai. "A Cult Site in the Samaria Mountains from the Period of the Judges" (in Hebrew). *Eretz-Israel* 16 (1982): 135-45. [Israel/Canaan]

Mazar, Amihai. *Mikdeshe Tel Kasilah.* 2 vols. Jerusalem: Hebrew University, 1977. [Israel/Canaan]

Mazar, Amihai. "A Philistine Temple at Tell Qasile." *BA* 36 (1973): 42-48. [Israel/Canaan]

Mazar, Amihai. "Tel Qasile." *RB* 82 (1975): 263-66. [Israel/Canaan]

Mazar, Benjamin. "The Archaeological Excavations near the Temple Mount." In *Jerusalem Revealed: Archaeology in the Holy City, 1968-1974,* edited by Yigael Yadin. 25-40. New Haven: Yale University Press, 1975. [Israel/Canaan]

Mazar, Benjamin. "Découverts archéologiques près des murs du Temple." *La Terre Sainte* 8-9 (1973): 222-32. [Israel/Canaan]

Mazar, Benjamin. *The Excavations in the Old City of Jerusalem near the Temple Mount: Preliminary Report of the Second and Third Seasons 1969-70.* Jerusalem: Israel Exploration Society, 1971. [Israel/Canaan]

Mazar, Benjamin. "Excavations near Temple Mount Reveal Splendors of Herodian Jerusalem." *BAR* 6/4 (1980): 44-59. [Israel/Canaan]

Mazar, Benjamin. "The Excavations South and West of the Temple Mount." *Ariel* 27 (1970): 11-19. [Israel/Canaan]

Mazar, Benjamin. "The Excavations South and West of the Temple Mount in Jerusalem: The Herodian Period." *BA* 33/2 (1970): 47-60. [Israel/Canaan]

Mazar, Benjamin. "Hebrew Inscription from the Temple Area in Jerusalem" (in Hebrew). *Qadmoniot* 3/4[12] (1970): 142-44. [Israel/Canaan]

Mazar, Benjamin. "Herodian Jerusalem in the Light of the Excavations South and Southwest of the Temple Mount." *IEJ* 28 (1978): 230-37. [Israel/Canaan]

Mazar, Benjamin. "Le mur du temple." *Bible et Terre Sainte* 122 (1970): 8-15. [Israel/Canaan]

Mazar, Benjamin. "The Royal Stoa on the Southern Part of the Temple Mount." In *Recent Archaeology in the Land of Israel,* edited by Hershel Shanks and Benjamin Mazar, 141-47. Washington, D.C.: Biblical Archaeology Society, 1984. [Israel/Canaan]

Mazar, Benjamin. "The Sanctuary of Arad and the Family of Hobab the Kenite" (in Hebrew; *English summary). *Eretz-Israel* 7 (1964): 1-5, *165. [Israel/Canaan]

Mazar, Benjamin, et al., eds. *The Mountain of the Lord.* Garden City: Doubleday, 1975. [Israel/Canaan]

Meinema, W. D. *De tempel van Salomo.* Netherlands: Delft, 1948. [Israel/Canaan]

Meiri, Menahem. *The Chosen House* (in Hebrew). 12 vols. Jerusalem: Yad ha-Rav Hertzog, 1963-74. [Israel/Canaan]

Meistermann, Barnabas. "Temple of Herod." In *The Catholic Encyclopedia*, edited by C. G. Herbermann et al. 15 vols. 14:502-4. New York: Encyclopedia, 1912. [Israel/Canaan]

Mendels, D. " 'On Kingship' in the 'Temple Scroll' and the Ideological Vorlage of the Seven Banquets in the 'Letter of Aristeas to Philocrates'." *Aegyptus* 59/1-2 (1979): 127-36. [Israel/Canaan]

Mendner, S. "Die Tempelreinigung." *ZNTW* 47 (1956): 93-112. [Israel/Canaan]

Menes, A. "Tempel und Synagogue." *ZAW* 50 (1932): 268-76. [Israel/Canaan]

Mensch, Ernst C. *King Solomon's 'First' Temple*. San Francisco: Mensch, 1947. [Israel/Canaan]

Mettinger, Tryggve N. D. "Den narvarande Guden: Om tempelteologi och gudsbild i Gamla Testamentet." *Svensk Exegetisk Årsbok* 47 (1982): 21-47. [Israel/Canaan]

Metzger, Martin. "Himmlische und irdische Wohnstatt Jahwes." In *Ugarit-Forschungen* 2 (1970):139-58. [Israel/Canaan]

Metzger, T. "Les objets du culte, le sanctuaire du désert et le temple de Jérusalem, dans les Bibles hébraïques médiévales enluminées, en Orient et en Espagne." *BJRL* 52-53 (1969-71): 397-436; 167-209. [Israel/Canaan]

Meyers, Carol L. "The Elusive Temple." *BA* 45 (1982): 33-41. [Israel/Canaan]

Meyers, Carol L. "Jachin and Boaz in Religious and Political Perspective." In *The Temple in Antiquity*, edited by Truman G. Madsen. 135-50. Provo: Brigham Young University Press, 1984. [Israel/Canaan]

Meyers, Carol L. "The Temple." In *Harper's Dictionary of the Bible*, 1021-32. [Israel/Canaan]

Meyers, Carol L. "Was There a Seven-Branched Lampstand in Solomon's Temple?" *BAR* 5/5 (1979): 46-57. [Israel/Canaan]

Michel, O., et al. "Der Tempel der goldenen Kuh." In *Gott und die Götter. Festgabe für Erich Fascher zum 60. Geburtstag*. 56-67. Berlin: Evangelische Verlagsanstatt, 1958. [Israel/Canaan]

Milgrom, Jacob. "Challenge to Sun-Worship Interpretation of Temple Scrolls Gilded Staircase." *BAR* 11/1 (1985): 70-73. [Israel/Canaan]

Milgrom, Jacob. "Day of Atonement." In *Encyclopaedia Judaica* 5:1384-87. [Israel/Canaan]

Milgrom, Jacob. "Further Studies in the Temple Scroll." *JQR* 71/1-2 (1980): 1-17; 89-106. [Israel/Canaan]

Milgrom, Jacob. "Kipper." In *Encyclopaedia Judaica* 10:1039-44. [Israel/Canaan]

Milgrom, Jacob. " 'Sabbath' and 'Temple City' in the Temple Scroll." *BASOR* 232 (1978): 25-27. [Israel/Canaan]

Milgrom, Jacob. "Studies in the Temple Scroll." *JBL* 97 (1978): 501-23. [Israel/Canaan]

Milgrom, Jacob. "The Temple in Biblical Israel: Kinships of Meaning." In *Reflections on Mormonism*, edited by Truman G. Madsen. 57-66. Provo: Brigham Young University Press, 1978. [Israel/Canaan]

Milgrom, Jacob. "Temple Scroll." *BA* 14/5 (1978): 105-20. [Israel/Canaan]

Miller, Patrick D. "Psalm 127—The House That Yahweh Builds." *Journal for the Study of the Old Testament* 22 (1982): 119-32. [Israel/Canaan]

Milson, D. "The Design of the Early Bronze Age Temples at Megiddo." *BASOR* 272 (1988): 75-78. [Israel/Canaan]

Milson, D. "The Design of the Temples and Gates at Shechem." *PEFQ* 119 (1987): 97-105. [Israel/Canaan]

Mink, H. A. "Die kol. III der Tempelrolle: Versuch einer Rekonstruktion." *Revue de Qumran* 11 (1983): 163-81. [Israel/Canaan]

Mink, H. A. "The Use of Scripture in the Temple Scroll and the Status of the Scroll as Law." *Scandinavian Journal of the Old Testament* 1 (1987): 20-50. [Israel/Canaan]

Mishelov, Isser. *Detailed Explanations to the Plan of the Temple* (in Hebrew). Haifa: Ben-Ariyeh, 1938. [Israel/Canaan]

Mistton, M. "On the Version of the Temple Scroll." *Tarbiz* 48/1-2 (1978-79): 173. [Israel/Canaan]

Moe, Olaf. "Das irdische und das himmlische Heiligtum: Zur Auslegung von Hebr. 9, 4f." *Theologische Zeischrift* 9 (1953): 23-29. [Israel/Canaan]

Möhlenbrink, Kurt. *Der Tempel Salomos*. Stuttgart: Kohlhammer, 1932. [Israel/Canaan]

Molin, G. "Ḥalonoth ʾaṭumoth bei Ezechiel." *Biblische Zeitschrift* 15 (1971): 250-53. [Israel/Canaan]

Montefiore, H. W. "Jesus and the Temple Tax." *NTS* 11 (October 1964): 60-71. [Israel/Canaan]

Montefiore, H. W. "Sulpicius Severus and Titus' Council of War." *Historia* 11 (1962): 156-70. [Israel/Canaan]

Moorhead, Walter J. "The Pharisees Reconsidered in Relation to the Temple Cultus and Early Christianity." Ph.D. diss., Southern Baptist Theological Seminary, 1960. [Israel/Canaan]

Moses ben Maimon. *The Book of Temple Service*, translated by M. Lewittes. In *Yale Judaica Series*, vol. 12. New Haven: Yale University Press, 1957. [Israel/Canaan]

Moses ben Maimon. *The Book of Temple Service* (in Hebrew), with commentary by S. D. Mendelson, Z. Sachs, and M. Reich. Jerusalem: Mossad Harav Kook, 1963. [Israel/Canaan]

Mowinckel, Sigmund. "The Copper Scroll: An Apocryphon?" *JBL* 76 (December 1957): 261-65. [Israel/Canaan]

Mowinckel, Sigmund. *Psalmenstudien*, 2 vols. Amsterdam: Schippers, 1966. [Israel/Canaan]

Mowinckel, Sigmund. "A quel moment le culte de Yahvé à Jérusalem est-il officiellement devenu un culte sans images?" *Revue d'histoire et de philosophie religieuses* (1929):197-216. [Israel/Canaan]

Mowinckel, Sigmund. "Wann wurde der Jahwäkultus in Jerusalem offiziell bildos?" *Acta Orientalia* 8 (1930): 257-79. [Israel/Canaan]

Muehsam, Alice. *Coin and Temple.* Leeds: Leeds University Oriental Society, 1966. [Israel/Canaan]

Mueller, J. R. "The Apocalypse of Abraham and the Destruction of the Second Jewish Temple." *SBLSP* 21 (1982): 341-49. [Israel/Canaan]

Mueller, J. R. "The Temple Scroll and the Gospel Divorce Texts." *Revue de Qumran* 10 (1980): 247-56. [Israel/Canaan]

Muilenburg, James. "The Site of Ancient Gilgal." *BASOR* 140 (1955): 11-27. [Israel/Canaan]

Mulder, M. J. "Einige Bemerkungen zur Beschreibung des Libanonwaldhauses in I Reg 7 2f." *ZAW* 88 (1976): 99-105. [Israel/Canaan]

Müller, Werner. *Die heilige Stadt: Roma Quadrata, himmlisches Jerusalem und die Mythe vom Weltnabel.* Stuttgart: Kohlammer, 1961. [Israel/Canaan]

Muntingh, L. M. " 'The City Which Has Foundations': Hebrews 11:8-10 in the Light of the Mari Texts." In *De fructo oris sui: Essays in Honour of Adrianus van Selms*, edited by I. H. Eybers. 108-20. Leiden: Brill, 1971. [Israel/Canaan]

Murphy, D. J. "Ezekiel and the New Temple." *Bible Today* 40 (1969): 2805-9. [Israel/Canaan]

Murphy, Frederick J. "The Temple in the Syriac Apocalypse of Baruch." *JBL* 106 (December 1987): 671-83. [Israel/Canaan]

Muuss, R. "Der Jahwetempel in Elephantine." *ZAW* 36 (1916): 81-107. [Israel/Canaan]

Myers, Jacob M. "Building the Temple." In Myers, *II Chronicles.* 8-44. Garden City: Doubleday, 1965. [Israel/Canaan]

Myers, Jacob M. "David and the Founding of the Temple." In *I Chronicles.* 77-200. Garden City: Doubleday, 1965. [Israel/Canaan]

Myres, J. L. "King Solomon's Temple and Other Buildings and Works of Art." *PEQ* 80 (1948): 14-41. [Israel/Canaan]

Narkiss, Bezalel. "The Scheme of the Sanctuary from the Time of Herod the Great." *Journal of Jewish Art* 1 (1974): 6-14. [Israel/Canaan]

Narkiss, Bezalel. "Temple: Temple in the Arts." In *Encyclopaedia Judaica* 15:984-88. [Israel/Canaan]

Nataf, G. "Les Zélotes et la chute du Temple." *Le Monde de la Bible* 13 (1980): 36-37. [Israel/Canaan]

Nebe, G. Wilhelm. "'DŠK 'Mass, Abmessung' in 11Q Tempelrolle XLI, 16." *Revue de Qumran* 11 (1983): 391-99. [Israel/Canaan]

Nedava, J. "The Destruction of the Second Temple" (in Hebrew). *Maḥanayim* 96 (1964): 56-63. [Israel/Canaan]

Negev, A. "Temples." In Negev, *Archaeological Encyclopedia of the Holy Land.* 310-13. New York: Putnam's Sons, 1972. [Israel/Canaan]

Neusner, Jacob. "Judaism after the Destruction of the Temple." In *Israelite and Judaean History*, edited by J. H. Hayes and M. Miller. 663-77. Philadelphia: Westminster, 1977. [Israel/Canaan]

Neusner, Jacob. "Judaism beyond Catastrophe: The Destruction of the Temple and the Renaissance of Torah." In Neusner, *Judaism in the Beginning of Christianity.* 89-99. Philadelphia: Fortress, 1984. [Israel/Canaan]

Neusner, Jacob. "Judaism in a Time of Crisis: Four Responses to the Destruction of the Second Temple." *Judaism* 21 (1972): 313-27. [Israel/Canaan]

Nibley, Hugh W. "Ancient Temples: What Do They Signify?" *Ensign* 2 (1972): 45-49. [Israel/Canaan]

Nibley, Hugh W. "Christian Envy of the Temple" *JQR* 50 (1959-60): 97-123; 229-40; reprinted in Nibley, *Mormonism and Early Christianity.* 391-434. Salt Lake City: Deseret Book and F.A.R.M.S., 1987. [Israel/Canaan]

Nicholson, Ernest W. "The Centralisation of the Cult in Deuteronomy." *VT* 13 (1963): 380-89. [Israel/Canaan]

Nicholson, Ernest W. "Josiah's Reformation and Deuteronomy." *Transactions of the Glasgow University Oriental Society* 20 (1965): 77-84. [Israel/Canaan]

Nickelsburg, G. W. E., and M. Stone. "Temple and Cult." In Nickelsburg and Stone, *Faith and Piety in Early Judaism: Texts and Documents.* 51-88. Philadelphia: Fortress, 1983. [Israel/Canaan]

Nickolsky, N. M. "Pascha im Kulte des jerusalemischen Tempels." *ZAW* 45 (1927): 171-90, 241-53. [Israel/Canaan]

Niditch, S. "Ezekiel 40-48 in a Visionary Context." *CBQ* 48 (1986): 208-24. [Israel/Canaan]

Nikiprowetzky, Valentin. "Le nouveau temple. A propos d'un ouvrage récent." *REJ* 130 (1971): 5-30. [Israel/Canaan]

Nikiprowetzky, Valentin. "Temple et communauté." *REJ* 126 (1967): 7-25. [Israel/Canaan]

Nodet, E. "Table delphique au temple." *RB* 96 (October 1989): 533-44. [Israel/Canaan]

Nolland, J. "A Misleading Statement of the Essene Attitude to the Temple (Josephus Antiquities, XViii, I, 5, 19)." *Revue de Qumran* 9 (1978): 555-62. [Israel/Canaan]

Nordström, C.-O. "Some Miniatures in Hebrew Bibles." In *Synthronon: Art et archéologie de la fin de l'antique et du moyen age.* 89-105. Paris: Klincksieck, 1968. [Israel/Canaan]

Northcote, H. "A Solution to the Chief Difficulties in Revelation XX-XXII." *ET* 26 (1914-15): 426-28. [Israel/Canaan]

Noth, Martin. "The Life of the Jerusalem Religious Community in the Persian Period." In *The History of Israel*, edited by P. Ackroyd, 2d ed. 337-45. New York: Harper and Row, 1960. [Israel/Canaan]

Noth, Martin. "The Re-establishment of the Sanctuary and the Cultus in Jerusalem." In *The History of Israel*, edited by P. Ackroyd, 2d ed. 300-16. New York: Harper and Row, 1960. [Israel/Canaan]

Noy, Dov. "The Foundation Stone and the Beginning of Creation" (in Hebrew). In *And to Jerusalem*. 360-94. Jerusalem: Union of Hebrew Writers of Israel, 1968. [Israel/Canaan]

Oesterley, William O. E. "Herod's Temple." In *A History of Israel*, vol. 2 of *From the Fall of Jerusalem, 586 B.C. to the Bar Kokhba Revolt, A.D. 135*, edited by T. H. Robinson and W. O. E. Oesterley. 376-78. Oxford: Clarendon, 1932. [Israel/Canaan]

Oesterley, William O. E. "The Temple." In *A Dictionary of Christ and the Gospels*, edited by James Hastings. vol. 2. 208-13. New York: Scribners & Sons, 1908. [Israel/Canaan]

Oestreicher, Theodor. *Reichstempel und Ortsheiligtümer in Israel*. Gütersloh: Bertelsmann, 1930. [Israel/Canaan]

Orchard, William E. *The Temple*. New York: Seabury Press, [1965]. [Israel/Canaan]

Oren, E. D. "Excavations at Qasrawet in NW Sinai." *IEJ* 32 (1982): 203-11. [Israel/Canaan]

Orlinsky, Harry M. "The Destruction of the First Temple and the Babylonian Exile in the Light of Archaeology." In *Essays in Biblical Culture and Bible Translation*. 144-61. New York: KTAV, 1974. [Israel/Canaan]

Orrieux, C. "Le Temple de Salomon." In *Temples et Sanctuaires: Seminaire de recherche 1981-1983*, edited by G. Roux. 51-59. Lyon: Maison de l'Orient, 1984. [Israel/Canaan]

Otto, Eckart. "El und JHWH in Jerusalem: Historische und theologische Aspekte einer Religionsintegration." *VT* 30 (1980): 316-29. [Israel/Canaan]

Ottosson, Magnus. "*hêkhal*." In *Theological Dictionary of the Old Testament* 3:382-88. [Israel/Canaan]

Ottosson, Magnus. *Temples and Cult Places in Palestine*. Stockholm: Almquist and Wiksell, 1980. [Israel/Canaan]

Ouellette, Jean. "*Atumim* in I Kings 6:4." *Bulletin of the Institute of Jewish Studies* (1974): 99-102. [Israel/Canaan]

Ouellette, Jean. "The Basic Structure of Solomon's Temple and Archaeological Research." In *The Temple of Solomon*, edited by J. Gutman. 1-20. Missoula: Scholars, 1976. [Israel/Canaan]

Ouellette, Jean. "Jachin and Boaz." In *The Interpreter's Dictionary of the Bible*, supp. vol., 469. [Israel/Canaan]

Ouellette, Jean. "The Solomonic *dᵉbîr* according to the Hebrew Text of I Kings 6." *JBL* 89 (1970): 338-43. [Israel/Canaan]

Ouellette, Jean. "Temple of Solomon." In *The Interpreter's Dictionary of the Bible*, supp. vol., 873-74. [Israel/Canaan]

Ouellette, Jean. "The Temple of Solomon: A Philological and Archaeological Study." Ph.D. diss., Hebrew Union College, 1966. [Israel/Canaan]

Ouellette, Jean. "Le vestibule du Temple de Salomon était-il un Beit Hilani?" *RB* 76 (1969): 365-78. [Israel/Canaan]

Ouellette, Jean. "The *Yāṣîaᶜ* and the *Ṣᵉlāᶜōt*: Two Mysterious Structures in Solomon's Temple." *JNES* 31 (1972): 187-91. [Israel/Canaan]

Pailloux, Xavier. *Monographie du Temple de Salomon.* Paris: Roger and Chernoviz, 1885. [Israel/Canaan]

Paine, Timothy O. *Solomon's Temple and Capitol, Ark of the Flood and Tabernacle; or, The Holy Houses of the Hebrew, Chaldee, Syriac, Samaritan, Septuagint, Coptic, and Itala Scriptures.* Boston: Houghton Mifflin, 1885. [Israel/Canaan]

Paine, Timothy O. *Solomon's Temple, including the Tabernacle.* Boston: Phinney, 1861. [Israel/Canaan]

Palmer, Martin. "The Cardinal Points in Psalm 48." *Biblica* 46 (1945): 357-58. [Israel/Canaan]

Parrot, André. *The Temple of Jerusalem.* New York: Philosophical Library, 1955. [Israel/Canaan]

Parunak, H. "Was Solomon's Temple Aligned to the Sun?" *PEQ* 110 (1978): 29-33. [Israel/Canaan]

Patai, Raphael. *Man and Temple in Ancient Jewish Myth and Ritual.* New York: Nelson, 1947. [Israel/Canaan]

Paton, Lewis B. "The Location of the Temple." In Paton, *Jerusalem in Bible Times.* 1-7. Chicago: University of Chicago Press, 1908. [Israel/Canaan]

Patrich, Joseph. "The *mesibbah* of the Temple according to the Tractate *Middot*." *IEJ* 36/3-4 (1986): 215-33. [Israel/Canaan]

Patrich, Joseph. "Reconstructing the Magnificent Temple Herod Built." *Bible Review* 4 (October 1988): 16-29. [Israel/Canaan]

Paul, S. M., and William G. Dever. "Cultic Structures." In *Biblical Archaeology*, edited by Geoffrey Wigoder. 54-83. New York: Quadrangle, 1974. [Israel/Canaan]

Pedersen, Johannes. "Feasts and Sacred Customs." In *Israel: Its Life and Culture*, translated by Annie E. Fausboll. 4 vols., 4:376-465. London: Oxford University Press, 1940. [Israel/Canaan]

Pedersen, Johannes. "Holy Places and Holy Things." In *Israel: Its Life and Culture*, translated by Annie E. Fausboll. 4 vols., 3:235-63. London: Oxford University Press, 1940. [Israel/Canaan]

Pelletier, André. "Le grand rideau du vestibule du Temple de Jérusalem." *Syria* 35 (1958): 218-26. [Israel/Canaan]

Pelletier, André. "Le 'voile du Temple' de Jérusalem en termes de métier." *Revue des études grecques* 77 (1964): 70-75. [Israel/Canaan]

Pelletier, André. "Le 'voile' du temple de Jérusalem est-il devenu la 'portière' du temple d' Olympie?" *Syria* 32 (1955): 289-307. [Israel/Canaan]

Peter, A. "Der Segensstrom des endzeitlichen Jerusalem: Herkunft und Bedeutung eines prophetischen symbols." In *Miscellanea Fuldensia: Beitrage aus Geschichte, Theologie, Seelsorge* (Festschrift Adolf Bolte), edited by Franz Scholz. 109-34. Fulda: Parzeller, 1966. [Israel/Canaan]

Peters, F. E. "Not a Stone upon a Stone: The Destruction of the Holy City." In Peters, *Jerusalem: The Holy City in the Eyes of Chroniclers, Visitors, Pilgrims, and Prophets from the Days of Abraham to the Beginnings of Modern Times*. 88-130. Princeton: Princeton University Press, 1985. [Israel/Canaan]

Peters, John P. "A Jerusalem Processional." *JBL* 39 (1920): 52-59. [Israel/Canaan]

Petersen, David L. "Zechariah's Visions: A Theological Perspective." *VT* 34 (April 1984): 195-206. [Israel/Canaan]

Petersen, David L. "Zerubbabel and Jerusalem Temple Reconstruction." *CBQ* 36 (July 1974): 366-72. [Israel/Canaan]

Petitjean, Albert. "La mission de Zorobabel et la reconstruction du Temple, Zach. iii, 8-10." *Ephemerides Theologicae Lovanienses* 42 (1966): 40-71. [Israel/Canaan]

Petitjean, Albert. *Les oracles du Proto-Zacharie*. Paris: Gabalda, 1969. [Israel/Canaan]

Pfeifer, C. J. "Ezekiel and the New Jerusalem." *Bible Today* 18 (1980): 22-27. [Israel/Canaan]

Phillips, C. R. "Julian's Rebuilding of the Temple: A Sociological Study of Religious Competiton." *SBLSP* 17 (1979): 167-72. [Israel/Canaan]

Pierik, Marie. *The Psalter in the Temple and the Church*. Washington, D.C.: Catholic University of America, 1957. [Israel/Canaan]

Pillet, Maurice. "Le Temple de Byblos." *Syria* 8 (1927): 105-12. [Israel/Canaan]

Plooij, D. "Jesus and the Temple." *Expository Times* 42 (1930-31): 36-40. [Israel/Canaan]

Poels, Henri. *Le sanctuaire de Kirjath-Jearim*. Louvain: Istas, 1894. [Israel/Canaan]

Pohl, A. "Das verschlossene Tor: Ez. 44:1-3." *Biblica* 13 (1932): 90-92, 201. [Israel/Canaan]

Portaleone, Abraham. *Shilṭe ha-Giborim.* Jerusalem: n.p., 1969/1970. [Israel/Canaan]

Portaleone, Abraham. *Ha-Shir sheba-Mikdash.* Jerusalem: Yefeh-nof, 1964/1965. [Israel/Canaan]

Porten, Bezalel. "The Structure and Orientation of the Jewish Temple at Elephantine—A Revised Plan of the Jewish District." *JAOS* 81 (1961): 38-42. [Israei/Canaan]

Porten, Bezalel. "Temple: Temple of Zerubbabel." In *Encyclopaedia Judaica* 15:955-58. [Israel/Canaan]

Porten, Bezalel, Yehoshua M. Grintz, Michael Avi-Yonah, and Shmuel Safrai. "Temple: Second Temple." In *Encyclopaedia Judaica* 15:955-83. [Israel/Canaan]

Potin, J. "Le Temple." *Bible et Terre Sainte* 20 (1959): 8-14. [Israel/Canaan]

Pratt, Richard L. "Royal Prayer and the Chronicler's Program." Th.D. diss., Harvard University, 1987. [Israel/Canaan]

Prescott, J. E. "On the Gate Beautiful of the Temple." *Journal of Sacred Literature* 5 ser. 2/3 (1867): 33-45. [Israel/Canaan]

Prestel, Jakob. *Die Baugeschichte des jüdischen Heiligthums und der Tempel Salomons.* Strassburg: Heitz, 1902. [Israel/Canaan]

Pronobis, C. "Der Tempel zu Jerusalem: Seine Masse und genaue Lage." *Das heilige Land* 70 (1926): 197-211; 71 (1927): 8-32. [Israel/Canaan]

Qimron, Elisha. "Column 14 of the *Temple Scroll*" (in Hebrew). *IEJ* 38/1-2 (1988): 44-46. [Israel/Canaan]

Qimron, Elisha. "Further New Readings in the Temple Scroll." *IEJ* 37 (1987): 31-35. [Israel/Canaan]

Qimron, Elisha. "New Readings in the Temple Scroll." *IEJ* 28 (1978): 161-72. [Israel/Canaan]

Qimron, Elisha. "Three Notes on the Text of the Temple Scroll" (in Hebrew; *English summary) *Tarbiz* 51 (1981): 135-37, *IX. [Israel/Canaan]

Rabe, Virgil W. "Israelite Opposition to the Temple." *CBQ* 29 (April 1967): 228-33. [Israel/Canaan]

Rabello, A. M. "The 'Lex de Templo Hierosolymitano' Prohibiting Gentiles from Entering Jerusalem's Sanctuary." *Christian News from Israel* 21/3 (1970): 28-32; 21/4 (1970): 28-32. [Israel/Canaan]

Rabina, M. "Music in the Temple" (in Hebrew). *Maḥanayim* 96 (1965): 44-49. [Israel/Canaan]

Ramaroson, L. "Contre les 'temples faits de mains d'homme.' " *Revue de Philosophie, Literature, et d'Histoire* 3/43 (1969): 217-38. [Israel/Canaan]

Redisch, Heinrich. "Der *bit hillani* und seine Verwendung bei den salomonischen Bauten." In *Festschrift Adolf Schwarz zum siebzigsten Geburtstage.* 13-27. Berlin: Löwit, 1917. [Israel/Canaan]

Reicke, Bo. "The Knowledge Hidden in the Tree of Paradise." *Journal of Semitic Studies* 1 (July 1956): 193-201. [Israel/Canaan]

Reinach, S. "L'Arc de Titus." *REJ* 20 (1890): lxv-xci. [Israel/Canaan]

Rengstorf, K. H. "Erwägungen zur Frage des Landbesitzes des zweiten Tempels in Judaea und seiner Verwaltung." In *Bible and Qumran (Festschrift Hans Bardtke)*, edited by S. Wagner. 156-76. Berlin: Evangelische Haupt-Bibelgesellschaft, 1968. [Israel/Canaan]

Renov, I. "A View of Herod's Temple from Nicanor's Gate in a Mural Panel of the Dura-Europos Synagogue." *IEJ* 20 (1970): 67-72. [Israel/Canaan]

Renwick, David A. "Paul the Temple, and the Presence of God." Ph.D. diss. Union Theological Seminary in Virginia, 1988. [Israel/Canaan]

Reynès-Monlaur, M. "Les vendeurs du Temple." In *Jérusalem*. 170-79. Paris: Plon, 1911. [Israel/Canaan]

Richardson, P. "Barnabas, Nerva, and the Yavnean Rabbis." *JTS* 34 (April 1983): 31-55. [Israel/Canaan]

Richardson, P., and M. Shukster. "Religion, Architecture and Ethics: Some First Century Case Studies." *Horizons in Biblical Theology: An International Dialogue* 10 (1988): 19-49. [Israel/Canaan]

Richter, G. "Die Kesselwagen des salomonischen Tempels." *ZDPV* 41 (1918): 1-34. [Israel/Canaan]

Ricke, Herbert. *Die Tempel Nektanebos' II in Elephantine und ihre Erweiterungen. Beiträge zur ägyptischen Bauforschung* 6 (1960). [Israel/Canaan]

Riis, Poul J. *Soukas I, The North East Sanctuary*. Copenhagen: Munksgaard, 1970. [Israel/Canaan]

Riley, W. "Temple Imagery and the Book of Revelation: Ancient Near Eastern Temple Ideology and Cultic Resonances in the Apocalypse." *Proceedings of the Irish Biblical Association* 6 (1982): 81-102. [Israel/Canaan]

Ritmeyer, K., and L. Ritmeyer. "Herod's Temple Mount—Stone by Stone." *BAR* 15/6 (1989): 23-53. [Israel/Canaan]

Robins, Edward D. *The Temple of Solomon*. London: Whittaker, 1887. [Israel/Canaan]

Rokéah, D. "The Temple Scroll, Philo, Josephus, and the Talmud." *JTS* 34 (1983): 515-26. [Israel/Canaan]

Romanoff, P. *Forms and Symbols in the Architecture of the Temple*, 1-14, 67-82, 133-58. New York: n.p., 1936. [Israel/Canaan]

Rops, D. "Les demeures de Dieu." In *La vie quotidienne en Palestine au temps de Jésus*. 436-55. Paris: Hachette, 1961. [Israel/Canaan]

Rosen, Debra, and Alison Salvesen. "A Note on the Qumran Temple Scroll 56:15-18 and Psalm of Solomon 17:33." *JJS* 38 (Spring 1987): 99-101. [Israel/Canaan]

Rosen, Georg. *Das Haram von Jerusalem und der Tempelplatz des Moria. Eine Untersuchung über die Identität beider Stätten.* Gotha: Besser, 1866. [Israel/Canaan]

Rosenau, Helen. "The Architecture of N. Lyra's Temple Illustrations and the Jewish Traditions." *JJS* 25 (1974): 294-304. [Israel/Canaan]

Rosenau, Helen. "Jacob Judah Leon Templo's Contribution to Architectural Imagery." *JJS* 23 (1972): 72-81. [Israel/Canaan]

Rosenau, Helen. "Some Aspects of the Pictorial Influence of the Jewish Temple." *PEFQ* 68 (1936): 157-62. [Israel/Canaan]

Rosenau, Helen. "The Synagogue and the Diaspora." *PEQ* 69 (1937): 196-202. [Israel/Canaan]

Rosenau, Helen. *Vision of the Temple.* London: Oresko Books, 1979. [Israel/Canaan]

Rosenau, W. "Harel und Ha-Ariel: Ezechiel 43:15-16." *MGWJ* 65 (1921): 350-56. [Israel/Canaan]

Ross, Theodore S. "The Attitude of the Rabbis toward the Destruction of the Second Temple." Ph.D. diss., Hebrew Union College, 1949. [Israel/Canaan]

Rost, P. "Der Altar Ezechiels, Kap. 43:13-17." In *Altorientalische Studien* (Festschrift Bruno Meissner). 170-74. Leipzig: Harrassowitz, 1928-29. [Israel/Canaan]

Roth, Cecil. "Cleansing of the Temple and Zechariah 14:21." *NT* 4 (1960): 174-81. [Israel/Canaan]

Rowe, Allan. *The Four Canaanite Temples of Bethshan,* vol. 1. Philadelphia: University Press for the University of Pennsylvania Museum, 1940. [Israel/Canaan]

Rowley, Harold H. "Hezekiah's Reform and Rebellion." *BJRL* 44 (1961-62): 395-431; and also in Rowley, *Men of God: Studies in Old Testament History and Prophecy.* 98-132. London: Nelson, 1963. [Israel/Canaan]

Rowley, Harold H. "Sanballat and the Samaritan Temple." *BJRL* 38 (1955-56): 166-98. [Israel/Canaan]

Rowton, M. B. "The Date of the Founding of Solomon's Temple." *BASOR* 119 (1950): 20-22. [Israel/Canaan]

Ruffini, Ernesto. "Il tempio di Gerusalemme." In Ruffini, *Conferenze bibliche.* 138-57. Rome: Libreria editrice Ancora, 1966. [Israel/Canaan]

Rüger, H. P. "Tempel." In *Biblisch-historisches Handwörterbuch,* edited by Bo Reicke and L. Rost. 3:1940-47. Göttingen: Vandenhoeck and Ruprecht, 1966. [Israel/Canaan]

Rupprecht, Konrad. "Nachrichten von Erweiterung und Renovierung des Tempels in 1 Könige 6." *ZDPV* 88 (1972): 38-52. [Israel/Canaan]

Rupprecht, Konrad. *Der Tempel von Jerusalem: Gründung Salomos oder jebusitisches Erbe.* Berlin: de Gruyter, 1976. [Israel/Canaan]

Rupprecht, Konrad. "Die Zuverlässigkeit der Überlieferung von Salomos Tempelgründung." *ZAW* 89 (1977): 205-14. [Israel/Canaan]

Sabourin, Léopold. "Novum Templum." *Verbum Domini* 47 (1969): 65-82. [Israel/Canaan]

Sabourin, Léopold. "The Temple and the Cult in Late Judaism." *Religious Studies Bulletin* 1 (1981): 33-37. [Israel/Canaan]

Safrai, Shmuel. "Contribution to the History of Ritual in the Second Temple" (in Hebrew). In *Yerushalayim.* 2 vols., 2:5:35-41. Jerusalem: Rabbi Kook Foundation, 1955. [Israel/Canaan]

Safrai, Shmuel. "The Divine Service in the Temple on the Day of Atonement" (in Hebrew). *Maḥanayim* 49 (1961): 122-25. [Israel/Canaan]

Safrai, Shmuel. "The Festival of Pentecost in the Time of the Second Temple" (in Hebrew). In *The Book of Festivals,* edited by Z. Ariel. 313-15. Tel-Aviv: Am Oved, 1967. [Israel/Canaan]

Safrai, Shmuel. "The Heavenly Jerusalem." *Ariel* 23 (1969): 11-16. [Israel/Canaan]

Safrai, Shmuel. "Jews of Eretz-Israel during the Second Commonwealth and the Talmudic Period." In *History of Eretz-Israel from Prehistory up to 1882,* edited by Joel Rappel. 291-304. Tel-Avi: Ministry of Defence, 1980. [Israel/Canaan]

Safrai, Shmuel. *Ha-Mikdash bi-Tekufat ha-Bayit ha-Sheni.* Jerusalem: ha-Sokhut ha-Yehudit, 1958/1959. [Israel/Canaan]

Safrai, Shmuel. "Die Stellung des Zweiten Tempels des Volkes." *Freiburger Rundbrief* 28/105-8 (1976): 158-65. [Israel/Canaan]

Safrai, Shmuel. "Das Synhedrion in der Zeit des zweiten Tempels." In *Das jüdische Volk im Zeitalter des zweiten Tempels.* 67-72. Neukirchen-Vluyn: Neukirchener, 1978. [Israel/Canaan]

Safrai, Shmuel. "Der Tempel." In *Das jüdische Volk im Zeitalter des zweiten Tempels.* 56-60. Neukirchen-Vluyn: Neukirchener, 1978. [Israel/Canaan]

Safrai, Shmuel. "The Temple." In *The Jewish People in the First Century* 2, edited by Shmuel Safrai and Michael Stern. 865-907. Assen: van Gorcum, 1976. [Israel/Canaan]

Safrai, Shmuel. "The Temple and the Divine Service." In *The World History of the Jewish People, 7: The Herodian Period,* edited by Michael Avi-Yonah. 282-337. Jerusalem: Massada, 1975. [Israel/Canaan]

Safrai, Shmuel. "Was There a Women's Gallery in the Synagogue of Antiquity?" (in Hebrew). *Tarbiz* 32 (1963): 329-38. [Israel/Canaan]

Saldarini, A. J. "Varieties of Rabbinic Response to the Destruction of the Temple." *SBLSP* 21 (1982): 437-58. [Israel/Canaan]

Saller, S. J. "Sacred Places and Objects of Ancient Palestine." *Liber Annuus* 14 (1963-64): 161-228. [Israel/Canaan]

Salzberger, Georg. *Salomos Tempelbau und Thron in der semitischen Sagenliteratur.* Berlin: Mayer and Müller, 1912. [Israel/Canaan]

Sarno, R. A. "Rebuilding the Temple." *The Bible Today* 45 (1969): 2799-804. [Israel/Canaan]

Sauer, Frank. *Die Tempeltheologie des Propheten Haggai.* Freiburg: Sauer, 1977. [Israel/Canaan]

Savignac, R., and G. Horsfield. "Le Temple de Ramm." *RB* 44 (1935): 245-78. [Israel/Canaan]

Sawyer, J. F. A. "The Temple at Jerusalem." In *From Moses to Patmos: New Perspectives in Old Testament Study.* 57-71. London: SPCK, 1977. [Israel/Canaan]

Schächter, J. "The Temple Site" (in Hebrew). In *Jerusalem Through the Ages— Two Chapters of Bibliography.* 21-98. Jerusalem: Yad Izhak Ben Zvi Publications, 1975. [Israel/Canaan]

Schäfer, P. "Tempel und Schöpfung: Zur Interpretation einiger Heiligtums-traditionen in der rabbinischen Literatur." In Schäfer, *Studien zur Geschichte und Theologie des rabbinischen Judentums.* 122-33. Leiden: Brill, 1978. [Israel/Canaan]

Schaffer, Shaul. *Bet ha-Mikdash.* Jerusalem: Yefeh-nof, 1968/1969. [Israel/Canaan]

Schaffer, Shaul. *Har ha-Bayit.* Jerusalem: Yefer-nof, 1968/1969. [Israel/Canaan]

Schaffer, Shaul. *Israel's Temple Mount: The Jews Magnificent Sanctuary—an Illustrated Compendium on the Holy Temples.* Jerusalem: Achva, 1975. [Israel/Canaan]

Schaffer (Shefer), Shaúl. *Ha-Mikdash ha-Shelishi.* Jerusalem: Yefeh-nof, 1963/64. [Israel/Canaan]

Schaffer, Shaul. *The Music of the Temple* (in Hebrew). Jerusalem: Yefeh-Nof, 1965. [Israel/Canaan]

Schaya, L. "The Meaning of the Temple." *Studies in Comparative Religion* 5 (1971): 241-46. [Israel/Canaan]

Schepansky, I. "The Site of the Temple and its Sanctity" (in Hebrew). In Schepansky, *Eretz-Israel in the Responsa Literature*, vol. 1, 425-33. Jerusalem: Mosad Harav Kook, 1966. [Israel/Canaan]

Schick, Conrad. "Ausdehnung der Stadt Jerusalem und ihre Einwohnerzahl zur Zeit des 2. Tempels." *Jerusalem* 1 (1881): 83-103. [Israel/Canaan]

Schick, Conrad. *Beit El Makdas.* Jerusalem: Syrisches Waisenhaus, 1887. [Israel/Canaan]

Schick, Conrad. *Die Stiftshütte, der Tempel in Jerusalem und der Tempelplatz der Jetztzeit.* Berlin: Weidmannsche Buchhandlung, 1896. [Israel/Canaan]

Schiller, E. "The Stone of Foundation." In *The Dome of the Rock and the Stone of Foundation.* 46-54. Jerusalem: Ariel, 1976. [Israel/Canaan]

Schmandt-Besserat, D. "Biblical Archaeologist's Guide to Artifacts: Tokens and Counting." *BA* 46 (1983): 117-20. [Israel/Canaan]

Schmid, H. "Der Tempelbau Salomos in religionsgeschichtlicher Sicht." In *Archäologie und altes Testament: Festschrift für Kurt Galling,* edited by Arnulf Kuschke and Ernst Kutsch. 241-50. Tübingen: Mohr, 1970. [Israel/Canaan]

Schmidt, Emanuel. "Solomon's Temple." *Biblical World* 14 (1899): 164-71. [Israel/Canaan]

Schmidt, Emanuel. *Solomon's Temple in the Light of Other Oriental Temples.* Chicago: Univeristy of Chicago Press, 1902. [Israel/Canaan]

Schmidt, H. "Die Tempelrolle vom Toten Meer." *Judaica* 34/4 (1978): 187-88. [Israel/Canaan]

Schmidt, Hans. "Der Fels im Tempel des Herodes." In Schmidt, *Der heilige Fels in Jerusalem—eine archäologische und religionsgeschichtliche Studie.* 17-39. Tübingen: Mohr, 1933. [Israel/Canaan]

Schmidt, Martin. *Prophet und Tempel.* Zurich: Evangelischer, 1948. [Israel/Canaan]

Schmidt, Paul F. *Temple Reflections.* Albuquerque: Hummingbird, 1980. [Israel/Canaan]

Schneider, H. "Das Jahubild im Tempel Salomos." *Memnon* 3 (1909): 159-62. [Israel/Canaan]

Schnellbächer, E. L. "The Temple as the Focus of Mark's Theology." *Horizons in Biblical Theology* 5/2 (1983): 95-112. [Israel/Canaan]

Schoeps, H.-J. "Die Tempelzerstörung des Jahres 70 in der jüdischen Religionsgeschichte." In *Coniectanea Neotestamentica,* vol. 6, pp. 1-45. Uppsala: Seminarium Neotestamentium Upsaliense, 1942; also in Schoeps, *Aus frühchristlicher Zeit.* 144-83. Tübingen: Mohr, 1950. [Israel/Canaan]

Schonberg, D. "The Temple." *Turtle—a New Jewish Arts Magazine* 4 (1972): 42-53. [Israel/Canaan]

Schreckenberg, H. "The Destruction of the Second Temple as Reflected in Christian Art: Jerusalem in the Second Temple Period." In *Jerusalem in the Second Temple Period: Abraham Schalit Memorial Volume* (in Hebrew; English summary), edited by A. Oppenheimer et al. 394-414. Jerusalem: Yad Izhaq Ben-Avi, 1980. [Israel/Canaan]

Schreiber, A. "La légende de l'emplacement du Temple de Jérusalem." *REJ* 109 (1949): 103-8. [Israel/Canaan]

Schreiner, Josef. *Sion-Jerusalem Jahwes Königssitz, Theologie der heiligen Stadt im alten Testament.* Munich: Köselverlag, 1963. [Israel/Canaan]

Schreiner, Josef. "Tempeltheologie im Streit der Propheten." *Biblische Zeitschrift* 31(1987): 1-14. [Israel/Canaan]

Schult, Hermann. "Zum Bauverfahren in 1 Könige 6, 7." *ZDPV* 88 (1972): 53-54. [Israel/Canaan]

Schunck, K. D. "Zentralheiligtum, Grenzheiligtum und Höhenheiligtum in Israel." *Numen* 18 (1971): 132-40. [Israel/Canaan]

Schürer, E. "Die *thura* oder *pulā hōraia* Act 3, 2 und 10." *ZNTW* 7 (1906): 51-68. [Israel/Canaan]

Schwartz, A. "Die Schatzkammer des Tempels in Jerusalem." *MGWJ* 63 (1919): 227-52. [Israel/Canaan]

Schwartz, Daniel R. "The Three Temples of 4 Q Florilegium." *Revue de Qumran* 10 (1979): 83-91. [Israel/Canaan]

Schwartz, Daniel R. "The Tribes of As. Mos. 4:7-9." *JBL* 99 (1980): 217-23. [Israel/Canaan]

Schwartz, Daniel R. "Viewing the Holy Utensils (P. Ox. V, 840)." *NTS* 32 (1986): 153-59. [Israel/Canaan]

Schwartz, J. "The *Encaenia* of the Church of the Holy Sepulchre, the Temple of Solomon and the Jews." *Theologische Zeitschrift* 43 (1987): 265-81. [Israel/Canaan]

Schwartzman, S. D. "How Well Did the Synoptic Evangelists Know the Synagogue (Temple)?" *HUCA* 24 (1952): 115-32. [Israel/Canaan]

Schwartzman, S. D. "The Jewish Institutions of Synagogue and Temple in the Synoptic Gospels." Ph.D. diss., Vanderbilt University, 1952. [Israel/Canaan]

Scott, R. B. Y. "The Pillars Jachin and Boaz." *JBL* 58 (1939): 143-49. [Israel/Canaan]

Sellin, Ernst. "Der Stein des Sacharja." *JBL* 50 (1931): 242-49. [Israel/Canaan]

Seow, Choon-Leong. "Ark Processions in the Politics of the Monarchy (Israel)." Ph.D. diss., Harvard University, 1984. [Israel/Canaan]

Seton-Williams, M. V. "Palestinian Temples." *Iraq* 11 (1949): 77-89. [Israel/Canaan]

Seybold, Klaus. *Bilder zum Tempelbau: Die Visionen des Propheten Sacharja.* Stuttgart: KBW, 1974. [Israel/Canaan]

Seyrig, Henri. "Antiquités Syriennes 17: Bas-reliefs monumentaux du temple de Bel à Palmyre." *Syria* 15 (1934): 155-86. [Israel/Canaan]

Shachor, M. L. "The Stone of Foundation" (in Hebrew). *B'shearayich* 6 (1970): 3-6. [Israel/Canaan]

Shalem, Raphael A. *The Temple, Drawing and Notes* (in Hebrew). Jerusalem: Shalem, 1967. [Israel/Canaan]

Shanks, Hershel, ed. "Temple Scroll Revisted—Three New Views." *BAR* 13/6 (1987): 21-37. [Israel/Canaan]

Sherlock, Charles. "Ezekiel 10: A Prophet Surprised." *Reformed Theological Review* 42 (1983): 42-44. [Israel/Canaan]

Shiloh, Y. "Iron Age Sanctuaries and Cult Elements in Palestine." In *Symposia,* edited by Frank M. Cross. 147-57. Cambridge: American Schools of Oriental Research, 1979. [Israel/Canaan]

Shupak, Nili. "Jachin and Boaz." In *Encyclopaedia Judaica* 9:1186-89. [Israel/Canaan]

Siebeneck, R. T. "The Messianism of Aggeus and Proto-Zacharias." *CBQ* 19 (1957): 312-28. [Israel/Canaan]

Simhoni, J. N. "The Destruction of the Second Temple" (in Hebrew). In *The Book of Festivals,* edited by Z. Ariel. 332-35. Tel-Aviv: Am Oved, 1967. [Israel/Canaan]

Simon, Marcel. "Le discours de Jésus sur la ruine du Temple." *RB* 56 (1949): 70-75. [Israel/Canaan]

Simon, Marcel. "La prophétie de Nathan et le temple." *Revue d'histoire et de philosophie religieuses* 32 (1952): 41-58. [Israel/Canaan]

Simon, Marcel. "Retour du Christ et reconstruction du Temple dans la pensée chrétienne primitive." In Simon, *Recherches d'histoire judéo-chrétienne.* 9-19. Paris: Mouton, 1962. [Israel/Canaan]

Simon, Marcel. "Saint Stephen and the Jerusalem Temple." *Journal of Ecclesiastical History* 2/2 (1951): 127-42. [Israel/Canaan]

Simons, Jan. "The Problem of the Temple." In Simons, *Jerusalem in the Old Testament: Researches and Theories,* 381-436. Leiden: Brill, 1952. [Israel/Canaan]

Simpson, J. "Where Are the Sacred Vessels of the Temple?" *PEQ* 29 (1897): 77-80. [Israel/Canaan]

Simpson, W. "Robinson's Arch." *PEFQ* 1-2 (1869-70): 46-48. [Israel/Canaan]

Simpson, W. "The Temple and the Mount of Olives." *PEFQ* 29 (1897): 307-8. [Israel/Canaan]

Sisti, A. "Le due alleanze (Gal 4, 21-31)." *Bibbia e Oriente* 11 (1969): 25-32. [Israel/Canaan]

Skehan, P. W. "Wisdom's House." *CBQ* 29 (1967): 468-86. [Israel/Canaan]

Smallwood, E. Mary. "The Chronology of Gaius' Attempt to Desecrate the Temple." *Latomus* 16 (1957): 3-17. [Israel/Canaan]

Smith, Arthur E. *The Temple and Its Teaching.* Chicago: Moody, 1956. [Israel/Canaan]

Smith, J. M. P. "The Jewish Temple at Elephantine." *The Biblical World* 31 (1908): 448-59. [Israel/Canaan]

Smith, Jonathan Z. "Earth and Gods." *Journal of Religion* 49 (1969): 103-27. [Israel/Canaan]

Smith, S. "Timber and Brick or Masonry Construction." *PEQ* 73 (1941): 5-17. [Israel/Canaan]

Snaith, Norman H. *The Jewish New Year Festival, Its Origin and Development.* London: Society for Promoting Christian Knowledge, 1947. [Israel/Canaan]

Snijders, L. A. "L'orientation du temple de Jerusalem." *Oudtestamentische Studiën* 14 (1965): 214-34. [Israel/Canaan]

Soares, T. G. "Ezekiel's Temple." *Biblical World* 14 (1899): 93-103. [Israel/Canaan]

Sperber, Daniel. "Social Legislation in Jerusalem during the Latter Part of the Second Temple Period." *Journal for the Study of Judaism* 6 (1975): 86-95. [Israel/Canaan]

Sperling, S. David. "Navel of the Earth." In *The Interpreter's Dictionary of the Bible*, supp. vol., 621-23. [Israel/Canaan]

Spiess, F. "Die königliche Halle des Herodes im Tempel von Jerusalem." *ZDPV* 15 (1892): 234-56. [Israel/Canaan]

Spiess, F. "Der Tempel nebst der Antonia." In Spiess, *Das Jerusalem des Josephus—Beitrag zur Topographie der heiligen Stadt.* 46-94. Berlin: Habel, 1881. [Israel/Canaan]

Spiess, F. *Der Tempel zu Jerusalem während des letzten Jahrhunderts seines Bestandes nach Josephus.* Berlin: Habel, 1880. [Israel/Canaan]

Stade, B. "Die Kesselwagen des salomonischen Tempels, 1 Kö. 7, 27-39." *ZAW* 21 (1901): 145-90. [Israel/Canaan]

Stade, B. "Der Text des Berichtes über Salomos Bauten, 1 Kö. 5-7." *ZAW* 3 (1883): 129-77. [Israel/Canaan]

Stager, L. E., and S. R. Wolff. "Production and Commerce in Temple Courtyards: An Olive Press in the Sacred Precinct at Tel Dan." *BASOR* 243 (1981): 95-102. [Israel/Canaan]

Stamm, Jakob J. "Zum Altargesetz im Bundesbuch." *Theologische Zeitschrift* 1 (1945): 304-6. [Israel/Canaan]

Starcky, J. "Le Temple hérodien et les sanctuaires orientaux." *Le Monde de la Bible* 13 (1980): 14-18. [Israel/Canaan]

Stauffer, Ethelbert. "Das Tor des Nikanor." *ZNTW* 44 (1953): 44-46. [Israel/Canaan]

Steck, O. H. "Zu Haggai 1:2-11." *ZAW* 83 (1971): 355-79. [Israel/Canaan]

Stegemann, Hartmut. "Is the Temple Scroll a Sixth Book of the Torah, Lost for 2500 Years?" *BAR* 13/6 (1987): 28-35. [Israel/Canaan]

Stein, M. "How Herod Moved Gigantic Blocks to Construct Temple Mount." *BAR* 7/3 (1981): 42-46. [Israel/Canaan]

Steinmueller, John E. "Temples." *New Catholic Encyclopedia* 13 (1968): 998-1000. [Israel/Canaan]

Stendebach, F. J. "Altarformen im kanaanäisch-israelitischen Raum." *Biblische Zeitschrift* 20 (1976): 180-96. [Israel/Canaan]

Stern, E. "A Favissa of a Phoenician Sanctuary from Tel Dor." *JJS* 33 (1982): 35-54. [Israel/Canaan]

Stern, Menahem. "The Period of the Second Temple. In *History of the Jewish People*, edited by H. H. Ben-Sasson. 183-303. Cambridge: Harvard Universty Press, 1976. [Israel/Canaan]

Stinespring, William F. "Temple, Jerusalem: The Temple of Solomon," "Temple, Jerusalem: The Temple of Zerubbabel," and "Temple, Jerusalem: The Temple of Herod." In *The Interpreter's Dictionary of the Bible* 4:534-60. [Israel/Canaan]

Stinespring, William F. "Temple Research in Jerusalem." *Duke Divinity School Review* 29 (1964): 85-101. [Israel/Canaan]

Stinespring, William F. "Wilson's Arch and the Masonic Hall." *BA* 30 (1967): 27-31. [Israel/Canaan]

Stinespring, William F. "Wilson's Arch Revisited." *BA* 29 (1966): 27-36. [Israel/Canaan]

Stockton, E. D. "Sacred Pillars in the Bible." *Australian Biblical Review* 20 (1972): 16-32. [Israel/Canaan]

Stolz, F. *Strukturen and Figuren in Kult von Jerusalem: Studien zur altorientalischen vor und frühisraelitischen Religion.* Berlin: de Gruyter, 1970. [Israel/Canaan]

Stone, Michael E. "Reactions to Destructions of the Second Temple: Theology, Perception, and Conversion." *Journal for the Study of Judaism* 12 (1981): 195-204. [Israel/Canaan]

Strange, James. "The Idea of Afterlife in Ancient Israel: Some Remarks of the Iconography in Solomon's Temple." *PEQ* 117 (1985): 35-40. [Israel/Canaan]

Stuhlmacher, Peter. "Die Stellung Jesu und des Paulus zu Jerusalem: Versuch einer Erinnerung." *Zeitschrift für Theologie und Kirche* 86 (1989): 140-56. [Israel/Canaan]

Sulley, Henry. *The Temple of Ezekiel's Prophecy: Being an Enlarged and Revised Edition of an Explanation of the Nature, Character, and Extent of the Building Which Is Shortly to Be Erected in the Land of Israel as "a House of Prayer for All People."* 3d rev. ed. London: Simpkin, Marshall, Hamilton, Kent, 1921. [Israel/Canaan]

Sweeney, Marvin A. "Midrashic Perspective in the *Torat ham-Melek* of the Temple Scroll." *Hebrew Studies* 28 (1987): 51-66. [Israel/Canaan]

Sweeney, Marvin A. "Sefirah at Qumran: Aspects of the Counting Formulas for the First-Fruits Festivals in the Temple Scroll." *BASOR* 251 (1983): 61-66. [Israel/Canaan]

Sylva, D. D. "The Cryptic Clause *en tois tou patros mou dei einai me* in Lk 2:49b." *ZNTW* 78/1-2 (1987): 132-40. [Israel/Canaan]

Sylva, D. D. "The Meaning and Function of Acts 7:46-50." *JBL* 106 (June 1987): 261-75. [Israel/Canaan]

Sylva, D. D. "The Temple Curtain and Jesus' Death in the Gospel of Luke." *JBL* 105 (1986): 239-50. [Israel/Canaan]

"Tamid, or the Continual Service, with the Commentary of Rabbi Obadiah of Bartenora." *PEFQ* (1886): 119-30, 213-23. [Israel/Canaan]

Taylor, Noel M. "The Place of the Temple in the New Testament." Ph.D. diss. Southern Baptist Theological Seminary, 1942 [Israel/Canaan]

Taylor, W. R. "A Jerusalem Forgery of the Balustrade Inscription of Herod's Temple." *JPOS* 13 (1933): 137-39. [Israel/Canaan]

Taylor, W. R. "A Second Forgery of the Balustrade Inscription of Herod's Temple." *JPOS* 16 (1936): 37-38. [Israel/Canaan]

Telford, W. R. *The Barren Temple and the Withered Tree.* Sheffield: JSOT, 1980. [Israel/Canaan]

Testa, Emmanuel. "La 'Gerusalemme celeste,' dall'antico oriente alla Bibbia e alla liturgia." *Bibbia e Oriente* 1 (1959): 47-50. [Israel/Canaan]

Testa, Emmanuel. "Lo schema letterario sulla distruzione del tempio e di Gerusalemme." *Liber Annuus* 24 (1974): 265-316. [Israel/Canaan]

Theissen, G. "Die Tempelweissagung Jesu: Prophetie im Spannungsfeld von Stadt und Land." *Theologische Zeitschrift* 32 (1976): 144-58. [Israel/Canaan]

Thiering, B. E. "Mebaqqer and Episkopos in Light of the Temple Scroll." *JBL* 100 (1981): 59-74. [Israel/Canaan]

Thoma, Clemens. "Die Zerstörung des Tempels von Jerusalem (70 n. Chr.) als Wende." In *Auf den Trümmern des Tempels*, edited by C. Thoma. 53-75. Vienna: Herder, 1968. [Israel/Canaan]

Thompson, H. O. "Tell el-Husn—Biblical Beth-shan." *BA* 30 (1967): 110-35. [Israel/Canaan]

Thompson, L. "Cult and Eschatology in the Apocalypse of John." *Journal of Religion* 49 (1969): 330-50. [Israel/Canaan]

Thompson, T. L. "The Dating of the Megiddo Temples in Strata XV-XIV." *ZDPV* 86 (1970): 38-49. [Israel/Canaan]

Thomsen, P. "Der Tempel." In *Denkmäler Palästinas aus der Zeit Jesu*, Heft 1. 26-33. Leipzig: Hinrichs, 1916. [Israel/Canaan]

Thomsen, P. "Vom Tempel: Inschriften vom Tempel, von Kirchen und Kapellen." *ZDPV* 44 (1921): 7-8. [Israel/Canaan]

Thomson, H. C. "The Right of Entry to the Temple in the Old Testament." *Transactions of the Glasgow University Oriental Society* 21 (1965/1966): 25-34. [Israel/Canaan]

Thomson, H. C. "A Row of Cedar Beams." *PEQ* 92 (1960): 57-63. [Israel/Canaan]

Thorion, Y. "Die Sprache der Tempelrolle und die Chronikbücher." *Revue de Qumran* 11 (1983): 423-26. [Israel/Canaan]

Thorion, Y. "Tempelrolle LIX, 8-11 und Babli, Sanhedrin 98ª." *Revue de Qumran* 11 (1983): 427-28. [Israel/Canaan]

Thorion, Y. "Zur Bedeutung von 'Gibbore Hayil Lamilhama' in 11Q T LVII, 9." *Revue de Qumran* 10 (1981): 597-98. [Israel/Canaan]

Thorion-Vardi, Talia. "The Personal Pronoun as a Syntactical Glide in the Temple Scroll and in the Masoretic Text." *Revue de Qumran* 12 (1986): 421-22. [Israel/Canaan]

Thüsing, W. "Die Vision des 'Neuen Jerusalem' (Apk 21, 1-22) als Verheissung und Gottesverkündigung." *Trierer Theologische Zeitschrift* 77 (1968): 17-34. [Israel/Canaan]

Todd, E. W. "The Reforms of Hezekiah and Josiah." *Scottish Journal of Theology* 9 (1956): 288-93. [Israel/Canaan]

Torrey, C. C. "The Foundry of the Second Temple at Jerusalem." *JBL* 55 (1936): 247-60. [Israel/Canaan]

Tov, E. "The 'Temple Scroll' and Old Testament Textual Criticism" (in Hebrew; *English summary). *Eretz-Israel* 16 (1982): 100-11, *255. [Israel/Canaan]

Townsend, J. T. "The Jerusalem Temple in New Testament Thought." Ph.D. diss., Harvard University, 1959. [Israel/Canaan]

Townsend, J. T. "The Jerusalem Temple in the First Century." In *God and His Temple*, edited by L. E. Frizzell. 48-65. South Orange, NJ: Seton Hall University Institute for Judaeo-Christian Studies, 1980. [Israel/Canaan]

Trocmé, É. "L'expulsion des marchands du Temple." *NTS* 15 (1968-69): 1-22. [Israel/Canaan]

Trocmé, E. "Jesus Christ et le Temple: éloge d'un naif." *Revue d'histoire et de philosophe Religieuses* 44 (1964): 245-51. [Israel/Canaan]

Tropper, D. "Bet Din shel Kohanim." *JQR* 63 (January 1973): 204-21. [Israel/Canaan]

Tucatzinsky, Jehiel M. *Ir ha-Kodesh veha-Mikdash.* 5 vols. Jerusalem: n.p., 1970. [Israel/Canaan]

Tufnell, Olga. *Lachish II, The Fosse Temple.* London: Oxford University Press, 1940. [Israel/Canaan]

Tur-Sinai, N. H. (Torczyner, Harry). "The Foundation Stone" (in Hebrew). *Leshonenu* 19 (1954): 124. [Israel/Canaan]

Ubigli, L. R. "Dalla 'Nuova Gerusalemme' alla 'Gerusalemme Celeste'— Contributo per la comprensiòne dell' Apocalittica." *Henoch* 3 (1981): 69-80. [Israel/Canaan]

Uhrbach, Ephraim M. "Heavenly and Earthly Jerusalem" (in Hebrew; *English summary). In *Jerusalem through the Ages*, edited by J. Aviram. 156-71, *64. Jerusalem: Israel Exploration Society, 1968. [Israel/Canaan]

Ulshoefer, H. K. "Nathan's Opposition to David's Intention to Build a Temple in the Light of Selected Ancient Near Eastern Texts." Ph.D. diss., Boston University, 1977. [Israel/Canaan]

Unger, M. F. "The Temple Vision of Ezekiel." *Bibliotheca Sacra* 105 (1948): 418-32; 106 (1949): 48-64. [Israel/Canaan]

Ussishkin, D. "Building Four in Hamath and the Temples of Solomon and Tell Tayanat." *IEJ* 16 (1966): 104-10. [Israel/Canaan]

Ussishkin, D. "The Date of the Judaean Shrine at Arad." *IEJ* 38 (1988): 142-57. [Israel/Canaan]

Ussishkin, D. "The Ghassulian Shrine at En-Gedi." *Tel Aviv* 7 (1980): 1-44. [Israel/Canaan]

Ussishkin, D. "The Ghassulian Temple in Ein Gedi and the Origin of the Hoard from Nahal Mishmar." *BA* 34 (February 1971): 23-39. [Israel/Canaan]

Ussishkin, D. "Solomon's Temple and the Temples of Hamath and Tell Tainat" (in Hebrew). *Yediot* 30 (1966): 76-84. [Israel/Canaan]

Vajda, G. "La description du Temple de Jérusalem d'après le K. al-masālik waʾl-mamālik d'Al-Muhallabī—ses éléments bibliques et rabbinques." *Journal Asiatique* 247 (1959): 193-202. [Israel/Canaan]

Valentine, James. "Theological Aspects of the Temple Motif in the Old Testament and Revelation." Ph.D. diss., Boston University, 1985. [Israel/Canaan]

Van den Bussche, H. "Le signe du Temple (Jean 2, 13-22)." *Bible et vie chrétienne* 20 (1957-58): 92-100. [Israel/Canaan]

Van der Born, A. "Zum Tempelweihspruch (I Kg VIII, 12f)." *Oudtestamentische Studiën* 14 (1965): 235-44. [Israel/Canaan]

Van der Waal, C. "The Temple in the Gospel according to Luke." In *Essays on the Gospel of Luke and Acts: Proceedings of the Ninth Meeting of Die Nuwe Testamentiese Werkgemeenskap van Suid Afrika*, edited by W. van Unnik, 49-59. Pretoria: University of Pretoria, 1973. [Israel/Canaan]

Van der Woude, Adam S. "Serubbabel und die messianischen Erwartungen des Propheten Sacharja." *ZAW* 100 (1988): 138-56. [Israel/Canaan]

Van der Woude, Adam S. "De Tempel van Qumran." *Nederlands Theologisch Tijdschrift* 34 (1980): 177-90, 281-93. [Israel/Canaan]

Vanhoye, Albert. "Le Christ, grand-prétre selon Héb. 2, 17-18." *La nouvelle revue théologique* 91 (1969): 449-74. [Israel/Canaan]

Vanhoye, Albert. " 'Par la tente plus grande et plus parfaite . . .' (He 9,11)." *Biblica* 46 (1965): 1-28. [Israel/Canaan]

Vanhoye, Albert. "L'utilisation du livre d'Ézechiel dans l'Apocalypse." *Biblica* 43 (1962): 436-76. [Israel/Canaan]

Vanni, Ugo. "Gerusalemme nell' Apocalisse," In *Gerusalemme. Atti della XXVI Settimana Biblica, Associazione Biblica Italiana*, edited by M. Borrmans. 27-52. Brescia: Paideia, 1982. [Israel/Canaan]

van Pelt, R. J. *Tempel van de Wereld: de Kosmische symboliek van de tempel van Salomo.* Utrecht: HES, 1984. [Israel/Canaan]

Vaux, Roland de. "Les décrets de Cyrus et de Darius sur la reconstruction du Temple." *RB* 46 (1937): 29-57; also in English as "The Decrees of Cyrus and Darius on the Rebuilding of the Temple." In de Vaux, *The Bible and the Ancient Near East,* translated by Damian McHugh. 63-96. Garden City: Doubleday, 1971. [Israel/Canaan]

Vaux, Roland de. "Le lieu que Yahwé a choisi pour y établir son nom." In *Das ferne und nahe Wort: Festschrift Leonhard Rost zur Vollendung seines 70. Geburtstages,* edited by Fritz Maass. 219-28. Berlin: Töpelmann, 1967. [Israel/Canaan]

Vaux, Roland de. "Notes sur le temple de Salomon." In de Vaux, *Bible et Orient.* 203-16. Paris: Cerf, 1967. [Israel/Canaan]

Vaux, Roland de. "Tempel von Jerusalem." In *Lexikon für Theologie und Kirche,* edited by Josef Höfer and Karl Rahner. 10 vols., 9:1355-58. Breiburg: Herder, 1964. [Israel/Canaan]

Vaux, Roland de. "The Temple at Jerusalem." In de Vaux, *Ancient Israel: Its Life and Institutions.* 312-30. New York: McGraw-Hill, 1961. [Israel/Canaan]

Vaux, Roland de. "Le temple de Jérusalem." In de Vaux, *Bible et Orient.* 303-15. Paris: Cerf, 1967. [Israel/Canaan]

Venetianer, Ludwig. *Ezekiels Vision and die salomonischen Wasserbecken.* Budapest: Nachfloger, 1906. [Israel/Canaan]

Vernes, M. "Notes sur les sanctuaires de la région chananéenne qui furent fréquentés concurrémment par les Israelites et les nations voisines." *RHR* 43 (1901): 352-54. [Israel/Canaan]

Vernes, M. "Les plus anciens sanctuaires des Israelites." *RHR* 5 (1882): 22-48. [Israel/Canaan]

Vilnay, Zev. *The Sacred Land: Vol. 1: Legends of Jerusalem.* 3 vols. Philadelphia: Jewish Publication Society of America, 1973. [Israel/Canaan]

Vincent, Louis-Hugues. "Abraham à Jérusalem." *RB* 58 (1951): 360-71. [Israel/Canaan]

Vincent, Louis-Hugues. "Une antéchambre du palais de Salomon." *RB* n.s. 2 (1905): 258-65. [Israel/Canaan]

Vincent, Louis-Hugues. "L'autel des holcaustes et le caractère du temple d'Ézéchiel." *Analecta Bollandiana* 67 (1949): 7-20. [Israel/Canaan]

Vincent, Louis-Hugues. "Les bassins roulants du temple de Salomon." In *Miscellanea Biblica B. Ubach. Scripta et Documenta.* 147-59. Montserrat: n.p., 1953. [Israel/Canaan]

Vincent, Louis-Hugues. "Le caractère du temple salomonien." In *Melanges bibliques rédigés en l'honneur de André Robert.* 137-48. Paris: Bloud and Gay, 1957. [Israel/Canaan]

Vincent, H. (Louis-Hugues). "La description du Temple de Salomon. Notes exégètiques sur I Rois VI." *RB* n.s. 4 (1907): 515-42. [Israel/Canaan]

Vincent, Louis-Hugues. "La notion biblique du Haut Lieu." *RB* 55 (1948): 245-78, 438-45. [Israel/Canaan]

Vincent, Louis-Hugues. "Le temple Hérodian d'après la Mishnah." *RB* 61 (1954): 5-35, 398-418. [Israel/Canaan]

Vincent, Louis-Hugues, and M.-A. Steve. "Le temple de Salomon." In *Jérusalem de l'Ancien Testament*, edited by Louis-Hugues Vincent and M.-A. Steve. 2 vols., 3 parts., pt. 2:373-431. Paris: Gabalda, 1954-56. [Israel/Canaan]

Vincent, Louis-Hugues, and M.-A. Steve. "Le temple d'Ézéchiel." In *Jérusalem de l'Ancien Testament*, edited by Louis-Hugues Vincent and M.-A. Steve. 2 vols., 3 parts., pt. 2:471-95. Paris: Gabalda, 1954-56. [Israel/Canaan]

Vincent, Louis-Hugues, and M.-A. Steve. "Le temple hérodien d'après la Mishnah." In *Jérusalem de l'Ancien Testament*, edited by Louis-Hugues Vincent and M.-A. Steve. 2 vols., 3 parts., pt. 2:496-525. Paris: Gabalda, 1954-56. [Israel/Canaan]

Vogelstein, H. "Einige Probleme der jüdischen Geschichte der Zeit des zweiten Tempels." In *Jewish Studies in Memory of Israel Abrahams.* 416-25. New York: Jewish Institute of Religion, 1927. [Israel/Canaan]

Vogt, E. "Von Tempel zum Felsendom." *Biblica* 55 (1974): 23-64. [Israel/Canaan]

Vogue, Charles J. M. *Le temple de Jérusalem.* Paris: Noblet and Baudry, 1864. [Israel/Canaan]

von Alten, Baron. "Die Antonia und ihre Umgebungen." *ZDPV* 1 (1878): 61-100. [Israel/Canaan]

Vriezen, Theodorus C. "Holy Places." In Vriezen, *The Religion of Ancient Israel.* 83-99, translated by Hubert Hoskins. Philadelphia: Westminster, 1967. [Israel/Canaan]

Wacholder, Ben Zion. "Calendar of Sabbatical Cycles during the Second Temple and the Early Rabbinic Period." *HUCA* 44 (1973): 153-96. [Israel/Canaan]

Wacholder, Ben Zion. *The Dawn of Qumran.* Cincinati: Hebrew Union College Press, 1983. [Israel/Canaan]

Wainwright, J. A. "Zoser's Pyramid and Solomon's Temple." *ET* 91 (1980): 137-40. [Israel/Canaan]

Walker, N. "Riddle of the Ass's Head, and the Question of a Trigram." *ZAW* 75 (1963): 225-27. [Israel/Canaan]

Walter, N. "Tempelzerstörung und synoptische Apokalypse." *ZNTW* 57/1-2 (1966): 38-49. [Israel/Canaan]

Walvoord, J. F. "Will Israel Build a Temple in Jerusalem?" *Bibliotheca Sacra* 125 (April-June 1968): 99-106. [Israel/Canaan]

Warren, Charles. "The Temple." In *Underground Jerusalem*, edited by Charles Warren. 58-81. London: Bentley, 1876. [Israel/Canaan]

Warren, Charles. "The Temple of Herod." *PEQ* 1 (1869): 23-26. [Israel/Canaan]

Warren, Charles. "The Temple of Herod." *PEQ* 7 (1875): 97-101. [Israel/Canaan]

Warren, Charles. *The Temple or the Tomb.* London: Bentley, 1880. [Israel/Canaan]

Warren, Charles. "The Temples of Coele-Syria." *PEQ* 1 (1869-70): 183-210. [Israel/Canaan]

Waterman, L. "The Damaged 'Blueprints' of the Temple." *JNES* 2 (1943): 284-94. [Israel/Canaan]

Waterman, L. "A Rebuttal [to G. Ernest Wright]." *JNES* 7 (1948): 54-55. [Israel/Canaan]

Waterman, L. "The Treasuries of Solomon's Chapel." *JNES* 6 (1947): 161-63. [Israel/Canaan]

Watson, Charles M. "The Site of the Temple." *PEQ* 28 (1896): 47-60. [Israel/Canaan]

Watson, W. "The New Jerusalem." *ET* 25 (1914): 454-57. [Israel/Canaan]

Watty, William W. "Jesus and the Temple—Cleansing or Cursing?" *ET* 93 (1982): 235-39. [Israel/Canaan]

Watzinger, Carl. "Herodes der Grosse." In *Denkmäler Palästinas,* edited by Carl Watzinger. 2 vols., 2:31-78. Leipzig: Hinrichs, 1935. [Israel/Canaan]

Weiler, I. "Titus und die Zerstörung des Tempels von Jerusalem—Absicht oder Zufall?" *Klio* 50 (1968): 139-58. [Israel/Canaan]

Weinberg, J. P. "*Nethinim* und 'Söhne der Sklaven Salomos' im 6-4," *ZAW* 87 (1975): 355-71. [Israel/Canaan]

Weinert, Francis D. "Luke, Stephen, and the Temple in Luke-Acts." *BTB* 17 (July 1987): 88-90. [Israel/Canaan]

Weinert, Francis D. "Luke, the Temple, and Jesus' Saying about Jerusalem's Abandoned House (Luke 13:34-35)." *CBQ* 44 (January 1982): 68-76. [Israel/Canaan]

Weinert, Francis D. "The Meaning of the Temple in Luke-Acts." *BTB* 11 (July 1981): 85-89. [Israel/Canaan]

Weinert, Francis D. "The Meaning of the Temple in the Gospel of Luke." Ph.D. diss., Fordham University, 1979. [Israel/Canaan]

Weinfeld, Moshe. "Cult Centralization in Israel in the Light of a Neo-Babylonian Analogy." *JNES* 23 (1964): 202-12. [Israel/Canaan]

Weinfeld, Moshe. "Zion and Jerusalem as Religious and Political Capital: Ideology and Utopia." In *The Poet and the Historian: Essays in Literary and Historical Criticism,* edited by R. E. Friedman. 75-115. Chico, CA: Scholars, 1983. [Israel/Canaan]

Weippert Helga. "Der Ort, den Jahwe erwählen wird, um dort seinen Namen wohnen zu lassen: Die Geschichte einer alttestamentlichen Formel." *Biblische Zeitschrift* 24 (1980): 76-94. [Israel/Canaan]

Weiser, Artur. "Die Tempelbaukrise unter David." *ZAW* 77 (1965): 153-68. [Israel/Canaan]

Weiser, Artur. "Zur Frage nach den Beziehungen der Psalmen zum Kult: Die Darstellung der Theophanie in dem Psalmen und im Festkult." In *Festschrift Alfred Bertholet zum 80. Geburtstag gewidmet von Kollegen und Freunden,* edited by Walter Baumgartner et al. 513-31. Tübingen: Mohr, 1950; also in *Glaube und Geschichte im Alten Testament,* edited by Artur Weiser. 303-21. Göttingen: Vandenhoeck and Ruprecht, 1961. [Israel/Canaan]

Weiss, M. *The Chosen House—The Second Temple as Described by the Sages of Blessed Memory* (in Hebrew). Jerusalem: Mosad Harav Kook, 1946. [Israel/Canaan]

Welch, Alford C. "When Was the Worship of Israel Centralised at the Temple?" *ZAW* 43 (1925): 250-55. [Israel/Canaan]

Welten, Peter. "Kulthöhe." In *Biblisches Reallexikon,* edited by Kurt Galling, 2d ed. 94-95. Tübingen: Mohr, 1977. [Israel/Canaan]

Welten, Peter. "Kulthöhe and Jahwetempel." *ZDPV* 88 (1972): 19-37. [Israel/Canaan]

Welten, Peter. "Lade-Tempel-Jerusalem: Zur Theologie der Chronikbücher." In *Textgemäss: Aufsätze und Beiträge zur Hermeneutik des alten Testaments: Festschrift für Ernst Würthwein zum 70. Geburtstag,* edited by A. H. J. Gunneweg and Otto Kaiser. 169-83. Göttingen: Vandenhoeck and Ruprecht, 1979. [Israel/Canaan]

Wenham, Gordon J. "Deuteronomy and the Central Sanctuary." *Tyndale Bulletin* 22 (1971): 103-18. [Israel/Canaan]

Wenschkewitz, Hans. "Die Spiritualisierung der Kultusbegriffe: Tempel, Priester, und Opfer im Neuen Testament." *Angelos: Archiv für neutesta-mentlich Zeitgeschichte und Kulturkunde* 4 (1932): 70-230. [Israel/Canaan]

Westphal, Gustav. *Jahwes Wohnstätten nach den Anschauungen der alten Hebraeer.* Giessan: Töpelmann, 1908. [Israel/Canaan]

Wheeler, Samuel B. "Prayer and Temple in the Dedication Speech of Solomon, 1 Kings 8:14-61." Ph.D. diss. Columbia University, 1977. [Israel/Canaan]

Whirley, Carlton F. "Significance of the Temple Cultus in the Background of the Gospel of John." Ph.D. diss., Southern Baptist Theological Seminary, 1958. [Israel/Canaan]

Whitaker, G. H. "The Building and the Body (Eph. 2:21f)." *Theology* 13 (1926): 335-36. [Israel/Canaan]

Wiesenberg, E. "The Nicanor Gate." *JJS* 3 (1952): 14-29. [Israel/Canaan]

Wilkinson, John D. "Jesus Comes to Jerusalem." In Wilkinson, *Jerusalem as Jesus Knew It.* 70-122. London: Thames and Hudson, 1978. [Israel/Canaan]

Wilkinson, John D. "Orientation, Jewish and Christian." *PEQ* 116 (1984): 16-30. [Israel/Canaan]

Willesen, F. "The Cultic Situation of Ps. LXXIV." *VT* 2 (1952): 289-306. [Israel/Canaan]

Wilson, A., and L. Wills. "Literary Sources of the Temple Scroll." *Harvard Theological Review* 75 (July 1982): 275-88. [Israel/Canaan]

Wilson, Charles W., et al. *The Recovery of Jerusalem—A Narrative of Exploration and Discovery in the City and the Holy Land.* London: Bentley, 1871. [Israel/Canaan]

Winer, Georg B. "Tempel-herodianischer." *Biblisches Realwoerterbuch,* edited by Georg B. Winer. 2 vols., 2:578-91. Leipzig: Reclam, 1848. [Israel/Canaan]

Wischnitzer, R. "Maimonides' Drawings of the Temples." *Journal of Jewish Art* 1 (1974): 16-27. [Israel/Canaan]

Wise, Michael O. "A New Manuscript Join in the 'Festival of Wood Offering.' " *JNES* 47 (April 1988): 113-21. [Israel/Canaan]

Wolcott, S. "The Land of Moriah." *Bibliotheca Sacra* 25 (1868): 765-79. [Israel/Canaan]

Wolff, Odilo. "Der Salomonische Tempelplatz und der heutige Haram zu Jerusalem." *ZDPV* 11 (1888): 60-67. [Israel/Canaan]

Wolff, Odilo. *Tempelmasse: Das Gesetz der Proportion in den antiken und altchristlichen Sakralbauten.* Vienna: Schroll, 1912. [Israel/Canaan]

Wolff, Odilo. *Der Tempel von Jerusalem.* Wein: Schroll, 1913. [Israel/Canaan]

Wolff, Odilo. *Der Tempel von Jerusalem und seine Masse.* Graz: Styria, 1887. [Israel/Canaan]

Wray, G. O. "Southern Projection from the Masjed al Aksa, Jerusalem." *PEQ* 23 (1891): 320-22. [Israel/Canaan]

Wright, George E. (Ernest). "Dr. Waterman's View Concerning the Solomonic Temple." *JNES* 7 (1948): 53-55. [Israel/Canaan]

Wright, G. (George) Ernest. "God Amidst His People: The Story of the Temple." In Wright, *Rule of God: Essays in Biblical Theology.* 57-76. Garden City, NY: Doubleday, 1960). [Israel/Canaan]

Wright, George E. (Ernest). "Solomon's Temple Resurrected." *BA* 4 (1941): 17-31. [Israel/Canaan]

Wright, George E. (Ernest). "The Stevens' Reconstruction of the Solomonic Temple." *BA* 18 (1955): 41-44. [Israel/Canaan]

Wright, George E. (Ernest). "The Temple in Palestine-Syria." *BA* 7 (1944): 41-44, 65-88. [Israel/Canaan]

Wright, G. R. H. "Bronze Age Temple at Amman." *ZAWT* 78 (1966): 351-59. [Israel/Canaan]

Wright, G. R. H. "Pre-Israelite Temples in the Land of Canaan." *PEQ* 103 (1971): 17-32. [Israel/Canaan]

Wright, G. R. H. "Shechem and League Shrines." *VT* 21 (1971): 572-603. [Israel/Canaan]

Wright, G. R. H. "Structure of the Qasr Bint Far'un: A Preliminary Review." *PEQ* 93 (1961): 8-37. [Israel/Canaan]

Wright, G. R. H. "Temples at Shechem." *ZAW* 80 (1968): 1-35. [Israel/Canaan]

Wright, G. R. H. "Temples at Shechem: A Detail." *ZAW* 87 (1975): 56-64. [Israel/Canaan]

Wright, John S. *The Building of the Second Temple.* London: Tyndale, 1958. [Israel/Canaan]

Wylie, C. C. "On King Solomon's Molten Sea." *BA* 12 (1949): 86-90. [Israel/Canaan]

Yaari, A. "Drawings of Jerusalem and the Temple Place as Ornament in Hebrew Books" (in Hebrew). *Kirjath Sepher* 15 (1938-39): 377-82. [Israel/Canaan]

Yadin, Yigael. "Beer-Sheba: The High Place Destroyed by King Josiah." *BASOR* 222 (1976): 5-17. [Israel/Canaan]

Yadin, Yigael. "The Gate of the Essenes and the Temple Scroll." In *Jerusalem Revealed: Archaeology in the Holy City, 1968-1974,* edited by Yigael Yadin. 90-91. New Haven: Yale University Press, 1976. [Israel/Canaan]

Yadin, Yigael. "The Gate of the Essenes and the Temple Scroll." *Qadmoniot* 5 (1972): 129-30. [Israel/Canaan]

Yadin, Yigael. "Le rouleau du Temple." In *Qumrân, Sa piété, sa théologie et son milieu,* edited by M. Delcor. 115-19. Paris: Duculot, 1978. [Israel/Canaan]

Yadin, Yigael. "The Temple" (in Hebrew). *Encyclopedia Hebraica* 8:555-91. Jerusalem: Mass, 1981. [Israel/Canaan]

Yadin, Yigael. "The Temple Scroll." *BA* 30 (1967): 135-39. [Israel/Canaan]

Yadin, Yigael. *The Temple Scroll.* 3 vols. Jerusalem: Israel Exploration Society, 1977-83. [Israel/Canaan]

Yadin, Yigael. *The Temple Scroll.* New York: Random House, 1985. [Israel/Canaan]

Yadin, Yigael. "The Temple Scroll, the Longest and Most Recently Discovered Dead Sea Scroll." *BAR* 10/5 (1984): 32-49. [Israel/Canaan]

Yeivin, S. "Casemated Walls and Sacred Areas." *Proceedings of the Fifth World Congress on Jewish Studies, August 3-11, 1969.* 62-68. Jerusalem: World Union of Jewish Studies, 1972. [Israel/Canaan]

Yeivin, S. "Jachin and Boaz." *PEQ* 91 (1959): 6-22. [Israel/Canaan]

Yeivin, S. "Solomon's Temple" (in Hebrew; *English summary). In *Jerusalem through the Ages*, edited by J. Aviram. 12-26, *58-59. Jerusalem: Israel Exploration Society, 1968. [Israel/Canaan]

Yeivin, S. "Was There a High Portal in the First Temple?" *VT* 14 (July 1964): 331-43. [Israel/Canaan]

Yerushalmi, Moses. *Yede Mosheh*. Jerusalem: Yeshivat Kodesh Hilulim, 1968/1969. [Israel/Canaan]

Yon, M. "Sanctuaires d'Ougarit." In *Temples et Sanctuaires: Seminaire de recherche 1981-1983*, edited by G. Roux. 37-50. Lyon: GIS - Maison de l'Orient, 1984. [Israel/Canaan]

Young, Francis M. "Temple Cult and Law in Early Christianity: A Study in the Relationship between Jews and Christians in the Early Centuries." *NTS* 19 (April 1973): 325-38. [Israel/Canaan]

Zarkowski, Zevi. *Kedushat Har*. Brooklyn: Balshon, 1971/1972. [Israel/Canaan]

Zeilinger, F. "Das himmlische Jerusalem: Untersuchungen zur Bildersprache der Johannesapokalypse und des Hebräerbriefes." In *Memoria Jerusalem: Freundesgabe Franz Sauer zum 70. Geburtstag*, edited by Johannes B. Bauer and Johannes Marböck. 143-65. Graz: Akademische, 1977. [Israel/Canaan]

Zeitlin, Solomon. "A Note on the Chronology of the Destruction of the Second Temple." *JQR* 37 (1946-47): 165-67. [Israel/Canaan]

Zeitlin, Solomon. "The Temple." In *The Rise and Fall of the Judaean State*. 2d ed. 3 vols., 1:256-68. Philadelphia: Jewish Publication Society of America, 1968. [Israel/Canaan]

Zeitlin, Solomon. "There Was No Court of Gentiles in the Temple Area." *JQR* 56 (1965-66): 88-89. [Israel/Canaan]

Zeitlin, Solomon. "There Was No Synagogue in the Temple." *JQR* 53 (1962-63): 168-69. [Israel/Canaan]

Zeitlin, Solomon. "Were There Three Torah-Scrolls in the Azarah?" *JQR* 56 (1965-66): 269-72. [Israel/Canaan]

Zilbershtain, Yesh'ay. *Ma'asei la-Melekh*. 2 vols. Vácz: Kahn, 1913. [Israel/Canaan]

Zimmer, R. G. "Temple of God." *Journal of the Evangelical Theological Society* 18 (1975): 41-46. [Israel/Canaan]

Zimmerli, Walther. *Ezechiel*. Neukirchen-Vluyn: Neukirchener, 1969. [Israel/Canaan]

Zimmerli, Walther. "Ezechieltempel und Salomostadt." In *Hebräische Wortforschung, Festschrift zum 80. Geburtstag von Walter Baumgartner*, edited by G. W. Anderson et al. 398-414. Leiden: Brill, 1967. [Israel/Canaan]

Zimmerli, Walther. "The Great Vision of the New Temple and the New Land." In *Ezekiel*, vol. 2 of *A Commentary on the Book of the Prophet Ezekiel*, 325-62. Philadelphia: Fortress, 1983. [Israel/Canaan]

Zimmerli, Walther. "Jerusalem in der Sicht des Ezechielbuches." In *The Word of the Lord Shall Go Forth: Essays in Honor of David Noel Freedman*, edited by C. L. Meyers and M. O'Connor. 415-26. Winona Lake: Eisenbrauns, 1983. [Israel/Canaan]

Zimmerli, Walther. "Planungen für den Wiederaufbau nach der Katastrophe von 587." *VT* 18 (1968): 229-55. [Israel/Canaan]

Zoref, Efrayim. "The Temple Mount and Foundation Stone" (in Hebrew). *Maḥanayim* 116 (1968): 22-33. [Israel/Canaan]

Temples of Mesopotamia

Andrae, Walter. *Der Anu-Adad-Tempel in Assur.* Leipzig: Hinrichs, 1909. [Mesopotamia]

Andrae, Walter. *Die archäischen Ischtar Tempel in Assur.* Leipzig: Hinrichs, 1922. [Mesopotamia]

Andrae, Walter. *Kultrelief aus dem Brunnen des Assurtempels zu Assur.* Liepzig: Hinrichs, 1931. [Mesopotamia]

Andrae, Walter. "Die Tempel der Assyrer." *ZDMG* 91 (1937): 49-57. [Mesopotamia]

Andrae, Walter. *Das wiedererstandene Assur,* 2d ed. Berlin: Propylaen, 1977. [Mesopotamia]

Banks, Edgar J. "The Bismya Temple." *Records of the Past* 5 (1906): 227-36. [Mesopotamia]

Barton, George A., ed. *Haverford Library Collection of Cuneiform Tablets or Documents from the Temple Archives of Telloh.* 3 vols. Philadelphia: Winston, 1905-14. [Mesopotamia]

Behrens, Emil. *Assyrisch-babylonische Briefe kultischen Inhalts aus der Sargonidenzeit.* Leipzig: Zentralantiquariat der DDR, 1968. [Mesopotamia]

Bittle, K. "Hittite Temples and High Places in Anatolia and North Syria." In *Temples and High Places in Biblical Times,* edited by Avraham Biran. 63-73. Jerusalem: Nelson Glueck School of Biblical Archaeology, 1981. [Mesopotamia]

Böhl, Franz. *Nieuwjaarsfeest en Koningsdag in Babylon en Israël.* Groningen: Woelters, 1927. [Mesopotamia]

Busink, Th. A. *De Babylonische tempeltoren: een archaeologische en stijlcritische studie.* Leiden: Brill, 1949. [Mesopotamia]

Busink, Th. A. *Sumerische en Babylonische tempelbouw.* Batavia: Noordhoff-Kolff, 1940. [Mesopotamia]

Busink, Th. A. "Tempelbouw in Oud-Mesopotame." *Ex Oriente Lux: Jaarbericht van het vooraziatisch-egyptisch Gezelschap* 5 (1937-38): 409-20. [Mesopotamia]

Charpin, D. "Temples à decouvrir en Syrie du Nord d'après des documents inédits de Mari." *Iraq* 45 (1983): 56-63. [Mesopotamia]

Charriere, G. "L'Orientation de quelques ziggurats et sanctuaries du Moyen-Orient." *Revue d'Assyriologie* 58 (1964): 9-22. [Mesopotamia]

Chiera, Edward. *Selected Temple Accounts from Telloh, Yokha and Drehem.* Princeton: Princeton University Press, 1922. [Mesopotamia]

Dandamayev, M. A. "State and Temple in Babylonia in the First Millennium B.C." In *State and Temple Economy in the Ancient Near East:*, edited by Edward Lipiński. 2 vols., 2:589-96. Louvain: Departement Orientalistiek, 1979. [Mesopotamia]

Dandamayev, M. A. "Tempelbauern in späten Babylonien." *Palestinski Sbornik* 17 (1967): 41-49. [Mesopotamia]

Dandamayev, M. A. "Temple and State in Babylonia." *Vestnik Drevnei Istorii* 4/98 (1966): 17-39. [Mesopotamia]

Delitzsch, F. "Esagila, the Babylonian Pantheon." *Records of the Past* 2 (1903): 322-31. [Mesopotamia]

Delougaz, Pinhas. *Pre-Sargonid Temples in the Diyala Region.* Chicago: University of Chicago Press, 1942. [Mesopotamia]

Delougaz, Pinhas. *The Temple Oval of Khafajah.* Chicago: University of Chicago, 1940. [Mesopotamia]

Dhorme, Édouard P. "Le plus ancien temple d'Ishtar à Ninive." *Revue de l'histoire des religions* 110 (1934): 140-56. [Mesopotamia]

Dhorme, Édouard P. *Les religions de babylonie et d'assyrie.* Paris, Presses universitaires de France, 1949. [Mesopotamia]

Dossin, Georges. "Un rituel du culte d'Ishtar provenant de Mari." *Revue d'Assyriologie et d'Archéologie Orientale* 35 (1938): 1-13. [Mesopotamia]

Ellis, Richard S. *Foundation Deposits in Ancient Mesopotamia.* New Haven: Yale University Press, 1968. [Mesopotamia]

Falkenstein, Adam. "La cité-temple sumérienne." *Journal of World History/Cahiers d'histoire mondiale* 1 (1954): 784-814; also in English as *The Sumerian Temple City*, translated by Maria Ellis. Malibu: Undena, 1974. [Mesopotamia]

Falkenstein, Adam. *Die Inschriften Gudeas von Lagash.* Rome: Pontifical Biblical Institute, 1966. [Mesopotamia]

Frankfort, Henri. *The Gimilsin Temple and the Palace of the Rulers at Tell Asmar.* Chicago: University of Chicago Press, 1940. [Mesopotamia]

Galter, H. D. "Die Bautätigkeit Sanheribs am Aššurtempel." *Orientalia* 53 (1984): 433-41. [Mesopotamia]

Golzio, Karl-Heinz. *Der Tempel im alten Mesopotamien und seine Parallelen in Indien.* Leiden: Brill, 1983. [Mesopotamia]

Gressmann, Hugo. *The Tower of Babel.* New York: Jewish Institute of Religion Press, 1928. [Mesopotamia]

Grice, Ettalene M. *Records from Ur and Larsa Dated in the Larsa Dynasty.* New Haven: Yale University Press, 1919. [Mesopotamia]

Gurney, Oliver R. "The Cult." In Gurney, *Some Aspects of Hittite Religion.* Oxford: Oxford University Press, 1977. [Mesopotomia]

Gustavs, A. "Religionsgeschictliches aus 'Koldewey, die Tempel von Babylon und Borsippa.' " *ZAW* 32 (1912): 65-68. [Mesopotamia]

Hackman, George G. *Temple Documents of the Third Dynasty of Ur from Umma.* London: Milford, 1937. [Mesopotamia]

Harris, Rivkah. "The Archive of the Sin Temple in Khafajah." *Journal of Cuneiform Studies* 9 (1955): 31-88. [Mesopotamia]

Harris, Rivkah. "Old Babylonian Temple Loans." *Journal of Cuneiform Studies* 14 (1960): 126-39. [Mesopotamia]

Heinrich, Ernst. *Kleinfunde aus den archaischen Tempelschichten in Uruk.* Berlin: Deutsche Forschungsgemeinschaft, 1936. [Mesopotamia]

Heinrich, Ernst. "Die Stellung der Uruktempel in der Baugeschichte." *Zeitschrift für Assyriologie* 49 (1949): 21-44. [Mesopotamia]

Heinrich, Ernst. *Die Tempel und Heiligtümer im alten Mesopotamien: Typologie, Morphologie, und Geschichte.* Berlin: de Gruyter, 1982. [Mesopotamia]

Henrickson, E. F. "House or Temples: Ubaid Tripartite Architecture in Mesopotamia." *AJA* 89 (1985): 333. [Mesopotamia]

Howard-Carter, T. "An Interpretation of the Sculptural Decoration of the 2nd Millennium Temple at Tell al-Rimah." *Iraq* 45 (1983): 64-72. [Mesopotamia]

Jastrow, Morris, Jr. "The Cosmology of the Babylonians." In *The Religion of Babylonia and Assyria.* 407-53. Boston: Ginn, 1898. [Mesopotamia]

Jastrow, Morris, Jr. "Did the Babylonian Temples have Libraries?" *JAOS* 27 (1906): 147-82. [Mesopotamia]

Jastrow, Morris, Jr. "The Temples and the Cult." In *The Religion of Babylonia and Assyria.* 612-89. Boston: Ginn, 1898. [Mesopotamia]

Kapelrud, Arvid S. "Temple Building, a Task for Gods and Kings." *Orientalia* 32 (1963): 56-62; also in Kapelrud, *God and His Friends in the Old Testament.* 184-90. Oslo: Universitetsforlaget, 1979. [Mesopotamia]

Keiser, Clarence E. *Selected Temple Documents of the Ur Dynasty.* New Haven: Yale University Press, 1919. [Mesopotamia]

Keiser, Helen. *Tempel und Türme in Sumer: Archäologen auf der Spur von Gilgamesch.* Freiburg: Walter, 1977. [Mesopotamia]

Koldewey, Robert. *Die Tempel von Babylon und Borsippa*. Osnabrück: Zeller, 1972. [Mesopotamia]

Korosec, V. "Einiges zur inneren Struktur hethitischer Tempel nach der Instruktion für Tempelleute." *Publication of the Institutes of History and Archaeology* 35 (1974): 165-74. [Mesopotamia]

Kramer, Samuel N. "The Temple in Sumerian Literature." In *Temple in Society*, edited by Michael V. Fox. 1-16. Winona Lake: Eisenbrauns, 1988. [Mesopotamia]

Kraus, F. R. "Le rôle des temples depuis la troisième dynastie d'Ur jusqu'a la première dynastie de Babylone." *Journal of World History/Cahiers d'histoire mondiale* 1 (1953-54): 518-45. [Mesopotamia]

Lambert, M. M. "En Marge du problème de al Siqquart. Les Pontifes du Temples d'En-Haut." *Sumer* 7 (1951): 58-65. [Mesopotamia]

Lau, Robert J. *Old Babylonian Temple Records*. New York: AMS, 1966. [Mesopotamia]

Lenzen, H. J. "Mesopotamische Tempelanlagen von der Frühzeit bis zum zweiten Jahrtausend." *Zeitschrift für Assyriologie* 51 (1955): 1-36. [Mesopotamia]

Lenzen, H. J. "Die Tempel der Schicht Archaisch IV in Uruk." *Zeitschrift für Assyriologie* 49/15 (1949): 1-20. [Mesopotamia]

Levine, Baruch A., and W. W. Hallo. "Offerings to the Temple Gates at Ur." *HUCA* 38 (1967): 17-58. [Mesopotamia]

Lipiński, Edward. "Les temples néo-assyriens et les origines du monnayage." In *State and Temple Economy in the Ancient Near East*, edited by Edward Lipiński. 2 vols., 2:565-88. Louvain: Departement Orientalistiek, 1979. [Mesopotamia]

Luckenbill, D. D. "The Temples of Babylonia and Assyria." *AJSL* 24 (1907/08): 291-322. [Mesopotamia]

Lutz, Henry F. *Sumerian Temple Records of the Late Ur Dynasty*. Berkeley: University of California Press, 1928. [Mesopotamia]

McEwan, Gilbert J. P. *Priest and Temple in Hellenistic Babylonia*. Wiesbaden: Steiner, 1981. [Mesopotamia]

Margueron, Jean. "Notes d'archéologie et d'architecture orientales." *Syria* 63/3-4 (1986): 257-303. [Mesopotamia]

Martiny, Günter. *Die Gegensätze im babylonischen und assyrischen Tempelbau*. Leipzig: Kraus Reprint, 1936. [Mesopotamia]

Mayassis, S. *Mystères et initiations dans la préhistoire et protohistoire, de l'antédiluvien à Sumer-Babylone*. Athens: B.A.O.A., 1961. [Mesopotamia]

Menzel, Brigitte. *Assyrische Tempel*. Rome: Pontifical Biblical Institute, 1981. [Mesopotamia]

Neve, Peter. "Die Kulträume in den hethitischen Tempeln Hattusas." In *Festschrift Heinrich Otten*, edited by Erich New and Christel Rüster. 253-72. Wiesbaden: Harrassowitz, 1973. [Mesopotamia]

Oppenheim, A. Leo. "The Mesopotamian Temple." *BA* 7 (1944): 54-63. [Mesopotamia]

Pallis, Svend A. *The Babylonian Akitu Festival.* Copenhagen: Bianco Lunos Bogtrykkeri, 1926. [Mesopotamia]

Parrot, André. *Le Temple d'Ishtar.* Paris: Geuthner, 1956. [Mesopotamia]

Parrot, André. "La Tour de Babel et les Ziggurats." *La Nouvelle Clio* 2 (1950): 153-61. [Mesopotamia]

Parrot, André. *The Tower of Babel,* translated by Edwin Hudson. London: SCM, 1955. [Mesopotamia]

Pinches, Theophilus G. "Assur and Nineveh." *Records of the Past* 12 (1913): 23-41. [Mesopotamia]

Postgate, J. N. "The *bit akiti* in Assyrian Nabu Temples." *Sumer* 30 (1974): 51-74. [Mesopotamia]

Postgate, J. N. "The Role of the Temple in the Mesopotamian Secular Community." In *Man, Settlement and Urbanism,* edited by Peter J. Ucko. 811-25. Cambridge: Schenkman, 1972. [Mesopotamia]

Renger, J. "Interaction of Temple, Palace, and 'Private Enterprise' in the Old Babylonian Economy." In *State and Temple Economy in the Ancient Near East,* edited by Edward Lipiński. 2 vols., 1:249-56. Louvain: Departement Orientalistiek, 1979. [Mesopotamia]

Salihi, W. "The Shrine of Nebo at Hatra." *British School of Archaeology in Iraq* 45 (1983): 140-45. [Mesopotamia]

Salvini, M. "Das *Susi*-Heiligtum vom Kamir-Blur und der Urartäische Turmtempel." *Archaeologische Mitteilungen aus Iran* 12 (1979): 249-69. [Mesopotamia]

Schneider, N. "Göttertempel in Ur III-Reich." *Orientalia* 19 (1950): 257-64. [Mesopotamia]

Sjoberg, Åke W., and E. Bergmann. *The Collection of the Sumerian Temple Hymns.* Locust Valley: Augustin, 1969. [Mesopotamia]

Smith, S. "The Babylonian Ritual for the Consecration and Induction of a Divine Statue." *Journal of the Royal Asiatic Society of Great Britain and Ireland* (1925): 37-60. [Mesopotamia]

Sollberger, E. "The Temple in Babylonia." In *Le temple et le culte: Compte rendu de la vingtième recontre assyriologique internationale organisée à Leiden du 3 au 7 juillet 1972.* 31-34. İstanbul: Nederlands Historisch-Archeologisch Instituut te Istambul 1975. [Mesopotamia]

Swetnam, Walter. "Selected Temple Documents of the Reign of Bur Sin of the Third Dynasty of Ur." Ph.D., diss., Hartford Seminary Foundation, 1930. [Mesopotamia]

Torczyner (Tur-Sinai), Harry. *Altbabylonische Tempelrechnungen.* Wien: Hölder, 1913. [Mesopotamia]

Van Buren, E. (Elizabeth) D. (Douglas). "The Building of a Temple Tower." *Revue d'Assyriologie et d'Archeologie Orientale* 46 (1952): 65-74. [Mesopotamia]

Van Buren, E. (Elizabeth Douglas). "Foundation Rites for a New Temple." *Orientalia* 21 (1952): 293-306. [Mesopotamia]

Vincent, Louis-Hugues. "De la tour de Babel au Temple." *RB* 53 (1946): 403-40. [Mesopotamia]

Widengren, Geo. "Aspetti simbolici dei templi e luoghi di culto del vicino oriente antico." *Numen* 7 (1960): 1-25; also in a slightly revised version in German as "Der Kultplatz: Symbolische Bedeutung des Heiligtums im alten Vorderen Orient." In Widengren, *Religionsphänomenologie*. 328-39. Berlin: de Gruyter, 1969. [Mesopotamia]

Wright, G. R. H. "Square Temples East and West." In *Memorial Volume of the Fifth International Congress of Iranian Art and Archaeology. Teheran-Isfahan-Shiraz, 11th-18th April 1968*. 2 vols., 1: 380-88. Teheran: Ministry of Culture and Arts, 1972. [Mesopotamia]

Xella, Paolo. "A proposito del sacrificio umano nel mondo mesopotamico." *Orientalia* 45 (1976): 185-96. [Mesopotamia]

Tabernacle of Moses

Abrahams, Israel. "Tabernacle." In *Encyclopaedia Judaica* 15:679-87. [Tabernacle]

Aharoni, Yohanan. "From Shiloh to Jerusalem" (in Hebrew; *English summary). In *Jerusalem through the Ages*, edited by Joseph Aviram. 85-95, *61. Jerusalem: Israel Exploration Society, 1968. [Tabernacle]

Ahlström, Gösta W. "The Travels of the Ark: A Religio-Political Composition." *JNES* 43 (1984): 141-49. [Tabernacle]

Albright, William F. "What Were the Cherubim?" *BA* 1 (1938): 1-3. [Tabernacle]

Alon, Gedalyahu. "The Festival of Tabernacles in Jerusalem in the Days of the Second Temple." In Alon, *Studies in Jewish History in the Times of the Second Temple, the Mishna and the Talmud* (in Hebrew). 2 vols., 1:77-82. Tel-Aviv: Hakubutz Hameuchad, 1957. [Tabernacle]

Alt, Albrecht. "Zelte und Hütten." In *Alttestamentliche Studien: Friedrich Nötscher zum sechzigsten Geburtstag*, edited by Hubert Junker and G. Johannes Botterweck. 16-25. Bonn: Hanstein, 1950; also in Alt, *Kleine Schriften zur Geschichte des Volkes Israel*. 3 vols., 3:233-42. Munich: Beck, 1959. [Tabernacle]

Andrews, S. J. "The Worship of the Tabernacle Compared with That of the Second Temple." *JBL* 6 (1886): 56-68. [Tabernacle]

Arnold, William R. *Ephod and Ark: A Study in the Records and Religion of the Ancient Hebrews.* Cambridge: Harvard University Press, 1917. [Tabernacle]

Atwater, Edward E. *History and Significance of the Sacred Tabernacle of the Hebrews.* New York: Dodd and Mead, 1875. [Tabernacle]

Baker, D. "Recreating the Divine Design: Tabernacle Furnishings." *Christianity Today* 15 (12 March 1971): 43. [Tabernacle]

Barnett, R. D. "Cherubim and the Temple of Solomon." In *Illustrations of Old Testament History,* 44-45. London: British Museum, 1966. [Tabernacle]

Beattie, K. M. *The Tabernacle: A Simplified Presentation.* London: Marshal, Morgan and Scott, 1962. [Tabernacle]

Ben-Ori, Z. "The Ark of Testimony and Its Parts" (in Hebrew). *Beth Mikra* 27 (1981-82): 214-21. [Tabernacle]

Ben-Ori, Z. "The Posts of the Tabernacle Court" (in Hebrew). *Beth Mikra* 26 (1981): 148-58. [Tabernacle]

Benzinger, Immanuel. "Tabernacle." In *Encyclopaedia Biblica* 4:4861-75. [Tabernacle]

Bernhardt, Karl-Heinz. "Lade." In *Biblisch-Historisches Handwörterbuch,* edited by Bo Reicke and Leonhard Rost. 4 vols., 2:1038-41. Göttingen: Vandenhoeck and Ruprecht, 1964. [Tabernacle]

Blenkinsopp, Joseph. "Gibeon and the Ark: A Hypothesis." In *Gibeon and Israel: The Role of Gibeon and the Gibeonites in the Political and Religious History of Early Israel,* edited by J. A. Emerton. 65-83. Cambridge: Cambridge University Press, 1972. [Tabernacle]

Blenkinsopp, Joseph. "Kiriath-Jearim and the Ark." *JBL* 88 (1969): 143-56. [Tabernacle]

Botterweck, G. Johannes. "*hêkhāl.*" In *Theological Dictionary of the Old Testament* 3:382-88. [Tabernacle]

Brinke, Georg R. *Die Symbolik der Stiftshütte.* Wuppertal: Brockhaus, 1956. [Tabernacle]

Brown, John Pairman. "The Ark of the Covenant and the Temple of Janus: The Magico-Military Numen of the State in Jerusalem and Rome." *Biblische Zeitschrift* 30 (1986): 20-35. [Tabernacle]

Budde, K. "Ephod und Lade." *ZAW* 39 (1921): 1-42. [Tabernacle]

Caldecott, William S. *The Tabernacle: Its History and Structure.* London: Religious Tract, 1904. [Tabernacle]

Campbell, Anthony F. *The Ark Narrative (1 Sam 4-6; 2 Sam 6): A Form-Critical and Traditio-Historical Study.* Missoula, MT: Scholars, 1975. [Tabernacle]

Carlyle, Thomas. *The Mosaic Tabernacle.* Glasgow: Hobbs, 1901. [Tabernacle]

Chase, Ira J. *The Jewish Tabernacle.* Cincinnati: Standard, 1883. [Tabernacle]

Cheyne, T. K. "Ark of the Covenant." In *Encyclopaedia Biblica*, 300-310. [Tabernacle]

Clifford, Richard J. "Tent of El and the Israelite Tent of Meeting." *CBQ* 33 (1971): 221-27. [Tabernacle]

Couard, Ludwig. "Die religiosnationale Bedeutung der Lade Jahves." *ZAW* 12 (1892): 53-90. [Tabernacle]

Cowan, Aldworth. *God's Tent*. Old Tappan: Revell, 1980. [Tabernacle]

Cross, Frank M. "The Cultus of the Israelite League." In Cross, *Canaanite Myth and Hebrew Epic*. 77-144. Cambridge: Harvard University Press, 1973. [Tabernacle]

Cross, Frank M. "The Priestly Tabernacle in the Light of Recent Research." In *Temples and High Places in Biblical Times*, edited by Avraham Biran. 169-80. Jerusalem: Nelson Glueck School of Biblical Archaeology, 1981; also in a slightly revised version in *The Temple in Antiquity*, edited by Truman G. Madsen. 91-105. Provo: Brigham Young University Press, 1984. [Tabernacle]

Cross, Frank M. "The Tabernacle: A Study from an Archaeological and Historical Approach." *BA* 10 (1947): 45-68; reprinted in slightly revised form as "The Priestly Tabernacle" In *Biblical Archaeologist Reader*, edited by G. Ernest Wright and D. N. Freedman. 201-28. New York: Anchor, 1961. [Tabernacle]

Daglin, Aharon Z. *Book of the Temple of Aaron: An Explanation of the Tabernacle and Its Vessels* (in Hebrew). Warsaw: Argelbrand Brothers, 1891. [Tabernacle]

Davies, G. Henton. "The Ark in the Psalms." In *Promise and Fulfillment, Essays Presented to S. H. Hooke in Celebration of His Ninetieth Birthday*, edited by F. F. Bruce. 51-61. Edinburgh: Clark, 1963. [Tabernacle]

Davies, G. Henton. "Ark of the Covenant." In *The Interpreter's Dictionary of the Bible* 1:222-26. [Tabernacle]

Davies, G. Henton. "The Ark of the Covenant." *Annual of the Swedish Theological Institute* 5 (1967): 30-47. [Tabernacle]

Davies, G. Henton. "Tabernacle." In *The Interpreter's Dictionary of the Bible* 4:498-506. [Tabernacle]

de Charms, George. *The Tabernacle of Israel*. New York: Pageant Press International, 1969. [Tabernacle]

Deglin, Selig H. *Mikdash Aharon*. C.-Ilerepóypr: n.p., 1894. [Tabernacle]

de Haan, Martin R. *The Tabernacle, The House of Blood* Grand Rapids: Zondervan, 1973. [Tabernacle]

de Tarragon, J. M. "David et l'arche: 2 Sam 6." *RB* 86 (1979): 514-23. [Tabernacle]

de Tarragon, J. M. "La *kapporet* est-elle une fiction ou un élément du culte tardif?" *RB* 88 (1981): 5-12. [Tabernacle]

Dhorme, Édouard (Paul). "Les Cherubins." *RB* 35 (1926): 328-58, 481-95.
[Tabernacle]

Dhorme, Édouard. "Le nom des Chérubins." In Dhorme, *Recueil Édouard Dhorme: Études et orientales.* 671-83. Paris: Imprimerie Nationale, 1951.
[Tabernacle]

Dibelius, Martin. *Die Lade Jahves: Eine religionsgeschichtliche Untersuching.* Göttingen: Vandenhoeck and Ruprecht, 1906. [Tabernacle]

Dombart, Theodor. "Der zweitürmige Tempel-Pylon altägyptischer Baukunst und seine religiöse Symbolik." *Egyptian Religion* 1 (1933): 87-98. [Tabernacle]

Dürr, Lorenz. "Ursprung und Bedeutung der Bundeslade." *Bonner Zeitschrift für Theologie und Seelsorge* 1 (1924): 17-24. [Tabernacle]

Dus, Jan. "Die Analyse zweier Ladeerzählungen des Josuabuches (Jos. 3-4 und 6)." *ZAW* 72 (1960): 107-34. [Tabernacle]

Dus, Jan. "Der Brauch der Ladewanderung im alten Israel." *Theologische Zeitschrift* 17 (1961): 1-16. [Tabernacle]

Dus, Jan. "The Dreros Bilingual and the Tabernacle of Ancient Israelites." *Journal of Semitic Studies* 10 (1965): 54-58. [Tabernacle]

Dus, Jan. "Die Erzählung über den Verlust der Lade, 1 Sam. IV." *VT* 13 (1963): 333-37. [Tabernacle]

Dus, Jan. "Herabfahrung Jahwes auf die Lade und Entziehung der Feuerwolke." *VT* 19 (1969): 290-311. [Tabernacle]

Dus, Jan. "Noch zum Brauch der 'Ladewanderung'." *VT* 13 (1963): 126-32.
[Tabernacle]

Dus, Jan. "Die Thron- und Bundeslade." *Theologische Zeitschrift* 20 (1964): 241-51. [Tabernacle]

Dus, Jan. "Zur bewegten Geschichte der israelitischen Lade." *Annali dell'Istituto Orientale di Napoli* 41 (1981): 351-83. [Tabernacle]

Eerdmans, B. D. "Sojourn in the Tent of Jahu." *Oudtestamentische Studien* 1 (1942): 1-16. [Tabernacle]

Eissfeldt, Otto. "Die Komposition der Sinai-Erzählung Exodus 19-34." *Forschungen und Fortschritte* 40 (1966): 213-15; also in *Kleine Schriften,* edited by Rudolf Sellheim and Fritz Maass. 6 vols., 4:231-37. Tübingen: Mohr, 1968. [Tabernacle]

Eissfeldt, Otto. "Kultzelt und Tempel." In *Wort und Geschichte: Festschrift für Karl Elliger zum 70. Geburtstag,* edited by Hartmut Gese et al. 51-55. Neukirchen-Vluyn: Neukirchener, 1973; also in *Kleine Schriften,* edited by Rudolf Sellheim and Fritz Maass. 6 vols. 6:1-7. Tübingen: Mohr, 1979.
[Tabernacle]

Eissfeldt, Otto. "Die Lade Jahwes in Geschichtserzählung, Sage und Lied." *Altertum* 14 (1968): 131-45; also in *Kleine Schriften,* edited by Rudolf Sellheim and Fritz Maass. 6 vols., 5:77-93. Tübingen: Mohr, 1973.
[Tabernacle]

Eissfeldt, Otto. "Lade und Gesetztafeln." *Theologische Zeitschrift* 16 (1960): 281-84; also in *Kleine Schriften*, edited by Rudolf Sellheim and Fritz Maass. 6 vols., 3:526-29. Tübingen: Mohr, 1966. [Tabernacle]

Eissfeldt, Otto. "Lade und Stierbild." *ZAW* 58 (1940-41): 190-215; also in *Kleine Schriften*, edited by Rudolf Sellheim and Fritz Maass. 6 vols., 2:282-305. Tübingen: Mohr, 1963. [Tabernacle]

Epstein, C. "Aspects of Symbolism in Chalcolithic Palestine." In *Archaeology in the Levant, Essays for Kathleen Kenyon*, edited by Roger Moorey. 23-35. Warminster: Aris and Phillips, 1978. [Tabernacle]

Epstein, E. M. *The Construction of the Tabernacle.* Chicago: Open Court, 1911. [Tabernacle]

Faber van der Meulen, H. E. "One or Two Veils in Front of the Holy of Holies?" *Theologia Evangelica* 18 (1985): 22-27. [Tabernacle]

Friedman, R. E. "The Tabernacle in the Temple." *BA* 43 (1980): 241-48. [Tabernacle]

Fuller, Charles E. *The Tabernacle in the Wilderness.* Westwood: Revell, 1955. [Tabernacle]

Galling, Kurt. "Lade Jahwes." In *Die Religion in Geschichte und Gegenwart*, edited by Alfred Bertholet et al. 5 vols., 3:1449-50. 2d ed. Tübingen: Mohr, 1929. [Tabernacle]

Goldman, Bernard. *The Sacred Portal*, 69-100. Detroit: Wayne State, 1966. [Tabernacle]

Goodenough, Erwin R. "The Menorah: The Menorah on the Monuments." In *Jewish Symbols in the Greco-Roman Period.* 13 vols., 4:71-77. New York: Pantheon Books, 1953-68. [Tabernacle]

Gooding, David W. *The Account of the Tabernacle.* Cambridge: Cambridge University Press, 1959. [Tabernacle]

Grintz, Yehoshua M. "Ark of the Covenant." In *Encyclopaedia Judaica* 3:459-65. [Tabernacle]

Guillebaud, M. L. G. "The Tent over the Tabernacle." *Evangelical Quarterly* 31 (1959): 90-98. [Tabernacle]

Gutmann, Joseph. "The History of the Ark." *ZAW* 83 (1971): 22-30. [Tabernacle]

Habershon, Ada R. *Outline Studies of the Tabernacle.* Grand Rapids: Kregel, 1974. [Tabernacle]

Hachlili, Rachel. "The Niche and the Ark in Ancient Synagogues." *BASOR* 223 (1976): 43-53. [Tabernacle]

Haldeman, Isaac M. *The Tabernacle, Priesthood and Offerings.* New York: Revell, 1925. [Tabernacle]

Haran, Menahem. "The Ark and the Cherubim: Their Symbolic Significance in Biblical Ritual." *IEJ* 9 (1959): 30-38, 89-94. [Tabernacle]

Haran, Menahem. "The Ark of the Covenant and the Cherubs" (in Hebrew; *English summary). *Eretz-Israel* 5 (1958): 83-90, *88. [Tabernacle]

Haran, Menahem. "The Complex of Ritual Acts Performed inside the Tabernacle." *Scripta Hierosolymitana* 8 (1961): 272-302. [Tabernacle]

Haran, Menahem. "Nature of the '^ɔOhel Mo^cedh' in Pentateuchal Sources." *Journal of Semitic Studies* 5 (1960): 50-65. [Tabernacle]

Haran, Menahem. "The Priestly Image of the Tabernacle." *HUCA* 36 (1965): 191-226. [Tabernacle]

Haran, Menahem. "Shiloh and Jerusalem" (in Hebrew). *Tarbiz* 31 (1961-62): 317-25. [Tabernacle]

Haran, Menahem. "The Tabernacle: A Graded Tabu of Holiness" (in Hebrew). In *Studies in the Bible, Presented to M. H. Segal*, edited by Jehoshua M. Grintz et al. 33-41. Jerusalem: Keriot Sefer, 1964): 33-41. [Tabernacle]

Haran, Menahem. "The Tabernacle and Ritualistic Interior Enclosure" (In Hebrew). Ph.D. diss., Hebrew University, 1955. [Tabernacle]

Haran, Menahem. "The Tabernacle in the Priestly Source: Its Technical and Material Gradations" (in Hebrew). In *Sefer Tur-Sinai Jubilee Volume*, edited by Menahem Haran. 27-42. Jerusalem: Ha-Hevrah leheker ha-Mikra be-Yisrael, 1960. [Tabernacle]

Haran, Menahem. "The Tent of Meeting." *Tarbiz* 25 (1955): 11-20. [Tabernacle]

Hart, I. "Preaching on the Account of the Tabernacle." *Evangelical Quarterly* 54 (1982): 111-16. [Tabernacle]

Hartmann, R. "Zelt und Lade." *ZAW* 37 (1917-18): 209-44. [Tabernacie]

Hewett, Louisa A. *Papers on the Tabernacle*. Glasgow: Hobbs, 1898. [Tabernacle]

Hillers, Delbert R. "Ritual Procession of the Ark and Psalm 132." *CBQ* 30 (1968): 48-55. [Tabernacle]

Hofius, Otfried. "Das 'erste' und das 'zweite' Zelt; ein Beitrag zur Auslegung von Heb 9:1-10." *ZNTW* 61/3-4 (1970): 271-77. [Tabernacle]

Hruby, Kurt. "La fête des tabernacles au temple, à la synagogue et dans le Nouveau Testament." *L'Orient Syrien* 7 (1962): 163-74. [Tabernacle]

Hurowitz, Victor (Avigdor). "The Priestly Account of Building the Tabernacle." *JAOS* 105 (1985): 21-30. [Tabernacle]

Ing, Anthony. *The Tabernacle*. Toronto: Good News, 1986. [Tabernacle]

Jehuda, Jacob. *Ha-Mishkan ve-Khelav*. Jerusalem: Kiryah ne^ɔemanah, 1965. [Tabernacle]

Jeremias, Jörg. "Lade und Zion: Zur Entstehung der Ziontradition." In *Probleme biblischer Theologie: Gerhard von Rad zum 70. Geburtstag*, edited by Hans W. Wolff. 183-98. Munich: Kaiser, 1971. [Tabernacle]

Kaufman, Asher S. "Fixing the Site of the Tabernacle at Shiloh." *BAR* 14/6 (1988): 46-52. [Tabernacle]

Kelchner, John W. *A Description of King Solomon's Temple and Citadel and the Tabernacle in the Wilderness.* Philadelphia: Holman, 1925. [Tabernacle]

Kelly, J. J. "The Sense of the Holy." *The Way* 13 (1973): 249-58. [Tabernacle]

Kelso, J. L. "The Hebrew Tabernacle as a Work of Literature." *Bibliotheca Sacra* 79 (1922): 62-71. [Tabernacle]

Kennedy, A. R. S. "Ark of the Covenant." In *Dictionary of the Bible* 1:149-51. [Tabernacle]

Kennedy, A. R. S. "Tabernacle." In *Dictionary of the Bible* 4:653-68. [Tabernacle]

Kennett, R. H. "Ark." In *Encyclopaedia of Religion and Ethics* 1:791-93. [Tabernacle]

Kiene, Paul F. *The Tabernacle of God in the Wilderness of Sinai.* Grand Rapids: Zondervan, 1977. [Tabernacle]

Kline, Meridith G. "Investiture with the Image of God." *Westminster Theological Journal* 40 (1977): 39-62. [Tabernacle]

Koch, K. "Die Eigenart der priesterschriftlichen Sinaigesetzgebung." *Zeitschrift für Theologie und Kirche* 55 (1958): 36-51. [Tabernacle]

Koch, K. "'ōhel." In *Theological Dictionary of the Old Testament* 1:118-30. [Tabernacle]

Koester, Craig R. *The Dwelling of God: The Tabernacle in the Old Testament, Intertestamental Jewish Literature, and the New Testament.* Washington, D.C.: Catholic Biblical Association of America, 1987. [Tabernacle]

Kristensen, William B. *De ark van Jahwe.* Amsterdam: Noord-Hollandsche Uitgevers-Maatschappij, 1933. [Tabernacle]

Kutsch, E. "Lade Jahwes." In *Die Religion in Geschichte und Gegenwart.* 7 vols., 4:197-99. 3d ed. Tübingen: Mohr, 1960. [Tabernacle]

Kutsch, E. "Zelt." In *Die Religion in Geschichte und Gegenwart.* 7 vols., 6:1893-94. 3d ed. Tübingen: Mohr, 1962. [Tabernacle]

Légasse, S. "Les voiles du temple de Jérusalem: Essai de parcours historique." *RB* 87 (1980): 560-89. [Tabernacle]

Lesêtre, Henri. "Arche d'Alliance." In *Dictionnaire de la Bible,* edited by F. Vigouroux. 5 vols., 1:912-23. Paris: Letouzey et Ané, 1895. [Tabernacle]

Lesêtre, Henri. "Tabernacle." In *Dictionnaire de la Bible,* edited by F. Vigouroux. 5 vols., 5:1951-61. Paris: Letouzey et Ané, 1895. [Tabernacle]

Levine, Baruch A. "The Descriptive Tabernacle Texts of the Pentateuch." *JAOS* 85 (1965): 307-18. [Tabernacle]

Levine, Moshe. *Melekhet ha-Mishkan: Tavnit ha-Mishkan ve-Khelav.* Tel Aviv: Melekhet ha-mishkan, 1968; also in English as *The Tabernacle: Its Structure and Utensils.* London: Soncino, 1970. [Tabernacle]

Lewis, George W. *The Tabernacle of the Testimony, from the Book of Exodus.* Cincinnati: Standard, 1925. [Tabernacle]

Lewis, J. "The Ark and the Tent." *Review and Expositor* 74 (1977): 537-48. [Tabernacle]

Lindeskog, G. "Veil." *Coniectanea Neotestamentica* 11 (1947): 132-37. [Tabernacle]

Little, David. *The Tabernacle in the Wilderness*. 2d ed. Neptune, NJ: Loizeaux Bros., 1989. [Tabernacle]

Lotz, Wilhelm. *Die Bundeslade*. Erlangen: Deichert, 1901. [Tabernacle]

Lotz, Wilhelm, M. G. Kyle, and C. E. Armerding. "Ark of the Covenant." In *International Standard Bible Encyclopedia*, edited by G. W. Bromily. 4 vols., 1:291-94. Grand Rapids: Eerdmans, 1979. [Tabernacle]

Martin, W. S., and A. Marshall, ed. *Tabernacle Types and Teachings*. London: Martin, 1924. [Tabernacle]

McGee, J. V. "The Theology of the Tabernacle." *Bibliotheca Sacra* 95 (1938): 22-39. [Tabernacle]

McKane, W. "The Earlier History of the Ark." *Transactions of the Glasgow University Oriental Society* 21 (1965/1966): 68-76. [Tabernacle]

Maclaren, Alexander. *The Holy of Holies*. London: Alexander and Shepheard, 1890. [Tabernacle]

Madsen, N. P. "Pneumatological Anthropology: A Proposal for a Theology of the Holy Spirit." *Reformed Review* 37 (1983): 13-24. [Tabernacle]

Maier, Johann. *Das altisraelitische Ladeheiligtum*. Berlin: Töpelmann, 1965. [Tabernacle]

May, Herbert G. "The Ark—a Miniature Temple." *AJSL* 52 (1936): 215-34. [Tabernacle]

Meyers, Carol L. "Menorah." In *The Interpreter's Dictionary of the Bible*, supp. vol., 586-87. [Tabernacle]

Meyers, Carol L. *The Tabernacle Menorah*. Missoula: Scholars, 1976. [Tabernacle]

Milgrom, Jacob. "Israel's Sanctuary: The Priestly 'Picture of Dorian Gray.' " *RB* 83 (1976): 390-99. [Tabernacle]

Milgrom, Jacob. "The Shared Custody of the Tabernacle and a Hittite Analogy." *JAOS* 90 (1970): 204-9. [Tabernacle]

Miller, Patrick D., and J. J. M. Roberts. *The Hand of the Lord: A Reassessment of the "Ark Narrative" of 1 Samuel*. Baltimore: Johns Hopkins University Press, 1977. [Tabernacle]

Moorehead, William G. *Studies in Mosaic Institutions: The Tabernacle, the Priesthood, the Sacrifices and the Feasts of Ancient Israel*. Dayton, OH: Shuey, 1896. [Tabernacle]

Morgenstern, Julian. "The Ark, the Ephod, and the 'Tent of Meeting'." *HUCA* 17 (1942-43): 153-266; 18 (1944): 1-52; also reprinted as *The Ark, the*

Ephod and the Tent of Meeting. Cincinnati: Hebrew Union College Press, 1945. [Tabernacle]

Morgenstern, Julian. "The Tent of Meeting." *JAOS* 38 (1918): 125-39. [Tabernacle]

Mudge, William. *The Tabernacle of Testimony in the Wilderness*. 3d ed. London Simpkin, Marshall, 1861. [Tabernacle]

Ness, Alex W. *Pattern for Living: The Tabernacle, Priesthood, Offerings, Feasts*. Downsview, Ontario: Christian Centre, 1979. [Tabernacle]

Newberry, Thomas. *The Tabernacle, the Temple, and the Offerings: Their Types and Spiritual Significance*. Kilmarnock: Ritchie, 1927. [Tabernacle]

Newton, Richard. *The Jewish Tabernacle and Its Furniture, in Their Typical Teachings*. New York: Carter, 1878. [Tabernacle]

Nielsen, E. "Some Reflections on the History of the Ark." In *International Organization for the Study of the Old Testament, Congress Volume, Oxford, 1959*. 61-74. Leiden: Brill, 1960. [Tabernacle]

Nixon, Hilary A. *Typology of the Mosaic Tabernacle*. Ann Arbor: University Microfilm, 1984. [Tabernacle]

Noll, S. F. "Tabernacle, Temple." In *Evangelical Dictionary of Theology*, edited by W. A. Elwell. 1067-69. Grand Rapids: Baker Book House, 1984. [Tabernacle]

Olford, Stephen F. *The Tabernacle: Camping with God*. Neptune: Loizeaux Brothers, 1971. [Tabernacle]

Otto, Eckart. "Silo und Jerusalem." *Theologische Zeitschrift* 32 (1976): 65-77. [Tabernacle]

Parker, Percy G. *The Tabernacle of Israel: Its History and Mystery*. London: Victory, 1932. [Tabernacle]

Percy, Emily C. *The Figures of the True*. London: Chiswick, 1903. [Tabernacle]

Pfeiffer, R. H. "Cherubim." *JBL* 41 (1922): 249-50. [Tabernacle]

Popper, Julius. *Der biblische Bericht über die Stiftshütte: Ein Beitrag zur Geschichte der Composition und Diaskeue des Pentateuch*. Leipzig: Hunger, 1862. [Tabernacle]

Porter, J. R. "Ark." In *Harper's Dictionary of the Bible*, 63-64. [Tabernacle]

Porter, J. R. "Tabernacle." In *Harper's Dictionary of the Bible*, 1013-14. [Tabernacle]

Proby, W. H. B. "Construction of the Tabernacle." *PEFQ* 28 (1896): 223-24. [Tabernacle]

Rabe, Virgil W. "The Identity of the Priestly Tabernacle." *JNES* 25 (1966): 132-34. [Tabernacle]

Rabe, Virgil W. "The Temple as Tabernacle." Ph.D. diss., Harvard University, 1963. [Tabernacle]

Rad, Gerhard von. "The Tent, the Ark, and the Glory of God." In Rad, *Old Testament Theology*. 2 vols., 1:234-41. New York: Harper 1962-65. [Tabernacle]

Rad, Gerhard von. "Zelt und Lade." *Kirchliche Zeitschrift* 42 (1931): 476-98. [Tabernacle]

Radius, Marianne C. V. *The Tent of God: A Journey through the Old Testament.* Grand Rapids: Eerdmans, 1968. [Tabernacle]

Randellini, L. "La tenda e l'arca nella tradizione del Vecchio Testamento." *Liber Annuus* 13 (1962-63): 163-89. [Tabernacle]

Reicke, Bo. "Stiftshütte." In *Biblisch-Historisches Handwörterbuch*, edited by Bo Reicke and Leonhard Rost. 4 vols., 3:1871-75. Göttingen: Vandenhoeck and Ruprecht, 1966. [Tabernacle]

Reimpell, W. "Der Ursprung der Lade Jahwes." *Orientalistische Literaturzeitung* 19 (1916): 326-31. [Tabernacle]

Ricchi, Immanuel H. *Maʿaseh Ḥoshev: ʿAl Melʾekhet ha-Mishkan*. Przemysl: Amkraut, 1883. [Tabernacle]

Rice, George E. "Hebrews 6:19: Analysis of Some Assumptions concerning *Katapetasma*." *Andrews University Seminary Studies* 25 (Spring 1987): 65-71. [Tabernacle]

Ridges, W. B. "On the Structure of the Tabernacle." *PEFQ* 28 (1896): 189. [Tabernacle]

Ridout, Samuel. *Lectures on the Tabernacle*. New York: Loizeaux, 1952. [Tabernacle]

Ritchie, John. *The Tabernacle in the Wilderness*. Grand Rapids: Kregal, 1982. [Tabernacle]

Rost, Leonhard. "Die Wohnstätte des Zeugnisses." In *Festschrift F. Baumgärtel, Erlanger Forschungen, Reihe A: Geisteswissenshaften, 10*, edited by J. Hermann, 158-65. Erlangen: n.p., 1959. [Tabernacle]

Schaffer (Shafer), Shaul. *Ha-Mishkan ve-Khelav*. Jerusalem: Yeteh-nof, 1964/1965. [Tabernacle]

Schick, Conrad. "Some Remarks on the Tabernacle Controversy." *PEFQ* 30 (1898): 241-44. [Tabernacle]

Schmidt, H. "Kerubenthron und Lade." In *Eucharisterion für H. Gunkel*, edited by H. Schmidt. 120-44. Göttingen: Vandenhoeck and Ruprecht, 1923. [Tabernacle]

Schmidt, Werner H. "*Mishkan* als Ausdruck Jerusalemer Kultsprache." *ZAW* 75 (1963): 91-92. [Tabernacle]

Schmitt, Rainer. *Zelt und Lade als Thema alttestamentlicher Wissenschaft.* Gutersloh: Mohn, 1972. [Tabernacle]

Schouten, Leendert. *De tabernakel, Gods heiligdom bij Israel.* Utrecht: Huinink, 1887. [Tabernacle]

Schult, Hermann. "Der Debir im salomonischen Tempel." *ZDPV* 80 (1964): 46-54. [Tabernacle]

Scott, John A. "The Pattern of the Tabernacle." Ph.D. diss., University of Pennsylvania, 1965. [Tabernacle]

Segal, M. H. "The Tent of Meeting." *Tarbiz* 25 (1956): 231-33. [Tabernacle]

Sellin, Ernst. "Das Zelt Jahwes." In *Alttestamentliche Studien für R. Kittel.* 168-92. Leipzig: Hinrichs, 1913. [Tabernacle]

Sevensma, Tietse P. *De ark Gods.* Amsterdam: Clausen, 1908. [Tabernacle]

Shea, W. H. "New Light on the Exodus and on Construction of the Tabernacle: Gerster's Protosinaitic Inscription No. 1." *Andrews University Seminary Studies* 25 (Spring 1987): 73-96. [Tabernacle]

Slemming, Charles W. *Made according to Pattern.* Fort Washington, PA: Christian Literature Crusade, 1971. [Tabernacle]

Soltau, Henry W. *The Tabernacle, the Priesthood and the Offerings.* London: Morgan and Scott, 1884. [Tabernacle]

Sperber, Daniel. "The History of the Menorah." *JJS* 16 (1965): 135-59. [Tabernacle]

Strong, J. "The Tabernacle." *Biblical World* 1 (1893): 270-77. [Tabernacle]

Strong, J. *The Tabernacle of Israel in the Desert.* Grand Rapids: Baker Book House, 1952. [Tabernacle]

Swetnam, J. " 'The Greater and More Perfect Tent'—A Contribution to the Discussion of Hebrews 9, 11." *Biblica* 47 (1966): 91-106. [Tabernacle]

Talbot, Lois T. *Christ in the Tabernacle.* Chicago: Moody, 1978. [Tabernacle]

Torczyner (Tur-Sinai), Harry. *Die Bundeslade und die Anfänge der Religion Israels,* 2d ed. Berlin: Philo, 1930. [Tabernacle]

Torczyner (Tur-Sinai), Harry. "Holy of Holies" (in Hebrew). *Encyclopedia Biblica* 1:538-50. [Tabernacle]

Tur-Sinai, N. H. (Torczyner, Harry). "The Ark of God at Beit Shemesh (1 Sam vi) and Peres ʿUzza (2 Sam vi; 1 Chron xiii)." *VT* 1 (1951): 275-86. [Tabernacle]

Tur-Sinai, N. H. (Torczyner, Harry). *Die Bundeslade und die Anfänge der Religion Israels.* Berlin: Philo, 1930. [Tabernacle]

Utzschneider, Helmut. *Das Heiligtum und das Gesetz: Studien zur Bedeutung der sinaitischen Heiligtumstexte (Ex 25-40; Lev 8-9).* Göttingen: Vandenhoeck & Ruprecht, 1988. [Tabernacle]

Vaux, Roland de. "Arche d'alliance et Tente de reunion." In *A la recontre de Dieu: Memorial Albert Gelin,* edited by André Barucq. 55-70. Le Puy: Editions Xavier Mappus, 1961; also in English as "Ark of the Covenant and Tent of Reunion." In de Vaux, *The Bible and the Ancient Near East.* 136-51. Garden City: Doubleday, 1971. [Tabernacle]

Vaux, Roland de. "Les chérubins et l'arche d'alliance, les sphinx gardiens et les trônes divins dans l'Ancien Orient." In de Vaux, *Bible et Orient.* 231-59. Paris: Cerf, 1967. [Tabernacle]

Vaux, Roland de. "The Desert Sanctuary: The Tent; The Ark of the Covenant." In de Vaux, *Ancient Israel: Its Life and Institutions.* 294-302. New York: McGraw-Hill, 1961. [Tabernacle]

Weimar, Peter. "Sinai und Schöpfung: Komposition und Theologie der priesterschriftlichen Sinaigeschichte." *RB* 95 (July 1988): 337-85. [Tabernacle]

Wiener, Harold M. "The Position of the Tent of Meeting." *Expositor* (1912): 476-80. [Tabernacle]

Worden, T. "The Ark of the Covenant." *Scripture* 5/4 (1952): 82-90. [Tabernacle]

Woudstra, Marten H. *The Ark of the Covenant from Conquest to Kingship.* Philadelphia: Presbyterian and Reformed, 1965. [Tabernacle]

Wright, Theodore F. "The Boards of the Tabernacle." *PEFQ* 31 (1899): 70. [Tabernacle]

Wright, Theodore F. "The Tabernacle Roof." *PEFQ* 29 (1897): 225-26. [Tabernacle]

Wright, Theodore F. "Was the Tabernacle Oriental?" *JBL* 18 (1899): 195-98. [Tabernacle]

Yarden, Leon. "Aaron, Bethel and the Priestly Menorah." *JJS* 26/1-2 (1975): 39-47. [Tabernacle]

Yarden, Leon. *The Tree of Light: A Study of the Menorah.* Ithaca: Cornell University Press, 1971. [Tabernacle]

Zehr, Paul M. *God Dwells with His People.* Scottsdale: Herald, 1981. [Tabernacle]

Zobel, Hans-Jürgen. "*arôn.*" In *Theological Dictionary of the Old Testament* 1:363-74. [Tabernacle]

Rituals and Symbols of the Temple
Arranged by Subject

Ablutions and Anointings

Aytoun, K. A. *The Mysteries of Baptism by Moses bar Kepha Compared with the Odes of Solomon*. In *The Syrian Churches Series*, edited by Jacob Vellian. vol. 6., pp. 1-15. Kottayam: CMS, 1973. [Ablutions/Anointings]

Birch, Bruce C. "The Development of the Tradition on the Anointing of Saul in 1 Sam 9:1-10:16." *JBL* 90 (1971): 55-68. [Ablutions/Anointings]

Blackman, Aylward M. "An Ancient Egyptian Foretaste of the Doctrine of Baptismal Regeneration." *Theology* 1 (1920): 134-42. [Ablutions/Anointings]

Blackman, Aylward M. "Some Notes on the Ancient Egyptian Practice of Washing the Dead." *JEA* 5 (1918): 117-24. [Ablutions/Anointings]

Bleeker, Claas J. "Guilt and Purification in Ancient Egypt." *Numen* 13 (1966): 81-87. [Ablutions/Anointings]

Bowman, W. D. "Anointing for Healing." *Brethren Life and Thought* 4 (1959): 54-62. [Ablutions/Anointings]

Brock, Sebastian. "Syrian Baptismal Ordines (With Special Reference to the Anointings)." *Studia Liturgica* 12 (1977): 177-83. [Ablutions/Anointings]

Castelot, John J. *Anointing in the Old Testament*. Washington: CUAP, 1950. [Ablutions/Anointings]

Daniélou, Jean. "Onction et baptême chez Gregoire de Nysse." *Ephemerides Liturgicae* 90 (1976): 440-45. [Ablutions/Anointings]

de la Potterie, I. "L'onction du chrétien par la foi." *Biblica* 40 (1959): 12-69. [Ablutions/Anointings]

Doeve, J. W. "Purification du Temple et desséchement du figuier—sur la structure du 21ème chapitre de Matthieu et parallèles." *NTS* 1 (1955): 297-308. [Ablutions/Anointings]

Elliott, J. K. "The Anointing of Jesus." *ET* 85 (1974): 105-7. [Ablutions/Anointings]

Empereur, James. L. *Prophetic Anointing: God's Call to the Sick, the Elderly, and the Dying.* Wilmington: Glazier, 1982. [Ablutions/Anointings]

Enright, Michael J. *Iona, Tara, and Soissons: the Origin of the Royal Anointing Ritual.* New York: de Gruyter, 1985. [Ablutions/Anointings]

Gardiner, Alan H. "The Baptism of Pharoah." *JEA* 36 (1950): 3-12. [Ablutions/Anointings]

Gero, S. "The So-Called Ointment Prayer in the Coptic Version of the Didache: A Re-evaluation." *Harvard Theological Review* 70 (1977): 67-84. [Ablutions/Anointings]

Harkins, P. W. "Pre-Baptismal Rites in Chrysostom's Baptismal Catecheses." In *Studia Patristica*, edited by F. L. Cross, 17 vols., 8:219-38. Berlin: Akademie-Verlag, 1966. [Ablutions/Anointings]

Hofmeister, Philipp. *Die heiligen Öle in der morgen- und abendländischen Kirche.* Würzburg: Augustinus, 1948. [Ablutions/Anointings]

Holst, R. "The One Anointing of Jesus: Another Application of the Form Critical Method." *JBL* 95 (1976): 435-46. [Ablutions/Anointings]

Malchow, B. V. "The Wisdom of the Anointed." *Lutheran Quarterly* 28 (1976): 70-82. [Ablutions/Anointings]

Martimort, Aimes G., ed. *L'église en prière.* Paris: Desclee, 1965. [Ablutions/Anointings]

Millard, A. R. "Saul's Shield Not Anointed with Oil." *BASOR* 230 (April 1978): 70. [Ablutions/Anointings]

Mitchell, Leonel L. *Baptismal Anointing.* London: University of Notre Dame Press, 1966. [Ablutions/Anointings]

Munro, W. "The Anointing in Mark 14:3-9 and John 12:1-8." *SBLSP* 16 (1979): 127-30. [Ablutions/Anointings]

Porter, H. B. "The Origin of the Medieval Rite for Anointing the Sick or Dying." *JTS* 7 (1956): 211-25. [Ablutions/Anointings]

Rabinowitz, Louis I. "Anointing." In *Encyclopedia Judaica* 3:27-31. [Ablutions/Anointings]

Strothmann, Werner. *Syrische Hymnen zur Myron-Weihe.* Wiesbaden: Harrassowitz, 1978. [Ablutions/Anointings]

Testa, Emmanuel. *L'huile de la foi.* Jerusalem: Studium Biblicum Franciscanum, 1967. [Ablutions/Anointings]

Thomson, Robert W. *The Teachings of St. Gregory.* Cambridge: Harvard University Press, 1970. [Ablutions/Anointings]

Torrance, Thomas F. "The Origins of Baptism." *Scottish Journal of Theology* 11 (1958): 158-71. [Ablutions/Anointings]

Van Engen, John. "Anoint, Anointing." In *Evangelical Dictionary of Theology*, edited by W. A. Elwell, 51-52. Grand Rapids: Baker Book House, 1984. [Ablutions/Anointings]

Vorgrimler, Herbert. *Busse und Krankensalbung*. Freiburg: Herder, 1978. [Ablutions/Anointings]

Weinel, Heinrich. *"MŠH* und seine Derivate." *ZAW* 18 (1898): 1-82. [Ablutions/Anointings]

Weisman, Z. "Anointing as a Motif in the Making of the Charismatic King." *Biblica* 57 (1976): 378-98. [Ablutions/Anointings]

Whitaker, E. C. "Unction in the Syrian Baptismal Rite." *Church Quarterly* 162 (1961): 176-87. [Ablutions/Anointings]

Widengren, Geo. "Baptism and Enthronement in Some Jewish-Christian Gnostic Documents." In *The Saviour God*, edited by Samuel G. F. Brandon. 205-17. New York: Barnes and Noble, 1963. [Ablutions/Anointings]

Wild, Robert A. *Water in the Cultic Worship of Isis and Sarapis*. Leiden: Brill, 1981. [Ablutions/Anointings]

Winkler, G. "Confirmation or Chrismation: A Study in Comparitive Liturgy." *Worship* 58 (January 1984): 2-17. [Ablutions/Anointings]

Winkler, G. "Original Meaning of Prebaptismal Anointing and Its Implications." *Worship* 52 (January 1978): 24-25. [Ablutions/Anointings]

Zuidhof, Albert. "King Solomon's Molten Sea and (*pi*)." *BA* 45 (1982): 179-84. [Ablutions/Anointings]

Covenant

Baltzer, Klaus. *The Covenant Formulary in Old Testament, Jewish, and Early Christian Writings*. Philadelphia: Fortress, 1971. [Covenant]

Beyerlin, Walter. *Origins and History of the Oldest Sinaitic Traditions*, translated by S. Rudman. Oxford: Blackwell, 1966. [Covenant]

Bishop, Jonathan. *The Covenant: A Reading*. Springfield: Templegate, 1982. [Covenant]

Brueggemann, Walter A. "Amos 4:4-13 and Israel's Covenant Worship." *VT* 15 (1965): 1-15. [Covenant]

Buchanan, George W. *The Consequences of the Covenant*. Leiden: Brill, 1970. [Covenant]

Cazelles, Henri. "La rupture de la berît selon les prophetes." *JJS* 33/1-2 (1982): 133-44. [Covenant]

Eakin, F. E. "Wisdom, Creation, and Covenant." *Perspectives in Religious Studies* 4 (1977): 226-39. [Covenant]

Elgvin, T. "The Qumran Covenant Festival and the Temple Scroll." *JJS* 36 (1985): 103-6. [Covenant]

Falk, Z. W. "Forms of Testimony." *VT* 11 (1961): 88-91. [Covenant]

Fensham, F. C. "Ps 21: A Covenant Song?" *ZAW* 77 (1965): 193-202. [Covenant]

Fuller, Daniel P. *Gospel and Law: Contrast or Continuum? The Hermeneutics of Dispensationalism and Covenant Theology.* Grand Rapids: Eerdmans, 1980. [Covenant]

Harris, J. G. "Covenant Concept among the Qumran Sectaries." *Evangelical Quarterly* 39 (1967): 86-92. [Covenant]

Hasel, Gerhard F. *Covenant in Blood.* Mountain View: Pacific, 1982. [Covenant]

Hillers, Delbert R. *Covenant: The History of a Biblical Idea.* Baltimore: Johns Hopkins University Press, 1969. [Covenant]

Hillers, Delbert R. *Treaty-Curses and Old Testament Prophets.* Rome: Pontifical Biblical Institute, 1964. [Covenant]

Kelley, P. H. "Israel's Tabernacling God." *Review and Expositor* 67 (1970): 485-94. [Covenant]

Kline, Meridith G. "Oath and Ordeal Signs." *Westminster Theological Journal* 27 (1965): 115-39; 28 (1965): 1-37. [Covenant]

Kraus, Hans-Joachim. "God's Covenant." *Reformed World* 35 (1979): 257-68. [Covenant]

Lang, G. H. "God's Covenants Are Conditional." *Evangelical Quarterly* 30 (1958): 86-97. [Covenant]

McCarthy, Dennis J. "*berît* in Old Testament History and Theology." *Biblica* 53 (1972): 110-21. [Covenant]

McCarthy, Dennis J. "Hosea 12:2: Covenant by Oil." *VT* 14 (1964): 215-21. [Covenant]

McCarthy, Dennis J. "Three Covenants in Genesis." *CBQ* 26 (1964): 179-89. [Covenant]

McCarthy, Dennis J. *Treaty and Covenant: A Study in Form in the Ancient Oriental Documents and in the Old Testament.* Rome: Pontifical Biblical Institute, 1978. [Covenant]

Mendenhall, George E. "Covenant Forms in Israelite Tradition." *BA* 17 (September 1954): 50-76. [Covenant]

Muilenburg, James. "The Form and Stucture of the Covenantal Formulations." *VT* 9 (1959): 347-65. [Covenant]

Newbigin, Lesslie B. "Politics and the Covenant." *Theology* 84 (1981): 356-63. [Covenant]

Newman, Murray L. *The People of the Covenant.* New York: Abingdon, 1962. [Covenant]

Nicholson, Ernest W. "Exodus, Covenant, and Treaty." In *Exodus and Sinai in History and Tradition: Growing Points in Theology.* 33-52. Oxford: Blackwell, 1973. [Covenant]

Petersen, David L. "Covenant Ritual: A Tradito-Historical Perspective." *Biblical Research* 22 (1977): 7-18. [Covenant]

Reumann, John H. P. "Oikonomia='Covenant': Terms for Heilsgeschichte in Early Christain Usage." *NT* 3 (1959): 282-92. [Covenant]

Rigby, P. "A Structural Analysis of Israelite Sacrifice and Its Other Institutions." *Église et Théologie* 11 (October 1980): 229-351. [Covenant]

Roehrs, W. R. "Covenant and Justification in the Old Testament." *Concordia Historical Institute Quarterly* 35 (October 1964): 583-602. [Covenant]

Stockton, E. D. "The Fortress Temple of Shechem and Joshua's Covenant." *Australian Journal of Biblical Archaeology* 1 (1968): 24-28. [Covenant]

Swain, Joseph C. *Covenants, Old, New, and Forever.* New York: United Presbyterian Church, 1972. [Covenant]

Thompson, John A. "Covenant Patterns in the Ancient Near East and Their Significance for Biblical Studies." *Reformed Theological Review* 18 (October 1959): 65-75. [Covenant]

Thompson, John A. "Cultic Credo and the Sinai Tradition." *Reformed Theological Review* 27 (1968): 53-64. [Covenant]

Trumbull, Henry C. *The Blood Covenant: A Primitive Rite and Its Bearing on Scripture.* New York: Scribner's, 1885. [Covenant]

Trumbull, Henry C. *The Threshold Covenant.* New York: Scribner's, 1896. [Covenant]

White, H. C. "The Divine Oath in Genesis." *JBL* 92 (1973): 165-79. [Covenant]

Creation and Cosmology

Alderink, L. J. "Cosmogonic Themes in Orphism." *SBLSP* 14 (1978): 121-35. [Creation/Cosmology]

Blacker, Carmen, and Michael Loewe, eds. *Ancient Cosmologies.* London: George Allen & Unwin, 1975. [Creation/Cosmology]

Bledstein, A. J. "Genesis of Humans: The Garden of Eden Revisited." *Judaica* 26 (1977): 187-200. [Creation/Cosmology]

Bleeker, Claas J. "L'idée de l'ordre cosmique dans l'ancienne Egypte." *Revue d'histoire et de philosophie religieuses* 42/2-3 (1962): 193-200. [Creation/Cosmology]

Brandon, Samuel G. F. *Creation Legends of the Ancient Near East.* London: Hodder and Stoughton, 1963. [Creation/Cosmology]

Buck, Harry M. "Creation Stories and Creation Science." *Anima* 8 (1982): 110-22. [Creation/Cosmology]

Burrows, E. "Some Cosmological Patterns in Babylonian Religion." In *The Labyrinth*, edited by Samuel H. Hooke, 45-69. London: Society for Promoting Christian Knowledge, 1935. [Creation/Cosmology]

Clifford, Richard J. "Cosmogonies in the Ugaritic Texts and in the Bible." *Orientalia* 53 (1984): 183-201. [Creation/Cosmology]

Culianu, Ioan P. " 'Démonisation du cosmos' et dualisme gnostique." *RHR* 196 (1979): 3-40. [Creation/Cosmology]

Derouche, M. "Contra Creation, Covenant, and Conquest (Jer. VIII. 13)." *VT* 30 (1980): 280-90. [Creation/Cosmology]

Eliade, Mircea. "Cosmogonic Myth and Sacred History." In Eliade, *The Quest: History and Meaning in Religion*. 72-87. Chicago: University of Chicago Press, 1969. [Creation/Cosmology]

Eliade, Mircea. *Cosmos and History: The Myth of the Eternal Return*. New York: Harper and Row, 1959. [Creation/Cosmology]

Eliade, Mircea. "The Myth of the Noble Savage or, the Prestige of the Beginning." In *Myths, Dreams and Mysteries: The Encounter between Contemporary Faiths and Archaic Reality*, translated by Philip Mairet. 39-58. New York: Harper and Row, 1960. [Creation/Cosmology]

Eliade, Mircea. "The Prestige of the Cosmogonic Myth." *Diogenes* 23 (1958): 1-13. [Creation/Cosmology]

Engnell, Ivan. " 'Knowledge' and 'Life' in the Creation Story." In *Wisdom in Israel in the Ancient Near East*, edited by M. Noth and D. Winton Thomas. 103-19. n.p., 1955. [Creation/Cosmology]

Fallon, Francis T. *The Enthronement of Sabaoth*. Leiden: Brill, 1978. [Creation/Cosmology]

Fisher, Loren R. "Creation at Ugarit and in the Old Testament." *VT* 15 (1965): 313-24. [Creation/Cosmology]

Fleury, H. "Cosmos in Stone." *Parabola* 3/1 (1978): 74-77. [Creation/Cosmology]

Fredriksen, P. "Hysteria and the Gnostic Myths of Creation." *Vigiliae Christianae* 33 (1979): 287-90. [Creation/Cosmology]

Friend, J. A. "Nature, Man, and God: A Temple Revisited." *Reformed Theological Review* 41 (1982): 34-41. [Creation/Cosmology]

Goldfless, Sanford K. "Babylonian Theogonies: Divine Origins in Ancient Mesopotamian Religion and Literature." Ph.D. diss., Harvard University, 1980. [Creation/Cosmology]

Hasel, Gerhard F. "Significance of the Cosmology in Genesis 1 in Relation to Ancient Near Eastern Parallels." *Andrews University Seminary Studies* 10 (1972): 1-20. [Creation/Cosmology]

James, Edwin O. *Creation and Cosmology.* Leiden: Brill, 1969. [Creation/ Cosmology]

Jordan-Smith, P. "War in Heaven." *Parabola* 7/4 (1982): 68-79. [Creation/ Cosmology]

Kearney, P. J. "Creation and Liturgy: The 'P' Redaction of Exodus 25-40." *ZAW* 89 (1977): 375-87. [Creation/Cosmology]

Keenan, Joseph J. "The Creation Motif: A Study of the Roman Catholic Mass Today in the Context of the History of Religions." Ph.D. diss., Catholic University of America, 1977. [Creation/Cosmology]

Keenan, Joseph J. "The Importance of the Creation Motif in a Eucharistic Prayer." *Worship* 53 (1979): 341-56. [Creation/Cosmology]

Lambert, W. G. "Kosmogonie." In *Reallexikon der Assyriologie,* edited by Erich Ebeling and Bruno Meissner. 7 vols., 6:218-22. Berlin: Walter de Gruyter, 1980-83. [Creation/Cosmology]

Lane, W. R. "Initiation of Creation." *VT* 13 (1963): 63-73. [Creation/ Cosmology]

Long, Charles H. *Alpha: The Myths of Creation.* New York: Braziller, 1963. [Creation/Cosmology]

Maclagan, David. *Creation Myths: Man's Introduction to the World.* London: Thames and Hudson, 1977. [Creation/Cosmology]

Petuchowski, Jakob J. "The Creation in Jewish Liturgy." *Judaica* 28 (Summer 1972): 309-15. [Creation/Cosmology]

Politella, Joseph. "Before Babel: The Puzzle of Ancient Cosmogonies." *Encounter* 29 (Summer 1968): 278-89. [Creation/Cosmology]

Prenter, Regin. "Worship and Creation." *Studia Liturgica* 2 (June 1963): 82-95. [Creation/Cosmology]

Wakeman, M. K. "Biblical Earth Monster in the Cosmogonic Combat Myth." *JBL* 88 (1969): 313-20. [Creation/Cosmology]

Wakeman, M. K. *God's Battle with the Monster: A Study in Biblical Imagery.* Leiden: Brill, 1973. [Creation/Cosmology]

Whybray, Roger N. "Proverbs 8:22-31 and Its Supposed Prototypes." *VT* 15 (October 1965): 504-14. [Creation/Cosmology]

Kingship and Coronation

Bentzen, Aage. *King and Messiah.* London: Lutterworth, 1955. [Kingship/ Coronation]

Bentzen, Aage. "King Ideology—'Urmensch'—'troonsbestijgingsfeest.' " *Studia Theologica* 3/2 (1949): 143-57. [Kingship/Coronation]

Bernhardt, Karl-Heinz. *Das Problem der altorientalischen Königsideologie im alten Testament unter besonderer Berücksichtigung der Geschichte der Psalmenexegese dargestellt und kritisch gewürdigt.* Leiden: Brill, 1961. [Kingship/Coronation]

Blair, H. J. "Kingship in Israel and Its Implications for the Lordship of Christ Today." *Evangelical Quarterly* 47 (1975): 70-77. [Kingship/Coronation]

Brandon, Samuel G. F. "Divine Kings and Dying Gods." *Hibbert Journal* 53 (1954-55): 327-33. [Kingship/Coronation]

Bouman, C. A. *Sacring and Crowning.* Groningen: Wolters, 1957. [Kingship/Coronation]

Briquel, Dominique. "Sur l'équipement royal indo-européen: données latines et grecques." *RHR* 200 (1983): 67-74. [Kingship/Coronation]

Brueggemann, Walter A. "From Dust to Kingship (1 Kings 16:2, Genesis 3:19)." *ZAW* 84 (1972): 1-18. [Kingship/Coronation]

Brueggemann, Walter A. "Kingship and Chaos: A Study in Tenth Century Theology." *CBQ* 33 (1971): 317-32. [Kingship/Coronation]

Buccellati, Giorgio. "The Enthronement of the King and the Capital City in Texts from Ancient Mesopotamia and Syria." In *Studies Presented to A. Leo Oppenheim.* 54-61. Chicago: Oriental Institute, 1964. [Kingship/Coronation]

Burgmann, E. H. "Royal Stole: An Inquiry." *Church Quarterly Review* 159 (1958): 408-14. [Kingship/Coronation]

Canney, M. A. "Ancient Conceptions of Kingship." In *Oriental Studies in Honour of Cursetji Erachji Pavry,* edited by Jal Dastur Cursetji Pavry. 63-75. London: Oxford University Press, 1933. [Kingship/Coronation]

Caquot, André. "Le Psaume LXVIII." *RHR* 177 (1970): 147-82. [Kingship/Coronation]

Cooke, G. "Israelite King as the Son of God." *ZAW* 73 (1961): 202-25. [Kingship/Coronation]

Cross, Frank M. "The Ideologies of Kingship in the Era of Empire: Conditional Covenant and Eternal Decree." In *Canaanite Myth and Hebrew Epic.* 219-73. Cambridge, MA: Harvard University Press, 1973. [Kingship/Coronation]

Davies, Robertson. "Nobility and Style." *Parabola* 7/3 (1982): 15-21. [Kingship/Coronation]

Dietrich, Walter. "Gott als König: Zur Frage nach der theologischen und politischen Legitimität religöser Begriffsbildung." *Zeitschrift für Theologie und Kirche* 77 (1980): 251-68. [Kingship/Coronation]

Dion, P. E. "Le role de la foi yahwiste dans la vie politique d'Israel." *Science et Espirit* 26 (1974): 173-203. [Kingship/Coronation]

Dumbrell, W. J. "Kingship and Temple in the Post-Exile Period." *Reformed Theological Review* 37 (1978): 33-42. [Kingship/Coronation]

Eaton, John H. *Kingship and the Psalms*. 2d ed. Sheffield: JSOT, 1986. [Kingship/Coronation]

Eissfeldt, Otto. "Jahwe als König." *ZAW* 46 (1928): 81-105; also in *Kleine Schriften*, edited by Rudolf Sellheim and Fritz Maass. 6 vols. 1:172-93. Tübingen: Mohr, 1962. [Kingship/Coronation]

Engnell, Ivan. *Studies in Divine Kingship in the Ancient Near East*. 2d ed. Oxford: Blackwell, 1967. [Kingship/Coronation]

Fairman, H. W. "The Kingship Rituals of Egypt." In *Myth, Ritual, and Kingship*, edited by Samuel H. Hooke. 74-104. Oxford: Clarendon, 1958. [Kingship/Coronation]

Ficker, R. "Kingship of God in the Psalms." *Bangalore Theological Forum* 12 (1980): 50-65. [Kingship/Coronation]

Fish, T. "Some Aspects of Kingship in the Sumerian City and Kingdom of Ur." *BJRL* 34 (1951): 37-43. [Kingship/Coronation]

Fisher, Loren R., and F. B. Knutson. "An Enthronment Ritual at Ugarit." *JNES* 28 (1969): 157-67. [Kingship/Coronation]

Frankfort, Henri. *Kingship and the Gods*. Chicago: University of Chicago Press, 1978. [Kingship/Coronation]

Frazer, James G. *Lectures on the Early History of the Kingship*. London: Macmillan, 1905. [Kingship/Coronation]

Friedrich, G. "Die Formale Struktur von Matt. 28:18-20." *Zeitschrift für Theologie und Kirche* 80 (1983): 137-83. [Kingship/Coronation]

Gardiner, Alan H. "The Coronation of King Haremhab." *JEA* 39 (1953): 13-31. [Kingship/Coronation]

Goodall, Terence. "Motifs of the Royal Ideology." In *Essays in Faith and Culture*, edited by N. Brown. 145-56. Sydney: Catholic Institute, 1979. [Kingship/Coronation]

Goodenough, Erwin R. "Kingship in Early Israel." *JBL* 48 (1929): 169-205. [Kingship/Coronation]

Gray, John. "Canaanite Kingship in Theory and Practice." *VT* 2 (1952): 193-220. [Kingship/Coronation]

Gray, John. "The Hebrew Conception of the Kingship of God: Its Origin and Development." *VT* 6 (1956): 268-85. [Kingship/Coronation]

Gray, John. "The Kingship of God in the Prophets and Psalms." *VT* 11 (1961): 1-29. [Kingship/Coronation]

Hallevy, R. "The Place of the Monarchy in Israelite Religion." *Tarbiz* 32 (1962-63): 215-24. [Kingship/Coronation]

Hanson, D. W. "The Ideology of Kingship in the Ancient Near East." Ph.D. diss., University of Utah, 1961. [Kingship/Coronation]

Hardy, E. R. "The Date of Psalm 110." *JBL* 64 (1945): 385-90. [Kingship/Coronation]

Harrison, Roland K. "Matriarchate and Hebrew Regal Succession." *Evangelical Quarterly* 29 (1957): 29-34. [Kingship/Coronation]

Hebert, A. G. "Idea of Kingship in the Old Testament." *Reformed Theological Review* 18 (1959): 34-45. [Kingship/Coronation]

Hiltebeital, A. "Nahusa in the Skies: A Human King of Heaven." *History of Religions* 16 (1977): 329-50. [Kingship/Coronation]

Hocart, Arthur M. "The Coronation Ceremony." *Ceylon Journal of Science, Section G* 1 (1924-28): 27-42. [Kingship/Coronation]

Hocart, Arthur M. *Kings and Councillors.* Cairo: Barbey, 1936. [Kingship/Coronation]

Hocart, Arthur M. *Kingship.* London: Oxford University Press, 1927. [Kingship/Coronation]

Honeyman, A. M. "The Evidence for Regnal Names among the Hebrews." *JBL* 67 (1948): 13-25. [Kingship/Coronation]

Ibrahim, Mohiy ed-Din. "Miscellaneous Passages about King and Kingship according to the Inscriptions of the Temple of Edfu." *ASAE* 60 (1968): 297-300. [Kingship/ Coronation]

Irwin, W. H. "Le sanctuaire central israélite avant l'établissement de la monarchie." *RB* 72 (1965): 161-84. [Kingship/Coronation]

Jacobsen, Thorkild. *The Sumerian King List.* Chicago: University of Chicago Press, 1939. [Kingship/Coronation]

James, Edwin O. "The Sacred Kingship and the Priesthood." In *The Sacral Kingship/La Regalità Sacra.* 63-70. Leiden: Brill, 1959. [Kingship/ Coronation]

Johnson, Aubrey R. "Divine Kingship and the Old Testament." *ET* 62 (1950-51): 36-42. [Kingship/Coronation]

Johnson, Aubrey R. "Hebrew Conceptions of Kingship." In *Myth, Ritual, and Kingship: Essays on the Theory and Practice of Kingship in the Ancient Near East and in Israel,* edited by S. H. Hooke. 204-35. Oxford: Clarendon, 1958. [Kingship/Coronation]

Johnson, Aubrey R. "The Role of the King in the Jerusalem Cultus." In *The Labyrinth: Further Studies in the Relation between Myth and Ritual in the Ancient World,* edited by S. H. Hooke. 71-111. London: SPCK, 1935. [Kingship/Coronation]

Johnson, Aubrey R. *Sacred Kingship in Ancient Israel.* Cardiff: University of Wales Press, 1967. [Kingship/Coronation]

Klauser, T. "Der Vorhang vor dem Thron Gottes." *Jahrbuch für Antike und Christentum* 3 (1960): 142-42. [Kingship/Coronation]

Klein, R. W. "Theology for Exiles: The Kingship of Yahweh." *Dialogue* 17 (1978): 128-34. [Kingship/Coronation]

Klimkeit, Hans J. "Manichaean Kingship: Gnosis at Home in the World." *Numen* 29 (1982): 17-32. [Kingship/Coronation]

Köhler, Ludwig. "*Jahwäh mālāk.*" *VT* 3 (1953): 188-89. [Kingship/Coronation]

Koolhaas, Antonie A. *Theocratie en monarchie in Israël.* Wageningen: Veenman, 1957. [Kingship/Coronation]

Kruse, H. "Psalm 132 and the Royal Zion Festival." *VT* 33 (1983): 279-97. [Kingship/Coronation]

Lifshitz, B. "Sur le culte dynastique des Séleucides." *RB* 70 (1963): 75-81. [Kingship/Coronation]

Lipiński, Edward. "Yāhweh Mâlâk." *Biblica* 44 (1963): 405-60. [Kingship/Coronation]

Lods, Adolphe. "La divinisation du roi dans l'Orient méditeranéen et ses répercussions dans l'ancien Israël." *Revue d'histoire et de philosophie religieuses* 10 (1930): 209-21. [Kingship/Coronation]

Longman, T. "1 Samuel 12:16-19: Divine Omnipotence or Covenant Curse?" *Westminster Theological Journal* 45 (1983): 168-71. [Kingship/Coronation]

L'Orange, H. P. *Studies on the Iconography of Cosmic Kingship in the Ancient World.* Oslo: Aschehoug, 1953. [Kingship/Coronation]

Maag, Victor. "Malkût Yhwh." In *International Organization for the Study of the Old Testament, Congress Volume, Oxford, 1959.* 129-53. Leiden: Brill, 1960. [Kingship/Coronation]

McCarthy, Dennis J. "Compact and Kingship: Stimuli for Hebrew Covenant Thinking." In *Studies in the Period of David and Solomon and Other Essays,* edited by T. Ishida. 75-92. Winona Lake, IN: Eisenbrauns, 1982. [Kingship/Coronation]

McCullough, W. Stewart. "Israel's Kings, Sacral and Otherwise." *ET* (1957): 144-48. [Kingship/Coronation]

McKenzie, John L. "Royal Messianism." *CBQ* 19 (1957): 25-52. [Kingship/Coronation]

Malamat, A. "Kingship and Council in Israel and Sumer: A Parallel." *JNES* 22 (1963): 247-53. [Kingship/Coronation]

Malchow, B. V. "A Manual for Future Monarchs (Proverbs 28-29)." *CBQ* 47 (1985): 238-45. [Kingship/Coronation]

Maly, E. H. "God and King in Ancient Israel." *Bible Today* 100 (1979): 1893-900. [Kingship/Coronation]

Mann, C. S. "Sacral Kingship: An Ashanti Footnote." *Journal of Semitic Studies* 5 (1960): 378-87. [Kingship/Coronation]

Matthiew, M. "A Note on the Coronation Rites in Ancient Egypt." *JEA* 16 (1930): 31-32. [Kingship/Coronation]

May, Herbert G. "The King in the Garden of Eden: A Study of Ezekiel 28:12-19." In *Israel's Prophetic Heritage,* edited by J. Muilenberg. 166-76. New York: Harper, 1962. [Kingship/Coronation]

Meeks, Wayne A. "Moses as God and King." In *Religions in Antiquity, Essays in Memory of E. R. Goodenough*, edited by Jacob Neusner. 354-71. Leiden: Brill, 1968. [Kingship/Coronation]

Meeks, Wayne A. *The Prophet King: Moses Traditions and the Johannine Christology.* Leiden: Brill, 1967. [Kingship/Coronation]

Mettinger, Tryggve N. D. *King and Messiah: The Civil and Sacral Legitimation of the Israelite Kings.* Lund: Gleerup, 1976. [Kingship/Coronation]

Mettinger, Tryggve N. D. "YHWH SABAOTH—The Heavenly King on the Cherubim Throne." In *Studies in the Period of David and Solomon and Other Essays*, edited by Tamoo Ishida. 109-38. Winona Lake: Eisenbrauns, 1982. [Kingship/Coronation]

Meyerowitz Eva L. R. *The Divine Kingship in Ghana and Ancient Egypt.* London: Faber and Faber, 1960. [Kingship/Coronation]

Moran, William L. "Enthronement Feast." In *New Catholic Encyclopedia*, 15 vols. 5:445-46. New York: McGraw-Hill, 1967. [Kingship/Coronation]

Moret, Alexandre. *Du caractère religieux de la royauté pharonique.* Paris: Leroux, 1902. [Kingship/Coronation]

Morgenstern, Julian. "The Cultic Setting of the Enthronement Psalms." *HUCA* 35 (1964): 1-42. [Kingship/Coronation]

Morgenstern, Julian. "The King-God among the Western Semites and the Meaning of Epiphanes." *VT* 10 (1960): 138-97. [Kingship/Coronation]

Mowinckel, Sigmund. "General Oriental and Specific Israelite Elements in the Israelite Conception of the Sacral Kingdom." In *The Sacral Kingship.* 283-93. Leiden: Brill, 1959. [Kingship/Coronation]

Mowinckel, Sigmund. *Zum israelitischen Neujahr und zur Deutung der Thronbesteigungspsalmen: Zwei Aufsätze.* Oslo: Dybwad, 1952. [Kingship/Coronation]

Muthunayagom, D. J. "Kingship of God and Creation in the Old Testament." *Bangalore Theological Forum* 15 (May-August 1983): 168-71. [Kingship/Coronation]

Nordheim, E. von. "König und Tempel: Der Hintergrund des Tempelbauverbotes in 2 Samuel 7." *VT* 27 (1977): 434-53. [Kingship/Coronation]

North, C. R. "The Religious Aspect of Hebrew Kingship." *ZAW* 50 (1932): 8-38. [Kingship/Coronation]

Noth, Martin. "God, King, and Nation in the Old Testament." In *The Laws in the Pentateuch and Other Studies.* 145-78. Edinburgh: Oliver and Boyd, 1966. [Kingship/Coronation]

Noth, Martin. "Gott, König, Volk im alten Testament." *Zeitschrift für Theologie und Kirche* 47 (1950): 157-91. [Kingship/Coronation]

Patai, Raphael. "Hebrew Installation Rites." *HUCA* 20 (1947): 143-225; also in Patai, *On Jewish Folklore.* 110-73. Detroit: Wayne State University Press, 1983. [Kingship/Coronation]

Pemberton, Joseph H. *The Coronation Service according to the Use of the Church of England.* London: Skeffington and Son, 1901. [Kingship/Coronation]

Perrin, N. "Interpretation of a Biblical Symbol." *Journal of Religions* 55 (July 1975): 348-70. [Kingship/Coronation]

Peters, T. "Monotheism and Kingship in Ancient Memphis: A Study in Egyptian Mythology." *Perspectives in Religious Studies* 4 (Summer 1977): 160-73. [Kingship/Coronation]

Pinches, T. G. "Notes on the Deification of Kings and Ancestor-Worship in Babylonia." *Proceedings of the Society of Biblical Archaeology* 37 (1915): 87-95, 126-34. [Kingship/Coronation]

Poulssen, Niek. *König und Tempel im Glaubenszeugnis des Alten Testamentes.* Stuttgart: Katholisches Bibelwerk, 1967. [Kingship/Coronation]

Poulssen, Niek. "Rex et templum in Israël." *Verbum Domini* 40 (1962): 264-69. [Kingship/Coronation]

Quintens, W. "La vie du roi dans le Psaume 21." *Biblica* 59 (1978): 516-41. [Kingship/Coronation]

Rad, Gerhard von. "Erwägungen zu den Königspsalmen." *ZAW* 57 (1940-41): 216-22. [Kingship/Coronation]

Rad, Gerhard von. "Das judäische Königsritual." *Theologische Literaturzeitung* 72 (1947): 211-18; also in English as "The Royal Ritual in Judah." In von Rad, *The Problem of the Hexateuch and Other Essays.* 222-31. New York: McGraw-Hill, 1966. [Kingship/Coronation]

Ratcliff, Edward C. *The English Coronation Service, Being the Coronation Service of King George V and Queen Mary, with Historical Introduction and Notes, Together with Extracts from Liber Regalis, Accounts of Coronations, etc.* London: Skeffington & Son, 1937. [Kingship/Coronation]

Rengstorf, K. H. "Old and New Testament Traces of a Formula of the Judean Royal Ritual." *NT* 5 (November 1962): 229-44. [Kingship/Coronation]

Ridderbos, J. "Jahwäh malak." *VT* 4 (1954): 87-89. [Kingship/Coronation]

Rodd, C. S. "Kingship and the Cult." *London Quarterly Historical Review* 185 (January 1959): 21-26. [Kingship/Coronation]

Runnalls, Donna. "The King as Temple Builder: A Messianic Typology." In *Spirit within Structure: Essays in Honor of George Johnston*, edited by E. J. Furcha. 15-37. Allison Park, PA: Pickwick, 1983. [Kingship/Coronation]

Schmidt, Werner H. *Königtum Gottes in Ugarit und Israel: Zur Herkunft der Königsprädikation Jahwes.* Berlin: Töpelmann, 1966. [Kingship/Coronation]

Schramm, Percy. *A History of the English Coronation.* Oxford: n.p., 1937. [Kingship/Coronation]

Seybold, Klaus. *Das davidische Königtum im Zeugnis der Propheten.* Göttingen: Vandenhoeck & Ruprecht, 1972. [Kingship/Coronation]

Shalit, Abraham. *King Herod: Portrait of a Ruler.* 2d ed. Jerusalem: Bialik Institute, 1964; also in German as *König Herodes: Der Mann und sein Werk.* Berlin: de Gruyter, 1969. [Kingship/Coronation]

Shorter, Alan W. "Reliefs Showing the Coronation of Ramses II." *JEA* 20 (1934): 18-19. [Kingship/Coronation]

Smith, G. V. "The Concept of God/the Gods as King in the Ancient Near East and the Bible." *Trinity Journal* 3 (1982): 1-38. [Kingship/Coronation]

Soggin, J. Alberto. "Gott als König in der biblischen Dichtung: Bemerkungen zu den *YHWH mlk*-Psalmen." In *Proceedings of the Fifth World Congress of Jewish Studies, Jerusalem, 1969.* 126-33. Jerusalem: World Union of Jewish Studies, 1972. [Kingship/Coronation]

Soggin, J. Alberto. *Das Königtum in Israel.* Berlin: Töpelmann, 1967. [Kingship/Coronation]

Stuhlmueller, C. "Yahweh-King and Deutero-Isaiah." *Biblical Research* 15 (1970): 32-45. [Kingship/Coronation]

Süring, Margit L. "The Horn-Motifs of the Bible and the Ancient Near East." *Andrews University Seminary Studies* 22 (1984): 327-40. [Kingship/Coronation]

Swanson, T. N. "The Kingship of God in Intertestamental Literature." *Bangalore Theological Forum* 12 (1980): 1-25. [Kingship/Coronation]

Thomasson, Gordon C. "Togetherness Is Sharing an Umbrella: Divine Kingship, The Gnosis, and Religious Syncretism." In *By Study and Also by Faith: Essays in Honor of Hugh W. Nibley,* edited by John M. Lundquist and Stephen D. Ricks. 2 vols, 1:523-61. Salt Lake City: Deseret Book and F.A.R.M.S. 1990. [Kingship/Coronation]

Thornton, T. C. G. "Charismatic Kingship in Israel and Judah." *JTS* 14 (April 1963): 1-11. [Kingship/Coronation]

Thurston, Herbert. *The Coronation Ceremonial: Its True History and Meaning.* 2d ed. London: Catholic Truth Society, 1911. [Kingship/Coronation]

Treves, M. "Reign of God in the Old Testament." *VT* 19 (April 1969): 230-43. [Kingship/Coronation]

Van Velduizen, Milo. "Moses: A Model of Hellenistic Philanthropia." *Reformed Review* 38 (1985): 215-24. [Kingship/Coronation]

Vaux, Roland de. "The King of Israel, Vassal of Yahweh." In *The Bible and the Ancient Near East.* 152-66. Garden City: Doubleday, 1971. [Kingship/Coronation]

Vaux, Roland de. "La regalità sacra—The Sacred Kingship." *RB* 68 (April 1961): 266-69. [Kingship/Coronation]

Vaux, Roland de. "Le roi d'Israël, vassal de Yahvé." In *Bible et Orient.* 287-301. Paris: Cerf, 1967. [Kingship/Coronation]

Weinfeld, Moshe. "The King as the Servant of the People: The Source of the Idea." *JJS* 33 (1982): 189-94. [Kingship/Coronation]

Westphal, M. "On Thinking of God as King." *Christian Scholars Review* 1 (1970): 27-34. [Kingship/Coronation]

Widengren, Geo. "Heavenly Enthronement and Baptism, Studies in Mandean Baptism." In *Religions in Antiquity, Essays in Memory of E. R. Goodenough,* edited by Jacob Neusner. 551-82. Leiden: Brill, 1968. [Kingship/Coronation]

Widengren, Geo. "King and Covenant." *Journal of Semitic Studies* 2 (1957): 1-32. [Kingship/Coronation]

Widengren, Geo. *The King and the Tree of Life in Ancient Near Eastern Religion (King and Saviour IV).* Leipzig: Harrassowitz, 1951. [Kingship/Coronation]

Widengren, Geo. "The Sacral Kingship of Iran." In *The Sacral Kingship/La Regalità Sacra.* 242-57 Leiden: Brill, 1959. [Kingship/Coronation]

Widengren, Geo. "Das sakrale Königtum." In Widengren, *Religionsphänomenologie.* 360-93. Berlin: de Gruyter, 1969. [Kingship/Coronation]

Widengren, Geo. *Sakrales Königtum im alten Testament und im Judentum.* Stuttgart: Kohlhammer, 1955. [Kingship/Coronation]

Woolley, Reginald M. *Coronation Rites.* Cambridge: Cambridge University Press, 1915. [Kingship/Coronation]

Zevit, Z. "Deuteronomistic Historiography in 1 Kings 12, 2 Kings 17 and the Reinvestiture of the Israelian Cult." *Journal for the Study of the Old Testament* 32 (1985): 57-73. [Kingship/Coronation]

Measurement and Plans

Bloch, Chaim. *The Form of the House: According to the Masters of the Talmud* (in Hebrew). Bretslavia: Shatzky, 1883. [Measurement]

Cases, Moses ben Samuel. *Commentary on the Treatise Midoth by Moses Cases, and with it Hanukath Ha'Baith—Descriptive Analysis of the Plans of the Temple by Malchiel Ashkenazi (Tedeschi)* (in Hebrew). Jerusalem: Schreiber, 1963. [Measurement]

Chaplin, T. "Middoth, or the Measurement of the Temple, with the Commentary of Rabbi Ohadiah of Bartenora." *PEQ* 18 (1886): 224-28; 19 (1887): 60-63, 116-28, 132. [Measurement]

Doctorowitz, Joseph. *Midot ha-Batim ʿal Masekhet Middot.* Brooklyn: n.p., 1937. [Measurement]

Emanuel, J. "The Measurements of the Herodian Temple, according to Tractate Middoth and the Writings of Flavius Josephus" (in Hebrew). *Ha Maayan* 15/2 (1975): 49-54. [Measurement]

Frankel, Joseph A. *Bet ha-middot.* Brooklyn: n.p., 1984-85. [Measurement]

Hildesheimer, Israel. *Die Beschreibung des herodianischen Tempels im Tractate Middoth und bei Flavius Josephus.* Jerusalem: Rabbiner-Seminar, 1877. [Measurement]

Hildesheimer, Israel. "The Herodian Temple, According to the Treatise Middoth and Flavius Josephus." *PEFQ* 18 (1886): 92-113. [Measurement]

Hildesheimer, Azriel (Israel). *Measurements of Herod's Temple in the Tractate 'Middot' and Josephus* (in Hebrew). Jerusalem: Friedman, 1974. [Measurement]

Hildesheimer, Israel. *Midot Bet ha-Mikdash shel Hordus be-Masekhet Middot uve-Khitve Yosef ben Matityahu.* Jerusalem: Nettler, 1973-74. [Measurement]

Kaufman, Asher S. "Determining the Length of the Medium Cubit." *PEQ* 116 (1984): 120-32. [Measurement]

Kaufman, Asher S. "New Light upon Zion: The Plan and Precise Location of the Second Temple." *Ariel* 43 (1977): 63-100. [Measurement]

Kaufman, Asher S. "New Light upon Zion: The Plan of the 'Hekhal' in the Second Temple." *Niv Hamidrashia* 15 (1980-81): 115-30. [Measurement]

Magen, Yizhaq. "The Gates of the Temple Mount according to Josephus and Mishnah (Middot)" (in Hebrew). *Cathedra: History of Eretz-Israel* 14 (1980): 41-53. [Measurement]

Mirusalayim, Aharon. *On the Measurements of the Temple* (in Hebrew). Jerusalem: HaLevi Tsukerman, 1906. [Measurement]

Shalem, Raphael A. *Plan of the Chosen House . . . according to Maimonides* (in Hebrew). Jerusalem: n.p., 1967. [Measurement]

"The Tract 'Middoth'—On the Measurements of the Temple, Literally Translated from the Mishna." *PEFQ* 4 (1872): 12-19. [Measurement]

Weinfeld, Shemuel. *The Writing of the Plan of the Chosen House* (in Hebrew). Jerusalem: Eshkol, 1966. [Measurement]

Mountains and High Places as Symbols of the Temple and Other Sacred Space

Abel, E. L. "The Nature of the Patriarchal God 'El Šadday.' " *Numen* 20 (1973): 48-59. [Mountain]

Aggoula, B. "Temple et agora à Hatra." *Annali dell'Istituto orientale di Napoli* 43 (1983): 407-28. [Mountain]

Albright, William F. "The Babylonian Temple-Tower and the Altar of Burnt-Offering." *JBL* 39 (1920): 137-42. [Mountain]

Anderson, R. T. "Mount Gerizim: Navel of the World." *BA* 43 (1980): 217-21. [Mountain]

Ap-Thomas, David R. "Elijah on Mount Carmel." *PEQ* 92 (1960): 146-55. [Mountain]

Barrick, W. B. "The Funerary Character of 'High Places' in Ancient Palestine: A Reassessment." *VT* 25 (1975): 565-95. [Mountain]

Barrick, W. B. "What Do We Really Know about High Places?" *Svensk Exegetisk Årsbok* 45 (1980): 50-57. [Mountain]

Bialoblocki, Samuel. "The Temple Mount and the Temple" (in Hebrew). In *Em la Masoret*, 42-68. Ramat-Gan: Bar-Ilan University, 1971. [Mountain]

Booij, Thijs. "Mountain and Theophany in the Sinai Narrative (Exodus 19-20, 24, 32-34)." *Biblica* 65 (1984): 1-26. [Mountain]

Canney, M. A. "The Primordial Mound." *Journal of the Manchester Egyptian and Oriental Society* 20 (1936): 25-40. [Mountain]

Cazelles, Henri. "David's Monarchy and the Gibeonite Claim (II Sam. xxi,1-14)." *PEQ* 87 (1955): 165-75. [Mountain]

Clifford, Richard J. "The Cosmic Mountain in Canaan and the Old Testament." *Biblica* 55 (1974): 443-46. [Mountain]

Clifford, Richard J. "The Temple and the Holy Mountain." In *The Temple in Antiquity*, edited by Truman G. Madsen. 107-24. Provo, UT: Brigham Young University Press, 1984. [Mountain]

Coats, G. W. "Conquest Traditions in the Wilderness Theme." *JBL* 95 (1976): 177-90. [Mountain]

Coats, G. W. "Moses in Midian." *JBL* 92 (1973): 3-10. [Mountain]

Cohn, Robert L. "The Mountains and Mount Zion." *Judaism* 26 (1977): 97-115. [Mountain]

Cohn, Robert L. *The Shape of Sacred Space: Four Biblical Studies*. Chico: Scholars, 1981. [Mountain]

Comay, Joan. *The Temple of Jerusalem*. New York: Holt, Rinehart and Winston, 1975. [Mountain]

Demsky, A. "The Trumpeter's Inscription from the Temple Mount" (in Hebrew; *English summary). *Eretz-Israel* 18 (1985): 40-42,*66. [Mountain]

Dumbrell, W. J. "The Role of Bethel in the Biblical Narratives from Jacob to Jeroboam I." *Australian Journal of Biblical Archaeology* 2/3 (1974-75): 65-76. [Mountain]

Edwards, Iorwerth E. S. *The Pyramids of Egypt*. London: Penguin Books, 1949. [Mountain]

Gaerte, W. "Komische Vorstellungen im Bilde prähistorischer Zeit: Erdberg, Himmelsberg, Erdnabel und Weltenströme." *Anthropos* 9 (1913): 956-79. [Mountain]

Gray, John. "Desert Sojourn of the Hebrews and the Sinai-Horeb Tradition." *VT* 4 (1954): 148-54. [Mountain]

Grintz, J. (Yehoshua) M. "Some Observations on the 'High-Place' in the History of Israel." *VT* 27 (January 1977): 111-13. [Mountain]

Gutmann, E. "The Mountain Concept in Israelite Religion." Ph.D. diss., Southern Baptist Seminary, 1982. [Mountain]

Hacohen, Mordecai. "Bibliography of the Temple Mount and Temple" (in Hebrew). *Morashah* 11 (1977): 97-100. [Mountain]

Haldar, Alfred. "Hermon, Mount." In *The Interpreter's Dictionary of the Bible* 2:585. [Mountain]

Hallencreutz, C. "Christ Is the Mountain." In *Religious Symbols and Their Functions*, edited by H. Biezais. 96-104. Uppsala: Almquist and Wiksell, 1979. [Mountain]

Hamlin, E. J. "The Meaning of 'Mountains and Hills' in Isaiah 41:14-16." *JNES* 13 (1954): 185-90. [Mountain]

Haran, Menahem. "Bamot and Miqdašim: From Arad to Dan." *Beth Mikra* 24 (1978): 94-105. [Mountain]

Haran, Menahem. "The Divine Presence in the Israelite Cult and the Cultic Institutions." *Biblica* 50 (1969): 251-67. [Mountain]

Holladay, W. L. "On Every High Hill and under Every Green Tree." *VT* 11 (1961): 170-76. [Mountain]

Horovicz, Jonathan. *Geschichte des Sch'thijasteines.* Frankfurt: Kauffmann, 1927. [Mountain]

Irwin, J. C. "The Sacred Hill and the Cult of the Primordial Mound." *History of Religions* 21 (1982): 339-60. [Mountain]

Iwry, S. "Maṣṣēbāh and Bāmāh in 1Q Isaiah[a] 6:13." *JBL* 76 (1957): 225-32. [Mountain]

Jasper, F. N. "Early Israelite Traditions and the Psalter." *VT* 17 (1967): 50-59. [Mountain]

Jeremias, Joachim. *Der Gottesberg, ein Beitrag zum Verständnis der biblischen Symbolsprache.* Gütersloh: Bertelmann, 1919. [Mountain]

Kanael, G. "The Temple Mount during the Period of the Second Temple" (in Hebrew). *Ha Umah* 6 (1967-68): 486-97. [Mountain]

Kaufmann, Yehezkel, and Clarence W. Efroymson, eds. *History of the Religion of Israel.* New York: KTAV, 1977. [Mountain]

Kimelman, A. "The Area of the Temple Mount and the Ḥel (Rampart), and the Laws Pertaining Thereto." *Ha-Maayan* 8/3 (1968): 3-32. [Mountain]

Kingsbury, E. C. "The Theophany Topos and the Mountain of God." *JBL* 86 (1967): 205-10. [Mountain]

McCown, C. C. "Hebrew High Places and Cult Remains." *JBL* 69 (1950): 205-19. [Mountain]

Mazar, Benjamin. "Excavations near the Temple Mount." *Qadmoniot* 5/3-4[19-20] (1972): 74-90. [Mountain]

Mazar, Benjamin. "Exploration of the Wilson Arch and the Northern Extension of the Western Wall." In *The Mountain of the Lord*, edited by Benjamin Mazar et al., 217-22. Garden City, Doubleday, 1975. [Mountain]

Mazar, Benjamin. "Herod's Temple/Functions of the Outer Walls and Gate of the Temple Mount." In *The Mountain of the Lord*, edited by Benjamin Mazar et al., 106-52. Garden City: Doubleday, 1975. [Mountain]

Mazar, Benjamin. "YHWH Came out from Sinai." In *Temples and High Place in Biblical Times*, edited by Avraham Biran, 5-9. Jerusalem: Jewish Institute of Religion, 1981. [Mountain]

Offord, Joseph. "The Mountain Throne of Jahveh." *PEFQ* 51 (1919): 39-45. [Mountain]

Parry, Donald W. "Sinai as Sanctuary and Mountain of God." In *By Study and Also by Faith: Essays in Honor of Hugh W. Nibley*, edited by John M. Lundquist and Stephen D. Ricks. 2 vols., 1:482-500. Salt Lake City: Deseret Book and F.A.R.M.S., 1990. [Mountain]

Reed, William L. "Mount, Mountain." In *The Interpreter's Dictionary of the Bible* 3:452. [Mountain]

Rofé, Yosef. "The Site of Our Holy Temple—the Location of the Temple at the Southern End of the Temple Mount" (in Hebrew; *English summary). *Niv ha-Midrashiyah* 13 (1978-79): 166-86, *105-13. [Mountain]

Talmon, Shemaryahu. *"har: Gibhʿāh."* In *Theological Dictionary of the Old Testament* 3:427-47. [Mountain]

Van Buren, E. (Elizabeth) D. (Douglas). "Mountain-Gods." *Orientalia* 12 (1943): 76-84. [Mountain]

Vaughan, Patrick H. *The Meaning of 'bāmâ' in the Old Testament: A Study of Etymologyical, Textual, and Archaeological Evidence.* Cambridge: Cambridge University Press, 1974. [Mountain]

Waldman, Nahum M. "The Wealth of Mountain and Sea: The Background of a Biblical Image." *JQR* 71 (1980-81): 176-80. [Mountain]

Wales, Horace G. Q. *The Mountain of God: A Study in Early Religion and Kingship.* London: Quaritch, 1953. [Mountain]

Wales, Horace G. Q. "The Sacred Mountain in the Old Asiatic Religion." *Journal of the Royal Asiatic Society* (1953): 23-30. [Mountain]

Whitney, J. T. "The Israelite 'bamah.' " Ph.D. diss., Nottingham University, 1974. [Mountain]

Wright, G. (George) Ernest. *Shechem: The Biography of a Biblical City.* New York: McGraw-Hill, 1965. [Mountain]

Wright, G. R. H. "The Mythology of Pre-Israelite Shechem." *VT* 20 (1970): 75-82. [Mountain]

Priesthood

Abba, Raymond. "Priests and Levites." In *The Interpreter's Dictionary of the Bible* 3:876-89. [Priesthood]

Abba, Raymond. "Priests and Levites in Deuteronomy." *VT* 27 (1977): 257-67. [Priesthood]

Abba, Raymond. "Priests and Levites in Ezechiel." *VT* 28 (1978): 1-9. [Priesthood]

Allan, N. "The Identity of the Jerusalem Priesthood during the Exile." *Heythrop Journal* 23 (1982): 259-69. [Priesthood]

Alon, Gedalyahu. "History of the High Priesthood at the End of the Second Temple Period" (in Hebrew). *Tarbiz* 13 (1942): 1-24. [Priesthood]

Armerding, Carl E. "Were David's Sons Really Priests?" In *Current Issues in Biblical and Patristic Interpretation: Studies in Honor of Merrill C. Tenney*, edited by Gerald F. Hawthorne, 75-86. Grand Rapids: Eerdmans, 1975. [Priesthood]

Bammel, Ernst. "Die Bruderfolge im Hochpriestertum der herodianisch-römischen Zeit." *ZDPV* 70 (1954): 147-53. [Priesthood]

Baudissin, W. "The Priesthood after OT Times." In *A Dictionary of the Bible*, edited by James Hastings. 4 vols. plus extra volume. 4:94-97. New York: Scribner's Songs, 1909. [Priesthood]

Belleli, L. "The High Priest's Procession on the Day of Atonement." *JQR* 17 (1904-5): 163-67. [Priesthood]

Berry, G. R. "Priests and Levites." *JBL* 42 (1923): 227-38. [Priesthood]

Bikler, Avraham. *The Priests and Their Service in the Jerusalem Temple in the Last Decade before the Destruction of the 2nd Temple* (in Hebrew). Jerusalem: Rav Kook, 1966. [Priesthood]

Bowman, John. "Ezekiel and the Zadokite Priesthood." *GUOST* 16 (1955-56): 1-14. [Priesthood]

Breasted, James H. "The Philosophy of a Memphite Priest." *ZÄS* 39 (1901): 39-54. [Priesthood]

Budd, P. J. "Priestly Instruction in Pre-Exilic Israel." *VT* 23 (1973): 1-14. [Priesthood]

Büchler, Adolph (Adolf). *Die Priester und der Cultus im letzten Jahrzehnt des jerusalemischen Tempels.* Wien: Israelitisch-theologische Lehranstalt, 1895. [Priesthood]

Cody, Aelred. *A History of Old Testament Priesthood.* Rome: Pontifical Biblical Institute, 1969. [Priesthood]

Cohen, Martin A. "The Role of the Shilonite Priesthood in the United Monarchy of Ancient Israel." *Hebrew Union College Annual* 35 (1965): 59-98. [Priesthood]

Corney, Richard W. "Zadok the Priest." In *The Interpreter's Dictionary of the Bible* 4:928-29. [Priesthood]

Crehan, J. H. "Priesthood, Kingship and Prophecy." *Theological Studies* 42 (1981): 216-31. [Priesthood]

Cross, Frank M. "The Priestly Houses of Early Israel." In *Canaanite Myth and Hebrew Epic*, 195-215. Cambridge: Harvard University Press, 1973. [Priesthood]

de Jonge, M., and Adam S. Van der Woude. "11Q Melchizedek and the New Testament." *NTS* 12 (1965-66): 301-26. [Priesthood]

Del Medico, H. E. "Melchisédech." *ZAW* 69 (1957): 160-70. [Priesthood]

Eastwood, Charles C. *The Royal Priesthood of the Faithful: An Investigation of the Doctrine from Biblical Times to the Reformation.* London: Epworth, 1963. [Priesthood]

Emerton, J. A. "Priests and Levites in Deuteronomy: An Examination of Dr. G. E. Wright's Theory." *VT* 12 (1962): 129-38. [Priesthood]

Falk, Zev. "The Law of Temple and Priests in the Halakah" (in Hebrew; *English summary). In *Proceedings of the Fifth World Congress of Jewish Studies, 1969*, edited by P. Peli. 1:105-9, *236-37. Jerusalem: World Union of Jewish Studies, 1972. [Priesthood]

Fitzmyer, J. " 'Now this Melchizedek. . .' (Heb. 7, 1)." *CBQ* 25 (1963): 305-21. [Priesthood]

Gammie, John. "Loci of the Melchizedek Tradition of Genesis 14:18-20." *JBL* 90 (1971): 385-96. [Priesthood]

Görg, Manfred. "Ein architektonischer Fachausdruck in der Priesterschrift: Zur Bedeutung von '*eden*." *VT* 33 (1983): 334-38. [Priesthood]

Graetz, Heinrich. "Die Bedeutung der Priesterschaft für die Gesetzgebung während des zweiten Tempelbestandes." *MGWJ* 36 (1887): 97-118. [Priesthood]

Graetz, Heinrich. "Zur Geschichte der nachexilischen Hohenpriester." *MGWJ* 30 (1881): 49-64. [Priesthood]

Greenberg, Moshe. "A New Approach to the History of the Israelite Priesthood." *JAOS* 70 (1950): 41-47. [Priesthood]

Greenwald, Leopold. *The History of the High Priests* (in Hebrew). New York: n.p., 1933. [Priesthood]

Griffith, Francis L. *Stories of the High Priests of Memphis: the Sethon of Herodotus and the Demotic Tales of Khamuas.* Oxford: Clarendon, 1900. [Priesthood]

Grünbaum, Paul. *Die Priestergesetze bei Flavius Josephus: Eine Parallele zu Bibel and Tradition.* Halle: n.p., 1887. [Priesthood]

Gunneweg, A. H. J. *Leviten und Priester: Hauptlinien der Traditionsbildung und Geschichte des israelitisch-jüdischen Kultpersonals.* Göttingen: Vandenhoeck and Ruprecht, 1965. [Priesthood]

Habermann, A. M. "Prayer in the Temple and the Prayer of the High Priest" (in Hebrew). *Maḥanayim* 96 (1964): 26-27. [Priesthood]

Haran, Menahem. "Priest, Temple and Worship." *Tarbiz* 48 (1978-79): 175-85. [Priesthood]

Haran, Menahem. "Priesthood, Temple, Divine Service: Some Observations on Institutions and Practices of Worship." *Hebrew Annual Review* 7 (1983): 121-35. [Priesthood]

Haran, Menahem. "Priests and Priesthood." In *Encyclopaedia Judaica* 13:1069-86. [Priesthood]

Haran, Menahem. "Shiloh and Jerusalem: The Origin of the Priestly Tradition in the Pentateuch." *JBL* 81 (1962): 14-24. [Priesthood]

Haran, Menachem. "Studies in the Bible: The Idea of Centralization of the Cult in the Priestly Apprehension" (in Hebrew; *English summary). *Beer-Sheva* 1 (1973): 114-21, *239. [Priesthood]

Hauer, Christian, Jr. "David and the Levites." *Journal for the Study of the Old Testament* 23 (1982): 33-54. [Priesthood]

Hauer, Christian, Jr. "Who Was Zadok?" *JBL* 82 (1963): 89-94. [Priesthood]

Hölscher, Gustav. *Die Hohenpriesterliste bei Josephus und die evangelische Chronologie.* Heidelberg: Winter, 1940. [Priesthood]

Hölscher, Gustav. "Sadduzäismus und Hohespriestertum." In *Der Sadduzäismus: Eine kritische Untersuchung zur späteren jüdischen Religionsgeschichte,* 37-84. Leipzig: Hinrichs, 1906. [Priesthood]

Hoonacker, Albin van. "Les Prêtres et les lévites dans le livre d'Ézéchiël." *Revue Biblique* 8 (1899): 177-205. [Priesthood]

Hoschander, Jacob. *The Priests and Prophets.* New York: Jewish Theological Seminary of America, 1938. [Priesthood]

James, Edwin O. *The Nature and Function of Priesthood: A Comparative and Anthropological Study.* New York: Vanguard, 1955. [Priesthood]

Judge, H. G. "Aaron, Zadok, and Abiathar." *JTS* 7 (1956): 70-74. [Priesthood]

Katzenstein, H. J. "Some Remarks on the Lists of the Chief Priests of the Temple of Solomon." *JBL* 81 (1962): 377-84. [Priesthood]

Katznelbogen, J. G. "The Status of the Levites in the Temple" (in Hebrew). *Maḥanayim* 96 (1964): 32-43. [Priesthood]

Kegel, Martin. *The History of the Israelitish Priesthood.* Dallas: South, Lamar & Barton, 1923. [Priesthood]

Kennett, R. H. "The Origin of the Aaronite Priesthood." *JTS* 9 (1905): 161-86. [Priesthood]

König, Eduard. "The Priests and Levites in Ezek. 44:7-15." *ET* 12 (1901): 300-303. [Priesthood]

Küper, Lic. *Das Priesterthum des alten Bundes.* Berlin: Hertz, 1866. [Priesthood]

Kuschke, Arnulf. "Die Lagervorstellung der priesterschriftlichen Erzählung." *ZAW* 63 (1951): 74-105. [Priesthood]

Levine, Baruch A. "Priests." In *The Interpreter's Dictionary of the Bible*, supp. vol., 687-90. [Priesthood]

Liver, Jacob, and Daniel Sperber. "Mishmarot and Maʿamadot," In *Encyclopaedia Judaica* 12:89-93. [Priesthood]

Luria, Ben-Zion. "The Cities of the Priests in the Days of the Second Temple" (in Hebrew). *HUCA* 44 (1973): 1-18. [Priesthood]

Mantel, Chaim D. (Hugo). "The Dichotomy of Judaism during the Second Temple." *HUCA* 44 (1973): 55-87. [Priesthood]

Mantel, Chaim D. (Hugo). "The High Priesthood and the Sanhedrin in the Time of the Second Temple." In *The World History of the Jewish People—The Herodian Period*, edited by M. Avi-Yonah, 7:264-81. Jerusalem: Massada, 1975. [Priesthood]

Mantel, Chaim D. "Ordination and Appointment in the Period of the Temple" (in Hebrew; *English summary). *Tarbiz* 32 (1963): 120-35, *II. [Priesthood]

Margueron, Jean, et al. *Sanctuaires et clergés.* Paris: Geuthner, 1985. [Priesthood]

Matthews, Charles D. "An Examination of the Character of the Jewish High Priesthood from Ezra to the New Testament Times." Ph.D. diss., Southern Baptist Seminary, 1945. [Priesthood]

Maybaum, Siegmund. *Die Entwickelung des altisraelitischen Priesterthums: Ein Beitrag zur Kritik der mittleren Bücher des Pentateuchs.* Breslau: Köbner, 1880. [Priesthood]

McCready, Wayne O. "Priests and Levites." In *The International Standard Bible Encyclopedia*, edited by G. W. Bromiley. 4 vols., 3:965-70. Grand Rapids: Eerdmans, 1986. [Priesthood]

Meek, Theophile J. "Aaronites and Zadokites." *AJSL* 45 (1929): 149-66. [Priesthood]

Meek, Theophile J. "The Origin of the Hebrew Priesthood." In *Hebrew Origins*, rev. ed. 119-47. New York: Harper, 1950. [Priesthood]

Möhlenbrink, Kurt. "Die levitischen Überlieferungen des Alten Testaments." *ZAW* 52 (1934): 184-231. [Priesthood]

Morgenstern, Julian. "A Chapter in the History of the High Priesthood." *AJSL* 55 (1938): 1-24, 183-97, 360-77. [Priesthood]

North, Francis S. "Aaron's Rise in Prestige." *ZAW* 66 (1954): 191-99. [Priesthood]

Olyan, Saul. "Zadok's Origins and the Tribal Politics of David." *JBL* 101 (1982): 177-93. [Priesthood]

Paton, Lewis B. "The Use of the Word 'Kohen' in the Old Testament." *JBL* 12 (1893): 1-14. [Priesthood]

Plöger, O. "Priester und Prophet." *ZAW* 63 (1951): 157-92. [Priesthood]

Polk, Timothy. "The Levites in the Davidic-Solomonic Empire." *Studia Biblica et Theologica* 9 (1979): 3-22. [Priesthood]

Porter, Joshua R. "Levites." In *Harper's Bible Dictionary*, 557-58. [Priesthood]

Rawlinson, A. E. J. "Priesthood and Sacrifice in Judaism and Christianity." *ET* 60 (1949): 116-21. [Priesthood]

Rehm, Merlin D. "Zadok the Priest." In *The Interpreter's Dictionary of the Bible*, supp. vol., 976-77. [Priesthood]

Reines, Chaim W. *Kohanim u-Nevi'im*. New York: n.p., 1945. [Priesthood]

Risikoff, Menachem. *Collection of Laws concerning the Priesthood, the Temple and Sacrifices* (in Hebrew). New York: n.p., 1948. [Priesthood]

Rowley, Harold H. "Melchizedek and Zadok (Gen 14 and Ps 110)." In *Festschrift Alfred Bertholet zum 80. Geburtstag gewidmet von Kollegen und Freunden*, edited by Walter Baumgartner et al., 461-72. Tübingen: Mohr, 1950. [Priesthood]

Rowley, Harold H. "Zadok and Nehushtan." *JBL* 58 (1939): 113-41. [Priesthood]

Sauneron, Serge. *The Priests of Ancient Egypt*. New York: Grove, 1960. [Priesthood]

Schiffman, Lawrence H. "Priests." In *Harper's Bible Dictionary*, 821-23. [Priesthood]

Sharwood Smith, John. *Temples, Priests and Worship*. London: Allen & Unwin, 1975. [Priesthood]

Smallwood, E. Mary. "High Priests and Politics in Roman Palestine." *JTS* n.s./13 (1962): 14-34. [Priesthood]

Staehelin, J. J. "Ueber die Wanderungen des Centralheiligthums der Hebraeer vom Tode des Hohenpriesters Eli bis auf die Erbauung des Tempels zu Jerusalem." *ZDMG* 11 (1857): 141-43. [Priesthood]

Stern, Menahem. "Priests and Priesthood—from the Beginning of the Hellenistic Era until the Destruction of the Temple." In *Encyclopaedia Judaica* 13:1086-88. [Priesthood]

Ta-Shema, I. "Levi." In *Encyclopaedia Hebraica* (in Hebrew). 32 vols., 21:366-71. Jerusalem: Encyclopaedia Hebraica, 1971. [Priesthood]

Torrance, Thomas F. *Royal Priesthood*. Edinburgh: Oliver and Boyd, 1955. [Priesthood]

Van der Woude, Adam S. "Melchizedek." In *The Interpreter's Dictionary of the Bible*, supp. vol., 585-86. [Priesthood]

Vogelstein, Hermann. *Der Kampf zwischen Priestern und Leviten seit den Tagen Ezechiels—eine historisch-kritische Untersuchung.* Stettin: Nagel, 1889. [Priesthood]

Wenham, Gordon J. "Were David's Sons Priests?" *ZAW* 87 (1975): 79-82. [Priesthood]

Zeitlin, Solomon. "The Titles High Priest and the Nasi of the Sanhedrin." *JQR* 48 (1957-58): 1-5. [Priesthood]

Ritual, Liturgy, and Worship

Abrahams, Roger D. *Rituals in Culture.* Bloomington: Folklore, 1974. [Ritual/Liturgy/Worship]

Akmar, Ernst. "Étude sur le rituel du culte divin." *Sphinx: Revue critique* 19 (1915): 65-80. [Ritual/Liturgy/Worship]

Amad, Gladys. *Le baiser rituel: Un geste de culte méconnu.* Beirut: Dar el-Machreq, 1973. [Ritual/Liturgy/Worship]

Amir, Yehoshua. "Philo's Version of the Pilgrimage to Jerusalem" (in Hebrew; English summary). In *Jerusalem in the Second Temple Period* (Abraham Schalit Memorial Volume), edited by A. Oppenheimer, U. Rappaport, and M. Stern. ix-x, 154-65. Jerusalem: Yad Izhak Ben-Zvi, 1980. [Ritual/Liturgy/Worship]

Backer, Émile de. *Sacramentum, le mot et l'idée représenté par lui dans les oeuvres de Tertullien.* Louvain: Bureau du Recueil, 1911. [Ritual/Liturgy/Worship]

Baly, T. J. "Notes on the Ritual of Opening the Mouth." *JEA* 16 (1930): 173-86. [Ritual/Liturgy/Worship]

Barta, Winfried. "Das Opferritual im täglichen Tempelkult." *Ex Oriente Lux: Jaarbericht van het vooraziatisch-egyptisch Gezelschap* 19 (1965-66): 457-631. [Ritual/Liturgy/Worship]

Barton, George A. "A Comparison of Some Features of Hebrew and Babylonian Ritual." *JBL* 46 (1927): 79-89. [Ritual/Liturgy/Worship]

Barton, George A. "A Liturgy for the Celebration of the Spring Festival at Jerusalem in the Age of Abraham and Melchizedek." *JBL* 53 (1934): 61-78. [Ritual/Liturgy/Worship]

Baumgarten, Joseph M. "Sacrifices and Worship among the Jewish Sectaries of the Dead Sea (Qumrân) Scrolls." *Harvard Theological Review* 46 (1953): 151-59. [Ritual/Liturgy/Worship]

Bell, Catherine. "Discourse and Dichotomies: The Structure of Ritual Theory." *Religion* 17 (April 1987): 95-118. [Ritual/Liturgy/Worship]

Bentzen, Aage. "The Cultic Use of the Story of the Ark in Samuel." *JBL* 67 (1948): 37-53. [Ritual/Liturgy/Worship]

Betz, H. "Fragments from a Catabasis Ritual in Greek Magical Papyrus." *History of Religions* 19 (May 1980): 287-95. [Ritual/Liturgy/Worship]

Bird, F. B. "The Nature and Function of Ritual Forms: A Sociological Discussion." *Studies in Religion* 9 (1980): 387-402. [Ritual/Liturgy/Worship]

Bjerke, S. "Remarks on the Egyptian Ritual of Opening the Mouth and Its Interpretation." *Numen* 12 (1965): 201-16. [Ritual/Liturgy/Worship]

Blackman, Aylward M. "Myth and Ritual in Ancient Egypt." In *Myth and Ritual*, edited by Samuel H. Hooke, 15-39. Oxford: Oxford University Press, 1953. [Ritual/Liturgy/Worship]

Blackman, Aylward M. "The Rite of Opening the Mouth in Ancient Egypt and Babylonia." *JEA* 10 (1924): 47-59. [Ritual/Liturgy/Worship]

Blackman, Aylward M. "Sacramental Ideas and Usages in Ancient Egypt." *Recueil de travaux relatifs à la philologie et à l'archéologie égyptiennes et assyriennes* 39 (1921): 44-78. [Ritual/Liturgy/Worship]

Blackman, Aylward M. "The Significance of Incense and Libations in Funerary and Temple Ritual." *ZÄS* 50 (1912): 69-75. [Ritual/Liturgy/Worship]

Blackman, Aylward M., et al. "Purification." In *Encyclopedia of Religion and Ethics* 10:476-90. [Ritual/Liturgy/Worship]

Bonsirven, Joseph. "Le Temple et ses liturgies." In *Le Judaisme au temps de Jésus-Christ.* 2:107-36. Paris: Beauchesne, 1935. [Ritual/Liturgy/Worship]

Bouyer, L. "Von der jüdischen zur christlichen Liturgie." *Internationale katholische Zeitschrift* 7 (1978): 509-20. [Ritual/Liturgy/Worship]

Brand, Joshua. "Pilgrimages and Their Organization" (in Hebrew). *Mayanot* 6 (1947): 66-79. [Ritual/Liturgy/Worship]

Bratcher, Dennis R. "Pilgrimage." In *Harper's Bible Dictionary*, 798-99. [Ritual/Liturgy/Worship]

Brightman, Frank E., ed. *Liturgies, Eastern and Western.* Oxford: Clarendon, 1965. [Ritual/Liturgy/Worship]

Broshi, M. "Pilgrimage to Jerusalem" (in Hebrew). In *Jerusalem—Ancient Sites.* 22-27. Tel Aviv: Tarbut ve Chinuch, 1967. [Ritual/Liturgy/Worship]

Brueggemann, Walter A. "A Form-Critical Study of the Cultic Material in Deuteronomy: An Analysis of the Nature of Cultic Encounter in the Mosaic Tradition." Ph.D. diss., Union Theological Seminary, 1961. [Ritual/Liturgy/Worship]

Brunner, H. "Magische, kultische und ethische Elemente ägyptischer Religiosität." *Antaios* 3 (1961): 534-43. [Ritual/Liturgy/Worship]

Buchanan, George W. "Worship, Feasts and Ceremonies in the Early Jewish-Christian Church." *NTS* 26 (1980): 279-97. [Ritual/Liturgy/Worship]

Burtchaell, J. T. "Rituals of Jesus, the Anti-Ritualist." *Journal of the American Academy of Religion* 39 (1971): 513-25. [Ritual/Liturgy/Worship]

Busse, Eduard. *Der Wein im Kult des Alten Testamentes.* Freiburg: Herder, 1922. [Ritual/Liturgy/Worship]

Caquot, André. "Pour une étude de l'initiation dans l'ancien Israël." In *Initiation,* edited by Claas J. Bleeker. 119-33. Leiden: Brill, 1965. [Ritual/Liturgy/Worship]

Casel, Odo. *Das christliche Kultmysterium.* Regensburg, Pustet, 1932. [Ritual/Liturgy/Worship]

Collins, M. "Ritual Symbols and the Ritual Process: The Work of Victor W. Turner." *Worship* 50 (1976): 336-46. [Ritual/Liturgy/Worship]

Corbin, Henry. "Ritual sabéen et exégèse ismaelienne du rituel." *Eranos Jahrbuch* 19 (1950): 181-246. [Ritual/Liturgy/Worship]

Cullmann, Oscar. *Early Christian Worship.* London: SCM, 1953. [Ritual/Liturgy/Worship]

Daniel, Suzanne. *Recherches sur le vocabulaire du culte dans la "Septante."* Paris: Klincksieck, 1966. [Ritual/Liturgy/Worship]

Dauenhauer, B. P. "Some Aspects of Language and Time in Ritual Worship." *International Journal for the Philosophy of Religion* 6 (1975): 54-62. [Ritual/Liturgy/Worship]

David, A. Rosalie. *A Guide to Religious Ritual at Abydos.* Warminster: Aris and Phillips, 1981. [Ritual/Liturgy/Worship]

Davies, John G. *A Dictionary of Liturgy and Worship.* New York: Macmillan, 1972. [Ritual/Liturgy/Worship]

Derchain, Philippe. *Le Papyrus Salt 825 (B.M. 10051), rituel pour la conservation de la vie en Égypte.* Brussels: Palais de Academies, 1965. [Ritual/Liturgy/Worship]

Derchain, Philippe. *Rites égyptiens.* Brussels: Fondation égyptologique reine Élisabeth, 1962. [Ritual/Liturgy/Worship]

Dooling, Dorothea M., ed. "Ceremonies." *Parabola* 7/3 (1982): 2-96. [Ritual/Liturgy/Worship]

Dowden, K. "Grades in the Eleusinian Mysteries." *RHR* 197 (1980): 409-27. [Ritual/Liturgy/Worship]

Drower, Ethel S. *Water into Wine: A Study of Ritual Idiom in the Middle East.* London: Murray, 1956. [Ritual/Liturgy/Worship]

Easton, B. S. "Jewish and Christian Ordination." *Anglican Theological Review* 5-6 (1922-23): 308-19; 285-95. [Ritual/Liturgy/Worship]

Eaton, E. "Towards Initiation." *Parabola* 1/3 (1976): 42-47. [Ritual/Liturgy/Worship]

Eaton, John H. *Vision in Worship: The Relation of Prophecy and Liturgy in the Old Testament.* London: SPCK, 1981. [Ritual/ Litrugy/Worship]

Ehrhardt, A. "Jewish and Christian Ordination." *Journal of Ecclesiastical History* 5 (1954): 125-38. [Ritual/Liturgy/Worship]

Ehrlich, E. L. *Die Kultsymbolik im Alten Testament und im nachbiblischen Judentum,* vol. 3. Stuttgart: Hiersemann, 1959. [Ritual/Liturgy/Worship]

Eisenhofer, Ludwig. *The Liturgy of the Roman Rite,* translated by A. J. Peeler. New York: Herder and Herder, 1961. [Ritual/Liturgy/Worship]

Eliade, Mircea. "History of Religions and 'Popular' Cultures." *History of Religions* 20 (1980): 1-26. [Ritual/Liturgy/Worship]

Eliade, Mircea. *Myths, Rites, Symbols.* New York: Harper and Colophon, 1976. [Ritual/Liturgy/Worship]

Eliade, Mircea. *Rites and Symbols of Initiation: The Mysteries of Birth and Rebirth,* translated by Willard R. Trask. New York: Harper & Row, 1975. [Ritual/Liturgy/Worship]

Elbogen, Ismar. *Der jüdische Gottesdienst in seiner geschichtlichen Entwicklung.* Leipzig: Fock, 1913. [Ritual/Liturgy/Worship]

Encausse, Jean d'. *De l'initiation.* Paris: le Courrier du livre, 1968. [Ritual/Liturgy/Worship]

Eshbach, W. M. "Another Look at John 13:1-20." *Brethren Life and Thought* 14 (1969): 117-25. [Ritual/Liturgy/Worship]

Fennelly, James M. "The Persepolis Ritual." *BA* 43 (1980): 135-62. [Ritual/Liturgy/ Worship]

Ferguson, Everett. "Jewish and Christian Ordination: Some Observations." *Harvard Theological Review* 56 (1963): 13-19. [Ritual/Liturgy/Worship]

Ferguson, Everett. "Selection and Installation to Office in Roman, Greek, Jewish, and Christian Antiquity." *Theologische Zeitschrift* 30 (1974): 273-84. [Ritual/Liturgy/Worship]

Finnestad, R. B. "The Meaning and Purpose of Opening the Mouth in Mortuary Contexts." *Numen* 25 (1978): 118-34. [Ritual/Liturgy/Worship]

Fisher, Loren R. "An Ugaritic Ritual and Genesis 1:1-5." *Ugaritica* 6 (1969): 197-205. [Ritual/Liturgy/Worship]

Fitzer, J. "Liturgy, Language and Mysticism." *Worship* 47 (1973): 66-79. [Ritual/Liturgy/Worship]

Fohrer, Georg. "Worship." In *History of Israelite Religion.* 195-214. Nashville: Abingdon, 1972. [Ritual/Liturgy/Worship]

Forster, Robert, and Orest Ranum. *Ritual, Religion, and the Sacred,* translated by Elborg Forster and Patricia M. Ranum. Baltimore: Johns Hopkins University Press, 1982. [Ritual/Liturgy/Worship]

Fried, Martha N., and Morton H. Fried. *Transitions: Four Rituals in Eight Cultures.* New York: Norton, 1980. [Ritual/Liturgy/Worship]

Gaster, Theodor H. "The Ritual Pattern of a Ras-Šamra Epic." *Archiv Orientàlni* 5 (1933): 118-23. [Ritual/Liturgy/Worship]

Gaster, Theodor H. *Thespis: Ritual, Myth, and Drama in the Ancient Near East.* New York: Harper and Row, 1950. [Ritual/Liturgy/Worship]

Gennep, Arnold van. *The Rites of Passage*, translated by Monika B. Vizedom and Gabrielle L. Caffe. Chicago: University of Chicago Press, 1960. [Ritual/Liturgy/Worship]

Gill, S. D. "Disenchantment." *Parabola* 1/3 (1976): 6-13. [Ritual/Liturgy/Worship]

Goetze, Albrecht, and E. H. Sturtevant, *The Hittite Ritual of Tunnawi.* New Haven: American Oriental Society, 1938. [Ritual/Liturgy/Worship]

Gonzenbach, Victorine von. *Untersuchungen zu den Knabenweihen im Isiskult der römischen Kaiserzeit.* Bonn: Habelt, 1957. [Ritual/Liturgy/Worship]

Goyon, J. C. "Une formule solennelle de purification des offrandes dans les temples ptolémaïques." *Chronique d'Égypte* 45 (1970): 267-81. [Ritual/Liturgy/Worship]

Grimes, Ronald L. *Ritual Criticism: Case Studies in Its Practice, Essays on Its Theory.* Columbia, SC: University of South Carolina Press, 1990. [Ritual/Liturgy/Worship]

Grimes, Ronald L. "Sources for the Study of Ritual." *Religious Studies Review* 10 (1984): 134-45. [Ritual/Liturgy/Worship]

Guénon, René. *Aperuçus sur l'initiation.* Paris: Editions Traditionelles, 1976. [Ritual/Liturgy/Worship]

Guénon, René. *Initiation et réalisation spirituelle.* Paris: Editions Traditionelles, 1975. [Ritual/Liturgy/Worship]

Guilmot, Max. *Les initiés et les rites initiatiques en Égypte ancienne.* Paris: Laffont, 1977. [Ritual/Liturgy/Worship]

Gurney, Oliver R. "Babylonian Prophylactic Figures and Their Rituals." *Annals of Archaeology and Anthropology* 22 (1935): 31-96. [Ritual/Liturgy/Worship]

Halpern, Baruch. "The Ritual Background of Zechariah's Temple Song." *CBQ* 40 (1978): 143-66. [Ritual/Liturgy/Worship]

Hamman, Gauthier A. *L'initiation chrétienne.* Paris: Bernard Grosset, 1963. [Ritual/Liturgy/Worship]

Haran, Menahem. "Priest, Temple and Worship" (in Hebrew; *English summary). *Tarbiz* 48/3-4 (1979): 175-85, *I. [Ritual/Liturgy/Worship]

Haran, Menahem. "The Uses of Incense in the Ancient Israelite Ritual." *VT* 10 (1960): 113-29. [Ritual/Liturgy/Worship]

Harrelson, Walter. *From Fertility Cult to Worship.* Garden City: Doubleday, 1969. [Ritual/Liturgy/Worship]

Harrelson, Walter. "Guilt and Rites of Purification Related to the Fall of Jerusalem in 587 B.C." In *Proceedings of the XIth International Congress of the International Association for the History of Religions.* 73-74. Leiden: Brill, 1968. [Ritual/Liturgy/Worship]

Harrelson, Walter. "Worship in Early Israel." *Biblical Research* 3 (1958): 1-14. [Ritual/Liturgy/Worship]

Haupt, Paul. "Babylonian Elements in Levitical Ritual." *JBL* 19 (1900): 55-61. [Ritual/Liturgy/Worship]

Heinemann, J. "Prayer in the Temple." In *Prayer in the Talmud: Forms and Patterns.* 123-38. Berlin and New York: de Gruyter, 1977. [Ritual/Liturgy/Worship]

Henderson, Joseph L. *Thresholds of Initiation.* Middletown, CT: Weslyan University Press, 1967. [Ritual/Liturgy/Worship]

Herbert, A. S. *Worship in Ancient Israel.* London: Lutterworth, 1959. [Ritual/Liturgy/Worship]

Hermission, Hans J. *Sprache und Ritus im altisraelitischen Kult.* Neukirchen-Vluyn: Neukirchener, 1965. [Ritual/Liturgy/Worship]

Hildebrand, D. R. "Temple Ritual: A Paradigm for Moral Holiness in Haggai ii 10-10." *VT* 39 (1989): 154-68. [Ritual/Liturgy/Worship]

Hochman, Joseph. *Jerusalem Temple Festivities.* London: Routledge, 1908. [Ritual/Liturgy/Worship]

Hooke, Samuel H., ed. *Myth and Ritual.* London: Oxford University Press, 1933. [Ritual/Liturgy/Worship]

Hooke, Samuel H., ed. *Myth, Ritual and Kingship.* Oxford: Clarendon, 1958. [Ritual/Liturgy/Worship]

Hooke, Samuel H. *The Origins of Early Semitic Ritual.* London: Oxford University Press, 1938. [Ritual/Liturgy/Worship]

Hooke, Samuel H. "The Theory and Practice of Substitution." *VT* 2 (1952): 2-17. [Ritual/Liturgy/Worship]

Hoonacker, Albin van. "La date de l'introduction de l'encens dans le culte de Jahvé." *RB* 11 (1914): 161-87. [Ritual/Liturgy/Worship]

Hoonacker, Albin van. *Le lieu du culte dans la législation rituelle des Hébreux.* Leipzig: Engelcke, 1894. [Ritual/Liturgy/Worship]

Idelsohn, Abraham Z. *Jewish Liturgy and Its Development.* New York: Schocken, 1967. [Ritual/Liturgy/Worship]

James, Edwin O. *Christian Myth and Ritual.* Cleveland: Meridian Books, 1965. [Ritual/Liturgy/Worship]

James, Edwin O. *Myth and Ritual in the Ancient Near East.* London: Thames and Hudson, 1958. [Ritual/Liturgy/Worship]

Jennings, T. W. "On Ritual Knowledge." *Journal of Religion* 62 (1982): 111-27. [Ritual/Liturgy/Worship]

Jones, B. H. "The Formation of the Nestorian Liturgy: The Great Conflation." *Anglican Theological Review* 48 (1966): 276-306. [Ritual/Liturgy/Worship]

Jones, B. H. "The Quest for the Origins of the Christian Liturgies." *Anglican Theological Review* 46 (1964): 5-21. [Ritual/Liturgy/Worship]

Jones, Cheslyn, ed. *The Study of Liturgy*. London: Clowes and Sons, 1978. [Ritual/Liturgy/Worship]

Jones, G. C. "Christian Initiation: New Wineskins for New Wine." *Religious Education* 74 (1979): 603-16. [Ritual/Liturgy/Worship]

Jones, Paul D. *Rediscovering Ritual*. New York: Newman, 1973. [Ritual/Liturgy/Worship]

Kapelrud, Arvid S. "The Role of the Cult in Old Israel." In *The Bible in Modern Scholarship*, edited by J. P. Hyatt. 45-56. Nashville: Abingdon, 1965. [Ritual/Liturgy/Worship]

Keet, Cuthbert C. *A Liturgical Study of the Psalter*. London: Allen & Unwin, 1928. [Ritual/Liturgy/Worship]

Kluckhohne, C. "Myths and Rituals: A General Theory." *Harvard Theological Review* 35 (1942): 45-79. [Ritual/Liturgy/Worship]

Koehl, R. B. "The Chieftan Cup: A Cretan Rite of Passage." *AJA* 89 (1985): 337. [Ritual/Liturgy/Worship]

Kraus, Hans-Joachim. "The Sanctuary and Its Worship." In Kraus, *Theology of the Psalms*, translated by Keith Crim. 73-106. Minneapolis: Augsburg Pub. House, 1986. [Ritual/Liturgy/Worship]

Kraus, Hans-Joachim. *Worship in Israel*, translated by G. Buswell. Richmond: John Know, 1966. [Ritual/Liturgy/Worship]

Laessøe, Jørgen. *Studies on the Assyrian Ritual and Series bît rimki*. Copenhagen: Munksgaard, 1955. [Ritual/Liturgy/Worship]

Lambert, W. G. "Myth and Ritual as Conceived by the Babylonians." *Journal of Semitic Studies* 13 (1968): 104-12. [Ritual/Liturgy/Worship]

Langdon, Stephen. *Babylonian Liturgies*. Paris: Geuthner, 1913. [Ritual/Liturgy/Worship]

Langdon, Stephen. *Sumerian Liturgical Texts*. Philadelphia: University Museum, 1917. [Ritual/Liturgy/Worship]

Langdon, Stephen. *Sumerian Liturgies and Psalms*. Philadelphia: University Museum, 1919. [Ritual/Liturgy/Worship]

Laperrousaz, E.-M. "Note à propos de la dotation du Rouleau du Temple et, plus généralement, des Manuscrits de la Mer Morte." *Revue de Qumran* 10 (1981): 447-52. [Ritual/Liturgy/Worship]

Laurentin, A. "Theatre and Liturgy." *Worship* 43 (1969): 382-406. [Ritual/Liturgy/Worship]

Lawler, M. G. "Christian Rituals: An Essay in Sacramental Symbolisms." *Horizons* 7 (1980): 7-35. [Ritual/Liturgy/Worship]

Lee, R. J. "Ritual and Theatre: An Overview." *Academy* 38/3-4 (1982): 132-49. [Ritual/Liturgy/Worship]

Lefebure, Francis. *Expériences initiatiques*. Antwerpen: Verrycken, 1978. [Ritual/Liturgy/Worship]

Lemaire, André. "Probable Head of Priestly Scepter from Solomon's Temple Surfaces in Jerusalem." *BAR* 10/1 (1984): 24-29. [Ritual/Liturgy/Worship]

Leslie, Elmer A. *The Psalms Translated and Interpreted in Light of Hebrew Life and Worship.* New York: Abingdon-Cokesbury, 1949. [Ritual/Liturgy/Worship]

Levine, Baruch A. "Cult." In *Encyclopaedia Judaica* 5:1155-62. [Ritual/Liturgy/Worship]

Lewis, P. B. "Indication of a Liturgical Source in the Gospel of Mark." *Encounter* 39 (1978): 385-94. [Ritual/Liturgy/Worship]

Lincoln, Bruce. "The Rape of Persephone: A Greek Scenario of Women's Initiation." *Harvard Theological Review* 72 (1979): 223-35. [Ritual/Liturgy/Worship]

Lohmeyer, Ernst. *Kultus und Evangelium.* Göttingen: Vandenhoeck and Ruprecht, 1942; also in English, *Lord of the Temple—a Study of the Relation between Cult and Gospel,* translated by S. Todd. Edinburgh: Oliver and Boyd, 1961. [Ritual/Liturgy/Worship]

McCarter, P. Kyle. "The Ritual Dedication of the City of David in 2 Samuel 6." In *The Word of the Lord Shall Go Forth: Essays in Honor of David Noel Freedman,* edited by C. L. Meyers and M. O'Connor. 273-78. Winona Lake: Eisenbrauns, 1983. [Ritual/Liturgy/Worship]

Macleod, D. "Dialogue of the Sanctuary." *Princeton Seminary Bulletin* 56 (1963): 15-32. [Ritual/Liturgy/Worship]

Maertens, Thierry. *A Feast in Honor of Yahweh: A Study of the Meaning of Worship,* translated by K. Sullivan. Notre Dame: Fides, 1965. [Ritual/Liturgy/Worship]

Martin-Achard, Robert. *Essai biblique sur les fêtes d'Israël.* Geneva: Labot et Fides, 1974. [Ritual/Liturgy/Worship]

Matthes, J. C. "Die Psalmen und der Tempeldienst." *ZAW* 22 (1902): 65-82. [Ritual/Liturgy/Worship]

Meier, G. "Die Ritualtafel der Serie 'Mundwaschung'." *Archiv für Orientforschung* 12 (1937): 40-45. [Ritual/Liturgy/Worship]

Michl, J. "Der Sinn der Fusswaschung (Jn 13)." *Biblica* 40 (1959): 697-708. [Ritual/Liturgy/Worship]

Miller, S. H. "Liturgy: Sign and Symbol." *Una Sancta* 25 (1968): 41-52. [Ritual/Liturgy/Worship]

Moraldi, Luigi. "Terminologia cultuale israelitica." *Rivista degli Studi Orientali* 32 (1957): 321-37. [Ritual/Liturgy/Worship]

Mowinckel, Sigmund. *Offersang og sangoffer.* Oslo: Aschehous, 1951; also in English as *The Psalms in Israel's Worship,* translated by D. R. Ap-Thomas. Oxford: Oxford University Press, 1962. [Ritual/Liturgy/Worship]

Mowinckel, Sigmund. *Religion og Kultus*. Oslo: Land og Kirke, 1950; also in English as *Religion and Cult*, translated by John F. X. Sheehan. Milwaukee: Marquette University, 1981. [Ritual/Liturgy/Worship]

Müller, Hans-Peter. "Die kultische Darstellung der Theophanie." *VT* 14 (1964): 183-91. [Ritual/Liturgy/Worship]

Murray, Grace A. *Ancient Rites and Ceremonies*. London: Rivers, 1929. [Ritual/Liturgy/Worship]

Murray, Robert. "Prophecy and the Cult." In *Israel's Prophetic Tradition: Essays in Honour of Peter R. Ackroyd*, edited by Richard Coggins, Anthony Phillips, and Michael Knibb. 200-226. Cambridge: Cambridge University Press, 1982. [Ritual/Liturgy/Worship]

Nibley, Hugh W. "The Early Christian Prayer Circle." *Brigham Young University Studies* 19 (1978): 41-78; also in Nibley, *Mormonism and Early Christianity*. 45-99. Salt Lake City: Deseret Book and F.A.R.M.S., 1987. [Ritual/Liturgy/Worship]

O'Connell, Laurence J., *The Book of Ceremonies*. Milwaukee: Bruce, 1943. [Ritual/Liturgy/Worship]

Oesterley, William O. E. "Early Hebrew Festival Rituals." In *Myth and Ritual*, edited by Samuel H. Hooke. 111-46. London: Oxford University Press, 1933. [Ritual/Liturgy/Worship]

Olsen, C. "The Closet, the House and the Sanctuary." *Christian Century* 98 (1981): 1285-89. [Ritual/Liturgy/Worship]

Otto, Eberhard. *Das ägyptische Mundöffnungsritual*. 2 vols. Wiesbaden: Harrassowitz, 1960. [Ritual/Liturgy/Worship]

Otto, Eberhard. *Gott und Mensch nach den ägyptischen Tempelinschriften der griechisch-römischen Zeit*. Heidelberg: Winter, 1964. [Ritual/Liturgy/Worship]

Pelletier, André. "Une particularité du rituel des 'pains d'oblation' conservée par la Septante (Lev. xxiv 8 & Ex. xxv 30)." *VT* 17 (1967): 364-67. [Ritual/Liturgy/Worship]

Petuchowski, Jacob J., ed. *Contributions to the Scientific Study of Jewish Liturgy*. New York: KTAV, 1970. [Ritual/Liturgy/Worship]

Power, David, ed. *Liturgy and Human Passage*. New York: Seabury, 1979. [Ritual/Liturgy/Worship]

Powers, J. M., and E. Kilmartin "Liturgical Theology." *Worship* 50 (July 1976): 307-15. [Ritual/Liturgy/Worship]

Poznanski, L. "À propos de la collation du nom dans le monde antique." *RHR* 194 (October 1978): 113-27. [Ritual/Liturgy/Worship]

Rattray, Susan. "Worship." In *Harper's Bible Dictionary*, 1143-47. [Ritual/Liturgy/Worship]

Reik, Theodor. *Mystery on the Mountain: The Drama of the Sinai Revelation*. New York: Harper and Row, 1959. [Ritual/Liturgy/Worship]

Reymond, Eve A. E. "Worship of the Ancestor Gods at Edfu." *Chronique d'Égypte* 38 (1963): 49-70. [Ritual/Liturgy/Worship]

Ridderbos, N. H. *Psalmen en Cultus.* Kampen: Kok, 1950. [Ritual/Liturgy/Worship]

Robertson, N. "The Ritual Background of the Dying God in Cyprus and Syro-Palestine." *Harvard Theological Review* 75 (July 1982): 313-59. [Ritual/Liturgy/Worship]

Roche de Coppens, Peter. *The Nature and Use of Ritual for Spiritual Attainment.* St. Paul: Llewellyn, 1985. [Ritual/Liturgy/Worship]

Rowley, Harold H. "Ritual and the Hebrew Prophets." *Journal of Semitic Studies* 1 (1956): 338-60. [Ritual/Liturgy/Worship]

Rowley, Harold H. *Worship in Ancient Israel.* Philadelphia: Fortress, 1967. [Ritual/Liturgy/Worship]

Rubenstein, Shmuel L. *The Service in the Beis HaMikdosh.* New York: Rubenstein, 1975. [Ritual/Liturgy/Worship]

Sabourin, Léopold. "Liturgie du Sanctuaire et de la Tente Véritable (Heb. viii, 2)." *NTS* 18 (1971-72): 87-90. [Ritual/Liturgy/Worship]

Sabourin, Léopold. "Sacrificium ut liturgia in Epistula ad Hebraeos." *Verbum Domini* 46 (1968): 235-58. [Ritual/Liturgy/Worship]

Safrai, Shmuel. "The Duty of Pilgrimage to Jerusalem and Its Performance during the Period of the Second Temple" (in Hebrew). *Zion* 25 (1960): 67-84. [Ritual/Liturgy/Worship]

Safrai, Shmuel. "Pilgrimage, Second Temple Period." In *Encyclopaedia Judaica* 13:510-14. [Ritual/Liturgy/Worship]

Safrai, Shmuel. "Pilgrimage to Jerusalem at the End of the Second Temple Period." In *Studies on the Jewish Background of the New Testament.* 12-21. Assen: van Gorcum, 1969. [Ritual/Liturgy/Worship]

Safrai, Shmuel. "Pilgrimage to the Temple at the Time of the Second Temple." *Emmanuel: Bulletin of Religious Thought and Research in Israel* 5 (1975): 51-62. [Ritual/Liturgy/Worship]

Safrai, Shmuel. *Pilgrimages during the Second Temple Period* (in Hebrew). Jerusalem: Hebrew University, 1958. [Ritual/Liturgy/Worship]

Safrai, Shmuel. "Pilgrims in Jerusalem in Second Temple Times" (in Hebrew). In *Jerusalem—the Holy City and the Temple.* 98-110. Jerusalem: Mossad Harav Kook and Jerusalem Municipality, 1977. [Ritual/Liturgy/Worship]

Safrai, Shmuel. *Pilgrims to Jerusalem during the Time of the Second Temple* (in Hebrew). Jerusalem: Ministry of Education and Culture, 1976. [Ritual/Liturgy/Worship]

Safrai, Shmuel. "The Ritual in the Second Temple." In *Sefer Yerushalayim,* edited by Michael Avi-Yonah. 369-91. Jerusalem and Tel-Aviv: Bialik Institute, 1956. [Ritual/Liturgy/Worship]

Safrai, Shmuel. *Wallfahrt im Zeitalter des zweiten Tempels.* Neukirchen-Vluyn: Neukirchener, 1981. [Ritual/Liturgy/Worship]

Schürer, Emil. "Priesthood and Temple Worship." In *The History of the Jewish People in the Age of Jesus Christ (175 B. C. - A. D. 135)*, edited and revised by Geza Vermes and Fergus Millar. 2 vols., 2:237-313. Edinburgh: Clark, 1973-79. [Ritual/Liturgy/Worship]

Segelberg, E. "The Ordination of the Mandaean *tarmida* and Its Relation to Jewish and Early Christian Ordination Rites." In *Studia Patristica*, vol. 10, edited by F. L. Cross. 419-25. Berlin: Akademie, 1970. [Ritual/Liturgy/Worship]

Shaughnessy, James D., ed. *The Roots of Ritual.* Grand Rapids: Eerdmans, 1973. [Ritual/Liturgy/Worship]

Shepherd, M. H. "Origin of the Church's Liturgy." *Studia Liturgica* 1 (1962): 83-100. [Ritual/Liturgy/Worship]

Shohat, A. "Pilgrimages to Jerusalem (up to the End of the Second Temple)" (in Hebrew). In *Jerusalem—Quarterly Devoted to the Study of Jerusalem and Its History*, vol. 1, pp. 21-37. Jerusalem: Mossad Harav Kook, 1948. [Ritual/Liturgy/Worship]

Smith, Jonathan Z. "The Bare Facts of Ritual." *History of Religions* 20/1-2 (1980): 112-27. [Ritual/Liturgy/Worship]

Snaith, Norman H. "The Sprinkling of Blood." *ET* 82 (1970-71): 23-24. [Ritual/Liturgy/Worship]

Snijders, L. A. "Het gebed naar de tempel toe: Over gebedsrichting in het Oude Testament." *Nederlands Theologisch Tijdschrift.* 19 (1964-65): 1-14. [Ritual/Liturgy/Worship]

Stricker, B. H. "De Pythagoreische Liturgie." *Oudheidkundige mededeelingen uit het rijksmuseum van oudheden te Leiden* 13 (1950): 72-117. [Ritual/Liturgy/Worship]

Swanston, H. F. G. "Liturgy as Paradise and Parousia." *Scottish Journal of Theology* 36 (1983): 505-19. [Ritual/Liturgy/Worship]

Thiering, B. E. "Qumran Initiation and New Testament Baptism." *NTS* 27 (October 1981): 615-31. [Ritual/Liturgy/Worship]

Thureau-Dangin, F. *Rituels accadiens.* Paris: Leroux, 1921. [Ritual/Liturgy/Worship]

Timpe, R. L. "Ritualizations and Ritualisms in Religious Development: A Psychosocial Perspective." *Journal of Psychological Theology* 11 (1983): 311-17. [Ritual/Liturgy/Worship]

Tippett, A. R. "Initiation Rites and Functional Substitutes." *Practical Anthropology* 10 (1963): 66-70. [Ritual/Liturgy/Worship]

Trathen, D. A. "Christian Initiation." *St. Mark's Review* 99 (1979): 1-31. [Ritual/Liturgy/Worship]

Turner, Victor W. "Center Out There: Pilgrim's Goal." *History of Religions* 12 (February 1973): 191-230. [Ritual/Liturgy/Worship]

Turner, Victor W. *The Ritual Process: Structure and Anti-Structure*. Chicago: Aldine, 1969. [Ritual/Liturgy/Worship]

Turner, Victor W. "Ritual, Tribal and Catholic." *Worship* 50 (November 1976): 504-26. [Ritual/Liturgy/Worship]

Turner, Victor W., ed. *Celebration: Studies in Festivity and Ritual.* Washington D.C.: Smithsonian Institution, 1982. [Ritual/Liturgy/Worship]

Uffenheimer, Benyamin. "On the Question of Centralisation of Worship in Ancient Israel." *Tarbiz* 28 (1958): 138-53. [Ritual/Liturgy/Worship]

Van Buren, E. (Elizabeth) D. (Douglas). "A Ritual Sequence." *Orientalia* 25 (1956): 39-41. [Ritual/Liturgy/Worship]

Vattioni, Francesco, ed. *Sangue e Antropologia nella Liturgia. Atti della IV Settimana (Roma, 21-26 Novembre 1983).* 3 vols. Rome: Ediz. Pia Unione Preziossimo Sangue, 1984. [Ritual/Liturgy/Worship]

Vieyra, M. "Rites de purification Hittites." *RHR* 119 (1939): 121-53. [Ritual/Liturgy/Worship]

Vizedom, Monika. *Rites and Relationships: Rites of Passage and Contemporary Anthropology*. Beverly Hills: Sage, 1976. [Ritual/Liturgy/Worship]

von Wellnitz, Marcus. "The Catholic Liturgy and the Mormon Temple." *Brigham Young University Studies* 21 (1981): 3-35. [Ritual/Liturgy/Worship]

Wainwright, Geoffrey. "Baptismal Eucharist before Nicaea: An Essay in Liturgical History." *Studia Liturgica* 4 (1965): 9-36. [Ritual/Liturgy/Worship]

Wainwright, Geoffrey. *Christian Initiation*. Richmond: John Knox, 1969. [Ritual/Liturgy/Worship]

Wainwright, Geoffrey. "Rites and Ceremonies of Christian Initiation: Developments in the Past." *Studia Liturgica* 10 (1974): 2-24. [Ritual/Liturgy/Worship]

Wellhausen, Julius. "History of the Ordinances of Worship," In Wellhausen, *Prolegomenon to the History of Ancient Israel.* New York: Meridian, 1957 (originally published in 1878). 17-167. [Ritual/Liturgy/Worship]

Widengren, Geo. *The Ascension of the Apostle and the Heavenly Book (King and Saviour III).* Uppsala: Lundequistska Bokhandeln, 1950. [Ritual/Liturgy/Worship]

Wijngaards, J. N. M. "The Adoption of Pagan Rites in Early Israelite Liturgy." In *God's Word among Men, Papers in Honor of Fr. Joseph Putz,* edited by G. Gispert Sauch. 247-56. Delhi: Vidyajyoti, 1973. [Ritual/Liturgy/Worship]

Wilkinson, John D. "Jewish Influences on the Early Christian Rite of Jerusalem." *Le Museon* 92/3-4 (1979): 347-59. [Ritual/Liturgy/Worship]

Wright, David P. *The Disposal of Impurity: Elimination Rites in the Bible and in Hittite and Mesopotamian Literature.* Atlanta: Scholars, 1987. [Ritual/Liturgy/Worship]

Yarnold, E. J. "The Ceremonies of Initiation in the *De Sacramentis* and *De Mysteriis* of S. Ambrose." In *Studia Patristica*, edited by F. L. Cross. 10:453-63. Berlin: Akademie-Verlag, 1970. [Ritual/Liturgy/Worship]

Young, Frank W. *Initiation Ceremonies*. Indianapolis: Bobbs-Merrill, 1965. [Ritual/Liturgy/Worship]

Zeitlin, Solomon. "The Temple and Worship." *JQR* 51 (1960-61): 209-41. [Ritual/Liturgy/Worship]

Sacred Space

Böhl, Felix, "Über das Verhältnis von Shetija-Stein und Nabel der Welt in der Kosmologonie der Rabbinen." *ZDMG* 124 (1974): 253-70. [Sacred Space]

Bokser, Baruch M. "Approaching Sacred Space." *Harvard Theological Review* 78/3-4 (1985): 279-99. [Sacred Space]

Caspari, Wilhelm. "*Tabur* (Nabel)." *ZDMG* 86 (1933): 49-65. [Sacred Space]

Corbin, Henry. *Temple et contemplation*. Paris: Flammarion, 1980; also in English as *Temple and Contemplation*, translated by Philip Sherrard. London: Islamic, 1986. [Sacred Space]

Eliade, Mircea. "Centre du monde, temple, maison." In *Le symbolisme cosmique des monuments religieux*, edited by Guiseppi Tucci. 57-82. Rome: Istituto Italiano par il Medio ed Estremo Oriente, 1957; also in a revised version as "Architecture sacrée et symbolisme." In *Mircea Eliade*, edited by Constantin Tacou. 141-56. Paris: L'Herne, 1978; also in English as "Sacred Architecture and Symbolism." In *Symbolism, the Sacred, and the Arts*, edited by Diana Apostolos-Cappadona. 105-29. New York: Crossroad, 1985. [Sacred Space]

Friedman, Irving. "The Sacred Space of Judaism." *Parabola* 3/1 (1978): 20-23. [Sacred Space]

Gawlikowski, Michel. "The Sacred Space in Ancient Arabic Religions." In *Studies in the History and Archaeology of Jordan 1*, edited by Adnan Hadidi. 301-3. Amman: Department of Antiquities, 1982. [Sacred Space]

Graves, Jennifer. "The Greek Omphalos: Its Symbolism and Significance." M.S. thesis, Brigham Young University, 1984. [Sacred Space]

Hofer Josef. "Zur Phänomenologie der Sakralraumer und sein Symbolismus im Alten Orient mit Berücksichtigung der Bauformen." Ph.D. diss., University of Vienna, 1969. [Sacred Space]

James, Edwin O. *From Cave to Cathedral: Temple and Shrines of Pre-historic, Classical, and Early Christian Times*. London: Thames and Hudson, 1965. [Sacred Space]

Lundquist, John M. "The Common Temple Ideology of the Ancient Near East." In *The Temple in Antiquity*, edited by Truman G. Madsen. 53-76. Provo: Brigham Young University Press, 1984. [Sacred Space]

Lundquist, John M. "The Legitimizing Role of the Temple in the Origin of the State." *SBLSP* 21 (1982): 271-97. [Sacred Space]

Lundquist, John M. "Studies on the Temple in the Ancient Near East." Ph.D. diss., University of Michigan, 1983. [Sacred Space]

Lundquist, John M. "What Is a Temple? A Preliminary Typology." In *The Quest for the Kingdom of God: Studies in Honor of George E. Mendenhall*, edited by H. B. Huffmon, F. A. Spina, and A. R. W. Green. 205-19. [Sacred Space]

Michel, O. "*naós.*" In *Theological Dictionary of the New Testament*, edited by G. Kittel. 880-90. Grand Rapids: Eerdmans, 1967. [Sacred Space]

Nibley, Hugh W. "The Idea of the Temple in History." *Millennial Star* 120 (1958): 228-37, 247-49; reprinted as "What Is a Temple." In Nibley, *Mormonism and Early Christianity*. 355-90. Salt Lake City: Deseret Book and F.A.R.M.S., 1987. [Sacred Space]

Nibley, Hugh W. "What Is a Temple? The Idea of the Temple in History." In Nibley, *Mormonism and Early Christianity*. 355-90. Salt Lake City: Deseret Book and F.A.R.M.S., 1987. [Sacred Space]

Nissen, Heinrich. *Orientation: Studien zur Geschichte der Religion*. Berlin: Weidmannsche, 1906. [Sacred Space]

Parry, Donald W. "The Garden of Eden: Sacred Space, Sanctuary, Temple of God." *Explorations: A Journal for Adventurous Thought* 5/4 (Summer 1987): 83-107. [Sacred Space]

Pummer, Reinhard. "Untersuchungen zur Omphalos-Vorstellung im alten Testament und im alten Orient." Ph.D. diss., Universität-Wien, Katholische Theologische Fakultät, 1974. [Sacred Space]

Raglan, Fitzroy R. S. *The Temple and the House*. New York: Norton, 1964. [Sacred Space]

Roscher, Wilhelm H. *Omphalos: Eine philologisch-archäologisch-volkskundliche Abhandlung über die Vorstellungen der Griechen und anderer Völker vom 'Nabel der Erde.'* In *Abhandlungen der philologisch-historischen Klasse der Königlichen sächsischen Gesellschaft der Wissenschaften* 29/9 (1913); also reprinted in Roscher, *Omphalos*. Hildesheim: Olms, 1974. [Sacred Space]

Roscher, Wilhelm H. *Der Omphalosgedanke bei verschiedenen Völkern, besonders den semitischen*. In *Berichte über die Verhandlungen der Sächsischen Gesellschaft der Wissenschaften zu Leipzig. Philologisch-historische Klasse* 70/2 (1918); also reprinted in Roscher, *Omphalos*. Hildesheim: Olms, 1974. [Sacred Space]

Talmon, Shemaryahu. "The 'Navel of the Earth' and the Comparative Method." In *Scripture in History and Theology: Essays in Honor of J. Coert Rylaarsdam*, edited by Arthur Merrill and Thomas Overholt. 243-68. Pittsburgh: Pickwick, 1977. [Sacred Space]

Terrien, Samuel. "The Omphalos Myth and Hebrew Religion." *VT* 20 (1970): 315-38. [Sacred Space]

Terrien, Samuel. *The Elusive Presence, Toward a New Biblical Theology.* New York: Harper & Row, 1978. [Sacred Space]

Turner, Harold W. "The New Temple of the New Testament." In Turner, *From Temple to Meetinghouse: The Phenomenology and Theology of Places of Worship.* 106-30. The Hague: Mouton, 1979. [Sacred Space]

Widengren, Geo. "Der Kultplatz." In Widengren, *Religionsphänomenologie.* 328-59. Berlin: de Gruyter, 1969. [Sacred Space]

Wright, G. R. H. "Joseph's Grave under the Tree by the Omphalos at Shechem." *VT* 22 (October 1972): 476-86. [Sacred Space]

Sacred Vestments

Ancessi, Victor A. *L'Égypte et Moïse.* Paris: Leroux, 1875. [Sacred Vestments]

Blumenthal, Israel C. *Bigde Kehunah.* Jerusalem: Orot, 1950. [Sacred Vestments]

Braun, Joseph. *Die liturgische Gewandung im Occident und Orient nach Ursprung und Entwicklung, Verwendung und Symbolik.* Freiburg im Breisgau: Herder, 1907. [Sacred Vestments]

Braun, Joseph. *Die pontificalen Gewänder des Abendlandes nach ihrer geschichtlichen Entwicklung.* Freiburg im Breisgau: Herder, 1893. [Sacred Vestments]

Braun, Joseph. *Die priesterlichen Gewänder des Abendlandes nach ihrer geschichtlichen Entwicklung.* Freiburg im Breisgau: Herder, 1897. [Sacred Vestments]

Chrysostomos, Archimandrite. "Historiographical Problematics in the Study of the Origin of Liturgical Vesture." *Greek Orthodox Theological Review* 26 (1981): 87-96. [Sacred Vestments]

Clapton, Edward. *The Precious Stones of the Bible—Descriptive and Symbolical,* 2d ed. London: Simpkin, Marshall, Hamilton, Kent, 1899. [Sacred Vestments]

Cooper, Charles W. *The Precious Stones of the Bible: With an Account of the Breastplate of the High Priest, the Ephod and Urim and Thummim.* London: Allenson, 1924. [Sacred Vestments]

Dean, Beryl. *Embroidery in Religion and Ceremonial.* London: Batsford, 1981. [Sacred Vestments]

Dolby, Anastasia M. *Church Embroidery, Ancient and Modern.* London: Chapman and Hall, 1867. [Sacred Vestments]

Dolby, Anastasia M. *Church Vestments: Their Origin, Use, and Ornament.* London: Chapman and Hall, 1868. [Sacred Vestments]

Elliger, Karl. "Ephod und Choschen: Ein Beitrag zur Entwicklungsgeschichte des hohepriesterlichen Ornats." *VT* 8 (1958): 19-35. [Sacred Vestments]

Foote, Theodore C. "The Ephod: Its Form and Use." Ph.D. diss., Johns Hopkins University, 1902. [Sacred Vestments]

Fortescue, Adrian. *The Vestments of the Roman Rite.* New York: Paulist, 1915. [Sacred Vestments]

González, Arthur E. J. "Byzantine Imperial Paradigm and Eastern Liturgical Vesture." *Greek Orthodox Theological Review* 17 (1972): 255-67. [Sacred Vestments]

Goodenough, Erwin R. "Symbolism of Dress." In Goodenough, *Jewish Symbols in the Greco-Roman Period.* 13 vols., 9:124-74. New York: Pantheon, 1953-68. [Sacred Vestments]

Grimme, Hubert. "Ephodentscheid und Prophetenrede." In *Orientalistische Studien: Fritz Hommel zum sechzigsten Geburtstag am 31. Juli 1914 gewidmet von Freunden, Kollegen und Schülern.* 316-27. Leipzig: Hinrichs, 1917. [Sacred Vestments]

Haran, Menahem. "The Ephod According to Biblical Sources." *Tarbiz* 24 (1955): 380-91. [Sacred Vestments]

Haran, Menahem. "Priestly Vestments." In *Encyclopaedia Judaica* 13:1063-69. [Sacred Vestments]

Haulotte, Edgar. *Symbolique du vêtement selon la Bible.* Paris: Aubier, 1966. [Sacred Vestments]

Higgins, Francis C. *The Apron: Its Traditions, History, and Secret Significances.* New York: Francis C. Higgins, 1914. [Sacred Vestments]

Hogg, James E. "The Inscription on Aaron's Head-dress." *JTS* 28 (1927): 287-88. [Sacred Vestments]

Hogg, James E. "A Note on Two Points in Aaron's Headdress." *JTS* 26 (1925): 72-75. [Sacred Vestments]

Hurvitz, Avi. "The Garments of Aharon and His Sons According to 1QM VII 9-10." In *Studies in Bible and the Ancient Near East: Presented to Samuel E. Loewenstamm on His Seventieth Birthday,* edited by Yitschak Avishur and Joshua Blau, 139-44. Jerusalem: Rubinstein, 1978. [Sacred Vestments]

Legg, John W. *Church Ornaments and Their Civil Antecedents.* Cambridge: Cambridge University Press, 1917. [Sacred Vestments]

Ludin Jansen, H. "The Consecration in the Eighth Chapter of Testamentum Levi." In *The Sacral Kingship/La Regalità Sacra.* 356-65. Leiden: Brill, 1959. [Sacred Vestments]

Macalister, Robert A. S. *Ecclesiastical Vestments: Their Development and History.* London: Stock, 1896. [Sacred Vestments]

May, Herbert G. "Ephod and Ariel." *AJSL* 56 (1939): 44-69. [Sacred Vestments]

Mayo, Janet. *A History of Ecclesiastical Dress.* New York: Holmes and Meier, 1984. [Sacred Vestments]

Norris, Herbert. *Church Vestments, Their Origin and Development.* London: Dent, 1949. [Sacred Vestments]

Oppenheim, A. Leo. "The Golden Garments of the Gods." *JNES* 8 (1949): 172-93. [Sacred Vestments]

Ostler, Blake. "Clothed Upon: A Unique Aspect of Christian Antiquity." *Brigham Young University Studies* 22 (1982): 31-45. [Sacred Vestments]

Parrot, André. "Cérémonie de la main et réinvestiture." In *Studia Mariana*, edited by André Parrot. 37-50. Leiden: Brill, 1950. [Sacred Vestments]

Rolfe, Clapton C. *The Ancient Use of Liturgical Colours.* Oxford: Parker, 1879. [Sacred Vestments]

Roulin, Eugène A. *Vestments and Vesture: A Manual of Liturgical Art,* translated by Dom J. McCann. Westminster, MD: Newman, 1950. [Sacred Vestments]

Schemel, Siegfried. *Die Kleidung der Juden im Zeitalter der Mischnah, nebst einem Anhange: Die Priesterkleidung.* Berlin: Itzkowski, 1912. [Sacred Vestments]

Scholem, Gershom G. *Jewish Gnosticism, Merkabah Mysticism, and Talmudic Tradition,* 2d ed., 59-61. New York: Jewish Theological Seminary of America, 1965. [Sacred Vestments]

Sellin, Ernst. *Das israelitische Ephod.* Giessen: Töpelmann, 1906. [Sacred Vestments]

Sellin, Ernst. "Ephod and Terafim." *JPOS* 14 (1934): 185-93. [Sacred Vestments]

Sellin, Ernst. "Noch einmal der alttestamentliche Efod." *JPOS* 17 (1937): 236-51. [Sacred Vestments]

Simon M. "On Josephus, Wars, V, 5, 7." *JQR* 13 (1901): 547-48. [Sacred Vestments]

Smith, Jonathan Z. "The Garments of Shame." In *History of Religions* 5 (1965): 217-38. [Sacred Vestments]

Tidwell, N. L. "The Linen Ephod: 1 Sam II 18 and 2 Sam VI 14." *VT* 24 (1974): 505-7. [Sacred Vestments]

Widengren, Geo. "Royal Ideology and the Testaments of the Twelve Patriarchs." In *Promise and Fulfillment: Essays Presented to S. H. Hooke*, edited by F. F. Bruce. 202-12. Edinburgh: Clark, 1963. [Sacred Vestments]

Sacrifice and Offerings

Abba, Raymond. "Origin and Significance of Hebrew Sacrifice." *BTB* 7 (1977): 123-38. [Sacrifice/Offerings]

Barta, Winfried. *Aufbau und Bedeutung der altägyptischen Opferformel.* Glückstadt: Augustin, 1968. [Sacrifice/Offerings]

Baumgarten, Joseph M. "The Laws of 'Orlah and First Fruits in the Light of Jubilees, the Qumran Writings, and Targum Ps. Jonathan." *JJS* 38 (Autumn 1987): 195-202. [Sacrifice/Offerings]

Baumgarten, Joseph M. "On the Non-Literal Use of maʿăśēr/dekatē." *JBL* 103 (1984): 245-51. [Sacrifice/Offerings]

Bertholet, Alfred. "Zum Verständnis des alttestamentlichen Opfergedankens." *JBL* 49 (1930): 218-33. [Sacrifice/Offerings]

Blome, Friedrich. *Die Opfermaterie in Babylonien und Israel.* Rome: Pontifical Biblical Institute, 1934. [Sacrifice/Offerings]

Brichto, H. C. "On Slaughter and Sacrifice, Blood and Atonement." *HUCA* 47 (1976): 19-55. [Sacrifice/Offerings]

Brown, James R. *Temple and Sacrifice in Rabbinic Judaism.* Evanston: Seabury-Western Theological Seminary, 1963. [Sacrifice/Offerings]

Brown, John Pairman. "The Sacrificial Cult and Its Critique in Greek and Hebrew." *Journal of Semitic Studies* 24 (1979): 159-73; 25 (1980): 1-21. [Sacrifice/Offerings]

Büchler, Adolph. "Private Sacrifices before the Jewish Day of Atonement." *Expositor* 22 (1911): 239-43. [Sacrifice/Offerings]

Canaan, Von T. "Das Opfer in palästinischen Sitten und Gebräuchen." *ZAW* 74 (1963): 31-44. [Sacrifice/Offerings]

Caquot, André. "Un sacrifice expiatoire à Ras Shamra." *Revue d'Histoire et de philosophie religieuses* 42 (1962): 201-11. [Sacrifice/Offerings]

Charbel, Antonio. "Introdução a Liturgia Sacrifical da Antiga e da Nova Aliança." *Revista de Cultura Teologica* 2 (1962): 41-52. [Sacrifice/Offerings]

Charbel, Antonio. "Offerta di prodotti vegetali nei sacrifici šᵉlāmîm." *Euntes Docete* 26 (1973): 398-403. [Sacrifice/Offerings]

Charbel, Antonio. "Positione degli šᵉlāmîm nella Scrittura." *Salesianum* 34 (1974): 431-42. [Sacrifice/Offerings]

Charbel, Antonio. "Il sacrificio di comunione presso i Greci." *Bibbia e Oriente* 16 (1974): 263-73. [Sacrifice/Offerings]

Charbel, Antonio. *Zeḇak Šᵉlāmîm: Sacrificio pacifico nei suoi riti e nel suo significato religioso e figurativo.* Jerusalem: n.p., 1967. [Sacrifice/Offerings]

Chelhod, Joseph. *Le sacrifice chez les Arabes; recherches sur l'évolution, la nature et la fonction des rites sacrificiels en Arabie Occidentale.* Paris: Presses universitaires de France, 1955. [Sacrifice/Offerings]

Chytraeus, David. *On Sacrifice: A Reformation Treatise in Biblical Theology.* St. Louis: Concordia, 1962. [Sacrifice/Offerings]

Collins, John J. "The Meaning of Sacrifice: A Contrast of Methods." *Biblical Research* 22 (1977): 19-34. [Sacrifice/Offerings]

Conybeare, Fred. "Les sacrifices d'animaux dans les anciennes églises chrétiennes." *RHR.* 44 (1901): 108-14. [Sacrifice/Offerings]

Cook, S. A. "The Theory of Sacrifice." *JTS* 22 (1921): 327-47. [Sacrifice/Offerings]

Dalman, Gustaf. "Der Felsen als Fundament des Altars." In *Neue Petra-Forschungen und der heilige Felsen von Jerusalem*, edited by Gustaf Dalman, 137-45. Leipzig: Hinrichs, 1912. [Sacrifice/Offerings]

Daly, Robert J. *Christian Sacrifice.* Washington, D.C.: Catholic University of America Press, 1978. [Sacrifice/Offerings]

Daly, Robert J. "New Testament Concept of Christian Sacrificial Activity." *BTB* 8 (1978): 99-107. [Sacrifice/Offerings]

Daly, Robert J. *The Origins of the Christian Doctrine of Sacrifice.* Philadelphia: Fortess, 1978. [Sacrifice/Offerings]

Daraki, Maria. "Aspects du sacrifice dionysiaque." *RHR* 197 (1980): 131-57. [Sacrifice/Offerings]

Davies, Douglas. "An Interpretation of Sacrifice in Leviticus." *ZAW* 89 (1977): 387-99. [Sacrifice/Offerings]

Davies, Douglas. "Sacrifice in Theology and Anthropology." *Scottish Journal of Theology* 35 (1982): 351-58. [Sacrifice/Offerings]

De Guglielmo, A. "A Sacrifice in the Ugaritic Texts." *CBQ* 17 (1955): 196-216. [Sacrifice/Offerings]

Detienne, Marcel, and J. P. Vernant. *La cuisine du sacrifice en pays grec.* Paris: Gallimard, 1979. [Sacrifice/Offerings]

Devries, L. F. "Incense Altars from the Period of the Judges and Their Significance." Ph.D. diss., Southern Baptist Theological Seminary, 1975. [Sacrifice/Offerings]

Dobbie, R. "Deuteronomy and the Prophetic Attitude to Sacrifice." *Scottish Journal of Theology* 12 (1959): 68-82. [Sacrifice/Offerings]

Durand, X. "Du rituel sacrificiel au sacrifice biblique." *Point* 24 (1977): 31-61. [Sacrifice/Offerings]

Dussaud, René. *Le sacrifice en Israel et chez les Phéniciens.* Paris: Levoux, 1914. [Sacrifice/Offerings]

Dussaud, René. *Les origines cananéennes du sacrifice israelite.* Paris: Leroux, 1921. [Sacrifice/Offerings]

Eisenstein, J. D. "Sacrifices." In *A Digest of Jewish Laws and Customs* (in Hebrew). 376-71. Tel-Aviv: Shoh, 1975. [Sacrifice/Offerings]

Feuchtwang, D. "Das Wasseropfer und die damit verbundenen Zeremonien." *MGWJ* 54 (1910): 535-52, 713-29; 55 (1911): 43-63. [Sacrifice/Offerings]

Fevrier, J. G. "L'évolution des rites sacrificiels à Carthage." *Bulletin archéologique* (1959-60): 22-27. [Sacrifice/Offerings]

Fevrier, J. G. "Les rites sacrificiels chez les Hébreux et à Carthage." *REJ* 4/3 (1964): 7-18. [Sacrifice/Offerings]

Fullerton, Kemper. "The Anti-sacrificial Psalms." In *Essays in Modern Theology and Related Subjects*. 49-63. New York: Scribner, 1911. [Sacrifice/Offerings]

Gadegaard, N. H. "On the So-Called Burnt Offering Altar in the Old Testament." *PEQ* 110 (1978): 35-45. [Sacrifice/Offerings]

Galling, Kurt. "Altar." In *The Interpreter's Dictionary of the Bible* 1:96-100. [Sacrifice/Offerings]

Galling, Kurt. *Der Altar in den Kulturen des alten Orients*. Berlin: Curtius, 1925. [Sacrifice/Offerings]

Galling, Kurt. "Incense Altar." In *The Interpreter's Dictionary of the Bible* 2:699-700. [Sacrifice/Offerings]

Gaster, Moses. "Sacrifice (Jewish)." In *Encyclopaedia of Religion and Ethics* 11:24-29. [Sacrifice/Offerings]

Gaster, Theodor H. "Sacrifices and Offerings." In *The Interpreter's Dictionary of the Bible* 4:147-59. [Sacrifice/Offerings]

Gates, Owen H. "The Relation of Priests to Sacrifices before the Exile." *JBL* 27 (1908): 67-92. [Sacrifice/Offerings]

Gayford, Sydney C. *Sacrifice and Priesthood, Jewish and Christian*. London: Methuen, 1924. [Sacrifice/Offerings]

Gerkan, Armin von. *Der Altar des Artemis-Tempels in Magnesia am Mäander*. Berlin: Schoetz, 1929. [Sacrifice/Offerings]

Goodsir, R. "Animal Sacrifice: Delusion or Deliverance?" *Studia Biblica* 1 (1978): 157-60. [Sacrifice/Offerings]

Gray, George B. "The Heavenly Temple and the Heavenly Altar." *Expositor* (1908-A): 385-402, 530-46. [Sacrifice/Offerings]

Gray, George B. *Sacrifice in the Old Testament*. Oxford: Clarendon, 1925; repr. New York, KTAV, 1971. [Sacrifice/Offerings]

Gray, John. "Cultic Affinities between Israel and Ras Shamra." *ZAW* 62 (1949-50): 207-20. [Sacrifice/Offerings]

Green, Alberto R. W. *The Role of Human Sacrifice in the Ancient Near East*. Missoula, MT: Scholars, 1975. [Sacrifice/Offerings]

Groot, Johannes de. *Die Altäre des salomonischen Tempelhofes*. Stuttgart: Kohlhammer, 1924. [Sacrifice/Offerings]

Guttman, A. "The End of the Jewish Sacrificial Cult." *HUCA* 38 (1967): 137-48. [Sacrifice/Offerings]

Hänel, John. "Das Recht des Opferschlachtens in der chronistischen Literatur." *ZAW* 55 (1937): 46-67. [Sacrifice/Offerings]

Haran, Menahem. "The Passover Sacrifice." In *Studies in the Religion of Ancient Israel*. 86-116. Leiden: Brill, 1972. [Sacrifice/Offerings]

Haran, Menahem. "*Zeḇaḥ Hayyamîm*." *VT* 19 (1969): 11-22. [Sacrifice/Offerings]

Harper, A. "The Prophets and Sacrifice." *Expositor* (1894-A): 241-53. [Sacrifice/Offerings]

Hecht, Richard D. "Studies on Sacrifice, 1970-1980." *Religious Studies Review* 8 (1982): 253-59. [Sacrifice/Offerings]

Henninger, Joseph. "Ist der sogenannte Nilus-Bericht eine brauchbare religionsgeschichtliche Quelle?" *Anthropos* 50 (1955): 81-148. [Sacrifice/Offerings]

Henninger, Joseph. "Menschenopfer bei den Arabern." *Anthropos* 53 (1958): 721-805. [Sacrifice/Offerings]

Henninger, Joseph. "Das Opfer in den altsüdarabischen Hochkulturen." *Anthropos* 37-40 (1942-45): 779-810. [Sacrifice/Offerings]

Henninger, Joseph. "Le sacrifice chez les Arabes." *Ethnos* 13/1-2 (1948): 1-16. [Sacrifice/Offerings]

Henninger, Joseph. "Über Menschenopfer bei den vorislamischen Arabern." In *Akten des 24. Internationalen Orientalisten-Kongresses, München, 18. August bis 4. September 1957*, edited by Herbert Franke. 244-46. Wiesbaden: Harrassowitz, 1957. [Sacrifice/Offerings]

Henninger, Joseph. "Die unblutige Tierweihe der vorislamischen Araber in ethnologischer Sicht." *Paideuma* 4 (1950): 179-90. [Sacrifice/Offerings]

Hentschke, Richard. "Opfer, 2: Im AT." In *Die Religion in Geschichte und Gegenwart*, 3d ed. 6 vols., 4:1641-47. Tübingen: Mohr, 1960. [Sacrifice/Offerings]

Hicks, Frederick C. N. *The Fullness of Sacrifice*. London: Macmillan, 1930. [Sacrifice/Offerings]

Hubert, Henri. *Sacrifice, Its Nature and Function*. Chicago: University of Chicago Press, 1964. [Sacrifice/Offerings]

James, Edwin O. *Origins of Sacrifice*. Port Washington: Kennikat Press, 1971. [Sacrifice/Offerings]

Schwartz, Daniel R. "Priesthood, Temple, Sacrifices: Opposition and Spiritualization in the Late Second Temple Period." Ph.D. diss., Hebrew University, 1979. [Sacrifice/Offerings]

Jones, D. "The Cessation of Sacrifice after the Destruction of the Temple in 586 B.C." *JTS* 14 (1963): 12-31. [Sacrifice/Offerings]

Kagan, Aaron. ʿ*Avodat ha-Korbanot*. New York: Binah, 1978 or 1979. [Sacrifice/Offerings]

Kaufman, Asher S. "The Quest of Scientific Methods to Fix the Position of the Altar in the Temple" (in Hebrew). *Torah u-Mada* 4 (1974): 37-38. [Sacrifice/Offerings]

Kellermann, Diether. "ʾāsham." In *Theological Dictionary of the Old Testament* 1:429-37. [Sacrifice/Offerings]

Kidner, D. "Sacrifice: Metaphors and Meaning." *Tyndale Bulletin* 33 (1982): 119-36. [Sacrifice/Offerings]

Kidner, Frank D. *Sacrifice in the Old Testament.* London: Tyndale, 1952. [Sacrifice/Offerings]

Kiuchi, N. *The Purification Offering in the Priestly Literature.* Sheffield: JSOT, 1987. [Sacrifice/Offerings]

Langhe, Robert de. *Het Gouden Altaar in de Israelietische Eredienst.* Brussels: Paleis der Academiën, 1952. [Sacrifice/Offerings]

Lattey, C. J. "The Prophets and Sacrifice: A Study in Biblical Relativity." *JTS* 42 (1941): 155-65. [Sacrifice/Offerings]

Laughlin, John C. H. "A Study of the Motif of Holy Fire in the Old Testament." Ph.D. diss., Southern Baptist Theological Seminary, 1975. [Sacrifice/Offerings]

Leibovitch, J. "Une scène de sacrifice rituel chez les anciens Égyptiens." *JNES* 12 (1953): 59-60. [Sacrifice/Offerings]

Lerner, M. B. "The Daily Whole-Offering in the Temple" (in Hebrew). *Maḥanayim* 96 (1965): 28-31. [Sacrifice/Offerings]

Lesêtre, Henri. "Sacrifice." In *Dictionnaire de la Bible*, edited by F. Vigouroux. 5 vols., 5:1311-37. Paris: Letouzey and Ané, 1922. [Sacrifice/Offerings]

Levine, Baruch A. *In the Presence of the Lord.* Leiden: Brill, 1974. [Sacrifice/Offerings]

Lichtenberger, Hermann. "Atonement and Sacrifice in the Qumran Community." In *Approaches to Ancient Judaism*, edited by William S. Green. 159-71. Chico, CA: Scholars, 1980. [Sacrifice/Offerings]

Lods, Adolphe. "Éléments anciens et éléments modernes dans le rituel de sacrifice israelite." *Revue d'histoire et de philosophie religieuses* 8 (1928): 399-411. [Sacrifice/Offerings]

Luria, Ben Zion. "You Shall Break Down Their Altars." *Beth Mikra* 95/4 (1983): 313-19. [Sacrifice/Offerings]

Lyonnet, Stanislas, and Léopold Sabourin. *Sin, Redemption, and Sacrifice: A Biblical and Patristic Study.* Rome: Pontifical Biblical Institute, 1970. [Sacrifice/Offerings]

Macalister, R. (Robert) A. Stewart. "Sacrifice (Semitic)." In *Encyclopaedia of Religion and Ethics* 11:31-38. [Sacrifice/Offerings]

McCarthy, Dennis J. "Further Notes on the Symbolism of Blood and Sacrifice." *JBL* 92 (1973): 205-10. [Sacrifice/Offerings]

McCarthy, Dennis J. "The Symbolism of Blood and Sacrifice." *JBL* 88 (1969): 166-76. [Sacrifice/Offerings]

MacLaurin, E. C. B. *The Origin of the Hebrew Sacrificial System*. Sydney: Sydney and Melbourne, 1948. [Sacrifice/Offerings]

Maimonides, Moses. *Commentar zum Tractate Tamid: Arabischer Text mit verbesserter hebraeischer Uebersetzung nebst Anmerkungen*. Frankfort: Kauffmann, 1903. [Sacrifice/Offerings]

Mayer, R. "Zum Problem des Opfers unmittelbar nach der Zerstörung des zweiten Tempels." In *Fourth World Congress of Jewish Studies: Papers*. 209-12. Jerusalem: World Union of Jewish Studies, 1968. [Sacrifice/Offerings]

Medebielle, Alexis. *L'expiation dans l'Ancien et le Nouveau Testament*. Rome: Pontifical Biblical Institute, 1923. [Sacrifice/Offerings]

Medebielle, Alexis. "Le symbolisme du sacrifice expiatoire en Israël." *Biblica* 2 (1921): 141-69, 273-302. [Sacrifice/Offerings]

Mehrs, M. "A Consideration and Comparison of Sacrificial Terminology and Practice in Ancient Israel and Ugarit." *Near East Archaeological Society Bulletin* 15-16 (1980): 5-21. [Sacrifice/Offerings]

Metzinger, Adalbert. "Die Substitutionstheorie und das alttestamentliche Opfer mit besonderer Beruecksichtigung von Lev 17,11." *Biblica* 21 (1940): 159-87, 353-77. [Sacrifice/Offerings]

Meyers, Carol L. "Altar." In *Harper's Dictionary of the Bible*, 22-24. [Sacrifice/Offerings]

Milgrom, Jacob. "Akkadian Confirmation for the Meaning of the Term *tĕrûmâ*" (in Hebrew). *Tarbiz* 44 (1974-75): 189; also in Milgrom, *Studies in Cultic Theology and Terminology*. 171-72. Leiden: Brill, 1983. [Sacrifice/Offerings]

Milgrom, Jacob. "The Alleged Wave-Offering in Israel and the Ancient Near East." *IEJ* 22 (1972): 33-38; also in Milgrom, *Studies in Cultic Theology and Terminology*. 133-38. Leiden: Brill, 1983. [Sacrifice/Offerings]

Milgrom, Jacob. "The Biblical Diet Laws as an Ethical System." *Interpretation* 17 (1963): 288-301; also in Milgrom, *Studies in Cultic Theology and Terminology*. 104-18. Leiden: Brill, 1983. [Sacrifice/Offerings]

Milgrom, Jacob. "Concerning Jeremiah's Repudiation of Sacrifice." *ZAW* 89 (1977): 274-75; also in Milgrom, *Studies in Cultic Theology and Terminology*. 119-21. Leiden: Brill, 1983. [Sacrifice/Offerings]

Milgrom, Jacob. "The Cultic *Šĕgāgāh* and Its Influence in Psalms and Job." *JQR* 58 (1967): 115-25; also in Milgrom, *Studies in Cultic Theology and Terminology*. 122-32. Leiden: Brill, 1983. [Sacrifice/Offerings]

Milgrom, Jacob. "The Functions of the *Hatta't* Sacrifice" (in Hebrew; *English summary). *Tarbiz* 40 (1970-71): 1-8, *I. [Sacrifice/Offerings]

Milgrom, Jacob. "*Hattĕnûpâ*." In Milgrom, *Studies in Cultic Theology and Terminology*. 139-58. Leiden: Brill, 1983. [Sacrifice/Offerings]

Milgrom, Jacob. "Israel's Sanctuary: The Priestly 'Picture of Dorian Gray.'" *RB* 83 (1976): 390-99; also in Milgrom, *Studies in Cultic Theology and Terminology*. 75-84. Leiden: Brill, 1983. [Sacrifice/Offerings]

Milgrom, Jacob. "The Paradox of the Red Cow (Nu. xix)." *VT* 31 (1931): 62-72; also in Milgrom, *Studies in Cultic Theology and Terminology*. 85-95. Leiden: Brill, 1983. [Sacrifice/Offerings]

Milgrom, Jacob. "A Prolegomenon to Leviticus 17:11." *JBL* 90 (1971): 149-56; also in Milgrom, *Studies in Cultic Theology and Terminology*. 96-103. Leiden: Brill, 1983. [Sacrifice/Offerings]

Milgrom, Jacob. "Sacrifices and Offerings, OT." In *The Interpreter's Dictionary of the Bible*, supp. vol., 763-71. [Sacrifice/Offerings]

Milgrom, Jacob. "Sancta Contagion and Altar/City/Asylum." In *International Organization for the Study of the Old Testament, Congress Volume, Vienna, 1980*, supplements to *VT*, 32:278-310. Leiden: Brill, 1981. [Sacrifice/Offerings]

Milgrom, Jacob. "Sin-offering or Purification-offering?" *VT* 21 (1971): 237-39; also in Milgrom, *Studies in Cultic Theology and Terminology*. 67-69. Leiden: Brill, 1983. [Sacrifice/Offerings]

Milgrom, Jacob. "The 'Šok hattĕrûmâ': A Chapter in Cultic History" (in Hebrew; *English summary). *Tarbiz* 42 (1972-73): 1-14, *I; also in Milgrom, *Studies in Cultic Theology and Terminology*. 159-70. Leiden: Brill, 1983. [Sacrifice/Offerings]

Milgrom, Jacob. *Studies in Levitical Terminology, I*. Berkeley: University of California Press, 1970. [Sacrifice/Offerings]

Milgrom, Jacob. "Two Kinds of ḥaṭṭāʾt." *VT* 26 (1976): 333-37; also in Milgrom, *Studies in Cultic Theology and Terminology*. 70-74. Leiden: Brill, 1983. [Sacrifice/Offerings]

Moraldi, Luigi. *Espiazione sacrificale e riti espiatori nell'ambiente biblico e nell'Antico Testamento*. Rome: Pontifical Biblical Institute, 1956. [Sacrifice/Offerings]

Moret, Alexandre. "Du sacrifice en Égypte." *RHR* 57 (1908): 81-101. [Sacrifice/Offerings]

Morgenstern, Julian. *The Fire upon the Altar*. Chicago: Quadrangle, 1963. [Sacrifice/Offerings]

Moses ben Maimon. *The Book of Offerings*, translated from Hebrew by H. Danby. In *Yale Judaica Series*, vol. 4. New Haven: Yale University Press, 1950. [Sacrifice/Offerings]

Moses ben Maimon. *The Book of Offerings* (in Hebrew), with commentary by Z. Sachs. Jerusalem: Mossad Harav Kook, 1960. [Sacrifice/Offerings]

Moule, C. F. D. "Sanctuary and Sacrifice in the Church of the New Testament." *JTS* 1 (1950): 29-41. [Sacrifice/Offerings]

Nelson, Richard D. "The Altar of Ahaz: A Revisionist View." *Hebrew Annual Review: A Journal of Studies in Bible, Hebrew Language and Literature* 10 (1986): 267-76. [Sacrifice/Offerings]

Neusner, Jacob. "Map without Territory: Mishnah's System of Sacrifice and Sanctuary." *History of Religions* 19 (1979): 103-27. [Sacrifice/Offerings]

Nicholson, Ernest W. "Blood-Spattered Altars?" *VT* 27 (January 1977): 113-17. [Sacrifice/Offerings]

Nikiprowetzky, Valentin. "La spiritualisation des sacrifices et le culte sacrificiel au temple de Jérusalem chez Philon d'Alexandrie." *Semitica* 17 (1967): 97-116. [Sacrifice/Offerings]

Obbink, H. Th. "The Horns of the Altar in the Semitic World, Especially in Jahwism." *JBL* 56 (1937): 43-49. [Sacrifice/Offerings]

Oesterley, William O. E. *Sacrifices in Ancient Israel: Their Origin, Purposes and Development.* London: Hodder and Stoughton, 1937. [Sacrifice/Offerings]

O'Rourke, William J. "Israelite Sacrifice." *American Ecclesistical Review* 149 (1963): 259-74. [Sacrifice/Offerings]

Paulme, Denise. "La notion de sacrifice chez un peuple 'fetichiste.' " *RHR* 132 (1946-B): 48-66. [Sacrifice/Offerings]

Pocknee, Cyril E. *The Christian Altar in History and Today.* London: Mowbray, 1963. [Sacrifice/Offerings]

Prince, J. Dyneley. "A Study of the Assyro-Babylonian Words Relating to Sacrifice." *JBL* (1907): 54-61. [Sacrifice/Offerings]

Rainey, A. F. "The Order of Sacrifices in Old Testament Ritual Texts." *Biblica* 51 (1970): 485-98. [Sacrifice/Offerings]

Reeves, John C. "What Does Noah Offer in 1QapGen X, 15?" *Revue de Qumran* 12 (December 1986): 415-19. [Sacrifice/Offerings]

Reinach, S. "Les sacrifices d'animaux dans l'église chrétienne." *Anthropologie* 14 (1903): 59-62. [Sacrifice/Offerings]

Rendtorff, Rolf. *Studien zur Geschichte des Opfers im alten Israel.* Neukirchen-Vluyn: Neukirchener, 1967. [Sacrifice/Offerings]

Ringgren, Helmer. *Sacrifice in the Bible.* London: Lutterworth, 1962. [Sacrifice/Offerings]

Robertson, E. "The Altar of Earth (Exodus 20:24-26)." *JJS* 1 (1948): 12-21. [Sacrifice/Offerings]

Robinson, H. W. "Hebrew Sacrifice and Prophetic Symbolism." *JTS* 43 (1942): 129-39. [Sacrifice/Offerings]

Rost, Leonhard. "Erwägungen zum israelitischen Brandopfer." In *Von Ugarit nach Qumran: Beiträge zur alttestamentlichen und altorientalischen Forschung: Otto Eissfeldt zum 1. September 1957 dargebracht von Freunden und Schulern,* edited by Johannes Hempel et al. 177-83. Berlin: Töpelmann, 1967. [Sacrifice/Offerings]

Rost, Leonhard. *Studien zum Opfer im alten Israel.* Stuttgart: Kohlhammer, 1981. [Sacrifice/Offerings]

Roth, Cecil. "The Debate on the Royal Sacrifices, A.D. 66." *Harvard Theological Review* 53 (1960): 93-97. [Sacrifice/Offerings]

Rothkoff, Aaron. "Sacrifice." In *Encylopaedia Judaica* 14:599-615. [Sacrifice/Offerings]

Rothkoff, Aaron. "Sacrifice: Second Temple Period." In *Encyclopaedia Judaica* 14:607-12. [Sacrifice/Offerings]

Rowley, Harold H. "The Meaning of Sacrifice in the Old Testament." *BJRL* 33 (February 1950): 74-110. [Sacrifice/Offerings]

Rutschmann, LaVerne A. "Altar and Sacrifice in the Old Testament Nomadic Period with Relation to Sacred Space and Sacred Time." Ph.D. diss., Southern California School of Theology at Claremont, 1962. [Sacrifice/Offerings]

Saydon, P. P. "Sin-Offering and Trepass-Offering." *CBQ* 8 (1946): 393-98. [Sacrifice/Offerings]

Scheneker, Adrien. "*Kōper* et expiation." *Biblica* 63 (1982): 32-46 [Sacrifice/Offerings]

Schmid, Rudolph. *Das Bundesopfer in Israel.* Munich: Koesel, 1964. [Sacrifice/Offerings]

Schoetz, Dionys. *Schuld und Sündopfer im alten Testament.* Breslau: Mueller and Sieffert, 1930. [Sacrifice/Offerings]

Scholander, Hans. *Det israelitiska offrets upploesning.* Lund: Ohlssons, 1909. [Sacrifice/Offerings]

Silverstein, Samuel H. *Korban Shemuel.* St. Louis: Quality, 1944. [Sacrifice/Offerings]

Sirard, L. "Sacrifices et rites sanglants dans l'ancien testament." *Science et Esprit* 15 (1963): 173-97. [Sacrifice/Offerings]

Snaith, Norman H. "The Altar at Gilgal: Joshua XXII:23-29." *VT* 28 (1978): 330-35. [Sacrifice/Offerings]

Snaith, Norman H. "Sacrifice in the Old Testament." *VT* 7 (1957): 308-17. [Sacrifice/Offerings]

Snaith, Norman H. "The Sin-Offering and the Guilt-Offering." *VT* 15 (1965): 73-80. [Sacrifice/Offerings]

Snaith, Norman H. "The Verbs *zābaḥ* and *šāḥaṭ*." *VT* 25 (1975): 242-46. [Sacrifice/Offerings]

Spoer, H. H. "Notes on Bloody Sacrifices in Palestine." *JAOS* 25 (1904): 312-13. [Sacrifice/Offerings]

Spoer, H. H. "On Bloody Sacrifices in Palestine." *JAOS* 27 (1906): 104. [Sacrifice/Offerings]

Steinmueller, John E. "Sacrificial Blood in the Bible." *Biblica* 40 (1959): 556-67. [Sacrifice/Offerings]

Stevenson, William B. "Hebrew ʿolah and Zebach Sacrifices." In *Festschrift Alfred Bertholet zum 80. Geburtstag gewidmet von Kollegen und Freunden,* edited by Walter Baumgartner et al. 488-97. Tübingen: Mohr, 1950. [Sacrifice/Offerings]

Swain, C. W. " 'For Our Sins': The Image of Sacrifice in the Thought of the Apostle Paul." *Interpretation* 17 (1963): 131-39. [Sacrifice/Offerings]

Swetnam, J. "Temple Sacrifices: Profile of a Theological Problem." *The Bible Today* 34 (1968): 2377-2380. [Sacrifice/Offerings]

Teicher, J. L. "Priests and Sacrifices in the Dead Sea Scrolls." *JJS* 5 (1954): 93-99. [Sacrifice/Offerings]

Tenz, J. M. "Position of the Altar of Burnt Sacrifice in the Temple of Jerusalem." *PEQ* 42 (1910): 137-39. [Sacrifice/Offerings]

Thoburn, C. Stanley. "Old Testament Sacrifice in the Light of Ugaritic Literature." Ph.D. diss., Boston University, 1954. [Sacrifice/Offerings]

Thompson, P. E. S. "The Anatomy of Sacrifice: A Preliminary Investigation." In *New Testament Christianity for Africa and the World,* edited by M. Glassnell and E. Fashole-Luke. 19-35. London: SPCK, 1974. [Sacrifice/Offerings]

Thompson, R. J. *Penitence and Sacrifice in Early Israel outside the Levitical Law.* London: Brill, 1963. [Sacrifice/Offerings]

Thomson, C. A. "The Necessity of Blood Sacrifice in Ezekiel's Temple." *Bibliotheca Sacra* 123 (1966): 237-48. [Sacrifice/Offerings]

Turner, V. "Sacrifice as Quintessential Process: Prophylaxis or Abandonment?" *History of Religions* 16 (1977): 189-215. [Sacrifice/Offerings]

Urie, D. M. L. "Sacrifice among the West Semites." *PEQ* 81 (1949): 67-82. [Sacrifice/Offerings]

Van Baal, J. "Offering, Sacrifice and Gift." *Numen* 23 (1976): 161-78. [Sacrifice/Offerings]

Van Seters, John. "The Religion of the Patriarchs in Genesis." *Biblica* 61 (1980): 220-33. [Sacrifice/Offerings]

Van Woerden, I. S. "The Iconography of the Sacrifice of Abraham." *Vigiliae Christianae* 15 (December 1961): 214-55. [Sacrifice/Offerings]

Vattioni, Francesco, ed. *Sangue e Antropologia Biblica nella Patristica. Atti della Settimana (Roma, 23-28 Novembre 1981).* 2 vols. Rome: Pia Unione Preziosissimo Sangue, 1982. [Sacrifice/Offerings]

Vattioni, Francesco, ed. *Sangue e Antropologia nella Letterature Cristiana. Atti della Settimana (Roma, 29 Novembre-4 Dicembre 1982).* 3 vols. Rome: Pia Unione Preziosissimo Sangue, 1983. [Sacrifice/Offerings]

Vattioni, Francesco, ed. *Settimana Sangue e Antropologia Biblica. Atti della Settimana Sangue e Antropologia Biblica (Roma, 10-15 Marzo 1980).* 2 vols. Roma: Pia unione Preziosissimo Sangue, 1981. [Sacrifice/Offerings]

Vaux, Roland de. "Le sacerdoce en Israël: Populus Dei, I." *Israel Cummunio* 10 (1969): 113-68. [Sacrifice/Offerings]

Vaux, Roland de. *Les sacrifices de l'Ancien Testament.* Paris: Gabalda, 1964; also in English as *Studies in Old Testament Sacrifice.* Cardiff: University of Wales, 1964. [Sacrifice/Offerings]

Vernant, Jean-Pierre. *Le sacrifice dans l'antiquité: Huit exposés suivis de discussions.* Genève: Fond Hardt, 1981. [Sacrifice/Offerings]

Vincent, A. "Les rites du balancement (tenouphah) et du prélèvement (teroumah) dans le sacrifice de communion de l'Ancien Testament." *Biblical Archaeology and History* 30 (1939): 267-72. [Sacrifice/Offerings]

Walfish, Jeroham J. L. *Gaḥale esh.* 2 vols. Warsaw: Bapmava, 1908. [Sacrifice/Offerings]

Wallace, D. H. "Essenes and Temple Sacrifice." *Theologische Zeitschrift* 13 (1957): 335-38. [Sacrifice/Offerings]

Watson, Charles M. "The Position of the Altar of Burnt Sacrifice in the Temple of Jerusalem." *PEFQ* 42 (1910): 15-22. [Sacrifice/Offerings]

Watteville, Jean. *Le sacrifice dans les textes eucharistiques des premiers siecles.* Paris: Delachaux and Niestle, 1966. [Sacrifice/Offerings]

Weinberg, Zwi. *Sacrifice in Israel according to the Priest Codex and the Customs of Other Mediterranean Peoples* (in Hebrew). Jerusalem: Mass, 1987. [Sacrifice/Offerings]

Wiener, Harold M. *The Altars of the Old Testament.* Leipzig: Hinrichs, 1927. [Sacrifice/Offerings]

Wendel, Adolf. *Das Opfer in der altisraelitischen Religion.* Leipzig: Pfeiffer, 1927. [Sacrifice/Offerings]

Wiesmann, Hermann. "Die 'opferfeindlichen' Psalmen." *Melanges Université Saint Joseph* 2 (1907): 321-35. [Sacrifice/Offerings]

Yerkes, Royden K. *Sacrifice in Greek and Roman Religions and Early Judaism.* New York: Scribner's, 1952. [Sacrifice/Offerings]

Young, F. "New Wine in Old Wineskins." *ET* 86 (1974-75): 305-9. [Sacrifice/Offerings]

Young, Frances M. *The Use of Sacrificial Ideas in Greek Chistian Writers from the New Testament in John Chrysostom.* Philadelphia: Patristic Foundation, 1979. [Sacrifice/Offerings]

Zawadski, S. "Neo-Assyrian Temple Sacrifices." *Rocznik Oriental* 41/2 (1980): 151-55. [Sacrifice/Offerings]

General Studies of Temples in the Ancient Near East and Mediterranean World Arranged by Author

Abba, Raymond. "Origin and Significance of Hebrew Sacrifice." *BTB* 7 (1977): 123-38. [Sacrifice/Offerings]

Abba, Raymond. "Priests and Levites." In *The Interpreter's Dictionary of the Bible* 3:876-89. [Priesthood]

Abba, Raymond. "Priests and Levites in Deuteronomy." *VT* 27 (1977): 257-67. [Priesthood]

Abba, Raymond. "Priests and Levites in Ezechiel." *VT* 28 (1978): 1-9. [Priesthood]

Abbott, E. A. "John 11:20." *Classical Review* 8 (1894): 89-93. [Israel/Canaan]

Abbott, Lyman. *The Temple.* New York: Macmillan, 1909. [Israel/Canaan]

Abd el-Raziq, Mahmud. *Die Darstellungen und Text des Sanktuars Alexanders des Grossen im Tempel von Luxor.* Mainz: von Zabern, 1984. [Egypt]

Abecassis, A. "Les Pharisiens et le temple." *Le Monde de la Bible* 13 (1980): 39-40. [Israel/Canaan]

Abel, E. L. "The Nature of the Patriarchal God 'El Šadday.'" *Numen* 20 (1973): 48-59. [Mountain]

Abel, Felix-Marie. "La reconstruction du temple de Jérusalem." In Abel, *Histoire de la Palestine, depuis la conquête d'Alexandre jusqu'à l'invasion arabe.* 2 vols., 1:372-79. Paris: Lecoffre, 1952. [Israel/Canaan]

Abel, Felix-Marie, and G. A. Barrois. "Dédicace d'un temple à Jérusalem." *RB* 40 (1931): 292-94. [Israel/Canaan]

Abrahams, Israel. "Tabernacle." In *Encyclopaedia Judaica* 15:679-87. [Tabernacle]

Abrahams, Roger D. *Rituals in Culture*. Bloomington: Folklore, 1974. [Ritual/Liturgy/Worship]

Ackroyd, Peter R. "The Temple Vessels—A Continuity Theme." In *Studies in the Religion of Ancient Israel*. 166-81. Leiden: Brill, 1972. [Israel/Canaan]

Adler, Yankel. "Borders of the Temple Mount" (in Hebrew). *The Spring* 9 (1969): 33-34. [Israel/Canaan]

Adrat, Abraham. "Destruction of the Second Temple" (in Hebrew). Ph.D. diss., Hebrew University, 1984. [Israel/Canaan]

Aggoula, B. "Temple et agora à Hatra." *Annali dell'Istituto orientale di Napoli* 43 (1983): 407-28. [Mountain]

Aharoni, Yohanan. "Arad: Its Inscriptions and Temple." *BA* 31 (1968): 2-32. [Israel/Canaan]

Aharoni, Yohanan. "The Building Activities of David and Solomon." *IEJ* 24 (1974): 13-16. [Israel/Canaan]

Aharoni, Yohanan. "Excavations at Tel Arad." *IEJ* 17 (1967): 247-49. [Israel/Canaan]

Aharoni, Yohanan. "From Shiloh to Jerusalem" (in Hebrew; *English summary). In *Jerusalem through the Ages*, edited by Joseph Aviram. 85-95, *61. Jerusalem: Israel Exploration Society, 1968. [Tabernacle]

Aharoni, Yohanan. "The Horned Altar of Beer-sheba." *BA* 37 (1974): 2-6. [Israel/Canaan]

Aharoni, Yohanan. "The Israelite Sanctuary at Arad." In *New Directions in Biblical Archaeology*, edited by David N. Freedman and Jonas C. Greenfield. 29-36. New York: Doubleday, 1969. [Israel/Canaan]

Aharoni, Yohanan. "Israelite Temples in the Period of the Monarchy." In *Proceedings of the Fifth World Congress of Jewish Studies, 1969*, edited by P. Peli. 69-74. Jerusalem: World Union of Jewish Studies, 1972. [Israel/Canaan]

Aharoni, Yohanan. "Lakhish." *RB* 75 (July 1968): 401-2. [Israel/Canaan]

Aharoni, Yohanan. "The Solomonic Temple, the Tabernacle and the Arad Sanctuary" (in Hebrew; *English summary). *Beer-Sheva* 1 (1973): 79-86, *240-41; also in English in *Orient and Occident: Essays Presented to Cyrus H. Gordon*, edited by Harry A. Hoffner, Jr. 1-8. Neukirchen-Vluyn: Neukirchen, 1973. [Israel/Canaan]

Aharoni, Yohanan. "Temples, Semitic." In *The Interpreter's Dictionary of the Bible*, supp. vol., 874-75. [Israel/Canaan]

Aharoni, Yohanan. "Trial Excavation in the 'Solar Shrine' at Lachish: Preliminary Report." *IEJ* 18 (1968): 157-69. [Israel/Canaan]

Ahlström, Gösta W. *Aspects of Syncretism in Israelite Religion*. Lund: Gleerup, 1963. [Israel/Canaan]

Ahlström, Gösta W. *Joel and the Temple Cult of Jerusalem*. Leiden: Brill, 1971. [Israel/Canaan]

Ahlström, Gösta W. "Der Prophet Nathan und der Tempelbau." *VT* 11 (April 1961): 113-27. [Israel/Canaan]

Ahlström, Gösta W. "Some Remarks on Prophet and Cult." In *Transitions in Biblical Scholarship. Essays in Divinity*, edited by J. Coert Rylaarsdam. 113-29. Chicago: University of Chicago Press, 1968. [Israel/Canaan]

Ahlström, Gösta W. "The Travels of the Ark: A Religio-Political Composition." *JNES* 43 (1984): 141-49. [Tabernacle]

Akmar, Ernst. "Étude sur le rituel du culte divin." *Sphinx: Revue critique* 19 (1915): 65-80. [Ritual/Liturgy/Worship]

Albeck, Hanoch. "The Sanhedrin and Its President" (in Hebrew). *Zion* 8/4 (1943): 165-78. [Israel/Canaan]

Albertson, F. "An Augustan Temple on a Julio-Claudian Relief." *AJA* 88 (April 1984): 236. [Greece/Rome]

Albright, William F. "The Babylonian Temple-Tower and the Altar of Burnt-Offering." *JBL* 39 (1920): 137-42. [Mountain]

Albright, William F. "The Place of the Temple of Solomon in the History of Israelite Religion." In *Archaeology and the Religion of Israel*. 5th ed. 138-50. Garden City: Doubleday, 1969. [Israel/Canaan]

Albright, William F. "Two Cressets from Marisa and the Pillars of Jachin and Boaz." *BASOR* 85 (1942): 18-27. [Israel/Canaan]

Albright, William F. "What Were the Cherubim?" *BA* 1 (1938): 1-3. [Tabernacle]

Albright, William F., and G. E. Wright. "Comments on Professor Garber's Article." *JBL* 77 (1958): 129-32. [Israel/Canaan]

Alderink, L. J. "Cosmogonic Themes in Orphism." *SBLSP* 14 (1978): 121-35. [Creation/Cosmology]

Allan, N. "The Identity of the Jerusalem Priesthood during the Exile." *Heythrop Journal* 23 (1982): 259-69. [Priesthood]

Alles, Gregory D. "Surface, Space, and Intention: the Parthenon and the Kandariya Mahadeva." *History of Religions* 28 (August 1988): 1-36. [Greece/Rome]

Alliot, Maurice. *Le Culte d'Horus à Edfou au temps des Ptolémées*. Beirut: Librairie du Liban, 1979. [Egypt]

Alon, Gedalyahu. "The Burning of the Temple." In Alon, *Jews, Judaism, and the Classical World: Studies in Jewish History in the Times of the Second Temple and Talmud*, translated by Israel Abrahams. 252-69. Jerusalem: Magnes, 1977. [Israel/Canaan]

Alon, Gedalyahu. "The Festival of Tabernacles in Jerusalem in the Days of the Second Temple." In Alon, *Studies in Jewish History in the Times of the Second Temple, the Mishna and the Talmud* (in Hebrew). 2 vols., 1:77-82. Tel-Aviv: Hakubutz Hameuchad, 1957. [Tabernacle]

Alon, Gedalyahu. "History of the High Priesthood at the End of the Second Temple Period" (in Hebrew). *Tarbiz* 13 (1942): 1-24. [Priesthood]

Alt, Albrecht. "Ägyptische Tempel in Palästina und die Landnahme der Philister." *ZDPV* 67 (1944-45): 1-20. [Egypt]

Alt, Albrecht. "Verbreitung und Herkunft des syrischen Tempeltypus." *Palästinajahrbuch* 35 (1939): 83-99. [Israel/Canaan]

Alt, Albrecht. "Zelte und Hütten." In *Alttestamentliche Studien: Friedrich Nötscher zum sechzigsten Geburtstag*, edited by Hubert Junker and G. Johannes Botterweck. 16-25. Bonn: Hanstein, 1950; also in Alt, *Kleine Schriften zur Geschichte des Volkes Israel*. 3 vols., 3:233-42. Munich: Beck, 1959. [Tabernacle]

Amad, Gladys. *Le baiser rituel: Un geste de culte méconnu*. Beirut: Dar el-Machreq, 1973. [Ritual/Liturgy/Worship]

Amiot, F. "Temple." In *Dictionary of Biblical Theology*, edited by Xavier Léon-Dufour. 594-97. New York: Seabury, 1973. [Israel/Canaan]

Amir, Yehoshua. "Philo's Version of the Pilgrimage to Jerusalem" (in Hebrew; English summary). In *Jerusalem in the Second Temple Period* (Abraham Schalit Memorial Volume), edited by A. Oppenheimer, U. Rappaport, and M. Stern. ix-x, 154-65. Jerusalem: Yad Izhak Ben-Zvi, 1980. [Ritual/Liturgy/Worship]

Amiran, Ruth. *Ancient Arad*. Jerusalem: Israel Museum, 1967. [Israel/Canaan]

Amiran, Ruth. "Tel Arad." *RB* 75 (July 1968): 388-92. [Israel/Canaan]

Ancessi, Victor A. *L'Égypte et Moïse*. Paris: Leroux, 1875. [Sacred Vestments]

Andersen, F. I. "Who Built the Second Temple?" *Australian Biblical Review* 6/1-4 (1958): 1-35. [Israel/Canaan]

Anderson, R. T. "Mount Gerizim: Navel of the World." *BA* 43 (1980): 217-21. [Mountain]

Andrae, Walter. *Der Anu-Adad-Tempel in Assur*. Leipzig: Hinrichs, 1909. [Mesopotamia]

Andrae, Walter. *Die archäischen Ischtar Tempel in Assur*. Leipzig: Hinrichs, 1922. [Mesopotamia]

Andrae, Walter. *Das Gotteshaus und die Urformen des Bauens im Alten Orient*. Berlin: Schötz, 1930. [Israel/Canaan]

Andrae, Walter. *Kultrelief aus dem Brunnen des Assurtempels zu Assur*. Liepzig: Hinrichs, 1931. [Mesopotamia]

Andrae, Walter. "Die Tempel der Assyrer." *ZDMG* 91 (1937): 49-57. [Mesopotamia]

Andrae, Walter. *Das wiedererstandene Assur*, 2d ed. Berlin: Propylaen, 1977. [Mesopotamia]

Andren, Arvid. *Architectural Terracottas from Etrusco-Italic Temples*. Lund: Gleerup, 1940. [Greece/Rome]

Andrews, S. J. "The Worship of the Tabernacle Compared with That of the Second Temple." *JBL* 6 (1886): 56-68. [Tabernacle]

Ap-Thomas, David R. "Elijah on Mount Carmel." *PEQ* 92 (1960): 146-55. [Mountain]

Arai, Sasagu. "Zum 'Tempelwort' Jesu in Apostelgeschichte 6:14." *NTS* 34 (1988): 397-410. [Israel/Canaan]

Arendt, Erich. *Griechische Tempel.* Leipzig: Insel, 1970. [Greece/Rome]

Armerding, Carl E. "Were David's Sons Really Priests?" In *Current Issues in Biblical and Patristic Interpretation: Studies in Honor of Merrill C. Tenney,* edited by Gerald F. Hawthorne, 75-86. Grand Rapids: Eerdmans, 1975. [Priesthood]

Arnold, Dieter. *Der Tempel des Königs Mentuhotep von Deir el-Bahari.* Cairo: Mainz, 1974. [Egypt]

Arnold, Dieter. *Der Tempel Qasr El-Sagha.* Mainz: von Zabern, 1979. [Egypt]

Arnold, Dieter. *Wandrelief und Raumfunktion in ägyptischen Tempeln des Neuen Reiches.* Berlin: Hessling, 1962. [Egypt]

Arnold, William R. *Ephod and Ark: A Study in the Records and Religion of the Ancient Hebrews.* Cambridge: Harvard University Press, 1917. [Tabernacle]

Arranz, S. J. Miguel. "La liturgie pénitentielle juive après la déstruction du temple." In *Liturgie et rémission des péchés. Conferences Saint-Serge, Paris, 1973,* edited by A. Pistoia. 39-55. Rome: Edizioni Liturgiche, 1975. [Israel/Canaan]

Artom, Menachem E. "Idee profetiche sul Santuario." *Annuario di Studi Ebraici* 2 (1964): 31-38. [Israel/Canaan]

Asami, S. "The Central Sanctuary in Israel in the Ninth Century B.C." Ph.D. diss., Harvard University, 1965. [Israel/Canaan]

Ashkenazi, Malchiel. *The Dedication of the Temple* (in Hebrew). Jerusalem: Hatchia, 1963. [Israel/Canaan]

Assaf, Simcha. *Sources and Research of Israel through the Ages* (in Hebrew). Jerusalem: Mosad ha-Rav Kook, 1946. [Israel/Canaan]

Atwater, Edward E. *History and Significance of the Sacred Tabernacle of the Hebrews.* New York: Dodd and Mead, 1875. [Tabernacle]

Aucler, P. "Le Temple de Jérusalem au temps de N.-S. Jésus-Christ: Critique des sources." *RB* 7 (1898): 193-206. [Israel/Canaan]

Audin, A. "Les piliers jumeaux dans le monde sémitique." *Archiv Orientální* 21 (1953): 430-39. [Israel/Canaan]

Auerbach, E. "Die Herkunft der Sadokiden." *ZAW* 49 (1931): 327-28. [Israel/Canaan]

Auerbach, Jacob, and Zvi Kaplan. "Temple-Mount." In *Encyclopaedia Judaica* 15:988-94. [Israel/Canaan]

Aviam, M. "The Roman Temple at Kedesh in the Light of Certain Northern Syrian City Coins." *Tel Aviv* 12 (1985): 212-14. [Greece/Rome]

Avigad, Nahman. "The Architecture of Jerusalem in the Second Temple Period" (in Hebrew). *Qadmoniot* 1/1-2 (1968): 28-36; also in English in *Jerusalem Revealed: Archaeology in the Holy City, 1968-1974*, edited by Yigael Yadin. 14-20. New Haven: Yale University Press, 1976. [Israel/Canaan]

Avi-Yonah, Michael. "The Facade of Herod's Temple: An Attempted Reconstruction." In *Religions in Antiquity—Essays in Memory of E. R. Goodenough*, edited by Jacob Neusner. 327-35. Leiden: Brill, 1968. [Israel/Canaan]

Avi-Yonah, Michael. "Jérusalem du temps d'Hérode." *Bible et Terre Sainte* 117 (1970): 7-13. [Israel/Canaan]

Avi-Yonah, Michael. "King Herod's Work on the Temple and Temple Mount." In *And to Jerusalem*. 318-24. Jerusalem: Union of Hebrew Writers in Israel, 1968. [Israel/Canaan]

Avi-Yonah, Michael. "Places of Worship in the Roman and Byzantine Periods." *Antiquity and Survival* 2 (1957): 262-72. [Israel/Canaan]

Avi-Yonah, Michael. "Reply to the Article by Joshua Brand" (in Hebrew). *Tarbiz* 29 (1960): 218-21. [Israel/Canaan]

Avi-Yonah, Michael. "The Second Temple" (in Hebrew). In *Sefer Yerushalayim*, edited by M. Avi-Yonah. 392-418. Jerusalem: Bialik Institute, 1956. [Israel/Canaan]

Avi-Yonah, Michael, and Menahem Stern. "Jerusalem: Second Temple Period." In *Encyclopaedia Judaica* 9:1384-405. [Israel/Canaan]

Ayali, Meir. "Gottes und Israels Trauer über die Zerstörung des Tempels." *Kairos* 23 (1981): 215-31. [Israel/Canaan]

Ayrton, Elisabeth. *The Doric Temple*. New York: Potter, 1961. [Greece/Rome]

Aytoun, K. A. *The Mysteries of Baptism by Moses bar Kepha Compared with the Odes of Solomon*. In *The Syrian Churches Series*, edited by Jacob Vellian. vol. 6., pp. 1-15. Kottayam: CMS, 1973. [Ablutions/Anointings]

Bachmann, Michael. *Jerusalem und der Tempel*. Stuttgart: Kohlhammer, 1980. [Israel/Canaan]

Backer, Émile de. *Sacramentum, le mot et l'idée représenté par lui dans les oeuvres de Tertullien*. Louvain: Bureau du Recueil, 1911. [Ritual/Liturgy/Worship]

Bacon, Benjamin W. "Among the Sun-Temples of Coele-Syria." *Records of the Past* 5 (1906): 67-83. [Israel/Canaan]

Badawy, Alexander M. "The Approach to the Egyptian Temple in the Late and Graeco-Roman Periods." *ZÄS* 102 (1975): 79-90. [Egypt]

Badawy, Alexander M. "Maru-Aten: Pleasure Resort or Temple?" *JEA* 42 (1956): 58-64. [Egypt]

Baer, Y. "Jerusalem in the Times of the Great Revolt (Based on Source Criticism of Josephus and Talmudic-Midrashic Legends of the Temple Destruction)" (in Hebrew; English summary). *Zion* 36 (1971): 127-90. [Israel/Canaan]

Bagatti, Bellarmino. "La posizione del tempio erodiano di Gerusalemme." *Biblica* 46 (1965): 428-44. [Israel/Canaan]

Bagatti, Bellarmino. *Recherches sur le site du temple de Jérusalem, Ier-VIIe siècle*. Jerusalem: Franciscan, 1979. [Israel/Canaan]

Bagatti, Bellarmino. "Il 'Tempio di Gerusalemme' dal II all' VIII secolo." *Biblica* 43 (1962): 1-21. [Israel/Canaan]

Baier, W. "Der zweite Tempel." In *Bibel-Lexikon*, edited by Herbert Haag. 1722-26. Zurich: Benzinger, 1968. [Israel/Canaan]

Baillet, J. "Le Temple d'Apet à Karnak." *Bibliothèque égyptologique* 16 (1905): 93-111. [Egypt]

Baker, D. "Recreating the Divine Design: Tabernacle Furnishings." *Christianity Today* 15 (12 March 1971): 43. [Tabernacle]

Bakry, H. S. K. "The Discovery of a Temple of Sobk in Upper Egypt." *MDAI.K* 27 (1969): 131-46. [Egypt]

Baltzer, Klaus. *The Covenant Formulary in Old Testament, Jewish, and Early Christian Writings*. Philadelphia: Fortress, 1971. [Covenant]

Baltzer, Klaus. "The Meaning of the Temple in the Lukan Writings." *Harvard Theological Review* 58 (1965): 262-77. [Israel/Canaan]

Baly, T. J. "Notes on the Ritual of Opening the Mouth." *JEA* 16 (1930): 173-86. [Ritual/Liturgy/Worship]

Bammel, Ernst. "Die Bruderfolge im Hochpriestertum der herodianisch-römischen Zeit." *ZDPV* 70 (1954): 147-53. [Priesthood]

Bammel, Ernst. "Nicanor and His Gate." *JJS* 7 (1956): 77-78. [Israel/Canaan]

Banks, Edgar J. "The Bismya Temple." *Records of the Past* 5 (1906): 227-36. [Mesopotamia]

Banvard, John. *The Origin of the Building of Solomon's Temple: An Oriental Tradition*. Boston: Gannett, 1880. [Israel/Canaan]

Barclay, Joseph. *The Talmud, with Illustrations and Plan of the Temple*. London: Murray, 1878. [Israel/Canaan]

Bardtke, H. "Der Tempel von Jerusalem." *Theologische Literaturzeitung* 97 (1972): 801-10. [Israel/Canaan]

Barguet, Paul. "Note sur le grand temple d'Aton à el-Amarna." *Revue d'Égyptologie* 28 (1976): 148-51. [Egypt]

Barguet, Paul. "La structure du temple Ipet-Sout d'Amon à Karnak du Moyen Empire à Aménophis II." *BIFAO* 52 (1953): 145-55. [Egypt]

Barnard, L. W. "The Testimonium Concerning the Stone in the New Testament and the Epistle of Barnabas." In *Studia Evangelica*, edited by F. L. Cross, vol. 3 of *Papers Presented to the Second International Congress on New Testament Studies, 2: The New Testament Message.* 306-13. Berlin: Akademie-Verlag, 1964. [Israel/Canaan]

Barnard, Will J. *De tempel van Herodes.* Amsterdam: Bijbelwerkplats i.o. Nederlandse Zondagsschool Vereniging, 1972. [Israel/Canaan]

Barnes, W. E. "Joachin and Boaz." *JTS* 5/19 (1904): 447-51. [Israel/Canaan]

Barnett, R. D. "Bringing the God into the Temple." In *Temples and High Places in Biblical Times,* edited by Avraham Biran. 10-20. Jerusalem: Nelson Glueck School of Biblical Archaeology, 1981. [Israel/Canaan]

Barnett, R. D. "Cherubim and the Temple of Solomon." In *Illustrations of Old Testament History,* 44-45. London: British Museum, 1966. [Tabernacle]

Barnett, R. D. "Reminiscences of Herod's Temple." *Christian News from Israel* 12/3 (1961): 13-24. [Israel/Canaan]

Barrett, C. K. "The House of Prayer and the Den of Thieves." In *Jesus und Paulus: Festschrift Georg Kümmel,* edited by E. Earle Ellis, 13-20. Göttingen: Vandenhoeck and Ruprecht, 1975. [Israel/Canaan]

Barrick, W. B. "The Funerary Character of 'High Places' in Ancient Palestine: A Reassessment." *VT* 25 (1975): 565-95. [Mountain]

Barrick, W. B. "What Do We Really Know about High Places?" *Svensk Exegetisk Årsbok* 45 (1980): 50-57. [Mountain]

Barrois, Georges A. "Cultes et sanctuaires Israélites: Les sanctuaires." In *Manuel d'archéologie biblique,* 2:426-56. Paris: Picard, 1953. [Israel/Canaan]

Barrois, Georges A. *Jesus Christ and the Temple.* Crestwood: St. Vladimir's Seminary, 1980. [Israel/Canaan]

Barrois, Georges A. "Le Temple d'Hérode." In *Manuel d'archéologie biblique,* 1:449-52. Paris: Picard, 1953. [Israel/Canaan]

Barta, Winfried. *Aufbau und Bedeutung der altägyptischen Opferformel.* Glückstadt: Augustin, 1968. [Sacrifice/Offerings]

Barta, Winfried. "Das Opferritual im täglichen Tempelkult." *Ex Oriente Lux: Jaarbericht van het vooraziatisch-egyptisch Gezelschap* 19 (1965-66): 457-631. [Ritual/Liturgy/Worship]

Bartlett, J. R. "Zadok and His Successors at Jerusalem." *JTS* 19 (1968): 1-18. [Israel/Canaan]

Barton, George A. "A Comparison of Some Features of Hebrew and Babylonian Ritual." *JBL* 46 (1927): 79-89. [Ritual/Liturgy/Worship]

Barton, George A. "A Liturgy for the Celebration of the Spring Festival at Jerusalem in the Age of Abraham and Melchizedek." *JBL* 53 (1934): 61-78. [Ritual/Liturgy/Worship]

Barton, George A. "Temple." In *The Jewish Encyclopedia* 12:81-101. [Israel/Canaan]

Barton, George A., ed. *Haverford Library Collection of Cuneiform Tablets or Documents from the Temple Archives of Telloh*. 3 vols. Philadelphia: Winston, 1905-14. [Mesopotamia]

Bar-Yosef, Mordechai. *Jerusalem and the Temple: Past and Present* (in Hebrew). Tel Aviv: Mordechai, 1974. [Israel/Canaan]

Baudissin, W. "The Priesthood after OT Times." In *A Dictionary of the Bible*, edited by James Hastings. 4 vols. plus extra volume. 4:94-97. New York: Scribner's Songs, 1909. [Priesthood]

Bauer, Johannes B. "Zion's Flüsse, Ps. 45 (46), 5." In *Memoria Jerusalem: Festschrift Franz Sauer zum 70. Geburtstag*, edited by Johannes B. Bauer and Johannes Marböck. 59-91. Graz: Akademische Druck- und Verlagsanstalt, 1977. [Israel/Canaan]

Baumgarten, Joseph M. "The Calendars of the Book of Jubilees and the Temple Scroll." *VT* 37 (January 1987): 71-78. [Israel/Canaan]

Baumgarten, Joseph M. "Exclusions from the Temple: Proselytes and Agrippa I." *JJS* 33 (1982): 215-25. [Israel/Canaan]

Baumgarten, Joseph M. "4Q500 and the Ancient Conception of the Lord's Vineyard." *JJS* 40 (Spring 1989): 1-6. [Israel/Canaan]

Baumgarten, Joseph M. "The Laws of 'Orlah and First Fruits in the Light of Jubilees, the Qumran Writings, and Targum Ps. Jonathan." *JJS* 38 (Autumn 1987): 195-202. [Sacrifice/Offerings]

Baumgarten, Joseph M. "On the Non-Literal Use of maʿăśēr/dekatē." *JBL* 103 (1984): 245-51. [Sacrifice/Offerings]

Baumgarten, Joseph M. "Sacrifices and Worship among the Jewish Sectaries of the Dead Sea (Qumrân) Scrolls." *Harvard Theological Review* 46 (1953): 151-59. [Ritual/Liturgy/Worship]

Beattie, K. M. *The Tabernacle: A Simplified Presentation*. London: Marshal, Morgan and Scott, 1962. [Tabernacle]

Beaucamp, Evode. "Psaume 87: A la Jérusalem nouvelle." *Laval théologique et philosophique* 35 (1979): 279-88. [Israel/Canaan]

Beet, J. A. "Another Solution of Revelation XX-XXII." *ET* 26 (1914-15): 217-20. [Israel/Canaan]

Behrens, Emil. *Assyrisch-babylonische Briefe kultischen Inhalts aus der Sargonidenzeit*. Leipzig: Zentralantiquariat der DDR, 1968. [Mesopotamia]

Bell, Catherine. "Discourse and Dichotomies: The Structure of Ritual Theory." *Religion* 17 (April 1987): 95-118. [Ritual/Liturgy/Worship]

Belleli, L. "The High Priest's Procession on the Day of Atonement." *JQR* 17 (1904-5): 163-67. [Priesthood]

Ben-Dov, Meir. "Daily Life in the Second Temple Period, Public Buildings and Institutions." In *In the Shadow of the Temple: The Discovery of Ancient Jerusalem*, 148-83. Jerusalem: Keter, 1985. [Israel/Canaan]

Ben-Dov, Meir. "Herod's Mighty Temple Mount." *BAR* 12/6 (1986): 40-49. [Israel/Canaan]

Ben-Dov, Meir. "Herod's Monumental Enterprise, The Walls of the Temple Mount, The First Overpass in History, The Gates of the Temple Mount." In *In the Shadow of the Temple: The Discovery of Ancient Jerusalem*, 148-83. Jerusalem: Keter, 1985. [Israel/Canaan]

Ben-Dov, Meir. "Temple of Herod." In *The Interpreter's Dictionary of the Bible*, supp. vol., 870-72. [Israel/Canaan]

Ben-Mordecai, C. A. "The Iniquity of the Sanctuary: A Study of the Hebrew Term 'āwôn.' " *JBL* 60 (1941): 310-14. [Israel/Canaan]

Ben-Ori, Z. "The Ark of Testimony and Its Parts" (in Hebrew). *Beth Mikra* 27 (1981-82): 214-21. [Tabernacle]

Ben-Ori, Z. "The Posts of the Tabernacle Court" (in Hebrew). *Beth Mikra* 26 (1981): 148-58. [Tabernacle]

Ben-Shammai, M. H. "The Legends of the Destruction of the Temple among the Paintings of the Dura Synagogue" (in Hebrew). *Bulletin of the Jewish Palestine Exploration Society* 9 (1942): 93-97. [Israel/Canaan]

Benson, Margaret. *The Temple of Mut in Asher.* London: Murray, 1899. [Egypt]

BenTor, A. "Plans of Dwellings and Temples in Early Bronze Age Palestine" (in Hebrew). *Eretz-Israel* 11 (1975): 92-98. [Israel/Canaan]

Bentzen, Aage. "The Cultic Use of the Story of the Ark in Samuel." *JBL* 67 (1948): 37-53. [Ritual/Liturgy/Worship]

Bentzen, Aage. *King and Messiah.* London: Lutterworth, 1955. [Kingship/Coronation]

Bentzen, Aage. "King Ideology—'Urmensch'—'troonsbestijgingsfeest.' " *Studia Theologica* 3/2 (1949): 143-57. [Kingship/Coronation]

Bentzen, Aage. "Zur Geschichte der Sadokiden." *ZAW* 51 (1933): 173-76. [Israel/Canaan]

Ben-Yashar, Menachem. "Noch zum Miqdaš ʾĀdām in 4 Q Florilegium." *Revue de Qumrân* 10 (1981): 587-88. [Israel/Canaan]

Benzinger, Immanuel. *Hebräische Archäologie.* Leipzig: Pfeiffer, 1927; repr. Hildescheim: Olms, 1974. [Israel/Canaan]

Benzinger, Immanuel. "Tabernacle." In *Encyclopaedia Biblica* 4:4861-75. [Tabernacle]

Benzinger, Immanuel. "Temple, Temple Service." In *Encyclopaedia Biblica* 4:4923-48, 4956. [Israel/Canaan]

Bergman, J., Helmer Ringgren, and B. Lang. "*zebhach.*" In *Theological Dictionary of the Old Testament* 4:8-29. [Israel/Canaan]

Bergquist, Birgitta. *The Archaic Greek Temenos.* Lund: Gleerup, 1967. [Greece/Rome]

Berkovits, E. "From the Temple to Synagogue and Back." *Judaica* 8 (1959): 303-11. [Israel/Canaan]

Bernhardt, Karl-Heinz. "Lade." In *Biblisch-Historisches Handwörterbuch*, edited by Bo Reicke and Leonhard Rost. 4 vols., 2:1038-41. Göttingen: Vandenhoeck and Ruprecht, 1964. [Tabernacle]

Bernhardt, Karl-Heinz. *Das Problem der altorientalischen Königsideologie im alten Testament unter besonderer Berücksichtigung der Geschichte der Psalmenexegese dargestellt und kritisch gewürdigt.* Leiden: Brill, 1961. [Kingship/Coronation]

Berry, G. R. "The Glory of Yahweh and the Temple." *JBL* 56 (1937): 115-17. [Israel/Canaan]

Berry, G. R. "Priests and Levites." *JBL* 42 (1923): 227-38. [Priesthood]

Bertholet, Alfred. "Die fertige Ordnung der künftigen Dinge (Hesekiels Verfassungsentwurf), Cap. 40-48." In *Das Buch Hesekiel.* 195-252. Freiburg: Mohr, 1897. [Israel/Canaan]

Bertholet, Alfred. "Zum Verständnis des alttestamentlichen Opfergedankens." *JBL* 49 (1930): 218-33. [Sacrifice/Offerings]

Berto, P. "Le temple de Jerusalem." *REJ* 59 (1910): 14-35, 161-87; 60 (1911): 1-23. [Israel/Canaan]

Bertrand, Alexandre. "L'enciente du Haram-Ech-Chérif et le temple de Salomon à Jérusalem." *Revue archéologique* n.s/7 (1863): 12-31. [Israel/Canaan]

Bertrand, Alexandre. "Le Temple de Jérusalem—opinion de M. de Vogüe," *Revue archéologique* n.s./9 (1864): 428-33. [Israel/Canaan]

Berve, Helmut. *Greek Temples, Theatres, and Shrines.* New York: Abrams, 1963. [Greece/Rome]

Betancourt, P. H. "An Aeolic Shrine in Philadelphia." *AJA* 75 (1971): 427-28. [Greece/Rome]

Betteridge, W. R. "The Builders of the Second Temple." *Bibliotheca Sacra* 53 (1896): 231-49. [Israel/Canaan]

Betz, H. "Fragments from a Catabasis Ritual in Greek Magical Papyrus." *History of Religions* 19 (May 1980): 287-95. [Ritual/Liturgy/Worship]

Betz, Otto. "Felsenmann und Felsengemeinde (Eine Paralle zu Mt. 16. 17-19 in den Qumranpsalmen)." *ZNTW* 48 (1957): 49-77. [Israel/Canaan]

Betz, Otto. "Le ministère cultuel dans la secte de Qumrân et dans le Christianisme." In *La secte de Qumrân et les origines du Christianisme*, 4:163-202. Paris: Descelée de Brouwer, 1959. [Israel/Canaan]

Betz, Otto. "The *Temple Scroll* and the Trial of Jesus." *Southwestern Journal of Theology* 30 (Summer 1988): 5-8. [Israel/Canaan]

Beuker, W. A. M. "God's Presence in Salem: A Study of Psalm 76." In *Loven en geloven* (Festschrift N. H. Ridderbos), edited by A. Ridderbos-Boersma. 135-50. Amsterdam: Ton Bolland, 1975. [Israel/Canaan]

Bewer, J. A. "Vision of the New Jerusalem." In *The Prophets. Harper's Annotated Bible Series*, 438-67. New York: Harper and Brothers, 1949. [Israel/Canaan]

Beyerlin, Walter. *Origins and History of the Oldest Sinaitic Traditions*, translated by S. Rudman. Oxford: Blackwell, 1966. [Covenant]

Bezzant, Reginald, and Reginald Poole-Pridham. *The Promise of Ezekiel's City.* Norwich: Jarrold and Sons, 1952. [Israel/Canaan]

Bialik, C. N., and Y. H. Ravnitzki. "The Second Temple—Its Structure and Services," and "The Destruction of the Second Temple" (in Hebrew). In *The Book of Legends.* 120-42. Tel Aviv: Dvir, 1955. [Israel/Canaan]

Bialoblocki, Samuel. "The Temple Mount and the Temple" (in Hebrew). In *Em la Masoret*, 42-68. Ramat-Gan: Bar-Ilan University, 1971. [Mountain]

Bianchi, R. S. "The Greek Temples of Sicily." *Archaeology* 37/2 (1984): 26-32. [Greece/Rome]

Biberfeld, Pinhas. "The Chosen House" (in Hebrew). In *Yad Shaul—Memorial Volume for S. Weingort.* 193-211. Tel Aviv: Ha-Merkaz, 1943. [Israel/Canaan]

Bic, M. "Betel—le sanctuaire du roi." *Archiv Orientální* 17 (1949): 46-63. [Israel/Canaan]

Bickerman, Elias J. "Héliodore au temple de Jérusalem." In *Studies in Jewish and Christian History.* 3 vols., 2:159-91. Leiden: Brill, 1980. [Israel/Canaan]

Bickerman, Elias J. (Bikerman, Elie). "Une proclamation seleucide relative au temple de Jerusalem." *Syria* 25 (1946-48): 67-85. [Israel/Canaan]

Bickerman, Elias J. "The Warning Inscriptions of Herod's Temple." *JQR* 37 (April 1947): 387-405. [Israel/Canaan]

Biguzzi, Giancarlo. "Mc 14, 58: Un tempio archeiropoiētos," *Rivista Biblica* 26 (1978): 225-40. [Israel/Canaan]

Bikler, Avraham. *The Priests and Their Service in the Jerusalem Temple in the Last Decade before the Destruction of the 2nd Temple* (in Hebrew). Jerusalem: Rav Kook, 1966. [Priesthood]

Bilde, Per. "The Roman Emperor Gaius (Caligula)'s Attempt to Erect His Statue in the Temple of Jerusalem." *Studia Theologica* 32 (1978): 67-93. [Israel/Canaan]

Billerbeck, P. "Ein Tempelgottesdienst in Jesu Tagen." *ZNTW* 55/1-2 (1964): 1-17. [Israel/Canaan]

Biran, Avraham. "An Israelite Horned Altar at Dan." *BA* 37 (1974): 106-7. [Israel/Canaan]

Biran, Avraham. "The Temenos at Dan" (in Hebrew; *English summary). *Eretz-Israel* 16 (1982): 15-43, *252-53. [Israel/Canaan]

Birch, Bruce C. "The Development of the Tradition on the Anointing of Saul in 1 Sam 9:1-10:16." *JBL* 90 (1971): 55-68. [Ablutions/Anointings]

Birch, W. F. "The Levelling of the Akra." *PEFQ* 35 (1903): 353-55. [Israel/Canaan]

Bird, F. B. "The Nature and Function of Ritual Forms: A Sociological Discussion." *Studies in Religion* 9 (1980): 387-402. [Ritual/Liturgy/Worship]

Birge, Darice E. "Sacred Groves in the Ancient Greek World." Ph.D. diss., University of California at Berkeley, 1982. [Greece/Rome]

Bishop, Jonathan. *The Covenant: A Reading.* Springfield: Templegate, 1982. [Covenant]

Bissing, Friedrich W. *Die Baugeschichte des südlichen Tempels von Buhen.* Munich: Bayerische Akademie der Wissenschaften, 1942. [Egypt]

Bissing, Friedrich W. "La chambre des trois saisons du sanctuaire solaire du roi Rathourès à Abousir." *ASAE* 53 (1955): 319-38. [Egypt]

Bissing, Friedrich W. *Das Re-Heiligtum des Königs Ne-woser-re (Rathures).* 3 vols. Berlin, 1905-23. [Egypt]

Bittle, K. "Hittite Temples and High Places in Anatolia and North Syria." In *Temples and High Places in Biblical Times,* edited by Avraham Biran. 63-73. Jerusalem: Nelson Glueck School of Biblical Archaeology, 1981. [Mesopotamia]

Bjerke, S. "Remarks on the Egyptian Ritual of Opening the Mouth and Its Interpretation." *Numen* 12 (1965): 201-16. [Ritual/Liturgy/Worship]

Blacker, Carmen, and Michael Loewe, eds. *Ancient Cosmologies.* London: George Allen & Unwin, 1975. [Creation/Cosmology]

Blackman, Aylward M. "An Ancient Egyptian Foretaste of the Doctrine of Baptismal Regeneration." *Theology* 1 (1920): 134-42. [Ablutions/Anointings]

Blackman, Aylward M. "A Group of Texts Inscribed on the Façade of the Sanctuary in the Temple of Horus at Edfou." *Miscellanea Gregoriana* 10 (1946): 397-428. [Egypt]

Blackman, Aylward M. "The House of the Morning." *JEA* 5 (1918): 148-65. [Egypt]

Blackman, Aylward M. *Luxor and Its Temples.* London: Black, 1923. [Egypt]

Blackman, Aylward M. "Myth and Ritual in Ancient Egypt." In *Myth and Ritual,* edited by Samuel H. Hooke, 15-39. Oxford: Oxford University Press, 1953. [Ritual/Liturgy/Worship]

Blackman, Aylward M. "The Rite of Opening the Mouth in Ancient Egypt and Babylonia." *JEA* 10 (1924): 47-59. [Ritual/Liturgy/Worship]

Blackman, Aylward M. "Sacramental Ideas and Usages in Ancient Egypt." *Recueil de travaux relatifs à la philologie et à l'archéologie égyptiennes et assyriennes* 39 (1921): 44-78. [Ritual/Liturgy/Worship]

Blackman, Aylward M. "The Significance of Incense and Libations in Funerary and Temple Ritual." *ZÄS* 50 (1912): 69-75. [Ritual/Liturgy/Worship]

Blackman, Aylward M. "Some Notes on the Ancient Egyptian Practice of Washing the Dead." *JEA* 5 (1918): 117-24. [Ablutions/Anointings]

Blackman, Aylward M. *The Temple of Bigeh.* Cairo: Imprimerie de l'Institut français d'archéologie orientale du Caire, 1915. [Egypt]

Blackman, Aylward M. *The Temple of Dendur.* Cairo: Imprimerie de l'Institut français d'archéologie orientale du Caire, 1911. [Egypt]

Blackman, Aylward M. *The Temple of Derr.* Imprimerie de l'Institut français d'archéologie orientale du Caire, 1913. [Egypt]

Blackman, Aylward M., and H. F. Fairman. "The Consecration of an Egyptian Temple according to the Use of Edfu." *JEA* 32 (1946): 75-91. [Egypt]

Blackman, Aylward M., et al. "Purification." In *Encyclopedia of Religion and Ethics* 10:476-90. [Ritual/Liturgy/Worship]

Blair, H. J. "Kingship in Israel and Its Implications for the Lordship of Christ Today." *Evangelical Quarterly* 47 (1975): 70-77. [Kingship/Coronation]

Blanchetière, F. "Julien Philhèllene, Philosémite, Antichrétien: L'affaire du Temple de Jerusalem." *JJS* 31 (1980): 61-81. [Israel/Canaan]

Bledstein, A. J. "Genesis of Humans: The Garden of Eden Revisited." *Judaica* 26 (1977): 187-200. [Creation/Cosmology]

Bleeker, Claas J. *Egyptian Festivals.* Leiden: Brill, 1967. [Egypt]

Bleeker, Claas J. "Guilt and Purification in Ancient Egypt." *Numen* 13 (1966): 81-87. [Ablutions/Anointings]

Bleeker, Claas J. "L'idée de l'ordre cosmique dans l'ancienne Egypte." *Revue d'histoire et de philosophie religieuses* 42/2-3 (1962): 193-200. [Creation/Cosmology]

Blenkinsopp, Joseph. "Gibeon and the Ark: A Hypothesis." In *Gibeon and Israel: The Role of Gibeon and the Gibeonites in the Political and Religious History of Early Israel,* edited by J. A. Emerton. 65-83. Cambridge: Cambridge University Press, 1972. [Tabernacle]

Blenkinsopp, Joseph. "Kiriath-Jearim and the Ark." *JBL* 88 (1969): 143-56. [Tabernacle]

Bloch, Chaim. *The Form of the House: According to the Masters of the Talmud* (in Hebrew). Bretslavia: Shatzky, 1883. [Measurement]

Blome, Friedrich. *Die Opfermaterie in Babylonien und Israel.* Rome: Pontifical Biblical Institute, 1934. [Sacrifice/Offerings]

Blum, Felix. *Le Sanhédrin ou Grand Conseil de Jérusalem.* Strassbourg: Dumont-Schauberg, 1889. [Israel/Canaan]

Blumenthal, Israel C. *Bigde Kehunah.* Jerusalem: Orot, 1950. [Sacred Vestments]

Boak, Arthur E. R., ed. *Karanis, the Temples, Coin Hoards, Botanical and Zoological Reports, Seasons 1924-31.* Ann Arbor: University of Michigan Press, 1933. [Egypt]

Bobichon, M. "Du temple au cénacle." *Bible et Terre Sainte* 98 (1968): 2-5. [Israel/Canaan]

Bockel, P. "Jésus et le Temple: Il parlait du sanctuaire de son corps." *Bible et Terre Sainte* 122 (1970): 16-18. [Israel/Canaan]

Bogaers, Julianus E. A. T. *De Gallo - Romeinse Tempels te Elst in de Over-Betuwe.* 'S-Gravenhage, Staatsdrukkerij-en Uitgeverijbedrijf, 1955. [Greece/Rome]

Böhl, Franz. *Nieuwjaarsfeest en Koningsdag in Babylon en Israël.* Groningen: Woelters, 1927. [Mesopotamia]

Böhl, Felix, "Über das Verhältnis von Shetija-Stein und Nabel der Welt in der Kosmologonie der Rabbinen." *ZDMG* 124 (1974): 253-70. [Sacred Space]

Bokser, Baruch M. "Approaching Sacred Space." *Harvard Theological Review* 78/3-4 (1985): 279-99. [Sacred Space]

Boling, R. G. "Bronze Age Buildings at the Shechem High Place." *BA* 32 (1969): 82-103. [Israel/Canaan]

Bonsirven, Joseph. "Le Temple et ses liturgies." In *Le Judaisme au temps de Jésus-Christ.* 2:107-36. Paris: Beauchesne, 1935. [Ritual/Liturgy/Worship]

Booij, Thijs. "Mountain and Theophany in the Sinai Narrative (Exodus 19-20, 24, 32-34)." *Biblica* 65 (1984): 1-26. [Mountain]

Bookidis, Nancy. "The Sanctuary of Demeter and Kore: An Archaeological Approach to Ancient Religion." *AJA* 91 (July 1987): 480-81. [Greece/Rome]

Borchardt, Ludwig. *Der ägyptische Tempel mit Umgang.* In *Beiträge zur ägyptischen Bauforschung and Altertumskunde* 2 (1938). [Egypt]

Borchardt, Ludwig. "Der Augustustempel auf Philae." *Jahrbuch des Deutschen Archäologischen Instituts* 18 (1903): 73-90. [Egypt]

Borchardt, Ludwig. *Zur Baugeschichte des Amonstempels von Karnak.* Leipzig: Hinrichs, 1905. [Egypt]

Boswell, R. B. "Destroying and Rebuilding the Temple." *ET* 26 (1914-15): 140-41. [Israel/Canaan]

Botterweck, G. Johannes. "*hêkhāl.*" In *Theological Dictionary of the Old Testament* 3:382-88. [Tabernacle]

Bouman, C. A. *Sacring and Crowning.* Groningen: Wolters, 1957. [Kingship/Coronation]

Bouyer, L. "Von der jüdischen zur christlichen Liturgie." *Internationale katholische Zeitschrift* 7 (1978): 509-20. [Ritual/Liturgy/Worship]

Bowman, J. "Temple and Festivals in the Persian Diatessaron." In *In Memoriam Paul Kahle,* edited by Matthew Black and Georg Fohrer. 53-61. Berlin: Töpelmann, 1968. [Israel/Canaan]

Bowman, John. "Ezekiel and the Zadokite Priesthood." *GUOST* 16 (1955-56): 1-14. [Priesthood]

Bowman, W. D. "Anointing for Healing." *Brethren Life and Thought* 4 (1959): 54-62. [Ablutions/Anointings]

Box, G. H. "The Temple Service." In *Encyclopaedia Biblica* 4:4948-56. [Israel/Canaan]

Brand, Joshua. "The Gates of Nicanor (a Contribution to Talmudic Archeology)" (in Hebrew). In *Minchah li-Yehudah* (Festschrift J. L. Zlotnik), edited by S. Assaf et al. 5-14. Jerusalem: Mossad Harav Kook, 1950. [Israel/Canaan]

Brand, Joshua. "Pilgrimages and Their Organization" (in Hebrew). *Mayanot* 6 (1947): 66-79. [Ritual/Liturgy/Worship]

Brand, Joshua. "Remarks on the Temple of Solomon" (in Hebrew). *Tarbiz* 34 (1964-65): 323-32. [Israel/Canaan]

Brand, Joshua. "Some Remarks on the Second Temple Edifice" (in Hebrew). *Tarbiz* 29 (1960): 210-17. [Israel/Canaan]

Brandon, Samuel G. F. *Creation Legends of the Ancient Near East.* London: Hodder and Stoughton, 1963. [Creation/Cosmology]

Brandon, Samuel G. F. "Divine Kings and Dying Gods." *Hibbert Journal* 53 (1954-55): 327-33. [Kingship/Coronation]

Brandon, Samuel G. F. *The Fall of Jerusalem and the Christian Church.* London: SPCK, 1957. [Israel/Canaan]

Bratcher, Dennis R. "Pilgrimage." In *Harper's Bible Dictionary*, 798-99. [Ritual/Liturgy/Worship]

Braun, F.-M. "L'expulsion des vendeurs du Temple (Mat., XXI, 12-17, 23-27, Mc., XI, 15-19, 27-33; Lc. XIX, 45-XX, 8; Jo., II, 13-22)." *RB* 38 (1929): 178-200. [Israel/Canaan]

Braun, Joseph. *Die liturgische Gewandung im Occident und Orient nach Ursprung und Entwicklung, Verwendung und Symbolik.* Freiburg im Breisgau: Herder, 1907. [Sacred Vestments]

Braun, Joseph. *Die pontificalen Gewänder des Abendlandes nach ihrer geschichtlichen Entwicklung.* Freiburg im Breisgau: Herder, 1893. [Sacred Vestments]

Braun, Joseph. *Die priesterlichen Gewänder des Abendlandes nach ihrer geschichtlichen Entwicklung.* Freiburg im Breisgau: Herder, 1897. [Sacred Vestments]

Braun, R. L. "The Message of Chronicles: Rally 'Round the Temple." *Concordia Theological Monthly* 42 (1971): 502-14. [Israel/Canaan]

Braun, R. L. "Solomon, the Chosen Temple Builder." *JBL* 95 (1976): 581-90. [Israel/Canaan]

Breasted, James H. "The Philosophy of a Memphite Priest." *ZÄS* 39 (1901): 39-54. [Priesthood]

Breasted, James H. *The Temples of Lower Nubia: Report of the Work of the Egyptian Expedition.* Chicago: Oriental Exploration Fund, 1906. [Egypt]

Brichto, H. C. "On Slaughter and Sacrifice, Blood and Atonement." *HUCA* 47 (1976): 19-55. [Sacrifice/Offerings]

Briend, Jacques. "Le Temple d' Hérode le Grand." *Le Monde de la Bible* 13 (1930): 12-13. [Israel/Canaan]

Bright, J. "The Restoration of the Jewish Community in Palestine, The Completion of the Temple." In *A History of Israel*, 3d ed. 360-72. Philadelphia: Westminster, 1981. [Israel/Canaan]

Brightman, Frank E., ed. *Liturgies, Eastern and Western*. Oxford: Clarendon, 1965. [Ritual/Liturgy/Worship]

Brin, Gershon. "Concerning Some of the Uses of the Bible in the *Temple Scroll*." *Revue de Qumran* 12 (November 1987): 519-28. [Israel/Canaan]

Brinke, Georg R. *Die Symbolik der Stiftshütte*. Wuppertal: Brockhaus, 1956. [Tabernacle]

Brinker, R. *The Influence of Sanctuaries in Early Israel*. Manchester: Manchester University Press, 1946. [Israel/Canaan]

Briquel, Dominique. "Sur l'équipement royal indo-européen: données latines et grecques." *RHR* 200 (1983): 67-74. [Kingship/Coronation]

Brock, Sebastian. "The Rebuilding of the Temple under Julian: A New Source." *PEQ* 108 (1976): 103-7. [Israel/Canaan]

Brock, Sebastian. "Syrian Baptismal Ordines (With Special Reference to the Anointings)." *Studia Liturgica* 12 (1977): 177-83. [Ablutions/Anointings]

Brodie, L. T. "A New Temple and a New Law: The Unity and Chronicler-Based Nature of Luke 1:1-4: 22a." *Journal for the Study of the New Testament* 5 (1979): 21-45. [Israel/Canaan]

Broneer, Oscar T. *Temple of Poseidon*. Princeton: American School of Classical Studies at Athens, 1971. [Greece/Rome]

Broneer, Oscar T. *Topography and Architecture*. Princeton: American School of Classical Studies at Athens, 1973. [Greece/Rome]

Broshi, M. "The Gigantic Dimensions of the Visionary Temple in the Temple Scroll." *BAR* 13/6 (1987): 36-37. [Israel/Canaan]

Broshi, M. "Pilgrimage to Jerusalem" (in Hebrew). In *Jerusalem—Ancient Sites*. 22-27. Tel Aviv: Tarbut ve Chinuch, 1967. [Ritual/Liturgy/Worship]

Broshi, M. "The Role of the Temple in the Herodian Economy." *JJS* 38 (Spring 1987): 31-37. [Israel/Canaan]

Brousseau, Gerald B. "The Source and Development of High Place Worship (Bamah) of Israel." Ph.D. diss., Ludwig Maximilian University, Munich, 1968. [Israel/Canaan]

Brown, D. "The Veil of the Temple Rent in Twain from the Top to the Bottom." *Expositor* 5 (1895): 158-60. [Israel/Canaan]

Brown, James R. *Temple and Sacrifice in Rabbinic Judaism*. Evanston: Seabury-Western Theological Seminary, 1963. [Sacrifice/Offerings]

174 A BIBLIOGRAPHY ON ANCIENT TEMPLES

Brown, John Pairman. "The Ark of the Covenant and the Temple of Janus: The Magico-Military Numen of the State in Jerusalem and Rome." *Biblische Zeitschrift* 30 (1986): 20-35. [Tabernacle]

Brown, John Pairman. "The Sacrificial Cult and Its Critique in Greek and Hebrew." *Journal of Semitic Studies* 24 (1979): 159-73; 25 (1980): 1-21. [Sacrifice/Offerings]

Bruce, F. F. "New Wine in Old Wine Skins: 3. The Corner Stone." *ET* 84 (1972-73): 231-35. [Israel/Canaan]

Brueggemann, Walter A. "Amos 4:4-13 and Israel's Covenant Worship." *VT* 15 (1965): 1-15. [Covenant]

Brueggemann, Walter A. "A Form-Critical Study of the Cultic Material in Deuteronomy: An Analysis of the Nature of Cultic Encounter in the Mosaic Tradition." Ph.D. diss., Union Theological Seminary, 1961. [Ritual/Liturgy/Worship]

Brueggemann, Walter A. "From Dust to Kingship (1 Kings 16:2, Genesis 3:19)." *ZAW* 84 (1972): 1-18. [Kingship/Coronation]

Brueggemann, Walter A. "Kingship and Chaos: A Study in Tenth Century Theology." *CBQ* 33 (1971): 317-32. [Kingship/Coronation]

Brueggemann, Walter A. "Presence of God, Cultic." In *The Interpreter's Dictionary of the Bible*, supp. vol., 680-83. [Israel/Canaan]

Brugsch, H. "Bau und Maasse des Tempels von Edfu." *ZÄS* 8 (1870): 153-61; 9 (1871): 32-45; 10 (1872): 1-16. [Egypt]

Brugsch, H. "Eine neue Bauurkunde des Tempels von Edfu." *ZÄS* 13 (1875): 113-23. [Egypt]

Brunner, A. "Die Sonnenbahn in ägyptischen Tempeln." In *Archäologie und Altes Testament, Festschrift für Kurt Galling*. 27-34. Tübingen: Mohr, 1970. [Egypt]

Brunner, H. "Magische, kultische und ethische Elemente ägyptischer Religiosität." *Antaios* 3 (1961): 534-43. [Ritual/Liturgy/Worship]

Bruston, C. "L'inscription des deux colonnes du temple de Salomon." *ZAW* 42 (1924): 153-54. [Israel/Canaan]

Buccellati, Giorgio. "The Enthronement of the King and the Capital City in Texts from Ancient Mesopotamia and Syria." In *Studies Presented to A. Leo Oppenheim*. 54-61. Chicago: Oriental Institute, 1964. [Kingship/Coronation]

Buchanan, George W. *The Consequences of the Covenant.* Leiden: Brill, 1970. [Covenant]

Buchanan, George W. "Mark 11:15-19: Brigands in the Temple." *HUCA* 30 (1959): 169-77; 31 (1960): 103-5. [Israel/Canaan]

Buchanan, George W. "Worship, Feasts and Ceremonies in the Early Jewish-Christian Church." *NTS* 26 (1980): 279-97. [Ritual/Liturgy/Worship]

Büchler, Adolph. "The Fore-Court of Women and the Brass Gate in the Temple of Jerusalem." *JQR* 10 (1898): 678-718. [Israel/Canaan]

Büchler, Adolph. "The Nicanor Gate and the Brass Gate." *JQR* 11 (1899): 46-63. [Israel/Canaan]

Büchler, Adolph. "On the History of the Temple Worship in Jerusalem." In *Studies in Jewish History—The Adolph Büchler Memorial Volume*, edited by I. Brodie and J. Rabbinowitz. 24-63. London: Oxford University Press, 1956. [Israel/Canaan]

Büchler, Adolph (Adolf). *Die Priester und der Cultus im letzten Jahrzehnt des jerusalemischen Tempels*. Vienna: Israelitisch-theologische Lehranstalt, 1895. [Priesthood]

Büchler, Adolph. "Private Sacrifices before the Jewish Day of Atonement." *Expositor* 22 (1911): 239-43. [Sacrifice/Offerings]

Büchler, Adolph. *Das Synedrion in Jerusalem und das grosse Beth-Din in der Quaderkammer des jerusalemischen Tempels*. Vienna: Israelitisch-Theologische Lehranstalt, 1902; reprinted in English as *The Sanhedrin in Jerusalem*. Jerusalem: Mossad Harav Kook, 1974. [Israel/Canaan]

Büchler, Adolph. "The Visits of Gentiles to the Temple." *JQR* 17 (1926-27): 31-38. [Israel/Canaan]

Büchler, Adolph. "Zur Geschichte der Tempelmusik und der Tempelpsalmen." *ZAW* 19 (1899): 96-133, 329-44; 20 (1900): 97-135. [Israel/Canaan]

Buck, Harry M. "Creation Stories and Creation Science." *Anima* 8 (1982): 110-22. [Creation/Cosmology]

Budd, P. J. "Priestly Instruction in Pre-Exilic Israel." *VT* 23 (1973): 1-14. [Priesthood]

Budde, K. "Das Deuteronomium und die Reform König Josias." *ZAW* 44 (1926): 177-224. [Israel/Canaan]

Budde, K. "Ephod und Lade." *ZAW* 39 (1921): 1-42. [Tabernacle]

Budde, K. "Die Herkunft Ṣadoḳ's." *ZAW* 52 (1934): 42-50. [Israel/Canaan]

Budde, K. "Die ursprüngliche Bedeutung Lade Jahwes." *ZAW* 21 (1901): 193-97. [Israel/Canaan]

Budde, K. "War die Lade Jahwes ein leerer Thron?" *Theologische Studien und Kritiken* 79 (1906): 489-507. [Israel/Canaan]

Budge, E. A. Wallis. *Liturgy of Funeral Offerings*. London: Paul, Trench, Trübner, 1909. [Egypt]

Budge, E. A. Wallis. *Osiris and the Egyptian Resurrection*. New York: Putman's Sons, 1911. [Egypt]

Buis, Pierre. "Écriture et prédication. 31-Le Seigneur libère et hommes: Psaume 76." *Études théologiques et religieuses* 55 (1980): 412-15. [Israel/Canaan]

Buis, Pierre. "Écriture et prédication. 43-Jérusalem, un chaudron rouillé. Ez. 24/3-14." *Études théologiques et religieuses* 56 (1981): 446-48. [Israel/Canaan]

Bull, R. J. "The Excavation of Tell er-Ras on Mt. Gerizim." *Biblical Archaeology* 31 (1968): 58-72. [Israel/Canaan]

Bull, R. J. "A Re-examination of the Shechem Temple." *BA* 23 (1960): 110-19. [Israel/Canaan]

Bultmann, R. "Die Frage nach der Echtheit von Mt. 16, 17-19." *Theologische Blätter* 20 (1941): 265-79. [Israel/Canaan]

Burch, V. "The 'Stone' and the 'Keys' (Mt. 16:18f)." *JBL* 52 (1933): 147-52. [Israel/Canaan]

Burdajewicz, M. "A propos des temples philistins de Qasileh." *RB* 93 (April 1986): 222-35. [Israel/Canaan]

Burgmann, E. H. "Royal Stole: An Inquiry." *Church Quarterly Review* 159 (1958): 408-14. [Kingship/Coronation]

Burkert, Walter. "The Meaning and Function of the Temple in Classical Greece." In *Temple in Society*, edited by Michael V. Fox. 27-47. Winona Lake: Eisenbrauns, 1988. [Greece/Rome]

Burkitt, F. C. "The Cleansing of the Temple." *JTS* 25 (1923-24): 386-90. [Israel/Canaan]

Burrows, E. "Some Cosmological Patterns in Babylonian Religion." In *The Labyrinth*, edited by Samuel H. Hooke, 45-69. London: Society for Promoting Christian Knowledge, 1935. [Creation/Cosmology]

Burtchaell, J. T. "Rituals of Jesus, the Anti-Ritualist." *Journal of the American Academy of Religion* 39 (1971): 513-25. [Ritual/Liturgy/Worship]

Buse, I. "The Cleansing of the Temple in the Synoptics and in John." *ET* 70 (1958): 22-24. [Israel/Canaan]

Busink, Th. A. *De Babylonische tempeltoren: een archaeologische en stijlcritische studie.* Leiden: Brill, 1949. [Mesopotamia]

Busink, Th. A. "Les Origines du Temple de Solomon." *Ex Oriente Lux: Jaarbericht van het vooraziatisch-egyptisch Gezelschap* 17 (1963): 165-92. [Israel/Canaan]

Busink, Th. A. *Sumerische en Babylonische tempelbouw.* Batavia: Noordhoff-Kolff, 1940. [Mesopotamia]

Busink, Th. A. "Tempelbouw in Oud-Mesopotame." *Ex Oriente Lux: Jaarbericht van het vooraziatisch-egyptisch Gezelschap* 5 (1937-38): 409-20. [Mesopotamia]

Busink, Th. A. *Der Tempel von Jerusalem*, 2 vols. Leiden: Brill, 1970-80. [Israel/Canaan]

Busse, Eduard. *Der Wein im Kult des Alten Testamentes.* Freiburg: Herder, 1922. [Ritual/Liturgy/Worship]

Busse, H. "Die arabischen Inschriften im und am Felsendom in Jerusalem." *Das heilige Land* 109/1-2 (1977): 8-24. [Israel/Canaan]

Caird, G. B. "The Mind of Christ, Christ's Attitude to Institutions: The Temple." *ET* 62 (1950-51): 259-61. [Israel/Canaan]

Caldecott, A. "The Significance of the Cleansing of the Temple." *JTS* 24 (1923): 382-86. [Israel/Canaan]

Caldecott, W. (William) Shaw. *Herod's Temple: Its New Testament Associations and Its Actual Structure.* Philadelphia: Union, [1914?]. [Israel/Canaan]

Caldecott, W. (William) Shaw. *The Second Temple in Jerusalem: Its History and Its Structure.* London: Murray, 1908. [Israel/Canaan]

Caldecott, W. (William) Shaw. *Solomon's Temple: Its History and Its Structure.* Philadelphia: Union, 1907. [Israel/Canaan]

Caldecott, William S. *The Tabernacle: Its History and Structure.* London: Religious Tract, 1904. [Tabernacle]

Caldecott, W. (William) Shaw. "The Temple Spoils Represented on the Arch of Titus." *PEFQ* 38 (1906): 306-15. [Israel/Canaan]

Caldecott, W. (William) Shaw, and J. Orr. "The Temple of Herod." In *The International Standard Bible Encyclopaedia,* edited by J. Orr. 5:2937-40. Michigan: Eerdmans, 1955. [Israel/Canaan]

Cali, François. *L'ordre grec: Essai sur le temple dorique.* Paris: Arthaud, 1958. [Greece/Rome]

Callaway, Phillip. "Exegetische Erwägungen zur Tempelrolle XXIX, 7-10." *Revue de Qumran* 12 (1985): 95-104. [Israel/Canaan]

Callaway, Phillip. "'Rbyh in the Temple Scroll 24, 8." *Revue de Qumran* 12 (1986): 269-70. [Israel/Canaan]

Callaway, Phillip. "Source Criticism of the Temple Scroll: The Purity Laws." *Revue de Qumran* 12 (1986): 213-22. [Israel/Canaan]

Calverley, Amice M. *The Temple of King Sethos I at Abydos,* edited by Alan H. Gardiner. Chicago: University of Chicago Press, 1933. [Egypt]

Caminos, Ricardo A. *The New Kingdom Temples of Buhen.* London: Oxford University Press, 1974. [Egypt]

Caminos, Ricardo A. *Two Stelae in the Kurnah Temple of Sethos I.* Berlin: Akademie, 1955. [Egypt]

Campbell, Anthony F. *The Ark Narrative (1 Sam 4-6; 2 Sam 6): A Form-Critical and Traditio-Historical Study.* Missoula, MT: Scholars, 1975. [Tabernacle]

Campbell, Anthony F. "Yahweh and the Ark: A Case Study in Narrative." *Journal of Biblical Literature* 98 (1979): 31-43. [Israel/Canaan]

Campbell, Edward F. "Jewish Shrines of the Hellenistic and Persian Periods." In *Symposia,* edited by Frank M. Cross. 159-67. Cambridge: American Schools of Oriental Research, 1979. [Israel/Canaan]

Campbell, Edward F., and G. Wright. "Tribal League Shrines in Amman and Shechem." *BA* 32 (1969): 104-16. [Israel/Canaan]

Campbell, K. M. "The New Jerusalem in Matthew 5:14." *Scottish Journal of Theology* 31 (1978): 335-63. [Israel/Canaan]

Canaan, Von T. "Das Opfer in palästinischen Sitten und Gebräuchen." *ZAW* 74 (1963): 31-44. [Sacrifice/Offerings]

Canney, M. A. "Ancient Conceptions of Kingship." In *Oriental Studies in Honour of Cursetji Erachji Pavry*, edited by Jal Dastur Cursetji Pavry. 63-75. London: Oxford University Press, 1933. [Kingship/Coronation]

Canney, M. A. "The Primordial Mound." *Journal of the Manchester Egyptian and Oriental Society* 20 (1936): 25-40. [Mountain]

Capart, Jean. *Abydos, Le temple de Seti Ier*. Brussels: Rossignol & Van den Bril, 1912. [Egypt]

Capart, Jean. *Le temple des muses*. Brussels: Musées royaux d'art et d'histoire, 1932; 2d ed., 1936. [Egypt]

Capt, E. Raymond. *King Solomon's Temple*. Thousand Oaks: Artisan Sales, 1979. [Israel/Canaan]

Caquot, André. "Pour une étude de l'initiation dans l'ancien Israël." In *Initiation*, edited by Claas J. Bleeker. 119-33. Leiden: Brill, 1965. [Ritual/Liturgy/Worship]

Caquot, André. "Le Psaume 47 et la royauté de Yahwe." *Revue d'histoire et de philosophie religieuses* 39 (1959): 311-37. [Israel/Canaan]

Caquot, André. "Le Psaume LXVIII." *RHR* 177 (1970): 147-82. [Kingship/Coronation]

Caquot, André. "Le Rouleau du Temple de Qumrân." *Etudes théologiques et religieuses* 53 (1978): 443-50. [Israel/Canaan]

Caquot, André. "Un sacrifice expiatoire à Ras Shamra." *Revue d'Histoire et de philosophie religieuses* 42 (1962): 201-11. [Sacrifice/Offerings]

Carlyle, Thomas. *The Mosaic Tabernacle*. Glasgow: Hobbs, 1901. [Tabernacle]

Carreira, José N. *A plano e a arquitectura do Templo de Salomâo à Luz dos paralelos orientais*. Porto: Livraria Tavares Martins, 1969. [Israel/Canaan]

Carter, Jane. "The Masks of Ortheia." *AJA* 91 (July 1987): 355-83. [Greece/Rome]

Carter, Joseph C. *The Sculpture of the Sanctuary of Athena Polias at Priene*. London: Thames and Hudson, 1983. [Greece/Rome]

Casalegno, Alberto. *Gesù e il Tempio: Studio redazionale di Luca-Atti*. Brescia: Morcelliana, 1984. [Israel/Canaan]

Casel, Odo. *Das christliche Kultmysterium*. Regensburg, Pustet, 1932. [Ritual/Liturgy/Worship]

Cases, Moses ben Samuel. *Be'ur 'al masekhet Middot.* Jerusalem: Hatchiya, 1963. [Israel/Canaan]

Cases, Moses ben Samuel. *Commentary on the Treatise Midoth by Moses Cases, and with it Hanukath Ha'Baith—Descriptive Analysis of the Plans of the Temple by Malchiel Ashkenazi (Tedeschi)* (in Hebrew). Jerusalem: Schreiber, 1963. [Measurement]

Caspari, Wilhelm. "*Tabur* (Nabel)." *ZDMG* 86 (1933): 49-65. [Sacred Space]

Cassano, R., et al. *Tempio di Adriano.* Roma: de Luca, 1982. [Greece/Rome]

Castelot, John J. *Anointing in the Old Testament.* Washington: CUAP, 1950. [Ablutions/Anointings]

Castelot, John J. "Religious Institutions of Israel." In *The Jerome Biblical Commentary,* edited by R. E. Brown, J. A. Fitzmyer, and R. E. Murphy. 703-35. Englewood Cliffs, NJ: Prentice-Hall, 1968. [Israel/Canaan]

Caton, Richard. *The Temples and Ritual of Asklepios at Epidauros and Athens.* London: Clay and Sons, 1900. [Greece/Rome]

Caubet-Iturbe, J. "Jerusalén y el Templo del Señor en los manuscriptos de Qumran y en el Nuevo Testamento." *Sacra Pagina: Miscellanea Biblica Congressus Internationalis Catholici de Re Biblica,* edited by J. Coppens, A. Descamps, and E. Massaux. 2 vols. 28-46. Paris: Gabalda, 1959. [Israel/Canaan]

Causse, Antonin. "De la Jérusalem terrestre à la Jérusalem céleste." *Revue d'histoire et de philosophie religieuses* 27 (1947): 12-36. [Israel/Canaan]

Causse, Antonin. *La vision de la Nouvelle Jérusalem.* Gembloux: n.p., 1939. [Israel/Canaan]

Cazelles, Henri. "David's Monarchy and the Gibeonite Claim (II Sam. xxi,1-14)." *PEQ* 87 (1955): 165-75. [Mountain]

Cazelles, Henri. "La rupture de la berît selon les prophetes." *JJS* 33/1-2 (1982): 133-44. [Covenant]

Cazelles, Henri. "Le Temple de Salomon." *Le Monde de la Bible* 13 (1980): 6-7. [Israel/Canaan]

Cenival, F. "Les associations dans les temples égyptiens d'après les données fournies par les papyrus démotiques." In *Religions en Egypte hellénistique et romaine, Colloque de Strasbourg, 16-18 mai 1967.* 5-19. Paris: Paris universitaires de France, 1969. [Egypt]

Chance, James B. "Jerusalem and the Temple in Lucan Eschatology." Ph.D. diss., Duke University, 1984. [Israel/Canaan]

Chaplin, T. "Middoth, or the Measurement of the Temple, with the Commentary of Rabbi Ohadiah of Bartenora." *PEQ* 18 (1886): 224-28; 19 (1887): 60-63, 116-28, 132. [Measurement]

Chaplin, T. "The Stone of Foundation and the Site of the Temple." *PEQ* 8 (1876): 23-28. [Israel/Canaan]

Charbel, Antonio. "Introdução a Liturgia Sacrifical da Antiga e da Nova Aliança." *Revista de Cultura Teologica* 2 (1962): 41-52. [Sacrifice/Offerings]

Charbel, Antonio. "Offerta di prodotti vegetali nei sacrifici *šelāmîm.*" *Euntes Docete* 26 (1973): 398-403. [Sacrifice/Offerings]

Charbel, Antonio. "Positione degli *šelāmîm* nella Scrittura." *Salesianum* 34 (1974): 431-42. [Sacrifice/Offerings]

Charbel, Antonio. "Il sacrificio di comunione presso i Greci." *Bibbia e Oriente* 16 (1974): 263-73. [Sacrifice/Offerings]

Charbel, Antonio. *Zebak Šelāmîm: Sacrificio pacifico nei suoi riti e nel suo significato religioso e figurativo.* Jerusalem: n.p., 1967. [Sacrifice/Offerings]

Charles, R. H. "A Solution of the Chief Difficulties in Revelation XX-XXII." *ET* 26 (1914-15): 54-57, 119-23. [Israel/Canaan]

Charpin, D. "Temples à decouvrir en Syrie du Nord d'après des documents inédits de Mari." *Iraq* 45 (1983): 56-63. [Mesopotamia]

Charriere, G. "L'Orientation de quelques ziggurats et sanctuaries du Moyen-Orient." *Revue d'Assyriologie* 58 (1964): 9-22. [Mesopotamia]

Chary, T. "Le Temple d'Ezéchiel." *Le Monde de la Bible* 40 (1985): 34-38. [Israel/Canaan]

Chase, Ira J. *The Jewish Tabernacle.* Cincinnati: Standard, 1883. [Tabernacle]

Chassinat, Émile. *Le mammisi d'Edfou.* Cairo: Imprimerie de l'Institut français d'archéologie orientale du Caire, 1939. [Egypt]

Chassinat, Émile. *Le temple de Dendara.* Cairo: Imprimerie de l'Institut français d'archéologie orientale du Caire, 1934. [Egypt]

Chassinat, Émile. *Le temple d'Edfou.* Cairo: Imprimerie de l'Institut français d'archéologie orientale du Caire, 1934. [Egypt]

Chavel, C. B. "An Additional Surname for the Sanctuary in Jerusalem" (in Hebrew). *Hadorom* 38 (1974): 45-46. [Israel/Canaan]

Cheetham, F. P. "Destroy This Temple and in Three Days I Will Raise It Up (St. John ii, 19)." *JTS* 24 (1922-23): 315-17. [Israel/Canaan]

Chelhod, Joseph. *Le sacrifice chez les Arabes; recherches sur l'évolution, la nature et la fonction des rites sacrificiels en Arabie Occidentale.* Paris: Presses universitaires de France, 1955. [Sacrifice/Offerings]

Chen, Doron. "The Design of the Dome of the Rock in Jerusalem." *PEQ* 112 (1980): 41-50. [Israel/Canaan]

Chevrier, Henri. *Le temple reposoir de Ramsès à Karnak.* Cairo: Imprimerie de l'Institut français d'archéologie orientale du Caire, 1933. [Egypt]

Chevrier, Henri. *Le temple reposoir de Seti II à Karnak.* Cairo: Imprimerie nationale, 1940. [Egypt]

Cheyne, T. K. "Ark of the Covenant." In *Encyclopaedia Biblica*, 300-310. [Tabernacle]

Chiera, Edward. *Selected Temple Accounts from Telloh, Yokha and Drehem*. Princeton: Princeton University Press, 1922. [Mesopotamia]

Chipiez, Charles. *Le Temple de Jérusalem et la Maison du Bois-Liban restitués d'après Ézéchiel et le livre des Rois*. Paris: Hachette, 1889. [Israel/Canaan]

Chopineau, J. "Les prophètes et le temple." *Le Monde de la Bible* 13 (1980): 10-13. [Israel/Canaan]

Chronis, H. L. "The Torn Veil: Cultus and Christology in Mark 15:37-39." *JBL* 101 (March 1982): 97-114. [Israel/Canaan]

Chrysostomos, Archimandrite. "Historiographical Problematics in the Study of the Origin of Liturgical Vesture." *Greek Orthodox Theological Review* 26 (1981): 87-96. [Sacred Vestments]

Chytraeus, David. *On Sacrifice: A Reformation Treatise in Biblical Theology*. St. Louis: Concordia, 1962. [Sacrifice/Offerings]

Cipriano, Palmira. *Templum*. Rome: Prima cattedra di glottologia Université "La Spienza," 1983. [Greece/Rome]

Clapton, Edward. *The Precious Stones of the Bible—Descriptive and Symbolical*, 2d ed. London: Simpkin, Marshall, Hamilton, Kent, 1899. [Sacred Vestments]

Clark, K. W. "Worship in the Jerusalem Temple after A.D. 70." *NTS* 6 (1960): 269-80. [Israel/Canaan]

Clements, Ronald E. "Deuteronomy and the Jerusalem Cult-Tradition." *VT* 15 (1965): 300-12. [Israel/Canaan]

Clements, Ronald E. "Temple and Land." *GUOST* 19 (1961/1962): 16-28. [Israel/Canaan]

Clermont-Ganneau, Charles. "Archaeological and Epigraphic Notes on Palestine: The 'Gate of Nicanor' in the Temple of Jerusalem." *PEQ* 35 (1903): 125-31. [Israel/Canaan]

Clermont-Ganneau, Charles. "A Column of Herod's Temple." In *Archaeological Researches in Palestine during the Years 1873-1874*, translated by Aubrey Stewart. 1:254-58. London: Palestine Exploration Fund, 1896. [Israel/Canaan]

Clermont-Ganneau, Charles. "Découverte à Jérusalem d'une synagogue de l'époque hérodienne." *Syria* 1 (1920): 190-97. [Israel/Canaan]

Clermont-Ganneau, Charles. "Discovery of a Tableau from Herod's Temple." *PEFQ* 3 (1871): 132-33. [Israel/Canaan]

Clermont-Ganneau, Charles. "La fausse stèle du Temple de Jérusalem." In Clermont-Ganneau, *Les fraudes archéologiques en Palestine*. 39-48. Paris: Leroux, 1885. [Israel/Canaan]

Clermont-Ganneau, Charles. "La Porte de Nicanor du temple de Jérusalem." *Recueil d'archeologie orientale* 5 (1903): 334-40. [Israel/Canaan]

Clermont-Ganneau, Charles. "The Statue of Hadrian Placed in the Temple of Jerusalem." *PEFQ* (1874): 207-10. [Israel/Canaan]

Clermont-Ganneau, Charles. "Une stèle du Temple de Jérusalem." *Revue archéologique* n.s./23 (1872): 214-34, 290-96. [Israel/Canaan]

Clermont-Ganneau, Charles. "The Veil of the Temple of Jerusalem at Olympia." *PEFQ* 10 (1878): 79-81. [Israel/Canaan]

Clermont-Ganneau, Charles. "The Veil of the Temple." In *The Survey of Western Palestine*, edited by C. Warren and C. R. Conder. 9 vols., 5:340-41. London: Palestine Exploration Fund, 1881-89. [Israel/Canaan]

Clermont-Ganneau, Charles, and C. Warren. "*Aven Hash-Sheteyah.*" *PEFQ* 7 (1875): 182-83. [Israel/Canaan]

Clifford, Richard J. "The Cosmic Mountain in Canaan and the Old Testament." *Biblica* 55 (1974): 443-46. [Mountain]

Clifford, Richard J. "Cosmogonies in the Ugaritic Texts and in the Bible." *Orientalia* 53 (1984): 183-201. [Creation/Cosmology]

Clifford, Richard J. "The Temple and the Holy Mountain." In *The Temple in Antiquity*, edited by Truman G. Madsen. 107-24. Provo, UT: Brigham Young University Press, 1984. [Mountain]

Clifford, Richard J. "The Temple in the Ugaritic Myth of Baal." In *Symposia*, edited by Frank M. Cross. 137-45. Cambridge: American Schools of Oriental Research, 1979. [Israel/Canaan]

Clifford, Richard J. "Tent of El and the Israelite Tent of Meeting." *CBQ* 33 (1971): 221-27. [Tabernacle]

Clowney, E. P. "The Final Temple." *Westminster Theological Journal* 35 (1973): 156-89. [Israel/Canaan]

Coats, G. W. "Conquest Traditions in the Wilderness Theme." *JBL* 95 (1976): 177-90. [Mountain]

Coats, G. W. "Moses in Midian." *JBL* 92 (1973): 3-10. [Mountain]

Cody, Aelred. *Heavenly Sanctuary and Liturgy in the Epistle to the Hebrews.* St. Meinrad, IN: Grail, 1960. [Israel/Canaan]

Cody, Aelred. *A History of Old Testament Priesthood.* Rome: Pontifical Biblical Institute, 1969. [Priesthood]

Cohen, J. "Les pélerinages au Temple de Jérusalem." *Le Monde de la Bible* 13 (1980): 29-32. [Israel/Canaan]

Cohen, Martin A. "The Role of the Shilonite Priesthood in the United Monarchy of Ancient Israel." *Hebrew Union College Annual* 35 (1965): 59-98. [Priesthood]

Cohen, Shaye J. D. "The Temple and the Synagogue." In *The Temple in Antiquity*, edited by Truman G. Madsen. 151-74. Provo: Brigham Young University Press, 1984. [Israel/Canaan]

Cohn, Erich W. "Second Thoughts about the Perforated Stone on the Haram of Jerusalem." *PEQ* 114 (1982): 143-46. [Israel/Canaan]

Cohn, Robert L. "The Mountains and Mount Zion." *Judaism* 26 (1977): 97-115. [Mountain]

Cohn, Robert L. *The Shape of Sacred Space: Four Biblical Studies.* Chico: Scholars, 1981. [Mountain]

Cohn-Wiener, Ernst. "Der Tempel des Herodes." In Cohn-Wiener, *Die jüdische Kunst, ihre Geschichte von den Anfängen bis zur Gegenwart.* 71-75. Berlin: Wasservogel, 1929. [Israel/Canaan]

Cole, Harold F. G. *Concerning Solomon's Temple.* London: Roberts, 1920. [Israel/Canaan]

Cole, Robert A. *The New Temple: A Study in the Origins of the Catechetical 'Form' of the Church in the New Testament.* London: Tyndale, 1950. [Israel/Canaan]

Collins, Alvin O. "The Significance of the Temple in the Religion of the Canonical Prophets." Ph.D. diss., Southern Baptist Theological Seminary, 1952. [Israel/Canaan]

Collins, John J. "The Meaning of Sacrifice: A Contrast of Methods." *Biblical Research* 22 (1977): 19-34. [Sacrifice/Offerings]

Collins, M. "Ritual Symbols and the Ritual Process: The Work of Victor W. Turner." *Worship* 50 (1976): 336-46. [Ritual/Liturgy/Worship]

Comay, Joan. *The Temple of Jerusalem.* New York: Holt, Rinehart and Winston, 1975. [Mountain]

Comblin, J. "La liturgie de la Nouvelle Jérusalem (Apoc. XXI, 1-XXII, 5)." *Ephemerides theologicae lovanienses* 29 (1953): 15-40. [Israel/Canaan]

Conder, Claude R. "Age of the Temple Wall: Pilasters of the West Haram Wall." *PEQ* 9 (1877): 135-37. [Israel/Canaan]

Conder, Claude R. "Herod's Temple." In *The City of Jerusalem.* 123-32. London: Murray, 1909. [Israel/Canaan]

Conder, Claude R. "The High Sanctuary of Jerusalem." *Transactions of the Royal Institute of British Architects* (1879): 25-60. [Israel/Canaan]

Conder, Claude R. "The Temple and Calvary." In *Tent Work in Palestine—A Record Discovery and Adventure.* 1:346-76. London: Bentley, 1879. [Israel/Canaan]

Congar, Yves M. *The Mystery of the Temple.* Westminster: Newman, 1962. [Israel/Canaan]

Conti, Flavio. *Shrines of Power,* translated by Pat Craegh. London: Cassell, 1978. [Greece/Rome]

Conybeare, Fred. "Les sacrifices d'animaux dans les anciennes églises chrétiennes." *RHR.* 44 (1901): 108-14. [Sacrifice/Offerings]

Cook, S. A. "The Synagogue of Theodotus at Jerusalem." *PEFQ* 53 (1921): 22-23. [Israel/Canaan]

Cook, S. A. "The Theory of Sacrifice." *JTS* 22 (1921): 327-47. [Sacrifice/Offerings]

Cooke, F. A. "The Cleansing of the Temple." *ET* 63/10 (1952): 321-22. [Israel/Canaan]

Cooke, G. "Israelite King as the Son of God." *ZAW* 73 (1961): 202-25. [Kingship/Coronation]

Cooke, George A. "Some Considerations on the Text and Teaching of Ezekiel 40-48." *ZAW* 42 (1924): 105-15. [Israel/Canaan]

Cooke, George A. "The Temple and the Community of the Future." In *A Critical and Exegetical Commentary on the Book of Ezekiel.* 425-541. Edinburgh: Clark, 1936. [Israel/Canaan]

Cooper, Charles W. *The Precious Stones of the Bible: With an Account of the Breastplate of the High Priest, the Ephod and Urim and Thummim.* London: Allenson, 1924. [Sacred Vestments]

Cooper, Frederick A. *The Temple of Apollo at Bassai: A Preliminary Study.* New York: Garland, 1978. [Greece/Rome]

Cooper, Frederick A., et al. *The Temple of Zeus at Nemea.* Athens: Benaki Museum, 1983. [Greece/Rome]

Coppens, J. "The Spiritual Temple in the Pauline Letters and Its Background." *Studia Evangelica* 6 (1973): 53-66. [Israel/Canaan]

Corbett, S. "Some Observations on the Gateways to the Herodian Temple in Jerusalem." *PEQ* 84 (1952): 7-14. [Israel/Canaan]

Corbin, Henry. "Ritual sabéen et exégèse ismaelienne du rituel." *Eranos Jahrbuch* 19 (1950): 181-246. [Ritual/Liturgy/Worship]

Corbin, Henry. *Temple et contemplation.* Paris: Flammarion, 1980; also in English as *Temple and Contemplation*, translated by Philip Sherrard. London: Islamic, 1986. [Sacred Space]

Corney, Richard W. "Zadok the Priest." In *The Interpreter's Dictionary of the Bible* 4:928-29. [Priesthood]

Cornfeld, Gaalyahu. *Bet ha-Mikdash Tamun mi-Darom le-Khipat ha-Selaᶜ.* Tel Aviv: Cornfeld, 1985/1987. [Israel/Canaan]

Cornfeld, Gaalyahu, ed. "Description of the Temple." In Josephus, *The Jewish War*, contributing editors Benjamin Mazar and Paul Maier. 346-64. Grand Rapids: Zondervan, 1982. [Israel/Canaan]

Cothenet, E. "Attitude de l'église naissante à l'égard du Temple de Jérusalem." In *Liturgie et l'église particulière et liturgie de l'église universelle. Conférences Saint-Serge XXIIe Semaine d'Études Liturgiques, Paris, 1975*, edited by A. Pistoia and A. M. Triacca. 89-111. Rome: Edizioni Liturgiche, 1977. [Israel/Canaan]

Couard, Ludwig. "Die religiosnationale Bedeutung der Lade Jahves." *ZAW* 12 (1892): 53-90. [Tabernacle]

Coulton, J. J. "Towards Understanding Greek Temple Design: General Considerations." *Annual of the British School at Athens* 70 (1975): 59-99. [Greece/Rome]

Couroyer, B. "Le temple de Yaho et l'orientation dans les papyrus araméens d'Éléphantine." *RB* 68 (1961): 525-40; 75 (January 1968): 80-85. [Israel/Canaan]

Cowan, Aldworth. *God's Tent.* Old Tappan: Revell, 1980. [Tabernacle]

Crehan, J. H. "Priesthood, Kingship and Prophecy." *Theological Studies* 42 (1981): 216-31. [Priesthood]

Cross, Frank M. "The Cultus of the Israelite League." In Cross, *Canaanite Myth and Hebrew Epic.* 77-144. Cambridge: Harvard University Press, 1973. [Tabernacle]

Cross, Frank M. "The Ideologies of Kingship in the Era of Empire: Conditional Covenant and Eternal Decree." In *Canaanite Myth and Hebrew Epic.* 219-73. Cambridge, MA: Harvard University Press, 1973. [Kingship/Coronation]

Cross, Frank M. "The Priestly Houses of Early Israel." In *Canaanite Myth and Hebrew Epic*, 195-215. Cambridge: Harvard University Press, 1973. [Priesthood]

Cross, Frank M. "The Priestly Tabernacle in the Light of Recent Research." In *Temples and High Places in Biblical Times*, edited by Avraham Biran. 169-80. Jerusalem: Nelson Glueck School of Biblical Archaeology, 1981; also in a slightly revised version in *The Temple in Antiquity*, edited by Truman G. Madsen. 91-105. Provo: Brigham Young University Press, 1984. [Tabernacle]

Cross, Frank M. "The Tabernacle: A Study from an Archaeological and Historical Approach." *BA* 10 (1947): 45-68; reprinted in slightly revised form as "The Priestly Tabernacle" In *Biblical Archaeologist Reader*, edited by G. Ernest Wright and D. N. Freedman. 201-28. New York: Anchor, 1961. [Tabernacle]

Culianu, Ioan P. " 'Démonisation du cosmos' et dualisme gnostique." *RHR* 196 (1979): 3-40. [Creation/Cosmology]

Cullmann, Oscar. *Early Christian Worship.* London: SCM, 1953. [Ritual/Liturgy/Worship]

Cullmann, Oscar. "A New Approach to the Interpretation of the Fourth Gospel." *ET* 71 (1959): 8-12, 39-43. [Israel/Canaan]

Cullmann, Oscar. "L'opposition contre le Temple de Jérusalem, motif commun de la théologie Johannique et du monde ambiant." *NTS* 5 (1958-59): 157-73. [Israel/Canaan]

Daglin, Aharon Z. *Book of the Temple of Aaron: An Explanation of the Tabernacle and Its Vessels* (in Hebrew). Warsaw: Argelbrand Brothers, 1891. [Tabernacle]

Dalmais, I. H. "Le souvenir du Temple dans la liturgie chrétienne." *Bible et Terre Sainte* 122 (1970): 6-7. [Israel/Canaan]

Dalman, Gustaf. "Der Felsen als Fundament des Altars." In *Neue Petra-Forschungen und der heilige Felsen von Jerusalem*, edited by Gustaf Dalman, 137-45. Leipzig: Hinrichs, 1912. [Sacrifice/Offerings]

Dalman, Gustaf. "Der östliche Stadthügel." In Dalman, *Jerusalem und sein Gelände*. 112-38. Hildesheim: Olms, 1972. [Israel/Canaan]

Dalman, Gustaf. "The Search for the Temple Treasure at Jerusalem." *PEQ* 44 (1912): 35-39. [Israel/Canaan]

Dalman, Gustaf. "Der zweite Tempel zu Jerusalem." *Palästinajahrbuch* 5 (1909): 29-57. [Israel/Canaan]

Daly, Robert J. *Christian Sacrifice*. Washington, D.C.: Catholic University of America Press, 1978. [Sacrifice/Offerings]

Daly, Robert J. "New Testament Concept of Christian Sacrificial Activity." *BTB* 8 (1978): 99-107. [Sacrifice/Offerings]

Daly, Robert J. *The Origins of the Christian Doctrine of Sacrifice*. Philadelphia: Fortess, 1978. [Sacrifice/Offerings]

Dandamayev, M. A. "State and Temple in Babylonia in the First Millennium B.C." In *State and Temple Economy in the Ancient Near East:*, edited by Edward Lipiński. 2 vols., 2:589-96. Louvain: Departement Orientalistiek, 1979. [Mesopotamia]

Dandamayev, M. A. "Tempelbauern in späten Babylonien." *Palestinski Sbornik* 17 (1967): 41-49. [Mesopotamia]

Dandamayev, M. A. "Temple and State in Babylonia." *Vestnik Drevnei Istorii* 4/98 (1966): 17-39. [Mesopotamia]

Daniel, Suzanne. *Recherches sur le vocabulaire du culte dans la "Septante."* Paris: Klincksieck, 1966. [Ritual/Liturgy/Worship]

Daniélou, Jean. "Onction et baptême chez Gregoire de Nysse." *Ephemerides Liturgicae* 90 (1976): 440-45. [Ablutions/Anointings]

Daniélou, Jean. *Le Signe du Temple*. Paris: Gallimard, 1942. [Israel/Canaan]

Daniélou, Jean. "La symbolique du temple de Jérusalem chez Philon et Josèphe." In *Le symbolisme cosmique des monuments religieux*. 83-90. Rome: Istituto Italiano par il Medio ed Estremo Oriente, 1957. [Israel/Canaan]

Dar, S., and J. Mintzker. "A Roman Temple at Senaim, Mount Hermon" (in Hebrew; *English summary). *Eretz-Israel* 19 (1987): 30-45, *74. [Greece/Rome]

Daraki, Maria. "Aspects du sacrifice dionysiaque." *RHR* 197 (1980): 131-57. [Sacrifice/Offerings]

Dauenhauer, B. P. "Some Aspects of Language and Time in Ritual Worship." *International Journal for the Philosophy of Religion* 6 (1975): 54-62. [Ritual/Liturgy/Worship]

Daumas, Francois. *Les mammisis des temples l'égyptiens.* Paris: Les belles lettres, 1958. [Egypt]

Daumas, Francois. "Les propylées du Temple d'Hathor à Philae et le culte de la déese." *ZÄS* 95 (1968): 1-17. [Egypt]

Daumas, Francois. "Les textes géographiques du Trésor D' du temple de Dendara." In *State and Temple Economy in the Ancient Near East,* edited by Edward Lipiński. 2 vols., 2:689-706. Louvain: Departement Orientalistiek, 1979. [Egypt]

Davey, C. J. "Temples of the Levant and the Buildings of Solomon." *Tyndale Bulletin* 31 (1980): 107-46. [Israel/Canaan]

David, A. Rosalie. *The Ancient Egyptians: Religious Beliefs and Practices.* London: Routledge and Kegan Paul, 1982. [Egypt]

David, A. Rosalie. *A Guide to Religious Ritual at Abydos.* Warminster: Aris and Phillips, 1981. [Ritual/Liturgy/Worship]

Davies, Douglas. "An Interpretation of Sacrifice in Leviticus." *ZAW* 89 (1977): 387-99. [Sacrifice/Offerings]

Davies, Douglas. "Sacrifice in Theology and Anthropology." *Scottish Journal of Theology* 35 (1982): 351-58. [Sacrifice/Offerings]

Davies, G. Henton. "The Ark in the Psalms." In *Promise and Fulfillment, Essays Presented to S. H. Hooke in Celebration of His Ninetieth Birthday,* edited by F. F. Bruce. 51-61. Edinburgh: Clark, 1963. [Tabernacle]

Davies, G. Henton. "Ark of the Covenant." In *The Interpreter's Dictionary of the Bible* 1:222-26. [Tabernacle]

Davies, G. Henton. "The Ark of the Covenant." *Annual of the Swedish Theological Institute* 5 (1967): 30-47. [Tabernacle]

Davies, G. Henton. "Presence of God." In *The Interpreter's Dictionary of the Bible* 3:874-75. [Israel/Canaan]

Davies, G. Henton. "Tabernacle." In *The Interpreter's Dictionary of the Bible* 4:498-506. [Tabernacle]

Davies, John G. *A Dictionary of Liturgy and Worship.* New York: Macmillan, 1972. [Ritual/Liturgy/Worship]

Davies, John G. *Temples, Churches, and Mosques—Religious Architecture.* New York: Pilgrim, 1982. [Greece/Rome]

Davies, N. de Garis. "Two Pictures of Temples." *JEA* 41 (1955): 80-82. [Egypt]

Davies, P. R. "The Ideology of the Temple in the Damascus Document." *JJS* 33/1-2 (1982): 287-301. [Israel/Canaan]

Davies, Robertson. "Nobility and Style." *Parabola* 7/3 (1982): 15-21. [Kingship/Coronation]

Davies, T. W. "Temple." In *Dictionary of the Bible* 4:695-716. [Israel/Canaan]

Davies, William D. *The Gospel and the Land: Early Christianity and Jewish Territorial Doctrine.* Los Angeles: University of California Press, 1974. [Israel/Canaan]

Davies, William D. "Jerusalem et la terre dans la tradition chretienne." *Revue de l'histoire et de philosophie religieuses* 55 (1975): 491-533. [Israel/Canaan]

Dawkins, Richard M. *The Sanctuary of Artemis Orthia at Sparta.* London: Council of the Society for the Promotion of Hellenic Studies, 1929. [Greece/Rome]

Dawsey, J. M. "Confrontation in the Temple (Luke 19:45–20:47)." *Perspectives in Religious Studies* 11 (1984): 153-65. [Israel/Canaan]

Dean, Beryl. *Embroidery in Religion and Ceremonial.* London: Batsford, 1981. [Sacred Vestments]

de Buck, Adriaan. *De Egyptische voorstellingen betreffende den Oerheuvel.* Leiden: Ijdo, 1922. [Egypt]

de Charms, George. *The Tabernacle of Israel.* New York: Pageant Press International, 1969. [Tabernacle]

Degardin, J. "Correspondances osiriennes entre les temples d'Opet et de Khonsou." *JNES* 44 (1985): 115-32. [Egypt]

Deglin, Selig H. *Mikdash Aharon.* C.-Ilerepóypr: n.p., 1894. [Tabernacle]

de Groot, J. *Die Altäre des salomonischen Tempelhofes: Beiträge zur Wissenschaft vom alten Testament.* Stuttgart: Kohlhammer, 1924. [Israel/Canaan]

De Guglielmo, A. "A Sacrifice in the Ugaritic Texts." *CBQ* 17 (1955): 196-216. [Sacrifice/Offerings]

de Haan, Martin R. *The Tabernacle, The House of Blood* Grand Rapids: Zondervan, 1973. [Tabernacle]

de Jonge, M. "Het motief van het gescheurde voorhangsel van der Tempel in een aantal vroegchristlijke geschriften." *Nederlands Theologisch Tijdschrift* 22 (1967): 257-76. [Israel/Canaan]

de Jonge, M., and Adam S. Van der Woude. "11Q Melchizedek and the New Testament." *NTS* 12 (1965-66): 301-26. [Priesthood]

Del Alamo, M. "Las medidas de la Jerusalem celeste (Apoc. 21, 16)." *Cultura biblica* 3 (1946): 136-38. [Israel/Canaan]

de Langhe, R. "L'autel d'or du Temple de Jérusalem." *Biblica* 40 (1959): 476-94. [Israel/Canaan]

de la Potterie, I. "L'onction du chrétien par la foi." *Biblica* 40 (1959): 12-69. [Ablutions/Anointings]

Delcor, Mathias. "Reflexions sur la fête de la xylophorie dans le *Rouleau du Temple* et les textes parallèles." *Revue de Qumran* 12 (November 1987): 561-69. [Israel/Canaan]

Delcor, Mathias. "Le statut du roi d'après le Rouleau du Temple." *Henoch* 3 (1981): 47-68. [Israel/Canaan]

Delcor, Mathias. "Le temple d'Onias en Égypte." *RB* 75 (1968): 188-203, with Post-Scriptum by Roland de Vaux, 204-5. [Israel/Canaan]

Delcor, Mathias. "Le trésor de la maison de Yahweh des origines à l'exil." *VT* 12 (1962): 353-77. [Israel/Canaan]

Delcourt, Marie. *Les grands sanctuaires de la Grèce.* Paris: Presses universitaires de France, 1947. [Greece/Rome]

Delekat, Lienhard. *Asylie und Schutzorakel am Zionheiligtum.* Leiden: Brill, 1967. [Israel/Canaan]

Delitzsch, F. "Esagila, the Babylonian Pantheon." *Records of the Past* 2 (1903): 322-31. [Mesopotamia]

Del Medico, H. E. "Melchisédech." *ZAW* 69 (1957): 160-70. [Priesthood]

Delougaz, Pinhas. *Pre-Sargonid Temples in the Diyala Region.* Chicago: University of Chicago Press, 1942. [Mesopotamia]

Delougaz, Pinhas. *The Temple Oval of Khafajah.* Chicago: University of Chicago, 1940. [Mesopotamia]

Demangel, Robert. *Le sanctuaire d'Athèna Pronaia.* Paris: de Boccard 1926. [Greece/Rome]

de Moor, F. "Le temple reconstruit par Zorobabel." *Le Muséon* 8 (1889): 364-371, 467-73, 514-51; 9 (1890): 5-15. [Israel/Canaan]

Demsky, A. "The Trumpeter's Inscription from the Temple Mount" (in Hebrew; *English summary). *Eretz-Israel* 18 (1985): 40-42,*66. [Mountain]

Demsky, A. "When the Priests Trumpeted the Onset of the Sabbath: A Monumental Hebrew Inscription from the Ancient Temple Mount Recalls the Sacred Signal." *BAR* 12/6 (1986): 50-52. [Israel/Canaan]

Derchain, Philippe. *Le Papyrus Salt 825 (B.M. 10051), rituel pour la conservation de la vie en Égypte.* Brussels: Palais de Academies, 1965. [Ritual/Liturgy/Worship]

Derchain, Philippe. *Rites égyptiens.* Brussels: Fondation égyptologique reine Élisabeth, 1962. [Ritual/Liturgy/Worship]

Derenbourg, J. "Une stèle du Temple d'Hérode." *Journal Asiatique* 6 (1872): 178-95. [Israel/Canaan]

Derfler, Steven. "A Terracotta Figurine from the Hellenistic Temple at Tel Beersheba." *IEJ* 31 (1981): 97-99. [Israel/Canaan]

Derouche, M. "Contra Creation, Covenant, and Conquest (Jer. VIII. 13)." *VT* 30 (1980): 280-90. [Creation/Cosmology]

Derrett, J. Duncan M. "No Stone upon Another: Leprosy and the Temple." *Journal for the Study of the New Testament* 30 (1987): 3-20. [Israel/Canaan]

Derrett, J. Duncan M. "The Zeal of the House and the Cleansing of the Temple." *Downside Review* 95/319 (1977): 79-94. [Israel/Canaan]

de Ruyt, C. "L'ordre de construction du temple périptère grec: état de la question et arguments nouveaux." *Les Études Classiques* 51 (1983): 63-70. [Greece/Rome]

de Salignac Fénelon, F. "Note on the Site of the Temple." *PEFQ* 31 (1899): 272. [Israel/Canaan]

de Tarragon, J. M. "David et l'arche: 2 Sam 6." *RB* 86 (1979): 514-23. [Tabernacle]

de Tarragon, J. M. "La *kapporet* est-elle une fiction ou un élément du culte tardif?" *RB* 88 (1981): 5-12. [Tabernacle]

Detienne, Marcel, and J. P. Vernant. *La cuisine du sacrifice en pays grec.* Paris: Gallimard, 1979. [Sacrifice/Offerings]

Dever, William G. "Monumental Architecture in Ancient Israel in the Period of the United Monarchy." In *Studies in the Period of David and Solomon,* edited by T. Ishida. 269-306. Winona Lake, IN: Eisenbrauns, 1982. [Israel/Canaan]

de Vogüe, M. "Note sur le temple de Jérusalem." *Revue archéologique* n.s./7 (1863): 281-92. [Israel/Canaan]

Devries, L. F. "Incense Altars from the Period of the Judges and Their Significance." Ph.D. diss., Southern Baptist Theological Seminary, 1975. [Sacrifice/Offerings]

de Wit, Constant. "Einige Bemerkungen zu den Inschriften des Epet-Tempels zu Karnak." *Wiener Zeitschrift für die Kunde des Morgenlandes* 54 (1957): 234-39. [Egypt]

de Wit, Constant. "Inscriptions dedicatoires du temple d'Edfou." *Chronique d'Égypte* 36 (1961): 56-97, 277-320. [Egypt]

de Wit, Constant. "Les inscriptions des lions-gargouilles du temple d'Edfou." *Chronique d'Égypte* 29 (1954): 29-45. [Egypt]

de Wit, Constant. *Les inscriptions du temple d'Opet à Karnak,* 3 vols. Brussels: Fondation de la Reine Élisabeth, 1958-68. [Egypt]

de Young, James C. *Jerusalem in the New Testament: The Significance of the City in the History of Redemption and in Eschatology.* Kampen: Kok, 1960. [Israel/Canaan]

Dhorme, Édouard (Paul). "Les Cherubins." *RB* 35 (1926): 328-58, 481-95. [Tabernacle]

Dhorme, Édouard. "Le nom des Chérubins." In Dhorme, *Recueil Édouard Dhorme: Études et orientales.* 671-83. Paris: Imprimerie Nationale, 1951. [Tabernacle]

Dhorme, Édouard P. "Le plus ancien temple d'Ishtar à Ninive." *Revue de l'histoire des religions* 110 (1934): 140-56. [Mesopotamia]

Dhorme, Édouard P. *Les religions de babylonie et d'assyrie.* Paris, Presses universitaires de France, 1949. [Mesopotamia]

Dibelius, Martin. *Die Lade Jahves: Eine religionsgeschichtliche Untersuching.* Göttingen: Vandenhoeck and Ruprecht, 1906. [Tabernacle]

Diebner, B. "Die Orientierung des Jerusalemer Tempels und die 'Sacred Direction' der frühchristlichen Kirchen." *ZDPV* 87 (1971): 153-66. [Israel/Canaan]

Dietrich, Walter. "Gott als König: Zur Frage nach der theologischen und politischen Legitimität religöser Begriffsbildung." *Zeitschrift für Theologie und Kirche* 77 (1980): 251-68. [Kingship/Coronation]

Dieulafoy, M. "Le rythme modulaire du temple de Salomon." *Comptes rendus des séances de l'Académie des Inscriptions et Belles Lettres* (1913): 332-47. [Israel/Canaan]

Dinsmoor, William B. *The Temple of Apollo at Bassae.* New York: Metropolitan Museum, 1933. [Greece/Rome]

Dion, P. E. "Early Evidence for the Ritual Significance of the "Base of the Altar." *JBL* 106 (1987): 487-90. [Israel/Canaan]

Dion, P. E. "Le role de la foi yahwiste dans la vie politique d'Israel." *Science et Espirit* 26 (1974): 173-203. [Kingship/Coronation]

Dobbie, R. "Deuteronomy and the Prophetic Attitude to Sacrifice." *Scottish Journal of Theology* 12 (1959): 68-82. [Sacrifice/Offerings]

Doctorowitz, Joseph. *Midot ha-Batim ʿal Masekhet Middot.* Brooklyn: n.p., 1937. [Measurement]

Doeve, J. W. "Le domaine du temple de Jérusalem." In *La Littérature Juive entre Tenach et Mischna*, edited by Willem C. Van Unnik. 9:118-63. Leiden: Brill, 1974. [Israel/Canaan]

Doeve, J. W. "Purification du Temple et desséchement du figuier—sur la structure du 21ème chapitre de Matthieu et parallèles." *NTS* 1 (1955): 297-308. [Ablutions/Anointings]

Dolby, Anastasia M. *Church Embroidery, Ancient and Modern.* London: Chapman and Hall, 1867. [Sacred Vestments]

Dolby, Anastasia M. *Church Vestments: Their Origin, Use, and Ornament.* London: Chapman and Hall, 1868. [Sacred Vestments]

Doll, Mary A. "The Temple: Symbolic Form in Scripture." *Soundings: An Interdisciplinary Journal* 70 (Spring-Summer 1987): 145-54. [Israel/Canaan]

Dombart, Theodor. "Der zweitürmige Tempel-Pylon altägyptischer Baukunst und seine religiöse Symbolik." *Egyptian Religion* 1 (1933): 87-98. [Tabernacle]

Donner, Herbert. "Der Felsen und der Tempel." *ZDPV* 93 (1977): 1-11. [Israel/Canaan]

Dooling, Dorothea M., ed. "Ceremonies." *Parabola* 7/3 (1982): 2-96. [Ritual/Liturgy/Worship]

Doran, Robert. *Temple Propaganda: The Purpose and Character of 2 Maccabbees.* Washington, D.C.: Catholic Bilbical Association of America, 1981. [Israel/Canaan]

Doran, Robert. "*T Mos* 4:8 and the Second Temple." *JBL* 106 (1987): 491-92. [Israel/Canaan]

Doresse, M. "Les temples atoniens de la région thébaine." *Orientalia* 24 (1955): 113-35. [Egypt]

Dossin, Georges. "Un rituel du culte d'Ishtar provenant de Mari." *Revue d'Assyriologie et d'Archéologie Orientale* 35 (1938): 1-13. [Mesopotamia]

Dothan, Trude, and Seymour Gitin. "Khirbet el-Muqannah (Migné-Ekrôn) 1985-1986." *RB* 95 (April 1988): 228-39. [Israel/Canaan]

Douglas, G. C. M. "Ezekiel's Temple." *ET* 9 (1897-98): 365-67, 420-22, 468-70, 515-18. [Israel/Canaan]

Douglas, G. C. M. "Ezekiel's Vision of the Temple." *ET* 14 (1902-3): 365-68; 424-27. [Israel/Canaan]

Doumato, Lamia. *The Temple of Athena Nike.* Monticello: Vance Bibliographies, 1980. [Greece/Rome]

Doumato, Lamia. *The Temple Ruins of Baalbek.* Monticello: Vance Bibliographies, 1979. [Israel/Canaan]

Dowda, Robert E. "The Cleansing of the Temple in the Synoptic Gospels." Ph.D. diss., Duke University, 1972. [Israel/Canaan]

Dowden, K. "Grades in the Eleusinian Mysteries." *RHR* 197 (1980): 409-27. [Ritual/Liturgy/Worship]

Downey, Robert R. *The Roman Temple on Hayling Island.* London: Robert Downey, 1977. [Greece/Rome]

Drioton, E. "Un temple égyptien." *Revue du Caire* 5 (1942): 132-43. [Egypt]

Drioton, E. *Le texte dramatique d'Edfou.* Cairo: Imprimerie de l'Institut français d'archéologie orientale du Caire, 1948. [Egypt]

Drower, Ethel S. *Water into Wine: A Study of Ritual Idiom in the Middle East.* London: Murray, 1956. [Ritual/Liturgy/Worship]

Dubarle, André-Marie. "Le signe du Temple (Jo ii, 19)." *RB* 48 (1939): 21-44. [Israel/Canaan]

Du Brul, P. "Jerusalem in the Apocalypse of John." In *Jerusalem: Seat of Theology. Yearbook of the Ecumenical Institute for Theological Research,* edited by D. Burrell, P. Du Brul, and W. Dalton. 55-77. Tantur, Jerusalem: Ecumenical Institute for Theological Research, 1982. [Israel/Canaan]

Du Buit, M. "Les rochers se fendirent." *Bible et Terre Sainte* 149 (1973): 7-8. [Israel/Canaan]

Dumbrell, W. J. "Kingship and Temple in the Post-Exile Period." *Reformed Theological Review* 37 (1978): 33-42. [Kingship/Coronation]

Dumbrell, W. J. "The Role of Bethel in the Biblical Narratives from Jacob to Jeroboam I." *Australian Journal of Biblical Archaeology* 2/3 (1974-75): 65-76. [Mountain]

Dümichen, Johannes. *Der ägyptische Felsentempel von Abu-Simbel und seine Bildwerke und Inschriften.* Berlin: Hempel, 1869. [Egypt]

Dümichen, Johannes. *Baugeschichte des Denderatempels und Beschreibung der einzelnen Theile des Bauwerkes nach den an seinen Mauern befindlichen Inschriften.* Strassburg: Trübner, 1877. [Egypt]

Dümichen, Johannes. *Bauurkunde der Tempelanlagen von Dendera.* Bad Honnef: LTR, 1982. [Egypt]

Dümichen, Johannes. *Die kalendarischen Opferfest-listen im Tempel von Medinet-Habu.* Leipzig: Hinrichs, 1881. [Egypt]

Dümichen, Johannes. *Über die Tempel und Gräber im alten Ägypten und ihre Bildwerke und Inschriften.* Strasburg: Trübner, 1872. [Egypt]

Dunand, M. "Byblos, Sidon, Jérusalem: Monuments apparentés des temps achémenides." In *International Organization for the Study of the Old Testament, Congress Volume, Rome 1968.* 64-70. Leiden: Brill, 1969. [Israel/Canaan]

Dunand, M. "Le temple d'Echmoun à Sidon." *Bulletin du Musée de Beyrouth* 26 (1973): 5-25. [Israel/Canaan]

Dunayevsky, I., and A. Kempinski. "The Megiddo Temples." *ZDPV* 89 (1973): 161-87. [Israel/Canaan]

Duncan, Alistair. *The Noble Sanctuary: Portrait of a Holy Place in Arab Jerusalem.* London: Longman, 1972. [Israel/Canaan]

Dunham, Dows. *The Barkal Temples.* Boston: Museum of Fine Arts, 1970. [Egypt]

Dupont, J. "Ruine du Temple et la fin des temps dans le discours de Marc 13." In *Apocalypses et théologie de l'espérance. Association Catholique Française pour l'Étude de la Bible, Congress de Toulouse, 1975* (Festschrift Louis Monoloubou), edited by Henri Cazelles. 207-69. Paris: Editions du Cerf, 1977. [Israel/Canaan]

Dupont-Sommer, A. " 'Maison de Yahvé' et vêtements sacrés à Éléphantine d'après un ostracon araméen du musée du Caire." *Journal asiatique* 235 (1946-47): 79-87. [Israel/Canaan]

Durand, X. "Du rituel sacrificiel au sacrifice biblique." *Point* 24 (1977): 31-61. [Sacrifice/Offerings]

Duri, Abdel Aziz. "Bayt al-Maqdis in Islam." In *Studies in the History and Archaeology of Jordan 1,* edited by Adnan Hadidi. 351-55. Amman: Department of Antiquities, 1982. [Israel/Canaan]

Dürr, Lorenz. "Ursprung und Bedeutung der Bundeslade." *Bonner Zeitschrift für Theologie und Seelsorge* 1 (1924): 17-24. [Tabernacle]

Dus, Jan. "Die Analyse zweier Ladeerzählungen des Josuabuches (Jos. 3-4 und 6)." *ZAW* 72 (1960): 107-34. [Tabernacle]

Dus, Jan. "Der Brauch der Ladewanderung im alten Israel." *Theologische Zeitschrift* 17 (1961): 1-16. [Tabernacle]

Dus, Jan. "The Dreros Bilingual and the Tabernacle of Ancient Israelites." *Journal of Semitic Studies* 10 (1965): 54-58. [Tabernacle]

Dus, Jan. "Die Erzählung über den Verlust der Lade, 1 Sam. IV." *VT* 13 (1963): 333-37. [Tabernacle]

Dus, Jan. "Herabfahrung Jahwes auf die Lade und Entziehung der Feuerwolke." *VT* 19 (1969): 290-311. [Tabernacle]

Dus, Jan. "Noch zum Brauch der 'Ladewanderung'." *VT* 13 (1963): 126-32. [Tabernacle]

Dus, Jan. "Die Thron- und Bundeslade." *Theologische Zeitschrift* 20 (1964): 241-51. [Tabernacle]

Dus, Jan. "Zur bewegten Geschichte der israelitischen Lade." *Annali dell'Istituto Orientale di Napoli* 41 (1981): 351-83. [Tabernacle]

Dussaud, René. "Des fouilles à entreprendre sur l'emplacement du Temple de Jérusalem." *RHR* 79 (1919): 319-27. [Israel/Canaan]

Dussaud, René. *Les origines cananéennes du sacrifice israelite.* Paris: Leroux, 1921. [Sacrifice/Offerings]

Dussaud, René. *Le sacrifice en Israel et chez les Phéniciens.* Paris: Levoux, 1914. [Sacrifice/Offerings]

Dussaud, René. "Le sanctuaire et les dieux phénicians de Ras Shamra." *RHR* 105 (1932): 245-302. [Israel/Canaan]

Dussaud, René. "Le temple de Jupiter damascénien et ses transformations aux époques chrétienne et musulmane." *Syria* 3 (1922): 219-50. [Greece/Rome]

Dussaud, René. "Temples et cultes de la triade héliopolitaine à Ba'albeck." *Syria* 23 (1942-43): 33-77. [Greece/Rome]

Dyggve, Ejnar. *Das Laphrion, der Tempelbezirk von Kalydon.* Copenhagen: Munksgaard, 1948. [Greece/Rome]

Eakin, F. E. "Wisdom, Creation, and Covenant." *Perspectives in Religious Studies* 4 (1977): 226-39. [Covenant]

Easton, B. S. "Jewish and Christian Ordination." *Anglican Theological Review* 5-6 (1922-23): 308-19; 285-95. [Ritual/Liturgy/Worship]

Eastwood, Charles C. *The Royal Priesthood of the Faithful: An Investigation of the Doctrine from Biblical Times to the Reformation.* London: Epworth, 1963. [Priesthood]

Eaton, E. "Towards Initiation." *Parabola* 1/3 (1976): 42-47. [Ritual/Liturgy/ Worship]

Eaton, John H. *Kingship and the Psalms.* 2d ed. Sheffield: JSOT, 1986. [Kingship/Coronation]

Eaton, John H. *Vision in Worship: The Relation of Prophecy and Liturgy in the Old Testament.* London: SPCK, 1981. [Ritual/ Litrugy/Worship]

Eckert, E. E. *Der Tempel Salomonis.* Prague: n.p., 1855. [Israel/Canaan]

Edersheim, Alfred. *The Temple, Its Ministry and Services as They Were at the Time of Jesus Christ.* Boston: Bradley and Woodruff, 1904; repr. Grand Rapids: Eerdmans, 1951. [Israel/Canaan]

Edwards, Iorwerth E. S. *The Pyramids of Egypt.* London: Penguin Books, 1949. [Mountain]

Eerdmans, B. D. "Sojourn in the Tent of Jahu." *Oudtestamentische Studien* 1 (1942): 1-16. [Tabernacle]

Efron, Y. "The Sanhedrin as an Ideal and as Reality in the Period of the Second Temple." *Immanuel* 2 (1973): 44-49. [Israel/Canaan]

Ehrhardt, A. "Jewish and Christian Ordination." *Journal of Ecclesiastical History* 5 (1954): 125-38. [Ritual/Liturgy/Worship]

Ehrlich, E. L. *Die Kultsymbolik im Alten Testament und im nachbiblischen Judentum,* vol. 3. Stuttgart: Hiersemann, 1959. [Ritual/Liturgy/Worship]

Eibschitz, E. "The Hekhal and the Ulam in the Second Temple" (in Hebrew). *Sinai* 87 (1980): 226-37. [Israel/Canaan]

Eichrodt, Walther. "Der neue Tempel in der Heilshoffnung Hesekiels." In *Das ferne und nahe Wort,* edited by Fritz Maass. 37-48. Berlin: Toepelmann, 1967. [Israel/Canaan]

Eichrodt, Walther. "Tempel und Tempelsatzungen, Land und Volk im Israel der Heilszeit." In *Der Prophet Hesekiel, Kapitel 19-48.* 372-421. Göttingen: Vandenhoeck & Ruprecht, 1966; also in English as "The Temple and Its Ordinances; The Land and the People in the New Israel of the Time of Salvation." In *Ezekiel: A Commentary,* translated by C. Quin. 530-94. Philadelphia: Westminster, 1970. [Israel/Canaan]

Eisenberg, Emmanuel. "The Temples at Tell Kittan." *BA* 40 (1977): 78-81. [Greece/Rome]

Eisenhofer, Ludwig. *The Liturgy of the Roman Rite,* translated by A. J. Peeler. New York: Herder and Herder, 1961. [Ritual/Liturgy/Worship]

Eisenstein, J. D. "Sacrifices." In *A Digest of Jewish Laws and Customs* (in Hebrew). 376-71. Tel-Aviv: Shoh, 1975. [Sacrifice/Offerings]

Eisenstein, J. D. "Temple, Administration and Service of." In *The Jewish Encyclopedia* 12:81-85. [Israel/Canaan]

Eisenstein, J. D. "Temple in Rabbinical Literature." In *The Jewish Encyclopedia* 12:92-97. [Israel/Canaan]

Eisenstein, J. D. "Temple, Plan of Second." In *The Jewish Encyclopedia* 12:89-92. [Israel/Canaan]

Eissfeldt, Otto. "Eine Einschmelzstelle am Tempel zu Jerusalem." *Forschungen und Fortschritte* 13 (1937): 165-64; also in *Kleine Schriften*, edited by Rudolf Sellheim and Fritz Maass. 6 vols., 2:107-9. Tübingen: Mohr, 1963. [Israel/Canaan]

Eissfeldt, Otto. "Der Gott Bethel." *Archiv für Religionswissenschaft* 28 (1938): 1-30; also in *Kleine Schriften*, edited by Rudolf Sellheim and Fritz Maass. 6 vols., 1:206-33. Tübingen: Mohr, 1962. [Israel/Canaan]

Eissfeldt, Otto. "Jahwe als König." *ZAW* 46 (1928): 81-105; also in *Kleine Schriften*, edited by Rudolf Sellheim and Fritz Maass. 6 vols. 1:172-93. Tübingen: Mohr, 1962. [Kingship/Coronation]

Eissfeldt, Otto. "Die Komposition der Sinai-Erzählung Exodus 19-34." *Forschungen und Fortschritte* 40 (1966): 213-15; also in *Kleine Schriften*, edited by Rudolf Sellheim and Fritz Maass. 6 vols., 4:231-37. Tübingen: Mohr, 1968. [Tabernacle]

Eissfeldt, Otto. "Kultzelt und Tempel." In *Wort und Geschichte: Festschrift für Karl Elliger zum 70. Geburtstag*, edited by Hartmut Gese et al. 51-55. Neukirchen-Vluyn: Neukirchener, 1973; also in *Kleine Schriften*, edited by Rudolf Sellheim and Fritz Maass. 6 vols. 6:1-7. Tübingen: Mohr, 1979. [Tabernacle]

Eissfeldt, Otto. "Die Lade Jahwes in Geschichtserzählung, Sage und Lied." *Altertum* 14 (1968): 131-45; also in *Kleine Schriften*, edited by Rudolf Sellheim and Fritz Maass. 6 vols., 5:77-93. Tübingen: Mohr, 1973. [Tabernacle]

Eissfeldt, Otto. "Lade und Gesetztafeln." *Theologische Zeitschrift* 16 (1960): 281-84; also in *Kleine Schriften*, edited by Rudolf Sellheim and Fritz Maass. 6 vols., 3:526-29. Tübingen: Mohr, 1966. [Tabernacle]

Eissfeldt, Otto. "Lade und Stierbild." *ZAW* 58 (1940-41): 190-215; also in *Kleine Schriften*, edited by Rudolf Sellheim and Fritz Maass. 6 vols., 2:282-305. Tübingen: Mohr, 1963. [Tabernacle]

Eissfeldt, Otto. "Tempel und Kulte syrischer Städte in hellenistisch-römischer Zeit." *Forschungen und Fortschritte* 17 (1941): 5-7; also in *Kleine Schriften*, edited by Rudolf Sellheim and Fritz Maass. 6 vols., 2:306-8. Tübingen: Mohr, 1963. [Greece/Rome]

El-Adly, Sanaa. A. "Das Gründungs- und Weiheritual des ägyptischen Tempels von der frühgeschichtlichen Zeit bis zum Ende des neuen Reiches," Ph.D. diss., Tübingen University, 1981. [Egypt]

Elbogen, Ismar. *Der jüdische Gottesdienst in seiner geschichtlichen Entwicklung*. Leipzig: Fock, 1913. [Ritual/Liturgy/Worship]

Elderkin, George W. *The First Three Temples at Delphi: Their Religious and Historical Significance*. Princeton: n.p., 1962. [Greece/Rome]

Elgvin, T. "The Qumran Covenant Festival and the Temple Scroll." *JJS* 36 (1985): 103-6. [Covenant]

Eliade, Mircea. "Centre du monde, temple, maison." In *Le symbolisme cosmique des monuments religieux*, edited by Guiseppi Tucci. 57-82. Rome: Istituto Italiano par il Medio ed Estremo Oriente, 1957; also in a revised version as "Architecture sacrée et symbolisme." In *Mircea Eliade*, edited by Constantin Tacou. 141-56. Paris: L'Herne, 1978; also in English as "Sacred Architecture and Symbolism." In *Symbolism, the Sacred, and the Arts*, edited by Diana Apostolos-Cappadona. 105-29. New York: Crossroad, 1985. [Sacred Space]

Eliade, Mircea. "Cosmogonic Myth and Sacred History." In Eliade, *The Quest: History and Meaning in Religion*. 72-87. Chicago: University of Chicago Press, 1969. [Creation/Cosmology]

Eliade, Mircea. *Cosmos and History: The Myth of the Eternal Return*. New York: Harper and Row, 1959. [Creation/Cosmology]

Eliade, Mircea. "History of Religions and 'Popular' Cultures." *History of Religions* 20 (1980): 1-26. [Ritual/Liturgy/Worship]

Eliade, Mircea. "The Myth of the Noble Savage or, the Prestige of the Beginning." In *Myths, Dreams and Mysteries: The Encounter between Contemporary Faiths and Archaic Reality*, translated by Philip Mairet. 39-58. New York: Harper and Row, 1960. [Creation/Cosmology]

Eliade, Mircea. *Myths, Rites, Symbols*. New York: Harper and Colophon, 1976. [Ritual/Liturgy/Worship]

Eliade, Mircea. "The Prestige of the Cosmogonic Myth." *Diogenes* 23 (1958): 1-13. [Creation/Cosmology]

Eliade, Mircea. *Rites and Symbols of Initiation: The Mysteries of Birth and Rebirth*, translated by Willard R. Trask. New York: Harper & Row, 1975. [Ritual/Liturgy/Worship]

Elliger, Karl. "Ephod und Choschen: Ein Beitrag zur Entwicklungsgeschichte des hohepriesterlichen Ornats." *VT* 8 (1958): 19-35. [Sacred Vestments]

Elliger, Karl. "Die grossen Tempelsakristeien im Verfassungsentwurf des Ezechiel (42: 1ff)." In *Geschichte und Alten Testament* (Festschrift Albrecht Alt). 79-102. Tübingen: Mohr, 1953. [Israel/Canaan]

Elliott, J. K. "The Anointing of Jesus." *ET* 85 (1974): 105-7. [Ablutions/ Anointings]

Ellis, Richard S. *Foundation Deposits in Ancient Mesopotamia*. New Haven: Yale University Press, 1968. [Mesopotamia]

El-Sawy, A. "The Nile-God: An Unusual Representation in the Temple of Sety I at Abydos." *Egitto e Vicino Oriente* 6 (1983): 7-13. [Egypt]

Eltester, W. "Der Siebenarmige Leuchter und der Titus-bogen." In *Judentum, Urchristentum, Kirche: Festschrift für Joachim Jeremias*, edited by Walter Eltester. 62-76. Berlin: Töpelmann, 1960. [Israel/Canaan]

Emanuel, J. "The Measurements of the Herodian Temple, according to Tractate Middoth and the Writings of Flavius Josephus" (in Hebrew). *Ha Maayan* 15/2 (1975): 49-54. [Measurement]

Emerton, J. A. "Priests and Levites in Deuteronomy: An Examination of Dr. G. E. Wright's Theory." *VT* 12 (1962): 129-38. [Priesthood]

Emery, D. L. "Ezra 4: Is Josephus Right After All?" *Journal of Northwest Semitic Languages* 13 (1987): 33-44. [Israel/Canaan]

Emmanuele da S. Marco. "Lo pseudo-Aristea e il Siracida (Ecclo 50) sulla cittadella e il tempio de Gerusalemme." In *La distruzione di Gerusalemme del 70: nei suoi riflessi storico-letterari. Atti del V. Convegno biblico francescano, Roma, 22 sett. 1969.* 194-207. Assisi: Studio Teologico "Porziuncolo," 1971. [Israel/Canaan]

Empereur, James. L. *Prophetic Anointing: God's Call to the Sick, the Elderly, and the Dying.* Wilmington: Glazier, 1982. [Ablutions/Anointings]

Encausse, Jean d'. *De l'initiation.* Paris: le Courrier du livre, 1968. [Ritual/Liturgy/Worship]

Engelbach, R. "A Foundation-Scene of the Second Dynasty." *JEA* 20 (1934): 183-84. [Egypt]

Engelkemper, Wilhelm. *Heiligtum und Opferstätten in den Gesetzen des Pentateuch.* Paderborn: Schöningh, 1908. [Israel/Canaan]

Engnell, Ivan. " 'Knowledge' and 'Life' in the Creation Story." In *Wisdom in Israel in the Ancient Near East,* edited by M. Noth and D. Winton Thomas. 103-19. n.p., 1955. [Creation/Cosmology]

Engnell, Ivan. *Studies in Divine Kingship in the Ancient Near East.* 2d ed. Oxford: Blackwell, 1967. [Kingship/Coronation]

Enright, Michael J. *Iona, Tara, and Soissons: the Origin of the Royal Anointing Ritual.* New York: de Gruyter, 1985. [Ablutions/Anointings]

Eppstein, V. "The Historicity of the Gospel Account of the Cleansing of the Temple." *ZNTW* 55 (1964): 42-58. [Israel/Canaan]

Epstein, C. "Aspects of Symbolism in Chalcolithic Palestine." In *Archaeology in the Levant, Essays for Kathleen Kenyon,* edited by Roger Moorey. 23-35. Warminster: Aris and Phillips, 1978. [Tabernacle]

Epstein, E. M. *The Construction of the Tabernacle.* Chicago: Open Court, 1911. [Tabernacle]

Epstein, J. N. "Die Zeiten des Holzopfers." *MGWJ* 78 (1934): 97-103. [Israel/Canaan]

Eshbach, W. M. "Another Look at John 13:1-20." *Brethren Life and Thought* 14 (1969): 117-25. [Ritual/Liturgy/Worship]

Etsyon, Yehuda. *Har ha-Bayit.* Jerusalem: n.p. 1984 or 1985. [Israel/Canaan]

Evans, J. A. S. "A Social and Economic History of an Egyptian Temple in Greco-Roman Period." *Yale Classical Studies* 17 (1961): 143-283. [Egypt]

Eybeschuetz, Jonathan. *Tavnit Binyan Bet ha-Mikdash shebi-Nevu'at Yeḥezk'el (40-43).* Jerusalem: Pe'er ha-Ḥasidut, 1965 or 1966. [Israel/Canaan]

Faber van der Meulen, H. E. "One or Two Veils in Front of the Holy of Holies?" *Theologia Evangelica* 18 (1985): 22-27. [Tabernacle]

Fairman, H. W. "The Kingship Rituals of Egypt." In *Myth, Ritual, and Kingship*, edited by Samuel H. Hooke. 74-104. Oxford: Clarendon, 1958. [Kingship/Coronation]

Fairman, H. W. "A Scene of the Offering of Truth in the Temple of Edfu." *MDAI.K* 16 (1958): 86-92. [Egypt]

Fairman, H. W. "Worship and Festivals in an Egyptian Temple." *BJRL* 37 (1954-55): 165-203. [Egypt]

Falk, Z. W. "Forms of Testimony." *VT* 11 (1961): 88-91. [Covenant]

Falk, Zev. "The Law of Temple and Priests in the Halakah" (in Hebrew; *English summary). In *Proceedings of the Fifth World Congress of Jewish Studies, 1969*, edited by P. Peli. 1:105-9, *236-37. Jerusalem: World Union of Jewish Studies, 1972. [Priesthood]

Falkener, Edward. *On the Hypaethron of Greek Temples*. London: Longmans, Green, and Roberts, 1861. [Greece/Rome]

Falkenstein, Adam. "La cité-temple sumérienne." *Journal of World History/Cahiers d'histoire mondiale* 1 (1954): 784-814; also in English as *The Sumerian Temple City*, translated by Maria Ellis. Malibu: Undena, 1974. [Mesopotamia]

Falkenstein, Adam. *Die Inschriften Gudeas von Lagash*. Rome: Pontifical Biblical Institute, 1966. [Mesopotamia]

Fallon, Francis T. *The Enthronement of Sabaoth*. Leiden: Brill, 1978. [Creation/Cosmology]

Farnell, Lewis R. *The Cults of the Greek States*, 5 vols. Chicago: Aegaean, 1971. [Greece/Rome]

Farrar, F. W. "The Last Nine Chapters of Ezekiel." *Expositor* 3/9 (1889): 1-15. [Israel/Canaan]

Fasolo, F., and Gullini, G. *Il sanctuario della Fortuna Primigenia a Palestrina*. Rome: Istituto di Archeologia, 1953. [Greece/Rome]

Faure, Paul. "Nouvelles recherches sur trois sortes de sanctuaries crétois." *BCH* 91 (1967): 114-50. [Greece/Rome]

Faure, Paul. "Sur trois sortes de sanctuaires crétois." *BCH* 93 (1969): 174-213. [Greece/Rome]

Fennelly, James M. "The Persepolis Ritual." *BA* 43 (1980): 135-62. [Ritual/Liturgy/ Worship]

Fennelly, James M. "The Temple of Dendur." *SBLSP* 21 (1982): 129-34. [Greece/Rome]

Fensham, F. C. "Ps 21: A Covenant Song?" *ZAW* 77 (1965): 193-202. [Covenant]

Ferguson, Everett. "Jewish and Christian Ordination: Some Observations." *Harvard Theological Review* 56 (1963): 13-19. [Ritual/Liturgy/Worship]

Ferguson, Everett. "Selection and Installation to Office in Roman, Greek, Jewish, and Christian Antiquity." *Theologische Zeitschrift* 30 (1974): 273-84. [Ritual/Liturgy/Worship]

Fergusson, James. "Herod's Temple." In Fergusson, *The Holy Sepulchre and the Temple at Jerusalem.* 91-97. London: Murray, 1865. [Israel/Canaan]

Fergusson, James. *The Temples of the Jews and the Other Buildings in the Haram Area at Jersualem.* London: Murray, 1878. [Israel/Canaan]

Fernández, A. "El Profeta Ageo 2, 15-18 y la fundación del segundo templo." *Biblica* 2 (1921): 206-15. [Israel/Canaan]

Feuchtwang, D. "Das Wasseropfer und die damit verbundenen Zeremonien." *MGWJ* 54 (1910): 535-52, 713-29; 55 (1911): 43-63. [Sacrifice/Offerings]

Feuillet, A. "Le discours de Jésus sur la ruine du Temple, d'après Marc xiii et Luc xxi:5-36." *RB* 55 (1948): 481-502; 56 (1949): 61-92. [Israel/Canaan]

Fevrier, J. G. "L'évolution des rites sacrificiels à Carthage." *Bulletin archéologique* (1959-60): 22-27. [Sacrifice/Offerings]

Fevrier, J. G. "Les rites sacrificiels chez les Hébreux et à Carthage." *REJ* 4/3 (1964): 7-18. [Sacrifice/Offerings]

Ficker, R. "Kingship of God in the Psalms." *Bangalore Theological Forum* 12 (1980): 50-65. [Kingship/Coronation]

Filson, Floyd V. "Temple, Synagogue and Church." *BA* 7/4 (1944): 66-88; also in *Biblical Archaeologist Reader*, edited by David N. Freedman. 3 vols., 1:185-200. Garden City: Doubleday, 1961. [Israel/Canaan]

Finegan, J. "The Pinnacle of the Temple," "The Double Gate," "The Triple Gate," "The Golden Gate," "Robinson's Arch," and "Wilson's Arch." In Finegan, *Archaeology of the New Testament: The Life of Jesus and the Beginnings of the Early Church.* 125-32. Princeton: Princeton University Press, 1969. [Israel/Canaan]

Finegan, J. "Plan of the Temple of Herod," and "Fragment of a Warning Inscription from Herod's Temple." In Finegan, *Archaeology of the New Testament: The Life of Jesus and the Beginnings of the Early Church.* 117-20. Princeton: Princeton University Press, 1969. [Israel/Canaan]

Finkel, Asher. "The Theme of God's Presence and the Qumrân Temple Scroll." In *God and His Temple*, edited by L. E. Frizzel. 39-47. South Orange, NJ: Seton Hall University Institute for Judaeo-Christian Studies, 1980. [Israel/Canaan]

Finn, E. A. "The Rock (Sakhrah) Foundation of Solomon's Temple." *PEQ* 21 (1889): 156-57. [Israel/Canaan]

Finnestad, R. B. "The Meaning and Purpose of Opening the Mouth in Mortuary Contexts." *Numen* 25 (1978): 118-34. [Ritual/Liturgy/Worship]

Fiorenza, E. S. "Cultic Language in Qumran and in the New Testament." *CBQ* 38 (1976): 159-77. [Israel/Canaan]

Fischer, M., et al. "The Roman Temple at Kedesh, Upper Galilee: A Preliminary Study." *Tel Aviv* 11 (1984): 146-72. [Greece/Rome]

Fish, T. "Some Aspects of Kingship in the Sumerian City and Kingdom of Ur." *BJRL* 34 (1951): 37-43. [Kingship/Coronation]

Fisher, Elliot. *The Temple as It Appeared in the Time of Our Saviour, with Full Description of Its Location, Construction and Service. To Accompany "The Temple in Miniature."* Rock Island, IL: Kramer, 1901. [Israel/Canaan]

Fisher, Loren R. "Creation at Ugarit and in the Old Testament." *VT* 15 (1965): 313-24. [Creation/Cosmology]

Fisher, Loren R. "The Temple Quarter," edited by C. F. Beckingham and E. Ullerdorf. *Journal of Semitic Studies* 8 (1963): 34-41. [Israel/Canaan]

Fisher, Loren R. "An Ugaritic Ritual and Genesis 1:1-5." *Ugaritica* 6 (1969): 197-205. [Ritual/Liturgy/Worship]

Fisher, Loren R., and F. B. Knutson. "An Enthronment Ritual at Ugarit." *JNES* 28 (1969): 157-67. [Kingship/Coronation]

Fitzer, J. "Liturgy, Language and Mysticism." *Worship* 47 (1973): 66-79. [Ritual/Liturgy/Worship]

Fitzmyer, J. " 'Now this Melchizedek. . .' (Heb. 7, 1)." *CBQ* 25 (1963): 305-21. [Priesthood]

Flanagan, N. M. "Mark and the Temple Cleansing." *Bible Today* 63 (1972): 980-84. [Israel/Canaan]

Fleming, J. "The Undiscovered Gate beneath Jerusalem's Golden Gate." *Biblical Archaeology Review* 9 (1983): 24-37. [Israel/Canaan]

Fleury, H. "Cosmos in Stone." *Parabola* 3/1 (1978): 74-77. [Creation/Cosmology]

Flusser, David. "Temple Scroll." *Numen* 26 (1979): 271-74. [Israel/Canaan]

Flusser, David. "The Temple Scroll from Qumran." *Immanuel* 9 (1979): 49-52. [Israel/Canaan]

Flusser, David. "Two Notes on the Midrash on 2 Sam. vii: 1. The Temple 'Not Made with Hands' in the Qumrân Doctrine." *IEJ* 9 (1959): 99-104. [Israel/Canaan]

Fohrer, Georg. "Jeremias Tempelwort 7:1-15." *Theologische Zeitschrift* 5 (1949): 401-17. [Israel/Canaan]

Fohrer, Georg. "Kritik an Tempel, Kultus und Kultusausübung in nachexilischer." In *Archäologie und altes Testament: Festschrift für Kurt Galling*, edited by Arnulf Kuschke and Ernst Kutsch. 101-16. Tübingen: Mohr, 1970. [Israel/Canaan]

Fohrer, Georg. "Worship." In *History of Israelite Religion*. 195-214. Nashville: Abingdon, 1972. [Ritual/Liturgy/Worship]

Foote, Theodore C. "The Ephod: Its Form and Use." Ph.D. diss., Johns Hopkins University, 1902. [Sacred Vestments]

Ford, J. M. "The Heavenly Jerusalem and Orthodox Judaism." In *Donum Gentilicium: New Testment Studies in Honour of David Daube*, edited by Ernst Bammel, C. K. Barrett, and W. D. Davies. 215-26. Oxford: Clarendon, 1978. [Israel/Canaan]

Forster, Robert, and Orest Ranum. *Ritual, Religion, and the Sacred*, translated by Elborg Forster and Patricia M. Ranum. Baltimore: Johns Hopkins University Press, 1982. [Ritual/Liturgy/Worship]

Fortescue, Adrian. *The Vestments of the Roman Rite*. New York: Paulist, 1915. [Sacred Vestments]

Fowden, Garth. "Bishops and Temples in the Eastern Roman Empire AD 320-435." *JTS* 29 (1978): 53-78. [Greece/Rome]

Fowler, Mervyn D. "A Closer Look at the 'Temple of El-berith' at Shechem." *PEQ* 115 (1983): 49-53. [Israel/Canaan]

Fraeyman, M. "La Spiritualisation de l'idée du Temple dans les épîtres pauliniennes." *Ephemerides theologicae lovanienses* 33 (1947): 378-412. [Israel/Canaan]

Frank, Zevi P. *Sefer Mikdash Melekh*. Jerusalem: Ya'ad Le'hotsa maran ha-Rav Tsevi Pesah Frank, 1967 or 1968. [Israel/Canaan]

Frankel, Joseph A. *Bet ha-middot*. Brooklyn: n.p., 1984-85. [Measurement]

Frankfort, Henri. *The Gimilsin Temple and the Palace of the Rulers at Tell Asmar*. Chicago: University of Chicago Press, 1940. [Mesopotamia]

Frankfort, Henri. *Kingship and the Gods*. Chicago: University of Chicago Press, 1978. [Kingship/Coronation]

Frankfort, Henri, et al. *The Cenotaph of Seti I at Abydos*. 2 vols. London: Egyptian Exploration Society, 1933. [Egypt]

Franklin, John H. *The Rebuilding of King Solomon's Temple*. Omaha: Douglas, 1910. [Israel/Canaan]

Fransen, I. "Jésus pontife parfait du parfait sanctuaire (Epitre aux Hebreux)." *Bible et vie chrétienne* 20 (1957-58): 79-91. [Israel/Canaan]

Fraser, P. M. "A Temple of Hathor at Kusae." *JEA* 42 (1956): 97-98. [Egypt]

Frazer, James G. *Lectures on the Early History of the Kingship*. London: Macmillan, 1905. [Kingship/Coronation]

Fredriksen, P. "Hysteria and the Gnostic Myths of Creation." *Vigiliae Christianae* 33 (1979): 287-90. [Creation/Cosmology]

Freedman, David N. "A Letter to the Readers." *BA* 40 (1977): 46-48. [Israel/Canaan]

Freedman, David N. "Temple without Hands." In *Temples and High Places in Biblical Times*, edited by Avraham Biran. Jerusalem: Jewish Institute of Religion, 1977. 21-30. [Israel/Canaan]

Fretheim, Terence E. "The Ark in Deuteronomy." *CBQ* 30 (1968): 1-14. [Israel/Canaan]

Fretheim, Terence E. "The Cultic Use of the Ark of the Covenant in the Monarchical Period." Th.D. diss., Princeton Theological Seminary, 1967. [Israel/Canaan]

Fretheim, Terence E. "The Priestly Document: Anti-Temple?" *VT* 18 (1968): 313-29. [Israel/Canaan]

Fried, Martha N., and Morton H. Fried. *Transitions: Four Rituals in Eight Cultures.* New York: Norton, 1980. [Ritual/Liturgy/Worship]

Friedman, Irving. "The Sacred Space of Judaism." *Parabola* 3/1 (1978): 20-23. [Sacred Space]

Friedman, R. E. "The Tabernacle in the Temple." *BA* 43 (1980): 241-48. [Tabernacle]

Friedrich, G. "Die Formale Struktur von Matt. 28:18-20." *Zeitschrift für Theologie und Kirche* 80 (1983): 137-83. [Kingship/Coronation]

Friend, J. A. "Nature, Man, and God: A Temple Revisited." *Reformed Theological Review* 41 (1982): 34-41. [Creation/Cosmology]

Fritz, Volkmar. "Der Tempel Salamos im Licht der neueren Forschung." *Mitteilungen der Deutschen Morgenländischen Gesellschaft* 112 (1980): 53-68. [Israel/Canaan]

Fritz, Volkmar. *Tempel und Zelt.* Neukirchen-Vluyn: Neukirchener, 1977. [Israel/Canaan]

Fritz, Volkmar. "Temple Architecture: What Can Archaeology Tell Us about Solomon's Temple." *BAR* 13/4 (1987): 38-49. [Israel/Canaan]

Frizzell, Lawrence E., ed. *God and His Temple.* South Orange: Institute of Judaeo-Christian Studies, 1981. [Israel/Canaan]

Fromer, Jacob. *Maimonides' Commentar zum Tractat Middoth mit der hebräischen Uebersetzung des Natanel Almoli* (in Hebrew). Breslau: Schatzky, 1898. [Israel/Canaan]

Fry, Euan. "The Temple in the Gospels and Acts." *Bible Translator* 38 (April 1987): 213-21. [Israel/Canaan]

Fry, V. R. L. "The Warning Inscriptions from the Herodian Temple." Ph.D. diss., Southern Baptist Theology Seminary, 1974. [Israel/Canaan]

Frymer-Kensky, Tivka. "Pollution, Purification, and Purgation in Biblical Israel." In *The Word of the Lord Shall Go Forth: Essays in Honor of David Noel Freedman,* edited by C. L. Meyers and M. O'Connor. 399-414. Winona Lake: Eisenbrauns, 1983. [Israel/Canaan]

Fujita, S. "Temple Theology in the Second Book of Maccabees." *Bible Today* 64 (1973): 1066-71. [Israel/Canaan]

Fujita, S. "The Temple Theology of the Qumran Sect and the Book of Ezekiel." Ph.D. diss., Princeton University, 1970. [Israel/Canaan]

Fuller, Charles E. *The Tabernacle in the Wilderness.* Westwood: Revell, 1955. [Tabernacle]

Fuller, Daniel P. *Gospel and Law: Contrast or Continuum? The Hermeneutics of Dispensationalism and Covenant Theology.* Grand Rapids: Eerdmans, 1980. [Covenant]

Fullerton, Kemper. "The Anti-sacrificial Psalms." In *Essays in Modern Theology and Related Subjects.* 49-63. New York: Scribner, 1911. [Sacrifice/Offerings]

Fullerton, Kemper. "The Stone of Foundation." *AJSL* 37 (1920-21): 1-12. [Israel/Canaan]

Furneaux, Rupert. *The Roman Siege of Jerusalem.* London: Hart-Davis MacGibbon, 1973. [Israel/Canaan]

Gabriel, Johann. *Zorobabel. Ein Beitrag zur Geschichte der Juden in der ersten Zeit nach dem Exil.* Wien: Mayer, 1927. [Israel/Canaan]

Gadegaard, N. H. "On the So-Called Burnt Offering Altar in the Old Testament." *PEQ* 110 (1978): 35-45. [Sacrifice/Offerings]

Gaechter, Paul. "The Original Sequence of Apocalypse 20-22." *Theological Studies* 10 (1949): 485-521. [Israel/Canaan]

Gaerte, W. "Komische Vorstellungen im Bilde prähistorischer Zeit: Erdberg, Himmelsberg, Erdnabel und Weltenströme." *Anthropos* 9 (1913): 956-79. [Mountain]

Galling, Kurt. "Das Allerheiligste im Salomos Tempel, ein christlicher 'Thoraschrein': Zwei archäologische Bemerkungen." *JPOS* 12 (1932): 43-46. [Israel/Canaan]

Galling, Kurt. "Altar." In *The Interpreter's Dictionary of the Bible* 1:96-100. [Sacrifice/Offerings]

Galling, Kurt. *Der Altar in den Kulturen des alten Orients.* Berlin: Curtius, 1925. [Sacrifice/Offerings]

Galling, Kurt. "Die Beschreibung des Kultortes." In *Hesekiel*, edited by Alfred Bertholet. 135-55. Tübingen: Mohr, 1936. [Israel/Canaan]

Galling, Kurt. "Die Halle des Schreibers." *Palästinajahrbuch* 27 (1931): 51-57. [Israel/Canaan]

Galling, Kurt. "Herodianischer Tempel." In *Die Religion in Geschichte und Gegenwart*, edited by H. Campenhausen et al. 6 vols., 5:1045-46. Tübingen: Mohr, 1931. [Israel/Canaan]

Galling, Kurt. "Incense Altar." In *The Interpreter's Dictionary of the Bible* 2:699-700. [Sacrifice/Offerings]

Galling, Kurt. "Königliche und nichtkönigliche Stifter beim Tempel von Jerusalem. *ZDPV* 68 (1950): 134-42. [Israel/Canaan]

Galling, Kurt. "Lade Jahwes." In *Die Religion in Geschichte und Gegenwart*, edited by Alfred Bertholet et al. 5 vols., 3:1449-50. 2d ed. Tübingen: Mohr, 1929. [Tabernacle]

Galling, Kurt. "Serubbabel und der Hohepriester beim Wiederaufbau des Tempels in Jerusalem." In Galling, *Studien zur Geschichte Israels im persischen Zeitalter.* 127-48. Tübingen: Mohr, 1964. [Israel/Canaan]

Galling, Kurt. "Serubbabel und der Wiederaufbau des Tempels in Jerusalem." In *Verbannung und Heimkehr: Beiträge zur Geschichte und Theologie Israels in 6. und 5. Jahrhundert v. Chr. Wilhelm Rudolph zum 70. Geburtstag,* edited by Arnulf Kuschke. 67-96. Tübingen: Mohr, 1961. [Israel/Canaan]

Galling, Kurt. "Tempel." In *Die Religion in Geschichte und Gegenwart,* edited by H. Campenhausen et al., 3d ed. 7 vols., 6:681-86. Tübingen: Mohr, 1962. [Israel/Canaan]

Galling, Kurt. "Tempelgeräte in Israel." In *Die Religion in Geschichte und Gegenwart,* edited by H. Campenhausen et al., 3d ed. 6 vols., 6:686-87. Tübingen: Mohr, 1962. [Israel/Canaan]

Galling, Kurt. "Tempel in Palästina." *ZDPV* 55 (1932): 245-50. [Israel/Canaan]

Galling, Kurt. "Der Tempelschatz nach Berichten und Urkunden im Buche Esra." *ZDPV* 60 (1937): 177-83. [Israel/Canaan]

Galling, Kurt. "Zur Lokalisierung von Debir." *ZDPV* 70 (1954): 135-41. [Israel/Canaan]

Galter, H. D. "Die Bautätigkeit Sanheribs am Aššurtempel." *Orientalia* 53 (1984): 433-41. [Mesopotamia]

Gamberoni, J. "Der nachexilische Tempel und der nachexilische Kult." *Bibel und Liturgie* 45 (1972): 94-108. [Israel/Canaan]

Gammie, John. "Loci of the Melchizedek Tradition of Genesis 14:18-20." *JBL* 90 (1971): 385-96. [Priesthood]

Garber, Paul L. "Reconsidering the Reconstruction of Solomon's Temple." *JBL* 77 (1958): 123-33. [Israel/Canaan]

Garber, Paul L. "Reconstructing Solomon's Temple." *BA* 14 (1951): 2-24. [Israel/Canaan]

Garber, Paul L. "A Reconstruction of Solomon's Temple." In *Archaeological Discoveries in the Holy Land.* 101-11. New York: Crowell, 1967. [Israel/Canaan]

Garber, Paul L. *Solomon's Temple.* Troy: Howland, 1950. [Israel/Canaan]

Garcia-Treto, F. O. "Bethel: The History and Traditions of an Israelite Sanctuary." Th.D diss., Princeton Theological Seminary, 1967. [Israel/Canaan]

García López, Félix. "Construction et destruction de Jérusalem: histoire et prophétie dans les cadres rédactionnels des Livres des Rois." *RB* 94 (April 1987): 222-32. [Israel/Canaan]

García Martínez, F. "El Rollo del Templo 11 Q Temple: Bibliografía sistemática." *Revue de Qumran* 12 (December 1986): 425-40. [Israel/Canaan]

García Martínez, F. "El Rollo de Templo: Traduccion y notas." *Estudios Bíblicos* 36 (1977): 247-92. [Israel/Canaan]

Gardiner, Alan H. "The Baptism of Pharoah." *JEA* 36 (1950): 3-12. [Ablutions/ Anointings]

Gardiner, Alan H. "The Coronation of King Haremhab." *JEA* 39 (1953): 13-31. [Kingship/Coronation]

Gardiner, Alan H. "The House of Life." *JEA* 24 (1938): 157-79. [Egypt]

Gardiner, Alan H. *The Temple of King Sethos I at Abydos.* Chicago: University of Chicago Press, 1933. [Egypt]

Gari-Jaune, L. " 'Desacralizzazione' neotestamentarie del tempio di Gerusalemme." In *La distruzione di Gerusalemme del 70: nei suoi riflessi storico-letterarie.* 135-44. Assisi: Studio Teologico, 1971. [Israel/Canaan]

Garland, David E. "Matthew's Understanding of the Temple Tax (Matt 17:24-27)." *SBLSP* 26 (1987): 190-209. [Israel/Canaan]

Gärtner, Bertil. *The Temple and the Community in Qumran and the New Testament,* edited by M. Black. Cambridge: Cambridge University Press, 1965. [Israel/Canaan]

Gasparri, Carlo. *Temple of Concord.* Rome: Instituto di studi romani, 1979. [Greece/Rome]

Gaster, Moses. "Sacrifice (Jewish)." In *Encyclopaedia of Religion and Ethics* 11:24-29. [Sacrifice/Offerings]

Gaster, Theodor H. "The Ritual Pattern of a Ras-Šamra Epic." *Archiv Orientàlni* 5 (1933): 118-23. [Ritual/Liturgy/Worship]

Gaster, Theodor H. "Sacrifices and Offerings." In *The Interpreter's Dictionary of the Bible* 4:147-59. [Sacrifice/Offerings]

Gaster, Theodor H. "The Service of the Sanctuary: A Study in Hebrew Survivals." In *A Mélanges syriens offerts à Monsieur René Dussaud,* II. 577-82. Paris: Geuthner, 1939. [Israel/Canaan]

Gaster, Theodor H. *Thespis: Ritual, Myth, and Drama in the Ancient Near East.* New York: Harper and Row, 1950. [Ritual/Liturgy/Worship]

Gaston, Lloyd. *No Stone on Another.* Leiden: Brill, 1970. [Israel/Canaan]

Gaston, Lloyd. "The Theology of the Temple: The New Testament Fulfillment of the Promise of Old Testament Heilsgeschichte." In *Oikonomia: Heilsgeschichte als Thema der Theologie. Festschrift Oscar Cullman.* 32-41. Hamburg: Herbert Reich, 1967. [Israel/Canaan]

Gates, Owen H. "The Relation of Priests to Sacrifices before the Exile." *JBL* 27 (1908): 67-92. [Sacrifice/Offerings]

Gatt, G. "Zion." *Das heilige Land* 25 (1881): 143-201. [Israel/Canaan]

Gauthier, Henri. *Les temples immergés de la Nubie. Le temple d'Amada.* Cairo: Imprimerie de l'Institut français d'archéologie orientale du Caire, 1913. [Egypt]

Gauthier, Henri. *Les temples immergés de la Nubie. Le temple de Kalabchah.* 2 vols. Cairo: Imprimerie de l'Institut français d'archéologie orientale du Caire, 1911-27. [Egypt]

Gawlikowski, Michel. "The Sacred Space in Ancient Arabic Religions." In *Studies in the History and Archaeology of Jordan 1*, edited by Adnan Hadidi. 301-3. Amman: Department of Antiquities, 1982. [Sacred Space]

Gawlikowski, Michel. *Le temple palmyrénien.* Warszawa: Editions scientifiques de Pologne, 1973. [Greece/Rome]

Gawlikowski, Michel, and M. Pietrzykiwski. "Les sculptures du temple de Baalshamin à Palmyre." *Syria* 57 (1980): 421-52. [Greece/Rome]

Gayford, Sydney C. *Sacrifice and Priesthood, Jewish and Christian.* London: Methuen, 1924. [Sacrifice/Offerings]

Gebhard, Elizabeth R. "The Early Sanctuary of Poseidon at Isthmia (Corinth, Greece)." *AJA* 91 (July 1987): 475-76. [Greece/Rome]

Geisinger, Marion. *The House of God.* New York: A and W, 1979. [Israel/Canaan]

Gelston, A. "The Foundations of the Second Temple." *VT* 16 (1966): 232-35. [Israel/Canaan]

Gennep, Arnold van. *The Rites of Passage*, translated by Monika B. Vizedom and Gabrielle L. Caffe. Chicago: University of Chicago Press, 1960. [Ritual/Liturgy/Worship]

Georgi, D. "Die Visionen vom himmlischen Jerusalem in Apk. 21 und 22." In *Kirche: Festschrift für Günther Bornkamm zum 75. Geburtstag*, edited by Dieter Lührmann and Georg Strecker. 351-72. Tübingen: Mohr, 1980. [Israel/Canaan]

Gerkan, Armin von. *Der Altar des Artemis-Tempels in Magnesia am Mäander.* Berlin: Schoetz, 1929. [Sacrifice/Offerings]

Gero, S. "The So-Called Ointment Prayer in the Coptic Version of the Didache: A Re-evaluation." *Harvard Theological Review* 70 (1977): 67-84. [Ablutions/Anointings]

Gervitz, S. "Jachin and Boaz." In *Harper's Dictionary of the Bible*, 443. [Israel/Canaan]

Gese, Hartmut. *Der Verfassungsentwurf des Ezechiel (Kap. 40-48) traditions-geschichtlichen Untersucht.* Tübingen: Mohr, 1957. [Israel/Canaan]

Gese, Hartmut. "Zur Geschichte der Kultsänger am zweiten Tempel." In *Abraham Unser Vater: Juden and Christen im Gesprach über die Bibel: Festschrift für Otto Michel*, edited by O. Betz. 222-34. Leiden: Brill, 1963. [Israel/Canaan]

Gessler-Löhr, Beatrix. *Die heiligen Seen ägyptischer Tempel.* Hildesheim: Gerstenberg, 1983. [Egypt]

Giblin, Charles H. *The Destruction of Jerusalem according to Luke's Gospel: A Historical-Theological Model.* Rome: Biblical Institute Press, 1985. [Israel/Canaan]

Gill, S. D. "Disenchantment." *Parabola* 1/3 (1976): 6-13. [Ritual/Liturgy/ Worship]

Gilliam, E. H. *The Archives of the Temple of Soknobraisis at Bacchias.* New Haven: Yale University Press, 1947. [Greece/Rome]

Gittlen, B. M. "Form and Function in the New Late Bronze Age Temple at Lachish." *Eretz-Israel* 16 (1982): 67-69. [Israel/Canaan]

Goedicke, H. "Cult-Temple and 'State' during the Old Kingdom in Egypt." In *State and Temple Economy in the Ancient Near East,* edited by Edward Lipiński. 2 vols., 1:113-32. Louvain: Departement Orientalistiek, 1979. [Egypt]

Goetze, Albrecht, and E. H. Sturtevant, *The Hittite Ritual of Tunnawi.* New Haven: American Oriental Society, 1938. [Ritual/Liturgy/Worship]

Goguel, M. "La parole de Jésus sur la déstruction et la reconstruction du Temple." In *Congrès d'Histoire du Christianisme.* 1:117-36. Paris: Éditions Rieder, 1928. [Israel/Canaan]

Goldberg, M. Y. "Greek Temples and Chinese Roofs." *AJA* 87 (1983): 305-10. [Greece/Rome]

Goldenberg, Robert. "Early Rabbinic Explanations for the Destruction of Jerusalem." *JJS* 33 (1982): 517-25. [Israel/Canaan]

Goldfless, Sanford K. "Babylonian Theogonies: Divine Origins in Ancient Mesopotamian Religion and Literature." Ph.D. diss., Harvard University, 1980. [Creation/Cosmology]

Goldman, Bernard. *The Sacred Portal,* 69-100. Detroit: Wayne State, 1966. [Tabernacle]

Goldschmidt-Lehmann, R. P. "The Second (Herodian) Temple: Selected Bibliography." *Jerusalem Cathedra* 1 (1981): 336-59. [Israel/Canaan]

Goldstein, N. "Worship at the Temple in Jerusalem—Rabbinic Interpretation and Influence" (in Hebrew). Ph.D. diss., Hebrew University, 1977. [Israel/Canaan]

Golzio, Karl-Heinz. *Der Tempel im alten Mesopotamien und seine Parallelen in Indien.* Leiden: Brill, 1983. [Mesopotamia]

Gonen, R. "Was the Site of the Jerusalem Temple Originally a Cemetery?" *BAR* 11/3 (1985): 44-55. [Israel/Canaan]

González, Arthur E. J. "Byzantine Imperial Paradigm and Eastern Liturgical Vesture." *Greek Orthodox Theological Review* 17 (1972): 255-67. [Sacred Vestments]

Gonzenbach, Victorine von. *Untersuchungen zu den Knabenweihen im Isiskult der römischen Kaiserzeit.* Bonn: Habelt, 1957. [Ritual/Liturgy/Worship]

Goodall, Terence. "Motifs of the Royal Ideology." In *Essays in Faith and Culture*, edited by N. Brown. 145-56. Sydney: Catholic Institute, 1979. [Kingship/Coronation]

Goodenough, Erwin R. "Kingship in Early Israel." *JBL* 48 (1929): 169-205. [Kingship/Coronation]

Goodenough, Erwin R. "The Menorah: The Menorah on the Monuments." In *Jewish Symbols in the Greco-Roman Period*. 13 vols., 4:71-77. New York: Pantheon Books, 1953-68. [Tabernacle]

Goodenough, Erwin R. "Symbolism of Dress." In Goodenough, *Jewish Symbols in the Greco-Roman Period*. 13 vols., 9:124-74. New York: Pantheon, 1953-68. [Sacred Vestments]

Gooding, David W. *The Account of the Tabernacle*. Cambridge: Cambridge University Press, 1959. [Tabernacle]

Gooding, David W. "An Impossible Shrine." *VT* 15 (1965): 405-20. [Israel/Canaan]

Gooding, David W. "Temple Specifications: A Dispute in Logical Arrangement between the MT and the LXX." *VT* 17 (1967): 143-72. [Israel/Canaan]

Goodsir, R. "Animal Sacrifice: Delusion or Deliverance?" *Studia Biblica* 1 (1978): 157-60. [Sacrifice/Offerings]

Goosens, G. "Le temple de Ptah à Memphis." *Chronique d'Égypt* 21 (1945): 49-53. [Egypt]

Görg, Manfred. "Ein architektonischer Fachausdruck in der Priesterschrift: Zur Bedeutung von 'eden." *VT* 33 (1983): 334-38. [Priesthood]

Görg, Manfred. "Die Gattung des sogenannten Tempelweihespruchs (I Kgs. 8, 12f)." In *Ugarit-Forschungen* 6 (1974): 55-63. [Israel/Canaan]

Görg, Manfred. "Lexikalisches zur Beschreibung des salomonischen Palastbezirks (I Kön 7, 1-12)." *Biblische Notizen: Beiträge zur exegetischen Diskussion* 11 (1980): 7-13. [Israel/Canaan]

Görg, Manfred. "Weiteres zur Gestalt des Tempelbaus." *Biblische Notizen: Beiträge zur exegetischen Diskussion* 13 (1980): 22-25. [Israel/Canaan]

Görg, Manfred. *Das Zelt der Begegnung*. Bonn: Hanstein, 1967. [Israel/Canaan]

Görg, Manfred. "Zur Dekoration der Tempelsäulen." *Biblische Notizen: Beiträge zur exegetischen Diskussion* 13 (1980): 17-21. [Israel/Canaan]

Görg, Manfred. "Zur Dekoration des Leuchters." *Biblische Notizen: Beiträge zur exegetischen Diskussion* 15 (1981): 21-29. [Israel/Canaan]

Görg, Manfred. "Zwei bautechnische Begriffe in I Kön 6, 9." *Biblische Notizen: Beiträge zur exegetischen Diskussion* 10 (1979): 12-15. [Israel/Canaan]

Gose, Erich. *Der Tempelbezirk des Lenus Mars in Trier*. Berlin: Mann, 1955. [Greece/Rome]

Gottlieb, Hans. "Amos und Jerusalem." *VT* 17 (1967): 430-63. [Israel/Canaan]

Goyon, J. C. "Une formule solennelle de purification des offrandes dans les temples ptolémaïques." *Chronique d'Égypte* 45 (1970): 267-81. [Ritual/Liturgy/Worship]

Graetz, Heinrich. "Die Bedeutung der Priesterschaft für die Gesetzgebung während des zweiten Tempelbestandes." *MGWJ* 36 (1887): 97-118. [Priesthood]

Graetz, Heinrich. *Dauer der gewaltsamen Hellenisierung der Juden und der Tempelentweihung durch Antiochus Epiphanes.* Breslau: Grass, Barth, 1864. [Israel/Canaan]

Graetz, Heinrich. "Die Höfe und Thore des zweiten Tempels." *MGWJ* 25 (1876): 385-97. [Israel/Canaan]

Graetz, Heinrich. "Die musikalischen Instrumente im jerusalemischen Tempel und der musikalische Chor der Leveiten." *MGWJ* 30 (1881): 241-59. [Israel/Canaan]

Graetz, Heinrich. "Die Tempelpsalmen." *MGWJ* 27 (1878): 217-22. [Israel/Canaan]

Graetz, Heinrich. "Zur Geschichte der nachexilischen Hohenpriester." *MGWJ* 30 (1881): 49-64. [Priesthood]

Graves, Jennifer. "The Greek Omphalos: Its Symbolism and Significance." M.S. thesis, Brigham Young University, 1984. [Sacred Space]

Gray, George B. "The Heavenly Temple and the Heavenly Altar." *Expositor* (1908-A): 385-402, 530-46. [Sacrifice/Offerings]

Gray, George B. *Sacrifice in the Old Testament.* Oxford: Clarendon, 1925; repr. New York, KTAV, 1971. [Sacrifice/Offerings]

Gray, John. "The Building and Dedication of the Temple." In *I and II Kings: A Commentary.* 2d ed. 149-238. London: SCM, 1970. [Israel/Canaan]

Gray, John. "Canaanite Kingship in Theory and Practice." *VT* 2 (1952): 193-220. [Kingship/Coronation]

Gray, John. "Cultic Affinities between Israel and Ras Shamra." *ZAW* 62 (1949-50): 207-20. [Sacrifice/Offerings]

Gray, John. "Desert Sojourn of the Hebrews and the Sinai-Horeb Tradition." *VT* 4 (1954): 148-54. [Mountain]

Gray, John. "Hazor." *VT* 16 (1966): 26-52. [Israel/Canaan]

Gray, John. "The Hebrew Conception of the Kingship of God: Its Origin and Development." *VT* 6 (1956): 268-85. [Kingship/Coronation]

Gray, John. "The Kingship of God in the Prophets and Psalms." *VT* 11 (1961): 1-29. [Kingship/Coronation]

Gray, L. "La ruïne du Temple par Titus." *RB* 55 (1948): 215-26. [Israel/Canaan]

Grdseloff, B. "Nouvelles données concernant la tente de purification." *ASAE* 51 (1951): 129-50. [Egypt]

Green, Alberto R. W. *The Role of Human Sacrifice in the Ancient Near East.* Missoula, MT: Scholars, 1975. [Sacrifice/Offerings]

Greenberg, Moshe. "The Design and Themes of Ezekiel's Program of Restoration." *Interpretation* 38 (1984): 181-208. [Israel/Canaan]

Greenberg, Moshe. "A New Approach to the History of the Israelite Priesthood." *JAOS* 70 (1950): 41-47. [Priesthood]

Greenwald, Leopold. *The History of the High Priests* (in Hebrew). New York: n.p., 1933. [Priesthood]

Greenwald, Leopold. *Le-Toldot ha-Sanhedrin bi-Yisrael.* New York: Shoulson, 1950. [Israel/Canaan]

Gregory, T. E. "Julian and the Last Oracle at Delphi." *Greek, Roman, and Byzantine Studies* 24 (1983): 355-66. [Greece/Rome]

Grelot, P. "La réconstruction du temple juif d'Éléphantine." *Orientalia* 36 (1967): 173-77. [Israel/Canaan]

Gressmann, Hugo. *Die Lade Jahves und das Allerheiligste des Salomonischen Tempels.* Berlin: Kohlhammer, 1920. [Israel/Canaan]

Gressmann, Hugo. *The Tower of Babel.* New York: Jewish Institute of Religion Press, 1928. [Mesopotamia]

Grice, Ettalene M. *Records from Ur and Larsa Dated in the Larsa Dynasty.* New Haven: Yale University Press, 1919. [Mesopotamia]

Griffith, Francis L. *Stories of the High Priests of Memphis: the Sethon of Herodotus and the Demotic Tales of Khamuas.* Oxford: Clarendon, 1900. [Priesthood]

Griffiths, Anna H. "Temple Treasures: A Study Based on the Works of Cicero and the Fasti of Ovid." Ph.D. diss., University of Philadelphia, 1943. [Greece/Rome]

Grigsby, Bruce. "Gematria and John 21:11—Another Look at Ezekiel 47:10." *ET* 95 (1984): 177-78. [Israel/Canaan]

Grimes, Ronald L. *Ritual Criticism: Case Studies in Its Practice, Essays on Its Theory.* Columbia, SC: University of South Carolina Press, 1990. [Ritual/Liturgy/Worship]

Grimes, Ronald L. "Sources for the Study of Ritual." *Religious Studies Review* 10 (1984): 134-45. [Ritual/Liturgy/Worship]

Grimme, Hubert. "Ephodentscheid und Prophetenrede." In *Orientalistische Studien: Fritz Hommel zum sechzigsten Geburtstag am 31. Juli 1914 gewidmet von Freunden, Kollegen und Schülern.* 316-27. Leipzig: Hinrichs, 1917. [Sacred Vestments]

Grinnell, Isabel H. *Greek Temples.* New York: Arno, 1943. [Greece/Rome]

Grintz, Yehoshua M. "Ark of the Covenant." In *Encyclopaedia Judaica* 3:459-65. [Tabernacle]

Grintz, J. (Yehoshua) M. "Some Observations on the 'High-Place' in the History of Israel." *VT* 27 (January 1977): 111-13. [Mountain]

Grintz, Yehoshua (Joshua) M. "The Temple" (in Hebrew). In *Encyclopaedia Hebraica*, edited by B. Natanyahu. 35 vols., 8:555-91. Jerusalem: Encyclopaedia Printing, 1957. [Israel/Canaan]

Grintz, Yehoshua M., and Yigael Yadin. "Temple: First Temple." In *Encyclopaedia Judaica* 15:943-55. [Israel/Canaan]

Groot, Johannes de. *Die Altäre des salomonischen Tempelhofes.* Stuttgart: Kohlhammer, 1924. [Sacrifice/Offerings]

Gros, Pierre. *Aurea Templa.* Rome: École française de Rome, 1976. [Greece/Rome]

Gros, Pierre. "Trois temples de la Fortune des Ier et IIe siècles de notre ere: Remarques sur l'origine des sanctuaires romains a abside." *Melita Historia* 79 (1967): 503-66. [Greece/Rome]

Gruben, Gottfried. *Die Tempel der Griechen.* Munich: Hirmer, 1980. [Greece/Rome]

Grünbaum, Paul. *Die Priestergesetze bei Flavius Josephus: Eine Parallele zu Bibel and Tradition.* Halle: n.p., 1887. [Priesthood]

Grünhut, L. "Der Raum des Tempels nach Estori hep-Parchi." *ZDPV* 31 (1908): 281-96. [Egypt]

Gry, L. "La ruine du temple par Titus—quelques traditions juives plus anciennes et primitives à la base de Pesikta Rabbathi xxvi." *RB* 55 (1948): 215-26. [Israel/Canaan]

Guénon, René. *Aperuçus sur l'initiation.* Paris: Editions Traditionelles, 1976. [Ritual/Liturgy/Worship]

Guénon, René. *Initiation et réalisation spirituelle.* Paris: Editions Traditionelles, 1975. [Ritual/Liturgy/Worship]

Guérin, Victor. "Jérusalem a l'epoche d'Hérode le Grand." In *La Terre Sainte—Jérusalem* . 63-76. Paris: Plon, 1897. [Israel/Canaan]

Guillebaud, M. L. G. "The Tent over the Tabernacle." *Evangelical Quarterly* 31 (1959): 90-98. [Tabernacle]

Guilmot, Max. *Les initiés et les rites initiatiques en Égypte ancienne.* Paris: Laffont, 1977. [Ritual/Liturgy/Worship]

Gulston, C. "Herod's Masterpiece." In *Jerusalem—the Tragedy and the Triumph.* 99-103 Michigan: Zondervan, 1978. [Israel/Canaan]

Gunneweg, A. H. J. *Leviten und Priester: Hauptlinien der Traditionsbildung und Geschichte des israelitisch-jüdischen Kultpersonals.* Göttingen: Vandenhoeck and Ruprecht, 1965. [Priesthood]

Gurney, Oliver R. "Babylonian Prophylactic Figures and Their Rituals." *Annals of Archaeology and Anthropology* 22 (1935): 31-96. [Ritual/Liturgy/Worship]

Gurney, Oliver R. "The Cult." In Gurney, *Some Aspects of Hittite Religion.* Oxford: Oxford University Press, 1977. [Mesopotomia]

Gustavs, A. "Religionsgeschictliches aus 'Koldewey, die Tempel von Babylon und Borsippa.' " *ZAW* 32 (1912): 65-68. [Mesopotamia]

Güterbock, H. G. "The Hittite Temple according to Written Sources." In *Le temple et le culte: Compte rendu de la vingtième recontre assyriologique internationale organisée à Leiden du 3 au 7 juillet 1972.* 125-32. Istanbul: Nederlands Historisch-Archeologisch Instituut te Istambul 1975. [Israel/Canaan]

Gutmann, E. "The Mountain Concept in Israelite Religion." Ph.D. diss., Southern Baptist Seminary, 1982. [Mountain]

Gutmann, Joseph. "The History of the Ark." *ZAW* 83 (1971): 22-30. [Tabernacle]

Gutmann, Joseph. "A Note on the Temple Menorah." *ZNTW* 60 (1969): 289-91. [Israel/Canaan]

Gutmann, Joseph, ed. *The Temple of Solomon.* Missoula: Scholars, 1976. [Israel/Canaan]

Gutmann, S. B. Z. *Ha-Kotel ha-Maʿaravi.* Tel-Aviv: Omonuth, 1929. [Israel/Canaan]

Guttman, A. "The End of the Jewish Sacrificial Cult." *HUCA* 38 (1967): 137-48. [Sacrifice/Offerings]

Haak, R. D. "The 'Shoulder' of the Temple." *VT* 33 (1983): 271-78. [Israel/Canaan]

Haase, Julius. *Der siebenarmige Leuchter des alten Bundes, seine Geschichte und Symbolik.* Munich: Asokthebu, 1922. [Israel/Canaan]

Habachi, Labib. *The Sanctuary of Heqaib.* Mainz am Rhein: von Zabern, 1985. [Egypt]

Habermann, A. M. "Prayer in the Temple and the Prayer of the High Priest" (in Hebrew). *Maḥanayim* 96 (1964): 26-27. [Priesthood]

Habershon, Ada R. *Outline Studies of the Tabernacle.* Grand Rapids: Kregel, 1974. [Tabernacle]

Hachlili, Rachel. "The Architecture of Nabataean Temples" (in Hebrew; *English summary). *Eretz-Israel* 12 (1975): 95-106, *121. [Israel/Canaan]

Hachlili, Rachel. "The Niche and the Ark in Ancient Synagogues." *BASOR* 223 (1976): 43-53. [Tabernacle]

Hachlili, Rachel, and R. Merhav. "The *Menorah* in First and Second Temple Times in the Light of the Sources and Archaeology" (in Hebrew; *English summary). *Eretz-Israel* 18 (1985): 256-67, *74. [Israel/Canaan]

Hackman, George G. *Temple Documents of the Third Dynasty of Ur from Umma.* London: Milford, 1937. [Mesopotamia]

Hacohen, Mordecai. *Ha-Bayit veha-ʿAliyah*. Jerusalem: Yad Ramah, 1978. [Israel/Canaan]

Hacohen, Mordecai. "Bibliography of the Temple Mount and Temple" (in Hebrew). *Morashah* 11 (1977): 97-100. [Mountain]

Hadey Jean. "Jéremie et la temple: le conflit de la parole prophétique et de la tradition religieuse: Jér. 7: 1-15; 26: 1-19." *Études théologiques et religieuses* 54 (1979): 438-43. [Israel/Canaan]

Haegg, R. "Mykenische Kultstätten im archäologischen Material." *Opuscula Atheniensia* 14 (1968): 39-60. [Greece/Rome]

Haeny, H. Gerhard. *Untersuchungen im Totentempel Amenophis III.* Wiesbaden: Steiner, 1981. [Egypt]

Hagg, Robin, and N. Marinatos, eds. *Sanctuaries and Cults in the Aegean Bronze Age*. Stockholm: Astroms, 1981. [Greece/Rome]

Haldar, Alfred. "Hermon, Mount." In *The Interpreter's Dictionary of the Bible* 2:585. [Mountain]

Haldeman, Isaac M. *The Tabernacle, Priesthood and Offerings*. New York: Revell, 1925. [Tabernacle]

Halevy, Yitshak. "The Sanhedrin in the Chamber of Hewn Stone." In Halevy, *Dorot Harishonim—Die Geschichte und Literatur Israels*, sect. 1, vol. 5 (in Hebrew). 112-16. Berlin: Harz, 1923. [Israel/Canaan]

Halivni, D. W. "Surrejoinder to E. Feldman." *Tradition: A Journal of Orthodox Jewish Thought* 23 (Winter 1988): 101-6. [Israel/Canaan]

Hallencreutz, C. "Christ Is the Mountain." In *Religious Symbols and Their Functions*, edited by H. Biezais. 96-104. Uppsala: Almquist and Wiksell, 1979. [Mountain]

Hallevy, R. "The Place of the Monarchy in Israelite Religion." *Tarbiz* 32 (1962-63): 215-24. [Kingship/Coronation]

Halpern, Baruch. "The Centralization Formula in Deuteronomy." *VT* 31 (1981): 20-38. [Israel/Canaan]

Halpern, Baruch. "The Ritual Background of Zechariah's Temple Song." *CBQ* 40 (1978): 143-66. [Ritual/Liturgy/Worship]

Hambridge, Jay. *The Parthenon and Other Greek Temples: Their Dynamic Symmetry*. New Haven: Yale University Press, 1924. [Greece/Rome]

Hamerton-Kelly, R. G. "The Temple and the Origins of Jewish Apocalyptic." *VT* 20 (1970): 1-15. [Israel/Canaan]

Hamilton, N. Q. "Temple Cleansing and Temple Bank." *JBL* 83 (1964): 365-72. [Israel/Canaan]

Hamilton, R. W. "Jerusalem: Patterns of Holiness." In *Archaeology in the Levant: Essays for Kathleen Kenyon*, edited by Roger Moorey and Peter Parr. 194-201. Warminster: Aris and Phillips, 1978. [Israel/Canaan]

Hamlin, E. J. "The Meaning of 'Mountains and Hills' in Isaiah 41:14-16." *JNES* 13 (1954): 185-90. [Mountain]

Hamman, Gauthier A. *L'initiation chrétienne.* Paris: Bernard Grosset, 1963. [Ritual/Liturgy/Worship]

Hanauer, J. E. "Julian's Attempt to Restore the Temple, and Other Notes." *PEQ* 34 (1902): 389-93. [Israel/Canaan]

Hänel, John. "Das Recht des Opferschlachtens in der chronistischen Literatur." *ZAW* 55 (1937): 46-67. [Sacrifice/Offerings]

Hani, Jean. *Le symbolisme du temple chrétien.* Paris: Tredaniel, 1978. [Israel/Canaan]

Hannay, T. "The Temple." *Scottish Journal of Theology* 3 (1950): 278-87. [Israel/Canaan]

Hanselman, Robert W. "An Architecturosymbolic Interpretation of the Ancient Jewish Temples." M.A. thesis, University of Florida, 1983. [Israel/Canaan]

Hanson, D. W. "The Ideology of Kingship in the Ancient Near East." Ph.D. diss., University of Utah, 1961. [Kingship/Coronation]

Hanson, John. A. *Roman Theater Temples.* Westport: Greenwood, 1978. [Greece/Rome]

Hanson, Richard P. C. "Transformation of Pagan Temples into Churches in the Early Christian Centuries." *Journal of Semitic Studies* 23 (1978): 257-67. [Greece/Rome]

Har, Moshe David. *The Temple and the Priests at the End of the 2nd Temple, According to Rabbinic Literature* (in Hebrew). Jerusalem: Hebrew University of Jerusalem, 1972 or 1973. [Israel/Canaan]

Haran, Menahem. "The Ark and the Cherubim: Their Symbolic Significance in Biblical Ritual." *IEJ* 9 (1959): 30-38, 89-94. [Tabernacle]

Haran, Menahem. "The Ark of the Covenant and the Cherubs" (in Hebrew; *English summary). *Eretz-Israel* 5 (1958): 83-90, *88. [Tabernacle]

Haran, Menahem. "Bamot and Miqdašim: From Arad to Dan." *Beth Mikra* 24 (1978): 94-105. [Mountain]

Haran, Menahem. "Biblical Studies: The Idea of the Divine Presence in Israelite Cult." *Tarbiz* 38 (1968): 105-19. [Israel/Canaan]

Haran, Menahem. "The Censer Incense and Tamid Incense." *Tarbiz* 26 (1956): 115-25. [Israel/Canaan]

Haran, Menahem. "The Complex of Ritual Acts Performed inside the Tabernacle." *Scripta Hierosolymitana* 8 (1961): 272-302. [Tabernacle]

Haran, Menahem. "The Disappearance of the Ark." *IEJ* 13 (1963): 46-58. [Israel/Canaan]

Haran, Menahem. "The Divine Presence in the Israelite Cult and the Cultic Institutions." *Biblica* 50 (1969): 251-67. [Mountain]

Haran, Menahem. "The Ephod According to Biblical Sources." *Tarbiz* 24 (1955): 380-91. [Sacred Vestments]

Haran, Menahem. "The Gibeonites, the Nethinim and the Servants of Solomon" (in Hebrew). In *Judah and Jerusalem: The Twelfth Archaeological Convention*. 37-45. Jerusalem: Israel Exploration Society, 1957. [Israel/Canaan]

Haran, Menahem. "Nature of the 'ʾOhel Moʿedh' in Pentateuchal Sources." *Journal of Semitic Studies* 5 (1960): 50-65. [Tabernacle]

Haran, Menahem. "The Passover Sacrifice." In *Studies in the Religion of Ancient Israel*. 86-116. Leiden: Brill, 1972. [Sacrifice/Offerings]

Haran, Menahem. "Priest, Temple and Worship" (in Hebrew; *English summary). *Tarbiz* 48/3-4 (1979): 175-85, *I. [Ritual/Liturgy/Worship]

Haran, Menahem. "Priesthood, Temple, Divine Service: Some Observations on Institutions and Practices of Worship." *Hebrew Annual Review* 7 (1983): 121-35. [Priesthood]

Haran, Menahem. "The Priestly Image of the Tabernacle." *HUCA* 36 (1965): 191-226. [Tabernacle]

Haran, Menahem. "Priestly Vestments." In *Encyclopaedia Judaica* 13:1063-69. [Sacred Vestments]

Haran, Menahem. "Priests and Priesthood." In *Encyclopaedia Judaica* 13:1069-86. [Priesthood]

Haran, Menahem. "Shiloh and Jerusalem" (in Hebrew). *Tarbiz* 31 (1961-62): 317-25. [Tabernacle]

Haran, Menahem. "Shiloh and Jerusalem: The Origin of the Priestly Tradition in the Pentateuch." *JBL* 81 (1962): 14-24. [Priesthood]

Haran, Menahem. "Studies in the Bible: The Idea of Centralization of the Cult in the Priestly Apprehension" (in Hebrew; *English summary). *Beer-Sheva* 1 (1973): 114-21, *239. [Priesthood]

Haran, Menahem. "The Tabernacle and Ritualistic Interior Enclosure" (In Hebrew). Ph.D. diss., Hebrew University, 1955. [Tabernacle]

Haran, Menahem. "The Tabernacle in the Priestly Source: Its Technical and Material Gradations" (in Hebrew). In *Sefer Tur-Sinai Jubilee Volume*, edited by Menahem Haran. 27-42. Jerusalem: Ha-Hevrah leheker ha-Mikra be-Yisrael, 1960. [Tabernacle]

Haran, Menahem. "The Tabernacle: A Graded Tabu of Holiness" (in Hebrew). In *Studies in the Bible, Presented to M. H. Segal*, edited by Jehoshua M. Grintz et al. 33-41. Jerusalem: Keriot Sefer, 1964): 33-41. [Tabernacle]

Haran, Menahem. "A Temple at Dor?" *IEJ* 27 (1977): 12-15. [Israel/Canaan]

Haran, Menahem. "Temple and Community in Ancient Israel." In *Temple in Society*, edited by Michael V. Fox. 17-25. Winona Lake: Eisenbrauns, 1988. [Israel/Canaan]

Haran, Menahem. *Temples and Temple-Service in Ancient Israel.* Oxford: Clarendon, 1977. [Israel/Canaan]

Haran, Menahem. "The Tent of Meeting." *Tarbiz* 25 (1955): 11-20. [Tabernacle]

Haran, Menahem. "The Uses of Incense in the Ancient Israelite Ritual." *VT* 10 (1960): 113-29. [Ritual/Liturgy/Worship]

Haran, Menahem. "*Zebah Hayyamîm.*" *VT* 19 (1969): 11-22. [Sacrifice/ Offerings]

Hardy, E. R. "The Date of Psalm 110." *JBL* 64 (1945): 385-90. [Kingship/ Coronation]

Harel, Menashe. "Water and the Temple in Jerusalem." *Ariel* 70 (1987): 71-88. [Israel/Canaan]

Harel, Menashe. "Water for Purification, Hygiene and Cult at the Temple in Jerusalem" (in Hebrew; *English summary). *Eretz-Israel* 19 (1987): 310-13, *82-83. [Israel/Canaan]

Harkins, P. W. "Pre-Baptismal Rites in Chrysostom's Baptismal Catecheses." In *Studia Patristica*, edited by F. L. Cross, 17 vols., 8:219-38. Berlin: Akademie-Verlag, 1966. [Ablutions/Anointings]

Harper, A. "The Prophets and Sacrifice." *Expositor* (1894-A): 241-53. [Sacrifice/Offerings]

Harrelson, Walter. *From Fertility Cult to Worship.* Garden City: Doubleday, 1969. [Ritual/Liturgy/Worship]

Harrelson, Walter. "Guilt and Rites of Purification Related to the Fall of Jerusalem in 587 B.C." In *Proceedings of the XIth International Congress of the International Association for the History of Religions.* 73-74. Leiden: Brill, 1968. [Ritual/Liturgy/Worship]

Harrelson, Walter. "Worship in Early Israel." *Biblical Research* 3 (1958): 1-14. [Ritual/Liturgy/Worship]

Harris, J. G. "Covenant Concept among the Qumran Sectaries." *Evangelical Quarterly* 39 (1967): 86-92. [Covenant]

Harris, Rivkah. "The Archive of the Sin Temple in Khafajah." *Journal of Cuneiform Studies* 9 (1955): 31-88. [Mesopotamia]

Harris, Rivkah. "Old Babylonian Temple Loans." *Journal of Cuneiform Studies* 14 (1960): 126-39. [Mesopotamia]

Harrison, Roland K. "Matriarchate and Hebrew Regal Succession." *Evangelical Quarterly* 29 (1957): 29-34. [Kingship/Coronation]

Hart, I. "Preaching on the Account of the Tabernacle." *Evangelical Quarterly* 54 (1982): 111-16. [Tabernacle]

Hartmann, R. "Zelt und Lade." *ZAW* 37 (1917-18): 209-44. [Tabernacle]

Hasel, Gerhard F. *Covenant in Blood.* Mountain View: Pacific, 1982. [Covenant]

Hasel, Gerhard F. "Significance of the Cosmology in Genesis 1 in Relation to Ancient Near Eastern Parallels." *Andrews University Seminary Studies* 10 (1972): 1-20. [Creation/Cosmology]

Hauer, Christian, Jr. "David and the Levites." *Journal for the Study of the Old Testament* 23 (1982): 33-54. [Priesthood]

Hauer, Christian, Jr. "Who Was Zadok?" *JBL* 82 (1963): 89-94. [Priesthood]

Haulotte, Edgar. *Symbolique du vêtement selon la Bible.* Paris: Aubier, 1966. [Sacred Vestments]

Haupt, Paul. "Babylonian Elements in Levitical Ritual." *JBL* 19 (1900): 55-61. [Ritual/Liturgy/Worship]

Hayes, W. C. "Royal Decrees from the Temple of Min at Coptus." *JEA* 32 (1946): 3-23. [Egypt]

Hayward, R. "The Jewish Temple at Leontopolis: A Reconsideration." *JJS* 33 (1982): 429-43. [Israel/Canaan]

Hebert, A. G. "Idea of Kingship in the Old Testament." *Reformed Theological Review* 18 (1959): 34-45. [Kingship/Coronation]

Hecht, Richard D. "Studies on Sacrifice, 1970-1980." *Religious Studies Review* 8 (1982): 253-59. [Sacrifice/Offerings]

Hedrick, Charles. W. "The Temple and Cult of Apollo Patroos in Athens." *AJA* 88 (1984): 247-48 (summary of a presentation); also in *AJA* 92 (1988): 185-210. [Greece/Rome]

Heinemann, J. "Prayer in the Temple." In *Prayer in the Talmud: Forms and Patterns.* 123-38. Berlin and New York: de Gruyter, 1977. [Ritual/Liturgy/Worship]

Heinrich, Ernst. *Kleinfunde aus den archaischen Tempelschichten in Uruk.* Berlin: Deutsche Forschungsgemeinschaft, 1936. [Mesopotamia]

Heinrich, Ernst. "Die Stellung der Uruktempel in der Baugeschichte." *Zeitschrift für Assyriologie* 49 (1949): 21-44. [Mesopotamia]

Heinrich, Ernst. *Die Tempel und Heiligtümer im alten Mesopotamien: Typologie, Morphologie, und Geschichte.* Berlin: de Gruyter, 1982. [Mesopotamia]

Helbig, Konrad. *Tempel Siziliens.* Frankfort: Insel, 1963. [Greece/Rome]

Hellstrom, Pontus. *The Temple of Zeus.* Lund: Aström, 1982. [Greece/Rome]

Henderson, Arthur E. "Temple of Diana." *Records of the Past* 8 (1909): 194-206. [Greece/Rome]

Henderson, Joseph L. *Thresholds of Initiation.* Middletown, CT: Weslyan University Press, 1967. [Ritual/Liturgy/Worship]

Hengel, Martin. "Der Eifer für die Reinheit des Heiligtums." In Hengel, *Die Zeloten—Untersuchungen zur jüdischen Freiheits-Bewegung in der Zeit von Herodes I. bis 70 N. Chr.* 211-29. Leiden: Brill, 1961. [Israel/Canaan]

Hengel, Martin, James H. Charlesworth, and D. Mendels. "The Polemical Character of 'On Kingship' in the Temple Scroll: An Attempt at Dating 11QTemple." *JJS* 37 (1986): 28-38. [Israel/Canaan]

Hennessy, Basil. "Amman." *RB* 73 (1966): 561-64. [Israel/Canaan]

Hennessy, J. B. "Excavation of a Late Bronze Age Temple at Amman." *PEQ* 98 (1966): 155-62. [Israel/Canaan]

Henninger, Joseph. "Ist der sogenannte Nilus-Bericht eine brauchbare religionsgeschichtliche Quelle?" *Anthropos* 50 (1955): 81-148. [Sacrifice/Offerings]

Henninger, Joseph. "Menschenopfer bei den Arabern." *Anthropos* 53 (1958): 721-805. [Sacrifice/Offerings]

Henninger, Joseph. "Das Opfer in den altsüdarabischen Hochkulturen." *Anthropos* 37-40 (1942-45): 779-810. [Sacrifice/Offerings]

Henninger, Joseph. "Le sacrifice chez les Arabes." *Ethnos* 13/1-2 (1948): 1-16. [Sacrifice/Offerings]

Henninger, Joseph. "Die unblutige Tierweihe der vorislamischen Araber in ethnologischer Sicht." *Paideuma* 4 (1950): 179-90. [Sacrifice/Offerings]

Henninger, Joseph. "Über Menschenopfer bei den vorislamischen Arabern." In *Akten des 24. Internationalen Orientalisten-Kongresses, München, 18. August bis 4. September 1957*, edited by Herbert Franke. 244-46. Wiesbaden: Harrassowitz, 1957. [Sacrifice/Offerings]

Henrickson, E. F. "House or Temples: Ubaid Tripartite Architecture in Mesopotamia." *AJA* 89 (1985): 333. [Mesopotamia]

Henson, Ralph B. "The Central Sanctuary in Ancient Israel." Th.D. diss., New Orleans Baptist Theological Seminary, 1984. [Israel/Canaan]

Hentschke, Richard. "Opfer, 2: Im AT." In *Die Religion in Geschichte und Gegenwart*, 3d ed. 6 vols., 4:1641-47. Tübingen: Mohr, 1960. [Sacrifice/Offerings]

Herbert, A. S. *Worship in Ancient Israel.* London: Lutterworth, 1959. [Ritual/Liturgy/Worship]

Herbert, Sharon C. "The Orientation of Greek Temples." *PEQ* 116 (1984): 31-34. [Greece/Rome]

Hermission, Hans J. *Sprache und Ritus im altisraelitischen Kult.* Neukirchen-Vluyn: Neukirchener, 1965. [Ritual/Liturgy/Worship]

"The Herodian Temple, according to the Treatise Middoth and Flavius Josephus." *PEFQ* 18 (1886): 92-113. [Israel/Canaan]

Herr, M. D. "Jerusalem, the Temple and Its Cult: Reality and Concepts in Second Temple Times—Jerusalem in the Second Temple Period." In *Jerusalem in the Second Temple Period: Abraham Schalit Memorial Volume* (in Hebrew; English summaries), edited by A. Oppenheimer et al. 166-67. Jerusalem: Yad Izhaq Ben-Avi, 1980. [Israel/Canaan]

Herrmann, Joseph. *Le temple de Jérusalem d'après les travaux des archéologues modernes.* Valenciennes: Prignet, 1882. [Israel/Canaan]

Herrmann, W. "Unknown Designs for the 'Temple of Jerusalem' by Claude Perrault." In *Essays in the History of Architecture Presented to Rudolf Wittkower,* edited by D. Fraser. 143-58. London: Phaidon, 1967. [Israel/Canaan]

Hertzberg, H. W. "Der heilige Fels und das Alte Testament." *JPOS* 12 (1932): 32-42. [Israel/Canaan]

Herzog, Ze'ev, Miriam Aharoni, and Anson F. Rainey. "Arad: An Ancient Israelite Fortress with a Temple to Yahweh." *BAR* 13 (1987): 16-35. [Israel/Canaan]

Herzog, Ze'ev, Miriam Aharoni, Anson F. Rainey, and S. Moshkovitz. "The Israelite Fortress at Arad." *BASOR* 254 (1984): 1-34. [Israel/Canaan]

Hewett, Louisa A. *Papers on the Tabernacle.* Glasgow: Hobbs, 1898. [Tabernacle]

Hicks, Frederick C. N. *The Fullness of Sacrifice.* London: Macmillan, 1930. [Sacrifice/Offerings]

Hiers, Richard. "Purification of the Temple: Preparation for the Kingdom of God." *JBL* 90 (1971): 82-90. [Israel/Canaan]

Higgins, Francis C. *The Apron: Its Traditions, History, and Secret Significances.* New York: Francis C. Higgins, 1914. [Sacred Vestments]

Hildebrand, D. R. "Temple Ritual: A Paradigm for Moral Holiness in Haggai ii 10-10." *VT* 39 (1989): 154-68. [Ritual/Liturgy/Worship]

Hildesheimer, Israel. *Die Beschreibung des herodianischen Tempels im Tractate Middoth und bei Flavius Josephus.* Jerusalem: Rabbiner-Seminar, 1877. [Measurement]

Hildesheimer, Israel. "The Herodian Temple, According to the Treatise Middoth and Flavius Josephus." *PEFQ* 18 (1886): 92-113. [Measurement]

Hildesheimer, Azriel (Israel). *Measurements of Herod's Temple in the Tractate 'Middot' and Josephus* (in Hebrew). Jerusalem: Friedman, 1974. [Measurement]

Hildesheimer, Israel. *Midot Bet ha-Mikdash shel Hordus be-Masekhet Middot uve-Khitve Yosef ben Matityahu.* Jerusalem: Nettler, 1973-74. [Measurement]

Hill, Bert H. *The Temple of Zeus at Nemea.* Princeton: American School of Classical Studies at Athens, 1966. [Greece/Rome]

Hillers, Delbert R. *Covenant: The History of a Biblical Idea.* Baltimore: Johns Hopkins University Press, 1969. [Covenant]

Hillers, Delbert R. "MŠKN 'Temple' in an Inscription from Hatra." *BASOR* 206 (1972): 54-56. [Israel/Canaan]

Hillers, Delbert R. "Ritual Procession of the Ark and Psalm 132." *CBQ* 30 (1968): 48-55. [Tabernacle]

Hillers, Delbert R. *Treaty-Curses and Old Testament Prophets.* Rome: Pontifical Biblical Institute, 1964. [Covenant]

Hiltebeital, A. "Nahusa in the Skies: A Human King of Heaven." *History of Religions* 16 (1977): 329-50. [Kingship/Coronation]

Himmelfarb, Martha. "Apocalyptic Ascent and the Heavenly Temple." *SBLSP* 26 (1987): 210-17. [Israel/Canaan]

Hirsch, S. A. "The Temple of Onias." In *Jews' College Jubilee Volume,* edited by I. Harris. 39-80. London: Luzac, 1906. [Israel/Canaan]

Hocart, Arthur M. "The Coronation Ceremony." *Ceylon Journal of Science, Section G* 1 (1924-28): 27-42. [Kingship/Coronation]

Hocart, Arthur M. *Kings and Councillors.* Cairo: Barbey, 1936. [Kingship/Coronation]

Hocart, Arthur M. *Kingship.* London: Oxford University Press, 1927. [Kingship/Coronation]

Hochman, Joseph. *Jerusalem Temple Festivities.* London: Routledge, 1908. [Ritual/Liturgy/Worship]

Hoenig, Sidney B. "The End of the Great Sanhedrin during the Second Temple Period" (in Hebrew). *Horeb* 3 (1936): 169-75. [Israel/Canaan]

Hoenig, Sidney B. "The Meeting Place." In *The Great Sanhedrin* (in Hebrew), 74-84. Philadelphia: Dropsie College, 1953. [Israel/Canaan]

Hoenig, Sidney B. "Suppositous Temple-Synagogue." *JQR* 54 (1963): 115-31. [Israel/Canaan]

Hofer Josef. "Zur Phänomenologie der Sakralraumer und sein Symbolismus im Alten Orient mit Berücksichtigung der Bauformen." Ph.D. diss., University of Vienna, 1969. [Sacred Space]

Hoffmann, Richard A. "Das Wort Jesu von der Zerstörung und dem Wiederaufbau des Tempels." In *Neustamentliche Studien Georg Heinrici zu seinem 70. Geburtstag.* 130-39. Leipzig: 1914. [Israel/Canaan]

Hofius, Otfried. "Das 'erste' und das 'zweite' Zelt; ein Beitrag zur Auslegung von Heb 9:1-10." *ZNTW* 61/3-4 (1970): 271-77. [Tabernacle]

Hofius, Otfried. *Der Vorhang vor dem Thron Gottes: Eine exegetisch-religionsgeschichtliche Untersuchung zu Hebräer 6, 19f und 10, 19f.* Tübingen: Mohr, 1972. [Israel/Canaan]

Hofmeister, Philipp. *Die heiligen Öle in der morgen- und abendländischen Kirche.* Würzburg: Augustinus, 1948. [Ablutions/Anointings]

Hogg, James E. "The Inscription on Aaron's Head-dress." *JTS* 28 (1927): 287-88. [Sacred Vestments]

Hogg, James E. "A Note on Two Points in Aaron's Headdress." *JTS* 26 (1925): 72-75. [Sacred Vestments]

Holladay, W. L. "On Every High Hill and under Every Green Tree." *VT* 11 (1961): 170-76. [Mountain]

Hollingshead, Mary B. B. *Legend, Cult, and Architecture at Three Sanctuaries of Artemis*. n.p., n.p., 1980. [Greece/Rome]

Hollis, C., and R. Brownrigg. "The Third Temple." In Hollis and Brownrigg, *Holy Places*, 52-54. New York: Praeger, 1969. [Israel/Canaan]

Hollis, F. J. *The Archaeology of Herods Temple*. London: Dent & Sons, 1934. [Israel/Canaan]

Hollis, F. J. "The Sun-Cult and the Temple at Jerusalem." In *Myth and Ritual*, edited by Samuel H. Hooke. 87-110. London: Oxford University Press, 1933. [Israel/Canaan]

Hölscher, Gustav. *Die Hohenpriesterliste bei Josephus und die evangelische Chronologie*. Heidelberg: Winter, 1940. [Priesthood]

Hölscher, Gustav. "Sadduzäismus und Hohespriestertum." In *Der Sadduzäismus: Eine kritische Untersuchung zur späteren jüdischen Religionsgeschichte*, 37-84. Leipzig: Hinrichs, 1906. [Priesthood]

Holscher, Uro. *Excavations at Ancient Thebes*. Chicago: University of Chicago Press, 1932. [Egypt]

Holscher, Uro. *The Mortuary Temple of Ramses III*. London: Cambridge University Press, 1940-45. [Egypt]

Holst, R. "The One Anointing of Jesus: Another Application of the Form Critical Method." *JBL* 95 (1976): 435-46. [Ablutions/Anointings]

Holtzmann, O. "Tore und Terrassen des herodianischen Tempels." *ZNTW* 8-9 (1908): 71-74. [Israel/Canaan]

Holzinger, H. "Der Schaubrottisch des Titusbogens." *ZAW* 21 (1901): 341-42. [Israel/Canaan]

Honeyman, A. M. "The Evidence for Regnal Names among the Hebrews." *JBL* 67 (1948): 13-25. [Kingship/Coronation]

Hood, S. "Minoan Town-Shrines." In *Greece and the Eastern Mediterranean in Ancient History and Prehistory. Studies Presented to Fritz Schachermeyr on the Occasion of His 80th Birthday*, edited by K. H. Kinzl. 156-72. Berlin: de Gruyter, 1977. [Greece/Rome]

Hooke, Samuel H. "The Corner-Stone of Scripture." In Hooke, *The Siege Perilous: Essays in Biblical Anthropology and Kindred Subjects*. 235-49. London: SCM, 1956. [Israel/Canaan]

Hooke, Samuel H. *The Origins of Early Semitic Ritual*. London: Oxford University Press, 1938. [Ritual/Liturgy/Worship]

Hooke, Samuel H. "The Theory and Practice of Substitution." *VT* 2 (1952): 2-17. [Ritual/Liturgy/Worship]

Hooke, Samuel H., ed. *Myth and Ritual*. London: Oxford University Press, 1933. [Ritual/Liturgy/Worship]

Hooke, Samuel H., ed. *Myth, Ritual and Kingship*. Oxford: Clarendon, 1958. [Ritual/Liturgy/Worship]

Hooker, Morna D. "Traditions about the Temple in the Sayings of Jesus." *BJRL* 70 (Spring 1988): 7-19. [Israel/Canaan]

Hoonacker, Albin van. "La date de l'introduction de l'encens dans le culte de Jahvé." *RB* 11 (1914): 161-87. [Ritual/Liturgy/Worship]

Hoonacker, Albin van. *Le lieu du culte dans la législation rituelle des Hébreux.* Leipzig: Engelcke, 1894. [Ritual/Liturgy/Worship]

Hoonacker, Albin van. "Les Prêtres et les lévites dans le livre d'Ézéchiël." *Revue Biblique* 8 (1899): 177-205. [Priesthood]

Hoonacker, Albin van. *Le sacerdoce lévitique dans la loi et dans l'histoire des Hebreux.* London: Williams and Norgate, 1899. [Israel/Canaan]

Hoonacker, Albin van. "Zorobabel et le second temple." *Le Muséon* 10 (1891): 379-97, 489-515, 634-44. [Israel/Canaan]

Hoonacker, Albin van. *Zorobabel et le second temple: Étude sur la chronologie des six premiers chapitres du livre d'Esdras.* Gand: Engelcke, 1892. [Israel/Canaan]

Horbury, William. "New Wine in Old Wine-Skins: IX. The Temple." *ET* 86 (1974): 36-42. [Israel/Canaan]

Horbury, William. "The Temple Tax." In *Jesus and the Politics of His Day*, edited by Ernst Bammel and C. F. D. Moule. 265-86. Cambridge: Cambridge University Press, 1984. [Israel/Canaan]

Horbury, William. *Templum Amicitiae: Essays on the Second Temple Presented to Ernst Bammel.* Sheffield: JSOT, 1990. [Israel/Canaan]

Hornblower, G. D. "Temples and Kings in Ancient Egypt." *Journal of Manchester Egyptian and Oriental Society* 17 (1932): 21-39. [Egypt]

Hornblower, G. D. "A Temple Seal and Its Connections." *ASAE* 34 (1934): 99-106. [Egypt]

Horne, Alexander. *King Solomon's Temple in the Masonic Tradition.* London: Aquarian, 1972. [Israel/Canaan]

Horovicz, Jonathan. *Geschichte des Sch'thijasteines.* Frankfurt: Kauffmann, 1927. [Mountain]

Horowitz, I. S. "The Temple Administration and the Divine Services" (in Hebrew). In *Jerusalem—a Geographical, Topographical, and Historical Encyclopaedia of Jerusalem.* 389-435. Jerusalem: Mass, 1964. [Israel/Canaan]

Horst, Friedrich. "Die Kultusreform des Königs Josia (II RG. 22-23)." *ZDMG* 77 (1923): 220-38. [Israel/Canaan]

Hoschander, Jacob. *The Priests and Prophets.* New York: Jewish Theological Seminary of America, 1938. [Priesthood]

Howard-Carter, T. "An Interpretation of the Sculptural Decoration of the 2nd Millennium Temple at Tell al-Rimah." *Iraq* 45 (1983): 64-72. [Mesopotamia]

Howie, C. G. "The East Gate of Ezekiel's Temple Enclosure and the Solomonic Gateway of Megiddo." *BASOR* 117 (1950): 13-19. [Israel/Canaan]

Howland, E. G. *Solomon's Temple.* Troy: Howland, 1950. [Israel/Canaan]

Hruby, Kurt. "La fête des tabernacles au temple, à la synagogue et dans le Nouveau Testament." *L'Orient Syrien* 7 (1962): 163-74. [Tabernacle]

Hubert, Henri. *Sacrifice, Its Nature and Function.* Chicago: University of Chicago Press, 1964. [Sacrifice/Offerings]

Hubmann, Franz D. "Der 'Weg' zum Zion: Literar- und stilkritische Beobachtungen zu Jes. 35: 8-10." In *Memoria Jerusalem: Freundesgabe Franz Sauer zum 70. Geburtstag,* edited by Johannes B. Bauer and Johannes Marböck. 29-41. Graz: Akademische Druck- und Verlagsanstalt, 1977. [Israel/Canaan]

Hudry-Clergeon, J. "Jésus et le Sanctuaire: Étude de Jn. 2, 12-22." *Nouvelle Revue Théologique* 105 (1983): 535-48. [Israel/Canaan]

Hull, E. "Where Are the Sacred Vessels of the Temples?" *PEFQ* 28 (1896): 344. [Israel/Canaan]

Hull, William E. "The Background of the New Temple Concept in Early Christianity." Ph.D. diss., Southern Baptist Theological Seminary, 1960. [Israel/Canaan]

Hummel, Charles. *Die dorischen Tempel Grossgriechenlands.* Basel: Vineta, 1951. [Greece/Rome]

Hurowitz, Victor (Avigdor). "The Priestly Account of Building the Tabernacle." *JAOS* 105 (1985): 21-30. [Tabernacle]

Hurowitz, Avigdor (Victor). "Temple Building in the Bible in Light of Mesopotamian and North-West Semitic Writings" (in Hebrew). Ph.D. diss., Hebrew University, 1983. [Israel/Canaan]

Hurst, L. D. "Eschatology and 'Platonism' in the Epistle to the Hebrews." *SBLSP* (1984): 41-74. [Israel/Canaan]

Hurvitz, Avi. "The Garments of Aharon and His Sons According to 1QM VII 9-10." In *Studies in Bible and the Ancient Near East: Presented to Samuel E. Loewenstamm on His Seventieth Birthday,* edited by Yitschak Avishur and Joshua Blau, 139-44. Jerusalem: Rubinstein, 1978. [Sacred Vestments]

Hurvitz, Avi. "The Term *lishkat sharîm* (Ezek. 40:44) and Its Position in the Cultic Terminology of the Temple" (in Hebrew; *English summary). *Eretz-Israel* 14 (1978): 100-104, *126. [Israel/Canaan]

Hussey, George B. "The Distribution of Hellenic Temples." *AJA* 6 (1890): 59-64. [Greece/Rome]

Hyatt, J. P. "The Deity Bethel and the Old Testament." *JAOS* 59 (1939): 81-98. [Israel/Canaan]

Hyldahl, N. "Die Versuchung auf der Zinne des Tempels (Matt. 4:5-7=Luke 4:9-12)." *Studia Theologica* 15 (1961): 113-27. [Israel/Canaan]

Ibrahim, Mohiy ed-Din. "The God of the Great Temple of Edfu." In *Orbis Aegyptiorum Speculum—Glimpses of Ancient Egypt: Studies in Honour of H. W. Fairman*, edited by Johann Ruffle, G. A. Gaballa, and K. A. Kitchen. 170-73. Warminster: Aris and Phillips, 1979. [Egypt]

Ibrahim, Mohiy ed-Din. "Miscellaneous Passages about King and Kingship according to the Inscriptions of the Temple of Edfu." *ASAE* 60 (1968): 297-300. [Kingship/ Coronation]

Idelsohn, Abraham Z. *Jewish Liturgy and Its Development.* New York: Schocken, 1967. [Ritual/Liturgy/Worship]

Idelsohn, Abraham Z. ". . .Second Temple. . ." In *Jewish Music in Its Historical Development.* 9-21. New York: Tudor, 1948. [Israel/Canaan]

Iliffe, J. H. "A Model Shrine of Phoenician Style." *Quarterly of the Department of Antiquities in Palestine* 11 (1945): 91-92. [Israel/Canaan]

Iliffe, J. H. "The Thanatos Inscription from Herod's Temple—Fragments of a Second Copy." *Quarterly of the Department of Antiquities in Palestine* 6 (1938): 1-3. [Israel/Canaan]

Imbert, J. "Le temple reconstruit par Zorobabel." *Le Muséon* 7 (1888): 77-87, 221-35, 302-14, 584-92; 8 (1889): 51-66, 520-21. [Israel/Canaan]

Ing, Anthony. *The Tabernacle.* Toronto: Good News, 1986. [Tabernacle]

Irshai, O. "Concerning the Purpose and Location of the Chamber of the Curtains in the Second Temple" (in Hebrew). *Morashah* 8 (1974): 56-65. [Israel/Canaan]

Irwin, J. C. "The Sacred Hill and the Cult of the Primordial Mound." *History of Religions* 21 (1982): 339-60. [Mountain]

Irwin, W. H. "Le sanctuaire central israélite avant l'établissement de la monarchie." *RB* 72 (1965): 161-84. [Kingship/Coronation]

Isaac, B. H. "A Donation for Herod's Temple in Jerusalem." *IEJ* 33/1-2 (1983): 86-92; also in Hebrew with *English summary in *Eretz-Israel* 18 (1985): 1-4, *65. [Israel/Canaan]

Isenberg, Sheldon R. "Power through Temple and Torah in Greco-Roman Palestine." In *Christianity, Judaism, and Other Greco-Roman Cults: Studies for Morton Smith at Sixty*, edited by Jacob Neusner. 3 vols., 2:24-52. Leiden: Brill, 1975. [Greece/Rome]

Ivry, A. L. "Nehemiah 6:10; Politics and the Temple." *Journal for the Study of Judaism* 3 (1974): 35-45. [Israel/Canaan]

Iwry, S. "Maṣṣēbāh and Bāmāh in 1Q Isaiah^a 6:13." *JBL* 76 (1957): 225-32. [Mountain]

Jacobsen, Thorkild. *The Sumerian King List.* Chicago: University of Chicago Press, 1939. [Kingship/Coronation]

Jacobson, D. M. "The Golden Section and the Design of the Dome of the Rock." *PEQ* 115 (1983): 145-77. [Israel/Canaan]

Jacobson, D. M. "Ideas Concerning the Plan of Herod's Temple." *PEQ* 112 (1980): 33-40. [Israel/Canaan]

Jacoby, Adolf. "Der angebliche Eselskult der Juden und Christen," *Archiv für Religionswissenschaft* 25 (1927): 264-82. [Israel/Canaan]

James, Edwin O. *Christian Myth and Ritual*. Cleveland: Meridian Books, 1965. [Ritual/Liturgy/Worship]

James, Edwin O. *Creation and Cosmology*. Leiden: Brill, 1969. [Creation/Cosmology]

James, Edwin O. *From Cave to Cathedral: Temple and Shrines of Pre-historic, Classical, and Early Christian Times*. London: Thames and Hudson, 1965. [Sacred Space]

James, Edwin O. *Myth and Ritual in the Ancient Near East*. London: Thames and Hudson, 1958. [Ritual/Liturgy/Worship]

James, Edwin O. *The Nature and Function of Priesthood: A Comparative and Anthropological Study*. New York: Vanguard, 1955. [Priesthood]

James, Edwin O. *Origins of Sacrifice*. Port Washington: Kennikat Press, 1971. [Sacrifice/Offerings]

James, Edwin O. "The Sacred Kingship and the Priesthood." In *The Sacral Kingship/La Regalità Sacra*. 63-70. Leiden: Brill, 1959. [Kingship/Coronation]

Janssen, J. J. "The Role of the Temple in the Egyptian Economy during the New Kingdom." In *State and Temple Economy in the Ancient Near East*, edited by Edward Lipiński. 2 vols., 2:505-16. Louvain: Departement Orientalistiek, 1979. [Egypt]

Japhet, Sara. "Sheshbazzar and Zerubbabel against the Background of the Historical and Religious Tendencies of Ezra-Nehemiah." *ZAW* 95 (1983): 218-29. [Israel/Canaan]

Jaritz, Horst. *Die Terrassen von den Tempeln des Chnum und der Satet*. Mainz: von Zabern, 1980. [Egypt]

Jasper, F. N. "Early Israelite Traditions and the Psalter." *VT* 17 (1967): 50-59. [Mountain]

Jastrow, Morris, Jr. "The Cosmology of the Babylonians." In *The Religion of Babylonia and Assyria*. 407-53. Boston: Ginn, 1898. [Mesopotamia]

Jastrow, Morris, Jr. "Did the Babylonian Temples have Libraries?" *JAOS* 27 (1906): 147-82. [Mesopotamia]

Jastrow, Morris, Jr. "The Temples and the Cult." In *The Religion of Babylonia and Assyria*. 612-89. Boston: Ginn, 1898. [Mesopotamia]

Jehuda, Jacob. *Ha-Mishkan ve-Khelav*. Jerusalem: Kiryah ne'emanah, 1965. [Tabernacle]

Jennings, T. W. "On Ritual Knowledge." *Journal of Religion* 62 (1982): 111-27. [Ritual/Liturgy/Worship]

Jequier, G. *L'architecture et la décoration dans l'ancienne Égypte: Les temples memphites et thébains des origines à la XVIII Dynastie.* Paris: Morancé, 1920. [Egypt]

Jeremias, Joachim. "Abba." In *Studien zur neutestamentlichen Theologie und Zeitgeschichte.* 353-60. Göttingen: Vandenhoeck and Ruprecht, 1966. [Israel/Canaan]

Jeremias, Joachim. "Der Eckstein." *Angelos* 1 (1925): 65-70. [Israel/Canaan]

Jeremias, Joachim. "Eckstein-Schlusstein." *ZTNW* 36 (1937): 154-60. [Israel/Canaan]

Jeremias, Joachim. *Der Gottesberg, ein Beitrag zum Verständnis der biblischen Symbolsprache.* Gütersloh: Bertelmann, 1919. [Mountain]

Jeremias, Joachim. "Hesekieltempel und Serubbabeltempel." *ZAW* 52 (1934): 109-12. [Israel/Canaan]

Jeremias, Joachim. *Jerusalem in the Time of Jesus.* London SCM, 1969. [Israel/Canaan]

Jeremias, Joachim. "*Kephalè gonìas-akrogoviaios.*" *ZNTW* 29 (1930): 264-80. [Israel/Canaan]

Jeremias, Joachim. "Lade und Zion: Zur Entstehung der Ziontradition." In *Probleme biblischer Theologie: Gerhard von Rad zum 70. Geburtstag,* edited by Hans W. Wolff. 183-98. Munich: Kaiser, 1971. [Israel/Canaan]

Jeremias, Joachim. "Die 'Zinne' des Tempels (Mt. 4. 5; Lk. 4.9)." *ZDPV* 59 (1936): 195-208. [Israel/Canaan]

Jeremias, Joachim, and A. M. Schneider. "Das westliche Südtor des herodianischen Tempels." *ZDPV* 65 (1942): 112-21. [Israel/Canaan]

Jeremias, Jörg. "Lade und Zion: Zur Entstehung der Ziontradition." In *Probleme biblischer Theologie: Gerhard von Rad zum 70. Geburtstag,* edited by Hans W. Wolff. 183-98. Munich: Kaiser, 1971. [Tabernacle]

Johns, C. N. "Excavations at the Citadel, Jerusalem: 1934-39." *PEQ* 72 (1940): 36-58. [Israel/Canaan]

Johnson, Aubrey R. "Divine Kingship and the Old Testament." *ET* 62 (1950-51): 36-42. [Kingship/Coronation]

Johnson, Aubrey R. "Hebrew Conceptions of Kingship." In *Myth, Ritual, and Kingship: Essays on the Theory and Practice of Kingship in the Ancient Near East and in Israel,* edited by S. H. Hooke. 204-35. Oxford: Clarendon, 1958. [Kingship/Coronation]

Johnson, Aubrey R. "The Role of the King in the Jerusalem Cultus." In *The Labyrinth: Further Studies in the Relation between Myth and Ritual in the Ancient World,* edited by S. H. Hooke. 71-111. London: SPCK, 1935. [Kingship/Coronation]

Johnson, Aubrey R. *Sacred Kingship in Ancient Israel.* Cardiff: University of Wales Press, 1967. [Kingship/Coronation]

Johnsson, William G. "The Cultus of Hebrews in Twentieth-Century Scholarship." *ET* 89 (1977-78): 104-8. [Israel/Canaan]

Jones, B. H. "The Formation of the Nestorian Liturgy: The Great Conflation." *Anglican Theological Review* 48 (1966): 276-306. [Ritual/Liturgy/Worship]

Jones, B. H. "The Quest for the Origins of the Christian Liturgies." *Anglican Theological Review* 46 (1964): 5-21. [Ritual/Liturgy/Worship]

Jones, Cheslyn, ed. *The Study of Liturgy.* London: Clowes and Sons, 1978. [Ritual/Liturgy/Worship]

Jones, D. "The Cessation of Sacrifice after the Destruction of the Temple in 586 B.C." *JTS* 14 (1963): 12-31. [Sacrifice/Offerings]

Jones, G. C. "Christian Initiation: New Wineskins for New Wine." *Religious Education* 74 (1979): 603-16. [Ritual/Liturgy/Worship]

Jones, Paul D. *Rediscovering Ritual.* New York: Newman, 1973. [Ritual/Liturgy/Worship]

Jongeling, B. "A propos de la colonne XXIII du rouleau du temple." *Revue de Qumran* 10 (1981): 593-95. [Israel/Canaan]

Jordan-Smith, P. "War in Heaven." *Parabola* 7/4 (1982): 68-79. [Creation/Cosmology]

Jouon, Paul. Les mots employes pour designer 'les temple' dans l'ancien testament, le Nouveau Testament et Josephe." *Recherches de science religieuse* 265 (1935): 329-43. [Israel/Canaan]

Judge, H. G. "Aaron, Zadok, and Abiathar." *JTS* 7 (1956): 70-74. [Priesthood]

Junker, Hermann. *Der grosse Pylon des Tempels der Isis in Philä.* Wien: Rohrer, 1958. [Egypt]

Junker, Hermann, ed. *Das Geburtshaus des Tempels der Isis in Philä.* Wien: Nachf, 1965. [Egypt]

Junker, Hubert. "Sancta Civitas, Jerusalem Nova: Eine formcritische und überlieferungsgeschichtliche Studie zu Is. 2." In *Ekklesia: Festschrift für Matthias Wehr,* edited by H. Gross and F. Musser. 17-33. Trier: Paulinus, 1962. [Israel/Canaan]

Kagan, Aaron. ʿAvodat ha-Korbanot. New York: Binah, 1978 or 1979. [Sacrifice/Offerings]

Kähler, Heinz. *Der griechische Tempel: Wesen und Gestalt.* Berlin: Mann, 1964. [Greece/Rome]

Kähler, Heinz. *Der römische Tempel.* Berlin: Mann, 1970. [Greece/Rome]

Kaiser, W., D. Bidoli, P. Grossmann, G. Haeny, H. Jaritz, and R. Stadelmann. "Stadt und Tempel von Elephantine: Dritter Grabungsbericht." *MDAI.K* 28 (1972): 157-200. [Egypt]

Kaiser, W., P. Grossmann, G. Haeny, and H. Jaritz. "Stadt und Tempel von Elephantine: Erster Grabungsbericht." *MDAI.K* 26 (1970): 87-167. [Egypt]

Kaiser, W., P. Grossmann, G. Haeny, H. Jaritz, and R. Stadelmann. "Stadt und Tempel von Elephantine: Zweiter Grabungsbericht." *MDAI.K* 27 (1971): 181-201. [Egypt]

Kanael, G. "The Temple Mount during the Period of the Second Temple" (in Hebrew). *Ha Umah* 6 (1967-68): 486-97. [Mountain]

Kapelrud, Arvid S. "The Gates of Hell and the Guardian Angels of Paradise." *JAOS* 70 (1950): 151-56. [Israel/Canaan]

Kapelrud, Arvid S. "The Role of the Cult in Old Israel." In *The Bible in Modern Scholarship*, edited by J. P. Hyatt. 45-56. Nashville: Abingdon, 1965. [Ritual/Liturgy/Worship]

Kapelrud, Arvid S. "Temple Building, a Task for Gods and Kings." *Orientalia* 32 (1963): 56-62; also in Kapelrud, *God and His Friends in the Old Testament.* 184-90. Oslo: Universitetsforlaget, 1979. [Mesopotamia]

Katzenstein, H. J. "Some Remarks on the Lists of the Chief Priests of the Temple of Solomon." *JBL* 81 (1962): 377-84. [Priesthood]

Katznelbogen, J. G. "The Status of the Levites in the Temple" (in Hebrew). *Maḥanayim* 96 (1964): 32-43. [Priesthood]

Kaufman, Asher S. "Determining the Length of the Medium Cubit." *PEQ* 116 (1984): 120-32. [Measurement]

Kaufman, Asher S. "The Eastern Wall of the Second Temple at Jerusalem Revealed." *BA* 44 (1981): 108-15. [Israel/Canaan]

Kaufman, Asher S. "Fixing the Site of the Tabernacle at Shiloh." *BAR* 14/6 (1988): 46-52. [Tabernacle]

Kaufman, Asher S. "New Light on the Ancient Temple of Jerusalem." *Christian News from Israel* 27/2 (1979): 54-58. [Israel/Canaan]

Kaufman, Asher S. "New Light upon Zion: The Plan and Precise Location of the Second Temple." *Ariel* 43 (1977): 63-100. [Measurement]

Kaufman, Asher S. "New Light upon Zion: The Plan of the 'Hekhal' in the Second Temple." *Niv Hamidrashia* 15 (1980-81): 115-30. [Measurement]

Kaufman, Asher S. "A Note on Artistic Representations of the Second Temple of Jerusalem." *BA* 47 (1984): 253-54. [Israel/Canaan]

Kaufman, Asher S. "The Quest of Scientific Methods to Fix the Position of the Altar in the Temple" (in Hebrew). *Torah u-Mada* 4 (1974): 37-38. [Sacrifice/Offerings]

Kaufman, Asher S. "The Second Temple—Description and Location." In *The Temple Mount—Its Locations and Limits* (in Hebrew). 39-46. Jerusalem: Municipality of Jerusalem, 1975. [Israel/Canaan]

Kaufman, Asher S. "Temple." In *Encyclopaedia Judaica* 17:577-80. [Israel/Canaan]

Kaufman, Asher S. "Temple." In *Encyclopaedia Judaica Yearbook, 1975/76.* 393-97. Jerusalem: Encyclopaedia Judaica, 1976. [Israel/Canaan]

Kaufman, Asher S. "Where the Ancient Temple of Jerusalem Stood." *BAR* 9/2 (1983): 40-59. [Israel/Canaan]

Kaufman, Stephen. "The Temple Scroll and Higher Criticism." *HUCA* 53 (1982): 29-43. [Israel/Canaan]

Kaufmann, Yehezkel. "The Cult." In *The Religion of Israel from the Beginnings to the Babylonian Exile,* translated and abridged by Moshe Greenberg. 101-21. Chicago: University of Chicago Press, 1960. [Israel/Canaan]

Kaufmann, Yehezkel. "Zerubabbel and the Building of the Temple," translated by Moshe Greenberg. In *The Religion of Israel.* 4 vols. 4:223-52. Chicago: University of Chicago Press, 1960. [Israel/Canaan]

Kaufmann, Yehezkel, and Clarence W. Efroymson, eds. *History of the Religion of Israel.* New York: KTAV, 1977. [Mountain]

Kearney, P. J. "Altar in the Bible." *New Catholic Encyclopedia* 1 (1967): 344-46. [Israel/Canaan]

Kearney, P. J. "Creation and Liturgy: The 'P' Redaction of Exodus 25-40." *ZAW* 89 (1977): 375-87. [Creation/Cosmology]

Keathley, Naymond H. "The Concept of the Temple in Luke-Acts." Th.D. diss., Southern Baptist Theological Seminary, 1971. [Israel/Canaan]

Kedar-Kopfstein, B., and G. Johannes Botterweck. "*chagh; hgg.*" In *Theological Dictionary of the Old Testament* 4:201-13. [Israel/Canaan]

Kee, H. C. "Tell-er-Ras and the Samaritan Temple." *NTS* 13 (1967): 401-2. [Israel/Canaan]

Keel, Othmar. "Kanaanäische Sühneriten auf ägyptischen Tempelreliefs." *VT* 25 (1975): 413-69. [Egypt]

Keel, Othmar. "The Temple: Place of Yahweh's Presence and Sphere of Life." In *Symbolism of the Biblical World: Ancient Near Eastern Iconography and the Book of Psalms.* 111-76. New York: Seabury, 1978. [Israel/Canaan]

Keenan, Joseph J. "The Creation Motif: A Study of the Roman Catholic Mass Today in the Context of the History of Religions." Ph.D. diss., Catholic University of America, 1977. [Creation/Cosmology]

Keenan, Joseph J. "The Importance of the Creation Motif in a Eucharistic Prayer." *Worship* 53 (1979): 341-56. [Creation/Cosmology]

Kees, Hermann. "Ein Sonnenheiligtum im Amonstempel von Karnak." *Orientalia* 18 (1949): 427-42. [Egypt]

Keet, Cuthbert C. *A Liturgical Study of the Psalter.* London: Allen & Unwin, 1928. [Ritual/Liturgy/Worship]

Kegel, Martin. *The History of the Israelitish Priesthood.* Dallas: South, Lamar & Barton, 1923. [Priesthood]

Keiser, Clarence E. *Selected Temple Documents of the Ur Dynasty.* New Haven: Yale University Press, 1919. [Mesopotamia]

Keiser, Helen. *Tempel und Türme in Sumer: Archäologen auf der Spur von Gilgamesch.* Freiburg: Walter, 1977. [Mesopotamia]

Kelchner, John W. *A Description of King Solomon's Temple and Citadel and the Tabernacle in the Wilderness.* Philadelphia: Holman, 1925. [Tabernacle]

Kelchner, John W. *Unequaled for 3000 Years: Reproduction of King Solomon's Temple and Citadel.* Chicago: Century of Progress Exposition, 1933. [Israel/Canaan]

Keller, C. A. "Über einige alttestamentliche Heiligtumslegenden." *ZAW* 67 (1955): 141-68. [Israel/Canaan]

Kellermann, Diether. "*ʾāsham.*" In *Theological Dictionary of the Old Testament* 1:429-37. [Sacrifice/Offerings]

Kelley, P. H. "Israel's Tabernacling God." *Review and Expositor* 67 (1970): 485-94. [Covenant]

Kelly, J. J. "The Sense of the Holy." *The Way* 13 (1973): 249-58. [Tabernacle]

Kelso, J. A. "The Unity of the Sanctuary in the Light of the Elephantine Papyri." *JBL* 28 (1909): 71-81. [Israel/Canaan]

Kelso, J. L. "The Hebrew Tabernacle as a Work of Literature." *Bibliotheca Sacra* 79 (1922): 62-71. [Tabernacle]

Kelso, James L. "Bethel (Sanctuary)." In *The Interpreter's Dictionary of the Bible,* 1:391-93. [Israel/Canaan]

Kempinski, A. "The Sin Temple at Khafaje and the En-Gedi Temple." *IEJ* 22 (1972): 10-15. [Israel/Canaan]

Kennard, Joseph S. *Jesus in the Temple.* Tokyo: n.p., 1935. [Israel/Canaan]

Kennedy, A. R. S. "Ark of the Covenant." In *Dictionary of the Bible* 1:149-51. [Tabernacle]

Kennedy, A. R. S. "Some Problems of Herod's Temple." *ET* 20 (1908-9): 24-27, 66-69, 181-83, 270-73. [Israel/Canaan]

Kennedy, A. R. S. "Tabernacle." In *Dictionary of the Bible* 4:653-68. [Tabernacle]

Kennedy, A. R. S., and N. H. Snaith. "Temple." In *Dictionary of the Bible,* 961-68 (1963 ed.). [Israel/Canaan]

Kennett, R. H. "Ark." In *Encyclopaedia of Religion and Ethics* 1:791-93. [Tabernacle]

Kennett, R. H. "The Origin of the Aaronite Priesthood." *JTS* 9 (1905): 161-86. [Priesthood]

Kenyon, Kathleen M. "New Evidence on Solomon's Temple." In *Mélanges offerts à M. Maurice Dunand,* 2. Beirut: Université Saint-Joseph, 1972. [Israel/Canaan]

Kenyon, Kathleen M. "Solomon and the Building of the Temple." In *Jerusalem: Excavating 3,000 Years of History*, edited by M. Wheeler. 54-62. New York: McGraw-Hill, 1967. [Israel/Canaan]

Kidner, D. "Sacrifice: Metaphors and Meaning." *Tyndale Bulletin* 33 (1982): 119-36. [Sacrifice/Offerings]

Kidner, Frank D. *Sacrifice in the Old Testament.* London: Tyndale, 1952. [Sacrifice/Offerings]

Kiene, Paul F. *The Tabernacle of God in the Wilderness of Sinai.* Grand Rapids: Zondervan, 1977. [Tabernacle]

Kimelman, A. "The Area of the Temple Mount and the Hel (Rampart), and the Laws Pertaining Thereto." *Ha-Maayan* 8/3 (1968): 3-32. [Mountain]

Kimura, Hiroshi. "Isaiah 6:1–9:6: A Theatrical Section of the Book of Isaiah." Ph.D. diss., Uppsala University, 1981. [Israel/Canaan]

King, James. *Recent Discoveries on the Temple Hill at Jerusalem.* London: The Religious Tract Society, 1884. [Israel/Canaan]

Kingsbury, E. C. "The Theophany Topos and the Mountain of God." *JBL* 86 (1967): 205-10. [Mountain]

Kirkbride, D. "Le temple nabatéen de Ramm: son évolution architecturale." *RB* 67 (1960): 65-92. [Israel/Canaan]

Kittel, R. "Der heilige Fels auf dem Moria: Seine Geschichte und seine Altäre." In Kittel, *Studien zur hebräischen Archäologie und Religionsgeschichte.* 1-96. Leipzig: Hinrichs, 1908. [Israel/Canaan]

Kittel, R. "Der herodianische Tempel." In *Realencyklopädie für protestantische Theologie und Kirche*, edited by A. Hauck. 24 vols., 19:498-500. Leipzig: Akademische, 1907. [Israel/Canaan]

Kiuchi, N. *The Purification Offering in the Priestly Literature.* Sheffield: JSOT, 1987. [Sacrifice/Offerings]

Klagsbald, Victor A. "The Menorah as Symbol: Its Meaning and Origin in Early Jewish Art." *Journal of Jewish Art* 12/13 (1987): 126-34. [Israel/Canaan]

Klamroth, Erich. *Lade und Tempel.* Gütersloh: Bertelsmann, 1932. [Israel/Canaan]

Klauser, T. "Der Vorhang vor dem Thron Gottes." *Jahrbuch für Antike und Christentum* 3 (1960): 142-42. [Kingship/Coronation]

Klausner, Joseph. *Ha-Bayit ha-Sheni bi-Gedulato.* Tel-Aviv: Devir, 1930. [Israel/Canaan]

Klausner, Joseph. *Historiyah shel ha-Bayit ha-Sheni.* 5 vols. Jerusalem: Ahi'asaf, 1949-51. [Israel/Canaan]

Klausner, Joseph. "Jesus in Jerusalem: the Cleansing of the Temple and the Debate in the Temple Courts." In *The World History of the Jewish People*, edited by Michael Avi-Yonah and Zvi Baras. Jerusalem: Massada, 1977. 227-33. [Israel/Canaan]

Klein, Mina C., and H. A. Klein. *Temple beyond Time: The Story of the Site of Solomon's Temple at Jerusalem.* New York: Van Nostrand Reinhold, 1970. [Israel/Canaan]

Klein, R. W. "Theology for Exiles: The Kingship of Yahweh." *Dialogue* 17 (1978): 128-34. [Kingship/Coronation]

Kliers, Moses. *Ha-Mikdash u-Kedoshav: Berurim ve-ʿIyunim ba-ʿAvodat Bet ha-Beḥirah ba-Zeman ha-Zeh.* Jerusalem: Mekhon Hari Fishel li-Derishat ha-Talmud u-Mishpat ha-Torah, 1970. [Israel/Canaan]

Klimkeit, Hans J. "Manichaean Kingship: Gnosis at Home in the World." *Numen* 29 (1982): 17-32. [Kingship/Coronation]

Klimkeit, Hans J. "Spatial Orientation in Mythical Thinking as Exemplified in Ancient Egypt: Considerations toward a Geography of Religions." *History of Religions* 14 (1975): 266-81. [Egypt]

Kline, Meridith G. "Investiture with the Image of God." *Westminster Theological Journal* 40 (1977): 39-62. [Tabernacle]

Kline, Meridith G. "Oath and Ordeal Signs." *Westminster Theological Journal* 27 (1965): 115-39; 28 (1965): 1-37. [Covenant]

Klingele, O. H. "Der Tempel von Jerusalem." *Das heilige Land* 90 (1958): 77-91. [Israel/Canaan]

Kluckhohne, C. "Myths and Rituals: A General Theory." *Harvard Theological Review* 35 (1942): 45-79. [Ritual/Liturgy/Worship]

Klyne, Sylvester S. "The Temple at Jerusalem—Its History and Its Influence on the Religion of the Hebrews." Ph.D. diss., Boston University, 1906. [Israel/Canaan]

Koch, Herbert. *Der griechisch-dorische Tempel.* Stuttgart: Metzler, 1951. [Greece/Rome]

Koch, Herbert. *Studien zum Theseustempel in Athen.* Berlin: Akademie, 1955. [Greece/Rome]

Koch, K. "Die Eigenart der priesterschriftlichen Sinaigesetzgebung." *Zeitschrift für Theologie und Kirche* 55 (1958): 36-51. [Tabernacle]

Koch, K. "ʾōhel." In *Theological Dictionary of the Old Testament* 1:118-30. [Tabernacle]

Koch, K. "Tempeleinlassliturgien und Dekaloge." In *Studien zur Theologie der alttestamentlichen Überlieferungen,* edited by Rolf Rendtorff and Klaus Koch, 45-60. Neukirchen-Vluyn: Neukirchener, 1961. [Israel/Canaan]

Koeberle, Justus. *Die Tempelsänger im alten Testament.* Erlangen: Junge, 1899. [Israel/Canaan]

Koehl, R. B. "The Chieftan Cup: A Cretan Rite of Passage." *AJA* 89 (1985): 337. [Ritual/Liturgy/Worship]

Koester, Craig R. *The Dwelling of God: The Tabernacle in the Old Testament, Intertestamental Jewish Literature, and the New Testament.* Washington, D.C.: Catholic Biblical Association of America, 1987. [Tabernacle]

Köhler, Ludwig. "*Jahwäh mālāk.*" *VT* 3 (1953): 188-89. [Kingship/Coronation]

Kolbe, Joshua J. *The Temple and City of Jerusalem.* London: Saunders Brothers, 1884. [Israel/Canaan]

Koldewey, Robert. *Die griechischen Tempel in Unteritalien und Sicilien.* Berlin: Asher, 1899. [Greece/Rome]

Koldewey, Robert. *Die Tempel von Babylon und Borsippa.* Osnabrück: Zeller, 1972. [Mesopotamia]

Kolenkow, Anitra B. "The Fall of the Temple and the Coming of the End: The Spectrum and Process of Apocalyptic Argument in 2 Baruch and Other Authors." *SBLSP* 21 (1982): 243-50. [Israel/Canaan]

Kon, Maximilian. "Jewish Art at the Time of the Second Temple." In *Jewish Art: An Illustrated History*, edited by Cecil Roth. 51-64. London: Allen, 1961. [Israel/Canaan]

Kon, Maximilian. "The Menorah of the Arch of Titus." *PEFQ* 82 (1950): 25-30. [Israel/Canaan]

König, Eduard. "The Priests and Levites in Ezek. 44:7-15." *ET* 12 (1901): 300-303. [Priesthood]

König, Eduard. *Zentralkultstätte und Kultuszentralisierung im alten Israel.* Gütersloh: Bertelsmann, 1931. [Israel/Canaan]

Koolhaas, Antonie A. *Theocratie en monarchie in Israël.* Wageningen: Veenman, 1957. [Kingship/Coronation]

Kopp, C. "Jerusalem I: The Temple." In *The Holy Places of the Gospels*, translated by Ronald Walls. 283-86. New York: Herder and Herder, 1963. [Israel/Canaan]

Kopp, C. "Der Tempelplatz unter Julian." *Das heilige Land* 91/1-2 (1959): 17-24. [Israel/Canaan]

Koren (Winkler), M. "Is the Zakrah the Foundation Stone?" (in Hebrew). *Ha-Maayan* 8/4 (1968): 27-31. [Israel/Canaan]

Kornfeld, W. "Der Symbolismus der Tempelsäulen." *ZAW* 74 (1962): 50-57. [Israel/Canaan]

Korosec, V. "Einiges zur inneren Struktur hethitischer Tempel nach der Instruktion für Tempelleute." *Publication of the Institutes of History and Archaeology* 35 (1974): 165-74. [Mesopotamia]

Kramer, Samuel N. "The Temple in Sumerian Literature." In *Temple in Society*, edited by Michael V. Fox. 1-16. Winona Lake: Eisenbrauns, 1988. [Mesopotamia]

Kraus, F. R. "Le rôle des temples depuis la troisième dynastie d'Ur jusqu'a la première dynastie de Babylone." *Journal of World History/Cahiers d'histoire mondiale* 1 (1953-54): 518-45. [Mesopotamia]

Kraus, Hans-Joachim. "God's Covenant." *Reformed World* 35 (1979): 257-68. [Covenant]

Kraus, Hans-Joachim. "The Sanctuary and Its Worship." In Kraus, *Theology of the Psalms*, translated by Keith Crim. 73-106. Minneapolis: Augsburg Pub. House, 1986. [Ritual/Liturgy/Worship]

Kraus, Hans-Joachim. *Worship in Israel*, translated by G. Buswell. Richmond: John Know, 1966. [Ritual/Liturgy/Worship]

Krauss, Samuel. "Die Synagoge auf dem Tempelberge." In *Synagogale Altertümer.* 66-72. Berlin-Wien: Harz, 1922. [Israel/Canaan]

Krauss, Samuel. "Der Tempel des Herodes." In *Jüdisches Lexikon*, edited by G. Herlitz and B. Kirschner. 4 vols. in 5, 4:2:915-17. Berlin: Jüdisch, 1930. [Israel/Canaan]

Krencker, Daniel M. *Römische Tempel in Syrien.* Berlin: de Gruyter, 1938. [Greece/Rome]

Krinetzki, Leo. "Zur Poetik und Exegese von Ps. 48." *Biblische Zeitschrift* 4 (1960): 70-97. [Israel/Canaan]

Krinsky, C. H. "Representations of the Temple of Jerusalem before 1500." *Journal of the Warburg and Courtauld Institutes* 33 (1970): 1-19. [Israel/Canaan]

Kristensen, William B. *De ark van Jahwe.* Amsterdam: Noord-Hollandsche Uitgevers-Maatschappij, 1933. [Tabernacle]

Kruse, H. "Psalm 132 and the Royal Zion Festival." *VT* 33 (1983): 279-97. [Kingship/Coronation]

Kühn, Ernst. "Ezechiels Gesicht vom Tempel der Vollendungszeit, Kap. 40-42; 43:13-17; 46:19-24." *Theologische Studien und Kritiken* 55 (1882): 601-88. [Israel/Canaan]

Kühnel, Bianca. "Jewish Symbolism of the Temple and the Tabernacle and Christian Symbolism of the Holy Sepulchre and the Heavenly Tabernacle." *Journal of Jewish Art* 12/13 (1987): 147-68. [Israel/Canaan]

Kumaki, Francis K. "The Temple Sermon: Jeremiah's Polemic against the Deuteronomists." Ph.D. diss, Union Theological Seminary, 1980. [Israel/Canaan]

Küper, Lic. *Das Priesterthum des alten Bundes.* Berlin: Hertz, 1866. [Priesthood]

Kurth, Dieter. *Die Dekoration der Säulen im Pronaos des Tempels von Edfou.* Wiesbaden: Harrassowitz, 1983. [Israel/Canaan]

Kurth, Dieter. *Edfu.* Wiesbaden: Harrassowitz, 1990. [Egypt]

Kurth, Dieter. *Den Himmel Stützen: Die "Tw3 pt"—Szenen in den ägyptischen Tempeln der griechisch-römischen Epoche.* Brussels: Fondation égyptologique Reine Elisabeth, 1975. [Egypt]

Kuschke, A. "Tempel." In *Biblisches Reallexikon*, edited by Kurt Galling. 333-42. Tübingen: Mohr, 1927. [Israel/Canaan]

Kuschke, Arnulf. "Der Tempel Salomos und der 'syrische Tempeltypus.' " In *Das ferne und nahe Wort*, edited by F. Maass. 124-32. Berlin: Töpelmann, 1967. [Israel/Canaan]

Kuschke, Arnulf. "Die Lagervorstellung der priesterschriftlichen Erzählung." *ZAW* 63 (1951): 74-105. [Priesthood]

Kutsch, E. "Lade Jahwes." In *Die Religion in Geschichte und Gegenwart*. 7 vols., 4:197-99. 3d ed. Tübingen: Mohr, 1960. [Tabernacle]

Kutsch, E. "Zelt." In *Die Religion in Geschichte und Gegenwart*. 7 vols., 6:1893-94. 3d ed. Tübingen: Mohr, 1962. [Tabernacle]

Labrousse, A. *Le temple haut du complexe funéraire du roi Ounas*. Cairo: Imprimerie de l'Institut français d'archéologie orientale du Caire, 1977. [Egypt]

Lacau, P. "Notes sur les plans des temples d'Edfou et de Kôm-Ombo." *ASAE* 52 (1954): 215-28. [Egypt]

Lachs, S. T. "Why Was the 'Amen' Response Interdicted in the Temple?" *Journal for the Study of Judaism in the Persian, Hellenistic and Roman Period* 19 (1988): 230-40. [Israel/Canaan]

Laconi, Mauro. "Gerusalemme e la liturgia del tempio nel quarto vangelo." In *Gerusalemme. Atti della XXVI Settimana Biblica. Associazione Biblica Italiana*, edited by M. Borrmans. 251-60. Brescia: Paideia, 1982. [Israel/Canaan]

Laessøe, Jørgen. *Studies on the Assyrian Ritual and Series bît rimki*. Copenhagen: Munksgaard, 1955. [Ritual/Liturgy/Worship]

Lagrange, F. J. "Comment s'est formée l'enceinte du Temple de Jérusalem." *RB* 2 (1893): 90-113. [Israel/Canaan]

Lamarche, P. "La mort du Christ et le voile du Temple selon Marc." *Nouvelle revue théologique* 96 (1974): 583-99. [Israel/Canaan]

Lambert, M. M. "En Marge du problème de al Siqquart. Les Pontifes du Temples d'En-Haut." *Sumer* 7 (1951): 58-65. [Mesopotamia]

Lambert, W. G. "Kosmogonie." In *Reallexikon der Assyriologie*, edited by Erich Ebeling and Bruno Meissner. 7 vols., 6:218-22. Berlin: Walter de Gruyter, 1980-83. [Creation/Cosmology]

Lambert, W. G. "Myth and Ritual as Conceived by the Babylonians." *Journal of Semitic Studies* 13 (1968): 104-12. [Ritual/Liturgy/Worship]

Lancellotti, A. "La distruzione di Gerusalemme e del suo tempio nel discorso eschatologico secondo una recente interpretatzione." In *La distruzione di Gerusalemme del 70: nei suoi riflessi storico-letterari*, edited by S. Gozzo. 69-78. Assisi: Studio teologico "porziuncolo." 1971. [Israel/Canaan]

Lande-Nash, I. "Der herodianische Tempel." In *3000 Jahre Jerusalem: Eine Geschichte der Stadt von den Anfängen bis zur Eroberung durch die Kreuzfahrer*. 101-11. Tübingen: Wasmuth, 1964. [Israel/Canaan]

Landsberger, F. "In the Days of the Second Temple." In *A History of Jewish Art.* 125-39. Cincinnati: Union of American Hebrew Congregations, 1946. [Israel/Canaan]

Lane, W. R. "Initiation of Creation." *VT* 13 (1963): 63-73. [Creation/ Cosmology]

Lang, G. H. "God's Covenants Are Conditional." *Evangelical Quarterly* 30 (1958): 86-97. [Covenant]

Langdon, Stephen. *Babylonian Liturgies.* Paris: Geuthner, 1913. [Ritual/Liturgy/ Worship]

Langdon, Stephen. *Sumerian Liturgical Texts.* Philadelphia: University Museum, 1917. [Ritual/Liturgy/Worship]

Langdon, Stephen. *Sumerian Liturgies and Psalms.* Philadelphia: University Museum, 1919. [Ritual/Liturgy/Worship]

Langhe, Robert de. *Het Gouden Altaar in de Israelietische Eredienst.* Brussels: Paleis der Academiën, 1952. [Sacrifice/Offerings]

Laperrousaz, E.-M. "Angle sud-est du 'Temple de Salomon' ou vestiges de l'Acra des Séleucides?" *Syria* 52 (1975): 241-59. [Israel/Canaan]

Laperrousaz, E.-M. "A-t-on dégagé l'angle sud-est du 'Temple de Salomon'?" *Syria* 50 (1973): 355-59. [Israel/Canaan]

Laperrousaz, E.-M. "La discontinuité *(seam, straight joint)* visible près de l'extrémité sud du mur oriental du Haram esh-Shérif marque-t-elle l'angle sud-est du 'temple de Salomon'?" *VT* 38 (October 1988): 399-406. [Israel/Canaan]

Laperrousaz, E.-M. "King Solomon's Wall Still Supports the Temple Mount." *BAR* 13/3 (1987): 34-44. [Israel/Canaan]

Laperrousaz, E.-M. "Note à propos de la dotation du Rouleau du Temple et, plus généralement, des Manuscrits de la Mer Morte." *Revue de Qumran* 10 (1981): 447-52. [Ritual/Liturgy/Worship]

Läpple, A. "Das neue Jerusalem: Die Eschatologie der Offenbarung des Johannes." *Bibel und Kirche* 39 (1984): 75-81. [Israel/Canaan]

Lattey, C. J. "The Prophets and Sacrifice: A Study in Biblical Relativity." *JTS* 42 (1941): 155-65. [Sacrifice/Offerings]

Lau, Robert J. *Old Babylonian Temple Records.* New York: AMS, 1966. [Mesopotamia]

Laughlin, John C. H. "The Remarkable Discoveries at Tel Dah." *Biblical Archaeology Review* 7 (1981): 20-37. [Israel/Canaan]

Laughlin, John C. H. "A Study of the Motif of Holy Fire in the Old Testament." Ph.D. diss., Southern Baptist Theological Seminary, 1975. [Sacrifice/ Offerings]

Launey, Marcel. *Le sanctuaire et le culte d'Héraklés à Thasos.* Paris: de Boccard, 1944. [Greece/Rome]

Laurentin, A. "Theatre and Liturgy." *Worship* 43 (1969): 382-406. [Ritual/ Liturgy/Worship]

Lauterbach, J. Z. "The Pharisees and Their Teachings." *HUCA* 6 (1929): 69-139. [Israel/Canaan]

Lauterbach, J. Z. "A Significant Controversy between the Sadducees and the Pharisees." In *Rabbinic Essays.* 51-83. Cincinnati: Hebrew Union College Press, 1951. [Israel/Canaan]

Lavas, Georg P. *Altgriechisches Temenos: Baukörper und Raumbildung: Ideogramma der baulichen Gruppenorganisation.* Basel: Birkhäuser, 1974. [Greece/Rome]

Lawler, M. G. "Christian Rituals: An Essay in Sacramental Symbolisms." *Horizons* 7 (1980): 7-35. [Ritual/Liturgy/Worship]

Le Bas, E. E. "Was the Corner-Stone of Scripture a Pyramidion?" *PEQ* 78 (1946): 103-15. [Israel/Canaan]

Le Bas, E. E. "Zechariah's Climax to the Career of the Corner-Stone." *PEQ* 83 (1951): 139-55. [Israel/Canaan]

Le Bas, E. E. "Zechariah's Enigmatical Contribution to the Corner-Stone." *PEQ* 82 (1950): 102-22. [Israel/Canaan]

Lee, R. J. "Ritual and Theatre: An Overview." *Academy* 38/3-4 (1982): 132-49. [Ritual/Liturgy/Worship]

Leeuwenburg, L. "Oversichten van de geschiedenis en opgravingen in het Nabije Oosten: Het tempel complex van Medinet Haboe." *Ex Oriente Lux: Jaarbericht van het vooraziatisch-egyptisch Gezelschap* 6 (1939): 43-59. [Egypt]

Lefebure, Francis. *Expériences initiatiques.* Antwerpen: Verrycken, 1978. [Ritual/Liturgy/Worship]

Légasse, S. "Les voiles du temple de Jérusalem: Essai de parcours historique." *RB* 87 (1980): 560-89. [Tabernacle]

Legg, John W. *Church Ornaments and Their Civil Antecedents.* Cambridge: Cambridge University Press, 1917. [Sacred Vestments]

Legrain, Georges A. *Les temples de Karnak.* Paris: Vromant, 1929. [Egypt]

Lehmann, M. R. "The Temple Scroll as a Source of Sectarian Halakhah." *Revue de Qumran* 9 (1978): 579-88. [Israel/Canaan]

Lehmann, Phyllis W. "The Setting of Hellenistic Temples." *Journal of the Society of Architectural Historians* 13/4 (1954): 15-20. [Greece/Rome]

Leibovitch, J. "Une scène de sacrifice rituel chez les anciens Égyptiens." *JNES* 12 (1953): 59-60. [Sacrifice/Offerings]

Lemaire, André. "Une inscription paléo-hébraïque sur grenade en ivoire." *RB* 88 (1981): 236-39. [Israel/Canaan]

Lemaire, André. "Probable Head of Priestly Scepter from Solomon's Temple Surfaces in Jerusalem." *BAR* 10/1 (1984): 24-29. [Ritual/Liturgy/ Worship]

Lenzen, H. J. "Mesopotamische Tempelanlagen von der Frühzeit bis zum zweiten Jahrtausend." *Zeitschrift für Assyriologie* 51 (1955): 1-36. [Mesopotamia]

Lenzen, H. J. "Die Tempel der Schicht Archaisch IV in Uruk." *Zeitschrift für Assyriologie* 49/15 (1949): 1-20. [Mesopotamia]

Léon-Dufour, Xavier. "Le signe du Temple selon saint Jean." *Revue des sciences religieuses* 39 (1951-52): 155-75. [Israel/Canaan]

Lerner, M. B. "The Daily Whole-Offering in the Temple" (in Hebrew). *Mahanayim* 96 (1965): 28-31. [Sacrifice/Offerings]

Lesêtre, Henri. "Arche d'Alliance." In *Dictionnaire de la Bible*, edited by F. Vigouroux. 5 vols., 1:912-23. Paris: Letouzey et Ané, 1895. [Tabernacle]

Lesêtre, Henri. "Sacrifice." In *Dictionnaire de la Bible*, edited by F. Vigouroux. 5 vols., 5:1311-37. Paris: Letouzey and Ané, 1922. [Sacrifice/Offerings]

Lesêtre, Henri. "Tabernacle." In *Dictionnaire de la Bible*, edited by F. Vigouroux. 5 vols., 5:1951-61. Paris: Letouzey et Ané, 1895. [Tabernacle]

Leslie, Elmer A. *The Psalms Translated and Interpreted in Light of Hebrew Life and Worship*. New York: Abingdon-Cokesbury, 1949. [Ritual/Liturgy/ Worship]

Levenson, David B. "A Source and Tradition Critical Study of the Stories of Julian's Attempt to Rebuild the Jerusalem Temple." Ph.D. diss, Harvard University, 1980. [Israel/Canaan]

Levenson, Jon D. "From Temple to Synagogue: I Kings 8." In *Traditions in Transformation: Turning Points in Biblical Faith*, edited by Baruch Halpern and Jon D. Levenson. 143-66. Winona Lake: Eisenbrauns, 1981. [Israel/ Canaan]

Levenson, Jon D. *Sinai and Zion*. Minneapolis: Winston, 1985. [Israel/Canaan]

Levenson, Jon D. "The Temple and the World." *Journal of Religion* 64 (1984): 275-98. [Israel/Canaan]

Levenson, Jon D. *Theology of the Program of Restoration of Ezekiel 40-48*, *Harvard Semitic Monographs*, vol. 10. Missoula, MT: Scholars, 1976. [Israel/Canaan]

Lévi, Israel. "Le temple du dieu Yahou et la colonie juive d'Éléphantine au Ve siècle avant l'ère chrétienne." *Revue des études juives* 54 (1907): 153-65; 56 (1908): 161-68. [Israel/Canaan]

Levine, Baruch A. "Cult." In *Encyclopaedia Judaica* 5:1155-62. [Ritual/Liturgy/ Worship]

Levine, Baruch A. "The Descriptive Tabernacle Texts of the Pentateuch." *JAOS* 85 (1965): 307-18. [Tabernacle]

Levine, Baruch A. *In the Presence of the Lord.* Leiden: Brill, 1974. [Sacrifice/Offerings]

Levine, Baruch A. "On the Presence of God in Biblical Religion." In *Religions in Antiquity: Essays in Memory of E. R. Goodenough,* edited by Jacob Neusner. 71-87. Leiden: Brill: 1968. [Israel/Canaan]

Levine, Baruch A. "Priests." In *The Interpreter's Dictionary of the Bible,* supp. vol., 687-90. [Priesthood]

Levine, Baruch A. "The Temple Scroll: Aspects of Its Historical Provenance and Literary Character." *BASOR* 232 (1978): 5-23. [Israel/Canaan]

Levine, Baruch A., and W. W. Hallo. "Offerings to the Temple Gates at Ur." *HUCA* 38 (1967): 17-58. [Mesopotamia]

Levine, Moshe. *Melekhet ha-Mishkan: Tavnit ha-Mishkan ve-Khelav.* Tel Aviv: Melekhet ha-mishkan, 1968; also in English as *The Tabernacle: Its Structure and Utensils.* London: Soncino, 1970. [Tabernacle]

Levinsky, Y.-T., ed. "The Destruction of the Temple" (in Hebrew). In *The Book of Festivals.* 8 vols., 7:207-452. Tel-Aviv: Dvir, 1957. [Israel/Canaan]

Levinson, N. Peter. "Tempel und Synagoge." In *Die Kultusymbolik im Alten Testament und im nachbiblischen Judentum. Symbolik der Religionen.* 17:15-45. Stuttgart: Hiersemann, 1972. [Israel/Canaan]

Levy, Abraham J., ed. *Rashi's Commentary on Ezekiel 40-48.* Philadelphia: Dropsie College, 1931. [Israel/Canaan]

Lewin, T. "Observations on the Probable Sites of the Jewish Temple and Antonia, and the Acra, with Reference to the Results of the Recent Palestine Explorations." *Archaeologia* 44 (1873): 17-62. [Israel/Canaan]

Lewis, George W. *From Bible Data of the House Which King Solomon Built for Jehovah.* Cincinnati: Standard, 1927. [Israel/Canaan]

Lewis, George W. *The Tabernacle of the Testimony, from the Book of Exodus.* Cincinnati: Standard, 1925. [Tabernacle]

Lewis, J. "The Ark and the Tent." *Review and Expositor* 74 (1977): 537-48. [Tabernacle]

Lewis, P. B. "Indication of a Liturgical Source in the Gospel of Mark." *Encounter* 39 (1978): 385-94. [Ritual/Liturgy/Worship]

Lewittes, M., tr. *The Book of Temple Service,* by Moses Maimonides. New Haven: Yale University Press, 1957. [Israel/Canaan]

Lewy, Julius. "The Šulmān Temple in Jerusalem." *JBL* 59 (1940): 519-22. [Israel/Canaan]

Lewy, Yohanan. "Julian the Apostate and the Building of the Temple." In *Jerusalem Cathedra,* edited by L. I. Levine, 3 vols., 3:70-96. Detroit: Wayne State University Press, 1983. [Israel/Canaan]

Licht, Jacob. "An Ideal Town Plan from Qumran—The Description of the New Jerusalem." *IEJ* 29 (1979): 45-59. [Israel/Canaan]

Lichtenberger, Hermann. "Atonement and Sacrifice in the Qumran Community." In *Approaches to Ancient Judaism*, edited by William S. Green. 159-71. Chico, CA: Scholars, 1980. [Sacrifice/Offerings]

Lieberman, S. "The Temple: Its Layout and Procedure." In *Hellenism in Jewish Palestine*. 164-79. New York: Jewish Theological Seminary of America, 1950. [Israel/Canaan]

Liebreich, Y. A. "The Psalms of the Levites for the Days of the Week" (in Hebrew). *Eretz-Israel* 3 (1954): 170-73. [Israel/Canaan]

Lifshitz, B. "Sur le culte dynastique des Séleucides." *RB* 70 (1963): 75-81. [Kingship/Coronation]

Lightfoot, R. H. "The Cleansing of the Temple in St. John's Gospel." *ET* 60/3 (1948): 64-68. [Israel/Canaan]

Lignée, Hubert. *The Living Temple*. Baltimore: Helicon, 1966. [Israel/Canaan]

Lignée, Hubert. *Zelt Gottes unter den Menschen: Welt der Bibel*. Duesseldorf: Patmos, 1961; also in English as *The Temple of Yahweh*. Baltimore: Helicon, 1966. [Israel/Canaan]

Lincoln, Bruce. "The Rape of Persephone: A Greek Scenario of Women's Initiation." *Harvard Theological Review* 72 (1979): 223-35. [Ritual/Liturgy/Worship]

Lindblom, J. "Theophanies in Holy Places in Hebrew Religion." *HUCA* 32 (1961): 91-106. [Israel/Canaan]

Lindeskog, G. "Veil." *Coniectanea Neotestamentica* 11 (1947): 132-37. [Tabernacle]

Lindeskog, G. "The Veil of the Temple." In *Coniectanea Neotestamentica, II: In Honorem A. Fridrichsen*. 132-37. Lund: Gleerup, 1947. [Israel/Canaan]

Lipinska, J. *Deir-el-Habhari II: The Temple of Tuthmosis III Architecture*. Warsaw: Naukowz, 1977. [Egypt]

Lipiński, Edward. "Beth-Schemisch und der Tempel der Herrin der Grabkammer in den Amaran-Briefen." *VT* 23 (1973): 443-45. [Israel/Canaan]

Lipiński, Edward. *La royauté de Yahwé dans la poésie et le culte de l'ancien Israel*. Brussels: Paleis der Academien, 1965. [Israel/Canaan]

Lipiński, Edward. "Les temples néo-assyriens et les origines du monnayage." In *State and Temple Economy in the Ancient Near East*, edited by Edward Lipiński. 2 vols., 2:565-88. Louvain: Departement Orientalistiek, 1979. [Mesopotamia]

Lipiński, Edward. "Yāhweh Mâlāk." *Biblica* 44 (1963): 405-60. [Kingship/Coronation]

Little, David. *The Tabernacle in the Wilderness*. 2d ed. Neptune, NJ: Loizeaux Bros., 1989. [Tabernacle]

Liver, Jacob, and Daniel Sperber. "Mishmarot and Maʿamadot," In *Encyclopaedia Judaica* 12:89-93. [Priesthood]

Lockyer, J. Norman. *The Dawn of Astronomy: A Study of the Temple-Worship and Mythology of the Ancient Egyptians.* London: Macmillan, 1894. [Egypt]

Lods, Adolphe. "Les cuisines du Temple de Jeursalem." *RHR* 127 (1944): 30-54. [Israel/Canaan]

Lods, Adolphe. "La divinisation du roi dans l'Orient méditeranéen et ses répercussions dans l'ancien Israël." *Revue d'histoire et de philosophie religieuses* 10 (1930): 209-21. [Kingship/Coronation]

Lods, Adolphe. "Éléments anciens et éléments modernes dans le rituel de sacrifice israelite." *Revue d'histoire et de philosophie religieuses* 8 (1928): 399-411. [Sacrifice/Offerings]

Lofthouse, W. F. "The City and the Sanctuary." *ET* 34 (1922-23): 198-202. [Israel/Canaan]

Lohmeyer, Ernst. *Kultus und Evangelium.* Göttingen: Vandenhoeck and Ruprecht, 1942; also in English, *Lord of the Temple—a Study of the Relation between Cult and Gospel*, translated by S. Todd. Edinburgh: Oliver and Boyd, 1961. [Ritual/Liturgy/Worship]

Lohmeyer, Ernst. "Die Reinigung des Tempels." *Theologische Blätter* 20 (1941): 257-64. [Israel/Canaan]

Lohse, Ernst. "Temple and Synagogue." In *Jesus in his Time*, edited by H. J. Schultz and translated by B. Watchorn. 75-83. Philadelpha: Fortress, 1971. [Israel/Canaan]

Long, Charles H. *Alpha: The Myths of Creation.* New York: Braziller, 1963. [Creation/Cosmology]

Longman, T. "1 Samuel 12:16-19: Divine Omnipotence or Covenant Curse?" *Westminster Theological Journal* 45 (1983): 168-71. [Kingship/Coronation]

L'Orange, H. P. *Studies on the Iconography of Cosmic Kingship in the Ancient World.* Oslo: Aschehoug, 1953. [Kingship/Coronation]

Losie, Lynn A. "The Cleansing of the Temple: A History of a Gospel Tradition in Light of Its Background in the Old Testament and in Early Judaism." Ph.D. diss., Fuller Theological Seminary, 1985. [Israel/Canaan]

Lotz, Wilhelm. *Die Bundeslade.* Erlangen: Deichert, 1901. [Tabernacle]

Lotz, Wilhelm, M. G. Kyle, and C. E. Armerding. "Ark of the Covenant." In *International Standard Bible Encyclopedia*, edited by G. W. Bromily. 4 vols., 1:291-94. Grand Rapids: Eerdmans, 1979. [Tabernacle]

Lowy, S. "The Confutation of Judaism in the Epistle of Barnabas." *JJS* 11 (1960): 1-33. [Israel/Canaan]

Luckenbill, D. D. "The Temples of Babylonia and Assyria." *AJSL* 24 (1907/08): 291-322. [Mesopotamia]

Ludin Jansen, H. "The Consecration in the Eighth Chapter of Testamentum Levi." In *The Sacral Kingship/La Regalità Sacra.* 356-65. Leiden: Brill, 1959. [Sacred Vestments]

Lugli, G. "Il culto ed i tempi di Apollo in Roma prima di Augusto." *MDAI.R* 58 (1943): 27-47. [Greece/Rome]

Lührmann, D. "Markus 14:55-64: Christologie und Zerstörung des Tempels im Markusevangelium." *NTS* 27 (1981): 457-74. [Israel/Canaan]

Luke, Harry C. *Ceremonies at the Holy Places.* Milwaukee: Morehouse, 1932. [Israel/Canaan]

Lundquist, John M. "The Common Temple Ideology of the Ancient Near East." In *The Temple in Antiquity*, edited by Truman G. Madsen. 53-76. Provo: Brigham Young University Press, 1984. [Sacred Space]

Lundquist, John M. "The Legitimizing Role of the Temple in the Origin of the State." *SBLSP* 21 (1982): 271-97. [Sacred Space]

Lundquist, John M. "Studies on the Temple in the Ancient Near East." Ph.D. diss., University of Michigan, 1983. [Sacred Space]

Lundquist, John M. "What Is a Temple? A Preliminary Typology." In *The Quest for the Kingdom of God: Studies in Honor of George E. Mendenhall*, edited by H. B. Huffmon, F. A. Spina, and A. R. W. Green. 205-19. [Sacred Space]

Luria, Ben Zion. "And a Fountain Shall Come Forth of the House of the Lord" (in Hebrew). *Beth Mikra* 15/40 (1970): 3-13. [Israel/Canaan]

Luria, Ben-Zion. "The Cities of the Priests in the Days of the Second Temple" (in Hebrew). *HUCA* 44 (1973): 1-18. [Priesthood]

Luria, Ben Zion. "Comments on the Scroll of the Sanctuary" (in Hebrew). *Beth Mikra* 74 (1978): 370-86. [Israel/Canaan]

Luria, Ben Zion. "Temple in the First Generation after the Exile." In *Proceedings, 8th World Congress of Jewish Studies, August 16-21, 1981.* 41-45. Jerusalem: World Union of Jewish Studies, 1982. [Israel/Canaan]

Luria, Ben Zion. "The Temple Mount at the Time of the Return to Zion" (in Hebrew). *Beth Mikra* 26 (1981): 206-18. [Israel/Canaan]

Luria, Ben Zion. "You Shall Break Down Their Altars." *Beth Mikra* 95/4 (1983): 313-19. [Sacrifice/Offerings]

Lutz, Henry F. *Sumerian Temple Records of the Late Ur Dynasty.* Berkeley: University of California Press, 1928. [Mesopotamia]

Lyonnet, Stanislas, and Léopold Sabourin. *Sin, Redemption, and Sacrifice: A Biblical and Patristic Study.* Rome: Pontifical Biblical Institute, 1970. [Sacrifice/Offerings]

Maag, Victor. "Erwägungen zur deuteronomischen Kultzentralisation." *VT* 6 (1956): 10-18. [Israel/Canaan]

Maag, Victor. "Malkût Yhwh." In *International Organization for the Study of the Old Testament, Congress Volume, Oxford, 1959.* 129-53. Leiden: Brill, 1960. [Kingship/Coronation]

Maas, Anthony J. *A Day in the Temple.* St. Louis, MO: Herder, 1892. [Israel/Canaan]

Macalister, R. (Robert) A. Stewart. "Sacrifice (Semitic)." In *Encyclopaedia of Religion and Ethics* 11:31-38. [Sacrifice/Offerings]

Macalister, Robert A. S. *A Century of Excavation in Palestine.* London: Religious Tract Society, 1925. [Israel/Canaan]

Macalister, Robert A. S. *Ecclesiastical Vestments: Their Development and History.* London: Stock, 1896. [Sacred Vestments]

McCall, Thomas S. *Israel and Tomorrow's Temple*, rev. ed. Chicago: Moody, 1977. [Israel/Canaan]

McCall, Thomas S., and Zola Levitt. *Satan in the Sanctuary: Israel's Four Temples.* Chicago: Moody, 1973. [Israel/Canaan]

McCarter, P. Kyle. "The Ritual Dedication of the City of David in 2 Samuel 6." In *The Word of the Lord Shall Go Forth: Essays in Honor of David Noel Freedman,* edited by C. L. Meyers and M. O'Connor. 273-78. Winona Lake: Eisenbrauns, 1983. [Ritual/Liturgy/Worship]

McCarthy, Dennis J. "*berît* in Old Testament History and Theology." *Biblica* 53 (1972): 110-21. [Covenant]

McCarthy, Dennis J. "Compact and Kingship: Stimuli for Hebrew Covenant Thinking." In *Studies in the Period of David and Solomon and Other Essays,* edited by T. Ishida. 75-92. Winona Lake, IN: Eisenbrauns, 1982. [Kingship/Coronation]

McCarthy, Dennis J. "Further Notes on the Symbolism of Blood and Sacrifice." *JBL* 92 (1973): 205-10. [Sacrifice/Offerings]

McCarthy, Dennis J. "Hosea 12:2: Covenant by Oil." *VT* 14 (1964): 215-21. [Covenant]

McCarthy, Dennis J. "The Symbolism of Blood and Sacrifice." *JBL* 88 (1969): 166-76. [Sacrifice/Offerings]

McCarthy, Dennis J. "Three Covenants in Genesis." *CBQ* 26 (1964): 179-89. [Covenant]

McCarthy, Dennis J. *Treaty and Covenant: A Study in Form in the Ancient Oriental Documents and in the Old Testament.* Rome: Pontifical Biblical Institute, 1978. [Covenant]

McConkie, Bruce R. "The Olivet Discourse: Jerusalem and the Temple." In McConkie, *The Mortal Messiah.* 4 vols, 3:421-35. Salt Lake City: Deseret Book, 1980. [Israel/Canaan]

McCown, C. C. "Hebrew High Places and Cult Remains." *JBL* 69 (1950): 205-19. [Mountain]

McCready, Wayne O. "Priests and Levites." In *The International Standard Bible Encyclopedia*, edited by G. W. Bromiley. 4 vols., 3:965-70. Grand Rapids: Eerdmans, 1986. [Priesthood]

McCready, Wayne O. "The Sectarian Status of Qumran: The Temple Scroll." *Revue de Qumran* 11 (1983): 183-91. [Israel/Canaan]

MacCulloch, J. A. "Temples." In *Encyclopaedia of Religion and Ethics.* 12:236-46. [Greece/Rome]

McCullough, W. Stewart. "Israel's Kings, Sacral and Otherwise." *ET* (1957): 144-48. [Kingship/Coronation]

McEwan, Gilbert J. P. *Priest and Temple in Hellenistic Babylonia.* Wiesbaden: Steiner, 1981. [Mesopotamia]

McGee, J. V. "The Theology of the Tabernacle." *Bibliotheca Sacra* 95 (1938): 22-39. [Tabernacle]

Macholz, G. Ch. "Noch Einmal: Planungen für den Wiederaufbau nach der Katastrophe von 587 (Erwägungen zum Schlussteil des sog. 'Verfassungsentwurfs des Hesekiel')." *VT* 19 (1969): 322-52. [Israel/Canaan]

Mackay, C. M. "The City and Sanctuary—Ezekiel 48." *Princeton Theological Review* 20 (1922): 399-417. [Israel/Canaan]

Mackay, C. M. "The City and the Sanctuary." *ET* 34 (1922-23): 475-76. [Israel/Canaan]

Mackay, C. M. "The City of Ezekiel's Oblation." *Princeton Theological Review* 21 (1923): 372-88. [Israel/Canaan]

Mackay, C. M. "The Key to the Old Testament (Ezek. 40-48)." *Church Quarterly Review* 199 (1935): 173-96. [Israel/Canaan]

Mackay, C. M. "Prolegomena to Ezekiel 40-48." *ET* 55 (1943-44): 292-95. [Israel/Canaan]

Mackay, C. M. "Zechariah's Relation to Ezek. 40-48." *Evangelical Quarterly* 40 (1968): 197-210. [Israel/Canaan]

McKane, W. "The Earlier History of the Ark." *Transactions of the Glasgow University Oriental Society* 21 (1965/1966): 68-76. [Tabernacle]

McKay, J. W. "Further Light on the Horses and Chariot of the Sun in the Jerusalem Temple (2 Kings 23:11)." *PEQ* 105 (1973): 167-69. [Israel/Canaan]

McKelvey, R. J. "Christ the Cornerstone." *NTS* 8 (1961-62): 352-59. [Israel/Canaan]

McKelvey, R. J. *The New Temple: The Church in the New Testament.* London: Oxford University Press, 1969. [Israel/Canaan]

McKelvey, R. J. " 'Temple' in the New Testament." In *The New Bible Dictionary*, edited by J. D. Douglas. 1247-50. Grand Rapids: Eerdmans, 1962. [Israel/Canaan]

McKenzie, John L. "The Presence in the Temple: God as Tenant." In *God and His Temple*, edited by L. E. Frizzell. 30-38. South Orange, NJ: Seton Hall University/Institute for Judaeo-Christian Studies, 1980. [Israel/Canaan]

McKenzie, John L. "Royal Messianism." *CBQ* 19 (1957): 25-52. [Kingship/ Coronation]

McKenzie, Leon. "Of Rocks and Stones and Temples Rare." *The Bible Today* 23 (1966): 1522-27. [Israel/Canaan]

Maclagan, David. *Creation Myths: Man's Introduction to the World*. London: Thames and Hudson, 1977. [Creation/Cosmology]

Maclaren, Alexander. *The Holy of Holies*. London: Alexander and Shepheard, 1890. [Tabernacle]

MacLaurin, E. C. B. *The Origin of the Hebrew Sacrificial System*. Sydney: Sydney and Melbourne, 1948. [Sacrifice/Offerings]

Macleod, D. "Dialogue of the Sanctuary." *Princeton Seminary Bulletin* 56 (1963): 15-32. [Ritual/Liturgy/Worship]

McNicol, A. J. "The Eschatological Temple in the Qumrân Pesher 4Q Florilegium 1: 1-7." *Ohio Journal of Religious Studies* 5 (1977): 133-41. [Israel/ Canaan]

McQueen, D. H. "The New Jerusalem and Town Planning." *Expositor* 9 (1924): 220-26. [Israel/Canaan]

MacQuitty, William. *Abu Simbel*. New York: Putnam, 1965. [Egypt]

MacRae, G. W. "Building of the House of the Lord." *American Ecclesiastical Review* 140 (1959): 361-76. [Israel/Canaan]

MacRae, G. W. "Heavenly Temple and Eschatology in the Letter to the Hebrews." *Semeia* 12 (1978): 179-99. [Israel/Canaan]

MacRae, G. W. "A Kingdom That Cannot Be Shaken: The Heavenly Jerusalem in the Letter to the Hebrews." In *Spirituality and Ecumenism. Yearbook of the Ecumenical Institute for Theological Research, 1979/1980*, edited by P. Bonnard, G. MacRae, and J. Cobb. 27-40. Tantur, Jerusalem: Ecumenical Institute for Theological Research, 1980. [Israel/Canaan]

MacRae, George. "The Temple as a House of Revelation in the Nag Hammadi Texts." In *The Temple in Antiquity*, edited by Truman G. Madsen. 175-90. Provo: Brigham Young University Press, 1984. [Egypt]

Madsen, N. P. "Pneumatological Anthropology: A Proposal for a Theology of the Holy Spirit." *Reformed Review* 37 (1983): 13-24. [Tabernacle]

Madsen, Truman G. "The Temple and the Restoration." In *The Temple in Antiquity*, edited by Truman G. Madsen. 1-18. Provo: Brigham Young University Press, 1984. [Israel/Canaan]

Maertens, Thierry. *A Feast in Honor of Yahweh: A Study of the Meaning of Worship*, translated by K. Sullivan. Notre Dame: Fides, 1965. [Ritual/ Liturgy/Worship]

Magen, Yizhaq. "*Bet Ha-Mesibah* in the Temple Scroll and in the Mishnah" (in Hebrew; *English summary). *Eretz-Israel* 17 (1984): 226-35, *10. [Israel/Canaan]

Magen, Yizhaq. "The Gates of the Temple Mount according to Josephus and Mishnah (Middot)" (in Hebrew). *Cathedra: History of Eretz-Israel* 14 (1980): 41-53. [Measurement]

Mah-Tov, G. *Ha-Mikdashim ve-Kodshehem: Korot, Toldot va-Atidot Har ha-Bayit, ha-Mishkan, Bate-ha-Mikdash, Kele ha-Mishkan veha-Mikdashim, ha-Korbanot, ha-Kotel ha-Maaravi ve-Sipure Pelaim odotehem be-Divre Yeme Yisrael.* Jerusalem: Oraita, 1983. [Israel/Canaan]

Maier, Johann. *Das altisraelitische Ladeheiligtum.* Berlin: Töpelmann, 1965. [Tabernacle]

Maier, Johann. "Gottesdienst in der Zeit des salomonischen Tempels." *Bibel und Liturgie* 44 (1971): 237-51. [Israel/Canaan]

Maier, Johann. "Die Hofanlagen im Tempel-Entwurf des Ezechiel im Licht der 'Tempelrolle' von Qumran." In *Prophecy: Essays Presented to Georg Fohrer,* edited by J. A. Emerton. 55-68. Berlin: de Gruyter, 1980. [Israel/Canaan]

Maier, Johann. "Religiongeschichtliche Aspekte frühjüdischer Institutionen: Tempel und Tempelkult." In *Literatur und Religion des Frühjudentums,* edited by J. Maier and J. Schreiner. 371-90. Würzburg: Echter, 1973. [Israel/Canaan]

Maier, Johann. *Die Tempelrolle vom Toten Meer.* Munich: Reinhardt, 1978; also in English as *The Temple Scroll.* Sheffield: JSOT, 1985. [Israel/Canaan]

Maigret, Jacques. "Le Temple au coeur de la Bible." *Le Monde de la Bible* 13 (1980): 3-5. [Israel/Canaan]

Maimonides, Moses. *Commentar zum Tractate Tamid: Arabischer Text mit verbesserter hebraeischer Uebersetzung nebst Anmerkungen.* Frankfort: Kauffmann, 1903. [Sacrifice/Offerings]

Malamat, A. "Kingship and Council in Israel and Sumer: A Parallel." *JNES* 22 (1963): 247-53. [Kingship/Coronation]

Malchow, B. V. "A Manual for Future Monarchs (Proverbs 28-29)." *CBQ* 47 (1985): 238-45. [Kingship/Coronation]

Malchow, B. V. "The Wisdom of the Anointed." *Lutheran Quarterly* 28 (1976): 70-82. [Ablutions/Anointings]

Mallakh, Kamal. *Treasures of the Nile.* New York: Newsweek, 1980. [Egypt]

Mallwitz, A. "Cella und Adyton des Apollontempels in Bassai." *MDAI.A* 77 (1962): 140-77. [Greece/Rome]

Maly, E. H. "God and King in Ancient Israel." *Bible Today* 100 (1979): 1893-900. [Kingship/Coronation]

Mann, C. S. "Sacral Kingship: An Ashanti Footnote." *Journal of Semitic Studies* 5 (1960): 378-87. [Kingship/Coronation]

Manson, T. W. "The Cleansing of the Temple." *BJRL* 33 (1950-51): 271-82. [Israel/Canaan]

Mantel, Chaim D. (Hugo). "The Dichotomy of Judaism during the Second Temple." *HUCA* 44 (1973): 55-87. [Priesthood]

Mantel, Chaim D. (Hugo). "The High Priesthood and the Sanhedrin in the Time of the Second Temple." In *The World History of the Jewish People—The Herodian Period*, edited by M. Avi-Yonah, 7:264-81. Jerusalem: Massada, 1975. [Priesthood]

Mantel, Chaim D. "Ordination and Appointment in the Period of the Temple" (in Hebrew; *English summary). *Tarbiz* 32 (1963): 120-35, *II. [Priesthood]

Mantel, Chaim D. (Hugo). *Studies in the History of the Sanhedrin*. Cambridge: Harvard University Press, 1961; also in Hebrew, *Studies in the History of the Sanhedrin*. Tel Aviv: Dvir, 1969. [Israel/Canaan]

Marböck, Johannes. "Das Gebet um die Rettung Zions Sir. 36, 1-22 (G: 33, 1-13a; 36, 16b-22) im Zusammenhang der Geschichtsschau Ben Siras." In *Memoria Jerusalem: Freundesgabe Franz Sauer zum 70. Geburtstag*, edited by Johannes B. Bauer and Johannes Marböck. 93-115. Graz: Akademische, 1977. [Israel/Canaan]

Margueron, Jean. "Notes d'archéologie et d'architecture orientales." *Syria* 63/3-4 (1986): 257-303. [Mesopotamia]

Margueron, Jean. "Les origins syriennes du Temple de Jérusalem." *Le Monde de la Bible* 20 (August-September 1981): 31-33. [Israel/Canaan]

Margueron, Jean, et al. *Sanctuaires et clergés*. Paris: Geuthner, 1985. [Priesthood]

Mariette, Auguste. *Abydos*, 2 vols. Paris: Frank, 1869-80. [Egypt]

Mariette, Auguste. *Dendérah: Description générale du grand Temple de cette ville*, 6 vols. Paris: Frank, 1870-73. [Egypt]

Mariette, Auguste. *Karnak*. Leipzig: Hinrichs, 1875. [Egypt]

Marquand, Allan. "Temple of Apollo." *Records of the Past* 4 (1905): 1-15. [Greece/Rome]

Martienssen, Rex D. *The Idea of Space in Greek Architecture*. Johannesburg: Witwatersrand University Press, 1958. [Greece/Rome]

Martimort, Aimes G., ed. *L'église en prière*. Paris: Desclee, 1965. [Ablutions/Anointings]

Martin, W. S., and A. Marshall, ed. *Tabernacle Types and Teachings*. London: Martin, 1924. [Tabernacle]

Martin-Achard, Robert. "Esaïe LIV et la nouvelle Jérusalem." In *International Organization for the Study of the Old Testament, Congress Volume, Vienna, 1980* 238-62. Leiden: Brill, 1981. [Israel/Canaan]

Martin-Achard, Robert. *Essai biblique sur les fêtes d'Israël*. Geneva: Labot et Fides, 1974. [Ritual/Liturgy/Worship]

Martiny, Günter. *Die Gegensätze im babylonischen und assyrischen Tempelbau.* Leipzig: Kraus Reprint, 1936. [Mesopotamia]

Martiny, V. G. "Le temple périptère en Égypt." *Chronique d'Égypte* 44 (1947): 305-8. [Egypt]

Maspero, G. "Le temple de louxor et ce qu'on apprend à le bien visiter." *Revue du Caire* 16 (1946): 308-29. [Egypt]

Matthes, J. C. "Die Psalmen und der Tempeldienst." *ZAW* 22 (1902): 65-82. [Ritual/Liturgy/Worship]

Matthews, Charles D. "An Examination of the Character of the Jewish High Priesthood from Ezra to the New Testament Times." Ph.D. diss., Southern Baptist Seminary, 1945. [Priesthood]

Matthiae, Paolo. "Unité et Développement du Temple dans la Syrie du Bronze Moyen." In *Le temple et le culte: Compte rendu de la vingtième recontre assyriologique internationale organisée à Leiden du 3 au 7 juillet 1972.* 43-72. Istanbul: Nederlands Historisch-Archeologisch Instituut te Istambul 1975. [Israel/Canaan]

Matthiew, M. "A Note on the Coronation Rites in Ancient Egypt." *JEA* 16 (1930): 31-32. [Kingship/Coronation]

May, G. L. "Temple or Shrine?" *ET* 62 (1950-51): 346-47. [Israel/Canaan]

May, Herbert G. "The Ark—a Miniature Temple." *AJSL* 52 (1936): 215-34. [Tabernacle]

May, Herbert G. "The Departure of the Glory of Yahweh." *JBL* 56 (1937): 309-21. [Israel/Canaan]

May, Herbert G. "Ephod and Ariel." *AJSL* 56 (1939): 44-69. [Sacred Vestments]

May, Herbert G. "Ezekiel, Exegesis: Vision of the Restored Community (40:1-48:35)." In *The Interpreter's Bible* 6:282-38. New York: Abingdon, 1956. [Israel/Canaan]

May, Herbert G. "The King in the Garden of Eden: A Study of Ezekiel 28:12-19." In *Israel's Prophetic Heritage*, edited by J. Muilenberg. 166-76. New York: Harper, 1962. [Kingship/Coronation]

May, Herbert G. "Ruth's Visit to the High Place at Bethlehem." *Journal of the Royal Asiatic Society* (1939): 75-78. [Israel/Canaan]

May, Herbert G. "Some Aspects of Solar Worship at Jerusalem." *ZAW* 55 (1937): 269-81. [Israel/Canaan]

May, Herbert G. "The Two Pillars before the Temple of Solomon." *BASOR* 88 (1942): 19-27. [Israel/Canaan]

Mayassis, S. *Le livre des morts de l'Égypte ancienne est un livre d'initiation.* Athens: B.A.O.A., 1955. [Egypt]

Mayassis, S. *Mystères et initiations dans la préhistoire et protohistoire, de l'anté-diluvien à Sumer-Babylone.* Athens: B.A.O.A., 1961. [Mesopotamia]

Mayassis, S. *Mystères et initiations de l'Égypte ancienne.* Athens: B.A.O.A., 1957. [Egypt]

Maybaum, Siegmund. *Die Entwickelung des altisraelitischen Priesterthums: Ein Beitrag zur Kritik der mittleren Bücher des Pentateuchs.* Breslau: Köbner, 1880. [Priesthood]

Mayer, H. "Das Bauholz des Tempels Salomos." *Biblische Zeitschrift* 11 (1967): 53-66. [Israel/Canaan]

Mayer, R. "Zum Problem des Opfers unmittelbar nach der Zerstörung des zweiten Tempels." In *Fourth World Congress of Jewish Studies: Papers.* 209-12. Jerusalem: World Union of Jewish Studies, 1968. [Sacrifice/Offerings]

Mayo, Janet. *A History of Ecclesiastical Dress.* New York: Holmes and Meier, 1984. [Sacred Vestments]

Mazar, Amihai. "Additional Philistine Temples at Tell Qasile." *BA* 40 (1977): 82-87. [Israel/Canaan]

Mazar, Amihai. "Bronze Bull Found in Israelite 'High Place' from the Time of the Judges." *BAR* 9 (1983): 34-40. [Israel/Canaan]

Mazar, Amihai. "A Cult Site in the Samaria Mountains from the Period of the Judges" (in Hebrew). *Eretz-Israel* 16 (1982): 135-45. [Israel/Canaan]

Mazar, Amihai. *Mikdeshe Tel Kasilah.* 2 vols. Jerusalem: Hebrew University, 1977. [Israel/Canaan]

Mazar, Amihai. "A Philistine Temple at Tell Qasile." *BA* 36 (1973): 42-48. [Israel/Canaan]

Mazar, Amihai. "Tel Qasile." *RB* 82 (1975): 263-66. [Israel/Canaan]

Mazar, Benjamin. "The Archaeological Excavations near the Temple Mount." In *Jerusalem Revealed: Archaeology in the Holy City, 1968-1974,* edited by Yigael Yadin. 25-40. New Haven: Yale University Press, 1975. [Israel/Canaan]

Mazar, Benjamin. "Découverts archéologiques près des murs du Temple." *La Terre Sainte* 8-9 (1973): 222-32. [Israel/Canaan]

Mazar, Benjamin. *The Excavations in the Old City of Jerusalem near the Temple Mount: Preliminary Report of the Second and Third Seasons 1969-70.* Jerusalem: Israel Exploration Society, 1971. [Israel/Canaan]

Mazar, Benjamin. "Excavations near the Temple Mount." *Qadmoniot* 5/3-4[19-20] (1972): 74-90. [Mountain]

Mazar, Benjamin. "Excavations near Temple Mount Reveal Splendors of Herodian Jerusalem." *BAR* 6/4 (1980): 44-59. [Israel/Canaan]

Mazar, Benjamin. "The Excavations South and West of the Temple Mount." *Ariel* 27 (1970): 11-19. [Israel/Canaan]

Mazar, Benjamin. "The Excavations South and West of the Temple Mount in Jerusalem: The Herodian Period." *BA* 33/2 (1970): 47-60. [Israel/Canaan]

Mazar, Benjamin. "Exploration of the Wilson Arch and the Northern Extension of the Western Wall." In *The Mountain of the Lord*, edited by Benjamin Mazar et al., 217-22. Garden City, Doubleday, 1975. [Mountain]

Mazar, Benjamin. "Hebrew Inscription from the Temple Area in Jerusalem" (in Hebrew). *Qadmoniot* 3/4[12] (1970): 142-44. [Israel/Canaan]

Mazar, Benjamin. "Herod's Temple/Functions of the Outer Walls and Gate of the Temple Mount." In *The Mountain of the Lord*, edited by Benjamin Mazar et al., 106-52. Garden City: Doubleday, 1975. [Mountain]

Mazar, Benjamin. "Herodian Jerusalem in the Light of the Excavations South and Southwest of the Temple Mount." *IEJ* 28 (1978): 230-37. [Israel/Canaan]

Mazar, Benjamin. "Le mur du temple." *Bible et Terre Sainte* 122 (1970): 8-15. [Israel/Canaan]

Mazar, Benjamin. "The Royal Stoa on the Southern Part of the Temple Mount." In *Recent Archaeology in the Land of Israel*, edited by Hershel Shanks and Benjamin Mazar, 141-47. Washington, D.C.: Biblical Archaeology Society, 1984. [Israel/Canaan]

Mazar, Benjamin. "The Sanctuary of Arad and the Family of Hobab the Kenite" (in Hebrew; *English summary). *Eretz-Israel* 7 (1964): 1-5, *165. [Israel/Canaan]

Mazar, Benjamin. "YHWH Came out from Sinai." In *Temples and High Place in Biblical Times*, edited by Avraham Biran, 5-9. Jerusalem: Jewish Institute of Religion, 1981. [Mountain]

Mazar, Benjamin, et al., eds. *The Mountain of the Lord*. Garden City: Doubleday, 1975. [Israel/Canaan]

Medebielle, Alexis. *L'expiation dans l'Ancien et le Nouveau Testament.* Rome: Pontifical Biblical Institute, 1923. [Sacrifice/Offerings]

Medebielle, Alexis. "Le symbolisme du sacrifice expiatoire en Israël." *Biblica* 2 (1921): 141-69, 273-302. [Sacrifice/Offerings]

Meek, Theophile J. "Aaronites and Zadokites." *AJSL* 45 (1929): 149-66. [Priesthood]

Meek, Theophile J. "The Origin of the Hebrew Priesthood." In *Hebrew Origins*, rev. ed. 119-47. New York: Harper, 1950. [Priesthood]

Meeks, D. "Les donations aux temples dans l'Égypte du Ier millénaire avant J.-C." In *State and Temple Economy in the Ancient Near East*, edited by Edward Lipiński. 2 vols., 2:605-88. Louvain: Departement Orientalistiek, 1979. [Egypt]

Meeks, Wayne A. "Moses as God and King." In *Religions in Antiquity, Essays in Memory of E. R. Goodenough*, edited by Jacob Neusner. 354-71. Leiden: Brill, 1968. [Kingship/Coronation]

Meeks, Wayne A. *The Prophet King: Moses Traditions and the Johannine Christology.* Leiden: Brill, 1967. [Kingship/Coronation]

Mees, M. "Der geistige Tempel: Einige Überlegungen zu Klemens von Alexandrien." *Vetera Christianorum* 1 (1964): 83-89. [Egypt]

Mehrs, M. "A Consideration and Comparison of Sacrificial Terminology and Practice in Ancient Israel and Ugarit." *Near East Archaeological Society Bulletin* 15-16 (1980): 5-21. [Sacrifice/Offerings]

Meier, G. "Die Ritualtafel der Serie 'Mundwaschung'." *Archiv für Orientforschung* 12 (1937): 40-45. [Ritual/Liturgy/Worship]

Meinema, W. D. *De tempel van Salomo.* Netherlands: Delft, 1948. [Israel/Canaan]

Meiri, Menahem. *The Chosen House* (in Hebrew). 12 vols. Jerusalem: Yad ha-Rav Hertzog, 1963-74. [Israel/Canaan]

Meistermann, Barnabas. "Temple of Herod." In *The Catholic Encyclopedia,* edited by C. G. Herbermann et al. 15 vols. 14:502-4. New York: Encyclopedia, 1912. [Israel/Canaan]

Melas, Evi, ed. *Tempel und Stätten der Götter Griechenlands.* Köln: Schauberg, 1970; also in English as *The Greek Experience: A Companion Guide to the Major Architectural Sites and an Introduction to Ancient History and Myth,* edited by Evi Melas and translated by F. Maxwell Brownjohn. New York: Dutton, 1974. [Greece/Rome]

Mendels, D. " 'On Kingship' in the 'Temple Scroll' and the Ideological Vorlage of the Seven Banquets in the 'Letter of Aristeas to Philocrates'." *Aegyptus* 59/1-2 (1979): 127-36. [Israel/Canaan]

Mendenhall, George E. "Covenant Forms in Israelite Tradition." *BA* 17 (September 1954): 50-76. [Covenant]

Mendner, S. "Die Tempelreinigung." *ZNTW* 47 (1956): 93-112. [Israel/Canaan]

Menes, A. "Tempel und Synagogue." *ZAW* 50 (1932): 268-76. [Israel/Canaan]

Mensch, Ernst C. *King Solomon's 'First' Temple.* San Francisco: Mensch, 1947. [Israel/Canaan]

Menzel, Brigitte. *Assyrische Tempel.* Rome: Pontifical Biblical Institute, 1981. [Mesopotamia]

Mertens, Dieter. *Der Tempel von Segesta und die dorische Tempelbaukunst des griechischen Westens in klassischer Zeit.* Mainz: Phillip von Zabern, 1984. [Greece/Rome]

Mertz, Barbara. *Temples, Tombs, and Hieroglyphs.* New York: Dodd, Mead, 1978. [Egypt]

Mettinger, Tryggve N. D. *King and Messiah: The Civil and Sacral Legitimation of the Israelite Kings.* Lund: Gleerup, 1976. [Kingship/Coronation]

Mettinger, Tryggve N. D. "Den narvarande Guden: Om tempelteologi och gudsbild i Gamla Testamentet." *Svensk Exegetisk Årsbok* 47 (1982): 21-47. [Israel/Canaan]

Mettinger, Tryggve N. D. "YHWH SABAOTH—The Heavenly King on the Cherubim Throne." In *Studies in the Period of David and Solomon and*

Other Essays, edited by Tamoo Ishida. 109-38. Winona Lake: Eisenbrauns, 1982. [Kingship/Coronation]

Metzger, Martin. "Himmlische und irdische Wohnstatt Jahwes." In *Ugarit-Forschungen* 2 (1970):139-58. [Israel/Canaan]

Metzger, T. "Les objets du culte, le sanctuaire du désert et le temple de Jérusalem, dans les Bibles hébraïques médiévales enluminées, en Orient et en Espagne." *BJRL* 52-53 (1969-71): 397-436; 167-209. [Israel/Canaan]

Metzinger, Adalbert. "Die Substitutionstheorie und das alttestamentliche Opfer mit besonderer Beruecksichtigung von Lev 17,11." *Biblica* 21 (1940): 159-87, 353-77. [Sacrifice/Offerings]

Meyerowitz Eva L. R. *The Divine Kingship in Ghana and Ancient Egypt.* London: Faber and Faber, 1960. [Kingship/Coronation]

Meyers, Carol L. "Altar." In *Harper's Dictionary of the Bible*, 22-24. [Sacrifice/Offerings]

Meyers, Carol L. "The Elusive Temple." *BA* 45 (1982): 33-41. [Israel/Canaan]

Meyers, Carol L. "Jachin and Boaz in Religious and Political Perspective." In *The Temple in Antiquity*, edited by Truman G. Madsen. 135-50. Provo: Brigham Young University Press, 1984. [Israel/Canaan]

Meyers, Carol L. "Menorah." In *The Interpreter's Dictionary of the Bible*, supp. vol., 586-87. [Tabernacle]

Meyers, Carol L. *The Tabernacle Menorah.* Missoula: Scholars, 1976. [Tabernacle]

Meyers, Carol L. "The Temple." In *Harper's Dictionary of the Bible*, 1021-32. [Israel/Canaan]

Meyers, Carol L. "Was There a Seven-Branched Lampstand in Solomon's Temple?" *BAR* 5/5 (1979): 46-57. [Israel/Canaan]

Michel, O. "naós." In *Theological Dictionary of the New Testament*, edited by G. Kittel. 880-90. Grand Rapids: Eerdmans, 1967. [Sacred Space]

Michel, O., et al. "Der Tempel der goldenen Kuh." In *Gott und die Götter: Festgabe für Erich Fascher zum 60. Geburtstag.* 56-67. Berlin: Evangelische Verlagsanstatt, 1958. [Israel/Canaan]

Michl, J. "Der Sinn der Fusswaschung (Jn 13)." *Biblica* 40 (1959): 697-708. [Ritual/Liturgy/Worship]

Milgrom, Jacob. "Akkadian Confirmation for the Meaning of the Term *tĕrûmā*" (in Hebrew). *Tarbiz* 44 (1974-75): 189; also in Milgrom, *Studies in Cultic Theology and Terminology.* 171-72. Leiden: Brill, 1983. [Sacrifice/Offerings]

Milgrom, Jacob. "The Alleged Wave-Offering in Israel and the Ancient Near East." *IEJ* 22 (1972): 33-38; also in Milgrom, *Studies in Cultic Theology and Terminology.* 133-38. Leiden: Brill, 1983. [Sacrifice/Offerings]

Milgrom, Jacob. "The Biblical Diet Laws as an Ethical System." *Interpretation* 17 (1963): 288-301; also in Milgrom, *Studies in Cultic Theology and Terminology*. 104-18. Leiden: Brill, 1983. [Sacrifice/Offerings]

Milgrom, Jacob. "Challenge to Sun-Worship Interpretation of Temple Scrolls Gilded Staircase." *BAR* 11/1 (1985): 70-73. [Israel/Canaan]

Milgrom, Jacob. "Concerning Jeremiah's Repudiation of Sacrifice." *ZAW* 89 (1977): 274-75; also in Milgrom, *Studies in Cultic Theology and Terminology*. 119-21. Leiden: Brill, 1983. [Sacrifice/Offerings]

Milgrom, Jacob. "The Cultic Šᵉgāgāh and Its Influence in Psalms and Job." *JQR* 58 (1967): 115-25; also in Milgrom, *Studies in Cultic Theology and Terminology*. 122-32. Leiden: Brill, 1983. [Sacrifice/Offerings]

Milgrom, Jacob. "Day of Atonement." In *Encyclopaedia Judaica* 5:1384-87. [Israel/Canaan]

Milgrom, Jacob. "The Functions of the Ḥaṭṭa't Sacrifice" (in Hebrew; *English summary). *Tarbiz* 40 (1970-71): 1-8, *I. [Sacrifice/Offerings]

Milgrom, Jacob. "Further Studies in the Temple Scroll." *JQR* 71/1-2 (1980): 1-17; 89-106. [Israel/Canaan]

Milgrom, Jacob. "*Hattĕnûpâ*." In Milgrom, *Studies in Cultic Theology and Terminology*. 139-58. Leiden: Brill, 1983. [Sacrifice/Offerings]

Milgrom, Jacob. "Israel's Sanctuary: The Priestly 'Picture of Dorian Gray.' " *RB* 83 (1976): 390-99. [Tabernacle]

Milgrom, Jacob. "Israel's Sanctuary: The Priestly 'Picture of Dorian Gray.' " *RB* 83 (1976): 390-99; also in Milgrom, *Studies in Cultic Theology and Terminology*. 75-84. Leiden: Brill, 1983. [Sacrifice/Offerings]

Milgrom, Jacob. "Kipper." In *Encyclopaedia Judaica* 10:1039-44. [Israel/Canaan]

Milgrom, Jacob. "The Paradox of the Red Cow (Nu. xix)." *VT* 31 (1931): 62-72; also in Milgrom, *Studies in Cultic Theology and Terminology*. 85-95. Leiden: Brill, 1983. [Sacrifice/Offerings]

Milgrom, Jacob. "A Prolegomenon to Leviticus 17:11." *JBL* 90 (1971): 149-56; also in Milgrom, *Studies in Cultic Theology and Terminology*. 96-103. Leiden: Brill, 1983. [Sacrifice/Offerings]

Milgrom, Jacob. " 'Sabbath' and 'Temple City' in the Temple Scroll." *BASOR* 232 (1978): 25-27. [Israel/Canaan]

Milgrom, Jacob. "Sacrifices and Offerings, OT." In *The Interpreter's Dictionary of the Bible*, supp. vol., 763-71. [Sacrifice/Offerings]

Milgrom, Jacob. "Sancta Contagion and Altar/City/Asylum." In *International Organization for the Study of the Old Testament, Congress Volume, Vienna, 1980*, supplements to *VT*, 32:278-310. Leiden: Brill, 1981. [Sacrifice/Offerings]

Milgrom, Jacob. "The Shared Custody of the Tabernacle and a Hittite Analogy." *JAOS* 90 (1970): 204-9. [Tabernacle]

Milgrom, Jacob. "The 'Šok hattĕrûmâ': A Chapter in Cultic History" (in Hebrew; *English summary). *Tarbiz* 42 (1972-73): 1-14, *I; also in Milgrom, *Studies in Cultic Theology and Terminology.* 159-70. Leiden: Brill, 1983. [Sacrifice/Offerings]

Milgrom, Jacob. "Sin-offering or Purification-offering?" *VT* 21 (1971): 237-39; also in Milgrom, *Studies in Cultic Theology and Terminology.* 67-69. Leiden: Brill, 1983. [Sacrifice/Offerings]

Milgrom, Jacob. *Studies in Levitical Terminology, I.* Berkeley: University of California Press, 1970. [Sacrifice/Offerings]

Milgrom, Jacob. "Studies in the Temple Scroll." *JBL* 97 (1978): 501-23. [Israel/Canaan]

Milgrom, Jacob. "The Temple in Biblical Israel: Kinships of Meaning." In *Reflections on Mormonism*, edited by Truman G. Madsen. 57-66. Provo: Brigham Young University Press, 1978. [Israel/Canaan]

Milgrom, Jacob. "Temple Scroll." *BA* 14/5 (1978): 105-20. [Israel/Canaan]

Milgrom, Jacob. "Two Kinds of *ḥaṭṭāʾt.*" *VT* 26 (1976): 333-37; also in Milgrom, *Studies in Cultic Theology and Terminology.* 70-74. Leiden: Brill, 1983. [Sacrifice/Offerings]

Millard, A. R. "Saul's Shield Not Anointed with Oil." *BASOR* 230 (April 1978): 70. [Ablutions/Anointings]

Miller, Patrick D. "Psalm 127—The House That Yahweh Builds." *Journal for the Study of the Old Testament* 22 (1982): 119-32. [Israel/Canaan]

Miller, Patrick D., and J. J. M. Roberts. *The Hand of the Lord: A Reassessment of the "Ark Narrative" of 1 Samuel.* Baltimore: Johns Hopkins University Press, 1977. [Tabernacle]

Miller, S. H. "Liturgy: Sign and Symbol." *Una Sancta* 25 (1968): 41-52. [Ritual/Liturgy/Worship]

Miller, Stephen G. *The Prytaneion: Its Function and Architectural Form.* Berkeley: University of California Press, 1978. [Greece/Rome]

Milson, D. "The Design of the Early Bronze Age Temples at Megiddo." *BASOR* 272 (1988): 75-78. [Israel/Canaan]

Milson, D. "The Design of the Temples and Gates at Shechem." *PEFQ* 119 (1987): 97-105. [Israel/Canaan]

Mink, H. A. "Die kol. III der Tempelrolle: Versuch einer Rekonstruktion." *Revue de Qumran* 11 (1983): 163-81. [Israel/Canaan]

Mink, H. A. "The Use of Scripture in the Temple Scroll and the Status of the Scroll as Law." *Scandinavian Journal of the Old Testament* 1 (1987): 20-50. [Israel/Canaan]

Mirusalayim, Aharon. *On the Measurements of the Temple* (in Hebrew). Jerusalem: HaLevi Tsukerman, 1906. [Measurement]

Mishelov, Isser. *Detailed Explanations to the Plan of the Temple* (in Hebrew). Haifa: Ben-Ariyeh, 1938. [Israel/Canaan]

Mistton, M. "On the Version of the Temple Scroll." *Tarbiz* 48/1-2 (1978-79): 173. [Israel/Canaan]

Mitchell, Leonel L. *Baptismal Anointing.* London: University of Notre Dame Press, 1966. [Ablutions/Anointings]

Moe, Olaf. "Das irdische und das himmlische Heiligtum: Zur Auslegung von Hebr. 9, 4f." *Theologische Zeischrift* 9 (1953): 23-29. [Israel/Canaan]

Möhlenbrink, Kurt. "Die levitischen Überlieferungen des Alten Testaments." *ZAW* 52 (1934): 184-231. [Priesthood]

Möhlenbrink, Kurt. *Der Tempel Salomos.* Stuttgart: Kohlhammer, 1932. [Israel/Canaan]

Molin, G. "Ḥalonoth ʾaṭumoth bei Ezechiel." *Biblische Zeitschrift* 15 (1971): 250-53. [Israel/Canaan]

Mond, Robert. *Temples of Armant.* London: Egypt Exploration Society, 1940. [Egypt]

Montefiore, H. W. "Jesus and the Temple Tax." *NTS* 11 (October 1964): 60-71. [Israel/Canaan]

Montefiore, H. W. "Sulpicius Severus and Titus' Council of War." *Historia* 11 (1962): 156-70. [Israel/Canaan]

Montet, Pierre. "Les divinités du temple de Behbeit el hagar." *Kêmi* 10 (1949): 43-49. [Egypt]

Montet, Pierre. "Le rituel de fondation des temples égyptiens." *Kêmi* 17 (1964): 74-100. [Egypt]

Moorehead, William G. *Studies in Mosaic Institutions: The Tabernacle, the Priesthood, the Sacrifices and the Feasts of Ancient Israel.* Dayton, OH: Shuey, 1896. [Tabernacle]

Moorhead, Walter J. "The Pharisees Reconsidered in Relation to the Temple Cultus and Early Christianity." Ph.D. diss., Southern Baptist Theological Seminary, 1960. [Israel/Canaan]

Moraldi, Luigi. *Espiazione sacrificale e riti espiatori nell'ambiente biblico e nell'Antico Testamento.* Rome: Pontifical Biblical Institute, 1956. [Sacrifice/Offerings]

Moraldi, Luigi. "Terminologia cultuale israelitica." *Rivista degli Studi Orientali* 32 (1957): 321-37. [Ritual/Liturgy/Worship]

Moran, William L. "Enthronement Feast." In *New Catholic Encyclopedia*, 15 vols. 5:445-46. New York: McGraw-Hill, 1967. [Kingship/Coronation]

Morenz, Siegfried. "Cult and Piety: The Conduct of Men." In Morenz, *Egyptian Religion*, translated by Ann E. Keep. 81-109. New York: Barnes and Noble, 1972. [Egypt]

Moret, Alexandre. *Du caractère religieux de la royauté pharonique.* Paris: Leroux, 1902. [Kingship/Coronation]

Moret, Alexandre. "Le rite de briser les vases rouges au temple de Louxor." *Revue d'Égyptologie* 3 (1938): 167. [Egypt]

Moret, Alexandre. *Le rituel de culte divin journalier en Égypte*. Paris: Leroux, 1902. [Egypt]

Moret, Alexandre. "Du sacrifice en Égypte." *RHR* 57 (1908): 81-101. [Sacrifice/Offerings]

Morgenstern, Julian. "The Ark, the Ephod, and the 'Tent of Meeting'." *HUCA* 17 (1942-43): 153-266; 18 (1944): 1-52; also reprinted as *The Ark, the Ephod and the Tent of Meeting*. Cincinnati: Hebrew Union College Press, 1945. [Tabernacle]

Morgenstern, Julian. "A Chapter in the History of the High Priesthood." *AJSL* 55 (1938): 1-24, 183-97, 360-77. [Priesthood]

Morgenstern, Julian. "The Cultic Setting of the Enthronement Psalms." *HUCA* 35 (1964): 1-42. [Kingship/Coronation]

Morgenstern, Julian. *The Fire upon the Altar*. Chicago: Quadrangle, 1963. [Sacrifice/Offerings]

Morgenstern, Julian. "The King-God among the Western Semites and the Meaning of Epiphanes." *VT* 10 (1960): 138-97. [Kingship/Coronation]

Morgenstern, Julian. "The Tent of Meeting." *JAOS* 38 (1918): 125-39. [Tabernacle]

Moses ben Maimon. *The Book of Offerings* (in Hebrew), with commentary by Z. Sachs. Jerusalem: Mossad Harav Kook, 1960. [Sacrifice/Offerings]

Moses ben Maimon. *The Book of Offerings*, translated from Hebrew by H. Danby. In *Yale Judaica Series*, vol. 4. New Haven: Yale University Press, 1950. [Sacrifice/Offerings]

Moses ben Maimon. *The Book of Temple Service* (in Hebrew), with commentary by S. D. Mendelson, Z. Sachs, and M. Reich. Jerusalem: Mossad Harav Kook, 1963. [Israel/Canaan]

Moses ben Maimon. *The Book of Temple Service*, translated by M. Lewittes. In *Yale Judaica Series*, vol. 12. New Haven: Yale University Press, 1957. [Israel/Canaan]

Moule, C. F. D. "Sanctuary and Sacrifice in the Church of the New Testament." *JTS* 1 (1950): 29-41. [Sacrifice/Offerings]

Mowinckel, Sigmund. "The Copper Scroll: An Apocryphon?" *JBL* 76 (December 1957): 261-65. [Israel/Canaan]

Mowinckel, Sigmund. "General Oriental and Specific Israelite Elements in the Israelite Conception of the Sacral Kingdom." In *The Sacral Kingship*. 283-93. Leiden: Brill, 1959. [Kingship/Coronation]

Mowinckel, Sigmund. *Offersang og sangoffer*. Oslo: Aschehous, 1951; also in English as *The Psalms in Israel's Worship*, translated by D. R. Ap-Thomas. Oxford: Oxford University Press, 1962. [Ritual/Liturgy/Worship]

Mowinckel, Sigmund. *Psalmenstudien*, 2 vols. Amsterdam: Schippers, 1966. [Israel/Canaan]

Mowinckel, Sigmund. "A quel moment le culte de Yahvé à Jérusalem est-il officiellement devenu un culte sans images?" *Revue d'histoire et de philosophie religieuses* (1929):197-216. [Israel/Canaan]

Mowinckel, Sigmund. *Religion og Kultus*. Oslo: Land og Kirke, 1950; also in English as *Religion and Cult*, translated by John F. X. Sheehan. Milwaukee: Marquette University, 1981. [Ritual/Liturgy/Worship]

Mowinckel, Sigmund. "Wann wurde der Jahwäkultus in Jerusalem offiziell bildos?" *Acta Orientalia* 8 (1930): 257-79. [Israel/Canaan]

Mowinckel, Sigmund. *Zum israelitischen Neujahr und zur Deutung der Thronbesteigungspsalmen: Zwei Aufsätze*. Oslo: Dybwad, 1952. [Kingship/Coronation]

Muchau, Hermann. *Pfahlhausbau und Griechentempel*. Jena: Costenolbe, 1909. [Greece/Rome]

Mudge, William. *The Tabernacle of Testimony in the Wilderness*. 3d ed. London Simpkin, Marshall, 1861. [Tabernacle]

Muehsam, Alice. *Coin and Temple*. Leeds: Leeds University Oriental Society, 1966. [Israel/Canaan]

Mueller, J. R. "The Apocalypse of Abraham and the Destruction of the Second Jewish Temple." *SBLSP* 21 (1982): 341-49. [Israel/Canaan]

Mueller, J. R. "The Temple Scroll and the Gospel Divorce Texts." *Revue de Qumran* 10 (1980): 247-56. [Israel/Canaan]

Muilenburg, James. "The Form and Stucture of the Covenantal Formulations." *VT* 9 (1959): 347-65. [Covenant]

Muilenburg, James. "The Site of Ancient Gilgal." *BASOR* 140 (1955): 11-27. [Israel/Canaan]

Mulder, M. J. "Einige Bemerkungen zur Beschreibung des Libanonwaldhauses in I Reg 7 2f." *ZAW* 88 (1976): 99-105. [Israel/Canaan]

Müller, Hans-Peter. "Die kultische Darstellung der Theophanie." *VT* 14 (1964): 183-91. [Ritual/Liturgy/Worship]

Müller, Werner. *Die heilige Stadt: Roma Quadrata, himmlisches Jerusalem und die Mythe vom Weltnabel*. Stuttgart: Kohlammer, 1961. [Israel/Canaan]

Munro, W. "The Anointing in Mark 14:3-9 and John 12:1-8." *SBLSP* 16 (1979): 127-30. [Ablutions/Anointings]

Muntingh, L. M. " 'The City Which Has Foundations': Hebrews 11:8-10 in the Light of the Mari Texts." In *De fructo oris sui: Essays in Honour of Adrianus van Selms*, edited by I. H. Eybers. 108-20. Leiden: Brill, 1971. [Israel/Canaan]

Murphy, D. J. "Ezekiel and the New Temple." *Bible Today* 40 (1969): 2805-9. [Israel/Canaan]

Murphy, Frederick J. "The Temple in the Syriac Apocalypse of Baruch." *JBL* 106 (December 1987): 671-83. [Israel/Canaan]

Murray, Grace A. *Ancient Rites and Ceremonies.* London: Rivers, 1929. [Ritual/Liturgy/Worship]

Murray, Margaret A. *Egyptian Temples.* London: Low, Marston, 1931. [Egypt]

Murray, Robert. "Prophecy and the Cult." In *Israel's Prophetic Tradition: Essays in Honour of Peter R. Ackroyd,* edited by Richard Coggins, Anthony Phillips, and Michael Knibb. 200-226. Cambridge: Cambridge University Press, 1982. [Ritual/Liturgy/Worship]

Mussche, H. F. *Religious Architecture.* Leiden: Brill, 1968. [Greece/Rome]

Muthunayagom, D. J. "Kingship of God and Creation in the Old Testament." *Bangalore Theological Forum* 15 (May-August 1983): 168-71. [Kingship/Coronation]

Muuss, R. "Der Jahwetempel in Elephantine." *ZAW* 36 (1916): 81-107. [Israel/Canaan]

Myers, Jacob M. "Building the Temple." In Myers, *II Chronicles.* 8-44. Garden City: Doubleday, 1965. [Israel/Canaan]

Myers, Jacob M. "David and the Founding of the Temple." In *I Chronicles.* 77-200. Garden City: Doubleday, 1965. [Israel/Canaan]

Myres, J. L. "King Solomon's Temple and Other Buildings and Works of Art." *PEQ* 80 (1948): 14-41. [Israel/Canaan]

Narkiss, Bezalel. "The Scheme of the Sanctuary from the Time of Herod the Great." *Journal of Jewish Art* 1 (1974): 6-14. [Israel/Canaan]

Narkiss, Bezalel. "Temple: Temple in the Arts." In *Encyclopaedia Judaica* 15:984-88. [Israel/Canaan]

Nataf, G. "Les Zélotes et la chute du Temple." *Le Monde de la Bible* 13 (1980): 36-37. [Israel/Canaan]

Naville, Edouard H. *The Temple of Deir el Bahari,* 6 vols. London: Egypt Exploration Fund, 1894-1908. [Egypt]

Nebe, G. Wilhelm. "ᵓDŠK 'Mass, Abmessung' in 11Q Tempelrolle XLI, 16." *Revue de Qumran* 11 (1983): 391-99. [Israel/Canaan]

Nedava, J. "The Destruction of the Second Temple" (in Hebrew). *Maḥanayim* 96 (1964): 56-63. [Israel/Canaan]

Negev, A. "Temples." In Negev, *Archaeological Encyclopedia of the Holy Land.* 310-13. New York: Putnam's Sons, 1972. [Israel/Canaan]

Nelson, Harold H. "The Egyptian Temple." *BA* 7 (1944): 44-53. [Egypt]

Nelson, Harold H. "The Identity of Amon Re of United-with-Eternity." *JNES* 1 (1942): 127-55. [Egypt]

Nelson, Harold H. *Key Plans Showing Locations of Theban Temple Decorations.* Chicago: University of Chicago Press, 1941. [Egypt]

Nelson, Harold H., et al. *Ramses III's Temple within the Great Inclosure of Amon.* Chicago: University of Chicago Press, 1936. [Egypt]

Nelson, Richard D. "The Altar of Ahaz: A Revisionist View." *Hebrew Annual Review: A Journal of Studies in Bible, Hebrew Language and Literature* 10 (1986): 267-76. [Sacrifice/Offerings]

Ness, Alex W. *Pattern for Living: The Tabernacle, Priesthood, Offerings, Feasts.* Downsview, Ontario: Christian Centre, 1979. [Tabernacle]

Neusner, Jacob. "Judaism after the Destruction of the Temple." In *Israelite and Judaean History*, edited by J. H. Hayes and M. Miller. 663-77. Philadelphia: Westminster, 1977. [Israel/Canaan]

Neusner, Jacob. "Judaism beyond Catastrophe: The Destruction of the Temple and the Renaissance of Torah." In Neusner, *Judaism in the Beginning of Christianity.* 89-99. Philadelphia: Fortress, 1984. [Israel/Canaan]

Neusner, Jacob. "Judaism in a Time of Crisis: Four Responses to the Destruction of the Second Temple." *Judaism* 21 (1972): 313-27. [Israel/Canaan]

Neusner, Jacob. "Map without Territory: Mishnah's System of Sacrifice and Sanctuary." *History of Religions* 19 (1979): 103-27. [Sacrifice/Offerings]

Neve, Peter. "Die Kulträume in den hethitischen Tempeln Hattusas." In *Festschrift Heinrich Otten*, edited by Erich New and Christel Rüster. 253-72. Wiesbaden: Harrassowitz, 1973. [Mesopotamia]

Newberry, Thomas. *The Tabernacle, the Temple, and the Offerings: Their Types and Spiritual Significance.* Kilmarnock: Ritchie, 1927. [Tabernacle]

Newbigin, Lesslie B. "Politics and the Covenant." *Theology* 84 (1981): 356-63. [Covenant]

Newman, Murray L. *The People of the Covenant.* New York: Abingdon, 1962. [Covenant]

Newton, Richard. *The Jewish Tabernacle and Its Furniture, in Their Typical Teachings.* New York: Carter, 1878. [Tabernacle]

Nibley, Hugh W. "Ancient Temples: What Do They Signify?" *Ensign* 2 (1972): 45-49. [Israel/Canaan]

Nibley, Hugh W. "Christian Envy of the Temple" *JQR* 50 (1959-60): 97-123; 229-40; reprinted in Nibley, *Mormonism and Early Christianity.* 391-434. Salt Lake City: Deseret Book and F.A.R.M.S., 1987. [Israel/Canaan]

Nibley, Hugh W. "The Early Christian Prayer Circle." *Brigham Young University Studies* 19 (1978): 41-78; also in Nibley, *Mormonism and Early Christianity.* 45-99. Salt Lake City: Deseret Book and F.A.R.M.S., 1987. [Ritual/Liturgy/Worship]

Nibley, Hugh W. "The Idea of the Temple in History." *Millennial Star* 120 (1958): 228-37, 247-49; reprinted as "What Is a Temple." In Nibley, *Mormonism and Early Christianity.* 355-90. Salt Lake City: Deseret Book and F.A.R.M.S., 1987. [Sacred Space]

Nibley, Hugh W. *The Message of the Joseph Smith Papyri: An Egyptian Endowment.* Salt Lake City: Deseret Book, 1975. [Egypt]

Nibley, Hugh W. "What Is a Temple? The Idea of the Temple in History." In Nibley, *Mormonism and Early Christianity.* 355-90. Salt Lake City: Deseret Book and F.A.R.M.S., 1987. [Sacred Space]

Nicholson, Ernest W. "Blood-Spattered Altars?" *VT* 27 (January 1977): 113-17. [Sacrifice/Offerings]

Nicholson, Ernest W. "The Centralisation of the Cult in Deuteronomy." *VT* 13 (1963): 380-89. [Israel/Canaan]

Nicholson, Ernest W. "Exodus, Covenant, and Treaty." In *Exodus and Sinai in History and Tradition: Growing Points in Theology.* 33-52. Oxford: Blackwell, 1973. [Covenant]

Nicholson, Ernest W. "Josiah's Reformation and Deuteronomy." *Transactions of the Glasgow University Oriental Society* 20 (1965): 77-84. [Israel/Canaan]

Nickelsburg, G. W. E., and M. Stone. "Temple and Cult." In Nickelsburg and Stone, *Faith and Piety in Early Judaism: Texts and Documents.* 51-88. Philadelphia: Fortress, 1983. [Israel/Canaan]

Nickolsky, N. M. "Pascha im Kulte des jerusalemischen Tempels." *ZAW* 45 (1927): 171-90, 241-53. [Israel/Canaan]

Niditch, S. "Ezekiel 40-48 in a Visionary Context." *CBQ* 48 (1986): 208-24. [Israel/Canaan]

Nielsen, E. "Some Reflections on the History of the Ark." In *International Organization for the Study of the Old Testament, Congress Volume, Oxford, 1959.* 61-74. Leiden: Brill, 1960. [Tabernacle]

Nikiprowetzky, Valentin. "Le nouveau temple. A propos d'un ouvrage récent." *REJ* 130 (1971): 5-30. [Israel/Canaan]

Nikiprowetzky, Valentin. "La spiritualisation des sacrifices et le culte sacrificiel au temple de Jérusalem chez Philon d'Alexandrie." *Semitica* 17 (1967): 97-116. [Sacrifice/Offerings]

Nikiprowetzky, Valentin. "Temple et communauté." *REJ* 126 (1967): 7-25. [Israel/Canaan]

Nissen, Heinrich. *Orientation: Studien zur Geschichte der Religion.* Berlin: Weidmannsche, 1906. [Sacred Space]

Nixon, Hilary A. *Typology of the Mosaic Tabernacle.* Ann Arbor: University Microfilm, 1984. [Tabernacle]

Nodet, E. "Table delphique au temple." *RB* 96 (October 1989): 533-44. [Israel/Canaan]

Noll, S. F. "Tabernacle, Temple." In *Evangelical Dictionary of Theology,* edited by W. A. Elwell. 1067-69. Grand Rapids: Baker Book House, 1984. [Tabernacle]

Nolland, J. "A Misleading Statement of the Essene Attitude to the Temple (Josephus Antiquities, XViii, I, 5, 19)." *Revue de Qumran* 9 (1978): 555-62. [Israel/Canaan]

Nordheim, E. von. "König und Tempel: Der Hintergrund des Tempelbauverbotes in 2 Samuel 7." *VT* 27 (1977): 434-53. [Kingship/Coronation]

Nordström, C.-O. "Some Miniatures in Hebrew Bibles." In *Synthronon: Art et archéologie de la fin de l'antique et du moyen age.* 89-105. Paris: Klincksieck, 1968. [Israel/Canaan]

Norman, Naomi J. *The 'Ionic' Cella: A Preliminary Study of Fourth Century B.C. Temple Architecture.* n.p., n.p., 1980. [Greece/Rome]

Norris, Herbert. *Church Vestments, Their Origin and Development.* London: Dent, 1949. [Sacred Vestments]

North, C. R. "The Religious Aspect of Hebrew Kingship." *ZAW* 50 (1932): 8-38. [Kingship/Coronation]

North, Francis S. "Aaron's Rise in Prestige." *ZAW* 66 (1954): 191-99. [Priesthood]

Northcote, H. "A Solution to the Chief Difficulties in Revelation XX-XXII." *ET* 26 (1914-15): 426-28. [Israel/Canaan]

Noth, Martin. "God, King, and Nation in the Old Testament." In *The Laws in the Pentateuch and Other Studies.* 145-78. Edinburgh: Oliver and Boyd, 1966. [Kingship/Coronation]

Noth, Martin. "Gott, König, Volk im alten Testament." *Zeitschrift für Theologie und Kirche* 47 (1950): 157-91. [Kingship/Coronation]

Noth, Martin. "The Life of the Jerusalem Religious Community in the Persian Period." In *The History of Israel*, edited by P. Ackroyd, 2d ed. 337-45. New York: Harper and Row, 1960. [Israel/Canaan]

Noth, Martin. "The Re-establishment of the Sanctuary and the Cultus in Jerusalem." In *The History of Israel*, edited by P. Ackroyd, 2d ed. 300-16. New York: Harper and Row, 1960. [Israel/Canaan]

Noy, Dov. "The Foundation Stone and the Beginning of Creation" (in Hebrew). In *And to Jerusalem.* 360-94. Jerusalem: Union of Hebrew Writers of Israel, 1968. [Israel/Canaan]

Obbink, H. Th. "The Horns of the Altar in the Semitic World, Especially in Jahwism." *JBL* 56 (1937): 43-49. [Sacrifice/Offerings]

O'Connell, Laurence J., *The Book of Ceremonies.* Milwaukee: Bruce, 1943. [Ritual/Liturgy/Worship]

Oesterley, William O. E. "Early Hebrew Festival Rituals." In *Myth and Ritual*, edited by Samuel H. Hooke. 111-46. London: Oxford University Press, 1933. [Ritual/Liturgy/Worship]

Oesterley, William O. E. "Herod's Temple." In *A History of Israel*, vol. 2 of *From the Fall of Jerusalem, 586 B.C. to the Bar Kokhba Revolt, A.D. 135,* edited by T. H. Robinson and W. O. E. Oesterley. 376-78. Oxford: Clarendon, 1932. [Israel/Canaan]

Oesterley, William O. E. *Sacrifices in Ancient Israel: Their Origin, Purposes and Development.* London: Hodder and Stoughton, 1937. [Sacrifice/Offerings]

Oesterley, William O. E. "The Temple." In *A Dictionary of Christ and the Gospels,* edited by James Hastings. vol. 2. 208-13. New York: Scribners & Sons, 1908. [Israel/Canaan]

Oestreicher, Theodor. *Reichstempel und Ortsheiligtümer in Israel.* Gütersloh: Bertelsmann, 1930. [Israel/Canaan]

Offord, Joseph. "The Mountain Throne of Jahveh." *PEFQ* 51 (1919): 39-45. [Mountain]

Olford, Stephen F. *The Tabernacle: Camping with God.* Neptune: Loizeaux Brothers, 1971. [Tabernacle]

Olsen, C. "The Closet, the House and the Sanctuary." *Christian Century* 98 (1981): 1285-89. [Ritual/Liturgy/Worship]

Olyan, Saul. "Zadok's Origins and the Tribal Politics of David." *JBL* 101 (1982): 177-93. [Priesthood]

Oppenheim, A. Leo. "The Golden Garments of the Gods." *JNES* 8 (1949): 172-93. [Sacred Vestments]

Oppenheim, A. Leo. "The Mesopotamian Temple." *BA* 7 (1944): 54-63. [Mesopotamia]

Orchard, William E. *The Temple.* New York: Seabury Press, [1965]. [Israel/Canaan]

Oren, E. D. "Excavations at Qasrawet in NW Sinai." *IEJ* 32 (1982): 203-11. [Israel/Canaan]

Orlandos, Anastasios K. *Les materiaux de construction et la technique architecturale des anciens Grecs.* Paris: de Boccard, 1966-68. [Greece/Rome]

Orlinsky, Harry M. "The Destruction of the First Temple and the Babylonian Exile in the Light of Archaeology." In *Essays in Biblical Culture and Bible Translation.* 144-61. New York: KTAV, 1974. [Israel/Canaan]

O'Rourke, William J. "Israelite Sacrifice." *American Ecclesistical Review* 149 (1963): 259-74. [Sacrifice/Offerings]

Orrieux, C. "Le Temple de Salomon." In *Temples et Sanctuaires: Seminaire de recherche 1981-1983,* edited by G. Roux. 51-59. Lyon: Maison de l'Orient, 1984. [Israel/Canaan]

Osburn, William, Jr. *The Monumental History of Egypt, as Recorded on the Ruins of Her Temples, Palaces and Tombs.* London: Trübner, 1854. [Egypt]

Osing, Jürgen. *Der Tempel Sethos I in Gurna.* Mainz: von Zabern, 1977. [Egypt]

Ostler, Blake. "Clothed Upon: A Unique Aspect of Christian Antiquity." *Brigham Young University Studies* 22 (1982): 31-45. [Sacred Vestments]

Otto, Eberhard. *Das ägyptische Mundöffnungsritual.* 2 vols. Wiesbaden: Harrassowitz, 1960. [Ritual/Liturgy/Worship]

Otto, Eberhard. *Gott und Mensch nach den ägyptischen Tempelinschriften der griechisch-römischen Zeit.* Heidelberg: Winter, 1964. [Ritual/Liturgy/Worship]

Otto, Eberhard. "Les Inscriptions du Temple d'Opet, à Karnak III: Traduction intégrale des texts rituels." *Biblitheca Orientalis* 28 (1971): 41-42. [Egypt]

Otto, Eberhard. *Osiris und Amon: Kult und heilige Stätten.* Munich: Hirmer, 1966; also in English as *Ancient Egyptian Art: The Cults of Osiris and Amon,* translated by Kate B. Griffiths. New York: Abrams, 1967. [Egypt]

Otto, Eckart. "El und JHWH in Jerusalem: Historische und theologische Aspekte einer Religionsintegration." *VT* 30 (1980): 316-29. [Israel/Canaan]

Otto, Eckart. "Silo und Jerusalem." *Theologische Zeitschrift* 32 (1976): 65-77. [Tabernacle]

Otto, Walter G. A. *Priester und Tempel im hellenistischen Ägypten,* 2 vols. Leipzig: Teubner, 1905-8. [Egypt]

Ottosson, Magnus. "*hêkhal.*" In *Theological Dictionary of the Old Testament* 3:382-88. [Israel/Canaan]

Ottosson, Magnus. *Temples and Cult Places in Palestine.* Stockholm: Almquist and Wiksell, 1980. [Israel/Canaan]

Ouellette, Jean. "*Atumim* in I Kings 6:4." *Bulletin of the Institute of Jewish Studies* (1974): 99-102. [Israel/Canaan]

Ouellette, Jean. "The Basic Structure of Solomon's Temple and Archaeological Research." In *The Temple of Solomon,* edited by J. Gutman. 1-20. Missoula: Scholars, 1976. [Israel/Canaan]

Ouellette, Jean. "Jachin and Boaz." In *The Interpreter's Dictionary of the Bible,* supp. vol., 469. [Israel/Canaan]

Ouellette, Jean. "The Solomonic *debîr* according to the Hebrew Text of I Kings 6." *JBL* 89 (1970): 338-43. [Israel/Canaan]

Ouellette, Jean. "Temple of Solomon." In *The Interpreter's Dictionary of the Bible,* supp. vol., 873-74. [Israel/Canaan]

Ouellette, Jean. "The Temple of Solomon: A Philological and Archaeological Study." Ph.D. diss., Hebrew Union College, 1966. [Israel/Canaan]

Ouellette, Jean. "Le vestibule du Temple de Salomon était-il un Beit Hilani?" *RB* 76 (1969): 365-78. [Israel/Canaan]

Ouellette, Jean. "The *Yāṣīaᶜ* and the *Ṣᵉlāᶜōt:* Two Mysterious Structures in Solomon's Temple." *JNES* 31 (1972): 187-91. [Israel/Canaan]

Pailloux, Xavier. *Monographie du Temple de Salomon.* Paris: Roger and Chernoviz, 1885. [Israel/Canaan]

Paine, Timothy O. *Solomon's Temple and Capitol, Ark of the Flood and Tabernacle; or, The Holy Houses of the Hebrew, Chaldee, Syriac, Samaritan, Septuagint, Coptic, and Itala Scriptures.* Boston: Houghton Mifflin, 1885. [Israel/Canaan]

Paine, Timothy O. *Solomon's Temple, including the Tabernacle.* Boston: Phinney, 1861. [Israel/Canaan]

Pallis, Svend A. *The Babylonian Akitu Festival.* Copenhagen: Bianco Lunos Bogtrykkeri, 1926. [Mesopotamia]

Pallu de Lessert, Augustin C. *De la formule 'Translata de sordentibus locis': trouvée sur des monuments de cherchel.* Paris: Leroux, 1888. [Greece/Rome]

Palmer, Martin. "The Cardinal Points in Psalm 48." *Biblica* 46 (1945): 357-58. [Israel/Canaan]

Paribeni, R. *I grandi santuari dell "Antica Grecia."* Milano: Societa editrice "Vita e pensiero," 1947. [Greece/Rome]

Parker, Percy G. *The Tabernacle of Israel: Its History and Mystery.* London: Victory, 1932. [Tabernacle]

Parrot, André. "Cérémonie de la main et réinvestiture." In *Studia Mariana*, edited by André Parrot. 37-50. Leiden: Brill, 1950. [Sacred Vestments]

Parrot, André. *Le Temple d'Ishtar.* Paris: Geuthner, 1956. [Mesopotamia]

Parrot, André. *The Temple of Jerusalem.* New York: Philosophical Library, 1955. [Israel/Canaan]

Parrot, André. "La Tour de Babel et les Ziggurats." *La Nouvelle Clio* 2 (1950): 153-61. [Mesopotamia]

Parrot, André. *The Tower of Babel*, translated by Edwin Hudson. London: SCM, 1955. [Mesopotamia]

Parry, Donald W. "The Garden of Eden: Sacred Space, Sanctuary, Temple of God." *Explorations: A Journal for Adventurous Thought* 5/4 (Summer 1987): 83-107. [Sacred Space]

Parry, Donald W. "Sinai as Sanctuary and Mountain of God." In *By Study and Also by Faith: Essays in Honor of Hugh W. Nibley*, edited by John M. Lundquist and Stephen D. Ricks. 2 vols., 1:482-500. Salt Lake City: Deseret Book and F.A.R.M.S., 1990. [Mountain]

Parunak, H. "Was Solomon's Temple Aligned to the Sun?" *PEQ* 110 (1978): 29-33. [Israel/Canaan]

Patai, Raphael. "Hebrew Installation Rites." *HUCA* 20 (1947): 143-225; also in Patai, *On Jewish Folklore.* 110-73. Detroit: Wayne State University Press, 1983. [Kingship/Coronation]

Patai, Raphael. *Man and Temple in Ancient Jewish Myth and Ritual.* New York: Nelson, 1947. [Israel/Canaan]

Paton, Lewis B. "The Location of the Temple." In Paton, *Jerusalem in Bible Times.* 1-7. Chicago: University of Chicago Press, 1908. [Israel/Canaan]

Paton, Lewis B. "The Use of the Word 'Kohen' in the Old Testament." *JBL* 12 (1893): 1-14. [Priesthood]

Patrich, Joseph. "The *mesibbah* of the Temple according to the Tractate *Middot.*" *IEJ* 36/3-4 (1986): 215-33. [Israel/Canaan]

Patrich, Joseph. "Reconstructing the Magnificent Temple Herod Built." *Bible Review* 4 (October 1988): 16-29. [Israel/Canaan]

Paul, S. M., and William G. Dever. "Cultic Structures." In *Biblical Archaeology,* edited by Geoffrey Wigoder. 54-83. New York: Quadrangle, 1974. [Israel/Canaan]

Paulme, Denise. "La notion de sacrifice chez un peuple 'fetichiste.' " *RHR* 132 (1946-B): 48-66. [Sacrifice/Offerings]

Pedersen, Johannes. "Feasts and Sacred Customs." In *Israel: Its Life and Culture,* translated by Annie E. Fausboll. 4 vols., 4:376-465. London: Oxford University Press, 1940. [Israel/Canaan]

Pedersen, Johannes. "Holy Places and Holy Things." In *Israel: Its Life and Culture,* translated by Annie E. Fausboll. 4 vols., 3:235-63. London: Oxford University Press, 1940. [Israel/Canaan]

Pelletier, André. "Le grand rideau du vestibule du Temple de Jérusalem." *Syria* 35 (1958): 218-26. [Israel/Canaan]

Pelletier, André. "Une particularité du rituel des 'pains d'oblation' conservée par la Septante (Lev. xxiv 8 & Ex. xxv 30)." *VT* 17 (1967): 364-67. [Ritual/Liturgy/Worship]

Pelletier, André. "Le 'voile du Temple' de Jérusalem en termes de métier." *Revue des études grecques* 77 (1964): 70-75. [Israel/Canaan]

Pelletier, André. "Le 'voile' du temple de Jérusalem est-il devenu la 'portière' du temple d' Olympie?" *Syria* 32 (1955): 289-307. [Israel/Canaan]

Pemberton, Joseph H. *The Coronation Service according to the Use of the Church of England.* London: Skeffington and Son, 1901. [Kingship/Coronation]

Percy, Emily C. *The Figures of the True.* London: Chiswick, 1903. [Tabernacle]

Pernier, Luigi. *Il tempio e l'altare di Apollo a Cirene.* Bergamo: Istituto Italiano d'arti grafiche, 1935. [Greece/Rome]

Perrin, N. "Interpretation of a Biblical Symbol." *Journal of Religions* 55 (July 1975): 348-70. [Kingship/Coronation]

Peter, A. "Der Segensstrom des endzeitlichen Jerusalem: Herkunft und Bedeutung eines prophetischen symbols." In *Miscellanea Fuldensia: Beitrage aus Geschichte, Theologie, Seelsorge* (Festschrift Adolf Bolte), edited by Franz Scholz. 109-34. Fulda: Parzeller, 1966. [Israel/Canaan]

Peters, F. E. "Not a Stone upon a Stone: The Destruction of the Holy City." In Peters, *Jerusalem: The Holy City in the Eyes of Chroniclers, Visitors, Pilgrims, and Prophets from the Days of Abraham to the Beginnings of*

Modern Times. 88-130. Princeton: Princeton University Press, 1985. [Israel/Canaan]

Peters, John P. "A Jerusalem Processional." *JBL* 39 (1920): 52-59. [Israel/Canaan]

Peters, T. "Monotheism and Kingship in Ancient Memphis: A Study in Egyptian Mythology." *Perspectives in Religious Studies* 4 (Summer 1977): 160-73. [Kingship/Coronation]

Petersen, David L. "Covenant Ritual: A Tradito-Historical Perspective." *Biblical Research* 22 (1977): 7-18. [Covenant]

Petersen, David L. "Zechariah's Visions: A Theological Perspective." *VT* 34 (April 1984): 195-206. [Israel/Canaan]

Petersen, David L. "Zerubbabel and Jerusalem Temple Reconstruction." *CBQ* 36 (July 1974): 366-72. [Israel/Canaan]

Peterson, B. J. *Fornegyptisk tempelarkitektur 3000-1000 F. K. R.* Stockholm: Medelhausmuseet, 1976. [Egypt]

Petitjean, Albert. "La mission de Zorobabel et la reconstruction du Temple, Zach. iii, 8-10." *Ephemerides Theologicae Lovanienses* 42 (1966): 40-71. [Israel/Canaan]

Petitjean, Albert. *Les oracles du Proto-Zacharie.* Paris: Gabalda, 1969. [Israel/Canaan]

Petrie, W. M. Flinders. *The Pyramids and Temples of Gizeh.* New York: Scribner & Welford, 1883. [Egypt]

Petrie, W. M. Flinders. *Six Temples at Thebes.* London: Quaritch, 1897. [Egypt]

Petuchowski, Jakob J. "The Creation in Jewish Liturgy." *Judaica* 28 (Summer 1972): 309-15. [Creation/Cosmology]

Petuchowski, Jacob J., ed. *Contributions to the Scientific Study of Jewish Liturgy.* New York: KTAV, 1970. [Ritual/Liturgy/Worship]

Pfeifer, C. J. "Ezekiel and the New Jerusalem." *Bible Today* 18 (1980): 22-27. [Israel/Canaan]

Pfeiffer, R. H. "Cherubim." *JBL* 41 (1922): 249-50. [Tabernacle]

Phillips, C. R. "Julian's Rebuilding of the Temple: A Sociological Study of Religious Competiton." *SBLSP* 17 (1979): 167-72. [Israel/Canaan]

Piankoff, Alexandre. *The Shrines of Tut-Ankh-Amon.* New York: Pantheon Books, 1955. [Egypt]

Pierik, Marie. *The Psalter in the Temple and the Church.* Washington, D.C.: Catholic University of America, 1957. [Israel/Canaan]

Pillet, Maurice. "Les scènes de naissance et de circoncision dans le temple nordest de Mout, a Karnak." *ASAE* 52 (1952): 77-104. [Egypt]

Pillet, Maurice. "Le Temple de Byblos." *Syria* 8 (1927): 105-12. [Israel/Canaan]

Pinches, T. G. "Notes on the Deification of Kings and Ancestor-Worship in Babylonia." *Proceedings of the Society of Biblical Archaeology* 37 (1915): 87-95, 126-34. [Kingship/Coronation]

Pinches, Theophilus G. "Assur and Nineveh." *Records of the Past* 12 (1913): 23-41. [Mesopotamia]

Plöger, O. "Priester und Prophet." *ZAW* 63 (1951): 157-92. [Priesthood]

Plommer, W. "The Temple of Poseidon on Cape Sunium: Some Further Questions." *Annual of the British School at Athens* 55 (1960): 218-33. [Greece/Rome]

Plooij, D. "Jesus and the Temple." *Expository Times* 42 (1930-31): 36-40. [Israel/Canaan]

Pocknee, Cyril E. *The Christian Altar in History and Today.* London: Mowbray, 1963. [Sacrifice/Offerings]

Poels, Henri. *Le sanctuaire de Kirjath-Jearim.* Louvain: Istas, 1894. [Israel/Canaan]

Pohl, A. "Das verschlossene Tor: Ez. 44:1-3." *Biblica* 13 (1932): 90-92, 201. [Israel/Canaan]

Politella, Joseph. "Before Babel: The Puzzle of Ancient Cosmogonies." *Encounter* 29 (Summer 1968): 278-89. [Creation/Cosmology]

Polk, Timothy. "The Levites in the Davidic-Solomonic Empire." *Studia Biblica et Theologica* 9 (1979): 3-22. [Priesthood]

Popper, Julius. *Der biblische Bericht über die Stiftshütte: Ein Beitrag zur Geschichte der Composition und Diaskeue des Pentateuch.* Leipzig: Hunger, 1862. [Tabernacle]

Portaleone, Abraham. *Shilṭe ha-Giborim.* Jerusalem: n.p., 1969/1970. [Israel/Canaan]

Portaleone, Abraham. *Ha-Shir sheba-Mikdash.* Jerusalem: Yefeh-nof, 1964/1965. [Israel/Canaan]

Porten, Bezalel. "The Structure and Orientation of the Jewish Temple at Elephantine—A Revised Plan of the Jewish District." *JAOS* 81 (1961): 38-42. [Israel/Canaan]

Porten, Bezalel. "Temple: Temple of Zerubbabel." In *Encyclopaedia Judaica* 15:955-58. [Israel/Canaan]

Porten, Bezalel, Yehoshua M. Grintz, Michael Avi-Yonah, and Shmuel Safrai. "Temple: Second Temple." In *Encyclopaedia Judaica* 15:955-83. [Israel/Canaan]

Porter, Bertha, and Rosalind L. B. Moss. *Topographical Bibliography of Ancient Egyptian Hieroglyphic Texts, Reliefs, and Paintings,* 2d ed. 7 vols. London: Oxford University Press, 1976-82. [Egypt]

Porter, H. B. "The Origin of the Medieval Rite for Anointing the Sick or Dying." *JTS* 7 (1956): 211-25. [Ablutions/Anointings]

Porter, Joshua R. "Ark." In *Harper's Dictionary of the Bible*, 63-64. [Tabernacle]

Porter, Joshua R. "Levites." In *Harper's Bible Dictionary*, 557-58. [Priesthood]

Porter, Joshua R. "Tabernacle." In *Harper's Dictionary of the Bible*, 1013-14. [Tabernacle]

Posener-Kriéger, Paule. *Les archives du temple funéraire de Néferirkarê-Kakäi.* Cairo: Imprimerie de l'Institut français d'archéologie orientale du Caire, 1976. [Egypt]

Posener-Kriéger, Paule. "Les papyrus d'Abousir et l'économie des temple funéraires de l'Ancien Empire." In *State and Temple Economy in the Ancient Near East*, edited by Edward Lipiński. 2 vols., 1:133-52. Louvain: Departement Orientalistiek, 1979. [Egypt]

Postgate, J. N. "The *bit akiti* in Assyrian Nabu Temples." *Sumer* 30 (1974): 51-74. [Mesopotamia]

Postgate, J. N. "The Role of the Temple in the Mesopotamian Secular Community." In *Man, Settlement and Urbanism*, edited by Peter J. Ucko. 811-25. Cambridge: Schenkman, 1972. [Mesopotamia]

Potin, J. "Le Temple." *Bible et Terre Sainte* 20 (1959): 8-14. [Israel/Canaan]

Poulssen, Niek. *König und Tempel im Glaubenszeugnis des Alten Testamentes.* Stuttgart: Katholisches Bibelwerk, 1967. [Kingship/Coronation]

Poulssen, Niek. "Rex et templum in Israël." *Verbum Domini* 40 (1962): 264-69. [Kingship/Coronation]

Powell, B. "The Temple of Apollo at Corinth." *AJA* 9 (1905): 44-63. [Greece/Rome]

Power, David, ed. *Liturgy and Human Passage.* New York: Seabury, 1979. [Ritual/Liturgy/Worship]

Powers, J. M., and E. Kilmartin "Liturgical Theology." *Worship* 50 (July 1976): 307-15. [Ritual/Liturgy/Worship]

Poznanski, L. "À propos de la collation du nom dans le monde antique." *RHR* 194 (October 1978): 113-27. [Ritual/Liturgy/Worship]

Pratt, Richard L. "Royal Prayer and the Chronicler's Program." Th.D. diss., Harvard University, 1987. [Israel/Canaan]

Prenter, Regin. "Worship and Creation." *Studia Liturgica* 2 (June 1963): 82-95. [Creation/Cosmology]

Prescott, J. E. "On the Gate Beautiful of the Temple." *Journal of Sacred Literature* 5 ser. 2/3 (1867): 33-45. [Israel/Canaan]

Prestel, Jakob. *Die Baugeschichte des jüdischen Heiligthums und der Tempel Salomons.* Strassburg: Heitz, 1902. [Israel/Canaan]

Prince, J. Dyneley. "A Study of the Assyro-Babylonian Words Relating to Sacrifice." *JBL* (1907): 54-61. [Sacrifice/Offerings]

Proby, W. H. B. "Construction of the Tabernacle." *PEFQ* 28 (1896): 223-24. [Tabernacle]

Pronobis, C. "Der Tempel zu Jerusalem: Seine Masse und genaue Lage." *Das heilige Land* 70 (1926): 197-211; 71 (1927): 8-32. [Israel/Canaan]

Pummer, Reinhard. "Untersuchungen zur Omphalos-Vorstellung im alten Testament und im alten Orient." Ph.D. diss., Universität-Wien, Katholische Theologische Fakultät, 1974. [Sacred Space]

Qimron, Elisha. "Column 14 of the *Temple Scroll*" (in Hebrew). *IEJ* 38/1-2 (1988): 44-46. [Israel/Canaan]

Qimron, Elisha. "Further New Readings in the Temple Scroll." *IEJ* 37 (1987): 31-35. [Israel/Canaan]

Qimron, Elisha. "New Readings in the Temple Scroll." *IEJ* 28 (1978): 161-72. [Israel/Canaan]

Qimron, Elisha. "Three Notes on the Text of the Temple Scroll" (in Hebrew; *English summary) *Tarbiz* 51 (1981): 135-37, *IX. [Israel/Canaan]

Quibell, James E. *Hierakonpolis.* London: Quaritch, 1900-1902. [Greece/Rome]

Quintens, W. "La vie du roi dans le Psaume 21." *Biblica* 59 (1978): 516-41. [Kingship/Coronation]

Rabe, Virgil W. "The Identity of the Priestly Tabernacle." *JNES* 25 (1966): 132-34. [Tabernacle]

Rabe, Virgil W. "Israelite Opposition to the Temple." *CBQ* 29 (April 1967): 228-33. [Israel/Canaan]

Rabe, Virgil W. "The Temple as Tabernacle." Ph.D. diss., Harvard University, 1963. [Tabernacle]

Rabello, A. M. "The 'Lex de Templo Hierosolymitano' Prohibiting Gentiles from Entering Jerusalem's Sanctuary." *Christian News from Israel* 21/3 (1970): 28-32; 21/4 (1970): 28-32. [Israel/Canaan]

Rabina, M. "Music in the Temple" (in Hebrew). *Maḥanayim* 96 (1965): 44-49. [Israel/Canaan]

Rabinowitz, Louis I. "Anointing." In *Encyclopedia Judaica* 3:27-31. [Ablutions/Anointings]

Rad, Gerhard von. "Erwägungen zu den Königspsalmen." *ZAW* 57 (1940-41): 216-22. [Kingship/Coronation]

Rad, Gerhard von. "Das judäische Königsritual." *Theologische Literaturzeitung* 72 (1947): 211-18; also in English as "The Royal Ritual in Judah." In von Rad, *The Problem of the Hexateuch and Other Essays.* 222-31. New York: McGraw-Hill, 1966. [Kingship/Coronation]

Rad, Gerhard von. "The Tent, the Ark, and the Glory of God." In Rad, *Old Testament Theology.* 2 vols., 1:234-41. New York: Harper 1962-65. [Tabernacle]

Rad, Gerhard von. "Zelt und Lade." *Kirchliche Zeitschrift* 42 (1931): 476-98. [Tabernacle]

Radius, Marianne C. V. *The Tent of God: A Journey through the Old Testament.* Grand Rapids: Eerdmans, 1968. [Tabernacle]

Raglan, Fitzroy R. S. *The Temple and the House.* New York: Norton, 1964. [Sacred Space]

Rainey, A. F. "The Order of Sacrifices in Old Testament Ritual Texts." *Biblica* 51 (1970): 485-98. [Sacrifice/Offerings]

Ramaroson, L. "Contre les 'temples faits de mains d'homme.' " *Revue de Philosophie, Literature, et d'Histoire* 3/43 (1969): 217-38. [Israel/Canaan]

Randall-MacIver, David, and A. C. Mace. *El Amrah and Abydos, 1899-1901.* London: Egypt Exploration Fund, 1902. [Egypt]

Randellini, L. "La tenda e l'arca nella tradizione del Vecchio Testamento." *Liber Annuus* 13 (1962-63): 163-89. [Tabernacle]

Ratcliff, Edward C. *The English Coronation Service, Being the Coronation Service of King George V and Queen Mary, with Historical Introduction and Notes, Together with Extracts from Liber Regalis, Accounts of Coronations, etc.* London: Skeffington & Son, 1937. [Kingship/Coronation]

Rattray, Susan. "Worship." In *Harper's Bible Dictionary*, 1143-47. [Ritual/Liturgy/Worship]

Rawlinson, A. E. J. "Priesthood and Sacrifice in Judaism and Christianity." *ET* 60 (1949): 116-21. [Priesthood]

Redisch, Heinrich. "Der *bit hillani* und seine Verwendung bei den salomonischen Bauten." In *Festschrift Adolf Schwarz zum siebzigsten Geburtstage.* 13-27. Berlin: Löwit, 1917. [Israel/Canaan]

Reed, William L. "Mount, Mountain." In *The Interpreter's Dictionary of the Bible* 3:452. [Mountain]

Reeves, John C. "What Does Noah Offer in 1QapGen X, 15?" *Revue de Qumran* 12 (December 1986): 415-19. [Sacrifice/Offerings]

Rehm, Merlin D. "Zadok the Priest." In *The Interpreter's Dictionary of the Bible*, supp. vol., 976-77. [Priesthood]

Reichel, Wolfgang. *Über vorhellenische Götterculte.* Vienna: Hölder, 1897. [Greece/Rome]

Reicke, Bo. "The Knowledge Hidden in the Tree of Paradise." *Journal of Semitic Studies* 1 (July 1956): 193-201. [Israel/Canaan]

Reicke, Bo. "Stiftshütte." In *Biblisch-Historisches Handwörterbuch*, edited by Bo Reicke and Leonhard Rost. 4 vols., 3:1871-75. Göttingen: Vandenhoeck and Ruprecht, 1966. [Tabernacle]

Reik, Theodor. *Mystery on the Mountain: The Drama of the Sinai Revelation.* New York: Harper and Row, 1959. [Ritual/Liturgy/Worship]

Reimpell, W. "Der Ursprung der Lade Jahwes." *Orientalistische Literaturzeitung* 19 (1916): 326-31. [Tabernacle]

Reinach, S. "L'Arc de Titus." *REJ* 20 (1890): lxv-xci. [Israel/Canaan]

Reinach, S. "Les sacrifices d'animaux dans l'église chrétienne." *Anthropologie* 14 (1903): 59-62. [Sacrifice/Offerings]

Reines, Chaim W. *Kohanim u-Nevi'im*. New York: n.p., 1945. [Priesthood]

Reisner, George A. *The Barkal Temples*. Boston: Museum of Fine Arts, 1970. [Egypt]

Reisner, George A. "The Barkal Temples in 1916." *JEA* 4 (1917): 213-27; 5 (1918): 99-112; 6 (1920): 247-64. [Egypt]

Reisner, George A. *Mycerinus. The Temples of the Third Pyramid at Giza*. Cambridge: Harvard University Press, 1931. [Egypt]

Rendtorff, Rolf. *Studien zur Geschichte des Opfers im alten Israel*. Neukirchen-Vluyn: Neukirchener, 1967. [Sacrifice/Offerings]

Renger, J. "Interaction of Temple, Palace, and 'Private Enterprise' in the Old Babylonian Economy." In *State and Temple Economy in the Ancient Near East*, edited by Edward Lipiński. 2 vols., 1:249-56. Louvain: Departement Orientalistiek, 1979. [Mesopotamia]

Rengstorf, K. H. "Erwägungen zur Frage des Landbesitzes des zweiten Tempels in Judaea und seiner Verwaltung." In *Bible and Qumran (Festschrift Hans Bardtke)*, edited by S. Wagner. 156-76. Berlin: Evangelische Haupt-Bibelgesellschaft, 1968. [Israel/Canaan]

Rengstorf, K. H. "Old and New Testament Traces of a Formula of the Judean Royal Ritual." *NT* 5 (November 1962): 229-44. [Kingship/Coronation]

Renov, I. "A View of Herod's Temple from Nicanor's Gate in a Mural Panel of the Dura-Europos Synagogue." *IEJ* 20 (1970): 67-72. [Israel/Canaan]

Renwick, David A. "Paul the Temple, and the Presence of God." Ph.D. diss. Union Theological Seminary in Virginia, 1988. [Israel/Canaan]

Reumann, John H. P. "Oikonomia='Covenant': Terms for Heilsgeschichte in Early Christain Usage." *NT* 3 (1959): 282-92. [Covenant]

Reuther, Oskar. *Der Heratempel von Samos: Der Bau seit der Zeit des Polykrates*. Berlin: Mann, 1957. [Greece/Rome]

Reymond, Eve A. "The Children of Tanen." *ZÄS* 96 (1969): 36-44. [Egypt]

Reymond, Eve A. *The Mythical Origin of the Egyptian Temple*. New York: Barnes and Noble, 1969. [Egypt]

Reymond, Eve A. E. "Worship of the Ancestor Gods at Edfu." *Chronique d'Égypte* 38 (1963): 49-70. [Ritual/Liturgy/Worship]

Reynès-Monlaur, M. "Les vendeurs du Temple." In *Jérusalem*. 170-79. Paris: Plon, 1911. [Israel/Canaan]

Rhodes, Robin F. "Early Corinthian Architecture and the Origins of the Doric Order." *AJA* 91 (July 1987): 477-80. [Greece/Rome]

Ricchi, Immanuel H. *Ma'aseh Ḥoshev: 'Al Mel'ekhet ha-Mishkan.* Przemysl: Amkraut, 1883. [Tabernacle]

Rice, George E. "Hebrews 6:19: Analysis of Some Assumptions concerning *Katapetasma.*" *Andrews University Seminary Studies* 25 (Spring 1987): 65-71. [Tabernacle]

Richard, Heinrich. *Vom Ursprung des dorischen Tempels.* Bonn: Habelt, 1970. [Greece/Rome]

Richardson, P. "Barnabas, Nerva, and the Yavnean Rabbis." *JTS* 34 (April 1983): 31-55. [Israel/Canaan]

Richardson, P., and M. Shukster. "Religion, Architecture and Ethics: Some First Century Case Studies." *Horizons in Biblical Theology: An International Dialogue* 10 (1988): 19-49. [Israel/Canaan]

Richter, G. "Die Kesselwagen des salomonischen Tempels." *ZDPV* 41 (1918): 1-34. [Israel/Canaan]

Ricke, Herbert. *Der Harmachistempel des Chefren in Giseh.* Wiesbaden: Steiner, 1970. [Egypt]

Ricke, Herbert. *Die Tempel Nektanebos' II in Elephantine und ihre Erweiterungen. Beiträge zur ägyptischen Bauforschung* 6 (1960). [Israel/Canaan]

Ricke, Herbert, G. R. Hughes, and E. F. Wente. *The Beit el-Wali Temple of Ramses II.* Chicago: University of Chicago Press, 1967. [Egypt]

Ridderbos, J. "Jahwäh malak." *VT* 4 (1954): 87-89. [Kingship/Coronation]

Ridderbos, N. H. *Psalmen en Cultus.* Kampen: Kok, 1950. [Ritual/Liturgy/Worship]

Ridges, W. B. "On the Structure of the Tabernacle." *PEFQ* 28 (1896): 189. [Tabernacle]

Ridout, Samuel. *Lectures on the Tabernacle.* New York: Loizeaux, 1952. [Tabernacle]

Riemann, Hans. "Zum griechischen Peripteraltempel; Seine Planidee und ihre Entwicklung bis zum Ende des 5. Jahrhunderts." Ph.D. diss., University of Frankfurt, 1935. [Greece/Rome]

Rigby, P. "A Structural Analysis of Israelite Sacrifice and Its Other Institutions." *Église et Théologie* 11 (October 1980): 229-351. [Covenant]

Rigsby, Kent J. "Megara and Tripodiscus." *Greek, Roman, and Byzantine Studies* 28 (Spring 1987): 93-102. [Greece/Rome]

Riis, Poul J. *Soukas I, The North East Sanctuary.* Copenhagen: Munksgaard, 1970. [Israel/Canaan]

Riley, W. "Temple Imagery and the Book of Revelation: Ancient Near Eastern Temple Ideology and Cultic Resonances in the Apocalypse." *Proceedings of the Irish Biblical Association* 6 (1982): 81-102. [Israel/Canaan]

Ringgren, Helmer. *Sacrifice in the Bible.* London: Lutterworth, 1962. [Sacrifice/Offerings]

Risikoff, Menachem. *Collection of Laws concerning the Priesthood, the Temple and Sacrifices* (in Hebrew). New York: n.p., 1948. [Priesthood]

Ritchie, John. *The Tabernacle in the Wilderness.* Grand Rapids: Kregal, 1982. [Tabernacle]

Ritmeyer, K., and L. Ritmeyer. "Herod's Temple Mount—Stone by Stone." *BAR* 15/6 (1989): 23-53. [Israel/Canaan]

Robertson, Donald. *A Handbook of Greek and Roman Architecture.* Cambridge: Cambridge University Press, 1959. [Greece/Rome]

Robertson, E. "The Altar of Earth (Exodus 20:24-26)." *JJS* 1 (1948): 12-21. [Sacrifice/Offerings]

Robertson, N. "The Ritual Background of the Dying God in Cyprus and Syro-Palestine." *Harvard Theological Review* 75 (July 1982): 313-59. [Ritual/Liturgy/Worship]

Robins, Edward D. *The Temple of Solomon.* London: Whittaker, 1887. [Israel/Canaan]

Robinson, H. W. "Hebrew Sacrifice and Prophetic Symbolism." *JTS* 43 (1942): 129-39. [Sacrifice/Offerings]

Roche de Coppens, Peter. *The Nature and Use of Ritual for Spiritual Attainment.* St. Paul: Llewellyn, 1985. [Ritual/Liturgy/Worship]

Rodd, C. S. "Kingship and the Cult." *London Quarterly Historical Review* 185 (January 1959): 21-26. [Kingship/Coronation]

Rodenwalt, Gerhart. *Die Bildwerke des Artemistempels.* Berlin: n.p., 1949. [Greece/Rome]

Rodenwaldt, Gerhart. *Griechische Tempel.* Munich: Deutscher Kunstverlag, 1951. [Greece/Rome]

Rodwell, Warwick, ed. *Temples, Churches, and Religion.* Oxford: BAR, 1980. [Greece/Rome]

Roehrs, W. R. "Covenant and Justification in the Old Testament." *Concordia Historical Institute Quarterly* 35 (October 1964): 583-602. [Covenant]

Rofé, Yosef. "The Site of Our Holy Temple—the Location of the Temple at the Southern End of the Temple Mount" (in Hebrew; *English summary). *Niv ha-Midrashiyah* 13 (1978-79): 166-86, *105-13. [Mountain]

Rokéah, D. "The Temple Scroll, Philo, Josephus, and the Talmud." *JTS* 34 (1983): 515-26. [Israel/Canaan]

Rolfe, Clapton C. *The Ancient Use of Liturgical Colours.* Oxford: Parker, 1879. [Sacred Vestments]

Romanoff, P. *Forms and Symbols in the Architecture of the Temple,* 1-14, 67-82, 133-58. New York: n.p., 1936. [Israel/Canaan]

Rops, D. "Les demeures de Dieu." In *La vie quotidienne en Palestine au temps de Jésus*. 436-55. Paris: Hachette, 1961. [Israel/Canaan]

Roscher, Wilhelm H. *Omphalos: Eine philologisch-archäologisch-volkskundliche Abhandlung über die Vorstellungen der Griechen und anderer Völker vom 'Nabel der Erde.'* In *Abhandlungen der philologisch-historischen Klasse der Königlichen sächsischen Gesellschaft der Wissenschaften* 29/9 (1913); also reprinted in Roscher, *Omphalos*. Hildesheim: Olms, 1974. [Sacred Space]

Roscher, Wilhelm H. *Der Omphalosgedanke bei verschiedenen Völkern, besonders den semitischen.* In *Berichte über die Verhandlungen der Sächsischen Gesellschaft der Wissenschaften zu Leipzig. Philologisch-historische Klasse* 70/2 (1918); also reprinted in Roscher, *Omphalos*. Hildesheim: Olms, 1974. [Sacred Space]

Rosen, Debra, and Alison Salvesen. "A Note on the Qumran Temple Scroll 56:15-18 and Psalm of Solomon 17:33." *JJS* 38 (Spring 1987): 99-101. [Israel/Canaan]

Rosen, Georg. *Das Haram von Jerusalem und der Tempelplatz des Moria. Eine Untersuchung über die Identität beider Stätten*. Gotha: Besser, 1866. [Israel/Canaan]

Rosenau, Helen. "The Architecture of N. Lyra's Temple Illustrations and the Jewish Traditions." *JJS* 25 (1974): 294-304. [Israel/Canaan]

Rosenau, Helen. "Jacob Judah Leon Templo's Contribution to Architectural Imagery." *JJS* 23 (1972): 72-81. [Israel/Canaan]

Rosenau, Helen. "Some Aspects of the Pictorial Influence of the Jewish Temple." *PEFQ* 68 (1936): 157-62. [Israel/Canaan]

Rosenau, Helen. "The Synagogue and the Diaspora." *PEQ* 69 (1937): 196-202. [Israel/Canaan]

Rosenau, Helen. *Vision of the Temple*. London: Oresko Books, 1979. [Israel/Canaan]

Rosenau, W. "Harel und Ha-Ariel: Ezechiel 43:15-16." *MGWJ* 65 (1921): 350-56. [Israel/Canaan]

Ross, Theodore S. "The Attitude of the Rabbis toward the Destruction of the Second Temple." Ph.D. diss., Hebrew Union College, 1949. [Israel/Canaan]

Rost, Leonhard. "Erwägungen zum israelitischen Brandopfer." In *Von Ugarit nach Qumran: Beiträge zur alttestamentlichen und altorientalischen Forschung: Otto Eissfeldt zum 1. September 1957 dargebracht von Freunden und Schulern*, edited by Johannes Hempel et al. 177-83. Berlin: Töpelmann, 1967. [Sacrifice/Offerings]

Rost, Leonhard. *Studien zum Opfer im alten Israel*. Stuttgart: Kohlhammer, 1981. [Sacrifice/Offerings]

Rost, Leonhard. "Die Wohnstätte des Zeugnisses." In *Festschrift F. Baumgärtel, Erlanger Forschungen, Reihe A: Geisteswissenshaften, 10*, edited by J. Hermann, 158-65. Erlangen: n.p., 1959. [Tabernacle]

Rost, P. "Der Altar Ezechiels, Kap. 43:13-17." In *Altorientalische Studien* (Festschrift Bruno Meissner). 170-74. Leipzig: Harrassowitz, 1928-29. [Israel/Canaan]

Roth, Cecil. "Cleansing of the Temple and Zechariah 14:21." *NT* 4 (1960): 174-81. [Israel/Canaan]

Roth, Cecil. "The Debate on the Royal Sacrifices, A.D. 66." *Harvard Theological Review* 53 (1960): 93-97. [Sacrifice/Offerings]

Rothkoff, Aaron. "Sacrifice." In *Encylopaedia Judaica* 14:599-615. [Sacrifice/Offerings]

Rothkoff, Aaron. "Sacrifice: Second Temple Period." In *Encyclopaedia Judaica* 14:607-12. [Sacrifice/Offerings]

Roulin, Eugène A. *Vestments and Vesture: A Manual of Liturgical Art*, translated by Dom J. McCann. Westminster, MD: Newman, 1950. [Sacred Vestments]

Rowe, Allan. *The Four Canaanite Temples of Bethshan*, vol. 1. Philadelphia: University Press for the University of Pennsylvania Museum, 1940. [Israel/Canaan]

Rowley, Harold H. "Hezekiah's Reform and Rebellion." *BJRL* 44 (1961-62): 395-431; and also in Rowley, *Men of God: Studies in Old Testament History and Prophecy.* 98-132. London: Nelson, 1963. [Israel/Canaan]

Rowley, Harold H. "The Meaning of Sacrifice in the Old Testament." *BJRL* 33 (February 1950): 74-110. [Sacrifice/Offerings]

Rowley, Harold H. "Melchizedek and Zadok (Gen 14 and Ps 110)." In *Festschrift Alfred Bertholet zum 80. Geburtstag gewidmet von Kollegen und Freunden*, edited by Walter Baumgartner et al., 461-72. Tübingen: Mohr, 1950. [Priesthood]

Rowley, Harold H. "Ritual and the Hebrew Prophets." *Journal of Semitic Studies* 1 (1956): 338-60. [Ritual/Liturgy/Worship]

Rowley, Harold H. "Sanballat and the Samaritan Temple." *BJRL* 38 (1955-56): 166-98. [Israel/Canaan]

Rowley, Harold H. *Worship in Ancient Israel.* Philadelphia: Fortress, 1967. [Ritual/Liturgy/Worship]

Rowley, Harold H. "Zadok and Nehushtan." *JBL* 58 (1939): 113-41. [Priesthood]

Rowton, M. B. "The Date of the Founding of Solomon's Temple." *BASOR* 119 (1950): 20-22. [Israel/Canaan]

Rubenstein, Shmuel L. *The Service in the Beis HaMikdosh.* New York: Rubenstein, 1975. [Ritual/Liturgy/Worship]

Ruffini, Ernesto. "Il tempio di Gerusalemme." In Ruffini, *Conferenze bibliche.* 138-57. Rome: Libreria editrice Ancora, 1966. [Israel/Canaan]

Rüger, H. P. "Tempel." In *Biblisch-historisches Handwörterbuch*, edited by Bo Reicke and L. Rost. 3:1940-47. Göttingen: Vandenhoeck and Ruprecht, 1966. [Israel/Canaan]

Ruggieri Tricoli, Maria C. *Acropoli e Mito*. Palermo: Flaccovio, 1979. [Greece/Rome]

Runnalls, Donna. "The King as Temple Builder: A Messianic Typology." In *Spirit within Structure: Essays in Honor of George Johnston*, edited by E. J. Furcha. 15-37. Allison Park, PA: Pickwick, 1983. [Kingship/Coronation]

Rupprecht, Konrad. "Nachrichten von Erweiterung und Renovierung des Tempels in 1 Könige 6." *ZDPV* 88 (1972): 38-52. [Israel/Canaan]

Rupprecht, Konrad. *Der Tempel von Jerusalem: Gründung Salomos oder jebusitisches Erbe*. Berlin: de Gruyter, 1976. [Israel/Canaan]

Rupprecht, Konrad. "Die Zuverlässigkeit der Überlieferung von Salomos Tempelgründung." *ZAW* 89 (1977): 205-14. [Israel/Canaan]

Rutschmann, LaVerne A. "Altar and Sacrifice in the Old Testament Nomadic Period with Relation to Sacred Space and Sacred Time." Ph.D. diss., Southern California School of Theology at Claremont, 1962. [Sacrifice/Offerings]

Sabourin, Léopold. "Liturgie du Sanctuaire et de la Tente Véritable (Heb. viii, 2)." *NTS* 18 (1971-72): 87-90. [Ritual/Liturgy/Worship]

Sabourin, Léopold. "Novum Templum." *Verbum Domini* 47 (1969): 65-82. [Israel/Canaan]

Sabourin, Léopold. "Sacrificium ut liturgia in Epistula ad Hebraeos." *Verbum Domini* 46 (1968): 235-58. [Ritual/Liturgy/Worship]

Sabourin, Léopold. "The Temple and the Cult in Late Judaism." *Religious Studies Bulletin* 1 (1981): 33-37. [Israel/Canaan]

Safrai, Shmuel. "Contribution to the History of Ritual in the Second Temple" (in Hebrew). In *Yerushalayim*. 2 vols., 2:5:35-41. Jerusalem: Rabbi Kook Foundation, 1955. [Israel/Canaan]

Safrai, Shmuel. "The Divine Service in the Temple on the Day of Atonement" (in Hebrew). *Mahanayim* 49 (1961): 122-25. [Israel/Canaan]

Safrai, Shmuel. "The Duty of Pilgrimage to Jerusalem and Its Performance during the Period of the Second Temple" (in Hebrew). *Zion* 25 (1960): 67-84. [Ritual/Liturgy/Worship]

Safrai, Shmuel. "The Festival of Pentecost in the Time of the Second Temple" (in Hebrew). In *The Book of Festivals*, edited by Z. Ariel. 313-15. Tel-Aviv: Am Oved, 1967. [Israel/Canaan]

Safrai, Shmuel. "The Heavenly Jerusalem." *Ariel* 23 (1969): 11-16. [Israel/Canaan]

Safrai, Shmuel. "Jews of Eretz-Israel during the Second Commonwealth and the Talmudic Period." In *History of Eretz-Israel from Prehistory up to 1882*, edited by Joel Rappel. 291-304. Tel-Avi: Ministry of Defence, 1980. [Israel/Canaan]

Safrai, Shmuel. *Ha-Mikdash bi-Tekufat ha-Bayit ha-Sheni.* Jerusalem: ha-Sokhut ha-Yehudit, 1958/1959. [Israel/Canaan]

Safrai, Shmuel. "Pilgrimage to Jerusalem at the End of the Second Temple Period." In *Studies on the Jewish Background of the New Testament.* 12-21. Assen: van Gorcum, 1969. [Ritual/Liturgy/Worship]

Safrai, Shmuel. "Pilgrimage, Second Temple Period." In *Encyclopaedia Judaica* 13:510-14. [Ritual/Liturgy/Worship]

Safrai, Shmuel. "Pilgrimage to the Temple at the Time of the Second Temple." *Emmanuel: Bulletin of Religious Thought and Research in Israel* 5 (1975): 51-62. [Ritual/Liturgy/Worship]

Safrai, Shmuel. *Pilgrimages during the Second Temple Period* (in Hebrew). Jerusalem: Hebrew University, 1958. [Ritual/Liturgy/Worship]

Safrai, Shmuel. "Pilgrims in Jerusalem in Second Temple Times" (in Hebrew). In *Jerusalem—the Holy City and the Temple.* 98-110. Jerusalem: Mossad Harav Kook and Jerusalem Municipality, 1977. [Ritual/Liturgy/Worship]

Safrai, Shmuel. *Pilgrims to Jerusalem during the Time of the Second Temple* (in Hebrew). Jerusalem: Ministry of Education and Culture, 1976. [Ritual/Liturgy/Worship]

Safrai, Shmuel. "The Ritual in the Second Temple." In *Sefer Yerushalayim,* edited by Michael Avi-Yonah. 369-91. Jerusalem and Tel-Aviv: Bialik Institute, 1956. [Ritual/Liturgy/Worship]

Safrai, Shmuel. "Die Stellung des Zweiten Tempels des Volkes." *Freiburger Rundbrief* 28/105-8 (1976): 158-65. [Israel/Canaan]

Safrai, Shmuel. "Das Synhedrion in der Zeit des zweiten Tempels." In *Das jüdische Volk im Zeitalter des zweiten Tempels.* 67-72. Neukirchen-Vluyn: Neukirchener, 1978. [Israel/Canaan]

Safrai, Shmuel. "Der Tempel." In *Das jüdische Volk im Zeitalter des zweiten Tempels.* 56-60. Neukirchen-Vluyn: Neukirchener, 1978. [Israel/Canaan]

Safrai, Shmuel. "The Temple." In *The Jewish People in the First Century* 2, edited by Shmuel Safrai and Michael Stern. 865-907. Assen: van Gorcum, 1976. [Israel/Canaan]

Safrai, Shmuel. "The Temple and the Divine Service." In *The World History of the Jewish People, 7: The Herodian Period,* edited by Michael Avi-Yonah. 282-337. Jerusalem: Massada, 1975. [Israel/Canaan]

Safrai, Shmuel. *Wallfahrt im Zeitalter des zweiten Tempels.* Neukirchen-Vluyn: Neukirchener, 1981. [Ritual/Liturgy/Worship]

Safrai, Shmuel. "Was There a Women's Gallery in the Synagogue of Antiquity?" (in Hebrew). *Tarbiz* 32 (1963): 329-38. [Israel/Canaan]

Saldarini, A. J. "Varieties of Rabbinic Response to the Destruction of the Temple." *SBLSP* 21 (1982): 437-58. [Israel/Canaan]

Salditt-Trappmann, Regina. *Tempel der ägyptischen Götter in Griechenland und an der Westküste Kleinasiens.* Leiden: Brill, 1970. [Greece/Rome]

Saleh, A. A. "The So-Called 'Primeval Hill' and Other Related Elevations in Ancient Egyptian Mythology." *MDAI.K* 25 (1969): 110-20. [Egypt]

Saleh, Janine M. "Les représentations de temples sur plates-formes à pieux, de la poterie gerzéenne d'Égypte." *BIFAO* 83 (1983): 263-96. [Egypt]

Salihi, W. "The Shrine of Nebo at Hatra." *British School of Archaeology in Iraq* 45 (1983): 140-45. [Mesopotamia]

Saller, S. J. "Sacred Places and Objects of Ancient Palestine." *Liber Annuus* 14 (1963-64): 161-228. [Israel/Canaan]

Salvini, M. "Das *Susi*-Heiligtum vom Kamir-Blur und der Urartäische Turmtempel." *Archaeologische Mitteilungen aus Iran* 12 (1979): 249-69. [Mesopotamia]

Salzberger, Georg. *Salomos Tempelbau und Thron in der semitischen Sagenliteratur.* Berlin: Mayer and Müller, 1912. [Israel/Canaan]

Sarno, R. A. "Rebuilding the Temple." *The Bible Today* 45 (1969): 2799-804. [Israel/Canaan]

Sauer, Frank. *Die Tempeltheologie des Propheten Haggai.* Freiburg: Sauer, 1977. [Israel/Canaan]

Sauneron, Serge. *Edfou et Philae.* Paris: Chene, 1975. [Egypt]

Sauneron, Serge. *Die letzten Tempel Ägyptens.* Zurich: Atlantis, 1978. [Egypt]

Sauneron, Serge. *The Priests of Ancient Egypt.* New York: Grove, 1960. [Priesthood]

Savignac, R., and G. Horsfield. "Le Temple de Ramm." *RB* 44 (1935): 245-78. [Israel/Canaan]

Sawyer, J. F. A. "The Temple at Jerusalem." In *From Moses to Patmos: New Perspectives in Old Testament Study.* 57-71. London: SPCK, 1977. [Israel/Canaan]

Saydon, P. P. "Sin-Offering and Trepass-Offering." *CBQ* 8 (1946): 393-98. [Sacrifice/Offerings]

Scenes and Inscriptions in the Court and the First Hypostyle Hall, vol. 1; *Temple of Khonsu—The Epigraphic Survey,* vol. 2. Chicago: Oriental Institute of the University of Chicago, 1979-81. [Egypt]

Schaber, Wilfried. *Die archäischen Tempel der Artemis von Ephesos.* Waldsassen-Bayern: Stiftland-verlag, 1982. [Greece/Rome]

Schächter, J. "The Temple Site" (in Hebrew). In *Jerusalem Through the Ages—Two Chapters of Bibliography.* 21-98. Jerusalem: Yad Izhak Ben Zvi Publications, 1975. [Israel/Canaan]

Schäfer, P. "Tempel und Schöpfung: Zur Interpretation einiger Heiligtums-traditionen in der rabbinischen Literatur." In Schäfer, *Studien zur*

Geschichte und Theologie des rabbinischen Judentums. 122-33. Leiden: Brill, 1978. [Israel/Canaan]

Schaffer, Shaul. *Bet ha-Mikdash*. Jerusalem: Yefeh-nof, 1968/1969. [Israel/Canaan]

Schaffer, Shaul. *Har ha-Bayit*. Jerusalem: Yefer-nof, 1968/1969. [Israel/Canaan]

Schaffer (Shefer), Shaúl. *Ha-Mikdash ha-Shelishi*. Jerusalem: Yefeh-nof, 1963/64. [Israel/Canaan]

Schaffer (Shafer), Shaul. *Ha-Mishkan ve-Khelav*. Jerusalem: Yeteh-nof, 1964/1965. [Tabernacle]

Schaffer, Shaul. *Israel's Temple Mount: The Jews Magnificent Sanctuary—an Illustrated Compendium on the Holy Temples*. Jerusalem: Achva, 1975. [Israel/Canaan]

Schaffer, Shaul. *The Music of the Temple* (in Hebrew). Jerusalem: Yefeh-Nof, 1965. [Israel/Canaan]

Schaya, L. "The Meaning of the Temple." *Studies in Comparative Religion* 5 (1971): 241-46. [Israel/Canaan]

Schemel, Siegfried. *Die Kleidung der Juden im Zeitalter der Mischnah, nebst einem Anhange: Die Priesterkleidung*. Berlin: Itzkowski, 1912. [Sacred Vestments]

Scheneker, Adrien. "*Kōper et expiation*." *Biblica* 63 (1982): 32-46 [Sacrifice/ Offerings]

Schepansky, I. "The Site of the Temple and its Sanctity" (in Hebrew). In Schepansky, *Eretz-Israel in the Responsa Literature*, vol. 1, 425-33. Jerusalem: Mosad Harav Kook, 1966. [Israel/Canaan]

Schick, Conrad. "Ausdehnung der Stadt Jerusalem und ihre Einwohnerzahl zur Zeit des 2. Tempels." *Jerusalem* 1 (1881): 83-103. [Israel/Canaan]

Schick, Conrad. *Beit El Makdas*. Jerusalem: Syrisches Waisenhaus, 1887. [Israel/Canaan]

Schick, Conrad. "Some Remarks on the Tabernacle Controversy." *PEFQ* 30 (1898): 241-44. [Tabernacle]

Schick, Conrad. *Die Stiftshütte, der Tempel in Jerusalem und der Tempelplatz der Jetztzeit*. Berlin: Weidmannsche Buchhandlung, 1896. [Israel/Canaan]

Schiffman, Lawrence H. "Priests." In *Harper's Bible Dictionary*, 821-23. [Priesthood]

Schiller, E. "The Stone of Foundation." In *The Dome of the Rock and the Stone of Foundation*. 46-54. Jerusalem: Ariel, 1976. [Israel/Canaan]

Schlatter, A. "Die Bauten am Tempel in der griechischen Zeit. In *Zur Topographie und Geschichte Palästinas*. 188-202. Stuttgart: Calwer, 1893. [Greece/Rome]

Schleif, Hans. *Der Artemistempel*. Berlin: Mann, 1940. [Greece/Rome]

Schmandt-Besserat, D. "Biblical Archaeologist's Guide to Artifacts: Tokens and Counting." *BA* 46 (1983): 117-20. [Israel/Canaan]

Schmid, H. "Der Tempelbau Salomos in religionsgeschichtlicher Sicht." In *Archäologie und altes Testament: Festschrift für Kurt Galling*, edited by Arnulf Kuschke and Ernst Kutsch. 241-50. Tübingen: Mohr, 1970. [Israel/Canaan]

Schmid, Rudolph. *Das Bundesopfer in Israel*. Munich: Koesel, 1964. [Sacrifice/Offerings]

Schmidt, Emanuel. "Solomon's Temple." *Biblical World* 14 (1899): 164-71. [Israel/Canaan]

Schmidt, Emanuel. *Solomon's Temple in the Light of Other Oriental Temples*. Chicago: Univeristy of Chicago Press, 1902. [Israel/Canaan]

Schmidt, H. "Kerubenthron und Lade." In *Eucharisterion für H. Gunkel*, edited by H. Schmidt. 120-44. Göttingen: Vandenhoeck and Ruprecht, 1923. [Tabernacle]

Schmidt, H. "Die Tempelrolle vom Toten Meer." *Judaica* 34/4 (1978): 187-88. [Israel/Canaan]

Schmidt, Hans. "Der Fels im Tempel des Herodes." In Schmidt, *Der heilige Fels in Jerusalem—eine archäologische und religionsgeschichtliche Studie*. 17-39. Tübingen: Mohr, 1933. [Israel/Canaan]

Schmidt, Martin. *Prophet und Tempel*. Zurich: Evangelischer, 1948. [Israel/Canaan]

Schmidt, Paul F. *Temple Reflections*. Albuquerque: Hummingbird, 1980. [Israel/Canaan]

Schmidt, Werner H. *Königtum Gottes in Ugarit und Israel: Zur Herkunft der Königsprädikation Jahwes*. Berlin: Töpelmann, 1966. [Kingship/Coronation]

Schmidt, Werner H. "*Mishkan* als Ausdruck Jerusalemer Kultsprache." *ZAW* 75 (1963): 91-92. [Tabernacle]

Schmitt, Rainer. *Zelt und Lade als Thema alttestamentlicher Wissenschaft*. Gutersloh: Mohn, 1972. [Tabernacle]

Schneider, H. "Das Jahubild im Tempel Salomos." *Memnon* 3 (1909): 159-62. [Israel/Canaan]

Schneider, N. "Göttertempel in Ur III-Reich." *Orientalia* 19 (1950): 257-64. [Mesopotamia]

Schnellbächer, E. L. "The Temple as the Focus of Mark's Theology." *Horizons in Biblical Theology* 5/2 (1983): 95-112. [Israel/Canaan]

Schoeps, H.-J. "Die Tempelzerstörung des Jahres 70 in der jüdischen Religionsgeschichte." In *Coniectanea Neotestamentica*, vol. 6, pp. 1-45. Uppsala: Seminarium Neotestamentium Upsaliense, 1942; also in Schoeps, *Aus frühchristlicher Zeit*. 144-83. Tübingen: Mohr, 1950. [Israel/Canaan]

Schoetz, Dionys. *Schuld und Sündopfer im alten Testament.* Breslau: Mueller and Sieffert, 1930. [Sacrifice/Offerings]

Scholander, Hans. *Det israelitiska offrets upploesning.* Lund: Ohlssons, 1909. [Sacrifice/Offerings]

Scholem, Gershom G. *Jewish Gnosticism, Merkabah Mysticism, and Talmudic Tradition,* 2d ed., 59-61. New York: Jewish Theological Seminary of America, 1965. [Sacred Vestments]

Schonberg, D. "The Temple." *Turtle—a New Jewish Arts Magazine* 4 (1972): 42-53. [Israel/Canaan]

Schott, Siegfried. *Die Reinigung Pharaohs in einem memphitischen Tempel.* Göttingen: Vandenhoeck and Ruprecht, 1957. [Egypt]

Schouten, Leendert. *De tabernakel, Gods heiligdom bij Israel.* Utrecht: Huinink, 1887. [Tabernacle]

Schramm, Percy. *A History of the English Coronation.* Oxford: n.p., 1937. [Kingship/Coronation]

Schreckenberg, H. "The Destruction of the Second Temple as Reflected in Christian Art: Jerusalem in the Second Temple Period." In *Jerusalem in the Second Temple Period: Abraham Schalit Memorial Volume* (in Hebrew; English summary), edited by A. Oppenheimer et al. 394-414. Jerusalem: Yad Izhaq Ben-Avi, 1980. [Israel/Canaan]

Schreiber, A. "La légende de l'emplacement du Temple de Jérusalem." *REJ* 109 (1949): 103-8. [Israel/Canaan]

Schreiner, Josef. *Sion-Jerusalem Jahwes Königssitz, Theologie der heiligen Stadt im alten Testament.* Munich: Köselverlag, 1963. [Israel/Canaan]

Schreiner, Josef. "Tempeltheologie im Streit der Propheten." *Biblische Zeitschrift* 31(1987): 1-14. [Israel/Canaan]

Schult, Hermann. "Der Debir im salomonischen Tempel." *ZDPV* 80 (1964): 46-54. [Tabernacle]

Schult, Hermann. "Zum Bauverfahren in 1 Könige 6, 7." *ZDPV* 88 (1972): 53-54. [Israel/Canaan]

Schunck, K. D. "Zentralheiligtum, Grenzheiligtum und Höhenheiligtum in Israel." *Numen* 18 (1971): 132-40. [Israel/Canaan]

Schürer, E. "Die *thura* oder *pulā hōraia* Act 3, 2 und 10." *ZNTW* 7 (1906): 51-68. [Israel/Canaan]

Schürer, Emil. "Priesthood and Temple Worship." In *The History of the Jewish People in the Age of Jesus Christ (175 B. C. - A. D. 135),* edited and revised by Geza Vermes and Fergus Millar. 2 vols., 2:237-313. Edinburgh: Clark, 1973-79. [Ritual/Liturgy/Worship]

Schwaller de Lubicz, R. A. *The Temple in Man: The Secrets of Ancient Egypt.* Brookline: Autumn, 1977. [Egypt]

Schwaller de Lubicz, R. A. *Les temples de Karnak.* Paris: Dervy-Livres, 1982. [Egypt]

Schwartz, A. "Die Schatzkammer des Tempels in Jerusalem." *MGWJ* 63 (1919): 227-52. [Israel/Canaan]

Schwartz, Daniel R. "Priesthood, Temple, Sacrifices: Opposition and Spiritualization in the Late Second Temple Period." Ph.D. diss., Hebrew University, 1979. [Sacrifice/Offerings]

Schwartz, Daniel R. "The Three Temples of 4 Q Florilegium." *Revue de Qumran* 10 (1979): 83-91. [Israel/Canaan]

Schwartz, Daniel R. "The Tribes of As. Mos. 4:7-9." *JBL* 99 (1980): 217-23. [Israel/Canaan]

Schwartz, Daniel R. "Viewing the Holy Utensils (P. Ox. V, 840)." *NTS* 32 (1986): 153-59. [Israel/Canaan]

Schwartz, J. "The *Encaenia* of the Church of the Holy Sepulchre, the Temple of Solomon and the Jews." *Theologische Zeitschrift* 43 (1987): 265-81. [Israel/Canaan]

Schwartzman, S. D. "How Well Did the Synoptic Evangelists Know the Synagogue (Temple)?" *HUCA* 24 (1952): 115-32. [Israel/Canaan]

Schwartzman, S. D. "The Jewish Institutions of Synagogue and Temple in the Synoptic Gospels." Ph.D. diss., Vanderbilt University, 1952. [Israel/Canaan]

Scott, John A. "The Pattern of the Tabernacle." Ph.D. diss., University of Pennsylvania, 1965. [Tabernacle]

Scott, R. B. Y. "The Pillars Jachin and Boaz." *JBL* 58 (1939): 143-49. [Israel/Canaan]

Scranton, R. L. "Interior Design of Greek Temples." *AJA* 50 (1946): 39-51. [Greece/Rome]

Scully, Vincent J. *The Earth, the Temple, and the Gods: Greek Sacred Architecture.* New Haven: Yale University Press, 1979. [Greece/Rome]

Segal, M. H. "The Tent of Meeting." *Tarbiz* 25 (1956): 231-33. [Tabernacle]

Segelberg, E. "The Ordination of the Mandaean *tarmida* and Its Relation to Jewish and Early Christian Ordination Rites." In *Studia Patristica*, vol. 10, edited by F. L. Cross. 419-25. Berlin: Akademie, 1970. [Ritual/Liturgy/Worship]

Seigne, Jacques. "Notes préliminaires sur l'évolution architecturale du Sanctuaire de Zeus à Jérash." *Syria* 62 (1985): 162-64. [Greece/Rome]

Seigne, Jacques. "Le sanctuaire de Zeus à Jérash: éléments de chronologie." *Syria* 62 (1985): 287-95. [Greece/Rome]

Sellin, Ernst. "Ephod and Terafim." *JPOS* 14 (1934): 185-93. [Sacred Vestments]

Sellin, Ernst. *Das israelitische Ephod.* Giessen: Töpelmann, 1906. [Sacred Vestments]

Sellin, Ernst. "Noch einmal der alttestamentliche Efod." *JPOS* 17 (1937): 236-51. [Sacred Vestments]

Sellin, Ernst. "Der Stein des Sacharja." *JBL* 50 (1931): 242-49. [Israel/Canaan]

Sellin, Ernst. "Das Zelt Jahwes." In *Alttestamentliche Studien für R. Kittel.* 168-92. Leipzig: Hinrichs, 1913. [Tabernacle]

Seow, Choon-Leong. "Ark Processions in the Politics of the Monarchy (Israel)." Ph.D. diss., Harvard University, 1984. [Israel/Canaan]

Sethe, Kurt. *Thebanische Tempelinschriften aus griechisch-römischer Zeit, I.* Berlin: Akademie, 1957. [Egypt]

Seton-Williams, M. V. "Palestinian Temples." *Iraq* 11 (1949): 77-89. [Israel/Canaan]

Seton-Williams, M. V. *Ptolemaic Temples.* London: Waterloo, 1978. [Egypt]

Sety, Omm, and Hanny El Zeini. *Abydos: Holy City of Ancient Egypt.* Los Angeles: L. L., 1981. [Egypt]

Sevensma, Tietse P. *De ark Gods.* Amsterdam: Clausen, 1908. [Tabernacle]

Seybold, Klaus. *Bilder zum Tempelbau: Die Visionen des Propheten Sacharja.* Stuttgart: KBW, 1974. [Israel/Canaan]

Seybold, Klaus. *Das davidische Königtum im Zeugnis der Propheten.* Göttingen: Vandenhoeck & Ruprecht, 1972. [Kingship/Coronation]

Seyrig, Henri. "Antiquités Syriennes 17: Bas-reliefs monumentaux du temple de Bel à Palmyre." *Syria* 15 (1934): 155-86. [Israel/Canaan]

Seyrig, Henri. *Le Temple de Bel à Palmyre.* 2 vols. Paris: Geuthner, 1975. [Greece/Rome]

Shachor, M. L. "The Stone of Foundation" (in Hebrew). *B'shearayich* 6 (1970): 3-6. [Israel/Canaan]

Shalem, Raphael A. *Plan of the Chosen House . . . according to Maimonides* (in Hebrew). Jerusalem: n.p., 1967. [Measurement]

Shalem, Raphael A. *The Temple, Drawing and Notes* (in Hebrew). Jerusalem: Shalem, 1967. [Israel/Canaan]

Shalit, Abraham. *King Herod: Portrait of a Ruler.* 2d ed. Jerusalem: Bialik Institute, 1964; also in German as *König Herodes: Der Mann und sein Werk.* Berlin: de Gruyter, 1969. [Kingship/Coronation]

Shanks, Hershel, ed. "Temple Scroll Revisted—Three New Views." *BAR* 13/6 (1987): 21-37. [Israel/Canaan]

Sharwood Smith, John. *Temples, Priests and Worship.* London: Allen & Unwin, 1975. [Priesthood]

Shaughnessy, James D., ed. *The Roots of Ritual.* Grand Rapids: Eerdmans, 1973. [Ritual/Liturgy/Worship]

Shaw, J. W. "Evidence for the Minoan Tripartite Shrine." *AJA* 82 (1978): 429-48. [Greece/Rome]

Shea, W. H. "New Light on the Exodus and on Construction of the Tabernacle: Gerster's Protosinaitic Inscription No. 1." *Andrews University Seminary Studies* 25 (Spring 1987): 73-96. [Tabernacle]

Shepherd, M. H. "Origin of the Church's Liturgy." *Studia Liturgica* 1 (1962): 83-100. [Ritual/Liturgy/Worship]

Sherlock, Charles. "Ezekiel 10: A Prophet Surprised." *Reformed Theological Review* 42 (1983): 42-44. [Israel/Canaan]

Shiloh, Y. "Iron Age Sanctuaries and Cult Elements in Palestine." In *Symposia*, edited by Frank M. Cross. 147-57. Cambridge: American Schools of Oriental Research, 1979. [Israel/Canaan]

Shohat, A. "Pilgrimages to Jerusalem (up to the End of the Second Temple)" (in Hebrew). In *Jerusalem—Quarterly Devoted to the Study of Jerusalem and Its History*, vol. 1, pp. 21-37. Jerusalem: Mossad Harav Kook, 1948. [Ritual/Liturgy/Worship]

Shorter, Alan W. "Reliefs Showing the Coronation of Ramses II." *JEA* 20 (1934): 18-19. [Kingship/Coronation]

Shupak, Nili. "Jachin and Boaz." In *Encyclopaedia Judaica* 9:1186-89. [Israel/Canaan]

Siebeneck, R. T. "The Messianism of Aggeus and Proto-Zacharias." *CBQ* 19 (1957): 312-28. [Israel/Canaan]

Silverstein, Samuel H. *Korban Shemuel*. St. Louis: Quality, 1944. [Sacrifice/Offerings]

Simhoni, J. N. "The Destruction of the Second Temple" (in Hebrew). In *The Book of Festivals*, edited by Z. Ariel. 332-35. Tel-Aviv: Am Oved, 1967. [Israel/Canaan]

Simon M. "On Josephus, Wars, V, 5, 7." *JQR* 13 (1901): 547-48. [Sacred Vestments]

Simon, Marcel. "Le discours de Jésus sur la ruine du Temple." *RB* 56 (1949): 70-75. [Israel/Canaan]

Simon, Marcel. "La prophétie de Nathan et le temple." *Revue d'histoire et de philosophie religieuses* 32 (1952): 41-58. [Israel/Canaan]

Simon, Marcel. "Retour du Christ et reconstruction du Temple dans la pensée chrétienne primitive." In Simon, *Recherches d'histoire judéo-chrétienne*. 9-19. Paris: Mouton, 1962. [Israel/Canaan]

Simon, Marcel. "Saint Stephen and the Jerusalem Temple." *Journal of Ecclesiastical History* 2/2 (1951): 127-42. [Israel/Canaan]

Simons, Jan. "The Problem of the Temple." In Simons, *Jerusalem in the Old Testament: Researches and Theories*, 381-436. Leiden: Brill, 1952. [Israel/Canaan]

Simpson, J. "Where Are the Sacred Vessels of the Temple?" *PEQ* 29 (1897): 77-80. [Israel/Canaan]

Simpson, W. "Robinson's Arch." *PEFQ* 1-2 (1869-70): 46-48. [Israel/Canaan]

Simpson, W. "The Temple and the Mount of Olives." *PEFQ* 29 (1897): 307-8. [Israel/Canaan]

Sirard, L. "Sacrifices et rites sanglants dans l'ancien testament." *Science et Esprit* 15 (1963): 173-97. [Sacrifice/Offerings]

Sisti, A. "Le due alleanze (Gal 4, 21-31)." *Bibbia e Oriente* 11 (1969): 25-32. [Israel/Canaan]

Sjoberg, Åke W., and E. Bergmann. *The Collection of the Sumerian Temple Hymns.* Locust Valley: Augustin, 1969. [Mesopotamia]

Skehan, P. W. "Wisdom's House." *CBQ* 29 (1967): 468-86. [Israel/Canaan]

Slemming, Charles W. *Made according to Pattern.* Fort Washington, PA: Christian Literature Crusade, 1971. [Tabernacle]

Smallwood, E. Mary. "The Chronology of Gaius' Attempt to Desecrate the Temple." *Latomus* 16 (1957): 3-17. [Israel/Canaan]

Smallwood, E. Mary. "High Priests and Politics in Roman Palestine." *JTS* n.s./13 (1962): 14-34. [Priesthood]

Smith, Arthur E. *The Temple and Its Teaching.* Chicago: Moody, 1956. [Israel/Canaan]

Smith, G. V. "The Concept of God/the Gods as King in the Ancient Near East and the Bible." *Trinity Journal* 3 (1982): 1-38. [Kingship/Coronation]

Smith, J. M. P. "The Jewish Temple at Elephantine." *The Biblical World* 31 (1908): 448-59. [Israel/Canaan]

Smith, James K. *The Temple of Zeus at Olympia.* Bergamo: n.p., 1924. [Greece/Rome]

Smith, Jonathan Z. "The Bare Facts of Ritual." *History of Religions* 20/1-2 (1980): 112-27. [Ritual/Liturgy/Worship]

Smith, Jonathan Z. "Earth and Gods." *Journal of Religion* 49 (1969): 103-27. [Israel/Canaan]

Smith, Jonathan Z. "The Garments of Shame." In *History of Religions* 5 (1965): 217-38. [Sacred Vestments]

Smith, Joseph L. *Tombs, Temples and Ancient Art.* Norman, OK: University of Oklahoma Press, 1956. [Egypt]

Smith, S. "The Babylonian Ritual for the Consecration and Induction of a Divine Statue." *Journal of the Royal Asiatic Society of Great Britain and Ireland* (1925): 37-60. [Mesopotamia]

Smith, S. "Timber and Brick or Masonry Construction." *PEQ* 73 (1941): 5-17. [Israel/Canaan]

Snaith, Norman H. "The Altar at Gilgal: Joshua XXII:23-29." *VT* 28 (1978): 330-35. [Sacrifice/Offerings]

Snaith, Norman H. *The Jewish New Year Festival, Its Origin and Development.* London: Society for Promoting Christian Knowledge, 1947. [Israel/Canaan]

Snaith, Norman H. "Sacrifice in the Old Testament." *VT* 7 (1957): 308-17. [Sacrifice/Offerings]

Snaith, Norman H. "The Sin-Offering and the Guilt-Offering." *VT* 15 (1965): 73-80. [Sacrifice/Offerings]

Snaith, Norman H. "The Sprinkling of Blood." *ET* 82 (1970-71): 23-24. [Ritual/Liturgy/Worship]

Snaith, Norman H. "The Verbs *zābaḥ* and *šāḥaṭ*." *VT* 25 (1975): 242-46. [Sacrifice/Offerings]

Snijders, L. A. "Het gebed naar de tempel toe: Over gebedsrichting in het Oude Testament." *Nederlands Theologisch Tijdschrift.* 19 (1964-65): 1-14. [Ritual/Liturgy/Worship]

Snijders, L. A. "L'orientation du temple de Jerusalem." *Oudtestamentische Studiën* 14 (1965): 214-34. [Israel/Canaan]

Soares, T. G. "Ezekiel's Temple." *Biblical World* 14 (1899): 93-103. [Israel/Canaan]

Soggin, J. Alberto. "Gott als König in der biblischen Dichtung: Bemerkungen zu den *YHWH mlk*-Psalmen." In *Proceedings of the Fifth World Congress of Jewish Studies, Jerusalem, 1969.* 126-33. Jerusalem: World Union of Jewish Studies, 1972. [Kingship/Coronation]

Soggin, J. Alberto. *Das Königtum in Israel.* Berlin: Töpelmann, 1967. [Kingship/Coronation]

Sollberger, E. "The Temple in Babylonia." In *Le temple et le culte: Compte rendu de la vingtième recontre assyriologique internationale organisée à Leiden du 3 au 7 juillet 1972.* 31-34. Istanbul: Nederlands Historisch-Archeologisch Instituut te Istambul 1975. [Mesopotamia]

Soltau, Henry W. *The Tabernacle, the Priesthood and the Offerings.* London: Morgan and Scott, 1884. [Tabernacle]

Spencer, A. J. "The Brick Foundations of Late Period Peripteral Temples and Their Mythological Origin." In *Orbis Aegyptiorum Speculum—Glimpses of Ancient Egypt: Studies in Honour of H. W. Fairman*, edited by Johann Ruffle, G. A. Gaballa, and K. A. Kitchen. 132-37. Warminster: Aris and Phillips, 1979. [Egypt]

Spencer, Patricia. *The Egyptian Temple: A Lexicographical Study.* Boston: Kegan Paul International, 1984. [Egypt]

Sperber, Daniel. "The History of the Menorah." *JJS* 16 (1965): 135-59. [Tabernacle]

Sperber, Daniel. "Social Legislation in Jerusalem during the Latter Part of the Second Temple Period." *Journal for the Study of Judaism* 6 (1975): 86-95. [Israel/Canaan]

Sperling, S. David. "Navel of the Earth." In *The Interpreter's Dictionary of the Bible*, supp. vol., 621-23. [Israel/Canaan]

Spiess, F. "Die königliche Halle des Herodes im Tempel von Jerusalem." *ZDPV* 15 (1892): 234-56. [Israel/Canaan]

Spiess, F. "Der Tempel nebst der Antonia." In Spiess, *Das Jerusalem des Josephus—Beitrag zur Topographie der heiligen Stadt.* 46-94. Berlin: Habel, 1881. [Israel/Canaan]

Spiess, F. *Der Tempel zu Jerusalem während des letzten Jahrhunderts seines Bestandes nach Josephus.* Berlin: Habel, 1880. [Israel/Canaan]

Spoer, H. H. "Notes on Bloody Sacrifices in Palestine." *JAOS* 25 (1904): 312-13. [Sacrifice/Offerings]

Spoer, H. H. "On Bloody Sacrifices in Palestine." *JAOS* 27 (1906): 104. [Sacrifice/Offerings]

Stade, B. "Die Kesselwagen des salomonischen Tempels, 1 Kö. 7, 27-39." *ZAW* 21 (1901): 145-90. [Israel/Canaan]

Stade, B. "Der Text des Berichtes über Salomos Bauten, 1 Kö. 5-7." *ZAW* 3 (1883): 129-77. [Israel/Canaan]

Staehelin, J. J. "Ueber die Wanderungen des Centralheiligthums der Hebraeer vom Tode des Hohenpriesters Eli bis auf die Erbauung des Tempels zu Jerusalem." *ZDMG* 11 (1857): 141-43. [Priesthood]

Stager, L. E., and S. R. Wolff. "Production and Commerce in Temple Courtyards: An Olive Press in the Sacred Precinct at Tel Dan." *BASOR* 243 (1981): 95-102. [Israel/Canaan]

Stamm, Jakob J. "Zum Altargesetz im Bundesbuch." *Theologische Zeitschrift* 1 (1945): 304-6. [Israel/Canaan]

Starcky, J. "Le Temple hérodien et les sanctuaires orientaux." *Le Monde de la Bible* 13 (1980): 14-18. [Israel/Canaan]

Stauffer, Ethelbert. "Das Tor des Nikanor." *ZNTW* 44 (1953): 44-46. [Israel/Canaan]

Steck, O. H. "Zu Haggai 1:2-11." *ZAW* 83 (1971): 355-79. [Israel/Canaan]

Stegemann, Hartmut. "Is the Temple Scroll a Sixth Book of the Torah, Lost for 2500 Years?" *BAR* 13/6 (1987): 28-35. [Israel/Canaan]

Stein, M. "How Herod Moved Gigantic Blocks to Construct Temple Mount." *BAR* 7/3 (1981): 42-46. [Israel/Canaan]

Steinmueller, John E. "Sacrificial Blood in the Bible." *Biblica* 40 (1959): 556-67. [Sacrifice/Offerings]

Steinmueller, John E. "Temples." *New Catholic Encyclopedia* 13 (1968): 998-1000. [Israel/Canaan]

Stendebach, F. J. "Altarformen im kanaanäisch-israelitischen Raum." *Biblische Zeitschrift* 20 (1976): 180-96. [Israel/Canaan]

Stern, E. "A Favissa of a Phoenician Sanctuary from Tel Dor." *JJS* 33 (1982): 35-54. [Israel/Canaan]

Stern, Menahem. "The Period of the Second Temple. In *History of the Jewish People*, edited by H. H. Ben-Sasson. 183-303. Cambridge: Harvard Universty Press, 1976. [Israel/Canaan]

Stern, Menahem. "Priests and Priesthood—from the Beginning of the Hellenistic Era until the Destruction of the Temple." In *Encyclopaedia Judaica* 13:1086-88. [Priesthood]

Stevenson, William B. "Hebrew ʿolah and Zebach Sacrifices." In *Festschrift Alfred Bertholet zum 80. Geburtstag gewidmet von Kollegen und Freunden*, edited by Walter Baumgartner et al. 488-97. Tübingen: Mohr, 1950. [Sacrifice/Offerings]

Stewart, A. F. "Some Observations on the West Akroteria of the Temple of Asklepios at Epidauros." *AJA* 88 (1984): 261. [Greece/Rome]

Stillwell, R. "The Siting of Classical Greek Temples." *Society of Architectural Historians Journal* 13/4 (1954): 3-8. [Greece/Rome]

Stinespring, William F. "Temple, Jerusalem: The Temple of Solomon," "Temple, Jerusalem: The Temple of Zerubbabel," and "Temple, Jerusalem: The Temple of Herod." In *The Interpreter's Dictionary of the Bible* 4:534-60. [Israel/Canaan]

Stinespring, William F. "Temple Research in Jerusalem." *Duke Divinity School Review* 29 (1964): 85-101. [Israel/Canaan]

Stinespring, William F. "Wilson's Arch and the Masonic Hall." *BA* 30 (1967): 27-31. [Israel/Canaan]

Stinespring, William F. "Wilson's Arch Revisited." *BA* 29 (1966): 27-36. [Israel/Canaan]

Stockton, E. D. "The Fortress Temple of Shechem and Joshua's Covenant." *Australian Journal of Biblical Archaeology* 1 (1968): 24-28. [Covenant]

Stockton, E. D. "Sacred Pillars in the Bible." *Australian Biblical Review* 20 (1972): 16-32. [Israel/Canaan]

Stoll, Heinrich A. *Griechische Tempel*. Leipzig: Köhler and Amelang, 1963. [Greece/Rome]

Stolz, F. *Strukturen and Figuren in Kult von Jerusalem: Studien zur altorientalischen vor und frühisraelitischen Religion*. Berlin: de Gruyter, 1970. [Israel/Canaan]

Stone, Michael E. "Reactions to Destructions of the Second Temple: Theology, Perception, and Conversion." *Journal for the Study of Judaism* 12 (1981): 195-204. [Israel/Canaan]

Strange, James. "The Idea of Afterlife in Ancient Israel: Some Remarks of the Iconography in Solomon's Temple." *PEQ* 117 (1985): 35-40. [Israel/Canaan]

Stricker, B. H. "De Pythagoreische Liturgie." *Oudheidkundige mededeelingen uit het rijksmuseum van oudheden te Leiden* 13 (1950): 72-117. [Ritual/Liturgy/Worship]

Strong, J. "The Tabernacle." *Biblical World* 1 (1893): 270-77. [Tabernacle]

Strong, J. *The Tabernacle of Israel in the Desert.* Grand Rapids: Baker Book House, 1952. [Tabernacle]

Strothmann, Werner. *Syrische Hymnen zur Myron-Weihe.* Wiesbaden: Harrassowitz, 1978. [Ablutions/Anointings]

Stuhlmacher, Peter. "Die Stellung Jesu und des Paulus zu Jerusalem: Versuch einer Erinnerung." *Zeitschrift für Theologie und Kirche* 86 (1989): 140-56. [Israel/Canaan]

Stuhlmueller, C. "Yahweh-King and Deutero-Isaiah." *Biblical Research* 15 (1970): 32-45. [Kingship/Coronation]

Suarès, André. *Temples Grecs; Maisons des dieux.* Paris: Dantan, 1937. [Greece/Rome]

Sulley, Henry. *The Temple of Ezekiel's Prophecy: Being an Enlarged and Revised Edition of an Explanation of the Nature, Character, and Extent of the Building Which Is Shortly to Be Erected in the Land of Israel as "a House of Prayer for All People."* 3d rev. ed. London: Simpkin, Marshall, Hamilton, Kent, 1921. [Israel/Canaan]

Süring, Margit L. "The Horn-Motifs of the Bible and the Ancient Near East." *Andrews University Seminary Studies* 22 (1984): 327-40. [Kingship/Coronation]

Swain, C. W. " 'For Our Sins': The Image of Sacrifice in the Thought of the Apostle Paul." *Interpretation* 17 (1963): 131-39. [Sacrifice/Offerings]

Swain, Joseph C. *Covenants, Old, New, and Forever.* New York: United Presbyterian Church, 1972. [Covenant]

Swanson, T. N. "The Kingship of God in Intertestamental Literature." *Bangalore Theological Forum* 12 (1980): 1-25. [Kingship/Coronation]

Swanston, H. F. G. "Liturgy as Paradise and Parousia." *Scottish Journal of Theology* 36 (1983): 505-19. [Ritual/Liturgy/Worship]

Sweeney, Marvin A. "Midrashic Perspective in the *Torat ham-Melek* of the Temple Scroll." *Hebrew Studies* 28 (1987): 51-66. [Israel/Canaan]

Sweeney, Marvin A. "Sefirah at Qumran: Aspects of the Counting Formulas for the First-Fruits Festivals in the Temple Scroll." *BASOR* 251 (1983): 61-66. [Israel/Canaan]

Swetnam, J. " 'The Greater and More Perfect Tent'—A Contribution to the Discussion of Hebrews 9, 11." *Biblica* 47 (1966): 91-106. [Tabernacle]

Swetnam, J. "Temple Sacrifices: Profile of a Theological Problem." *The Bible Today* 34 (1968): 2377-2380. [Sacrifice/Offerings]

Swetnam, Walter. "Selected Temple Documents of the Reign of Bur Sin of the Third Dynasty of Ur." Ph.D., diss., Hartford Seminary Foundation, 1930. [Mesopotamia]

Sylva, D. D. "The Cryptic Clause *en tois tou patros mou dei einai me* in Lk 2:49b." *ZNTW* 78/1-2 (1987): 132-40. [Israel/Canaan]

Sylva, D. D. "The Meaning and Function of Acts 7:46-50." *JBL* 106 (June 1987): 261-75. [Israel/Canaan]

Sylva, D. D. "The Temple Curtain and Jesus' Death in the Gospel of Luke." *JBL* 105 (1986): 239-50. [Israel/Canaan]

Talbot, Lois T. *Christ in the Tabernacle.* Chicago: Moody, 1978. [Tabernacle]

Talmon, Shermaryahu. "*har: Gibh'āh.*" In *Theological Dictionary of the Old Testament* 3:427-47. [Mountain]

Talmon, Shemaryahu. "The 'Navel of the Earth' and the Comparative Method." In *Scripture in History and Theology: Essays in Honor of J. Coert Rylaarsdam*, edited by Arthur Merrill and Thomas Overholt. 243-68. Pittsburgh: Pickwick, 1977. [Sacred Space]

"Tamid, or the Continual Service, with the Commentary of Rabbi Obadiah of Bartenora." *PEFQ* (1886): 119-30, 213-23. [Israel/Canaan]

Ta-Shema, I. "Levi." In *Encyclopaedia Hebraica* (in Hebrew). 32 vols., 21:366-71. Jerusalem: Encyclopaedia Hebraica, 1971. [Priesthood]

Tataki, A. B. *Sounion.* Athens: Ekdotike Athenon, 1978. [Greece/Rome]

Taylor, George. *The Roman Temples of Lebanon.* Beirut: Darel-Mashreq, 1971. [Greece/Rome]

Taylor, Noel M. "The Place of the Temple in the New Testament." Ph.D. diss. Southern Baptist Theological Seminary, 1942 [Israel/Canaan]

Taylor, W. R. "A Jerusalem Forgery of the Balustrade Inscription of Herod's Temple." *JPOS* 13 (1933): 137-39. [Israel/Canaan]

Taylor, W. R. "A Second Forgery of the Balustrade Inscription of Herod's Temple." *JPOS* 16 (1936): 37-38. [Israel/Canaan]

Teicher, J. L. "Priests and Sacrifices in the Dead Sea Scrolls." *JJS* 5 (1954): 93-99. [Sacrifice/Offerings]

Teichmann, Frank. *Der Mensch und sein Tempel: Ägypten.* Stuttgart: Urachhaus, 1978. [Egypt]

Telford, W. R. *The Barren Temple and the Withered Tree.* Sheffield: JSOT, 1980. [Israel/Canaan]

Le Temple: Representations de l'architecture sacrée. Paris: Ministère de la Culture, 1982. [Greece/Rome]

Tenz, J. M. "Position of the Altar of Burnt Sacrifice in the Temple of Jerusalem." *PEQ* 42 (1910): 137-39. [Sacrifice/Offerings]

Terrien, Samuel. *The Elusive Presence, Toward a New Biblical Theology.* New York: Harper & Row, 1978. [Sacred Space]

Terrien, Samuel. "The Omphalos Myth and Hebrew Religion." *VT* 20 (1970): 315-38. [Sacred Space]

Testa, Emmanuel. "La 'Gerusalemme celeste,' dall'antico oriente alla Bibbia e alla liturgia." *Bibbia e Oriente* 1 (1959): 47-50. [Israel/Canaan]

Testa, Emmanuel. *L'huile de la foi*. Jerusalem: Studium Biblicum Franciscanum, 1967. [Ablutions/Anointings]

Testa, Emmanuel. "Lo schema letterario sulla distruzione del tempio e di Gerusalemme." *Liber Annuus* 24 (1974): 265-316. [Israel/Canaan]

Theissen, G. "Die Tempelweissagung Jesu: Prophetie im Spannungsfeld von Stadt und Land." *Theologische Zeitschrift* 32 (1976): 144-58. [Israel/Canaan]

Theuer, Max. *Der griechisch-dorische Peripteral Tempel*. Berlin: Wasmuth, 1918. [Greece/Rome]

Thiering, B. E. "Mebaqqer and Episkopos in Light of the Temple Scroll." *JBL* 100 (1981): 59-74. [Israel/Canaan]

Thiering, B. E. "Qumran Initiation and New Testament Baptism." *NTS* 27 (October 1981): 615-31. [Ritual/Liturgy/Worship]

Thiersch, H. "Ein altmediterraner Tempeltyp." *ZAW* 50 (1932): 73-86. [Greece/Rome]

Thoburn, C. Stanley. "Old Testament Sacrifice in the Light of Ugaritic Literature." Ph.D. diss., Boston University, 1954. [Sacrifice/Offerings]

Thoma, Clemens. "Die Zerstörung des Tempels von Jerusalem (70 n. Chr.) als Wende." In *Auf den Trümmern des Tempels*, edited by C. Thoma. 53-75. Vienna: Herder, 1968. [Israel/Canaan]

Thomasson, Gordon C. "Togetherness Is Sharing an Umbrella: Divine Kingship, The Gnosis, and Religious Syncretism." In *By Study and Also by Faith: Essays in Honor of Hugh W. Nibley*, edited by John M. Lundquist and Stephen D. Ricks. 2 vols, 1:523-61. Salt Lake City: Deseret Book and F.A.R.M.S. 1990. [Kingship/Coronation]

Thompson, H. O. "Tell el-Husn—Biblical Beth-shan." *BA* 30 (1967): 110-35. [Israel/Canaan]

Thompson, John A. "Covenant Patterns in the Ancient Near East and Their Significance for Biblical Studies." *Reformed Theological Review* 18 (October 1959): 65-75. [Covenant]

Thompson, John A. "Cultic Credo and the Sinai Tradition." *Reformed Theological Review* 27 (1968): 53-64. [Covenant]

Thompson, L. "Cult and Eschatology in the Apocalypse of John." *Journal of Religion* 49 (1969): 330-50. [Israel/Canaan]

Thompson, P. E. S. "The Anatomy of Sacrifice: A Preliminary Investigation." In *New Testament Christianity for Africa and the World*, edited by M. Glassnell and E. Fashole-Luke. 19-35. London: SPCK, 1974. [Sacrifice/Offerings]

Thompson, R. J. *Penitence and Sacrifice in Early Israel outside the Levitical Law*. London: Brill, 1963. [Sacrifice/Offerings]

Thompson, T. L. "The Dating of the Megiddo Temples in Strata XV-XIV." *ZDPV* 86 (1970): 38-49. [Israel/Canaan]

Thomsen, P. "Der Tempel." In *Denkmäler Palästinas aus der Zeit Jesu*, Heft 1. 26-33. Leipzig: Hinrichs, 1916. [Israel/Canaan]

Thomsen, P. "Vom Tempel: Inschriften vom Tempel, von Kirchen und Kapellen." *ZDPV* 44 (1921): 7-8. [Israel/Canaan]

Thomson, C. A. "The Necessity of Blood Sacrifice in Ezekiel's Temple." *Bibliotheca Sacra* 123 (1966): 237-48. [Sacrifice/Offerings]

Thomson, H. C. "The Right of Entry to the Temple in the Old Testament." *Transactions of the Glasgow University Oriental Society* 21 (1965/1966): 25-34. [Israel/Canaan]

Thomson, H. C. "A Row of Cedar Beams." *PEQ* 92 (1960): 57-63. [Israel/Canaan]

Thomson, Robert W. *The Teachings of St. Gregory*. Cambridge: Harvard University Press, 1970. [Ablutions/Anointings]

Thorion, Y. "Die Sprache der Tempelrolle und die Chronikbücher." *Revue de Qumran* 11 (1983): 423-26. [Israel/Canaan]

Thorion, Y. "Tempelrolle LIX, 8-11 und Babli, Sanhedrin 98^a." *Revue de Qumran* 11 (1983): 427-28. [Israel/Canaan]

Thorion, Y. "Zur Bedeutung von 'Gibbore Hayil Lamilhama' in 11Q T LVII, 9." *Revue de Qumran* 10 (1981): 597-98. [Israel/Canaan]

Thorion-Vardi, Talia. "The Personal Pronoun as a Syntactical Glide in the Temple Scroll and in the Masoretic Text." *Revue de Qumran* 12 (1986): 421-22. [Israel/Canaan]

Thornton, T. C. G. "Charismatic Kingship in Israel and Judah." *JTS* 14 (April 1963): 1-11. [Kingship/Coronation]

Thüsing, W. "Die Vision des 'Neuen Jerusalem' (Apk 21, 1-22) als Verheissung und Gottesverkündigung." *Trierer Theologische Zeitschrift* 77 (1968): 17-34. [Israel/Canaan]

Thureau-Dangin, F. *Rituels accadiens*. Paris: Leroux, 1921. [Ritual/Liturgy/Worship]

Thurston, Herbert. *The Coronation Ceremonial: Its True History and Meaning*. 2d ed. London: Catholic Truth Society, 1911. [Kingship/Coronation]

Tidwell, N. L. "The Linen Ephod: 1 Sam II 18 and 2 Sam VI 14." *VT* 24 (1974): 505-7. [Sacred Vestments]

Timpe, R. L. "Ritualizations and Ritualisms in Religious Development: A Psychosocial Perspective." *Journal of Psychological Theology* 11 (1983): 311-17. [Ritual/Liturgy/Worship]

Tippett, A. R. "Initiation Rites and Functional Substitutes." *Practical Anthropology* 10 (1963): 66-70. [Ritual/Liturgy/Worship]

Todd, E. W. "The Reforms of Hezekiah and Josiah." *Scottish Journal of Theology* 9 (1956): 288-93. [Israel/Canaan]

Tomlinson, Richard A. *Greek Sanctuaries*. London: Elek, 1976. [Greece/Rome]

Torczyner (Tur-Sinai), Harry. *Altbabylonische Tempelrechnungen*. Wien: Hölder, 1913. [Mesopotamia]

Torczyner (Tur-Sinai), Harry. *Die Bundeslade und die Anfänge der Religion Israels*, 2d ed. Berlin: Philo, 1930. [Tabernacle]

Torczyner (Tur-Sinai), Harry. "Holy of Holies" (in Hebrew). *Encyclopedia Biblica* 1:538-50. [Tabernacle]

Torrance, Thomas F. "The Origins of Baptism." *Scottish Journal of Theology* 11 (1958): 158-71. [Ablutions/Anointings]

Torrance, Thomas F. *Royal Priesthood*. Edinburgh: Oliver and Boyd, 1955. [Priesthood]

Torrey, C. C. "The Foundry of the Second Temple at Jerusalem." *JBL* 55 (1936): 247-60. [Israel/Canaan]

Tov, E. "The 'Temple Scroll' and Old Testament Textual Criticism" (in Hebrew; *English summary). *Eretz-Israel* 16 (1982): 100-11, *255. [Israel/Canaan]

Townsend, J. T. "The Jerusalem Temple in New Testament Thought." Ph.D. diss., Harvard University, 1959. [Israel/Canaan]

Townsend, J. T. "The Jerusalem Temple in the First Century." In *God and His Temple*, edited by L. E. Frizzell. 48-65. South Orange, NJ: Seton Hall University Institute for Judaeo-Christian Studies, 1980. [Israel/Canaan]

"The Tract 'Middoth'—On the Measurements of the Temple, Literally Translated from the Mishna." *PEFQ* 4 (1872): 12-19. [Measurement]

Trathen, D. A. "Christian Initiation." *St. Mark's Review* 99 (1979): 1-31. [Ritual/Liturgy/Worship]

Trell, Bluma L. *The Temple of Artemis at Ephesos*. New York: American Numismatic Society, 1945. [Greece/Rome]

Trendelenburg, Adolf. *Der grosse Altar des Zeus in Olympia*. Berlin: Gaertners, 1902. [Greece/Rome]

Treves, M. "Reign of God in the Old Testament." *VT* 19 (April 1969): 230-43. [Kingship/Coronation]

Trocmé, É. "L'expulsion des marchands du Temple." *NTS* 15 (1968-69): 1-22. [Israel/Canaan]

Trocmé, E. "Jesus Christ et le Temple: éloge d'un naif." *Revue d'histoire et de philosophe Religieuses* 44 (1964): 245-51. [Israel/Canaan]

Tropper, D. "Bet Din shel Kohanim." *JQR* 63 (January 1973): 204-21. [Israel/Canaan]

Trumbull, Henry C. *The Blood Covenant: A Primitive Rite and Its Bearing on Scripture*. New York: Scribner's, 1885. [Covenant]

Trumbull, Henry C. *The Threshold Covenant*. New York: Scribner's, 1896. [Covenant]

Tucatzinsky, Jehiel M. *Ir ha-Kodesh veha-Mikdash*. 5 vols. Jerusalem: n.p., 1970. [Israel/Canaan]

Tufnell, Olga. *Lachish II, The Fosse Temple.* London: Oxford University Press, 1940. [Israel/Canaan]

Tur-Sinai, N. H. (Torczyner, Harry). "The Ark of God at Beit Shemesh (1 Sam vi) and Peres ʿUzza (2 Sam vi; 1 Chron xiii)." *VT* 1 (1951): 275-86. [Tabernacle]

Tur-Sinai, N. H. (Torczyner, Harry). *Die Bundeslade und die Anfänge der Religion Israels.* Berlin: Philo, 1930. [Tabernacle]

Tur-Sinai, N. H. (Torczyner, Harry). "The Foundation Stone" (in Hebrew). *Leshonenu* 19 (1954): 124. [Israel/Canaan]

Turner, Harold W. "The New Temple of the New Testament." In Turner, *From Temple to Meetinghouse: The Phenomenology and Theology of Places of Worship.* 106-30. The Hague: Mouton, 1979. [Sacred Space]

Turner, V. "Sacrifice as Quintessential Process: Prophylaxis or Abandonment?" *History of Religions* 16 (1977): 189-215. [Sacrifice/Offerings]

Turner, Victor W. "Center Out There: Pilgrim's Goal." *History of Religions* 12 (February 1973): 191-230. [Ritual/Liturgy/Worship]

Turner, Victor W. *The Ritual Process: Structure and Anti-Structure.* Chicago: Aldine, 1969. [Ritual/Liturgy/Worship]

Turner, Victor W. "Ritual, Tribal and Catholic." *Worship* 50 (November 1976): 504-26. [Ritual/Liturgy/Worship]

Turner, Victor W., ed. *Celebration: Studies in Festivity and Ritual.* Washington D.C.: Smithsonian Institution, 1982. [Ritual/Liturgy/Worship]

Ubigli, L. R. "Dalla 'Nuova Gerusalemme' alla 'Gerusalemme Celeste'— Contributo per la comprensiòne dell' Apocalittica." *Henoch* 3 (1981): 69-80. [Israel/Canaan]

Uffenheimer, Benjamin. "On the Question of Centralisation of Worship in Ancient Israel." *Tarbiz* 28 (1958): 138-53. [Ritual/Liturgy/Worship]

Uhrbach, Ephraim M. "Heavenly and Earthly Jerusalem" (in Hebrew; *English summary). In *Jerusalem through the Ages,* edited by J. Aviram. 156-71, *64. Jerusalem: Israel Exploration Society, 1968. [Israel/Canaan]

Ulshoefer, H. K. "Nathan's Opposition to David's Intention to Build a Temple in the Light of Selected Ancient Near Eastern Texts." Ph.D. diss., Boston University, 1977. [Israel/Canaan]

Unger, M. F. "The Temple Vision of Ezekiel." *Bibliotheca Sacra* 105 (1948): 418-32; 106 (1949): 48-64. [Israel/Canaan]

Uphill, Eric P. *The Temples of Per Rameses.* Warminster: Aris and Phillips, 1984. [Egypt]

Urie, D. M. L. "Sacrifice among the West Semites." *PEQ* 81 (1949): 67-82. [Sacrifice/Offerings]

Ussishkin, D. "Building Four in Hamath and the Temples of Solomon and Tell Tayanat." *IEJ* 16 (1966): 104-10. [Israel/Canaan]

Ussishkin, D. "The Date of the Judaean Shrine at Arad." *IEJ* 38 (1988): 142-57. [Israel/Canaan]

Ussishkin, D. "The Ghassulian Shrine at En-Gedi." *Tel Aviv* 7 (1980): 1-44. [Israel/Canaan]

Ussishkin, D. "The Ghassulian Temple in Ein Gedi and the Origin of the Hoard from Nahal Mishmar." *BA* 34 (February 1971): 23-39. [Israel/Canaan]

Ussishkin, D. "Solomon's Temple and the Temples of Hamath and Tell Tainat" (in Hebrew). *Yediot* 30 (1966): 76-84. [Israel/Canaan]

Utzschneider, Helmut. *Das Heiligtum und das Gesetz: Studien zur Bedeutung der sinaitischen Heiligtumstexte (Ex 25-40; Lev 8-9)*. Göttingen: Vandenhoeck & Ruprecht, 1988. [Tabernacle]

Vajda, G. "La description du Temple de Jérusalem d'après le K. al-masālik wa'l-mamālik d'Al-Muhallabī—ses éléments bibliques et rabbinques." *Journal Asiatique* 247 (1959): 193-202. [Israel/Canaan]

Valentine, James. "Theological Aspects of the Temple Motif in the Old Testament and Revelation." Ph.D. diss., Boston University, 1985. [Israel/Canaan]

Van Baal, J. "Offering, Sacrifice and Gift." *Numen* 23 (1976): 161-78. [Sacrifice/Offerings]

Van Buren, E. (Elizabeth) D. (Douglas). "The Building of a Temple Tower." *Revue d'Assyriologie et d'Archeologie Orientale* 46 (1952): 65-74. [Mesopotamia]

Van Buren, E. (Elizabeth Douglas). "Foundation Rites for a New Temple." *Orientalia* 21 (1952): 293-306. [Mesopotamia]

Van Buren, Elizabeth (Douglas). *Greek Fictile Revêtments in the Archaic Period*. London: Murray, 1926. [Greece/Rome]

Van Buren, E. (Elizabeth) D. (Douglas). "Mountain-Gods." *Orientalia* 12 (1943): 76-84. [Mountain]

Van Buren, E. (Elizabeth) D. (Douglas). "A Ritual Sequence." *Orientalia* 25 (1956): 39-41. [Ritual/Liturgy/Worship]

Van den Bussche, H. "Le signe du Temple (Jean 2, 13-22)." *Bible et vie chrétienne* 20 (1957-58): 92-100. [Israel/Canaan]

Van der Born, A. "Zum Tempelweihspruch (I Kg VIII, 12f)." *Oudtestamentische Studiën* 14 (1965): 235-44. [Israel/Canaan]

Van der Waal, C. "The Temple in the Gospel according to Luke." In *Essays on the Gospel of Luke and Acts: Proceedings of the Ninth Meeting of Die Nuwe Testamentiese Werkgemeenskap van Suid Afrika*, edited by W. van Unnik, 49-59. Pretoria: University of Pretoria, 1973. [Israel/Canaan]

Van der Woude, Adam S. "Melchizedek." In *The Interpreter's Dictionary of the Bible*, supp. vol., 585-86. [Priesthood]

Van der Woude, Adam S. "Serubbabel und die messianischen Erwartungen des Propheten Sacharja." *ZAW* 100 (1988): 138-56. [Israel/Canaan]

Van der Woude, Adam S. "De Tempel van Qumran." *Nederlands Theologisch Tijdschrift* 34 (1980): 177-90, 281-93. [Israel/Canaan]

Van Engen, John. "Anoint, Anointing." In *Evangelical Dictionary of Theology*, edited by W. A. Elwell, 51-52. Grand Rapids: Baker Book House, 1984. [Ablutions/Anointings]

Vanhoye, Albert. "Le Christ, grand-prêtre selon Héb. 2, 17-18." *La nouvelle revue théologique* 91 (1969): 449-74. [Israel/Canaan]

Vanhoye, Albert. " 'Par la tente plus grande et plus parfaite . . .' (He 9,11)." *Biblica* 46 (1965): 1-28. [Israel/Canaan]

Vanhoye, Albert. "L'utilisation du livre d'Ézechiel dans l'Apocalypse." *Biblica* 43 (1962): 436-76. [Israel/Canaan]

Vanni, Ugo. "Gerusalemme nell' Apocalisse," In *Gerusalemme. Atti della XXVI Settimana Biblica, Associazione Biblica Italiana*, edited by M. Borrmans. 27-52. Brescia: Paideia, 1982. [Israel/Canaan]

van Pelt, R. J. *Tempel van de Wereld: de Kosmische symboliek van de tempel van Salomo.* Utrecht: HES, 1984. [Israel/Canaan]

Van Seters, John. "The Religion of the Patriarchs in Genesis." *Biblica* 61 (1980): 220-33. [Sacrifice/Offerings]

Van Siclen, Charles C. *Two Theban Monuments from the Reign of Amenhotep II.* San Antonio: Van Siclen Books, 1982. [Egypt]

Van Velduizen, Milo. "Moses: A Model of Hellenistic Philanthropia." *Reformed Review* 38 (1985): 215-24. [Kingship/Coronation]

Van Woerden, I. S. "The Iconography of the Sacrifice of Abraham." *Vigiliae Christianae* 15 (December 1961): 214-55. [Sacrifice/Offerings]

Varille, A. "La grande porte du temple d'Apet à Karnak." *ASAE* 53 (1956): 79-118. [Egypt]

Vattioni, Francesco, ed. *Sangue e Antropologia Biblica nella Patristica. Atti della Settimana (Roma, 23-28 Novembre 1981).* 2 vols. Rome: Pia Unione Preziosissimo Sangue, 1982. [Sacrifice/Offerings]

Vattioni, Francesco, ed. *Sangue e Antropologia nella Letterature Cristiana. Atti della Settimana (Roma, 29 Novembre-4 Dicembre 1982).* 3 vols. Rome: Pia Unione Preziosissimo Sangue, 1983. [Sacrifice/Offerings]

Vattioni, Francesco, ed. *Sangue e Antropologia nella Liturgia. Atti della IV Settimana (Roma, 21-26 Novembre 1983).* 3 vols. Rome: Ediz. Pia Unione Preziossimo Sangue, 1984. [Ritual/Liturgy/Worship]

Vattioni, Francesco, ed. *Settimana Sangue e Antropologia Biblica. Atti della Settimana Sangue e Antropologia Biblica (Roma, 10-15 Marzo 1980).* 2 vols. Roma: Pia unione Preziosissimo Sangue, 1981. [Sacrifice/Offerings]

Vaughan, Patrick H. *The Meaning of 'bāmâ' in the Old Testament: A Study of Etymologyical, Textual, and Archaeological Evidence.* Cambridge: Cambridge University Press, 1974. [Mountain]

Vaux, Roland de. "Arche d'alliance et Tente de reunion." In *A la recontre de Dieu: Memorial Albert Gelin*, edited by André Barucq. 55-70. Le Puy: Editions Xavier Mappus, 1961; also in English as "Ark of the Covenant and Tent of Reunion." In de Vaux, *The Bible and the Ancient Near East.* 136-51. Garden City: Doubleday, 1971. [Tabernacle]

Vaux, Roland de. "Les chérubins et l'arche d'alliance, les sphinx gardiens et les trônes divins dans l'Ancien Orient." In de Vaux, *Bible et Orient.* 231-59. Paris: Cerf, 1967. [Tabernacle]

Vaux, Roland de. "Les décrets de Cyrus et de Darius sur la reconstruction du Temple." *RB* 46 (1937): 29-57; also in English as "The Decrees of Cyrus and Darius on the Rebuilding of the Temple." In de Vaux, *The Bible and the Ancient Near East*, translated by Damian McHugh. 63-96. Garden City: Doubleday, 1971. [Israel/Canaan]

Vaux, Roland de. "The Desert Sanctuary: The Tent; The Ark of the Covenant." In de Vaux, *Ancient Israel: Its Life and Institutions.* 294-302. New York: McGraw-Hill, 1961. [Tabernacle]

Vaux, Roland de. "The King of Israel, Vassal of Yahweh." In *The Bible and the Ancient Near East.* 152-66. Garden City: Doubleday, 1971. [Kingship/Coronation]

Vaux, Roland de."Le lieu que Yahwé a choisi pour y établir son nom." In *Das ferne und nahe Wort: Festschrift Leonhard Rost zur Vollendung seines 70. Geburtstages*, edited by Fritz Maass. 219-28. Berlin: Töpelmann, 1967. [Israel/Canaan]

Vaux, Roland de. "Notes sur le temple de Salomon." In de Vaux, *Bible et Orient.* 203-16. Paris: Cerf, 1967. [Israel/Canaan]

Vaux, Roland de. "La regalità sacra—The Sacred Kingship." *RB* 68 (April 1961): 266-69. [Kingship/Coronation]

Vaux, Roland de. "Le roi d'Israël, vassal de Yahvé." In *Bible et Orient.* 287-301. Paris: Cerf, 1967. [Kingship/Coronation]

Vaux, Roland de. "Le sacerdoce en Israël: Populus Dei, I." *Israel Cummunio* 10 (1969): 113-68. [Sacrifice/Offerings]

Vaux, Roland de. *Les sacrifices de l'Ancien Testament.* Paris: Gabalda, 1964; also in English as *Studies in Old Testament Sacrifice.* Cardiff: University of Wales, 1964. [Sacrifice/Offerings]

Vaux, Roland de. "Tempel von Jerusalem." In *Lexikon für Theologie und Kirche*, edited by Josef Höfer and Karl Rahner. 10 vols., 9:1355-58. Breiburg: Herder, 1964. [Israel/Canaan]

Vaux, Roland de. "The Temple at Jerusalem." In de Vaux, *Ancient Israel: Its Life and Institutions.* 312-30. New York: McGraw-Hill, 1961. [Israel/Canaan]

Vaux, Roland de. "Le temple de Jérusalem." In de Vaux, *Bible et Orient.* 303-15. Paris: Cerf, 1967. [Israel/Canaan]

Venetianer, Ludwig. *Ezekiels Vision and die salomonischen Wasserbecken.* Budapest: Nachfloger, 1906. [Israel/Canaan]

Ventura, Raphael. "Bent Axis or Wrong Direction? Studies on the Temple of Serabit el-Khadim." *IEJ* 38/3 (1988): 128-38. [Egypt]

Vernant, Jean-Pierre. *Le sacrifice dans l'antiquité: Huit exposés suivis de discussions.* Genève: Fond Hardt, 1981. [Sacrifice/Offerings]

Vernes, M. "Notes sur les sanctuaires de la région chananéenne qui furent fréquentés concurrémment par les Israelites et les nations voisines." *RHR* 43 (1901): 352-54. [Israel/Canaan]

Vernes, M. "Les plus anciens sanctuaires des Israelites." *RHR* 5 (1882): 22-48. [Israel/Canaan]

Vieyra, M. "Rites de purification Hittites." *RHR* 119 (1939): 121-53. [Ritual/Liturgy/Worship]

Vilnay, Zev. *The Sacred Land: Vol. 1: Legends of Jerusalem.* 3 vols. Philadelphia: Jewish Publication Society of America, 1973. [Israel/Canaan]

Vincent, A. "Les rites du balancement (tenouphah) et du prélèvement (teroumah) dans le sacrifice de communion de l'Ancien Testament." *Biblical Archaeology and History* 30 (1939): 267-72. [Sacrifice/Offerings]

Vincent, Louis-Hugues. "Abraham à Jérusalem." *RB* 58 (1951): 360-71. [Israel/Canaan]

Vincent, Louis-Hugues. "Une antéchambre du palais de Salomon." *RB* n.s. 2 (1905): 258-65. [Israel/Canaan]

Vincent, Louis-Hugues. "L'autel des holcaustes et le caractère du temple d'Ézéchiel." *Analecta Bollandiana* 67 (1949): 7-20. [Israel/Canaan]

Vincent, Louis-Hugues. "Les bassins roulants du temple de Salomon." In *Miscellanea Biblica B. Ubach. Scripta et Documenta.* 147-59. Montserrat: n.p., 1953. [Israel/Canaan]

Vincent, Louis-Hugues. "Le caractère du temple salomonien." In *Melanges bibliques rédigés en l'honneur de André Robert.* 137-48. Paris: Bloud and Gay, 1957. [Israel/Canaan]

Vincent, Louis-Hugues. "De la tour de Babel au Temple." *RB* 53 (1946): 403-40. [Mesopotamia]

Vincent, H. (Louis-Hugues). "La description du Temple de Salomon. Notes exégètiques sur I Rois VI." *RB* n.s. 4 (1907): 515-42. [Israel/Canaan]

Vincent, Louis-Hugues. "La notion biblique du Haut Lieu." *RB* 55 (1948): 245-78, 438-45. [Israel/Canaan]

Vincent, Louis-Hugues. "Le temple Hérodian d'après la Mishnah." *RB* 61 (1954): 5-35, 398-418. [Israel/Canaan]

Vincent, Louis-Hugues, and M.-A. Steve. "Le temple d'Ézéchiel." In *Jérusalem de l'Ancien Testament,* edited by Louis-Hugues Vincent and M.-A. Steve. 2 vols., 3 parts., pt. 2:471-95. Paris: Gabalda, 1954-56. [Israel/Canaan]

Vincent, Louis-Hugues, and M.-A. Steve. "Le temple de Salomon." In *Jérusalem de l'Ancien Testament,* edited by Louis-Hugues Vincent and M.-A. Steve. 2 vols., 3 parts., pt. 2:373-431. Paris: Gabalda, 1954-56. [Israel/Canaan]

Vincent, Louis-Hugues, and M.-A. Steve. "Le temple hérodien d'après la Mishnah." In *Jérusalem de l'Ancien Testament*, edited by Louis-Hugues Vincent and M.-A. Steve. 2 vols., 3 parts., pt. 2:496-525. Paris: Gabalda, 1954-56. [Israel/Canaan]

Vizedom, Monika. *Rites and Relationships: Rites of Passage and Contemporary Anthropology*. Beverly Hills: Sage, 1976. [Ritual/Liturgy/Worship]

Vogelstein, H. "Einige Probleme der jüdischen Geschichte der Zeit des zweiten Tempels." In *Jewish Studies in Memory of Israel Abrahams*. 416-25. New York: Jewish Institute of Religion, 1927. [Israel/Canaan]

Vogelstein, Hermann. *Der Kampf zwischen Priestern und Leviten seit den Tagen Ezechiels—eine historisch-kritische Untersuchung*. Stettin: Nagel, 1889. [Priesthood]

Vogt, E. "Von Tempel zum Felsendom." *Biblica* 55 (1974): 23-64. [Israel/Canaan]

Vogue, Charles J. M. *Le temple de Jérusalem*. Paris: Noblet and Baudry, 1864. [Israel/Canaan]

von Alten, Baron. "Die Antonia und ihre Umgebungen." *ZDPV* 1 (1878): 61-100. [Israel/Canaan]

von Wellnitz, Marcus. "The Catholic Liturgy and the Mormon Temple." *Brigham Young University Studies* 21 (1981): 3-35. [Ritual/Liturgy/Worship]

Vorgrimler, Herbert. *Busse und Krankensalbung*. Freiburg: Herder, 1978. [Ablutions/Anointings]

Vriezen, Theodorus C. "Holy Places." In Vriezen, *The Religion of Ancient Israel*. 83-99, translated by Hubert Hoskins. Philadelphia: Westminster, 1967. [Israel/Canaan]

Wacholder, Ben Zion. "Calendar of Sabbatical Cycles during the Second Temple and the Early Rabbinic Period." *HUCA* 44 (1973): 153-96. [Israel/Canaan]

Wacholder, Ben Zion. *The Dawn of Qumran*. Cincinati: Hebrew Union College Press, 1983. [Israel/Canaan]

Wainwright, Geoffrey. "Baptismal Eucharist before Nicaea: An Essay in Liturgical History." *Studia Liturgica* 4 (1965): 9-36. [Ritual/Liturgy/Worship]

Wainwright, Geoffrey. *Christian Initiation*. Richmond: John Knox, 1969. [Ritual/Liturgy/Worship]

Wainwright, Geoffrey. "Rites and Ceremonies of Christian Initiation: Developments in the Past." *Studia Liturgica* 10 (1974): 2-24. [Ritual/Liturgy/Worship]

Wainwright, J. A. "Zoser's Pyramid and Solomon's Temple." *ET* 91 (1980): 137-40. [Israel/Canaan]

Wakeman, M. K. "Biblical Earth Monster in the Cosmogonic Combat Myth." *JBL* 88 (1969): 313-20. [Creation/Cosmology]

Wakeman, M. K. *God's Battle with the Monster: A Study in Biblical Imagery.* Leiden: Brill, 1973. [Creation/Cosmology]

Waldman, Nahum M. "The Wealth of Mountain and Sea: The Background of a Biblical Image." *JQR* 71 (1980-81): 176-80. [Mountain]

Wales, Horace G. Q. *The Mountain of God: A Study in Early Religion and Kingship.* London: Quaritch, 1953. [Mountain]

Wales, Horace G. Q. "The Sacred Mountain in the Old Asiatic Religion." *Journal of the Royal Asiatic Society* (1953): 23-30. [Mountain]

Walfish, Jeroham J. L. *Gaḥale esh.* 2 vols. Warsaw: Bapmava, 1908. [Sacrifice/Offerings]

Walker, N. "Riddle of the Ass's Head, and the Question of a Trigram." *ZAW* 75 (1963): 225-27. [Israel/Canaan]

Wallace, D. H. "Essenes and Temple Sacrifice." *Theologische Zeitschrift* 13 (1957): 335-38. [Sacrifice/Offerings]

Walter, N. "Tempelzerstörung und synoptische Apokalypse." *ZNTW* 57/1-2 (1966): 38-49. [Israel/Canaan]

Walvoord, J. F. "Will Israel Build a Temple in Jerusalem?" *Bibliotheca Sacra* 125 (April-June 1968): 99-106. [Israel/Canaan]

Warren, Charles. "The Temple." In *Underground Jerusalem*, edited by Charles Warren. 58-81. London: Bentley, 1876. [Israel/Canaan]

Warren, Charles. "The Temple of Herod." *PEQ* 1 (1869): 23-26. [Israel/Canaan]

Warren, Charles. "The Temple of Herod." *PEQ* 7 (1875): 97-101. [Israel/Canaan]

Warren, Charles. *The Temple or the Tomb.* London: Bentley, 1880. [Israel/Canaan]

Warren, Charles. "The Temples of Coele-Syria." *PEQ* 1 (1869-70): 183-210. [Israel/Canaan]

Waterman, L. "The Damaged 'Blueprints' of the Temple." *JNES* 2 (1943): 284-94. [Israel/Canaan]

Waterman, L. "A Rebuttal [to G. Ernest Wright]." *JNES* 7 (1948): 54-55. [Israel/Canaan]

Waterman, L. "The Treasuries of Solomon's Chapel." *JNES* 6 (1947): 161-63. [Israel/Canaan]

Watson, Charles M. "The Position of the Altar of Burnt Sacrifice in the Temple of Jerusalem." *PEFQ* 42 (1910): 15-22. [Sacrifice/Offerings]

Watson, Charles M. "The Site of the Temple." *PEQ* 28 (1896): 47-60. [Israel/Canaan]

Watson, W. "The New Jerusalem." *ET* 25 (1914): 454-57. [Israel/Canaan]

Watteville, Jean. *Le sacrifice dans les textes eucharistiques des premiers siecles.* Paris: Delachaux and Niestle, 1966. [Sacrifice/Offerings]

Watty, William W. "Jesus and the Temple—Cleansing or Cursing?" *ET* 93 (1982): 235-39. [Israel/Canaan]

Watzinger, Carl. "Herodes der Grosse." In *Denkmäler Palästinas*, edited by Carl Watzinger. 2 vols., 2:31-78. Leipzig: Hinrichs, 1935. [Israel/Canaan]

Weiler, I. "Titus und die Zerstörung des Tempels von Jerusalem—Absicht oder Zufall?" *Klio* 50 (1968): 139-58. [Israel/Canaan]

Weimar, Peter. "Sinai und Schöpfung: Komposition und Theologie der priesterschriftlichen Sinaigeschichte." *RB* 95 (July 1988): 337-85. [Tabernacle]

Weinberg, J. P. "*Nethinim* und 'Söhne der Sklaven Salomos' im 6-4," *ZAW* 87 (1975): 355-71. [Israel/Canaan]

Weinberg, Zwi. *Sacrifice in Israel according to the Priest Codex and the Customs of Other Mediterranean Peoples* (in Hebrew). Jerusalem: Mass, 1987. [Sacrifice/Offerings]

Weinel, Heinrich. "*MŠH* und seine Derivate." *ZAW* 18 (1898): 1-82. [Ablutions/Anointings]

Weinert, Francis D. "Luke, Stephen, and the Temple in Luke-Acts." *BTB* 17 (July 1987): 88-90. [Israel/Canaan]

Weinert, Francis D. "Luke, the Temple, and Jesus' Saying about Jerusalem's Abandoned House (Luke 13:34-35)." *CBQ* 44 (January 1982): 68-76. [Israel/Canaan]

Weinert, Francis D. "The Meaning of the Temple in Luke-Acts." *BTB* 11 (July 1981): 85-89. [Israel/Canaan]

Weinert, Francis D. "The Meaning of the Temple in the Gospel of Luke." Ph.D. diss., Fordham University, 1979. [Israel/Canaan]

Weinfeld, Moshe. "Cult Centralization in Israel in the Light of a Neo-Babylonian Analogy." *JNES* 23 (1964): 202-12. [Israel/Canaan]

Weinfeld, Moshe. "Instructions for Temple Visitors in the Bible and in Ancient Egypt." In *Scripta Hierosolymitana*, edited by Sarah Israel-Groll, vol. 28. Jerusalem: Magnes Press, 1984. [Egypt]

Weinfeld, Moshe. "The King as the Servant of the People: The Source of the Idea." *JJS* 33 (1982): 189-94. [Kingship/Coronation]

Weinfeld, Moshe. "Zion and Jerusalem as Religious and Political Capital: Ideology and Utopia." In *The Poet and the Historian: Essays in Literary and Historical Criticism*, edited by R. E. Friedman. 75-115. Chico, CA: Scholars, 1983. [Israel/Canaan]

Weinfeld, Shemuel. *The Writing of the Plan of the Chosen House* (in Hebrew). Jerusalem: Eshkol, 1966. [Measurement]

Weippert Helga. "Der Ort, den Jahwe erwählen wird, um dort seinen Namen wohnen zu lassen: Die Geschichte einer alttestamentlichen Formel." *Biblische Zeitschrift* 24 (1980): 76-94. [Israel/Canaan]

Weiser, Artur. "Die Tempelbaukrise unter David." *ZAW* 77 (1965): 153-68. [Israel/Canaan]

Weiser, Artur. "Zur Frage nach den Beziehungen der Psalmen zum Kult: Die Darstellung der Theophanie in dem Psalmen und im Festkult." In *Festschrift Alfred Bertholet zum 80. Geburtstag gewidmet von Kollegen und Freunden,* edited by Walter Baumgartner et al. 513-31. Tübingen: Mohr, 1950; also in *Glaube und Geschichte im Alten Testament,* edited by Artur Weiser. 303-21. Göttingen: Vandenhoeck and Ruprecht, 1961. [Israel/Canaan]

Weisman, Z. "Anointing as a Motif in the Making of the Charismatic King." *Biblica* 57 (1976): 378-98. [Ablutions/Anointings]

Weiss, M. *The Chosen House—The Second Temple as Described by the Sages of Blessed Memory* (in Hebrew). Jerusalem: Mosad Harav Kook, 1946. [Israel/Canaan]

Welch, Alford C. "When Was the Worship of Israel Centralised at the Temple?" *ZAW* 43 (1925): 250-55. [Israel/Canaan]

Weller, Charles H. *Athens and Its Monuments.* New York: Macmillan, 1913. [Greece/Rome]

Wellhausen, Julius. "History of the Ordinances of Worship," In Wellhausen, *Prolegomenon to the History of Ancient Israel.* New York: Meridian, 1957 (originally published in 1878). 17-167. [Ritual/Liturgy/Worship]

Welten, Peter. "Kulthöhe." In *Biblisches Reallexikon,* edited by Kurt Galling, 2d ed. 94-95. Tübingen: Mohr, 1977. [Israel/Canaan]

Welten, Peter. "Kulthöhe and Jahwetempel." *ZDPV* 88 (1972): 19-37. [Israel/Canaan]

Welten, Peter. "Lade-Tempel-Jerusalem: Zur Theologie der Chronikbücher." In *Textgemäss: Aufsätze und Beiträge zur Hermeneutik des alten Testaments: Festschrift für Ernst Würthwein zum 70. Geburtstag,* edited by A. H. J. Gunneweg and Otto Kaiser. 169-83. Göttingen: Vandenhoeck and Ruprecht, 1979. [Israel/Canaan]

Wendel, Adolf. *Das Opfer in der altisraelitischen Religion.* Leipzig: Pfeiffer, 1927. [Sacrifice/Offerings]

Wenham, Gordon J. "Deuteronomy and the Central Sanctuary." *Tyndale Bulletin* 22 (1971): 103-18. [Israel/Canaan]

Wenham, Gordon J. "Were David's Sons Priests?" *ZAW* 87 (1975): 79-82. [Priesthood]

Wenschkewitz, Hans. "Die Spiritualisierung der Kultusbegriffe: Tempel, Priester, und Opfer im Neuen Testament." *Angelos: Archiv für neutesta-mentlich Zeitgeschichte und Kulturkunde* 4 (1932): 70-230. [Israel/Canaan]

Werbrouck, Marcelle. *Le Temple de Hatshepsut à Deir-el-Bahari.* Brussels: Fondation ègyptologique reine Elisabeth, 1949. [Egypt]

Westphal, Gustav. *Jahwes Wohnstätten nach den Anschauungen der alten Hebraeer.* Giessan: Töpelmann, 1908. [Israel/Canaan]

Westphal, M. "On Thinking of God as King." *Christian Scholars Review* 1 (1970): 27-34. [Kingship/Coronation]

Wheeler, Samuel B. "Prayer and Temple in the Dedication Speech of Solomon, 1 Kings 8:14-61." Ph.D. diss. Columbia University, 1977. [Israel/Canaan]

Whirley, Carlton F. "Significance of the Temple Cultus in the Background of the Gospel of John." Ph.D. diss., Southern Baptist Theological Seminary, 1958. [Israel/Canaan]

Whitaker, E. C. "Unction in the Syrian Baptismal Rite." *Church Quarterly* 162 (1961): 176-87. [Ablutions/Anointings]

Whitaker, G. H. "The Building and the Body (Eph. 2:21f)." *Theology* 13 (1926): 335-36. [Israel/Canaan]

White, H. C. "The Divine Oath in Genesis." *JBL* 92 (1973): 165-79. [Covenant]

Whitehorne, J. E. G. "New Light on Temple and State in Roman Egypt." *Journal of Religious History* 11 (December 1980): 218-26. [Egypt]

Whitney, J. T. "The Israelite '*bamah.*' " Ph.D. diss., Nottingham University, 1974. [Mountain]

Whybray, Roger N. "Proverbs 8:22-31 and Its Supposed Prototypes." *VT* 15 (October 1965): 504-14. [Creation/Cosmology]

Widengren, Geo. *The Ascension of the Apostle and the Heavenly Book (King and Saviour III)*. Uppsala: Lundequistska Bokhandeln, 1950. [Ritual/Liturgy/Worship]

Widengren, Geo. "Aspetti simbolici dei templi e luoghi di culto del vicino oriente antico." *Numen* 7 (1960): 1-25; also in a slightly revised version in German as "Der Kultplatz: Symbolische Bedeutung des Heiligtums im alten Vorderen Orient." In Widengren, *Religionsphänomenologie*. 328-39. Berlin: de Gruyter, 1969. [Mesopotamia]

Widengren, Geo. "Baptism and Enthronement in Some Jewish-Christian Gnostic Documents." In *The Saviour God*, edited by Samuel G. F. Brandon. 205-17. New York: Barnes and Noble, 1963. [Ablutions/Anointings]

Widengren, Geo. "Heavenly Enthronement and Baptism, Studies in Mandean Baptism." In *Religions in Antiquity, Essays in Memory of E. R. Goodenough*, edited by Jacob Neusner. 551-82. Leiden: Brill, 1968. [Kingship/Coronation]

Widengren, Geo. "King and Covenant." *Journal of Semitic Studies* 2 (1957): 1-32. [Kingship/Coronation]

Widengren, Geo. *The King and the Tree of Life in Ancient Near Eastern Religion (King and Saviour IV)*. Leipzig: Harrassowitz, 1951. [Kingship/Coronation]

Widengren, Geo. "Der Kultplatz." In Widengren, *Religionsphänomenologie*. 328-59. Berlin: de Gruyter, 1969. [Sacred Space]

Widengren, Geo. "Royal Ideology and the Testaments of the Twelve Patriarchs." In *Promise and Fulfillment: Essays Presented to S. H. Hooke*, edited by F. F. Bruce. 202-12. Edinburgh: Clark, 1963. [Sacred Vestments]

Widengren, Geo. "The Sacral Kingship of Iran." In *The Sacral Kingship/La Regalità Sacra.* 242-57 Leiden: Brill, 1959. [Kingship/Coronation]

Widengren, Geo. "Das sakrale Königtum." In Widengren, *Religions-phänomenologie.* 360-93. Berlin: de Gruyter, 1969. [Kingship/Coronation]

Widengren, Geo. *Sakrales Königtum im alten Testament und im Judentum.* Stuttgart: Kohlhammer, 1955. [Kingship/Coronation]

Wiener, Harold M. *The Altars of the Old Testament.* Leipzig: Hinrichs, 1927. [Sacrifice/Offerings]

Wiener, Harold M. "The Position of the Tent of Meeting." *Expositor* (1912): 476-80. [Tabernacle]

Wiesenberg, E. "The Nicanor Gate." *JJS* 3 (1952): 14-29. [Israel/Canaan]

Wiesmann, Hermann. "Die 'opferfeindlichen' Psalmen." *Melanges Université Saint Joseph* 2 (1907): 321-35. [Sacrifice/Offerings]

Wijngaards, J. N. M. "The Adoption of Pagan Rites in Early Israelite Liturgy." In *God's Word among Men, Papers in Honor of Fr. Joseph Putz*, edited by G. Gispert Sauch. 247-56. Delhi: Vidyajyoti, 1973. [Ritual/Liturgy/Worship]

Wild, Robert A. *Water in the Cultic Worship of Isis and Sarapis.* Leiden: Brill, 1981. [Ablutions/Anointings]

Wilkinson, John D. "Jesus Comes to Jerusalem." In Wilkinson, *Jerusalem as Jesus Knew It.* 70-122. London: Thames and Hudson, 1978. [Israel/Canaan]

Wilkinson, John D. "Orientation, Jewish and Christian." *PEQ* 116 (1984): 16-30. [Israel/Canaan]

Wilkinson, John D. "Jewish Influences on the Early Christian Rite of Jerusalem." *Le Museon* 92/3-4 (1979): 347-59. [Ritual/Liturgy/Worship]

Will, Ernest. "Un problème d'*interpretatio graeca*: la pseudo-tribune d'Echmoun à Sidon." *Syria* 62/1-2 (1985): 105-24. [Greece/Rome]

Willesen, F. "The Cultic Situation of Ps. LXXIV." *VT* 2 (1952): 289-306. [Israel/Canaan]

Wilson, A., and L. Wills. "Literary Sources of the Temple Scroll." *Harvard Theological Review* 75 (July 1982): 275-88. [Israel/Canaan]

Wilson, Charles W., et al. *The Recovery of Jerusalem—A Narrative of Exploration and Discovery in the City and the Holy Land.* London: Bentley, 1871. [Israel/Canaan]

Winer, Georg B. "Tempel-herodianischer." *Biblisches Realwoerterbuch*, edited by Georg B. Winer. 2 vols., 2:578-91. Leipzig: Reclam, 1848. [Israel/Canaan]

Winkler, G. "Confirmation or Chrismation: A Study in Comparitive Liturgy." *Worship* 58 (January 1984): 2-17. [Ablutions/Anointings]

Winkler, G. "Original Meaning of Prebaptismal Anointing and Its Implications." *Worship* 52 (January 1978): 24-25. [Ablutions/Anointings]

Winlock, H. E. *The Temple of Hibis in el Khargeh Oasis.* New York: Arno, 1973. [Egypt]

Winter, Eric. *Untersuchungen zu den ägyptischen Tempelreliefs der griechisch-römischen Zeit.* Wien: Bohlau in Kommissions, 1968. [Egypt]

Wischnitzer, R. "Maimonides' Drawings of the Temples." *Journal of Jewish Art* 1 (1974): 16-27. [Israel/Canaan]

Wise, Michael O. "A New Manuscript Join in the 'Festival of Wood Offering.' " *JNES* 47 (April 1988): 113-21. [Israel/Canaan]

Wolcott, S. "The Land of Moriah." *Bibliotheca Sacra* 25 (1868): 765-79. [Israel/Canaan]

Wolf, W. *Das schöne Fest von Opet: Die Festzugsdarstellungen im grossen römischen Säulengang des Tempels von Luksor.* Wien: Böhlav, 1931. [Egypt]

Wolfer-Sulzer, Lucie. *Das geometrische Prinzip der griechischdorischen Tempel.* Winterthur: Vogel, 1939. [Greece/Rome]

Wolff, Odilo. "Der Salomonische Tempelplatz und der heutige Haram zu Jerusalem." *ZDPV* 11 (1888): 60-67. [Israel/Canaan]

Wolff, Odilo. *Tempelmasse: Das Gesetz der Proportion in den antiken und altchristlichen Sakralbauten.* Vienna: Schroll, 1912. [Israel/Canaan]

Wolff, Odilo. *Der Tempel von Jerusalem.* Wein: Schroll, 1913. [Israel/Canaan]

Wolff, Odilo. *Der Tempel von Jerusalem und seine Masse.* Graz: Styria, 1887. [Israel/Canaan]

Woolley, Reginald M. *Coronation Rites.* Cambridge: Cambridge University Press, 1915. [Kingship/Coronation]

Worden, T. "The Ark of the Covenant." *Scripture* 5/4 (1952): 82-90. [Tabernacle]

Woudstra, Marten H. *The Ark of the Covenant from Conquest to Kingship.* Philadelphia: Presbyterian and Reformed, 1965. [Tabernacle]

Wray, G. O. "Southern Projection from the Masjed al Aksa, Jerusalem." *PEQ* 23 (1891): 320-22. [Israel/Canaan]

Wright, David P. *The Disposal of Impurity: Elimination Rites in the Bible and in Hittite and Mesopotamian Literature.* Atlanta: Scholars, 1987. [Ritual/Liturgy/Worship]

Wright, G. R. H. "Bronze Age Temple at Amman." *ZAWT* 78 (1966): 351-59. [Israel/Canaan]

Wright, G. R. H. "Joseph's Grave under the Tree by the Omphalos at Shechem." *VT* 22 (October 1972): 476-86. [Sacred Space]

Wright, G. R. H. *Kalabsha: The Preserving of the Temple.* Berlin: Mann, 1972. [Egypt]

Wright, G. R. H. "The Mythology of Pre-Israelite Shechem." *VT* 20 (1970): 75-82. [Mountain]

Wright, G. R. H. "Pre-Israelite Temples in the Land of Canaan." *PEQ* 103 (1971): 17-32. [Israel/Canaan]

Wright, G. R. H. "Shechem and League Shrines." *VT* 21 (1971): 572-603. [Israel/Canaan]

Wright, G. R. H. "Square Temples East and West." In *Memorial Volume of the Fifth International Congress of Iranian Art and Archaeology. Teheran-Isfahan-Shiraz, 11th-18th April 1968.* 2 vols., 1: 380-88. Teheran: Ministry of Culture and Arts, 1972. [Mesopotamia]

Wright, G. R. H. "Structure of the Qasr Bint Far'un: A Preliminary Review." *PEQ* 93 (1961): 8-37. [Israel/Canaan]

Wright, G. R. H. "Temples at Shechem." *ZAW* 80 (1968): 1-35. [Israel/Canaan]

Wright, G. R. H. "Temples at Shechem: A Detail." *ZAW* 87 (1975): 56-64. [Israel/Canaan]

Wright, George E. (Ernest). "Dr. Waterman's View Concerning the Solomonic Temple." *JNES* 7 (1948): 53-55. [Israel/Canaan]

Wright, G. (George) Ernest. "God Amidst His People: The Story of the Temple." In Wright, *Rule of God: Essays in Biblical Theology.* 57-76. Garden City, NY: Doubleday, 1960). [Israel/Canaan]

Wright, G. (George) Ernest. *Shechem: The Biography of a Biblical City.* New York: McGraw-Hill, 1965. [Mountain]

Wright, George E. (Ernest). "Solomon's Temple Resurrected." *BA* 4 (1941): 17-31. [Israel/Canaan]

Wright, George E. (Ernest). "The Stevens' Reconstruction of the Solomonic Temple." *BA* 18 (1955): 41-44. [Israel/Canaan]

Wright, George E. (Ernest). "The Temple in Palestine-Syria." *BA* 7 (1944): 41-44, 65-88. [Israel/Canaan]

Wright, James C. "The Old Temple Terrace at the Argive Heraeum and the Early Cult of Hera in the Argolid." *Journal of Hellenic Studies* 102 (1982): 186-201. [Greece/Rome]

Wright, John S. *The Building of the Second Temple.* London: Tyndale, 1958. [Israel/Canaan]

Wright, Theodore F. "The Boards of the Tabernacle." *PEFQ* 31 (1899): 70. [Tabernacle]

Wright, Theodore F. "The Tabernacle Roof." *PEFQ* 29 (1897): 225-26. [Tabernacle]

Wright, Theodore F. "Was the Tabernacle Oriental?" *JBL* 18 (1899): 195-98. [Tabernacle]

Wylie, C. C. "On King Solomon's Molten Sea." *BA* 12 (1949): 86-90. [Israel/Canaan]

Xella, Paolo. "A proposito del sacrificio umano nel mondo mesopotamico." *Orientalia* 45 (1976): 185-96. [Mesopotamia]

Yaari, A. "Drawings of Jerusalem and the Temple Place as Ornament in Hebrew Books" (in Hebrew). *Kirjath Sepher* 15 (1938-39): 377-82. [Israel/Canaan]

Yadin, Yigael. "Beer-Sheba: The High Place Destroyed by King Josiah." *BASOR* 222 (1976): 5-17. [Israel/Canaan]

Yadin, Yigael. "The Gate of the Essenes and the Temple Scroll." *Qadmoniot* 5 (1972): 129-30. [Israel/Canaan]

Yadin, Yigael. "The Gate of the Essenes and the Temple Scroll." In *Jerusalem Revealed: Archaeology in the Holy City, 1968-1974*, edited by Yigael Yadin. 90-91. New Haven: Yale University Press, 1976. [Israel/Canaan]

Yadin, Yigael. "Le rouleau du Temple." In *Qumrân, Sa piété, sa théologie et son milieu*, edited by M. Delcor. 115-19. Paris: Duculot, 1978. [Israel/Canaan]

Yadin, Yigael. "The Temple" (in Hebrew). *Encyclopedia Hebraica* 8:555-91. Jerusalem: Mass, 1981. [Israel/Canaan]

Yadin, Yigael. "The Temple Scroll." *BA* 30 (1967): 135-39. [Israel/Canaan]

Yadin, Yigael. *The Temple Scroll.* 3 vols. Jerusalem: Israel Exploration Society, 1977-83. [Israel/Canaan]

Yadin, Yigael. *The Temple Scroll.* New York: Random House, 1985. [Israel/Canaan]

Yadin, Yigael. "The Temple Scroll, the Longest and Most Recently Discovered Dead Sea Scroll." *BAR* 10/5 (1984): 32-49. [Israel/Canaan]

Yarden, Leon. "Aaron, Bethel and the Priestly Menorah." *JJS* 26/1-2 (1975): 39-47. [Tabernacle]

Yarden, Leon. *The Tree of Light: A Study of the Menorah.* Ithaca: Cornell University Press, 1971. [Tabernacle]

Yarnold, E. J. "The Ceremonies of Initiation in the *De Sacramentis* and *De Mysteriis* of S. Ambrose." In *Studia Patristica*, edited by F. L. Cross. 10:453-63. Berlin: Akademie-Verlag, 1970. [Ritual/Liturgy/Worship]

Yeivin, S. "Casemated Walls and Sacred Areas." *Proceedings of the Fifth World Congress on Jewish Studies, August 3-11, 1969.* 62-68. Jerusalem: World Union of Jewish Studies, 1972. [Israel/Canaan]

Yeivin, S. "Jachin and Boaz." *PEQ* 91 (1959): 6-22. [Israel/Canaan]

Yeivin, S. "Solomon's Temple" (in Hebrew; *English summary). In *Jerusalem through the Ages*, edited by J. Aviram. 12-26, *58-59. Jerusalem: Israel Exploration Society, 1968. [Israel/Canaan]

Yeivin, S. "Was There a High Portal in the First Temple?" *VT* 14 (July 1964): 331-43. [Israel/Canaan]

Yerkes, Royden K. *Sacrifice in Greek and Roman Religions and Early Judaism.* New York: Scribner's, 1952. [Sacrifice/Offerings]

Yerushalmi, Moses. *Yede Mosheh.* Jerusalem: Yeshivat Kodesh Hilulim, 1968/1969. [Israel/Canaan]

Yon, M. "Sanctuaires d'Ougarit." In *Temples et Sanctuaires: Seminaire de recherche 1981-1983,* edited by G. Roux. 37-50. Lyon: GIS - Maison de l'Orient, 1984. [Israel/Canaan]

Young, F. "New Wine in Old Wineskins." *ET* 86 (1974-75): 305-9. [Sacrifice/ Offerings]

Young, Francis M. "Temple Cult and Law in Early Christianity: A Study in the Relationship between Jews and Christians in the Early Centuries." *NTS* 19 (April 1973): 325-38. [Israel/Canaan]

Young, Frances M. *The Use of Sacrificial Ideas in Greek Chistian Writers from the New Testament in John Chrysostom.* Philadelphia: Patristic Foundation, 1979. [Sacrifice/Offerings]

Young, Frank W. *Initiation Ceremonies.* Indianapolis: Bobbs-Merrill, 1965. [Ritual/Liturgy/Worship]

Žabkar, L. V. "Adaptation of Ancient Egyptian Texts to the Temple Ritual of Philae." *JEA* 66 (1980): 127-35. [Egypt]

Žabkar, L. V. "A Hymn to Osiris Pantocrator at Philae." *ZÄS* 108 (1981): 141-71. [Egypt]

Žabkar, L. V. "Six Hymns to Isis in the Sanctuary of Her Temple at Philae and Their Theological Significance." *JEA* 69 (1983): 115-37. [Egypt]

Zarkowski, Zevi. *Kedushat Har.* Brooklyn: Balshon, 1971/1972. [Israel/ Canaan]

Zawadski, S. "Neo-Assyrian Temple Sacrifices." *Rocznik Oriental* 41/2 (1980): 151-55. [Sacrifice/Offerings]

Zehr, Paul M. *God Dwells with His People.* Scottsdale: Herald, 1981. [Tabernacle]

Zeilinger, F. "Das himmlische Jerusalem: Untersuchungen zur Bildersprache der Johannesapokalypse und des Hebräerbriefes." In *Memoria Jerusalem: Freundesgabe Franz Sauer zum 70. Geburtstag,* edited by Johannes B. Bauer and Johannes Marböck. 143-65. Graz: Akademische, 1977. [Israel/Canaan]

Zeitlin, Solomon. "A Note on the Chronology of the Destruction of the Second Temple." *JQR* 37 (1946-47): 165-67. [Israel/Canaan]

Zeitlin, Solomon. "The Temple." In *The Rise and Fall of the Judaean State.* 2d ed. 3 vols., 1:256-68. Philadelphia: Jewish Publication Society of America, 1968. [Israel/Canaan]

Zeitlin, Solomon. "The Temple and Worship." *JQR* 51 (1960-61): 209-41. [Ritual/Liturgy/Worship]

Zeitlin, Solomon. "There Was No Court of Gentiles in the Temple Area." *JQR* 56 (1965-66): 88-89. [Israel/Canaan]

Zeitlin, Solomon. "There Was No Synagogue in the Temple." *JQR* 53 (1962-63): 168-69. [Israel/Canaan]

Zeitlin, Solomon. "The Titles High Priest and the Nasi of the Sanhedrin." *JQR* 48 (1957-58): 1-5. [Priesthood]

Zeitlin, Solomon. "Were There Three Torah-Scrolls in the Azarah?" *JQR* 56 (1965-66): 269-72. [Israel/Canaan]

Zevit, Z. "Deuteronomistic Historiography in 1 Kings 12, 2 Kings 17 and the Reinvestiture of the Israelian Cult." *Journal for the Study of the Old Testament* 32 (1985): 57-73. [Kingship/Coronation]

Zilbershtain, Yeshʿay. *Maʿasei la-Melekh.* 2 vols. Vácz: Kahn, 1913. [Israel/Canaan]

Zimmer, R. G. "Temple of God." *Journal of the Evangelical Theological Society* 18 (1975): 41-46. [Israel/Canaan]

Zimmerli, Walther. *Ezechiel.* Neukirchen-Vluyn: Neukirchener, 1969. [Israel/Canaan]

Zimmerli, Walther. "Ezechieltempel und Salomostadt." In *Hebräische Wortforschung, Festschrift zum 80. Geburtstag von Walter Baumgartner,* edited by G. W. Anderson et al. 398-414. Leiden: Brill, 1967. [Israel/Canaan]

Zimmerli, Walther. "The Great Vision of the New Temple and the New Land." In *Ezekiel,* vol. 2 of *A Commentary on the Book of the Prophet Ezekiel,* 325-62. Philadelphia: Fortress, 1983. [Israel/Canaan]

Zimmerli, Walther. "Jerusalem in der Sicht des Ezechielbuches." In *The Word of the Lord Shall Go Forth: Essays in Honor of David Noel Freedman,* edited by C. L. Meyers and M. O'Connor. 415-26. Winona Lake: Eisenbrauns, 1983. [Israel/Canaan]

Zimmerli, Walther. "Planungen für den Wiederaufbau nach der Katastrophe von 587." *VT* 18 (1968): 229-55. [Israel/Canaan]

Zinserling, G. "Griechische Tempel als Raumschöpfungen." *Annales archéologiques arabes de Syrie* 21 (1971): 293-300. [Greece/Rome]

Zinserling, G. "Zeus-Tempel zu Olympia und Parthenon zu Athen—Kulttempel?: Ein Beitrag zum Raumproblem griechischer Architektur." *Acta Antiqua* 13 (1965): 41-80. [Greece/Rome]

Zobel, Hans-Jürgen. "arôn." In *Theological Dictionary of the Old Testament* 1:363-74. [Tabernacle]

Zoref, Efrayim. "The Temple Mount and Foundation Stone" (in Hebrew). *Maḥanayim* 116 (1968): 22-33. [Israel/Canaan]

Zuidhof, Albert. "King Solomon's Molten Sea and (*pi*)." *BA* 45 (1982): 179-84. [Ablutions/Anointings]

ANCIENT NEAR EASTERN TEXTS AND STUDIES